PROGRAMMING AND PROBLEM SOLVING

WITH

JAVA

SECOND EDITION

NELL DALE
University of Texas, Austin

CHIP WEEMS
University of Massachusetts, Amherst

JONES AND BARTLETT PUBLISHERS

Sudbury, Massachusetts

BOSTON   TORONTO   LONDON   SINGAPORE

World Headquarters

Jones and Bartlett Publishers
40 Tall Pine Drive
Sudbury, MA 01776
978-443-5000
info@jbpub.com
www.jbpub.com

Jones and Bartlett Publishers Canada
6339 Ormindale Way
Mississauga, Ontario L5V 1J2
CANADA

Jones and Bartlett Publishers International
Barb House, Barb Mews
London W6 7PA
UK

Jones and Bartlett's books and products are available through most bookstores and online booksellers. To contact Jones and Bartlett Publishers directly, call 800-832-0034, fax 978-443-8000, or visit our website, www.jbpub.com.

Substantial discounts on bulk quantities of Jones and Bartlett's publications are available to corporations, professional associations, and other qualified organizations. For details and specific discount information, contact the special sales department at Jones and Bartlett via the above contact information or send an email to specialsales@jbpub.com.

Production Credits
Chief Executive Officer: Clayton Jones
Chief Operating Officer: Don W. Jones, Jr.
President, Higher Education and Professional Publishing: Robert W. Holland, Jr.
V.P., Sales and Marketing: William J. Kane
V.P., Design and Production: Anne Spencer
V.P., Manufacturing and Inventory Control: Therese Connell
Acquisitions Editor: Timothy Anderson
Production Director: Amy Rose
Marketing Manager: Andrea DeFronzo
Editorial Assistant: Laura Pagluica
Photo Research: Christine McKeen
Composition: Northeast Compositors, Inc.
Cover Design: Kristin E. Ohlin
Cover Image: © Babusi Octavian Florentin/ShutterStock, Inc.
Texture used for the Graphical User Interface element: © Daniel Kvarfordt/Shutterstock, Inc.
Wrench used for the Software Maintenance Case Study element: © Celso Pupo/ShutterStock, Inc.
Printing and Binding: Replika Press Put. Ltd.
Cover Printing: Replika Press Put. Ltd.

Library of Congress Cataloging-in-Publication Data
Dale, Nell B.
 Programming and problem solving with Java / Nell Dale and Chip Weems.
-- 2nd ed.
   p. cm.
 ISBN-13: 978-0-7637-3402-2
 ISBN-10: 0-7637-3402-0
 1. Java (Computer program language) I. Title.
 QA76.73.J38D346 2007
 005.13'3--dc22
                      2006035893

6048

Printed in India
12 11 10 09 08   10 9 8 7 6 5 4 3 2

This book is dedicated to you, and to all of our other students for whom it was begun and without whom it would never have been completed.

To quote Mephistopheles, one of the chief devils, and tempter of Faust,
…My friend, I shall be pedagogic,
And say you ought to start with Logic…
…Days will be spent to let you know
That what you once did at one blow,
Like eating and drinking so easy and free,
Can only be done with One, Two, Three.
Yet the web of thought has no such creases
And is more like a weaver's masterpieces;
One step, a thousand threads arise,
Hither and thither shoots each shuttle,
The threads flow on, unseen and subtle,
Each blow effects a thousand ties.
The philosopher comes with analysis
And proves it had to be like this;
The first was so, the second so,
And hence the third and fourth was so,
And were not the first and second here,
Then the third and fourth could never appear.
That is what all the students believe,
But they have never learned to weave.

As you study this book, do not let the logic of algorithms bind your imagination, but rather make it your tool for weaving masterpieces of thought.

J. W. von Goethe, Faust, Walter Kaufman trans., New York, Anchor/Doubleday: 1963.

Contents

Chapter 7   **Additional Control Structures   338**

Chapter 8   **Object-Oriented Software Engineering   394**

Preface

Programming and Problem Solving with Java, Second Edition, represents a major revision in both the organization and the approach of the text. These changes are based on our experience with teaching this material, feedback from users and non-users regarding the first edition, and our ever-present desire to improve the introductory programming experience for students.

Approach

Many instructors have encountered difficulties in teaching Java to novices, and we believe that the approach presented here will make the job considerably easier. Introductory Java books tend to be characterized as falling into one of two camps: "early objects," meaning that object-oriented design and syntax are presented as the initial focus, or "late objects," where the emphasis is on traditional procedural programming, followed by introduction of object-oriented design. This book belongs to neither of these camps. Instead, we might describe our approach as "progressive objects."

The book begins by introducing some very simple but highly useful class designs. All of the early classes are immutable and use a minimum of syntax. The designs follow common patterns so that students can gain confidence in their ability to generate their own classes. Reading class code also becomes easier as students gain more experience.

The steady progression in development of relatively simple classes proceeds in parallel with the introduction of Java's basic data types, arithmetic operations, control structures, and file I/O. These more traditional topics provide students with increasing algorithmic capabilities for subsequent use in their class methods. At the same time, new elements of object-oriented design are added both directly and through the development of new classes in each case study.

Over the course of the book, students can readily see how their library of objects grows increasingly larger, enabling them to develop ever-more-sophisticated applications through reuse of these objects. Then, in the later chapters, we are able to focus on inheritance and polymorphism, using the firm foundation that has been laid by our slow but steady development of numerous simpler classes in the early part of the book.

To summarize the philosophy of this edition, we want students to feel that objects are the natural means of expressing problem solutions, that simple classes are intuitive and easy to build, and that adding greater capabilities to objects goes hand-in-hand with gradually learning more about both algorithms and object-oriented design. We do not try to immediately awe students with the many wonders of full-blown object-oriented design, nor do we allow them to fall into procedural programming habits before introducing them to object-oriented design.

Another major innovation in this edition is the Software Maintenance Case Study. In industry, it has become quite rare for programmers to begin with a clean-sheet design. Instead, most programmers' efforts involve penetrating legacy code. Of course, as soon as a programmer has written any piece of code, the debugging process involves the application of many of the same skills used in software maintenance. One of our "aha" moments was our realization that the lack of these skills is a significant impediment to the success of beginners in an introductory course. To help students overcome this obstacle, most chapters in the second edition now include one or more short case studies that explicitly explain and demonstrate these very basic and essential techniques, which are traditionally assumed to be implicit in learning to write code.

We have also continued to provide Problem-Solving Case Studies that illustrate the analysis of a realistic problem, followed by object-oriented design of its solution, implementation of that solution, and testing. The case studies continue to use the CRC card notation for the design process, but we also introduce UML Class Diagrams for documenting our implementations.

While we have retained our easy-to-read writing style, we also recognize that students often learn as much from seeing an example as from reading a clear explanation. For this reason, we have added a large number of "demo programs" to the second edition. These minimal drivers illustrate the use of some new piece of syntax, without the conceptual overhead of solving a real problem (as is done in the case studies). The result is that the students see how to use each new Java topic both in isolation and in a realistic context.

In the first edition, we introduced graphical user interface (GUI) programming in Chapter 8 and then employed it in later chapters. With this revision, the main thread of the text uses `System` I/O with the `Scanner` class throughout. Beginning in Chapter 4, however, a parallel (and optional) GUI thread is offered. The GUI coverage starts with the easy-to-use `JOptionPane` dialogs, adds `JFileChooser`, and then moves on in the later part of the text to include event-based I/O with `JFrame` and associated components. Thus each new aspect of GUI programming is presented after the main thread has covered all of the underlying principles that are needed to appreciate what is happening.

The optional GUI thread is an example of a broader goal of this revision—namely, to provide greater flexibility in how instructors can use the text. Other examples include the way that the chapters on recursion and applets are structured to allow coverage at different points in the chapter sequence, the fact that the discussions of algorithmic complexity and computing history appear in optional features so that they may be skipped if desired, and the new organization of the chapter on additional control structures. While we still firmly believe that branching and looping are best introduced using only one syntactic structure of each type (as shown in research by Soloway), Chapter 7 is designed so that those instructors who prefer to introduce *switch* with *if-then*, or *for* and *do* with *while*, may easily do so by assigning the relevant sections. This chapter also follows immediately after the chapter covering loops, which makes alternative orders of presentation seem more natural.

Chapter Coverage

Chapter 1 begins with basic definitions and computer concepts, the software life cycle, a discussion of compilation versus interpretation, problem-solving techniques including object-oriented problem solving, and a Problem-Solving Case Study that results in an object-oriented algorithm. The first Java program is encountered in a Software Maintenance Case Study, where the focus is on learning to enter existing code and verify that it is operating as specified before making a simple change. The chapter contains much material that is meant to enrich the students' understanding of the computer milieu, for instructors who prefer to gradually ease into the technical aspects of programming. At the same time, by treating this material as optional and moving quickly to the Software Maintenance Case Study, the chapter also serves the interests of instructors who prefer to dive more directly into programming.

Chapter 2 examines the `char` type, the `String` class, declarations, assignment, and expressions. These concepts are difficult—yet essential for beginners to grasp. Chapter 2 also covers simple output to `System.out`, and string input via the combination of `System.in` and `Scanner`. Students get off to a quick start with a simple working application and then move past the mechanics of program entry and execution. In writing this chapter, we faced the conundrum that students do not yet know enough to understand object classes, but they need practice in working with Java syntax and tools. At the same, we did not want to develop procedural programming habits by presenting a Problem-Solving Case Study that arrives at a solution without using object-oriented design. For this reason, we provide a Software Maintenance Case Study that emphasizes reading code and breaking it down into logical chunks so that we can extend it with new functionality. At this stage, it is more effective for students to focus on developing skills for reading code, and becoming comfortable with the editor and compiler, than it is to demand that they create new code.

Chapter 3 makes the leap from reading code to writing it, and does so in the context of developing classes and methods. Here students get their first taste of algorithmic problem solving and code development in direct connection with object-oriented design. We make a special effort to explain the crucial distinction between class and instance attributes. We also distinguish clearly between the design and implementation phases, and emphasize the differing terminology that applies in each phase (attributes and responsibilities versus fields and methods). Returning to the topic of data types, we examine the difference between simple and reference types. We then move into implementation of responsibilities with methods, including value-returning, void, constructor, and helper methods. The chapter concludes with the development of a complete library class, plus reimplementation of the application from Chapter 2 using this new class. This chapter also includes a section on ethics that is designed so that it can be covered at any point in the course that the instructor prefers.

With *Chapter 4,* we turn to the numeric types and expression syntax. We cover type conversions, precedence rules, and the use of numeric types with `String` objects. Further practice with value-returning methods is provided as we explore using numeric return types. Now that our applications are becoming nontrivial, we also discuss code formatting and test plans. Another library class—this time emphasizing the numeric types—is developed and used with the class from Chapter 3 to solve our first realistic problem. The GUI thread also appears here for the first time, with the introduction of the simplest `JOptionPane` dialog.

Chapter 5 introduces branching control flow. The Boolean type and expressions are covered extensively in preparation for branching. Next, the *if-else* statement is introduced as the general branching structure, and the *if* statement is presented as a special instance of it. Instructors who prefer to immediately contrast this statement with the *switch* statement may do so by assigning the first part of Chapter 7 at this point. Once students are comfortable with the idea of branching in the control flow, it is time to take a closer look at algorithm development. Thus the second part of Chapter 5 explores functional decomposition as a way of organizing the creation of algorithms for responsibilities, along with their natural translation into code as methods. We also expand the discussion of test plans to include the testing of branching algorithms. The GUI thread takes its next step in Chapter 5 as well, by adding options for customizing the appearance of message dialogs.

Chapter 6 brings us to loops and file I/O. As in our other textbooks, we introduce all of the basic loop algorithms with one loop construct, the *while* loop. We prefer to focus on looping algorithms, while introducing only the minimum syntax necessary. That way, students don't develop the misperception that common algorithms are bound to specific syntactic structures in a language. This approach also ensures that students don't become caught up in choosing among different looping statements while they are still unsure of which underlying algorithm is needed. For instructors who prefer to immediately contrast the different forms of looping syntax, the second part of Chapter 7, which introduces *for* and *do* loops, can be covered directly following the first part of Chapter 6. In the Problem-Solving Case Study, we add another class to our library, which we then combine with our two earlier classes to create our first problem-specific class. Previous problems were simple enough that we could solve them by using our general-purpose classes (`Name`, `Time`, `Address`) directly in a driver. Now we see the distinction between these "library" classes and classes that are designed for a specific use. Finally, the GUI thread moves from message-only dialogs to interactive dialogs that enable the user to respond to a query by clicking a button.

Chapter 7 is the "ice cream and cake" chapter of the book, covering the additional control structures that make the coding of certain algorithms easier. In addition to the *switch*, *do*, and *for* statements, Chapter 7 introduces the concept of exception handling. We show students how to use a *try-catch* statement to catch exceptions and how to throw a predefined exception. A new class, `Phone`, is developed to illustrate exception handling and then used in a case study that employs all three kinds of loops, plus a *switch*, to search a file. An optional section introduces the basic ideas of algorithmic complexity analysis. In the GUI thread, we move into general input dialogs.

Chapter 8 takes a break from the introduction of significant amounts of new syntax and focuses on object-oriented software engineering. We begin with a discussion of abstraction and encapsulation, then delve into the use of CRC card notation and UML Class Diagrams. Since the early chapters, students have been using the CRC approach of brainstorming initial classes, filtering the initial list, and then developing the responsibilities and collaborations for these and other classes that they discover through a series of scenarios. In Chapter 8, we introduce the formal notation for recording this process. In fact, the only new Java syntax covered in Chapter 8 is the named package and the enum type. Packages add a new dimension for organizing classes, and enumerations provide a good example of abstraction. As another example of abstraction at work, our GUI thread adds `JFileChooser` to the GUI programmer's toolkit.

In *Chapter 9,* the basic concept of a composite structure is introduced and illustrated with the Java array. We then extend the discussion of arrays to multiple dimensions. Because so many new algorithmic concepts emerge in our discussion of arrays of one and multiple dimensions, this chapter provides two Problem-Solving Case Studies. In the GUI thread, this chapter marks the beginning of our coverage of general event-based user interfaces. In terms of GUI functionality, we take one step back and two steps forward: Although we gain greater flexibility in how output is displayed by using a `JFrame`, we temporarily hold off from covering the more complex mechanisms required to take input in response to an event.

Chapter 10 represents a conceptual step upward in our use of object-oriented design. In this chapter, we bring together all of the previous discussion of classes and objects in the context of an object hierarchy with inheritance and polymorphism. Students learn how to read the documentation for a class hierarchy and how to identify the inherited members of a class. They also see how the classes are related through Java's scope rules. In this way, students are brought to the point of being armed with essentially all of Java's object-oriented tools, including abstract classes and interfaces. Our first demonstration of a subclass involves the definition of a new exception class that we can throw and catch. The Problem-Solving Case Study extends one of our existing classes and shows how dynamic binding enables us to search through a file containing objects of different subclasses. In the GUI thread, we add the ability to input a value and handle an event from a button. Auto-boxing and unboxing of the numeric wrapper classes is covered here as well.

In *Chapter 11,* we apply the object-oriented design techniques from Chapter 10 by showing how an array can be used to implement a general-purpose list class. We begin with a simple, unsorted list. Sorting is added as an operation in a derived class. As a separate branch of the list hierarchy, we derive a new sorted list class that maintains its ordering through insertions and deletions. Algorithms for sequential and binary searching are shown and contrasted. After working through a case study that applies a list, we note that the original organization of the hierarchy leads us down a blind alley; we therefore refactor the hierarchy to start from an abstract list class that defines operations common to sorted and unsorted lists. Chapter 11 also makes use of the `Comparable` interface in showing how to move from a list of strings to a list containing elements of class `Object`. We then provide a preview of the Java Collections Framework and generics, which are covered in more detail in Chapter 12. The GUI thread expands event handling to deal with events from multiple buttons. We see how to use a separate instantiation of a handler for each source, and we consider how to have a single handler identify the event source.

Having seen how to implement lists with arrays, we advance to developing linked implementations of lists in *Chapter 12.* As part of this development process, we introduce Java's generic class facility. We then present a general discussion of additional data structures, including stacks, queues, trees, and hash tables, before covering their implementation in Java's Collections Framework. This chapter is not meant to provide comprehensive coverage of data structures and algorithms; for that, we recommend the sequel to this book, *Object-Oriented Data Structures Using Java, Second Edition*. Instead, our goal here is to supply a high-level introduction to the topic, and to enable the student to solve problems using the Java library classes that represent common data structures.

Chapter 13 provides a quick tour of the concept of recursion and some example algorithms. As in our previous textbooks, this chapter is designed so that it can be assigned for reading along with earlier chapters. The first half of the chapter can be covered after Chapter 6; the second half of the chapter can be read after Chapter 9, as it applies recursion to arrays.

The book closes with *Chapter 14,* which is devoted to the implementation of Java applets. We specifically chose to use only applications in the first part of the text because of their more general applicability, their ability to use console I/O, and our desire to avoid issues related to portability across browsers in different environments. Of course, we recognize that many students are interested in Web programming and are curious to learn how to write applets. Chapter 14 serves this interest.

Chapter Features

∎ Goals

Each chapter begins with a list of learning objectives for the student, divided into knowledge goals and skill goals. These goals are reinforced and tested in the end-of-chapter exercises.

∎ Timeline

An illustrated timeline on computer history extends throughout the course of the book and appears on the opening pages of each chapter. This timeline highlights important moments in computer history and identifies key players in the development of computer technology.

∎ Software Maintenance Case Studies

Some of the most important skills for success in programming are those that are used for maintenance. Critical skills involve reading code with the goal of breaking it into logical chunks, isolating methods and individual statements that are related to specific application behaviors, using test data to establish patterns associated with errors, and so on. Many of the chapters now provide short case studies that explicitly demonstrate how to use these skills. Through these studies we are able to offer additional examples of Java applications that the students can study and draw upon for their later work.

∎ Problem Solving Case Studies

A full solution of a problem—that is, from its initial statement to the implementation of a working Java application—is developed over the course of the book in the Problem Solving Case Studies. The CRC card design strategy is employed throughout to develop object-oriented designs, which are then translated into code. Beginning in Chapter 10, we introduce the formal CRC card notation together with the UML Class Diagram. Test plans and sample test data are also presented for many of these case studies.

∎ Testing and Debugging

These sections consider the implications of the chapter material with regard to testing of applications or classes. They conclude with a list of testing and debugging hints.

∎ Graphical User Interfaces

Beginning with Chapter 4, a separate, optional thread introduces GUI programming. The main thread is not at all dependent on this material. The GUI coverage, however, is meant to complement the chapter material. It proceeds very gradually so that it never gets ahead of the level of Java fluency that the students have already achieved. By the end of the text, however, students who follow this thread should be able to develop modern event-based user interfaces.

■ Quick Checks

These questions test students' recall of major points associated with the chapter goals. Upon reading each question, students should immediately know the answer, which they can verify by glancing at the answer at the end of the section. The page number on which the concept is discussed also appears at the end of each question so that students can review the material in the event of an incorrect response.

■ Exam Preparation Exercises

To help students prepare for tests, these questions usually have objective answers and are designed to be answerable with a few minutes of work. Answers are provided in the Instructor's Guide.

■ Programming Warm-Up Exercises

These questions provide students with experience in writing Java code fragments. Students can practice the syntactic constructs in each chapter without the burden of writing a complete program.

■ Programming Problems

These exercises require students to design solutions and write complete Java applications.

■ Case Study Follow-Up Exercises

Much of modern programming practice involves reading and modifying existing code. These exercises provide students with an opportunity to strengthen this critical skill by answering questions about, or making changes to, the code in the case studies.

Supplements

■ Online Instructor's ToolKit

Available to adopters on request from the publisher is a powerful teaching tool entitled Online Instructor's ToolKit. This download contains an electronic version of the computerized test bank, PowerPoint lecture presentations, answers to the exercises, and the complete programs from the text. To download your copy, visit `http://computerscience.jbpub.com/ppsjava`.

■ Student Resource Disk for Java

The Student Resource Disk for Java contains the link to the most recent versions of Sun Java™ 2 SDK Standard Edition v. 6.0, a link to the Eclipse IDE download page, Eclipse™ SDK 3.2.1, and the text's Eclipse source code. Your copy of the Student Resource Disk is included free of charge with the purchase of your new textbook.

■ Programs

The programs contain the source code for all of the complete Java applications and stand-alone classes that are found within the textbook. They are available in the Online Instructor's ToolKit and as a free download for instructors and students from the publisher's website: `http://computerscience.jbpub.com/ppsjava`. The programs from all of the case studies, plus several programs that appear in the chapter bodies, are included. Fragments or snippets of code are not included, nor are the solutions to the chapter-ending Programming Problems. These application files can be viewed or edited using any standard text editor; to compile and run the applications, a Java compiler must be used. The programs have been tested with Eclipse, X-Code, and Blue-J, and on Windows, Linux, and OS-X.

■ Student Lecture Companion: A Note-Taking Guide

Adapted from the PowerPoint presentation developed for this text, the downloadable Student Lecture Companion is an invaluable tool for learning. The notebook is designed to encourage students to focus their energies on listening to the lecture as they fill in additional details. The skeletal outline concept helps students organize their notes and readily recognize the important concepts in each chapter.

■ *A Laboratory Course for Programming with Java*

Written by Nell Dale, this lab manual follows the organization of the text. The lab manual is designed to allow the instructor maximum flexibility and may be used in both open and closed laboratory settings. Each chapter contains three types of activities: Prelab, Inlab, and Postlab. Each lesson is broken into exercises that thoroughly demonstrate the concept covered in the chapter.

Acknowledgments

Many individuals have helped us in the preparation of this text. We are indebted to the members of the faculties of the Computer Science Departments at the University of Texas at Austin and the University of Massachusetts at Amherst.

The numerous respondents to our online survey provided us with valuable advice and insight into the teaching and learning that goes into their computer programming courses.

A special thanks to Jeff Brumfield for developing the syntax template metalanguage and allowing us to use it in this text. We also thank Tim Richards for testing the portability of the code and capturing the screen shots.

For their many helpful suggestions, we thank the lecturers, teaching assistants, consultants, and student proctors who run the courses for which this book was written, as well as the students themselves. We offer particular thanks to Ivan Bolz-Reynolds, Hana Keys, and Gabriel Smith for their feedback on an earlier version of the manuscript.

We are grateful to the following people who took the time to review the manuscript at various stages in its development:

Reviewers for the Second Edition:

Kevin Bierre, Rochester Institute of Technology
Robert Burton, Brigham Young University
Teresa Cole, Boise State University
Jose Cordova, University of Louisiana at Monroe
Adrienne Decker, State University of New York at Buffalo
Barbara Guillot, Louisiana State University at Baton Rouge
E. T. Hammerand, Arkansas State University
Christopher Merlo, Nassau Community College
Shyamal Mitra, University of Texas at Austin
Jun Ni, University of Iowa
Timothy Richards, University of Massachusetts at Amherst
Robert Rokey, University of Cincinnati
Jeffrey Six, University of Delaware
David Vineyard, Kettering University
Guangming Xing, Western Kentucky University

Reviewers for the First Edition:

Rama Chakrapani, Tennessee Technological University
Ilyas Cicekli, University of Central Florida
Jose Cordova, University of Louisiana at Monroe
Mike Litman, Western Illinois University
Rathika Rajaravivarma, Central Connecticut State University

Thanks to the many people at Jones and Bartlett Publishers who contributed so much, especially Tim Anderson, Amy Rose, Laura Pagluica, Anne Spencer, Mike Boblitt, Therese Connell, and Andrea DeFronzo. We also thank Mike and Sigrid Wile at Northeast Compositors, Inc.

Anyone who has ever written a book—or is related to someone who has—can appreciate the amount of time involved in such a project. To our families—all the Dale clan and the extended Dale family (too numerous to name); to Lisa, Charlie, and Abby—thanks for your tremendous support and indulgence.

N. D.
C. W.

1

Introduction to Object-Oriented Programming and Problem Solving

Goals

Knowledge Goals

To:

- Understand what a computer program is
- Know the three phases of the software life cycle
- Understand what an algorithm is
- Learn what a high-level programming language is
- Understand the difference between machine code and Bytecode
- Understand the compilation, execution, and interpretation processes
- Learn what the major components of a computer are and how they work together
- Understand the concept of an object in the context of computer problem solving

Skill Goals

To be able to:

- List the basic stages involved in writing a computer application
- Distinguish between hardware and software
- List the ways of structuring code in a Java application
- Name several problem-solving techniques
- Choose an applicable problem-solving technique
- Identify the objects in a problem statement

3000 BC
The precursor to today's wire-and-bead abacus was invented in Babylonia

1612–1614
John Napier conceives "Napier's Bones," ivory rods that served as an early calculator

1622
The slide rule is invented by the great mathematician William Oughtred

1642–1643
Blaise Pascal invents one of the first mechanical calculators, the Pascalene

1801
Punch-card-controlled Jacquard's Loom is invented.

1820
The first mass-produced calculator, the Thomas Arithmometer, is introduced to the world

Introduction

com·put·er \kəm-pyoo'tər\ *n. often attrib* (1646): one that computes; *specif*: a programmable electronic device that can store, retrieve, and process data[1]

What a brief definition for something that has, in just a few decades, changed the way of life in industrialized societies! Computers touch all areas of our lives: paying bills, driving cars, using the telephone, shopping. In fact, it might be easier to list those areas of our lives in which we do not use computers. You are probably most familiar with computers through the use of games, word processors, web browsers, and other applications. But there is a big difference between knowing how to use a computer, and knowing how to program one! In this book, we'll show you how to write your own programs using the Java programming language.

---

1. By permission. From *Merriam-Webster's Collegiate Dictionary*, tenth edition © 1994 by Merriam-Webster, Inc.

1822
Charles Babbage formulates his design for the Difference Engine

1842–1843
Augusta Ada Byron earns her designation as the first computer programmer with her notes on the Analytical Engine

1844
Samuel F. B. Morse successfully transmits a telegraph message across a wire from Washington to Baltimore

1854
George Boole's famous paper "An Investigation of the Laws of Thought" is published

1858
The first transatlantic telegraphic communication takes place

1868
Christopher Sholes creates the QWERTY keyboard for the early typewriter

1.1 : Overview of Object-Oriented Programming

Learning to program a computer is a matter of training yourself to solve problems in a very detailed and organized manner. You already know how to solve problems intuitively. Now you'll learn the skills necessary to solve a problem in terms of objects and actions that the computer can work with. In this chapter we begin developing these skills by answering some of the most commonly asked questions about programming. We then look at formal techniques for solving problems.

■ What Is Programming?

Much of human behavior and thought is characterized by logical sequences of actions involving objects. For example, to make a call, you press a sequence of digits on your cell phone and then the "Send" key. Since infancy, you have been learning how to act, how to do things. And you have learned to expect certain behaviors from everything you encounter in the world around you.

A lot of what you do every day you do automatically. Fortunately, you do not need to consciously think of every step involved in a process as simple as turning a page by hand:

1. Lift hand.
2. Move hand to right side of book.
3. Grasp top-right corner of page.
4. Move hand from right to left until page is positioned so that you can read what is on the other side.
5. Release page.

Think how many neurons must fire and how many muscles must respond, all in a certain order or sequence, to move your arm and hand. Yet you move them without conscious thought. When we program a computer, however, we often find ourselves trying to analyze our unconscious solutions to problems. Suppose you are programming a computer to direct a robot to turn a page in a book. You would spend a good deal of time watching how your own hands accomplish the task before you could write the steps for the robot to follow.

On a broader scale, mathematics never could have been developed without logical sequences of steps for manipulating symbols to solve problems and prove theorems. Mass-produced goods are possible because an assembly line operates on component parts in a certain order. Our entire civilization is based on the order of actions, the logical arrangement of things, and their interactions.

We create order, both consciously and unconsciously, through a process called **programming**. This book is concerned with the programming of one particular tool—the **computer**.

Just as a concert program lists the pieces to be performed in the order that the players will perform them, a computer program lists the objects needed to solve a prob-

> **Programming** Writing out instructions for solving a problem or performing a task
>
> **Computer** A programmable device that can store, retrieve, and process data

lem and orchestrates their interactions. From now on, when we use the words "programming" and "program," we mean **computer programming** and **computer program**, respectively.

The computer allows us to perform tasks more efficiently, quickly, accurately, and consistently than we could by hand—if we could do them by hand at all. For this powerful machine to be a useful tool, however, it must first be programmed. That is, we must specify what we want done and how. We do so through programming.

<aside>
Computer programming The process of specifying objects and the ways in which those objects interact to solve a problem

Computer program Instructions defining a set of objects and orchestrating their interactions to solve a problem
</aside>

■ How Do We Write a Program?

A computer is not intelligent. It cannot analyze a problem and come up with a solution. A human (the programmer) must analyze the problem, develop a general solution for the problem, and then write the solution in terms of objects and instructions the computer can work with. Once we have written a solution for the computer, the computer can repeat the solution very quickly and consistently, again and again. In this way, the computer frees people from repetitive and boring tasks.

To write a program for a computer to follow, we must go through a two-phase process: problem solving and implementation (see Figure 1.1).

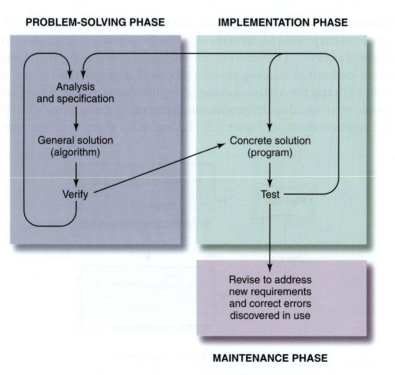

FIGURE 1.1   Programming Process (Waterfall Model)

Problem-Solving Phase

1. *Analysis and specification.* Understand (define) the problem and identify what the solution must do.
2. *General solution (design).* Specify the objects and their interactions to solve the problem.
3. *Verify.* Follow the steps exactly to see if the solution really does solve the problem.

Implementation Phase

1. *Concrete solution (program).* Translate the object specifications (the general solution) into a programming language.
2. *Test.* Have the computer carry out the solution and then check the results. If you find errors, analyze the code and the general solution to determine the source of the errors, and then make corrections.

Once a program has been written, it enters a third phase: maintenance.

Maintenance Phase

1. *Use.* Use the program.
2. *Maintain.* Modify the program to meet changing requirements, to enhance its functionality, or to correct any errors that show up in using it.

Computer scientists refer to this as the waterfall model of the program's life cycle. Like water falling, the development process begins at the top of the list of phases and proceeds to the bottom. Understanding and analyzing a problem take up much more time than Figure 1.1 implies. Indeed, these tasks form the heart of the programming process. The programmer begins the programming process by analyzing the problem and identifying the objects that are present in the problem.

Some people try to speed up the programming process by going directly from the problem definition to implementation (see Figure 1.2). Taking such a shortcut is very tempting and, at

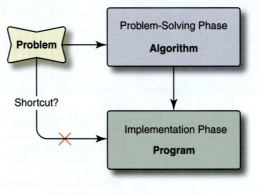

FIGURE 1.2   Programming Shortcut

first glance, seems to save a lot of time. However, for many reasons that will become obvious as you read this book, this "shortcut" actually consumes more time and requires more effort. It's like taking a shortcut in a car, which looks good on the map, only to discover that the road is so full of holes that it takes far more time than going the "long" way.

Developing a general solution before you write a Java program will help you manage the problem, keep your thoughts straight, and avoid mistakes. If you don't take the time at the beginning to think out and polish your solution, you'll spend a lot of extra time fixing your program. So think first and program later! The sooner you start programming, the longer it will take to write an application that works correctly.

Once a Java application has been put into use, it often becomes necessary to modify it later. Modification may involve fixing an error that is discovered during use of the application or changing the program in response to changes in the user's requirements. Each time the program is modified, the programmer should repeat the problem-solving and implementation phases for those aspects of the application that change. Then the programmer should check that the changed sections still work with the other parts of the application.

This phase of the programming process, known as maintenance, actually accounts for the majority of the effort expended on most applications. For example, an application that is implemented in a few months may need to be maintained over a period of many years. For this reason, it is a cost-effective investment of time to carefully develop the initial problem solution and algorithm implementation. Together, the problem-solving, implementation, and maintenance phases constitute the application's life cycle.

In addition to solving the problem, implementing the algorithm, and maintaining the program, **documentation** is an important part of the programming process. Documentation includes written explanations of the problem at hand, the organization of the solution, explanatory comments embedded within the program itself, and user manuals that describe how to use the program. Many different people are likely to work on an application over its lifetime. Each of those individuals must be able to read the code underlying the application and understand it.

> **Documentation** The written text and comments that make an application easier for others to understand, use, and modify

1.2 : Are There Other Ways to Develop a Program?

Because each phase of development in the waterfall model is completed before the next phase begins, the requirements must all be defined in advance, and the design must be completed before implementation begins. This approach is especially appropriate for the kinds of programming problems that you encounter in an introductory programming course.

Other models of the programming process exist, although we do not describe them in detail in this text. For example, the spiral model of the program life cycle begins with a partial specification of the problem, proceeds to a partial implementation, then refines the specification, and finally resumes implementation. The specification and implementation cycle may be repeated many times, and this pattern continues into the maintenance phase. The spiral model is appropriate in developing large software systems where the requirements are expected to evolve over the course of months or years while the project is going on.

In the disposable prototype model, a solution is developed and implemented quickly, with no concern for maintenance. As soon as it is working, this solution is thrown away. Then, based on the lessons learned, a new solution is created. Poor decisions made with the prototype are rectified in the second implementation, producing a better solution.

Paired programming is a technique that can be applied to any of the programming models. It is an example of the old saying, "Two heads are better than one." Two programmers work together to solve the problem, with one programmer writing the solution and the second programmer looking over his or her shoulder. The observer's job is to understand what the writer is doing. By questioning the approach of the writer, the observer often identifies problems with the design. In reading the work of the writer, the observer also tends to spot simple mistakes such as typographical errors. The result is that both the general solution and the implementation have fewer errors.

Object-oriented programming is an approach to problem solving and implementation that focuses on the objects in the problem and the ways in which they interact. The goal is to develop the solution and the implementation in terms of small, easy-to-manage pieces that represent those objects and their actions.

■ How Can a Computer Work with Objects?

A key word in the definition of a computer is data. Computers manipulate data. **Data** is information in a form that the computer can use—for example, numbers and letters. **Information** is any knowledge that can be communicated, including abstract ideas and concepts such as "the Earth is round."

Data Information in a form that a computer can use

Information Any knowledge that can be communicated

Object A collection of data values and associated operations

When you write a program (instructions) for a computer, you specify the properties of the data and the operations that can be applied to it. In computer science, we refer to the combination of the data and its associated operations as an **object**, because that is how we represent the objects that exist in the problems we are solving. The objects we represent can be physical objects from the real world, such as products in an inventory; abstract objects, such as mathematical constructs; or anything in between. Our computer representations of these objects are then programmed to interact with each other to solve a problem.

Data comes in many different forms: letters, words, integer numbers, real numbers, dates, times, coordinates on a map, and so on. In the absence of operations that manipulate the data, however, these forms are essentially meaningless. For example, the number 7.5 has no meaning out of context. In the context of an operation that computes it from a measurement of a person's head, however, it becomes a hat size (see Figure 1.3). By combining data with related operations, it becomes possible to represent information as objects in the computer. Virtually any kind of information and its related operations can be represented as such an object.

Let's consider some examples of what we mean by "object" in this context. Suppose you are filling out a job application form. The form asks for your name, address, and phone number. When the data from your form is entered into the computer, it is stored in objects representing the name, address, and phone number.

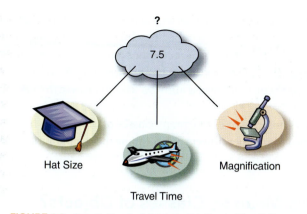

FIGURE 1.3   Data Is Meaningful Only in Relation to What It Represents

Let's now take a closer look at the Name object. What kind of data would it store? Probably a first name, a last name, and a middle name. It might also include a prefix, such as Ms. or Dr. And it might allow a suffix, such as Jr. or Esq. Now that we have a sense of the data in a Name object, what sort of operations should it have? Well, we need to be able to create a Name object from the different pieces. Beyond that, we likely want the ability to retrieve each individual piece (get the first name, get the last name, get the middle name, get the prefix, get the suffix).

So far, the Name object is just a convenient way to hold the pieces of a name in one place. What operations could we add that would make it more useful? How about an operation that returns the full name, neatly formatted for displaying on the screen, as shown in Figure 1.4?

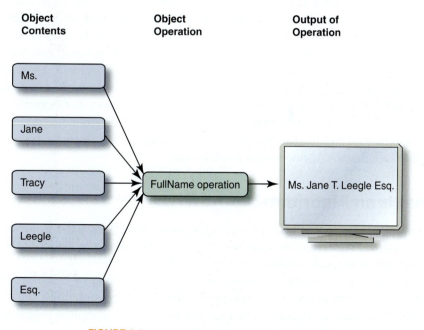

FIGURE 1.4   An Operation Associated with a Name Object

The Address and Phone Number objects would have a similar structure and corresponding operations. The three objects might be grouped together in a Job Application Form object that provides operations to get each object that it contains and to display the form on the screen. A collection of Job Application Form objects might be stored in an Application List object that sorts the forms into alphabetical order and allows a user to browse through the list, adding and deleting forms.

As you can see, it is possible to define many classes of objects. By having objects work together or using objects within other objects, we combine their capabilities and create even more powerful objects.

■ What Do We Mean by Classes of Objects?

It is quite common for a problem to include multiple objects that have the same properties. For example, our Job Application Form might include several names: the applicant's name, the names of references, and so on. Rather than writing a specification for each individual object, we write a specification for the particular *kind* of object. In our example, instead of writing a specification for each name, we write a specification for how names are represented in general. Such a specification defines a **class** of objects. Once we've defined the representation for a Name class, we can easily tell the computer to create any number of Name objects.

> **Class** A specification of the representation of a particular kind of object, in terms of data and operations
>
> **Algorithm** Instructions for solving a problem in a finite amount of time using a finite amount of data

The distinction between a class and an object is an important one. A class is like the blueprint for a house design. We can build any number of houses from the blueprint, just as we can create any number of objects from the class specification. The class specifies what all of the objects have in common. Carrying this analogy a bit further, even though the houses built from the same design look alike, different people live in them. Likewise, even though each object of a given class has the same representation, it contains different data values. On the Job Application Form, one Name object contains the applicant's name and other Name objects contain the names of references.

As we noted previously, each object has an associated set of operations. The programmer determines which operations will be available for each type of object. For example, the operations for an ATM card object in a banking system would be chosen to mimic the actions that are applied to the real ATM card. Once an operation is defined for an object, we write an algorithm that specifies how the operation is carried out.

■ What Is an Algorithm?

For each operation associated with an object, the programmer writes the sequence of steps (called an **algorithm**) required to perform the operation. The operations associated with all of the objects combine to create a solution to the original problem.

More generally, an algorithm is a verbal or written description of a logical set of actions involving objects. We use algorithms every day. Recipes, knitting instructions, and driving directions are all examples of algorithms that are not programs. A computer program is an algorithm translated into a programming language for a computer to execute. We generally refer to Java programs as applications.[2]

When you start your car, for example, you follow a step-by-step set of actions involving various objects. The algorithm might look something like this (we've highlighted the objects in the algorithm):

Objects: Key, Transmission, Gas Pedal, Engine, Phone

1. Insert the key.
2. Make sure the transmission is in Park (or Neutral).
3. Depress the gas pedal.
4. Turn the key to the start position.
5. If the engine starts within six seconds, release the key.
6. If the engine doesn't start within six seconds, release the key and gas pedal, wait ten seconds, and repeat Steps 3 through 6, but not more than five times.
7. If the car doesn't start, phone your mechanic.

Without the phrase "but not more than five times" in Step 6, you could be stuck trying to start the car forever. Why? Because if something is wrong with the car, repeating Steps 3 through 6 over and over will not start it. This kind of never-ending situation is called an *infinite loop*. If we leave the phrase "but not more than five times" out of Step 6, the procedure doesn't fit our definition of an algorithm. An algorithm must terminate in a finite amount of time for all possible conditions.

Suppose a programmer needs an algorithm to determine an employee's weekly wages. The algorithm reflects what would be done by hand (objects are again highlighted):

Objects: Employee Record, Personnel Database, Employee ID, Time Card, Pay Rate, Hours Worked, Regular Wages, Overtime Wages, Total Wages

1. The Personnel Database gets the Employee Record, using the Employee ID from the Time Card.
2. The Employee Record provides its Pay Rate.
3. The Time Card provides the Hours Worked during the week.
4. If the number of Hours Worked is less than or equal to 40, multiply it by the Pay Rate to calculate the Regular Wages.
5. If the number of Hours Worked is greater than 40, multiply 40 by the Pay Rate to calculate the Regular Wages, and then multiply the Hours Worked minus 40 by 1 ½ times the Pay Rate to calculate the Overtime Wages.
6. Add the Regular Wages to the Overtime Wages (if any) to determine the Total Wages for the week.

The steps the computer follows are often the same steps you would follow to do the calculations by hand.

---

2. Java supports two types of programs: applications and applets. An applet is a restricted form of application that can be executed by a web browser.

After developing a general solution, the programmer tests the algorithm by "walking through" each step mentally or manually with paper and pencil. If the algorithm doesn't work, the programmer repeats the problem-solving process, analyzing the problem again and coming up with another algorithm. Often the second algorithm is simply a variation of the first. Once we have a working algorithm, we can implement it in a programming language.

1.3 : What Is a Programming Language?

When the programmer is satisfied with the algorithm, he or she translates it into **statements** in a **programming language**, such as Java.

A programming language is a simplified form of English (with math symbols) that adheres to a strict set of grammatical rules. English is far too complicated and ambiguous a language for today's computers to follow. Programming languages, which have a limited vocabulary and grammar, are much simpler.

Although a programming language is simple in form, it is not always easy to use. Try giving a friend directions to pick someone up at the nearest airport using a vocabulary of only 25 words, and you begin to see the problem. When your vocabulary is so limited, directions that you can easily express in unrestricted English, such as "go west on highway 27 to exit 14 and follow the signs for arriving flights," must to be written out as many simpler steps. Furthermore, words like "go" are ambiguous because they do not indicate a specific means of transportation. Here are airport directions in a program-like form:

> Start with car at parking lot exit.
>
> Turn car left.
>
> Drive 3.2 miles.
>
> Turn car left.
>
> Drive 12.35 miles.
>
> Bear right.
>
> Drive 1.61 miles.
>
> Turn car right.
>
> Drive 0.34 miles.
>
> Bear right.
>
> Stop car at open place by curb.

Statements Specific combinations of symbols and special words that are defined by a programming language to be complete units within a program; analogous to sentences in a human language

Programming language A set of rules, symbols, and special words used to construct a computer program

Code Instructions for a computer that are written in a programming language

Computer programming requires us to write very simple, exact instructions that consist only of operations that a computer can perform.

Translating an algorithm into a programming language is called coding, or implementing the algorithm. **Code** is the product of translating an algorithm into a programming language. The term "code" can refer to a complete program or to any portion of a program. As we see later in the chapter, this term originated with early computer languages that were much more cryptic— like writing in a secret code. Modern languages are much closer to English and, therefore, easier to read.

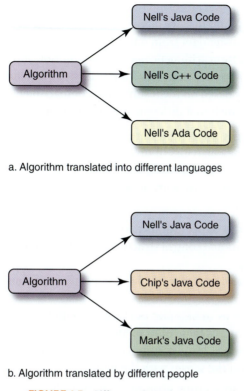

a. Algorithm translated into different languages

b. Algorithm translated by different people

FIGURE 1.5   Differences in Implementation

A program is tested by running (executing) it on the computer. If the program fails to produce the desired results, the programmer must debug it—that is, determine what is wrong and then modify the program, or even revise the algorithm, to fix it. The process of coding and testing the algorithm takes place during the implementation phase.

There is no single way to implement an algorithm. For example, an algorithm can be translated into more than one programming language (see Figure 1.5a). When two people translate an algorithm into the same programming language, they often come up with different implementations (see Figure 1.5b). Why? Because a programming language gives the programmer flexibility in translating an algorithm. Given this flexibility, people adopt their own styles in writing programs, just as they do in writing short stories, essays, or novels. Once you have some programming experience, you will develop a style of your own. Throughout this book, we offer tips on good programming style.

■ What Kinds of Instructions Can Be Written in a Programming Language?

The instructions in a programming language reflect the basic operations a computer can perform:

- A computer can input (accept) data from an input device (a keyboard or mouse, for example) and output (send) data to an output device (a screen, for example).

- A computer can store data into and retrieve data from its memory and secondary storage (parts of a computer that we discuss in the next section).
- A computer can transfer data from one place to another within its memory.
- A computer can perform arithmetic operations (addition and subtraction, for example).
- A computer can compare data values for equality or inequality and other relationships and make decisions based on the result of the comparison.
- A computer can branch to a different section of the instructions.

Programming languages use certain statements called *control structures* to organize the instructions that specify the behaviors of objects. In most programming languages, these behaviors can be organized in four ways: sequentially, conditionally, repetitively, and with subprograms. Java adds a fifth way: asynchronously (see Figure 1.6). Here are some key concepts related to control structures:

- A sequence is a series of operations that are executed one after another.
- Selection, the conditional control structure, executes different operations depending on certain conditions.
- The repetitive control structure, the loop, repeats operations as long as certain conditions are met.
- Subprograms allow us to organize our code into units that correspond to specific object behaviors; Java calls these units methods.
- Asynchronous control lets us write code that handles events, such as the user clicking a button on the screen with the mouse.

Each of these ways of structuring operations controls the order in which the computer executes the operations, which is why they are called control structures. To get a sense of how these work, let's examine some analogies from everyday experience.

Suppose you're driving a car. Going down a straight stretch of road is like following a sequence of instructions. When you come to a fork in the road, you must decide which way to go and then take one or the other branch of the fork. The computer does something similar when it encounters a selection control structure (sometimes called a branch or decision) in a program. Sometimes you have to drive around the block several times to find a place to park your car. The computer does the same sort of thing when it encounters a loop.

A subprogram is a named sequence of instructions written as a separate unit. Suppose, for example, that every day you go to work at an office. The directions for getting from home to work form a method called "Go to the office." It makes sense, then, for someone to give you directions to a meeting by saying, "Go to the office, then go four blocks west"—without repeating all the steps needed to get to the office.

Responding to asynchronous events is like working as a pizza delivery person. You wait around the dispatch station with all of the other delivery people. The dispatcher calls your name and gives you some pizzas and a delivery address. You deliver the pizzas and return to the dispatch station. At the same time, other delivery people may be out driving.[3] The term "asynchronous" means

---

3. Java actually allows us to write more general asynchronous programs using a construct called a thread. Threaded programs are beyond the scope of this text. We restrict our use of asynchronous structures to handling events.

SEQUENCE

SELECTION (also called *branch* or *decision*)
IF condition THEN statement1 ELSE statement2

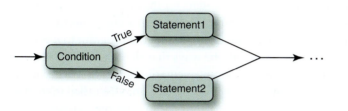

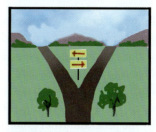

LOOP (also called *repetition* or *iteration*)
WHILE condition DO statement1

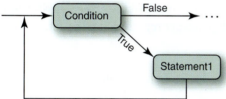

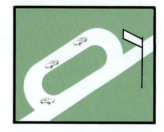

SUBPROGRAM (also called *method, procedure, function,* or *subroutine*)

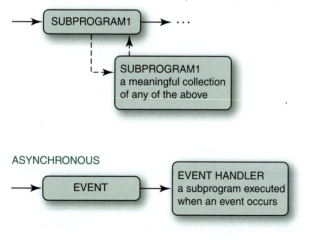

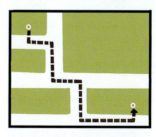

ASYNCHRONOUS

EVENT → EVENT HANDLER
a subprogram executed
when an event occurs

FIGURE 1.6 Basic Control Structures of Programming Languages

"not at the same time." In this context, it refers to the fact that the user can, for example, click the mouse on the screen at any time while the application is running. The mouse click does not have to happen at some particular time corresponding to certain instructions within the code.

As we saw in the software life cycle, after a solution to a problem has been implemented—in a programming language—it enters a new phase—maintenance.

1.4 : What Is Software Maintenance?

In the life cycle of a program, the maintenance phase accounts for the majority of a typical program's existence. As we said earlier, programs are initially written in a fairly short time span and used for many years thereafter. The original designers develop the program to meet a set of specifications, but they cannot possibly foresee all the ways that the program will be used in the future. Decisions that were made in the initial implementation may prove to be inadequate to support some future use, and a new team of programmers may be called in to modify the program. After going through many modifications, the code may become so complicated that it is difficult to identify the purpose of some of the original instructions.

For example, at the turn of the millennium, the software industry faced a major maintenance effort known collectively as the "Y2K Problem." For much of the preceding fifty years, programmers had been encoding dates with a two-digit integer representing the year, as shown here:

```
Year      Actual
Code       Year

 00        1900
 01        1901
  .          .
  .          .
  .          .
 64        1964
  .          .
  .          .
  .          .
 99        1999
```

There was no way for these programs to make the transition to the new millennium and be able to distinguish a year such as 2005 from 1905. Dire predictions foretold the failure of much of our modern infrastructure, such as the shutdown of the electric power grid, the telecommunication networks, and the banking system.

In the end, the software industry spent billions of dollars finding all of the places in which programs used a two-digit year and changing the code to use four digits. Some of this code dated back to the 1960s, and the original programmers were not available to help with the conversion. A new generation of programmers had to read and understand the programs well enough to make the necessary changes.

While the rest of the world was celebrating New Year's Eve in 1999, many of these programmers were sitting at their computers, watching nervously as the date ticked over to 2000, just in case they had missed something. Although a few problems were encountered, the vast majority of computers made the transition without skipping a beat.

In retrospect, it is easy to find fault with the decisions of the original programmers to use a two-digit date. But at the time, computers had very small memories (in the 1960s a large computer could hold only 65,000 letters or digits in main memory), and saving even a digit or two in representing a date could make the difference between a working program and one that wouldn't fit in memory. None of those programmers expected their code to be used for forty years. By the same token, it is impossible to know which programming decisions are being made today that will turn out to be problematic in the future.

Successive attempts to extend the capabilities of a program will often produce errors because programmers fail to comprehend the ways in which earlier changes to the program will interact with new changes. In some cases, testing fails to reveal those errors before the modified program is released, and it is the user who discovers the error. Then fixing the bugs becomes a new maintenance task and the corrections are usually done hastily because users are clamoring for their software to work. The result is that the code becomes even harder to understand. Over time, the software grows so complex that attempts to fix errors frequently produce new errors. In some cases the only solution is to start over, rewriting much of the software anew with a clean design.

SOFTWARE MAINTENANCE CASE STUDY

An Introduction to Software Maintenance

The preceding discussion illustrates the importance of developing skills not just in writing new code, but also in working with existing code. These Software Maintenance Case Study sections walk you through the process of typical maintenance tasks. Unlike the Problem-Solving Case Study sections, in which we begin with a problem, solve it, and then code a program, here we begin with a program and see how to understand what it does before making some change.

Let's start with something extremely simple, just to get a sense of what we'll be doing in future Software Maintenance Case Study sections. We'll keep this example so simple that you don't even have to know anything about Java to follow what's happening. Even so, in following our steps through this process, you'll get a sense of what's involved in working with programs.

Maintenance Task: Enter the "Hello World" application program, changing it to output "Hello Universe" instead.

Existing Code

```java
public class HelloWorld
{
   public static void main(String[] args)
   {
      System.out.println("Hello World!");
   }
}
```

Discussion: The classic first application that is written by many beginners is generically known as "Hello World." Its sole purpose is to print out a greeting from the computer to the programmer and then quit. Many variations of the message exist, but the traditional one is "Hello World!" Here, we are being asked to change the existing message to "Hello Universe!"

   Looking at this code, you can immediately see the message, printed in blue. Your first temptation would be to just change the word "World" to "Universe." (Even without knowing any Java, you're already programming!) In a simple case like this, that strategy may be adequate; with a larger application, however, such an approach could result in the creation of more problems. With any maintenance effort, we must first observe and record the current behavior of the application. If it isn't working initially, you may think that your changes are the source of what is actually a pre-existing problem and spend many hours in a futile attempt to fix the problem by correcting your changes.

   Thus the first step in this maintenance task is to enter the application exactly as it is written and run it to ensure that it works. Unless you've written programs before, it is difficult to appreciate how precisely you must type Java code. Every letter, every capitalization, every punctuation mark is significant. There are exceptions, which we'll see later, but for now it is good practice to enter this application exactly as it appears above. For example, can you spot the error in the following version of the code that fails to run? All you have to do is compare it, letter by letter, with the preceding version, to find the difference.[4]

```java
public class HelloWorld
{
   public static void main(String[] args)
   {
      System.Out.println("Hello World!");
   }
}
```

Once we are sure that the program works as claimed, we can change it with the knowledge that any new problems are associated with our modifications.

   Entering an application involves typing it into the computer with an editor, which is just a program that lets us record our typing in a file. A word processor is an example of an editor.

---

4. In the fifth line, the word "out" has been capitalized instead of being typed entirely in lowercase.

Most programming systems use a specialized code editor that has features to help us enter programs. For example, a code editor will indent the lines of an application automatically in a pattern similar to that shown in the preceding example, and it may color-code certain elements of the program to help us locate them more easily. When we run the application, if an error occurs, the editor shows us the point at which the error was detected in the code. Here's what one code editor window looks like:

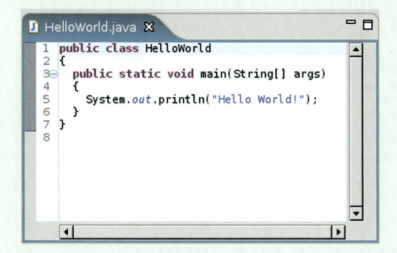

Depending on the programming system that you are using, you may need to begin by creating a new "project," which is the system's way of organizing the information it keeps about your application. Typically, creating a new project involves selecting the "New Project" item from the File menu of the programming system, and then entering a name for the project in a dialog box that appears.

In another programming system, you may need to create a new file directory manually and then tell the editor to store your code file there. There are too many different Java programming systems for us to show them all here. You should consult the manual or help screens for your particular system to learn the specifics for it.

Once you type the application into the editor window, you need to save it (with another menu selection) and then run it. Here's what happens when we try to run the erroneous version of the "Hello World" program. Notice that a mark appears in the margin next to the line with the offending name. Sometimes an explanatory message is also displayed, such as, "cannot resolve symbol: variable Out."

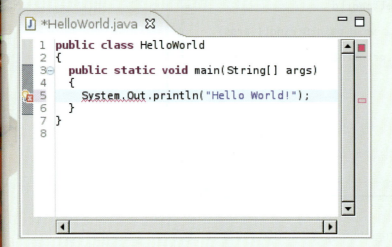

Every programmer encounters errors such as these. After all, very few of us are perfect typists! Rather than being afraid of seeing such messages, we just come to expect them, and we are pleasantly surprised on the rare occasions when we discover that we've entered a long stretch of code without any errors. Usually, we enter some code, look it over carefully for mistakes, and run it to see if the computer finds any more. We then use the error markers and messages to help us find remaining typos and fix them. Here's what happens when the application is at last correct:

Now we know that the program works as advertised, and we can start changing it. Of the seven lines in this application, only three contain instructions to the computer. The other four contain braces, which are a form of punctuation in a Java application.

```java
public class HelloWorld
{
  public static void main(String[] args)
  {
    System.out.println("Hello World!");
  }
}
```

Let's try making our change. Here's the editor window showing the revised application, with "Universe" substituted for "World."

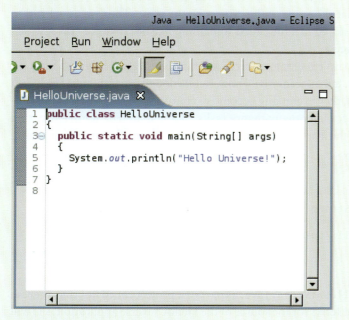

Running this application produces just the result that we desire:

Is that it? Could it really be as simple as changing one word? Actually, no. We edited our existing "Hello World" code file, and when we saved it, we overwrote the existing application, so we no longer have the original code. It's always a good idea to keep the working version of a program separate from a new version. That way, we have a working baseline program to compare against the new version. And if things really go wrong with our modifications, we have a place to go back to and start over.

To correct this situation, we really should have created a new project, perhaps called HelloUniverse, and copied the code from our existing project into the new one. Then we can edit the fifth line and save the change without affecting the original program.

Creating a new project seems simple enough. Is that all it takes? Unfortunately, the answer is still no. As we'll see in the next chapter, the first line of the code defines the name of the application, and most Java systems expect that the code will be stored in a file with the same name. They may also require that the name of the project be the same. Thus we now have an application called `HelloWorld`, stored in a file called something like `HelloWorld.java`, which is in a project called `HelloUniverse`.

Even if this inconsistency doesn't generate an error message, we are still leaving a mess for future programmers to deal with. It may seem trivial now, but if enough programmers leave such inconsistencies in an application, they eventually become so confusing that it can be almost impossible to understand the code for later maintenance tasks. Doing maintenance in a way that results in clean, consistent code is the mark of the true software professional. Thus we must change our application's name as follows:

```java
public class HelloUniverse
{
  public static void main(String[] args)
  {
    System.out.println("Hello Universe!");
  }
}
```

We also save it in a file called `HelloUniverse.java`, as part of a project called `HelloUniverse`. Now, when another programmer looks for the source of the HelloUniverse application, she will be able to spot it just from its file name.

Software Maintenance Tips

1. Check that the existing code works as claimed.
2. Make changes to a copy of the existing code.
3. A maintenance task isn't necessarily complete once the desired functionality has been achieved. Change related aspects of the program to leave clean, consistent code for the next programmer who has to do maintenance.
4. Keeping backup copies of code is also useful in developing new programs—before making any significant change in a program that you're developing, save a copy of the current version so that you can go back to it if necessary.

1.5 : How It All Works

We've now seen an example of a simple Java program, and we have a sense of how we might write one. But what really goes on inside the computer when we try to run the program? It's not magic, although sometimes it may seem that way. In this section, we pull back the curtain on the inner workings of the machine and reveal that there's no wizardry involved—just a lot of technology that has been built up over many years. To understand what's happening, we return to the beginning of computer programming and explore the basic nature of the computer.

Theoretical Foundations

Q.E.D

Binary Representation of Data

In a computer, data are represented electronically by pulses of electricity. Electric circuits, in their simplest form, are either on or off. A circuit that is on represents the number 1; a circuit that is off represents the number 0. Any kind of data can be represented by combinations of enough 1s and 0s. We simply have to choose which combination represents each piece of data we are using. For example, we could arbitrarily choose the pattern 1101000110 to represent the name "Java."

Data represented by 1s and 0s are in binary form. The binary, or base-2, number system uses only 1s and 0s to represent numbers. (The decimal, or base-10, number system uses the digits 0 through 9.) The word "bit" (short for <u>bi</u>nary di<u>git</u>) refers to a single 1 or 0. Thus the pattern 1101000110 has 10 bits. A binary number with 3 bits can represent 2^3, or eight, different patterns. The eight patterns are shown here, together with some examples of base-2 arithmetic:

Binary	Decimal Equivalent	Examples of Binary Addition	Decimal Equivalent
000	0	001 + 001 = 010	1 + 1 = 2
001	1	011 + 010 = 101	3 + 2 = 5
010	2	111 + 001 = 1000	7 + 1 = 8
011	3		
100	4	**Examples of Binary Subtraction**	
101	5	011 − 011 = 000	3 − 3 = 0
110	6	110 − 010 = 100	6 − 2 = 4
111	7	101 − 011 = 010	5 − 3 = 2

A 10-digit binary number can represent 2^{10} (1024) distinct patterns. Thus you can use your fingers to count in binary from 0 to 1023! A byte is a group of 8 bits; it can represent 2^8 (256) patterns. Inside the computer, each character (such as the letter *A*, the letter *g*,

Theoretical Foundations

the digit *7*, a question mark, or a blank) is usually represented by either one or two bytes.[5] For example, in one scheme 01001101 represents *M* and 01101101 represents *m* (look closely—the third bit from the left is the only difference). Groups of 16, 32, and 64 bits are generally referred to as words (the terms "short word" and "long word" sometimes are used to refer to 16-bit and 64-bit groups, respectively).

The process of assigning bit patterns to pieces of data is called coding—the same name we give to the process of translating an algorithm into a programming language. The names are the same because the first computers recognized only one language—which was binary in form. Thus, in the early days of computers, programming meant translating both data and algorithms into patterns of 1s and 0s. The programs that resulted looked like messages in a secret code that were being passed from the programmer to the computer. It was very difficult for one programmer to understand a program written by another programmer. In fact, after leaving a program alone for a while, many programmers could not even understand their own programs!

The patterns of bits that represent data vary from one family of computers to another. Even on the same computer, different programming languages may use different binary representations for the same data. A single programming language may even use the same pattern of bits to represent different things in different contexts. (People do this, too: The four letters that form the word *tack* have different meanings depending on whether you are talking about upholstery, sailing, sewing, paint, or horseback riding.) The point is that patterns of bits by themselves are meaningless. Rather, it is the way in which the patterns are used that gives them their meaning. That's why we combine data with operations to form meaningful objects.

Fortunately, we no longer have to work with binary coding schemes. Today, the process of coding is usually just a matter of writing down the data in letters, numbers, and symbols. The computer automatically converts these letters, numbers, and symbols into binary form. Still, as you work with computers, you will continually run into numbers that are related to powers of 2—numbers like 256, 32,768, and 65,536. They are reminders that the binary number system is lurking somewhere in the background.

■ How Does a Computer Run a Program?

Machine language
The language, made up of binary-coded instructions, that is used directly by the computer

In the computer, instructions are stored and used in binary (base-2) codes, consisting of strings of 1s and 0s. When computers were first developed, the only programming language available was the primitive (binary) instruction set built into each machine—the **machine language** (also known as machine code).

---

5. Most programming languages use the American Standard Code for Information Interchange (ASCII) to represent the English alphabet and other symbols. Each ASCII character is stored in a single byte. Java recognizes both ASCII and a newer standard called Unicode, which includes the alphabets of many other languages. A single Unicode character takes up two bytes in the computer's memory.

When programmers used machine language for programming, they had to enter the binary codes for the various instructions, a tedious process that was prone to error. Moreover, their programs were difficult to read and modify. In time, **assembly languages** were developed to make the programmer's job easier.

Instructions in an assembly language are in an easier-to-remember form called a mnemonic (pronounced "ni-mon′-ik"). Typical instructions for addition and subtraction might look like this:

> **Assembly language**
> A low-level programming language in which a mnemonic represents each machine language instruction for a particular computer

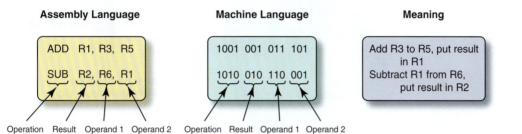

Although humans find it easier to work with assembly language, the computer cannot directly execute the instructions. Instead, they must be converted from assembly language into machine language. How is this done?

If you looked at the binary codes representing instructions and data in memory, you could not tell the difference between them; they differ only in how the computer uses them. This fact enables the computer to process its own instructions as a form of data. As a consequence, it is possible to write a program to translate assembly language instructions into machine code instructions.

Such a program is called an **assembler**. The name comes from the fact that much of what an assembler does is to look up the pieces of an instruction in a table to find the corresponding binary code (such as ADD = 1001, R1 = 001, R3 = 011, R5 = 101), and then assemble these binary-coded pieces of the instruction into a complete machine language instruction (1001 001 011 101). The assembler also puts the instructions together in the specified sequence to create a complete program.

> **Assembler** A program that translates an assembly language program into machine code
>
> **Compiler** A program that translates code written in a high-level language into machine code

Assembly language represents a step in the right direction, but it still forces programmers to think in terms of individual machine instructions. Eventually, computer scientists developed high-level programming languages. These languages are easier to use than assembly languages or machine code because they are closer to English and other natural languages (see Figure 1.7). For example, the preceding pair of instructions might appear in a Java program as follows:

```
taxOwed = calculatedTax - (payments + credits);
```

■ How Does Java Run on a Computer?

A program called a **compiler** translates instructions written in high-level languages (Java, C++, Visual Basic, and Ada, for example) into machine language. As you might expect, this is a more complicated process than what an assembler does. Unlike assembly language instructions, high-level language instructions don't convert directly into matching machine language instructions.

FIGURE 1.7 Levels of Abstraction

Even though most computers perform the same kinds of operations, their designers choose different sets of binary codes for each instruction. As a result, code written in the machine language for one family of computers can't be run on another family of computers.

In contrast, if you write an application in a high-level language, you can run it on any computer that has the appropriate compiler. This portability is possible because high-level languages are not tied to a particular machine instruction set, and because most high-level languages are standardized, which means that an official definition of the language exists that every manufacturer adheres to.

The text of an algorithm written in a high-level language is called **source code**. To the compiler, source code is just input data—letters, numbers, and special symbols. The compiler translates the source code into a machine language form called **object code**. Figure 1.8 shows this process for a program written in the C++ programming language. Many other programming languages use the same approach, but as we explain later, Java does it differently.

As Figure 1.8 emphasizes, the same C++ application can be run on different machines. However, a C++ program must be put through a different compiler for each machine to produce compatible machine language. With the development of the World Wide Web, it became desirable to include programs within web pages to give them greater capabilities. But every kind of computer connects to the Web, which means that a web-page program must be translated into every machine language. Companies don't want to send their source code over the Web, where a competitor might intercept it, nor do they want to have to compile it for every machine.

Java was developed, in part, to solve this problem. It takes a different approach to satisfy the portability requirements of the Web, while still protecting the source code. How does it achieve this goal? Java source code is translated into a standardized machine language called **Bytecode**.

> **Source code** Instructions written in a high-level programming language
>
> **Object code** A machine language version derived from source code
>
> **Bytecode** A standardized machine language into which Java source code is compiled

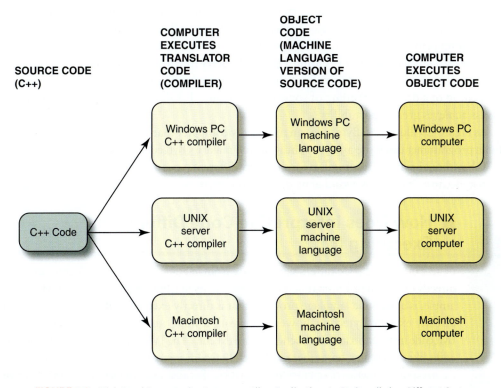

FIGURE 1.8 High-Level Programming Languages Allow Applications to Be Compiled on Different Systems

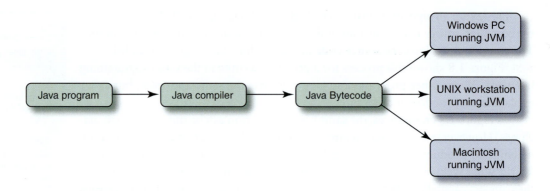

FIGURE 1.9   A Java Compiler Produces Bytecode That Can Be Run on Any Machine with a JVM

No computers actually use Bytecode as their machine language. Instead, for a computer to run Bytecode, it must have another program called the Java Virtual Machine (JVM) that serves as a language interpreter for the Bytecode (we will explain the meaning of the term "virtual machine" shortly). Just as an interpreter of human languages listens to words spoken in one language and then speaks a translation of them in a language that another person understands, so the JVM reads the Bytecode instructions and translates them one-by-one into machine language operations that the particular computer executes. The code is then executed.

In this way, the Bytecode is interpreted, one instruction at a time. This process is not the same as compilation, which is a separate step that translates all of the source code instructions in a program prior to their execution. The difference between compilation and interpretation is like the difference between translating a book of poetry into another language (say, translating Goethe's *Faust* from German to English) and having a human interpreter provide a live interpretation of a dramatic reading of some poems. Figure 1.9 shows how the Java translation process achieves greater portability.

As Figure 1.9 illustrates, Bytecode can run on any computer that has a JVM to interpret for it. Thus a programmer can write a Java application and make its Bytecode available to the public via the Web without having to recompile it for the many different types of computers that may be used to run it. Because Bytecode is a kind of machine language, the source code also remains protected.

■ How Does Interpreting Code Differ from Executing It?

Direct execution   The process by which a computer performs the actions specified in a machine language program

Interpretation   The translation, while a program is running, of non-machine language instructions (such as Bytecode) into executable operations

Direct execution of code differs significantly from **interpretation** of code. A computer can directly execute a program that is compiled into its machine language. The JVM, for example, is a machine language program that is directly executed. The computer cannot directly execute Bytecode, however. Instead, it must run the JVM to interpret each Bytecode instruction into instructions it can execute. The JVM does not produce machine code, like a compiler, but rather reads each Bytecode instruction and gives the computer a corresponding series of operations to perform. Because each Bytecode instruction must first be interpreted, the computer cannot run Bytecode as quickly as it can execute machine language. Slower execution is the price we pay for increased portability.

■ How Is Compilation Related to Interpretation and Execution?

It is important to understand that compilation, interpretation, and execution are distinct processes. During compilation, the computer runs the compiler, which translates a program into Bytecode or machine language. *Execution* refers to the computer following machine language instructions. The JVM is a machine language program that executes directly on the computer; its job is to take Bytecode instructions and interpret them into machine language instructions that are then executed.

With Java, during compilation, the computer executes the compiler program, which takes Java source code as input and produces Bytecode as output. The compiler is then replaced by the JVM in the computer's memory, and the JVM is executed with the Bytecode as its input. The effect is that the computer carries out the operations specified by the Bytecode, just as if it could execute the Bytecode directly. Figure 1.10 illustrates this process.

The output from a compiler can be saved for future use. Thus, once a Java application has been compiled, it can be used repeatedly without being recompiled. For example, the JVM is a program that was compiled by someone else, which you simply use whenever you need to run some Bytecode.

Viewed from a different perspective, the JVM makes the computer look like a different computer, one that has Bytecode as its machine language. The computer itself hasn't changed—it remains the same collection of electronic circuits—but the JVM makes it act like a different machine. When a program is used to make one computer act like another, we call it a **virtual machine**. For convenience, we may refer to the computer as "executing a Java application," but keep in mind this is just shorthand for saying that "the computer is executing the JVM running a Java application."

> **Virtual machine** A program that makes one computer act like another

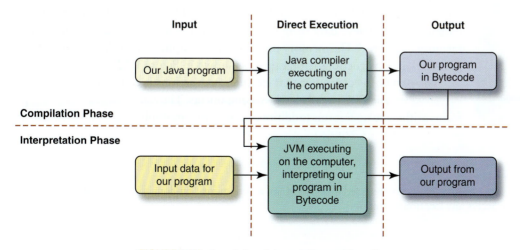

FIGURE 1.10　Compilation, Interpretation, and Execution

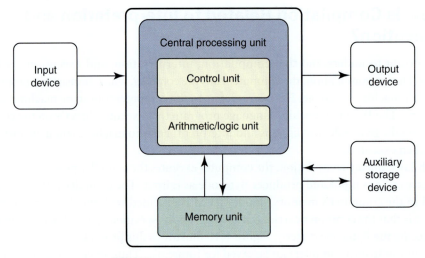

FIGURE 1.11 Basic Components of a Computer

1.6 : What's Inside the Computer?

Memory unit Internal data storage in a computer

Central processing unit (CPU) The part of the computer that executes the instructions (object code) stored in memory; made up of the arithmetic/logic unit and the control unit

Arithmetic/logic unit (ALU) The component of the central processing unit that performs arithmetic and logical operations

You can learn how to use a programming language, write applications, and run (execute) these applications without knowing much about computers. If you know something about the parts of a computer, however, you can better understand the effect of each instruction in a programming language.

Most computers have six basic components: the memory unit, the arithmetic/logic unit, the control unit, input devices, output devices, and auxiliary storage devices. Figure 1.11 shows a stylized diagram of the basic components of a computer.

The **memory unit** is an ordered sequence of storage cells, each capable of holding a piece of data. Each memory cell has a distinct address to which we refer to store data into it or retrieve data from it. These storage cells are called memory cells, or memory locations.[6] The memory unit holds data (input data or the product of computation) and instructions (programs), as shown in Figure 1.12.

The part of the computer that executes instructions is called the **central processing unit (CPU)**. The CPU usually has two components. The **arithmetic/logic unit (ALU)** performs arithmetic operations (addition, subtraction, multiplication, and division) and

---

6. The memory unit is also referred to as RAM, an acronym for "random access memory" (because we can access any location at random).

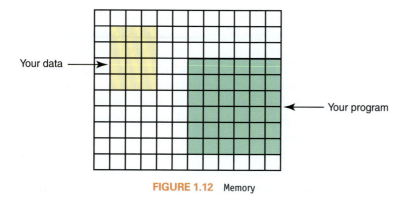

FIGURE 1.12   Memory

logical operations (comparing two values). The **control unit** manages the actions of the other components so that program instructions execute in the correct order.

To use computers, we must have some way of getting data into and out of them. **Input/output (I/O) devices** accept data to be processed (input) and present data that have been processed (output). Common input devices include keyboards, mice, other "pointing" devices, and bar-code scanners. Common output devices are printers and liquid crystal display (LCD) screens.

For the most part, computers simply move and combine data in memory. The many types of computers differ primarily in terms of the size of their memory, the speed with which data can be recalled, the efficiency with which data can be moved or combined, and limitations on I/O devices.

Computers support a wide variety of **peripheral devices**, which include input and output devices and auxiliary storage devices. An **auxiliary storage device**, or secondary storage device, holds coded data and instructions (programs) for the computer until we actually want to use them. Instead of inputting data every time, we can input it once and have the computer store it onto an auxiliary storage device. Then, whenever we need to use the data, we simply tell the computer to transfer the data from the auxiliary storage device to its memory. An auxiliary storage device therefore serves as both an input device and an output device.

Typical auxiliary storage devices include various types of disk drives. A hard disk is like a cross between a compact disc player and a tape recorder. It uses a thin disk made out of magnetic material. A read/write head (similar to the record/playback head in a tape recorder) travels across the spinning disk, retrieving or recording data stored as magnetic spots on the surface of the disk.

Unlike the memory unit, which loses its contents when the computer's power is turned off, the data on the hard disk is preserved even when the computer is shut down. Have you ever been typing a report in your word processor and lost all of your work because of a power failure? If so, you've experienced the temporary nature of the memory unit. But saving your work regularly to the hard disk helps prevent a complete loss of your work, as the copy on disk will survive the power loss. Because the hard disk uses magnetism to store data, it can be sensitive to stray magnetic fields.

Control unit   The component of the central processing unit that controls the actions of the other components so that instructions (the object code) execute in the correct sequence

Input/output (I/O) devices   The parts of the computer that accept data to be processed (input) and present the results of that processing (output)

Peripheral device   An input, output, or auxiliary storage device attached to a computer

Auxiliary storage device   A device that stores data and programs in encoded form outside the computer's main memory

Hardware The physical components of a computer

Software Computer programs; the set of all programs available on a computer

Clock An electrical circuit that sends out a train of pulses to coordinate the actions of the computer's hardware components; its speed is measured in hertz (cycles per second)

In contrast to magnetic storage, a CD-ROM or DVD-ROM drive uses a laser to read information stored optically on a plastic disk. Some forms of CDs and DVDs can also be used to store (write) data. Optical storage is immune to stray magnetic fields, but CDs and DVDs can warp if they get too warm, and the writable ones can be damaged by prolonged exposure to strong sunlight.

A magnetic tape drive was a typical auxiliary storage device in the early days of computing. It is still used to back up (make a copy of) the data on a disk in case the disk becomes damaged.

Collectively, all of these physical components are known as **hardware**. The programs that allow the hardware to operate are called **software**. Hardware usually is fixed in design; in contrast, software is easily changed. In fact, the ease with which software can be manipulated is what makes the computer such a versatile, powerful tool.

Background Information

What Makes One Computer Faster Than Another?

The faster a computer is, the more quickly it responds to our commands and the more work it can do in less time. But what factors affect the speed of a computer? The answer is quite complex, but let's consider some of the essential issues.

In computer advertising, you often see numbers such as 3.2 GHz, and the ads clearly want you to believe that they are an important contributor to speed. But what does such a number really mean? The abbreviation GHz is short for gigahertz, which means billions of cycles per second. What's cycling at this speed is the pulse of the computer—an electrical signal called the **clock**, which generates a continuous sequence of precisely regulated on/off pulses that are used to coordinate all of the actions of the other circuitry within the computer. It's called a clock because it bears a similarity to the steady ticking of a mechanical clock. But if you want a better sense of what it does, think of the clock as akin to the rhythmic swinging of an orchestra conductor's baton, which keeps all of the instruments playing in time with one another.

The clock ensures that all components of the computer do their jobs in unison. It's clear that the faster the clock, the faster the components work. But that's just one factor that affects speed.

Although we write our programs as if the computer always fetches just one instruction at a time and executes that instruction to completion before fetching the next one, modern computers are not so simple. They often fetch and execute multiple instructions at once (for example, most can simultaneously do integer and real arithmetic, while retrieving values from memory). In addition, they start fetching the next instruction from memory while executing prior instructions. The number of instructions that the computer can execute simultaneously also has a significant effect on speed.

A computer may also have multiple "cores," which is a way of saying that it has more than one CPU. Each core can run a program, so a computer with dual cores can run two

Background Information

programs at once. In most cases, the individual programs do not run any faster. If the computer has multiple programs to execute, however, it can run the set of programs in less time.

Different computers also work with data broken into chunks of different sizes. The computer in a microwave oven may work with 8 bits at a time, whereas a laptop typically handles 32 bits at once. Higher-performance machines work with data in units of 64 bits. The more data the computer can process at once, the faster it will be, assuming that the application has a need to work with larger quantities of data. The computer in the microwave is plenty fast enough to do its job—your popcorn would not pop any faster if it had a 64-bit processor!

It is not uncommon to see, for example, a 2.4 GHz, 64-bit computer that can process many instructions at once, which is significantly faster than a 3.2 GHz, 32-bit computer that handles fewer instructions in parallel. The only way to accurately judge the speed of a computer is to run an application on it and measure the time it takes to execute.

Other major hardware factors that affect speed are the amount of memory (RAM) and speed of the hard disk. When a computer has more memory, it can hold more programs and data in its memory. With less memory, it must keep more of the programs and data on the hard disk drive, shuffling them between disk and memory as it needs them. The hard disk takes as much as a million times longer to access data than RAM does, so you can see that a computer with too little RAM can be slowed down tremendously. Disks themselves vary significantly in the speed with which they access data.

Software also affects speed. As we will see in later chapters, problems can be solved more or less efficiently. A program that is based on an inefficient solution can be vastly slower than one that is more efficient. Different compilers do a better job of translating high-level instructions into efficient machine code, which also affects speed. And operating systems (which we explain next) also vary in their efficiency. The raw speed of the hardware is masked by the overall efficiency of the software. As a programmer, you can therefore have a strong influence on how fast the computer seems to be.

1.7 : What Is System Software?

In addition to the software that we write or purchase, some programs in the computer are designed to simplify the **user/computer interface**, making it easier for humans to use the machine. The interface between the user and the computer consists of a set of I/O devices and associated software that allows the user to communicate with the computer. We work with the keyboard, mouse, and screen on our side of the interface boundary; wires attached to the keyboard and the screen carry the electronic pulses that the computer manipulates on its side of the interface boundary. At the boundary itself is a mechanism that translates information for the two sides.

User/computer interface A connecting link that translates between the computer's internal representation of data and representations that humans are able to work with

When we communicate directly with the computer through an interface, we use an **interactive system**. Interactive systems allow direct entry of source code and data and provide immediate feedback to the user. You're probably most familiar with interactive processing—you use the mouse to click a button on a web page, which then asks you for some information that you enter through the keyboard, and you click another button when you're done.

In contrast, batch systems require that all data be entered before an application runs, and they provide feedback only after an application has been executed—for example, an electric company runs a batch program to print out the millions of bills that it mails to its customers each month. In this book we focus largely on interactive systems, although in Chapter 6 we discuss file-oriented applications, which share certain similarities with batch systems.

The set of programs that simplifies the user/computer interface and improves the efficiency of processing is called **system software**. It includes the JVM and the Java compiler as well as the operating system and the editor (see Figure 1.13). The **operating system** manages all of the computer's resources. It can input programs, call the compiler, execute object code, and carry out any other system commands.

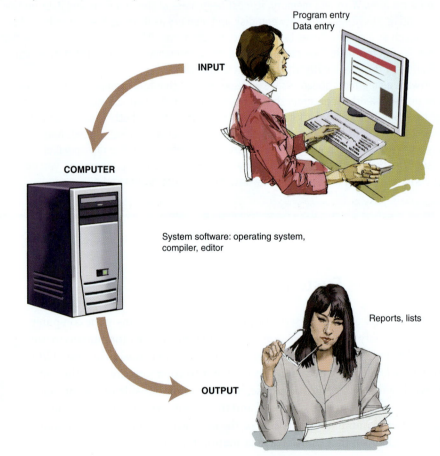

FIGURE 1.13   User/Computer Interface

1.8 : Problem-Solving Techniques

We solve problems every day, often remaining unaware of the process we are going through. In a learning environment, we usually are given most of the information we need: a clear statement of the problem, the necessary input, and the required output. In real life, of course, the process is not so simple. We often have to define the problem ourselves and then decide which objects we should work with and what their behaviors should be.

After we understand and analyze a problem, we must come up with a potential solution—a set of objects and the algorithms for their operations. Although we solve problems all the time, we typically do so intuitively. We don't really think about how to fit the groceries into the refrigerator or how to fit an appointment into our schedule. In the problem-solving phase of computer programming, however, we explicitly design such problem solutions.

For example, each item in our grocery bag is an object with certain properties (dimensions, whether it has to remain upright, and so on) and the refrigerator is an object that contains additional objects and empty spaces. We need to develop an algorithm that lets us find an empty space in the refrigerator into which we can fit each grocery object. We may also need an algorithm for rearranging the contents of the fridge, so as to create a larger space.

As you can see, programming requires us to become conscious of the strategies we use intuitively to solve problems. Of course, some programming problems will be completely new to us. In those cases, formal problem-solving techniques can help us tackle the problem. Here we look at some specific approaches.

■ Ask Questions

If you are given a task orally, you ask questions—When? Why? Where?—until you understand exactly what you have to do. If your instructions are written, you might put question marks in the margin, underline a word or a sentence, or indicate in some other way that the task is not clear. Your questions may be answered by a later paragraph, or you might have to discuss them with the person who assigned you the task.

Here are some of the questions you might ask in the context of programming:

- What do I have to work with—that is, which objects does the problem require?
- What do the objects look like?
- What tasks do the objects perform on their data?
- How much input is there?
- How do I know when I have input the last value?
- What should my output look like?
- How do the objects work together to solve the problem?
- What special error conditions might come up?

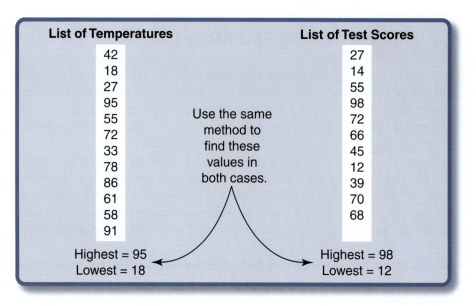

FIGURE 1.14 Look for Things That Are Familiar

■ Look for Things That Are Familiar

Never reinvent the wheel. If a solution already exists, use it. If you've solved the same or a similar problem before, just repeat or modify your solution. In fact, people are good at recognizing similar situations. Once we've learned how to go to the store to buy milk, we don't need to learn how to go to the store again when we need to buy eggs or candy. In programming, certain problems occur again and again in different guises. A good programmer recognizes when an existing class of objects can be plugged into the solution directly, or with some modification. For example, finding the daily high and low temperatures is really the same problem as finding the highest and lowest grades on a test. You want the largest and smallest values in a collection of numbers (see Figure 1.14).

When we recognize an object that we've seen before, we reuse it in the new problem. Even if an existing class isn't exactly what we need, it can serve as the starting point for a new class. In Chapter 10, we see how we can implement this problem-solving strategy in Java by using a mechanism called *inheritance,* which allows us to define a new object that adds to and perhaps modifies the capabilities of an existing object.

■ Solve by Analogy

Often a problem may remind you of one you have seen before. You may find solving the problem at hand easier if you remember how you solved the other problem. In other words, you can draw an analogy between the two problems. For example, a solution to a perspective projection problem from an art class might help you figure out how to compute the distance to a landmark when you are on a cross-country hike. As you work your way through the new prob-

FIGURE 1.15 Analogy

lem, you may come across things that differ from the old problem, but usually you can deal with these minor details one at a time.

Analogy is really just a broader application of the strategy of looking for things that are familiar. When you are trying to find an algorithm for solving a problem, don't limit yourself to computer-oriented solutions. Step back and try to get a larger view of the problem. Don't worry if your analogy doesn't match perfectly—the only reason for starting with an analogy is that it gives you a place to start (see Figure 1.15). The best programmers are people who have broad experience solving all kinds of problems.

■ Means-Ends Analysis

Often the beginning state and the ending state are given, but the problem requires you to define a set of interactions between objects that takes you from one state to the other. Suppose you want to go from Boston, Massachusetts, to Austin, Texas. You know the beginning state (you are in Boston) and the ending state (you want to be in Austin). The problem is how to get from one place to the other.

In this example, you have lots of options. You can take a plane, walk, hitchhike, ride a bike, or whatever. The method you choose depends on your circumstances. If you're in a hurry, you'll probably decide to fly.

Once you've identified the essential objects and their capabilities (airplane; fly between cities), you have to work out the details. It may help to establish intermediate goals that are easier to meet than the overall goal. Suppose a really cheap, direct flight to Austin goes out of Newark, New Jersey. You might decide to divide the trip into legs: Boston to Newark, and then Newark to Austin. Your intermediate goal is to get from Boston to Newark. Now you merely have to examine the means of meeting that intermediate goal (see Figure 1.16). Is there an object (airplane) that has the necessary capabilities (fly between Boston and Newark)?

The overall strategy of means-ends analysis is to define the ends and then to analyze your means of achieving them. This process translates easily to computer programming. That is, you begin by writing down what the input is and what the output should be. Then you consider the available objects and the actions they can perform, and you design a set of interactions among those objects that can transform the input into the desired results. If no appropriate object is available, then you may have to create a new one.

Start: Boston **Goal**: Austin	**Means**: *Fly*, walk, hitchhike, bike, drive, sail, bus
Start: Boston **Goal**: Austin	**Revised Means**: Fly to Chicago and then to Austin; *fly to Newark and then to Austin:* fly to Atlanta and then to Austin
Start: Boston **Intermediate Goal**: Newark **Goal**: Austin	**Means to Intermediate Goal**: *Commuter flight*, walk, hitchhike, bike, drive, sail, bus
Solution: Take commuter flight to Newark and then catch cheap flight to Austin	

FIGURE 1.16 Means-Ends Analysis

■ Divide and Conquer

We often break up large problems into smaller units that are easier to handle. Cleaning the whole house may seem overwhelming; cleaning each room, one at a time, seems much more manageable. The same principle applies to programming. We break up a large problem into smaller pieces that we can solve individually (see Figure 1.17). We divide the problem into its compo-

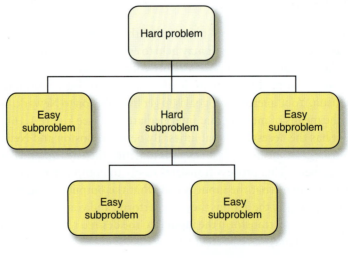

FIGURE 1.17 Divide and Conquer

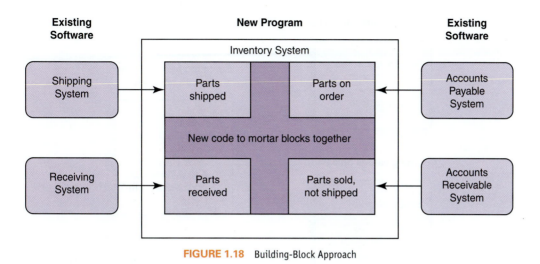

FIGURE 1.18 Building-Block Approach

nent objects, and for each class of objects we define a set of capabilities. Of course, the working pieces must be assembled and integrated into a working solution.

■ The Building-Block Approach

Another way of attacking a large problem is to see if any solutions for smaller pieces of the problem already exist. It may be possible to combine these solutions to solve most of the big problem. This strategy is just a combination of the look-for-familiar-things and divide-and-conquer approaches. You look at the big problem and see that it can be divided into smaller problems for which solutions already exist. Solving the big problem is then just a matter of putting the existing solutions together, like mortaring together blocks to form a wall (see Figure 1.18).

With an object-oriented programming language, the building blocks are classes. We often solve a problem by looking in the class library to see which solutions have been developed previously; we then write a small amount of additional code to put the pieces together.

■ Merging Solutions

Another way to combine existing solutions is to merge them on a step-by-step basis. For example, to compute the average of a list of values, we must both sum and count the values. If we already have separate solutions for summing values and for counting the number of values, we can combine them. If we first do the summing and then do the counting, however, we have to read the list twice. We can save steps by merging these two solutions: read a value and then

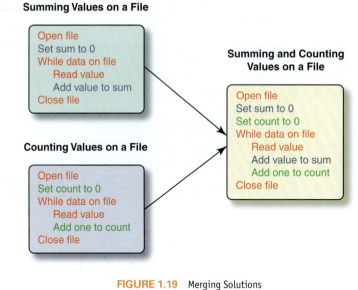

FIGURE 1.19 Merging Solutions

add it to the running total and add 1 to our count before going on to the next value. Figure 1.19 shows the common steps in red, and the differing steps in blue and green, with the merged solution containing just one copy of the common steps. When you're writing an operation for a class, and existing operations can be used but partially duplicate each other's actions, think about merging the steps they perform instead of simply using them one after the other.

■ Object-Oriented Problem Solving

Brainstorming Freely listing all the objects that may contribute to the solution of a problem

Filtering Reviewing the initial list of objects to identify duplicate and unnecessary objects

The initial step in solving many problems is to identify the objects. Some of these will be obvious from the problem description (an application of the "look for things that are familiar" strategy). For others, you may have to do some **brainstorming**. For example, in a datebook application, it is obvious that objects representing dates, times, and event names are needed. With some brainstorming, however, we might also conjecture that having a calendar, location name, event duration, and weekly (versus unique) event objects would be useful. Here, we are using the analogy of a physical datebook to guide our design.

Our initial list is just a first attempt to identify the objects. It gives us a place to begin. After freely listing all the objects we can think of, we review the list and look for duplicate objects and objects that aren't really needed. This **filtering** step produces a smaller list of distinct objects that we believe are sufficient to solve the problem. As part of the filtering stage, we may recognize alternative approaches and choose one set of objects over another set.

As an example, in a highway traffic management system we may list managers, drivers, lights, and cars as objects. In filtering the list, we see that the problem can be solved either by representing managers and drivers or by representing lights and cars, but we don't need both. We may also find that the Java class library contains objects that we can use to implement items on our list. For example, we could use Java classes for representing various forms of dates and times with the datebook problem.

Starting with the filtered list, we use role-playing to identify which operations are associated with the objects and how they interact. We call the operations **responsibilities**, and the interactions **collaborations**. For example, we may start with the scenario of adding a new event to our datebook. As we go through the new-event process, we identify the objects that are involved and determine which operations we expect them to supply, such as deciding that a date object should have an operation that lets us set the month, day, and year to values input by the user. A scenario often involves means-ends analysis, as we identify the available means (operations) and define new operations that need to be developed.

After the object responsibilities are identified, we design the algorithm for each one. For example, we may need a way to compute the number of days between two dates. In designing the algorithm, we must decide how data is represented within the object. A date could be represented in several ways:

September 28, 2007	Words and numbers
9, 28, 2007	Three numbers
2453879	Number of days since an arbitrary date

We refer to the ways in which the data values are represented as the **attributes** of the object.

Once the objects are designed, we write a **driver** program that begins the processing by instantiating objects and coordinating their interactions.

In this book, we introduce you to Java's object classes and operations in a gradual manner. In each chapter, we add to our knowledge of Java so that we can tackle a growing range of problems. We also gradually build up a set of our own classes that we use repeatedly in successive chapters. At first the problems may seem trivial, but we have much to learn before we can write more sophisticated programs. Soon, however, we encounter problems that require thoughtful use of these problem-solving techniques. By reusing the classes that we have developed in earlier chapters, we will be able to write much more sophisticated applications in later chapters.

Coming up with a solution for a particular problem is not always a cut-and-dried process. Just the opposite, in fact—it is usually a trial-and-error process requiring several attempts and refinements. We test each attempt to see if it really solves the problem. If it does, that's great. If it doesn't, we try again. We typically use a combination of the techniques we've described to solve any nontrivial problem.

■ Mental Blocks: The Fear of Starting

Writers are all too familiar with the experience of staring at a blank page, not knowing where to begin. Programmers often have the same difficulty when they first tackle a big problem. They look at the problem and it seems overwhelming (see Figure 1.20).

Responsibilities The operations associated with a class of objects

Collaborations The interactions between the classes that are needed to solve a problem

Attributes The values defined by a class that are used to represent its objects

Driver A program for creating the objects and coordinating their collaborations to solve the problem

FIGURE 1.20   Mental Block

Remember that you always have a place to begin when trying to solve any problem: Write the problem down on paper in your own words so that you understand it. Once you paraphrase the problem, you can focus on each of the subparts individually instead of trying to tackle the entire problem at once. This process gives you a clearer picture of the overall problem. It helps you see pieces of the problem that look familiar or that are analogous to other problems you have solved in the past. It also pinpoints areas where something is unclear, where you need more information.

As you write down a problem, you tend to group things together into small, understandable chunks of data and operations, which may be natural candidates for objects. Your description of the problem may collect all of the information about data and results into one place for easy reference. Then you can see the beginning and ending states necessary for means-ends analysis.

Most mental blocks are caused by a failure to truly understand the problem. Writing down the problem in your own words is a good way to focus on the subparts of the problem, one at a time, and to understand what is required for a solution.

Party Planning

Problem: You and some friends want to have a party on Saturday night, and you need to get ready for it.

Brainstorming the Initial Objects: You're familiar with this problem from having attended other parties. Here, we apply object-oriented problem solving to the planning process, to see how it works. Let's start by brainstorming the objects needed for a good party. You need a good location, a sound system, some music, room to dance, and snacks. Anything else? People, of course! We tend not to think of our friends as "objects," but in this case they are part of our solution. Here is the initial list:

Location
Sound system
Music
Room to dance
Snacks
People

Now you filter this list. "Room to dance" is an attribute of "a good location," so you can drop it from the list, although you may make a note that it is one attribute of the location. The filtered list is

Location with room to dance
Sound system
Music
Snacks
People

Initial Responsibilities: Next, you develop the list of responsibilities and collaborations for each object. You have an apartment with a big living room that can serve as the location. But you need to rearrange the furniture. Here is our first class, with its initial responsibilities:

Location with room to dance
Rearrange furniture

One of your friends, James, has a sound system and a great music collection. You need to move it from his apartment, across town, and set it up in your living room. After the party, it needs to be taken apart and returned. Another friend, Sally, has a car that you can use to move the sound system. James will arrange the songs and play them. Snacks need to be purchased and set out. Here are those classes and their responsibilities.

Sound system

- Move to location via car
- Set up
- Break down

Music

- Arrange playlist
- Play songs

Snacks

- Purchase
- Set out

Scenario: Based on your experiences with parties that have gone well (looking for things that are familiar), you and your friends go through a dry run of the party: invite people, get food, move furniture, move the sound system, choose music, set up the sound system, welcome guests, have snacks available, dance for most of the evening, wind down with some party games, say goodbye to guests as they leave, take down the sound system and move it back, move the furniture back.

Now it's time to divide and conquer all of this work by assigning the responsibilities. At this point you realize that your initial list of objects isn't appropriate (this happens quite a lot in programming). The objects are really you, Sally, and James. The guests don't have any responsibilities other than to have a good time! The location, sound system, and food aren't active in the process. Rather, they are really analogous to the passive data values of a program.

Sally can get the food and help James deliver the sound system. James can set up the sound system and select the music. You can invite the people and move the furniture. Sally can purchase the food. On the evening of the party, you can answer the doorbell, James can run the sound system and lead the games, and Sally can take care of the food. After the party, you can move the furniture back, and Sally can help James return the sound system to his apartment.

Here is a list of the "objects" we've identified and their responsibilities:

You

- Invite guests
- Move furniture
- Answer doorbell
- Say goodbye to leaving guests
- Move furniture back

Sally

- Buy food
- Help James deliver the sound system
- Take care of food at party
- Help James return the sound system

James

Select music and gather it together
Deliver and set up sound system
Run sound system
Lead games
Return sound system

Each of these responsibilities requires further expansion—for example, it takes James several steps to set up the sound system. The responsibilities are just high-level solutions. Developing a complete solution requires working out all of the details. Computers require such complete solutions. Fortunately, for party planning, you can count on your friends to work out the details.

Our collection of objects needs to be coordinated in carrying out their responsibilities. We don't just perform these steps in random fashion. In programming, such a coordinating plan is the driver. We write a series of steps that refers to each object and its responsibility as necessary. For example:

You: Call guests.

Sally: Buy food.

James: Select music. Deliver sound system (collaborate with Sally for delivery).

You: Move furniture. Welcome guests.

Sally: Take care of food.

James: Run sound system. Help lead games.

You: Say goodbye to guests. Move furniture back (collaborate with Sally and James).

James: Return sound system (collaborate with Sally).

As we will see, Java uses a similar mechanism (known as a method call) for naming an object and one of its responsibilities to get the object to carry out an action. Over the next few chapters you will gain a great deal of experience with writing and calling methods.

We've illustrated problem solving in a noncomputer context to show that these techniques are very general. Even if your career takes you in a direction that doesn't require computer programming, the skills that you learn in this course can be applied in many different situations. In learning to program, you will hone your problem-solving abilities to a high degree.

1.9 : Testing and Debugging

Even the best-laid plans sometimes go awry. Along the way, we will offer tips on what to do when things don't work as expected. We will also offer advice on how to avoid problems (programming bugs) in the first place.

Testing and Debugging Hints

1. Be sure to understand the problem before you start trying to solve it.
2. Note anything that is unclear and ask questions to clarify the problem.
3. Rewrite the problem statement in your own words.
4. Identify the required objects and their responsibilities.
5. Use the problem-solving techniques discussed in this chapter to help develop your solution.
6. Keep in mind the actions that a computer can perform when developing solutions for it.

Summary

We think nothing of turning on a television and sitting down to watch it. Television is a complex communication tool that we use easily. Today, computers are nearly as common as televisions—that is, just a normal part of our lives. Like televisions, computers are based on complex principles but are designed for easy use.

Computers are dumb; they must be told what to do. A true computer error is extremely rare (and usually crops up because of a component malfunction or an electrical fault). Because we tell the computer what to do, most errors in computer-generated output are really human errors.

Computer programming is the process of developing a problem solution for a computer to execute. It encompasses a problem-solving phase as well as an implementation phase. After analyzing a problem, we develop and test a general solution (a design). This general solution becomes a concrete solution—a program—when we write it in a high-level programming language. A program coordinates the actions of a set of objects (data and associated operations) that collaborate to solve the problem.

A class is a specification for creating an object. It provides a way to indicate the types of values that the object may hold and the operations that can be applied to the object. Once a class has been defined, any number of objects can be created from it.

The instructions that make up the program (the source code) are either compiled into machine code (the language used by the computer) or Bytecode (the language used by the Java Virtual Machine). After we correct any errors or "bugs" that show up during testing, the program is ready to use.

Once we begin to use the program, it enters the maintenance phase. Maintenance involves correcting any errors discovered by users and changing the program to reflect changes in the users' requirements.

Data and instructions are represented as binary numbers (numbers consisting of just 1s and 0s) in electronic computers. The process of converting data and instructions into a form usable by the computer is called coding.

A programming language reflects the range of operations that a computer can perform. In this book, you will learn to write application programs in the high-level programming language called Java. The basic control structures in the Java programming language—sequence, selection, loop, subprogram, and asynchronous control—are based on the fundamental operations of the computer. Java provides the ability to collect data and operations into objects, as specified by classes, which other applications can then reuse.

Computers are composed of six basic parts: the memory unit, the arithmetic/logic unit, the control unit, input devices, output devices, and auxiliary storage devices. The arithmetic/logic unit and control unit together form the central processing unit. The physical parts of the computer constitute hardware. The programs that are executed by the computer are called software. System software is a set of programs designed to simplify the user/computer interface. It includes the compiler, the operating system, the JVM, and the editor.

The most important phase of any programming project is the development of the initial solution to the problem. Object-oriented problem solving focuses on the objects in the problem, and their responsibilities and collaborations. We use problem-solving techniques such as analogy, means-ends analysis, divide and conquer, building blocks, and merging solutions to help us organize our efforts in this phase.

Today computers are widely used in science, engineering, business, government, medicine, production of consumer goods, and the arts. Learning to program in Java can help you use these powerful tools more effectively. In addition, the problem-solving skills that you develop through programming can be applied in many noncomputer contexts.

LEARNING Portfolio

Quick Check

Quick Check exercises are intended to help you decide whether you've met the goals set forth at the beginning of each chapter. If you understand the material in the chapter, the answer to each question should be fairly obvious. After reading a question, check your response against the answers listed at the end of the Quick Check. If you don't know an answer or don't understand the answer that's provided, turn to the page(s) listed at the end of the question to review the material.

1. What is a computer program? (p. 5)
2. What are the three phases in a program's life cycle? (pp. 5–7)
3. Is an algorithm the same as a program? (pp. 10–12)
4. What are the advantages of using a high-level programming language? (pp. 25–27)
5. What is the difference between machine code and Bytecode? (pp. 27–28)

6. What part does the Java Virtual Machine play in the compilation and interpretation process? (pp. 28–29)

7. What are the six basic components of a computer? (pp. 29–32)

8. What is meant by the term object, in the context of programming? (pp. 8–10)

9. Name the five basic ways of structuring statements in Java. (pp. 13–15)

10. What is the difference between hardware and software? (p. 32)

11. What should you do before you begin to code a problem solution in Java? (pp. 5–7, 35)

12. Name the problem-solving technique in which we break the problem into more manageable chunks. (pp. 38–39)

13. Which problem-solving technique would be a natural choice in planning a hike between two campgrounds? (pp. 37–38)

14. In the following problem statement, what are the objects: "Compute the area of a circle, given its radius." (pp. 40–41)

Answers

1. A computer program is a list of instructions performed by a computer. 2. The three phases of a program's life cycle are problem solving, implementation, and maintenance. 3. No. A program is an algorithm written in a programming language. All programs are algorithms, but not all algorithms are programs. 4. A high-level programming language is easier to use than an assembly language or a machine language. Also, programs written in a high-level language can be run on many different computers. 5. Machine code is the native binary language that is directly executed by any particular computer. Bytecode is a standardized portable machine language that is executed by the Java Virtual Machine, but it is not directly executed by the computer. 6. It translates the Bytecode instructions into operations that are executed by the computer. 7. The basic components of a computer are the memory unit, arithmetic/logic unit, control unit, input devices, output devices, and auxiliary storage devices. 8. A collection of data and associated operations that can be applied to the data. 9. Sequence, selection, loop, subprogram, and asynchronous. 10. Hardware comprises the physical components of the computer; software is the collection of programs that run on the computer. 11. Understand the problem and develop an algorithmic solution to the problem. 12. Divide and conquer. 13. Means-ends analysis. 14. Area, circle, and radius are the obvious objects.

Exam Preparation Exercises

1. Explain why the following series of steps is not an algorithm, then rewrite the series so that it is.

   Shampooing

   1. Rinse.

   2. Lather.

   3. Repeat.

2. Describe the input and output files used by a compiler.

3. In the following recipe for chocolate pound cake, identify the steps that are branches (selection) and loops, and the steps that make references to subalgorithms outside the algorithm.

Preheat the oven to 350 degrees

Line the bottom of a 9-inch tube pan with wax paper

Sift 2 ¾ c flour, ¾ t cream of tartar, ½ t baking soda, 1 ½ t salt, and 1 ¾ c
   sugar into a large bowl

Add 1 c shortening to the bowl

If using butter, margarine, or lard, then
 add ⅔ c milk to the bowl,
else
 (for other shortenings) add 1 c minus 2 T of milk to the bowl

Add 1 t vanilla to the mixture in the bowl

If mixing with a spoon, then
 see the instructions in the introduction to the chapter on cakes
else
 (for electric mixers) beat the contents of the bowl for 2 minutes at medium
    speed, scraping the bowl and beaters as needed

Add 3 eggs plus 1 extra egg yolk to the bowl

Melt 3 squares of unsweetened chocolate and add it to the mixture in the bowl

Beat the mixture for 1 minute at medium speed

Pour the batter into the tube pan

Put the pan into the oven and bake for 1 hour 10 minutes

Perform the test for doneness described in the introduction to the chapter on cakes

Repeat the test once each minute until the cake is done

Remove the pan from the oven and allow the cake to cool for 2 hours

Follow the instructions for removing the cake from the pan, given in the introduction to
    the chapter on cakes

Sprinkle powdered sugar over the cracks on top of the cake just before serving

4. Put a check next to each of the following items that is a peripheral device.

_____ **a.** Disk drive

_____ **b.** Arithmetic/logic unit

_____ **c.** Magnetic tape drive

_____ **d.** Printer

_____ **e.** CD-ROM drive

_____ **f.** Memory

_____ **g.** Auxiliary storage device

_____ **h.** Control unit

_____ **i.** LCD display

_____ **j.** Mouse

5. Next to each of the following items, indicate whether it is hardware (H) or software (S).

_____ **a.** Disk drive

_____ **b.** Memory

LEARNING / Portfolio

_____ **c.** Compiler

_____ **d.** Arithmetic/logic unit

_____ **e.** Editor

_____ **f.** Operating system

_____ **g.** Object program

_____ **h.** Java Virtual Machine

_____ **i.** Central processing unit

6. Distinguish between information and data.

7. You are planning a trip. Which problem-solving strategy would you use?

8. You are designing a house. Which problem-solving strategy would you use?

9. You are lost on a hike. Which problem-solving strategies would you use?

10. Identify the obvious objects in the recipe in Exercise 3.

11. What is Bytecode?

12. How does interpretation differ from direct execution?

13. Which of the following converts a source program in a high level-language into machine language?

    a. JVM

    b. Assembler

    c. Editor

    d. Compiler

    e. Operating system

14. What are the two major components of the CPU?

15. How does storing data in RAM (main memory) differ from storing it on a disk?

Programming Warm-Up Exercises

1. Look up a recipe for angel food cake in a cookbook. Identify the obvious objects in the recipe. Then identify which portions of this algorithm consist of a sequence of instructions, where branches occur, where loops occur, and where subprograms are called.

2. Find a set of instructions for operating an appliance that requires you to set the date and time, such as a DVD player, microwave oven, clock radio, or a computer. Identify the obvious objects in the instructions. Then identify which portions of this algorithm consist of a sequence of instructions, where branches occur, where loops occur, and where subprograms are called.

3. Music notation works much like a programming language. Identify the symbols and notation in music that indicate a unit of music in a sequence of such units, that indicate repetition of a section of music, that indicate a choice between endings of a song, and that

indicate a separate section to be played or sung at a given point. If you aren't familiar with musical notation, you'll need to do some research in books on basic musicianship.

4. Browse through the next several chapters of this book and identify Java statements that are used for branching and looping. (*Hint:* Look in the table of contents.)

Programming Problems

1. Write an algorithm for driving from where you live to the nearest airport that has regularly scheduled flights. Restrict yourself to a vocabulary of 20 words plus numbers and place names. You must select the appropriate set of words for this task. The purpose of this exercise is to give you practice in writing simple, exact instructions with a small vocabulary, just as a computer programming language requires you to do.

2. Write an algorithm for making a peanut butter and jelly sandwich, using a vocabulary of just 20 words (you choose the words). Assume that all ingredients are available in the cabinet or refrigerator and that the necessary tools are in a drawer under the kitchen counter. The instructions must be very simple and exact because the person making the sandwich has no knowledge of food preparation and takes every word literally.

3. Write an algorithm for doing your laundry, using a vocabulary of just 20 words (you choose the words). Assume that you have the detergent, bleach, fabric softener, and any other objects needed to do the laundry, and that the starting state is you standing before a washing machine with your laundry and these objects. The ending state is a set of clean, neatly folded laundry items (no starch in the socks, please).

Case Study Follow-Up

1. Expand the instructions for Sally's responsibility to make the shopping list. It may help to imagine that you are writing the instructions for someone else to follow.

2. You have another friend who plays guitar and sings. How might you change the plan for the party and reassign the responsibilities?

3. This occasion marks the first time you've ever given a party, and you're unsure of your plans. How could you check them out before the party to confirm that you've covered everything that needs to be done?

2 The Elements of Java

Goals

Knowledge Goals

To:

- Understand the difference between syntax and semantics
- Understand the distinction between built-in types and objects
- Recognize how the `char` type and `String` class are related and differ
- See the difference between objects in general and their use in Java
- Understand the difference between a named constant and a variable
- See why it is important to use meaningful identifiers in Java
- Understand what happens in an assignment operation
- Recognize how `void` and value-returning methods differ in their use

Skill Goals

To be able to:

- Read and understand the formal syntax rules governing Java programs
- Distinguish between reserved words and identifiers
- Create and recognize legal Java identifiers
- Write simple output statements using the `System.out` class
- Construct a Java application
- Declare fields of type `char` and `String`
- Assign values to variables
- Construct string expressions
- Use comments to clarify programs
- Instantiate a `Scanner` object
- Write `String` input operations using the `Scanner` class
- Design an interactive user interface

1876
Alexander Graham Bell invents the telephone, and obtains one of the most valuable patents in history

1882
William S. Burroughs leaves his job at a bank to pursue the invention of an accurate and efficient adding machine

1889
Herman Hollerith patents his Tabulating Machine, which is used to expedite the processing of census data in 1890

1895
Italian inventor Guglielmo Marconi sends and receives his first radio signal, demonstrating the feasibility of wireless communication

1901
The keypunch, which cuts holes or notches in a punch card, emerges in the form it remains for the next 50 years

1904
John A. Fleming builds on Thomas Edison's work, and invents the diode vacuum tube, which converts AC signals to DC signals

Introduction

Now that we have a general sense of what computer programming and problem solving involve, it's time to get down to the business of actually writing a Java application. In this chapter we introduce enough of the Java programming language to enable us to write a simple application that does something interesting. We'll be working with data in the form of strings of characters.

We begin the chapter by introducing some notation that helps us see how to write Java code. Next we look specifically at some basic Java elements. Once we have all of the necessary pieces, we put them together into an application, and then briefly review the mechanics of getting an application to run on the computer.

1906
The National Electrical Signaling Company's radio station in Massachusetts hosts the first broadcast radio program of speech and music on Christmas Eve

1911
The Calculating, Tabulating, and Recording Company (CTR) is established

1915
Physicist Manson Benedicks discovers that AC can be converted to DC using the germanium crystal, providing the basis for microchips

1919
W. H. Eccles and F. W. Jordan invent the electronic trigger circuit, or today's flip-flop switching circuit

1920–1921
Playwright Karl Capek introduces the word "robot" in his work "Rossum's Universal Robots"

1924
The Calculating, Tabulating, and Recording Company is renamed by T. J. Watson to International Business Machines, or IBM

53

2.1 : Learning a Language: Grammar and Words

If you've ever studied a foreign language, you know that it takes more than memorizing vocabulary to master use of the language. There are also grammar rules that explain how to connect the words to form meaningful sentences. Computer languages are much the same. They must be more precisely defined than human languages, however, because the computer lacks the intelligence to "make sense" of anything. The "sentences" we write in a computer language are merely instructions that trigger the operation of electronic circuits. In this section we look at some notation that allows us to write the rules of Java with the necessary precision. We then examine an example: the rule for writing new words.

We've already seen one working program: the `HelloWorld` program from Chapter 1.

```java
public class HelloWorld
{
  public static void main(String[] args)
  {
    System.out.println("Hello World!");
  }
}
```

We were able to change the message output by this program simply by substituting "Universe" in place of "World." But what do all of those other words mean? Why are there so many braces, parentheses, and brackets mixed in among them? And what's going on with the periods that have other words jammed up against them? We're about to find out the answers to those questions and more, and the answers all have to do with what we call syntax and semantics.

■ Syntax and Semantics

A programming language is a set of rules, symbols, and special words used to construct a program. A language is defined by both **syntax** (grammar) and **semantics** (meaning).

Syntax is a formal set of rules that defines exactly which combinations of letters, numbers, and symbols can be used in a programming language. The syntax of a programming language leaves no room for ambiguity. To avoid ambiguity, syntax rules themselves must be written in a very simple, precise, formal language called a **metalanguage**.

> **Syntax** The formal rules governing how valid instructions are written in a programming language
>
> **Semantics** The set of rules that determines the meaning of instructions written in a programming language
>
> **Metalanguage** A language that is used to write the syntax rules for another language

Learning to read a metalanguage is like learning to read the playbook for a sport. Once you understand the notation, you can learn the plays that give a team its competitive edge. It's true that many people learn a sport simply by watching others play, but what they learn is usually just enough to allow them to take part in casual games. You could learn Java by following the examples in this book, but a serious programmer, like a serious athlete, must take the time to read and understand the rules and to see how they are applied.

Syntax rules show us how the elements of a programming language—the basic building blocks of code—can be assembled into useful constructs. If our code violates any of the rules of the language—by misspelling a crucial word or leaving out an important comma, for instance—the program is said to have *syntax errors*. The compiler will be unable to fully translate the program until we fix them.

Theoretical Foundations

Q.E.D

Metalanguages

Metalanguage is the word *language* with the prefix *meta*, which means "beyond" or "more comprehensive." In other words, a metalanguage is a language that goes beyond a normal language by allowing us to speak precisely about that language. It is a language for talking about languages.

One of the first computer-oriented metalanguages was the *Backus-Naur Form* (*BNF*), which is named for John Backus and Peter Naur, who developed it in 1960. BNF is an extremely simple language. When we say simple, however, we mean that the metalanguage itself has very few symbols and rules. Unfortunately, that simplicity forces each syntax definition to be written using many symbols, so that it becomes long and difficult to read. In this book, we use another metalanguage, called a syntax template. Syntax templates show at a glance the form of a Java construct.

One final note: Metalanguages show only how to write instructions that the compiler can translate. They do not define what those instructions do (their semantics). Formal languages for defining the semantics of a programming language exist, but they are beyond the scope of this text. Throughout this book, we will describe the semantics of Java in English.

■ Syntax Templates

In this book we write the syntax rules for Java using a metalanguage called a *syntax template*. A syntax template is a generic example of the Java construct being defined. Colored shading shows which portions are optional and an ellipsis (. . .) indicates an item that can be repeated. A color word or symbol is written in Java code just as it is in the template. A black word is defined by another template.

Let's look at an example. Here are a pair of syntax templates that specify a set of rules for the children's game, Simon Says:

Simon Says

```
  Simon says   Action   · · ·
```

Action

```
  any of

    move forward
    move backward
    touch nose
    rub tummy
    pat head
    jump up and down
```

The first template shows that a Simon Says consists of the specific (colored) words, Simon says, which are optional (because they have shading around them), followed by an Action (which is defined in another template). The ellipsis indicates that the combination within the box can be repeated as many times as desired. In the second template, we see that Action is defined as any one of six items, each of which is a specific set of words.

■ Words That Java Supplies: Reserved Words

In syntax templates, any words or symbols shown in color are meant to be written exactly as you see them. If you were to look at a complete set of Java syntax templates, you would find only 52 distinct words (plus some special symbols) that appear in color. Those words are Java's predefined vocabulary.

Java programs would be pretty limited if those were the only words we could use. As we see in the next section, most of the words that appear in our Java programs are ones that we (or other programmers) define. But those 52 words are reserved for use by Java, and we are not allowed to redefine them. For obvious reasons, such words are called reserved words.

> **Reserved word** A word that has a specific pre-defined meaning in Java

Appendix A lists all of the reserved words in Java. Throughout this text, we use the color red to distinguish reserved words within the text and in programs. Here again is `HelloWorld`, with the reserved words highlighted:

```java
public class HelloWorld
{
    public static void main(String[] args)
    {
        System.out.println("Hello World!");
    }
}
```

There are half a dozen of the reserved words that you won't see in this text, because they apply to features of Java that are beyond an introductory programming course. We'll gradually introduce the others in the chapters to come. In addition to `public`, `class`, `static`, and `void`, in this chapter you'll learn about `private`, `package`, `new`, `char`, and `final`.

■ Words That We Make Up: Identifiers

We mainly use reserved words to specify actions in a program or in defining new words that represent classes, objects, operations, and other elements of our programs. New words that we define are called *identifiers* (we formally define this term shortly). Reserved words cannot be used as identifiers. The restriction that an identifier cannot be the same as a reserved word is an example of a semantic rule. The syntax templates alone won't tell us this. Now, let's see what they do tell us.

The following template defines a Java identifier. Remember that black words refer to another template, so there must be two more templates, Letter and Digit.

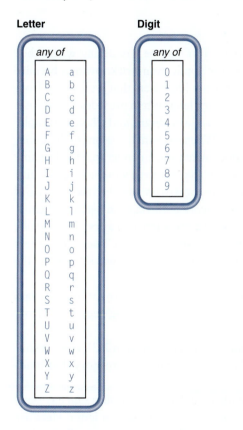

We read the template for an identifier as follows: It begins with a letter or an underscore or a dollar sign. It may then optionally have a letter, a digit, an underscore, or a dollar sign. After that, there may optionally appear any number of letters, digits, underscores, and dollar signs.

Remember that Letter and Digit represent additional templates. You can probably guess what they are, but we show them here for completeness:

Letter

any of

A a
B b
C c
D d
E e
F f
G g
H h
I i
J j
K k
L l
M m
N n
O o
P p
Q q
R r
S s
T t
U u
V v
W w
X x
Y y
Z z

Digit

any of

0
1
2
3
4
5
6
7
8
9

Thus a letter can be any one of the uppercase or lowercase letters, and a digit can be any of the numeric characters 0 through 9. Because all of the symbols in these templates are in color, we don't have to refer to any other templates to complete the definition of Identifier. Here are some examples of valid identifiers:

```
SomeName    easy_to_read    OkBuThArDtOrEaD    _Not_a_good_idea    $4_the_system
```

It's clear that the syntax rules do not prevent us from making up meaningless or unreadable names. Whether a program is readable depends on the care that we put into writing it. Readability has a big impact on the amount of work that it takes to maintain a program. The last two examples also hint at another semantic rule: Identifiers that start with an underscore or dollar sign have special uses, and we should avoid them in our programs.

Let's take another look at `HelloWorld` and see which parts are reserved words and which are identifiers. We highlight the reserved words in blue and the identifiers in yellow. As you can see, most of the program is made up of identifiers and reserved words.

```java
public class HelloWorld
{
    public static void main(String[] args)
    {
        System.out.println("Hello World!");
    }
}
```

The code for `HelloWorld` includes seven identifiers. You may be wondering where they came from. It's obvious that `HelloWorld` is the name of the application (we know that because we made that one up). `String`, `System`, `out`, and `println` are identifiers that were taken from the Java *library*, a large collection of object classes that every Java system provides for our use.

Programmers at Sun Microsystems developed the original Java library, and when they implemented those classes, they made up the identifiers for them. When we want to use one of these convenient predefined classes, we look it up in the library documentation and refer to it by the name the original programmers gave it. Predefined identifiers aren't like reserved words: We could give our own identifiers the same names, but we usually don't want to do so because then the same word would have two meanings (and Java will make us do extra work to distinguish between them).

> **Identifier** A name associated with a package, class, method, or field and used to refer to that element
>
> **Method** A subprogram in Java
>
> **Field** A named place in memory that holds data

The remaining two identifiers in `HelloWorld` are `main` and `args`. Technically, Java considers them to be identifiers that we've chosen. But, as we'll see shortly, this part of the program is really following a required pattern, so we always "choose" the same identifiers here.

Later in the chapter, we see how to define our own identifiers for holding data values. In the meantime, we'll be able to do quite a bit by just using ones we get from the library. Now it's time for some formal definitions.

An **identifier** can be the name of a package (defined in Section 2.3), class, a subprogram (called a **method** in Java), or a place in the computer's memory that holds data (called a **field** in Java).

As we've noted, identifiers beginning with an underscore or dollar sign have special meaning in some Java systems, so it is best to begin an identifier with a letter. Here are some additional examples of valid identifiers that are more like those you typically see in a program:

```
sum_of_squares    J9    box_22A    getData    MAXIMUM    Bin3D4    count    Count
```

Note that the Java compiler considers the last two identifiers—`count` and `Count`—to be completely different names. The uppercase and lowercase forms of a letter are two distinct characters to the computer. Here are some examples of invalid identifiers and the reasons they are invalid:

Invalid Identifier	Explanation
40Hours	Identifiers cannot begin with a digit
Get Data	Blanks are not allowed in identifiers
box-22	The hyphen (–) is a math symbol (minus) in Java
empty_?	Special symbols such as **?** are not allowed (other than **$** and **_**)
char	The word **char** is a reserved word

Now that we've seen how to write identifiers, let's look at some of the things that Java allows us to name.

Matters of Style

Using Meaningful, Readable Identifiers

The names we use to refer to things in our code are totally irrelevant to the computer. The computer behaves in the same way whether we call a value 3.14159265, `pi`, or `cake`, as long as we always call it the same thing. Of course, it is much easier for someone to understand your code if the names chosen for identifiers describe what they represent. Choose a name that will be meaningful when others read it.

As mentioned earlier, Java is a case-sensitive language, which means that it sees uppercase letters as different from lowercase letters. The identifiers listed below represent five distinct names and are not interchangeable.

```
PRINTTOPPORTION   printtopportion   pRiNtToPpOrTiOn   printTopPortion
```

The last of these forms is the easiest to read. In this book, we use combinations of uppercase letters, lowercase letters, and underscores in identifiers. Many Java programmers use different capitalizations of identifiers as a way to indicate what they represent. Later in this chapter, we show you the conventions that we—and many other Java programmers—use.

2.2 : Building Blocks: Types, Classes, and Objects

■ Standard Types in Java

In Chapter 1, we saw that objects in a computer program consist of data and associated operations. Both data values and operations can be named with identifiers. Each piece of data within an object has a specific data type. The data type determines how the data is represented in the

> **Standard (built-in) type**
> A data type that is automatically available for use in every Java program
>
> **Primitive type** Any of the built-in types that represent integral, real, character, or Boolean values
>
> **Character set** A list of letters, digits, and symbols with corresponding binary representations in the computer

computer and the kinds of processing that can be applied to it. As part of specifying an identifier to represent a data value, we must indicate the type of the data.

Because some types of data are used very frequently, Java provides them for us. These data types are called **standard** (or **built-in**) **types**. You are already familiar with most of them from everyday life: integer numbers, real numbers, and characters. In this chapter we focus on character data. In Chapter 4, we examine the integer types `int` and `long`, and the real types `float` and `double`. By the end of Chapter 5, you'll be equally familiar with one more type, `boolean`. Java refers to all of these as **primitive types** because they are fully defined by the language itself. Objects, by contrast, are defined by the programmer. Java calls objects *reference types*, and we will see where this name comes from later in this chapter.

The `char` Data Type The built-in type `char` describes data consisting of one alphanumeric character—a letter, a digit, or a special symbol. Java uses a particular **character set**, or set of alphanumeric characters. Java's character set, which is called Unicode, includes characters for many written languages. In this book, we use a subset of Unicode that corresponds to an older character set called the American Standard Code for Information Interchange (ASCII). ASCII consists of the alphabet for the English language, plus numbers and symbols.

Here are some example values of type `char`:

```
'A'    'a'    '8'    '2'    '+'    '-'    '$'    '?'    '*'    ' '
```

Notice that each character is enclosed in single quotes (apostrophes). The Java compiler needs the quotes to be able to differentiate between the character data and other Java elements. For example, the quotes around the characters `'A'` and `'+'` distinguish them from the identifier A and the addition sign. Notice also that the blank, `' '`, is a valid character.

How do we write the single quote itself as a character? If we write `'''`, Java complains that we have made a syntax error. The second quote indicates the end of the (empty) character value, and the third quote starts a new character value. To deal with this problem, Java provides a special *escape sequence* that allows us to write a single quote as a character. That is, Java treats the sequence of two characters `\'` as a single character representing the quote. Thus, when we want to write the quote as a character in Java, we write

```
'\''
```

Notice that we use the backward slash, or backslash (\), as the escape character rather than the forward slash (/). As we will see in Chapter 4, Java uses the forward slash as a division sign, so it is important to recognize that the two slashes are different. A moment's thought reveals that this scheme introduces a new problem: How do we write the backslash as a character? The answer is that Java provides a second escape sequence, \\, that allows us to write a backslash. Thus we write the `char` value of the backslash in Java as follows:

```
'\\'
```

Be careful that you don't confuse this sequence with the // sequence, which begins a comment in Java (we look at comments a little later in this chapter).

In Chapter 5, we will see how Java provides operations that allow us to compare data values of type char. The Unicode character set uses a **collating sequence**, which is the predefined ordering of all the characters. In Unicode, 'A' compares as less than 'B', 'B' as less than 'C', and so forth. Also, '1' compares as less than '2', '2' as less than '3', and so on.

The type char is one of Java's primitive types. The String class, which allows us to work with collections of characters, such as words and sentences, is one of the classes provided for us in Java. Notice that char is in red because it is a reserved word. String is not in red because it is not a reserved word but a library class. To this point, we've discussed classes and objects in the abstract sense as part of the problem-solving process. Now we explore them in the sense of Java syntax and semantics, so that we can better appreciate the String class.

> **Collating sequence** The ordering of characters, with respect to one another, within a character set

Background Information

Data Storage

Where does our code get the data it needs to operate? Data is stored in the computer's memory. Memory is divided into a large number of separate locations or cells, each of which can hold a piece of data. Each memory location has a unique address we refer to when we store or retrieve data. We can visualize memory as a set of post office boxes, with the box numbers serving as the addresses used to designate particular locations.

Of course, the actual address of each memory location is a binary number in machine language. In Java, we use identifiers to name memory locations; the compiler and the Java Virtual Machine (JVM) then translate those identifiers into binary form for us. This translation represents one of the advantages provided by a high-level programming language: It frees us from having to keep track of the numeric addresses of the memory locations in which our data and instructions are stored.

■ Classes and Objects

In Chapter 1, we identified two phases of programming: problem solving and implementation. Often the same vocabulary is used in different ways in the two phases.

In the problem-solving phase, for example, an object is an entity or some thing that makes sense in the context of the problem at hand. A class is a description of a group of objects with similar attributes and behaviors.

In the implementation phase, a `class` is a Java construct that allows the programmer to describe an object. A `class` contains fields (data) and methods (subprograms) that define the behavior of the object. Think of a class in the general sense as a pattern for what an object looks like and how it behaves, and a Java `class` as the construct that allows you to simulate the object in code.

If a `class` is a description of an object, how do we get an object that fits the description? We use an operator called `new`, which takes the class name and returns an object of the kind defined by the class (we see how to do this later). The object that is returned is said to be an `instance` of the class. The act of creating an object from a class is thus called `instantiation`.

The `String` Class Whereas a value of type `char` is limited to a single character, a *string* (in the general sense) is a sequence of characters, such as a word, name, or sentence, enclosed in double quotes. In Java, a string is an object, an instance of the `String` class. For example, the following are strings in Java:

```
"Introduction to "   "Programming and Problem Solving"   " with Java "   "."
```

A string must be typed entirely on one line. For example, the string

```
"This string is invalid because it
is typed on more than one line."
```

is not valid because it is split across two lines before the closing double quote. In this situation, the Java compiler will issue an error message at the first line because it fails to find a matching quote. The message may say something like "unclosed string literal," depending on the particular compiler.

The quotes are not considered to be part of the string but are simply there to distinguish the string from other parts of a Java class. For example, the symbols `"12345"` represent a string made up of the characters 1, 2, 3, 4, and 5 in that order. If we write `12345` without the quotes, it is an integer quantity that can be used in calculations. Notice that we use the color blue for data values written in our code, regardless of whether they are string values, `char` values, or numeric values.

A string containing no characters is called the empty string. We write the empty string using two double quotes with nothing (not even spaces) between them:

```
""
```

The empty string is not equivalent to a string of spaces; rather, it is a special string that contains no characters.

To write a double quote within a string, we use another escape sequence, \". Here is a string containing both quotation marks and the escape sequence for a backslash:

```
"She said, \"Don't forget that \\ is not the same as the / character.\""
```

The value of this string is

```
She said, "Don't forget that \ is not the same as the / character."
```

Notice that we do not have to use the escape sequence \' to represent a single quote within a string. Similarly, we can write the double quote as a value of type char ('"') without using an escape sequence. In contrast, we have to use \\ to write a backslash as a char value or within a string. If you look again at HelloWorld, you can now appreciate that it contains a Java string (which we highlight):

```
public class HelloWorld
{
  public static void main(String[] args)
  {
    System.out.println("Hello World!");
  }
}
```

Java provides operations for joining strings, comparing strings, copying portions of strings, changing the case of letters in strings, converting numbers to strings, and converting strings to numbers. We will look at some of these operations later in this chapter and then cover the remaining operations in subsequent chapters.

At this point, you can identify each individual piece of HelloWorld as either a reserved word, an identifier, or a string. So much for basic vocabulary—now it's time to move on to sentences. We'll start with the one that displays the output in the HelloWorld application:

```
System.out.println("Hello World!");
```

In learning how this works, we'll introduce a little more syntax, but mainly we will focus on semantics.

■ Output Using System.out

Early computers used printers to display their output. Older programming languages included output statements, such as *print* or *write*, that would type information on the printer. When display screens replaced printers, output still appeared on the screen as if it was being typed by a printer, line by line. In the 1970s, however, computer scientists at the Xerox Palo Alto Research Center developed the idea of display windows, which opened up a new era in the design of user interfaces.

Today, virtually every computer operating system supports a graphical user interface (GUI) based on windows. Such interfaces make it much easier for people to use programs, but they require more work on the part of the programmer than did the old-fashioned printer-style output. Because Java was developed after the GUI became popular, it includes built-in features that support GUI output. Even so, the programming of such a user interface can still be rather complicated, so we defer coverage of this topic until we've explored more of the basics of programming.

Here we introduce a very simple way of writing messages on the screen that is similar to the technique used in older languages. To do so, we use an operation (method) associated with an output object called `System.out`.

> **Call** A statement that causes a method to be executed; in Java we call a method by writing its name, followed by a list of arguments enclosed in parentheses
>
> **Argument** An expression used for communicating values to a method

Calling Methods Methods provide the operations associated with objects. To use a method, we **call** it. A call to a method is a statement in Java that causes the method to be executed. We code the call statement simply by writing the name of the method, followed by a list of **arguments** enclosed in parentheses. The call causes the computer to jump to the instructions in the method, which use the values given as arguments. When the method has completed its task, the computer returns to the statement following the call. We'll revisit this mechanism in greater detail in Chapter 3. At this point, our goal is just to appreciate that wherever you write a method call in your code, work is done by a subprogram.

Here is the syntax template for a call statement:

Call

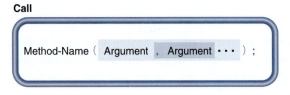

```
Method-Name ( Argument , Argument ••• ) ;
```

As you examine the template, note that the arguments in a call are optional, but the parentheses are required. We often write call statements of the following form:

```
methodName();
```

A synonym for the term "call" is *invoke*. That is, saying that a method is invoked is another way of saying that it is called.

We've said that a method is associated with an object. But how do we know which object? We precede the call with the name of an object. Sometimes a method is associated with a class itself, in which case we precede the call with the name of the class. The object name or class name is separated from the call by a dot. Let's take another look at the output statement from `HelloWorld`:

```
System.out.println("Hello World");
```

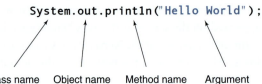

Class name   Object name   Method name   Argument

`System` is the name of a class, `out` is the name of an object that is contained within `System`, and `println` is the name of a method associated with `out`. Within the parentheses, the string `"Hello World!"` is an argument to that method. The `println` method is a subprogram that displays the value of the argument on the screen.

Now, let's take a closer look at output methods.

`print` and `println` Methods Java provides an object that represents an output device—by default, the screen. We invoke methods associated with this object, asking it to print something on the screen. The name of the object is `out`. Because it is contained in a class called `System`, we refer to it using the combination of the class name and the object name, joined by a dot: `System.out`. The methods associated with `System.out` are `print` and `println`. For example,

```
System.out.print("Susy Sunshine");
```

prints

```
Susy Sunshine
```

in a window on the screen. There are several things to notice about this statement. First, the method is invoked (called) by placing the method name (`print`) next to the object name (`out`) with a dot in between. Second, the "something" to be printed is a string that serves as an argument to the method. Notice that the string appears within the parentheses. What do you think the next code fragment prints?

```
System.out.print("Susy");
System.out.print(" ");
System.out.print("Sunshine");
```

If you said that the two code fragments print the same thing, you would be correct. Successive messages sent via the `print` method print the strings next to each other on the same line. If you want to go to the next line after the string is printed, you must use the `println` (pronounced "print line") method. For example, the code fragment

```
System.out.println("Susy");
System.out.println(" ");
System.out.println("Sunshine");
```

prints

```
Susy

Sunshine
```

Note that the `println` method does not go to the next line until *after* the string is printed. The second line contains a blank—it is not the empty string.

Before we move on, we should say just a bit more about `System.out`. As we've seen, `System` specifies the library class and `out` is the name of the actual object. Java calls `System.out` a qualified identifier. Qualification is what enables us to define an identifier in our program that is the same as one in the Java class library. Remember how we said that Java makes us do extra work to distinguish between the two meanings when we have this kind of duplication? Typing the class name and a period before the object name is that extra work. `System.out` and `out` (without qualification) are two different identifiers to Java. We'll see many examples in which we write calls to library methods using qualified names.

2.3 : Putting the Pieces Together: Application Construction

So far in this chapter, we have looked at the basic elements of Java code: reserved words, identifiers, and method calls. Now let's see how to collect these elements into an application.

■ Application Syntax and Semantics

Here's the syntax template for a Java application, which is identical to the template for a Java class:

Class

Import-Declaration ; · · ·

Class-Modifiers   · · ·   `class` Identifier

{

　Class-Declaration · · ·

}

> **Package**   A named collection of classes in Java that can be imported by a program

What does this template tell us? The first line says that a Java application may optionally begin with a series of Import-Declarations, each of which ends in a semicolon. Import-Declaration is defined in another template, but here we explain what it means. Java's library contains so many classes that they must be organized into groups called **packages**. Import declarations are statements that tell the Java compiler which library packages our program uses. We look at how to write import declarations shortly, but for now let's continue with our examination of this syntax template.

The next line may optionally begin with a series of Class-Modifiers (defined in another template), which are then followed by the word `class` and an identifier. This line is called the *heading* of the class. A Java application is a collection of elements that are grouped together into a class. The heading gives the class a name (the identifier) and may optionally specify some general properties of the class (the class modifiers).

The last three lines of the template show that the heading is followed by an open brace, an optional series of Class-Declarations, and a closing brace. These three elements make up the *body* of the class. The braces indicate where the body begins and ends, and the Class-Declarations contain all of the statements that tell the computer what to do. Here is the Java code for a class that omits all of the optional parts in the template:

```
class NothingExtra
{
}
```

Method main   For a class to be an application (a program), the class declarations must include the definition of a method called `main`. Here's the code for declaring a `main` method that doesn't do anything:

```
public static void main(String[] args)
{
}
```

We'll soon see what these words and symbols mean, but for now, just think of this as a formula for writing the outline of `main`. If we insert this method as a class declaration within the application, we get the simplest Java application we can write:

```
class DoNothing
{
  public static void main(String[] args)
  {
  }
}
```

As its name implies, this program does absolutely nothing. It is simply an empty shell of an application. Your job as a programmer is to add useful instructions inside this shell.

You may be wondering, "Am I going to have to memorize all of these special words and symbols?" The answer is yes. When you study any language, you must memorize both its vocabulary and its grammar. The best way to memorize Java syntax is to practice. Write down the code for the main method a few times, until you are able to write it without referring to this book. If there were a *Tourist's Book of Phrases for the Java Language*, the code for `main` would be right on the first page!

Class Modifiers   Now let's take a closer look at class modifiers. We use this set of keywords to specify certain properties of classes. Java defines quite a few class modifiers, but the only ones we need to be concerned with at this point are `public` and `private`. As the heading for `main` illustrates, the same modifiers are also used in declaring identifiers within classes, and we'll explore their meaning further when we see how to do that. For now, all of our classes have the modifier `public`; we won't define any `private` classes.

Class-Modifiers

any of
```
private

public
```

Access modifiers
Reserved words in Java
that specify where a
class, method, or field
may be accessed; two
examples are `public` and
`private`

The modifiers `public` and `private` are more precisely called **access modifiers** because they specify whether elements outside of the class can use the class. What's considered to be outside of the class? Any of the packages that we list in `import` declarations, any other class that imports the class being defined, and the JVM. The last of these is the one that's significant for applications—the JVM needs to access an application class to run it. Thus, we always write the word `public` in the heading for an application.

`import` **Declarations**   We've informally described `import` declarations. Here is the formal syntax diagram:

Import-Declaration

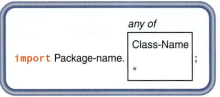

As the template shows, an `import` declaration begins with the keyword `import`, the name of a package, and a dot (period). Following the period, we can either write the name of a class in the package or type an asterisk (`*`). The declaration ends with a semicolon. If we want to use exactly one class from a particular package, then we simply give its name (Class-Name). More often, however, we want to use multiple classes in a package, and the asterisk is a shorthand notation to the compiler that says, "Import whatever classes from this package that this class uses." Here are some examples of `import` declarations, together with comments that explain them:

```
import java.util.Scanner;   // Import class Scanner in the java.util package
import java.io.*;           // Import additional input/output classes
```

Why would we ever want to use the first form, when the asterisk has the same effect and is easier to type? The first form documents the specific class that we intend to use (`Scanner`, in this example), and it causes the compiler to warn us if we mistakenly attempt to use another class from the package. In this book, we often use the asterisk instead of the Class-Name.

■ An Example Application: `PrettyPrint`

Enough of `HelloWorld`! Now that we've seen all of the syntax necessary to write an application, let's go ahead and try it out. One advantage of learning a computer language compared with learning a foreign language is that when we make a mistake, we don't have to worry about offending the computer. We can just keep trying until we get it right.

Suppose you want to write an application to print out a pretty pattern on the screen—something like:

```
   *       *       *       *
 *   *   *   *   *   *   *   *
*  *  *  *  *  *  *  *  *  *  *
 *   *   *   *   *   *   *   *
   *       *       *       *
```

Because this application is so simple, we don't need to apply our object-oriented problem-solving techniques, except to note that we can represent each of these lines with a string, which is an object. Thus we know that we need to output the following strings, one per line, in the order shown.

```
"   *       *       *       *"
" *   *   *   *   *   *   *   *"
"*  *  *  *  *  *  *  *  *  *  *"
" *   *   *   *   *   *   *   *"
"   *       *       *       *"
```

The method that outputs a string on a line by itself is `System.out.println`. We can therefore write these steps as:

```java
System.out.println("   *       *       *       *");
System.out.println(" *   *   *   *   *   *   *   *");
System.out.println("*  *  *  *  *  *  *  *  *  *  *");
System.out.println(" *   *   *   *   *   *   *   *");
System.out.println("   *       *       *       *");
```

We need to place this code within the `main` method:

```java
public static void main(String[] args)
{
  System.out.println("   *       *       *       *");
  System.out.println(" *   *   *   *   *   *   *   *");
  System.out.println("*  *  *  *  *  *  *  *  *  *  *");
  System.out.println(" *   *   *   *   *   *   *   *");
  System.out.println("   *       *       *       *");
}
```

Finally, we put the `main` method within a class, which we call `PrettyPrint`:

```java
public class PrettyPrint
{
  public static void main(String[] args)
  {
    System.out.println("   *       *       *       *");
    System.out.println(" *   *   *   *   *   *   *   *");
    System.out.println("*  *  *  *  *  *  *  *  *  *  *");
    System.out.println(" *   *   *   *   *   *   *   *");
    System.out.println("   *       *       *       *");
  }
}
```

And that is all it takes to write a Java application that outputs a nice pattern of stars!

■ Compiling and Running an Application

Once your application is stored in a file, you compile it by issuing a command to run the Java compiler. The compiler translates the application and then stores the Bytecode version into a new file. Sometimes the compiler may display a window with messages indicating errors in the application. Some systems let you click on an error message to automatically position the cursor in the editor window at the point where the error was detected.

If the compiler finds errors in your application (*syntax errors*), you must determine their cause, return to the editor and fix them, and then run the compiler again. Once your application compiles without errors, you can run (execute) it.

Some systems automatically run an application when it compiles successfully. On other systems, you must issue a separate command to run the application. Whatever series of commands your system uses, the result is the same: Your application is loaded into memory and executed by the JVM. The compiled version of your program that the JVM executes is stored in a file with `.class` appended to the class name.

Even though an application runs, it still may have errors in its design. After all, the computer does exactly what you tell it to do—even if that's not what you intended. If your application doesn't do what it should (*logic error*), you must revise the algorithm, return to the editor, and fix the code. Then you must compile and run the code again. This *debugging* process is repeated until the application works as planned (see Figure 2.1).

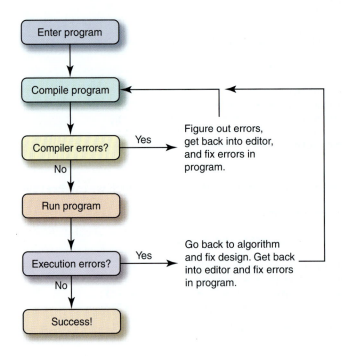

FIGURE 2.1 The Debugging Process

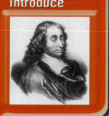

Blaise Pascal

One of the great historical figures in the world of computing was the French mathematician and religious philosopher Blaise Pascal (1623–1662), the inventor of one of the earliest known mechanical calculators.

Pascal's father, Etienne, was a noble in the French court, a tax collector, and a mathematician. His mother died when Pascal was three years old. Five years later, the family moved to Paris, where Etienne took over the education of the children. Pascal quickly showed a talent for mathematics. When he was only 17, he published a mathematical essay that earned the jealous envy of René Descartes, one of the founders of modern geometry. (Pascal's work actually had been completed before he was 16.) Pascal's essay was based on a theorem, which he called the *hexagrammum mysticum* (mystic hexagram), that described the inscription of hexagons in conic sections (parabolas, hyperbolas, and ellipses). In addition to the theorem (now called Pascal's theorem), the essay included more than 400 corollaries.

When Pascal was about 20 years old, he constructed a mechanical calculator that performed addition and subtraction of eight-digit numbers. His calculator required the user to dial in the numbers to be added or subtracted; the sum or difference then appeared in a set of windows. Pascal's motivation for building this machine may have been to aid his father in collecting taxes. The earliest version of the machine does, indeed, split the numbers into six decimal digits and two fractional digits, as would be used for calculating sums of money. It was hailed by his contemporaries as a great advance in mathematics, and Pascal built several more forms of his calculator. It achieved such popularity that many fake, nonfunctional copies were built by others and displayed as novelties. Several of Pascal's calculators still exist in various museums.

Pascal's box, as it is called, was long believed to be the first mechanical calculator. However, in 1950, a letter from Wilhelm Shickard to Johannes Kepler written in 1624 was discovered. This letter described an even more sophisticated calculator built by Shickard 20 years prior to Pascal's box. Unfortunately, the machine was destroyed in a fire and never rebuilt.

During his twenties, Pascal solved several difficult problems related to the cycloid curve, indirectly contributing to the development of differential calculus. Working with Pierre de Fermat, he laid the foundation of the calculus of probabilities and combinatorial analysis. One result of this work came to be known as Pascal's triangle, which simplifies the calculation of the coefficients of the expansion of $(X + Y)^N$, where N is a positive integer.

Pascal also published a treatise on air pressure and conducted experiments showing that barometric pressure decreases with altitude, helping to confirm theories that had been proposed by Galileo and Torricelli. His work on fluid dynamics forms a significant part of the foundation of that field. Among the most famous of his contributions is Pascal's law, which states that pressure applied to a fluid in a closed vessel is transmitted uniformly throughout the fluid.

When Pascal was 23, his father became ill, and the family was visited by two disciples of Jansenism, a reform movement in the Catholic Church that had begun six years earlier.

May We Introduce

The family converted, and five years later one of his sisters entered a convent. Initially, Pascal was not so taken with the new movement, but by the time he was 31, his sister had persuaded him to abandon the world and devote himself to religion. His religious works are considered no less brilliant than his mathematical and scientific writings. Some consider *Provincial Letters*, his series of 18 essays on various aspects of religion, to be the beginning of modern French prose.

Pascal returned briefly to mathematics when he was 35, but a year later his health, which had always been poor, took a turn for the worse. Unable to perform his usual work, he devoted himself to helping the less fortunate. Three years later, he died while staying with his sister, having given his own house to a poor family.

2.4 : Extending the Java Dictionary

■ How We Define New Words: Declarations

> **Declaration** A statement that associates an identifier with a field, a method, a class, or a package so that the programmer can refer to the item by name

How do we tell the computer what an identifier represents? We use a **declaration**, a statement that associates a name (an identifier) with a description of an element in a Java program (just as a dictionary definition associates a name with a description of the thing being named). In a declaration, we both name the identifier and indicate what it represents.

When we declare an identifier, the compiler picks a location in memory to be associated with it. We don't have to know the actual address of the memory location because the computer automatically keeps track of it for us.

To see how this process works, suppose that when we mail a letter, we have to put only a person's name on it and the post office will look up the address. Of course, everyone in the world would need a different name with such a system; otherwise, the post office wouldn't be able to figure out whose address was whose. The same is true in Java. Each identifier can represent just one thing. Every identifier you use in your code must be different from all others (except under special circumstances, such as qualified identifiers).

The syntax template for an application shows that Class-Declarations appear between the braces that indicate the start and end of the body of the class. Class declarations include method declarations (such as `main`) and field declarations. Let's take a look at field declarations.

■ Creating Words to Represent Values

Classes are made up of methods and fields. We've already heard that methods are operations. Fields are the components of a class that represent the values we work with. Values in a class can be of any type, including the primitive types or objects.

We use identifiers to refer to fields. In Java, you must declare every identifier before it can be used. The compiler can then verify that the use of the identifier is consistent with its declaration. If you declare an identifier to hold a `char` value and later try to store a number into it, for example, the compiler will detect this inconsistency and issue an error message.

A field can be either a constant or a variable. In other words, a field identifier can be the name of a memory location whose contents are not allowed to change or it can be the name of a memory location whose contents can change. First we'll look at declaring variables; then we'll see how to give them values. After that, we'll return to constants.

Variables Data is stored in memory. While an application is executing, different values may be stored in the same memory location at different times. This kind of memory location is called a **variable**, and its contents are the *variable value*. The symbolic name that we associate with a memory location is the *variable identifier* or *variable name*. In practice, we often refer to the variable name more briefly as the *variable*.

> **Variable** A location in memory, referenced by an identifier, that contains a data value that can be changed

Declaring a variable means specifying both its identifier and its data type or class. This specification tells the compiler to associate an identifier with a memory location and what kind of information it represents (for example, `char` or `String`). The following statement declares `myChar` to be a variable of type `char`:

```
char myChar;
```

Notice that this declaration does not specify a value to be stored in `myChar`. Rather, it specifies that the name `myChar` can hold a value of type `char`. At this point, `myChar` has been reserved as a place in memory but it contains no data. Soon, we will see how to actually put a value into a variable. (See Figure 2.2.)

Here are two example variable declarations:

```
String firstName;
char   middleInitial;
```

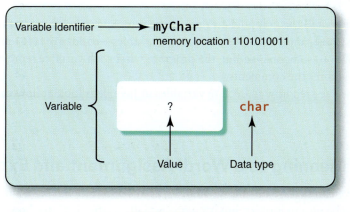

FIGURE 2.2 Variable

Here's the syntax template for a variable declaration:

Variable-Declaration

Modifiers Type-Name Identifier , Identifier • • • ;

In this template, modifiers specify additional properties of the variable. We'll see an example of one when we look at constants, and we'll introduce additional modifiers later as needed. Note that the modifiers are optional—we don't have to use any of them. Type-Name is the name of a type or class such as `char` or `String`. Notice also that a declaration always ends with a semicolon.

From the syntax template, you can see that we can declare several variables in one statement:

```
char letter, middleInitial, ch;
String firstname, lastName, title;
```

Here, three variables are declared to be `char` variables and three variables are declared to be `String` variables. Our preference, though, is to declare each variable with a separate statement because we can attach comments to the right of each declaration. As shown below, comments are words to the right of the characters `//`. Notice that we use the color green to distinguish comments in our code.

```
String firstName;        // A person's first name
String lastName;         // A person's last name
String title;            // A person's title, such as Dr.
char middleInitial;      // A person's middle initial
char myChar;             // A place to store one letter
```

These declarations tell the compiler to reserve memory space for three `String` variables—`firstName`, `lastName`, and `title`—and two `char` variables—`middleInitial` and `myChar`. The comments explain to someone reading the program what each variable represents. The compiler, however, ignores the comments.

Now that we've seen how to declare variables in Java, let's look at how to give them values.

■ Giving Meaning to a Word: Assignment and Expressions

At this point, we can declare an empty variable. That's a bit like having a car with an empty gas tank: It may be nice to look at, but it's not especially useful. Let's see how to fill it up.

Assignment   We set or change the value of a variable through an **assignment statement**. For example,

```
lastName = "Lincoln";
```

assigns the string value `"Lincoln"` to the variable `lastName` (that is, it stores the sequence of characters "Lincoln" into the memory associated with the variable named `lastName`).

Here's the syntax template for an assignment statement:

Assignment-Statement

Variable = Expression ;

The semantics (meaning) of the assignment operator (=) are "is set equal to" or "gets"; the variable is *set equal to* the value of the **expression**. Any previous value in the variable is replaced by the value of the expression.

Only one variable can appear on the left side of an assignment statement. An assignment statement is *not* like a math equation ($x + y = z + 4$). Instead, the expression (what is on the right side of the assignment operator) is **evaluated**, and the resulting value is stored into the single variable to the left of the assignment operator. A variable keeps its assigned value until another statement stores a new value into it.

The value assigned to a variable must be of the same type as the variable. For example, given the declarations

```
String firstName;
String middleName;
String lastName;
String title;
char middleInitial;
char myChar;
```

the following assignment statements are valid:

```
firstName = "Abraham";      // String value assigned to string variable
middleName = firstName;     // String variable assigned to string variable
middleName = "";            // String value assigned to string variable
lastName = "Lincoln";       // String value assigned to string variable
title = "President";        // String value assigned to string variable
middleInitial = ' ';        // char value assigned to char variable
myChar = 'B';               // char value assigned to char variable
```

Java is a **strongly typed** language, which means that a field can contain a value only of the type or class specified in its declaration.[1] For example, because of the preceding declaration,

---

1. Many early programming languages—some of which are still in use today—allow a value of any type to be stored in a variable. This weak typing was inherited from assembly language programming and has been a source of many programming errors. Most modern languages check that variables contain proper values, thereby helping us to avoid such errors.

Assignment statement
A statement that stores the value of an expression into a variable

Expression   An arrangement of identifiers, values, and operators that can be evaluated to compute a value of a given type

Evaluate   To compute a new value by performing a specified set of operations on given values

Strongly typed
A property of a programming language in which the language allows a variable to contain only values of the specified type or class

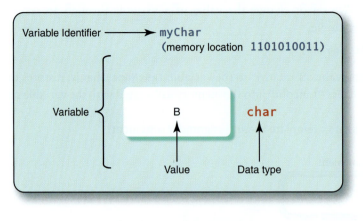

FIGURE 2.3 Variable with Value

the variable `myChar` can contain only a `char` value. If the Java compiler comes across an instruction that tries to store a value of the wrong type, it gives an error message, usually something like "Cannot assign String to char."

The following assignments are *not* valid:

Invalid Assignment Statement	**Explanation**
`middleInitial = "A.";`	`middleInitial` is of type `char`; `"A."` is a string
`myChar = firstName;`	`myChar` is of type `char`; `firstName` is of type `String`
`myChar = " ";`	`myChar` is of type `char`; `" "` is a one-character literal string
`firstName = Thomas;`	`Thomas` is an undeclared identifier
`"Edison" = lastName;`	Only a variable can appear to the left of `=`
`lastName = ;`	The expression to the right of `=` is missing

Figure 2.3 shows the variable `myChar` with the letter B stored in it.

String Expressions   Although we can't perform arithmetic on strings, Java provides the `String` class with a special string operation, called *concatenation*, that uses the + operator. Concatenating (joining) two strings yields a new string containing copies of the characters from both strings. For example, given the following declarations and assignment statements

```
String bookTitle;
String phrase1;
String phrase2;

phrase1 = "Introduction to Programming and Problem Solving ";
phrase2 = "with Java";
```

we could write

```
bookTitle = phrase1 + phrase2;
```

This results in **bookTitle** being set equal to the character string

`"Introduction to Programming and Problem Solving with Java"`

The order of the strings in the expression determines how they appear in the resulting string. If, for example, we write

`bookTitle = phrase2 + phrase1;`

then **bookTitle** is set equal to the string

`"with Java Introduction to Programming and Problem Solving "`

Concatenation works with string values as well as **String** variables. For example, suppose we have performed the following assignments:

```
word1 = "Introduction";
word3 = "Programming";
```

Then we could write the following statement:

`bookTitle = word1 + " to " + word3;`

As a result, **bookTitle** is assigned the following string:

`"Introduction to Programming"`

Occasionally we need to assign a string value that is too long to fit on one line. Then a concatenation expression is necessary, as in the following statement:

```
longSentence = "The Red-Wing Blackbird hovered precariously in the gusty " +
               "breeze as he tried to display his brilliant red and " +
               "yellow epaulets to his rival suitor. ";
```

Sometimes we may encounter a situation in which we want to add some characters to an existing string value. Suppose that **bookTitle** already contains `"Introduction to Programming"` and that we wish to complete the title. We could use a statement of the form

`bookTitle = bookTitle + " and Problem Solving with Java";`

This statement retrieves the value of **bookTitle** from memory, concatenates the string `" and Problem Solving with Java"` to form a new string, and then assigns the new string back to **bookTitle**. The new string replaces the old value of **bookTitle** (which is destroyed).

Theoretical Foundations

Assignment of Primitive Types Versus Objects

After reading the preceding discussion of assignment statements and expressions, you may wonder what really happens inside the computer when assignment occurs. For Java's primitive types that represent values such as characters and numbers, the answer is straightforward: The value on the right side of the equals sign (assignment operator) is stored in the memory location corresponding to the identifier on the left side of the equals sign.

But what about objects such as strings? Surely they can't fit into a single memory location? The answer is no, they can't. So how does assignment work in that case?

Assignment of objects is done indirectly. A variable of the object data type contains a value that identifies the memory address where the actual object is stored. When Java needs to operate on an object, it uses the value stored in the variable to find the object in memory. We say that the value *refers* to another location. This is why Java calls objects **reference types**.

> **Reference type**   A data type that holds a value representing a memory address (a reference) that refers to a place in memory where additional information is stored

This process takes place automatically, so we don't have to worry about it. With respect to assignment, however, it means that assigning one object variable to another works just the same as assigning one integer variable to another. The value contained in one variable is copied from its memory location into the location associated with the other variable. For an object, this value is an address in memory.

In Chapter 3, we return to this topic and note that it has some additional consequences. In the meantime, we will avoid situations where this issue might cause problems.

Initializer Expressions   Now that we have defined expressions, we can generalize the variable declaration syntax to allow for the use of an expression in initializing the field. We call this a field declaration.

Field-Declaration

> Modifiers   Type-Name   Identifier = Expression , Identifier = Expression ;

The following declarations are, therefore, legal:

```
String word1 = "Introduction";
String word3 = "Java " + word1;
String word5 = "Design " + word3;
```

They store `"Design Java Introduction"` as the initial value of variable `word5`.

Constants In Java, as in mathematics, a constant is something whose value never changes. A data value that is written directly in our code is called a **literal constant** (or *literal*). All single characters (enclosed in single quotes) and strings (enclosed in double quotes) are literal constants.

```
'A'   '@'   "Howdy boys"   "Please enter an employee number:"
```

An alternative to the literal constant is the **named constant** (or **symbolic constant**), which is introduced in a declaration statement. A named constant is just another way of representing a literal value. Instead of using the literal value directly in our code, we give the literal value a name in a declaration statement, and then we use that name in the code.

Here are two examples of named constant declarations:

```
final String BORDER = "+++++++++++++++++++++";
final char BLANK = ' ';
```

> **Literal constant** Any value written directly in Java
>
> **Named (symbolic) constant** A location in memory, referenced by an identifier, that contains a data value that cannot be changed

The only difference between declaring a constant and a variable is that, when declaring a constant, we include the modifier `final`, a reserved word, and follow the identifier with an initializer expression. The `final` modifier tells the Java compiler that this value is the last and only value that this identifier should have.

We have put the identifier names in all uppercase to help the reader quickly distinguish between variable names and constants. Using the literal value of a constant may seem easier than giving it a name and then referring to it by that name. In fact, named constants make a program easier to read, because they make the meaning of literal constants clearer. Also, named constants make it easier to change a program later on.

■ Where We Write Our Declarations

In the preceding discussion we have seen how to write individual declarations, but we haven't talked about where they go in our applications. As we've seen, a class contains class declarations, which can appear in any order. Thus we can mix fields and methods in any order. We find it easier to understand how a class works, however, when all of the field declarations appear before the method declarations; thus, we'll use that style throughout the text. Here is an example:

```java
public class SomeClass
{
  char someChar;
  final char BLANK = ' ';
  String someString = "2B || !2B";
  public static void main(String[] args)
  {
    .
    .
    .
```

Class Fields Versus Instance Fields   To keep matters simple, we've been ignoring an important point about the class fields. We've avoided modifiers other than `final` and `public` in all of our declarations. In fact, fields have a property that is distinguished by another modifier, `static`. As we'll see in Chapter 3, some fields are associated with individual objects, whereas others are associated with an entire class of objects. The former are called *instance fields* and the latter are called *class fields* (we formally define these terms in the next chapter).

We use the `static` modifier to specify that a field belongs to a class. If we omit this modifier, the field becomes an instance field. Thus all of the field declarations we've shown so far are actually for instance fields. At this point, we aren't ready to write classes from which we can create individual objects, so until we reach Chapter 3, all of our field declarations should include the `static` modifier. For instance, we should really write the preceding example as follows:

```
public class SomeClass
{
  static char someChar;
  static final char BLANK = ' ';
  static String someString = "2B || !2B";
  public static void main(String[] args)
  {
    .
    .
    .
```

Note that we've been using `static` with `main` all along. Just like fields, methods can be associated with objects or classes. From this, you can infer that `main` is an example of a class method. In the next chapter we'll see what all of this means and learn when it is appropriate to write class declarations without `static`. Until then, you should include the `static` modifier in any class declarations that you write.

Class Declarations Versus Local Declarations   In addition to class declarations, Java lets us declare variables and constants within methods. These declarations are called **local declarations**. In this case, Java does place a restriction on the placement of declarations: A declaration of a local identifier must appear prior to any statement that uses it. Here's an example showing the difference in placement of class and local declarations.

> **Local declaration**
> A declaration that appears within a method

```
public class Example
{
  static final char BLANK = ' ';                    // Class declaration
  public static void main(String[] args)
  {
    String firstName = "Sally";                      // Local declaration
    System.out.println(firstName);
```

Notice that the local declaration doesn't include any modifiers. Local fields cannot be associated with objects, so there is no need to use `static` to indicate this fact. Also, local fields cannot be `public`—they are available for use only within the method. The only modifier allowed with a local field declaration is `final`. That is, we can declare local variables and local constants.

Why would we want to declare a variable or constant in a method? Fields declared in the class declarations can be used within any method. Local fields can be used only within the method where they are declared. Sometimes you may want to make certain values available for use by all methods. At other times, a value is needed only within a particular method.

One final note about class declarations and class fields. Because Java uses the same word (class) to name both of these items, it is easy to confuse them. Class declarations are declarations that appear within a class, but outside of any method. Class fields are those fields declared in the class declarations using the `static` modifier.

Matters of Style

Capitalization Conventions

Programmers often use capitalization to provide a quick, visual clue as to what an identifier represents. Different programmers adopt different conventions for using uppercase letters and lowercase letters. Some use only lowercase letters, separating the English words in an identifier with the underscore character:

```
pay_rate    emp_num   pay_file
```

The convention used by many Java programmers and the one we use in this book is the following:

- Variables and methods begin with a lowercase letter and capitalize each successive English word.

  ```
  lengthInYards   middleInitial   hours
  ```

- Class names begin with an uppercase letter but are capitalized the same as variable names thereafter.

  ```
  PayRollFrame   Sample   MyDataType   String
  ```

  Capitalizing the first letter allows a person reading the code to tell at a glance that an identifier represents a class name rather than a variable or method. Java's reserved words use all lowercase letters, so the type `char` is lowercase. `String` is a class, so it begins with a capital letter.

- Identifiers representing named constants are all uppercase with underscores used to separate the English words.

  ```
  BOOK_TITLE   OVERTIME   MAX_LENGTH
  ```

These conventions are simply that—conventions. Java does not require this particular style of capitalizing identifiers. You may wish to write your identifiers in a different fashion. But whatever method you use, it is essential that you maintain a consistent style throughout your code.

■ Saying What We Really Mean: Documenting Code

All you need to create a working application is the correct combination of declarations and executable statements. The compiler ignores comments, but this kind of documentation is of enormous help to anyone who must read the code. Comments can appear anywhere in your code except in the middle of an identifier, a reserved word, or a literal constant.

Java comments come in two forms. The first is any sequence of characters enclosed by the `/*  */` pair. The compiler ignores anything within the pair. Here's an example:

```
String idNumber;    /* Identification number of the aircraft */
```

One special note about using this form of comment: When the first character of the comment is an asterisk, the comment takes on a special meaning that indicates it should be used by an automatic documentation generation program called **javadoc**. For now, we recommend that you avoid comments that start with `/**`.

The second, and more common form of comment, which we have already seen in several examples, begins with two slashes (`//`) and extends to the end of that line of the program:

```
String idNumber;    // Identification number of the aircraft
```

The compiler ignores anything after the two slashes to the end of the line.

Writing fully commented code is good programming style. A comment should appear at the beginning of an application or class to explain what it does:

```
// This application computes the weight and balance of a Beechcraft
// Starship-1 airplane, given the amount of fuel, number of
// passengers, and weight of luggage in fore and aft storage.
// It assumes that there are two pilots and a standard complement
// of equipment, and that passengers weigh 170 pounds each.
```

Another good place for comments is in field declarations, where comments can explain how each identifier is used. In addition, they should introduce each major step in a long code segment and should explain anything that is unusual or difficult to read (for example, a lengthy formula).

You should keep your comments concise and arrange them in the code so that they are easy to see and it is clear what they document. If comments are too long or crowd the statements, they make the code more difficult to read—just the opposite of what you intended!

2.5 ⋮ Opening the Door to User Input

An application needs data on which to operate. So far, we have written data only in the code itself, in literal and named constants. If this were the sole means by which we could enter data, we would have to change our code for each different set of values. In this section we look at ways of entering data into an application while it is running.

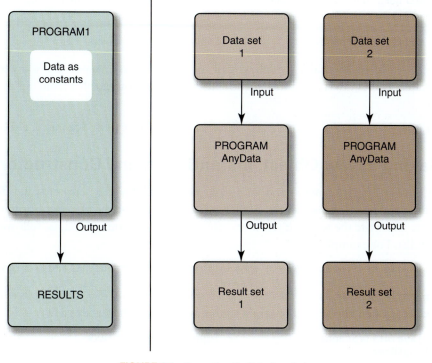

FIGURE 2.4 Separating the Data from Code

■ Input

One of the major advantages associated with computers is that an application can be used with many different sets of data. To do so, the data must be kept separate from the code until the code executes. Then method calls can copy values from the data set into variables in the application. Once values are in variables, the code can process them (see Figure 2.4).

The process of placing values from an outside data set into variables in an application is called *input*. The data for the application can come from an input device or from a file on an auxiliary storage device. We look at file input in detail in Chapter 6; here we consider only the standard input window, represented by the object `System.in`.

■ The `Scanner` **Class**

Unfortunately, Java doesn't make it quite as simple to input data from `System.in` as it does to output data to `System.out`. `System.in` is a very primitive object that is designed to serve as the basis for building more sophisticated objects. With `System.in`, we can input a single byte or a series of bytes (recall from Chapter 1 that a byte is eight binary bits). To be useful to us, this data must be converted into a string. The Java library contains a `Scanner` class that has a method called `nextLine`, which can be used to get a string from `System.in`. Other methods in class `Scanner` allow us to input numeric values, as we will see in Chapter 4.

We first need to bring class `Scanner` into our application by importing it from the package `java.util`:

```
import java.util.Scanner;          // Import Scanner class
```

Next, we declare a variable (which we call `in`) to be of class `Scanner`. It is okay to use `in` here, because `System.in` is a qualified identifier, so Java can distinguish it from our own identifier `in`.

```
Scanner in;                        // A variable of class Scanner, called in
```

■ Making a New Object: Instantiation and Constructors

We now have an empty `Scanner` variable, and we need to fill it with a `Scanner` value. To do so, we must instantiate a `Scanner` object. Earlier we said that we use the `new` operator to instantiate objects. We write the reserved word `new`, followed by the name of a class, followed by an argument list. For example:

```
in = new Scanner(System.in); // Instantiate a Scanner object and assign to in
```

In the same statement, we assign the new object to the variable `in`. Let's put these pieces together into a skeleton of an application program so that we can see where they go:

```
import java.util.Scanner;          // Import Scanner class
class InputDemo
{
  public static void main (String[] args)
  {
    Scanner in;                    // A variable of class Scanner, called in
    in = new Scanner(System.in);   // Instantiate a Scanner object and assign
                                   //    to in
    .
    .
    .
  }
}
```

The code following `new` looks very much like a method call. In fact, it is a call to a special kind of method called a constructor. Every class has at least one constructor method. The purpose of a constructor is to prepare a new object for use. The `new` operator creates an empty object of the given class and then calls the constructor, which can fill in fields of the object or take any other steps needed to make the object usable. For example, the constructor for class `Scanner` tells the new object to use `System.in` as its input source. Constructors are called only via the `new` operator; we cannot write them as normal method calls.

Constructors have a special property that requires some further explanation. The call to the constructor isn't preceded by an object name or a class name. If you stop to consider that the constructor creates an object before it is assigned to a field, you realize that it can't be associated with a particular object name. We don't have to precede the constructor name with the class name because the constructor always has the same name as the class, and that tells Java which class it belongs to.

The capitalization of a constructor doesn't follow our usual rule of starting a method name with a lowercase letter. Because we begin class names with an uppercase letter, and the constructor name must be spelled exactly the same, it follows the capitalization of its class.

■ The `nextLine` Method

The class `Scanner` provides us with a useful method called `nextLine`. Its name is descriptive of its function: The computer "reads" what we type into it on one line and returns the characters we type as a string. Here is an example of using `nextLine`:

```
String oneLineOfTyping;                 // A variable of class String
System.out.println("Enter a line of typing");  // Prompt the user to type a
                                        //   line
oneLineOfTyping = in.nextLine();        // Input what was typed
```

Now `oneLineOfTyping` contains whatever the user typed.

■ Value-Returning and `void` Methods

A call to `nextLine` is quite different from a call to `println`. We call `println` as a separate statement:

```
System.out.println("Enter a line of typing");
```

In contrast, `nextLine` is called from within an expression. In our example, the expression is part of an assignment statement.

```
oneLineOfTyping = in.nextLine();
```

Java supports two kinds of methods: **value-returning methods** and **void methods**. These methods are distinguished by how they are called. A value-returning method, such as `nextLine`, is called within an expression. When it returns, the value that it has computed takes its place in the expression, where it can be used for further computation. A `void` method, such as `println`, doesn't return a value. We call it as a separate statement and, when it has finished, execution picks up with the statement that follows it.

> **Value-returning method** A method that is called from within an expression and returns a value that can be used in the expression
>
> **void method** A method that is called as a separate statement; when it returns, processing continues with the next statement

■ Some Input and Output Etiquette

When an application inputs and outputs values that a human user supplies and reads, it performs interactive input/output. To make the application user-friendly, the programmer has to consider additional information that the user needs beyond the raw input and output. For example, the user must be prompted to enter values; otherwise, he or she won't know when or where to type the input. When the application outputs its results, it must label them so that they are meaningful. Labeling output also helps the user to distinguish among different values displayed by the application.

The following application uses `System.out.print` to display a prompting message, calls `nextLine` to read the name, and then outputs the name as part of a greeting, with a border above and below.

```java
//*********************************************************************
// Example.java
// Example Application that inputs from the screen and outputs to the
// screen.
//*********************************************************************
import java.util.Scanner;    // Import class Scanner
public class Example
{
  // Class declarations
  static final String BORDER = "+++++++++++++++++++++++"; // Message border
  static final char BLANK = ' ';                          // One blank

  public static void main(String[] args)
  {
    // Local declarations
    String firstName;                        // A string for first name
    Scanner in;                              // A Scanner for input
    // Actions
    in = new Scanner(System.in);             // Instantiate Scanner object
    System.out.println("Please enter your first name:");    // Prompt
    firstName = in.nextLine();               // Read in the name
    System.out.println(BORDER);              // Print the border
    System.out.print("Good morning");        // Print a message
    System.out.println(BLANK + firstName);   // Print a blank and the name
    System.out.println(BORDER);              // Print the border again
  }
}
```

If the user types in the name "Mary," the output screen would appear as shown here:

2.6 : An Example Application: `PrintName`

Here's another example of an application. The programmer selects the name for the application class; here we chose `PrintName`. Because an application is a class, we begin the name with an uppercase P.

```java
//*******************************************************************
// PrintName application
// This application inputs a name and prints it in two different formats
//*******************************************************************
import java.util.Scanner;

public class PrintName
{
  static final char COMMA = ',';
  static final char BLANK = ' ';

  public static void main(String[] args)
  {
    String first;                    // Person's first name
    String last;                     // Person's last name
    String middle;                   // Person's middle initial
    String firstLast;                // Name in first-last format
    String lastFirst;                // Name in last-first format
    Scanner in;                      // Input object

    in = new Scanner(System.in);
    System.out.print("Enter first name: ");    // Prompt for first name
    first = in.nextLine();                      // Get first name
    System.out.print("Enter last name: ");      // Prompt for last name
    last = in.nextLine();                       // Get last name
    System.out.print("Enter middle initial: ");// Prompt for middle initial
    middle = in.nextLine();                     // Get middle initial
    firstLast = first + BLANK + last;           // Generate first format
    System.out.println("Name in first-last format is " + firstLast);
    lastFirst = last + COMMA + BLANK            // Generate second format
                    + first + COMMA + BLANK;
    System.out.println("Name in last-first-initial format is "
                    + lastFirst + middle + ".");
  }
}
```

Now let's examine the `PrintName` application in detail. The application begins with a comment that explains what it does. Next comes an `import` declaration that tells the compiler we will use class `Scanner` from package `java.util`.

The `import` declaration is followed by the class heading and an open brace that begins the body of the class. The class contains class declarations of two constants and the method `main`. The first line of the method is its heading.

The body of the method contains local declarations of five `String` variables (`first`, `last`, `middle`, `firstLast`, and `lastFirst`) and a `Scanner` variable (`in`). A series of assignment and call statements follow.

We use spacing in the `PrintName` application to make it easy for someone else to read. Blank lines separate declarations and statements into related groups, and we indent the entire body of the class and the `main` method. The compiler doesn't require us to format the code this way; we do so only to make our program more readable. We will have more to say in subsequent chapters about formatting code.

Here is what the program displays on the screen when it executes:

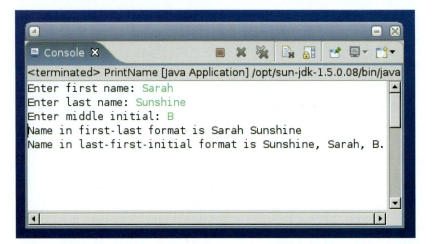

2.7 : A Last Word About Blocks

The body of a method is an example of what Java calls a *block*. The syntax template for a block is

Block

```
{
    Statement  . . .
}
```

A block is just a sequence of zero or more executable statements enclosed (delimited) by a `{}` pair. Now we can redefine a method declaration as a heading followed by a block:

Method-Declaration

```
Heading
Block
```

In later chapters, we will define the syntax of a method heading in greater detail.

Here is the syntax template for executable statements within a block, limited to the Java statements discussed in this chapter:

Statement

```
Null-Statement
Local-Field-Declaration
Assignment-Statement
Method-Call
Block
```

A statement can be empty (the *null statement*). The null statement is just a semicolon (;):

;

It does absolutely nothing at execution time; execution just proceeds to the next statement. The null statement is rarely used.

The syntax template shows that a Local-Field-Declaration (a declaration within a method) is an executable statement. Local field declarations wait until run time to associate an identifier with a type. That is, declarations in a method are not made by the compiler but rather by the JVM. In contrast, class declarations are non-executable, because they are handled by the compiler.

As the syntax template shows, we can use an entire block wherever a single statement is allowed. In later chapters, when we introduce the syntax for branching and looping structures, this fact will prove very important.

We use blocks often, especially as parts of other statements. Leaving out a { } pair can dramatically change both the meaning and the execution of an application. That explains why we always indent the statements inside a block—the indentation makes a block easy to spot in a long, complicated section of code.

Notice that the syntax templates for Block and Statement do not mention semicolons. Yet the **PrintName** and **Example** applications contain many semicolons. If you look back at the templates for a field declaration, assignment statement, and method call, you will see that a semicolon is required at the end of each kind of statement. The syntax template for a block, however, shows no semicolon after the right brace. The rule for using semicolons in Java, then, is quite simple: Terminate each statement except a block with a semicolon.

One more thing about local declarations: They can appear anywhere in a block, as long as the declaration of an item comes before the item is used. In this book, we group the declarations together at the beginning of the block because we think it is easier to read and, therefore, better style.

SOFTWARE MAINTENANCE CASE STUDY

Adding Titles to Names

In Chapter 1, we saw the essential steps of any software maintenance process:

1. Check the operation of the existing code.
2. Understand sufficiently how the code works to do the maintenance task.
3. Create a working copy of the code.
4. Make the modifications.
5. Test the new code.
6. Clean up any inconsistencies and update any related documentation.

For the `HelloWorld` program in Chapter 1, the code was so trivial that we could understand its operation and make the changes without any knowledge of Java syntax. In the following scenario, the code is not so simple. We'll need to study it more conscientiously to discover how it works and what needs to be changed.

Maintenance Task: Add support for a title such as "Dr." or "Ms." to the `PrintName` application.

Existing Code

```java
//************************************************************************
// PrintName application
// This application inputs a name and prints it in two different formats
//************************************************************************

import java.util.Scanner;
public class PrintName
{
  static final char COMMA = ' ';
  static final char BLANK = ' ';

  public static void main(String[] args)
  {
    String first;                        // Person's first name
    String last;                         // Person's last name
    String middle;                       // Person's middle initial
    String firstLast;                    // Name in first-last format
    String lastFirst;                    // Name in last-first format
    Scanner in;                          // Input stream for strings

    in = new Scanner(System.in);                // Instantiate Scanner
    System.out.print("Enter first name: ");     // Prompt for first name
    first = in.nextLine();                       // Get first name
    System.out.print("Enter last name: ");      // Prompt for last name
    last = in.nextLine();                        // Get last name
    System.out.print("Enter middle initial: "); // Prompt for middle initial
    middle = in.nextLine();                      // Get middle initial
    firstLast = first + BLANK + last;            // Generate first format
    System.out.println("Name in first-last format is " + firstLast);
    lastFirst = last + COMMA + BLANK             // Generate second format
                   + first + COMMA + BLANK;
```

```java
        System.out.println("Name in last-first-initial format is "
                        + lastFirst + middle + ".");
    }
}
```

Code Analysis: To understand any sizeable piece of code, we look for recognizable chunks into which we can partition it. One of our goals is to set aside portions that are unlikely to be related to our maintenance task. In this case, we see that there are opening comments:

```java
//***********************************************************************
// PrintName application
// This application inputs a name and prints it in two different formats
//***********************************************************************
```

There are two class constants and a class declaration that surrounds `main`, but does nothing else:

```java
import java.util.Scanner;               // Scanner class

public class PrintName
{
    final static char COMMA = ',';
    final static char BLANK = ' ';
```

Because the heading of `main` simply follows the standard formula, we can set aside that line of code and its associated braces. Thus the portion of this application that we must focus on is the block within `main`. That block can be further partitioned into a section of declarations:

```java
    String first;                       // Person's first name
    ...
    Scanner in;                         // Input stream for strings
```

Then a section that initializes a file variable and reads the three parts of the name from the keyboard:

```java
    in = new Scanner(System.in);              // Instantiate Scanner
    ...
    middle = in.nextLine();                   // Get middle initial
```

And a final section that generates and prints each of the two name formats:

```java
    firstLast = first + BLANK + last;         // Generate first format
    ...
    System.out.println("Name in last-first-initial format is "
                    + lastFirst + middle + ".");
```

Thus, the major steps in the application are: declarations, input, and output.

Solution: Our task is to modify the application to incorporate a title in each of the formats. How will we achieve this? We must begin with the problem-solving technique of asking questions.

How do we get the title? We need to ask the user to enter the title, and then read the response. From this requirement, we can see that the input section of the code must be changed to prompt for the title and read it into a variable. What variable do we read it into? We have to change the declaration section to provide a new `String` variable. Let's call it `title`. We add the following lines to the appropriate sections:

```java
String title;                           // Person's title

System.out.print("Enter title: ");      // Prompt for title
title = in.nextLine();                  // Get title
```

How is the title to be incorporated into the formats? For the first format, it simply appears at the beginning of the name—for example, Dr. Margaret Sklaznic. For the second format, it appears after the last name—for example, Sklaznic, Dr. Margaret, C.

Now we must decide how to accomplish this task within the application. There are two places where we could add the title to each format. One place is within the assignment statements that generate the formats.

```java
firstLast = title + BLANK + first + BLANK + last;   // Generate first format
```

The other is within the output statements that print the names.

```java
System.out.println("Name in first-last format is " +
                    title + BLANK + firstLast);
```

With the second format, the change is not so simple, because the title must be inserted between the names. We could still change the output statement, but it would not make use of the contents of `lastFirst`, which would be wasteful.

In this short application, it doesn't really matter which approach we choose. In a larger application, however, we would need to check whether the `firstLast` and `lastFirst` variables are used elsewhere. If they are, then we must understand how they are used. In this case, let's simply insert the title into the assignment statements.

Revised Code: Here is a listing of the revised application, with the inserted or modified code highlighted.

```java
import java.util.Scanner;
public class PrintName
{
  static final char COMMA = ',';
  static final char BLANK = ' ';
```

```java
public static void main(String[] args)
{
  String first;                                // Person's first name
  String last;                                 // Person's last name
  String middle;                               // Person's middle initial
  String title;                                // Person's title
  String firstLast;                            // Name in first-last format
  String lastFirst;                            // Name in last-first format
  Scanner in;                                  // Input stream for strings

  in = new Scanner(System.in);                 // Instantiate Scanner
  System.out.print("Enter first name: ");      // Prompt for first name
  first = in.nextLine();                       // Get first name
  System.out.print("Enter last name: ");       // Prompt for last name
  last = in.nextLine();                        // Get last name
  System.out.print("Enter middle initial: ");  // Prompt for middle initial
  middle = in.nextLine();                      // Get middle initial
  System.out.print("Enter title: ");           // Prompt for title
  title = in.nextLine();                       // Get title
  firstLast = title + BLANK + first + BLANK + last;
                                               // Generate first format
  System.out.println("Name in first-last format is " + firstLast);
                                               // Generate second format
  lastFirst = last + COMMA + BLANK + title + BLANK + first + COMMA + BLANK;
  System.out.println("Name in last-first-initial format is " +
                     lastFirst + middle + ".");
}
}
```

As you can see, the actual changes are quite small. By analyzing the original code and breaking it into meaningful sections, we were able to isolate the steps that required modification. It was then obvious how and where to make each of the changes.

Testing: Here is a sample run of this program.

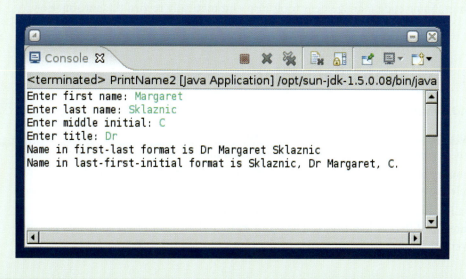

```
Console
<terminated> PrintName2 [Java Application] /opt/sun-jdk-1.5.0.08/bin/java
Enter first name: Margaret
Enter last name: Sklaznic
Enter middle initial: C
Enter title: Dr
Name in first-last format is Dr Margaret Sklaznic
Name in last-first-initial format is Sklaznic, Dr Margaret, C.
```

94

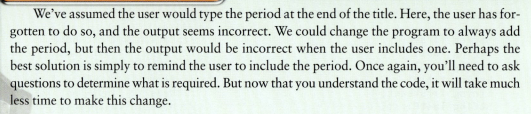

We've assumed the user would type the period at the end of the title. Here, the user has forgotten to do so, and the output seems incorrect. We could change the program to always add the period, but then the output would be incorrect when the user includes one. Perhaps the best solution is simply to remind the user to include the period. Once again, you'll need to ask questions to determine what is required. But now that you understand the code, it will take much less time to make this change.

Software Maintenance Tips

1. Break a long block of code into smaller chunks that have distinct purposes.
2. Identify portions of the code that you are sure you can ignore.
3. Focus on the code sections that are clearly related to the maintenance task.
4. Make sure that you understand what changes are required. Ask questions about anything that is unclear. Formally, this information would be written as a specification document.
5. Consider the major steps that you've identified in the existing code, and then establish how you would solve the maintenance task within that overall approach. For example, in a simple application whose steps are input, process, and output, think about how the task relates to each of these steps. It doesn't help to develop a solution for a maintenance task that takes a completely different approach from the existing code. You must work within the given context.
6. Consider how your changes might affect other parts of the application. If you're changing the content of an existing variable, check whether it is used elsewhere, and determine precisely how it is used.
7. Document your changes. In our example, we highlighted the updated code. Some companies have standards regarding how code changes are recorded. For example, each line may have a comment that identifies the programmer and the date of the change. Some code management tools also automatically record this information.

2.8 : Testing and Debugging

Testing and Debugging Hints

1. You must declare every identifier that isn't a Java reserved word or a predefined term. If you use a name that hasn't been declared, you will receive an error message.
2. If you try to declare an identifier that is the same as a reserved word in Java, you will receive an error message from the compiler. See Appendix A for a list of reserved words.
3. Java is a case-sensitive language, so two identifiers that are capitalized differently are treated as different identifiers. The word `main` and all Java reserved words use only lowercase letters.

4. Check for mismatched quotes in `char` and `String` literals. Each `char` literal begins and ends with an apostrophe (single quote). Each `String` literal begins and ends with a double quote.

5. Use only the apostrophe (`'`) to enclose `char` literals. Most keyboards include a reverse apostrophe (`` ` ``) that is easily confused with the apostrophe. If you use the reverse apostrophe, the compiler will issue an error message.

6. To use a double quote within a literal string, use the two symbols `\"` in a row. If you use just a double quote, it ends the string, and the compiler then sees the remainder of the string as an error. Similarly, to write a single quote in a `char` literal, use the two symbols `\'` without any space between them (that is, `'\''` is the `char` literal for a single quote).

7. In an assignment statement, make sure that the identifier to the left of = is a variable and not a named constant.

8. When assigning a value to a `String` variable, the expression to the right of = must be a `String` expression or a literal string.

9. In a concatenation expression, at least one of the two operands of + must be of the class `String`.

10. Make sure your statements end with semicolons (except blocks, which do not have a semicolon after the right brace).

11. On most Java systems, the file name that holds a class must be the same as the name of the class, but with the extension `.java`. For example, the application `PrintName` is stored in a file called `PrintName.java` and a class called `Name` would be stored in `Name.java`. Using another name will produce an error message from the compiler. The compiled code will be stored in the file with the public class name and a `.class` extension.

12. Be careful when using the `/* */` pair to delimit comments. If you forget the `*/`, then everything that follows until the end of the next `/* */` comment (or the end of your program) will be treated as a comment. Also, remember to avoid starting comments of this form with two asterisks (`/**`) because comments of that form are used by the `javadoc` program.

13. Confirm that every open brace (`{`) in your program is matched by a close brace (`}`) in the appropriate place. Braces determine the beginning and end of blocks in Java, and their placement affects the structure of the program. Similarly, it is always wise to confirm that parentheses are used in matched pairs in your program.

14. Instantiate objects by using `new`.

15. When instantiating an object in an argument list, include the `new` operator before the class name.

16. Objects to which methods are being applied must have the method name appended to the object name with a dot in between.

Summary

The syntax (grammar) of the Java language is defined by a metalanguage. In this book, we use a form of metalanguage called syntax templates. We describe the semantics (meaning) of Java statements in English.

Identifiers are used in Java to name things. Some identifiers, called reserved words, have predefined meanings in the language; others are created by the programmer. The identifiers you invent are restricted to those not reserved by the Java language. (Reserved words are listed in Appendix A.)

Identifiers are associated with memory locations through declarations. A declaration may give a name to a location whose value does not change (a constant) or to a location whose value can change (a variable). Every constant and variable has an associated data type or class. Java provides many predefined data types and classes. In this chapter, we examined the `char` type and the `String` class. A class contains fields and methods that describe the behavior of an object. An object is an instance of the class that describes it.

You use the assignment operator to change the value of a variable by assigning the value of an expression to it. At execution time, the expression is evaluated and the result is stored into the variable. With the `String` class, the plus sign (+) is an operator that concatenates two strings. A string expression can concatenate any number of strings to form a new `String` value.

Simple output to the screen is accomplished by using the `System.out` object that is provided in Java. Two methods are defined on this object: `print` and `println`. `System.out.print("A string")` prints whatever value is between the parentheses. `println` behaves in exactly the same way as `print`, except that `println` goes to the next line after it finishes the printing. String input is accomplished through the `Scanner` class method `nextLine`, which returns the next line of input from the screen. Class `Scanner` is instantiated using `System.in` as an argument.

A Java application is a `public` class containing fields and methods. One of the methods *must* be named `main`. Execution of an application class always begins with the `main` method. A class may begin with `import` declarations if it uses outside packages. It must have a heading, followed by a block that may contain class declarations, fields, and methods.

LEARNING **Portfolio**

Quick Check

1. What is syntax? (p. 54)

2. Why do we write meaningful identifiers in our code? (p. 59)

3. What is stored in a variable that is of a primitive type? (p. 78)

4. How does a class in Java differ from a class in the abstract sense? (p. 62)

5. How do objects in the general sense differ from objects in Java? (p. 62)

6. Is `char` an object or a primitive type? (p. 61)

7. What distinguishes a named constant from a variable field? (pp. 73–79)

8. When an object is assigned to a variable, what is actually stored there? (p. 78)

9. What happens when a `void` method is called? (p. 85)

10. What are the essential components of a Java application? (pp. 66–68)

11. Use the following syntax template to decide whether your last name is a valid Java identifier. (pp. 56–59)

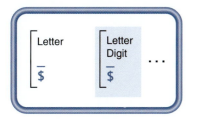

12. Write a Java constant declaration that gives the name ZED to the value `'Z'`. (p. 79)

13. Declare a `char` variable named `letter` and a `String` variable named `street`. (pp. 73–74)

14. Assign the value `"Elm"` to the `String` variable `street`. (pp. 74–76)

15. Add the value `" Street"` to the value in `street`. (pp. 76–77)

16. Write an output statement that displays the title of this book (*Introduction to Programming and Problem Solving with Java*) on `System.out`. (pp. 63–66)

17. The following code is incorrect. Rewrite it, using correct comment syntax. (p. 82)

```
String address;      / Employee's street address,

                     / including apartment
```

18. What does the following code segment output on the screen? (pp. 76–77)

```
String str;

str = "Abraham";

System.out.println("The answer is " + str + " Lincoln");
```

Answers

1. Syntax is the set of rules that defines valid constructs in a programming language. 2. Meaningful identifiers make the code easier to debug and maintain. 3. The actual value of the primitive type is stored in the variable. 4. A class in Java defines an object that can be instantiated. In the abstract sense, a class describes an object in a problem. 5. Objects in Java represent objects in the general sense through code that simulates their behavior. 6. It is a primitive type. 7. The use of the reserved word `final`. 8. The memory address where the object's data is stored. 9. The argument values are copied into the parameter variables of the method and the method is executed. When it returns, execution resumes with the next statement. 10. A public class containing a method named `main`. 11. Unless your last name is hyphenated, it probably is a valid Java identifier. 12. `final char ZED = 'Z';`

13. `char letter;`
    `String street;`
14. `street = "Elm";`
15. `street = street + " Street";`
16. `System.out.print("Introduction to Programming and Problem Solving with Java");`

17. `String address;` `// Employee's street address,`
    `// including apartment`

    or

    `String address;` `/* Employee's street address,`
    `including apartment     */`

18. `The answer is Abraham Lincoln`

Exam Preparation Exercises

1. Mark the following identifiers as either valid or invalid.

	Valid	Invalid
a. `item#1`	_____	_____
b. `data`	_____	_____
c. `y`	_____	_____
d. `3Set`	_____	_____
e. `PAY_DAY`	_____	_____
f. `bin-2`	_____	_____
g. `num5`	_____	_____
h. `Sq Ft`	_____	_____

2. Given these four syntax templates:

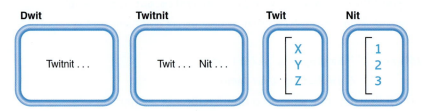

mark the following "Dwits" as either valid or invalid.

	Valid	Invalid
a. XYZ	_____	_____
b. 123	_____	_____
c. X1	_____	_____
d. 23Y	_____	_____
e. XY12	_____	_____
f. Y2Y	_____	_____
g. ZY2	_____	_____
h. XY23X1	_____	_____

3. Match each of the following terms with the correct definition (1 through 15) given. There is only one correct definition for each term.

_____ **a.** program   _____ **c.** compiler

_____ **b.** algorithm   _____ **d.** identifier

	e. compilation phase		**i.** memory
	f. execution phase		**j.** syntax
	g. variable		**k.** semantics
	h. constant		**l.** block

(1) A symbolic name made up of letters, digits, underscores, and dollar signs, but not beginning with a digit

(2) A place in memory where a data object that cannot be changed is stored

(3) A program that takes a program in a high-level language and translates it into machine code or Bytecode

(4) An input device

(5) The time spent planning a program

(6) Grammar rules

(7) A sequence of statements enclosed by braces

(8) Meaning

(9) A program that translates assembly language instructions into machine code

(10) When the compiled version of a program is being run

(11) A place in memory where a data value that can be changed is stored

(12) When a program in a high-level language is converted into machine code or Bytecode

(13) A part of the computer that can hold both programs and data

(14) Instructions for solving a problem in a finite amount of time with a finite amount of data

(15) Data type specifications and instructions used by a computer to solve a problem

4. Which of the following are reserved words and which are programmer-defined identifiers? (Note that we purposely print all the words in black so that you can't use color to identify reserved words in this exercise—you may need to look them up.)

	Reserved	Programmer-Defined
a. `char`		
b. `sort`		
c. `INT`		
d. `new`		
e. `Public`		

5. Reserved words can be used as variable names. (True or False?)

6. In a Java application containing just one method, that method can be named either `main` or `Main`. (True or False?)

7. If `s1` and `s2` are `String` variables containing `"blue"` and `"bird"`, respectively, what does each of the following statements print?

a. `System.out.println("s1 = " + s1 + "s2 = " + s2);`

    b. `System.out.println("Result:" + s1 + s2);`

    c. `System.out.println("Result:    " + s1 + s2);`

    d. `System.out.println("Result:    " + s1 + ' ' + s2);`

8. Show precisely what is output by the following statement:

```
System.out.println("A rolling" +
    "stone" +
    "gathers" +
    "no" +
    "moss");
```

9. How many characters can be stored into a variable of type `char`?

10. How many characters are in the empty string?

11. A variable of the class `String` can be assigned to a variable of type `char`. (True or False?)

12. A literal string can be assigned to a variable of the class `String`. (True or False?)

13. What is the difference between the literal string `"computer"` and the identifier `computer`?

14. What is output by the following code segment? (All variables are of the class `String`.)

```
street = "Elm St.";
address = "1425B";
city = "Amaryllis";
state = "Iowa";
streetAddress = address + " " + street;
System.out.println(streetAddress);
System.out.println(city);
System.out.println(", " + state);
```

15. Correct the following program so that it displays `"Martin Luther King Jr."`

```
// This application is full of errors
class LotsOfErrors;
{
   void main (string args[]);
   {
      constant String FIRST : Martin";
      constant String MID : "Luther;
      constant String LAST : King

      String name;
      character initial;
      name = Martin + Luther + King;
      initial = MID;
      LAST = "King Jr.";
      System.out.println('Name = ' + name));
      System.out.println(mid
   }
}
```

16. How do you invoke an instance method?

17. Name two methods associated with the `System.out` object.

18. What does the expression "invoking a method" mean?

19. Describe the role of a parameter list.

20. What do we call a `public` class that contains a method called `main`?

21. What is the function of the `nextLine` method of the class `Scanner`?

22. We have used the convention that method names begin with a lowercase letter. Why does a constructor have to begin with an uppercase letter?

Programming Warm-Up Exercises

1. Write the output statement that prints your name.

2. Write three consecutive output statements that print the following three lines.

```
The moon
is
blue.
```

3. Write declaration statements to declare three variables of the class `String` and two variables of type `char`. The `String` variables should be named `make`, `model`, and `color`. The `char` variables should be named `plateType` and `classification`.

4. Write a series of output statements that display the values in the variables declared in Exercise 3. Each value should be preceded by an identifying message.

5. Change the `PrintName` application (pp. 92–93) so that it also prints the name in the following format

First-name Middle-initial. Last-name

Define a new `String` variable to hold the name in the new format and assign it the string using the existing variables, any literal strings that are needed for punctuation and spacing, and concatenation operations. Print the string, labeled appropriately.

6. Write code to print the following groups of text.

a. `Four score`
`and seven years ago`

b. `Four score`
`and seven`
`years ago`

c. `Four score`
`and`
`seven`
`years ago`

   d. Four
      score
      and
      seven
      years
      ago

7. Write the declarations and statements necessary to input a string from `System.in`.

8. Enter and run the following application. Be sure to type it exactly as it appears here.

```java
//******************************************************************
// HelloWorld application
// This application displays two simple messages
//******************************************************************
public class HelloWorld
{
  public static void main(String args[])
  {
    final String MSG1 = "Hello world.";
    String msg2;

    System.out.println(MSG1);
    msg2 = MSG1 + " " + MSG1 + " " + MSG1;
    System.out.println(msg2);
  }
}
```

Programming Problems

1. Write a Java application that displays a series of Haiku poems. A Haiku poem is written in three phrases. The first phrase has five syllables, the second phase has seven syllables, and the third phrase has five syllables. For example:

Bright flash then silence

My expensive computer

Has gone to heaven

Your program should input three strings with five syllables and two strings of seven syllables. Output every possible 5–7–5 permutation of these phrases. Do not use the same phrase twice in any poem. See if you can create phrases that make sense together in every permutation. Be sure to include appropriate comments in your code, choose meaningful identifiers, and use indentation as shown in the code in this chapter.

2. Write a program that simulates the children's game called "My Grandmother's Trunk." In this game, the players sit in a circle, and the first player names something that goes in the trunk: "In my grandmother's trunk, I packed a pencil." The next player restates the sentence and adds something new to the trunk: "In my grandmother's trunk, I packed a pencil and a red ball." Each player in turn adds something to the trunk, attempting to keep track of all the items that are already there.

Your program should simulate five turns in the game. Starting with the empty string, simulate each player's turn by reading and concatenating a new word or phrase to the existing string, and print the result.

3. Write a program that prints its own grading form. The program should output the name and number of the class, the name and number of the programming assignment, your name and student number, and labeled spaces for scores reflecting correctness, quality of style, late deduction, and overall score. Have the program input the name, ID number, and assignment number as strings. An example of such a form is the following:

```
CS-101 Introduction to Programming and Problem Solving


Programming Assignment 1


Sally A. Student    ID Number 431023877


Grade Summary:


Program Correctness:     Quality of Style:
Late Deduction:          Overall Score:
Comments:
```

Case Study Follow-Up

1. Change the `PrintName` application so that it also takes a suffix, such as Jr. or Esq.

2. We chose to modify the assignment statements in `PrintName` to generate the formats with the titles. At that time, we said that we could instead change the output statements. Start from the original version of `PrintName` and figure out how to solve the problem this way.

3. Add a third format to the `PrintName` application that displays the name as just the first and last names, without the middle initial.

4. In the original `PrintName` application, what is output if the user enters the first and last names in reverse order?

3 Classes and Methods

Goals

Knowledge Goals

To:

- Appreciate the difference between a class in the abstract sense and a class as a Java construct
- Know what attributes are
- Know what responsibilities are
- Know how assignment of an object reference differs from assignment of a standard type
- Appreciate how aliases can lead to errors
- Know what garbage collection is
- Understand the distinction between instance methods and class methods
- Know what a constructor does
- Appreciate the differences between void and value-returning methods
- Understand what immutability is

Skill Goals

To be able to:

- Determine the attributes and responsibilities of a class
- Write the heading for a new class
- Write the class declarations for a new class
- Write an instance method
- Write a class method
- Write a constructor
- Write a helper method
- Write a value-returning method
- Assemble class declarations into a working class

1927
First public demonstration of television in the U.S. takes place: a speech in D.C. is broadcast in New York

1929
Experimentation with color television begins; Bell Laboratories is the first in the U.S. to demonstrate the technology

1935
The IBM 601 punch-card machine and the electric typewriter are introduced

1935
IBM graduates its first class of female service technicians

1936
Konrad Zuse begins developing the first binary digital computer to help automate engineering and architectural drawing

1937
Howard Aiken proposes a calculating machine that can carry out operations in a predetermined sequence

Introduction

In this chapter, we go beyond a basic application by defining classes that represent objects in a problem. Creating a new class is the essential skill that you need for object-oriented programming. After you've learned to do that, everything else we'll cover in the remainder of the book is just a matter of gradually learning how to give your objects more sophisticated abilities.

1937
George Stibitz develops the "Model K," the prototype binary adder circuit

1937
Alan Turing introduces the idea of his "Turing Machine," a theoretical model for a general purpose computer

1938
Bill Hewlett and Dave Packard begin Hewlett-Packard in a garage with $538 in capital

1939
John Vincent Atanasoff and Cliff Berry create a model for the electronic-digital computer

1943
Construction of the ENIAC (Electronic Numerical Integrator and Computer) begins at the Moore School of Electrical Engineering in Philadelphia

1943
Invention of the first all-electronic calculating device, the Collosus, used by England during World War II to decrypt secret messages

3.1 ⋮ Defining New Classes of Objects

We've now seen how to write an application class that has just the required method, `main`. This kind of coding resembles the programs written in older languages that lacked support for object-oriented programming. Of course, as problem complexity grows, the number of statements likewise grows. Eventually, such applications become so immense that it is nearly impossible to maintain them. To avoid this complexity, we break the problem up into classes that are small enough to be easily understood and that we can test and debug independently. In this section, we see how problem solving incorporates classes other than an application class, and methods other than `main`.

■ Classes of Objects

In Chapter 2, we worked with `char` and `String` values. It is important to recognize the underlying distinction between these two kinds of values. The former is a primitive type in Java, and the latter is an object defined by a class. In Java, primitive data types are completely predefined by the language, whereas classes are defined by the programmer. In many cases you will use classes that are defined by other programmers (such as `String`); in other cases, you must define new classes.

Figure 3.1 shows the syntax for defining a new class, which is the same as the syntax for an application. As we noted in Chapter 2, an application is just a class that has a `main` method. So what's special about a class that defines objects? Other than the absence of a `main` method, there aren't any syntactic differences. The distinction is that an object class has a design that specifies a set of attributes and responsibilities.

■ Class Design

Attributes and responsibilities are part of the abstract definition of a class. Before we implement the class, we first design it in the problem-solving phase using abstract terms. This approach allows us to focus on what its objects represent (attributes) and what they need to do (respon-

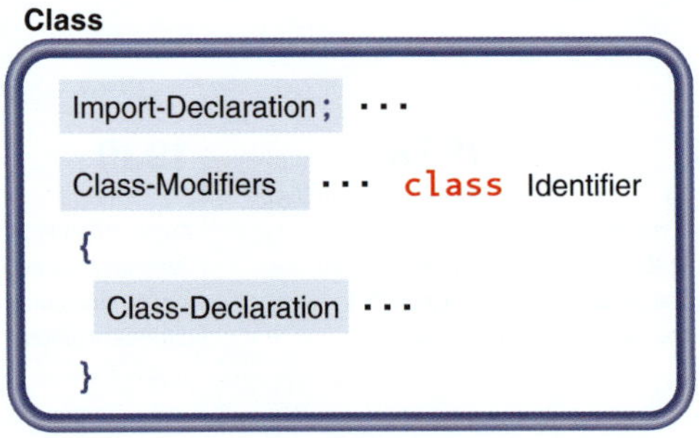

FIGURE 3.1 Class Syntax

sibilities) in solving the problem. When those aspects of the design are clear, we have a definition of the class that guides our implementation.

We typically begin the design process by looking carefully at the problem to identify potential objects. For example, if the problem is to make robots weld seams on car bodies, then we might guess that a robot, a seam, and a car body are objects we need to model in our solution. We could design a robot class and use it to create objects that model each of the robots on the assembly line.

After identifying a class that's part of a problem solution, we specify what objects of the class represent and what they do. In the case of the robot class, we would look carefully at how a robot (like the one shown in Figure 3.2) is built and how it operates. In our design, we would then specify the attributes (number of joints, range of joint angles, etc.) and responsibilities (actions for moving the robot, turning on the welder, etc.) that are needed to model a robot so that we can direct its actions.

Once we are satisfied with the initial design, we check it by running through a set of processing scenarios in which we pretend to be the computer solving the problem. With each scenario, we decide which objects are involved, and we determine how to carry out the scenario using them. If we discover that an object is lacking some ability, we add a new responsibility to its definition (it's much easier to do this at the abstract definition stage than after coding has started). Once we know that the available objects can carry out all of the scenarios, we are reasonably confident that we have a complete problem solution. Only then do we turn to implementation.

Now that we've seen where classes, attributes, and responsibilities originate in a problem, let's take a closer look at some important properties of attributes and responsibilities that affect our design decisions.

FIGURE 3.2   An Industrial Robot

■ Attributes of a Class

We say that an object is represented by its attributes, but what does that mean? What are attributes? Each object in a problem solution represents some entity within the problem. For example, in a check-printing application, we have objects that represent checks. A check object contains additional objects to represent entities such as the date, the numerical amount of the check, the amount in words, and the name of the payee.

Each entity has one or more values associated with it. The numerical amount may be a single real number, while the date may be represented by the month, day, and year. As part of the design process, we select the Java data types or classes that are suited to holding these values. Sometimes the choice is clear, as when we use one of Java's numeric types to represent a real number in the problem. In other cases, we may need to choose between alternatives. For example, the date could be stored either as a string or as three numbers, and the choice of representation depends on how we expect to use the date.

Each object that represents an entity keeps its own value or set of values. For example, the numerical amount for check number 785 holds the amount of that check ($89.54), while check number 799 has its own numerical amount that holds a different value ($39.95).

When a value is associated with a specific object, we say that it is an **instance value** (recall from Chapter 2 that each object is said to be an *instance* of its class). Thus the numerical amount in a check object is an instance value, because it is specific to that check.

Sometimes values are associated with an entire class of objects. For example, suppose that our application places a limit on the amount of a check. This limit applies to every check, so every object of the check class has the same limit value. Because the value isn't unique to each object, it is not an instance value. Rather, we say that it is a **class value**.

Together, class values and instance values make up the **attributes** of a class. They specify all of the values defined by the class that make up the representation of its objects. Figure 3.3 illustrates the relationship between a class and instances of the class in terms of the actual objects being modeled.

Attributes are implemented as variables and constants in the class declarations. As an example, here are the class declarations that might be used in defining a `Check` class. (We will explain type `double` in Chapter 4.)

> **Instance value** A value that is associated with a specific object
>
> **Class value** A value that is associated with a class and is the same for every object of that class
>
> **Attributes** The values defined by a class that are used to represent its objects; the combination of instance and class values

```java
public class Check
{
    static double limit = 10000.0;        // A class variable
    String dateOfIssue;                   // Instance variables
    String payee;
    String amountInWords;
    double amount;
```

We first saw the `static` modifier in Chapter 2, where we recommended using it with all class declarations until we could explore it further in Chapter 3. Now we can explain it. We use `static` to distinguish between class and instance values. Part of the design process involves deciding which attributes represent class values and which represent instance values. For each value, you must determine whether it is the same for all objects (class value) or potentially different for each object (instance value).

Another important concept to appreciate here is the difference in where class and instance fields are stored. The compiler gives a `static` field a specific memory location within a class. But an instance field can exist only within a specific object. Until an object of the class is instantiated with the `new` operator, no place has been set aside to hold the instance values. As `new` creates an object, it allocates memory space for instance values. Instance field declarations are therefore merely a pattern that `new` uses in creating each object. For each additional object that is instantiated, an additional set of instance fields is created within that object.

To illustrate this distinction between class and instance fields let's look at an example. If we execute the following instantiation operations for the `Check` class, then we have the relationship shown in Figure 3.4.

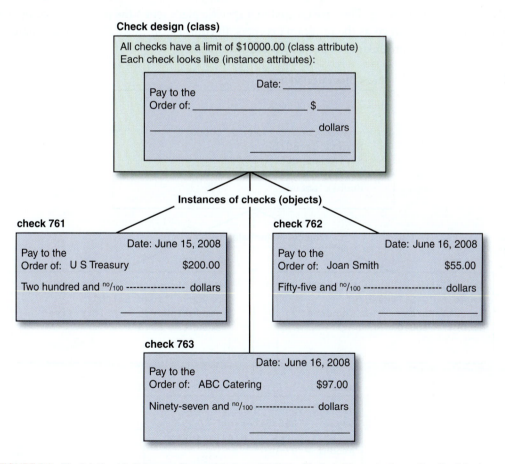

FIGURE 3.3 The Relationship Between a Class and Instance Attributes Illustrated by an Analogy with a Check Design and Individual Checks

```
Check check761 = new Check("June 15, 2008", "U.S. Treasury", "Two hundred", 200.0);
Check check762 = new Check("June 16, 2008", "Joan Smith", "Fifty-five", 55.0);
Check check762 = new Check("June 16, 2008", "ABC Catering", "Ninety-seven", 97.0);
```

In Figure 3.4, you can see that the **static** variable limit exists in just one place (the class) and has a value stored in it. The instance field declarations are just patterns that new uses to create each object. Before any objects are created, only the patterns exist. No memory locations are associated with them that could be used to hold instance values. After three objects have been instantiated, however, the instance fields exist in three different places, all of which are capable of holding distinct values.

Syntactically, Java lets us assign an initial value to an instance field as part of the declaration. If the field doesn't exist until it is instantiated, how can it have a value? The answer is that the declaration keeps the value as part of the pattern; when new eventually creates the corresponding field within the object, it assigns a copy of that value from the pattern to the field.

The use of the word "static" as a reserved word in Java is meant to convey the sense that class fields are unmoving. They are created in a specific place when the program is compiled and do not come and go as the program executes. In contrast, instance fields are dynamic in the sense that they are created as needed, in different places.

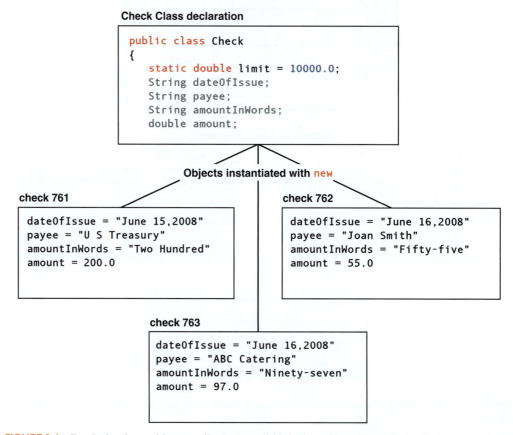

FIGURE 3.4 Class Declarations and Corresponding Instance Fields in Three Objects (Gray indicates that no memory space is provided for a field at that point.)

Now we turn our attention to the operations that can be applied to the attributes—that is, the responsibilities of the class.

■ Responsibilities of a Class

In the last section, we saw how classes use instance and class values, stored in variables and constants, to represent the data aspect of an object. From Chapters 1 and 2, we know that an object also combines data with operations that can be applied to that data. In the problem-solving phase, we refer to these operations as **responsibilities**.

Just as we can have instance values and class values, so we can have **instance responsibilities** and **class responsibilities**. An instance responsibility is an operation that is performed with respect to a specific object. For example, printing a `Check` object is an operation that takes place for a specific check. A class responsibility is an operation that is associated with a class and does not refer to a specific object. An example of a class responsibility would be an operation that sets the class variable `limit` to a different value, so that all checks have a new limit.

As we've already seen, in Java we use methods to implement operations. Not surprisingly, when a method represents an instance responsibility, we call it an **instance method**. Similarly a method that implements a class responsibility is a **class method**.

You may be wondering why we would go to so much trouble to distinguish between responsibilities and methods, when both are merely different ways of referring to operations supplied by a class. The reason is that we want to design a class in an abstract sense to solve part of our problem, and then move on to the implementation. If we use Java terminology at the problem-solving phase, it is far too easy to slip directly into writing code, where we might get bogged down in Java details and lose sight of the actual problem.

In Chapter 2, we saw one other type of method, the constructor, which has a corresponding responsibility in the problem-solving phase. Constructors help with the instantiation process, often by setting the attributes to initial values using either values specified in the declarations or values supplied through arguments.

Because objects are created while the program is running, and because each object can have unique values in its instance attributes, we typically want to supply some or all of those values when the object is instantiated. For example, when we create check number 799, we want to give it an amount, a date, and a payee. The job of the check constructor is to take those values and place them in the empty instance variables for the new check object. Figure 3.5 shows how the constructor fits into this process.

You might think that a constructor is an *example* of an instance method, because it seems to be associated with a specific object. But that's incorrect: When we call it, the object does not yet exist! The constructor is *part* of the instantiation process. You can think of it as analogue to a midwife assisting in the birth of a baby. After the baby is born, the midwife moves on to help with the next delivery, rather than staying with that baby for the rest of its life. Similarly, once an object is instantiated, we never need to call its constructor again.

The preceding discussion has shown that a class may have two kinds of attributes (class, instance) and three kinds of responsibilities (class, instance, constructor). Part of the class de-

> **Responsibilities** The operations that are provided by a class of objects
>
> **Instance responsibility** An operation performed with respect to a specific object
>
> **Class responsibility** An operation performed with respect to a class of objects
>
> **Instance method** A method that implements an instance responsibility
>
> **Class method** A method that implements a class responsibility

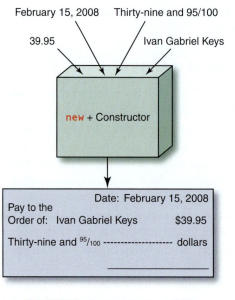

FIGURE 3.5 Constructor Responsibility

sign process is being conscious of which kind is which as you define each attribute and responsibility. Now, let's look at an example of a class design.

■ The Name Class Design

One object in our check-printing example is the name of the payee. To keep the example simple, we showed an implementation using a String variable. Many data processing problems include the storage and output of names. Although the output format varies from one application to the next, most English-language names consist of a first, middle, and last name. Here we develop a design for a Name class that can be used in many different situations.

We begin by identifying the attributes of a name. It's obvious that we should have a first, middle, and last name as attributes. What about titles and suffixes? We could include them as additional attributes, but let's keep this example class simple. Once we see how to design a basic Name class, adding those extensions should be easy. Each of these attributes should be able to hold a different value for any given name, so they all represent instance values. Here is our list of attributes:

Attributes

First (instance)

Last (instance)

Middle (instance)

What responsibilities should a Name object have? Let's tackle this part of the design by assuming that our goal is to simplify the implementation of the PrintName application from

Chapter 2. Recall that the application prints a name in two different formats. Thus our design could include responsibilities for printing the name in each of these formats. These formats are specific to the `PrintName` application, however; so they might not be useful elsewhere. Such a class design is application-specific, and our goal is to create a general-purpose `Name` class.

To make the class more widely usable, we could try to imagine all of the different name formats that people might want and create a responsibility for each one. But that would be a very long list! And as soon as we had them all coded, someone would surely come up with one we hadn't thought of.

Another approach to achieving generality is simply to store the parts of a name and supply them for use whenever they are requested. We can let the user worry about how to format them for output. Here are two lists of responsibilities that we might brainstorm for the `Name` class, showing the difference between a general version and a specialized version:

General Version of Name	Specialized Version of Name
Create an empty Name	Create an empty Name
Create a Name with a value	Create a Name with a value
Return First Name	Prompt user and read a Name from a Scanner object
Return Middle Name	Output Name in first format to System.out
Return Last Name	Output Name in second format to System.out

Usually, the less specialized that we make the class, the more widely it can be reused. If we write a `Name` class that directly addresses the needs of `PrintName`, we'll have to change it to work in any other program that needs a name. For example, if the requirements for `PrintName` were changed to include a third format, we would have to add another responsibility to the specialized `Name` class. With the general `Name` class, there is no need to change the class; only the client code would change.

From our brainstorming we can see that the class has five responsibilities: The two that create a `Name` should be constructors, and the three that return parts of a `Name` are instance methods. Notice that we specified a constructor to create an empty name. On the surface, this operation seems fairly useless, so why did we do it? Here we see how our choice of a programming language sometimes drives part of a design.

For a variety of reasons, Java needs to have a **default constructor** for every class. This method is a constructor that Java can count on being present. In fact, if we don't include a default constructor in a class, Java automatically supplies one for us. So why don't we just let Java handle this task? Many programmers do. However, we feel it is better programming style to explicitly write the default constructor. That way, we know exactly what happens when Java calls the default constructor. Also, someone reading our code will know that we took time to think about the default constructor, rather than simply forgetting it and letting Java supply something.

> **Default constructor** A constructor that has no parameters; Java automatically supplies one for each class if we do not do so

To summarize our design so far, our `Name` class has three attributes and five responsibilities. One of the responsibilities is the default constructor. The other four responsibilities create a name and return its three attributes. We now have a design for a very simple but general `Name` class. The implementation of the attributes is quite easy. We just need to declare three `String` variables to hold the parts of a name. These are class declarations from which we omit the `static` modifier because they are instance variables.

```
class Name
{
  String first;                         // Person's first name
  String last;                          // Person's last name
  String middle;                        // Person's middle initial
  // Responsibilities will go here
}
```

Before we can implement the responsibilities, we must learn more about writing methods. We also need to take a closer look at Java's data types, so that we can get a better sense of how objects are stored and assigned to variables. Understanding the object assignment mechanism is a key part of knowing what happens when we pass objects as arguments to methods.

Background Information

History of Programming Languages

Computer programming did not begin with the object-oriented approach. In this section, we trace the history of programming languages, to see how we got to this point.

In the beginning, programming primarily used data types such as integers and real numbers, whose operations are defined by mathematics. These types were built directly into a language and were the only ones supported. These kinds of programming languages are known as **procedural languages** because they focus on processing values, rather than defining different kinds of data.

As programmers gained more experience, they soon realized that complex problems are more easily solved if we can define new types of data—such as names, addresses, dates, and times—that are not built into a programming language. Each new kind of data is said to have a specific **data type**.

Procedural language A programming language that focuses on the processing procedures that are applied to built-in types of data (unlike languages that facilitate the representation of new types of data)

Data type The specification in a programming language of how information is represented in the computer as data and the set of operations that can be applied to it

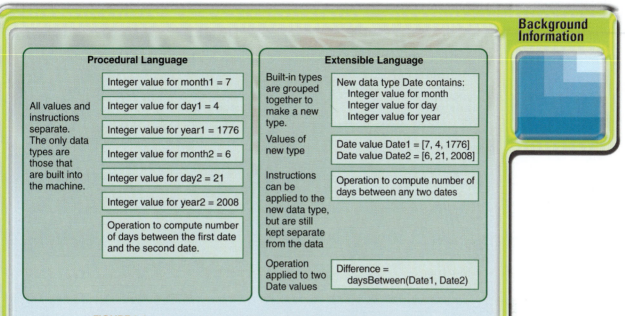

FIGURE 3.6 Procedural Programming Languages Versus Extensible Languages

Over time, procedural languages were extended to have the ability to define new data types and hence became known as **extensible languages**. The data and operations, however, remained separate parts of the program, as shown in Figure 3.6. A programmer could define a new data type to represent a date and then write a subprogram to compute the number of days between two dates, for example, but could not indicate that the values and the operation were related.

Object-oriented languages allow us to collect data and its associated operations into a class (see Figure 3.7). Given a class, we can easily create any number of objects within a program. Because the data and operations are bundled together, each class is a complete, self-contained unit that can be reused in other applications. This reusability enables us to write more code by using existing classes, thereby saving a considerable amount of time and effort.

Extensible language
A procedural programming language that allows the definition of new data types.

Object-oriented language A programming language in which new data types can be defined so that they include the data representation and the operations for the type in a self-contained unit called an object

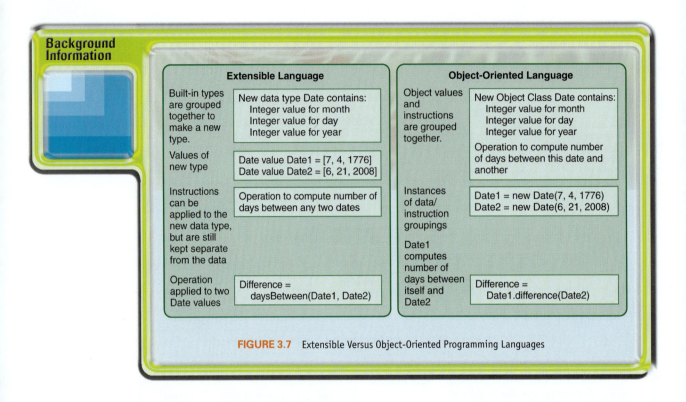

Background Information

Extensible Language	

Built-in types are grouped together to make a new type.	New data type Date contains:
	    Integer value for month
	    Integer value for day
	    Integer value for year

Values of new type	Date value Date1 = [7, 4, 1776] Date value Date2 = [6, 21, 2008]
Instructions can be applied to the new data type, but are still kept separate from the data	Operation to compute number of days between any two dates
Operation applied to two Date values	Difference = daysBetween(Date1, Date2)

Object-Oriented Language	

Object values and instructions are grouped together.	New Object Class Date contains:
	    Integer value for month
	    Integer value for day
	    Integer value for year
	Operation to compute number of days between this date and another

Instances of data/ instruction groupings Date1 computes number of days between itself and Date2	Date1 = new Date(7, 4, 1776) Date2 = new Date(6, 21, 2008)
	Difference = Date1.difference(Date2)

FIGURE 3.7   Extensible Versus Object-Oriented Programming Languages

3.2 ⋮ Overview of Java Data Types

In Chapter 2, we informally discussed the distinctions among Java's data types. Now it is time to make this intuitive understanding more formal. Java's built-in data types are organized into primitive types and reference types (see Figure 3.8).

Notice that the familiar `String` from Chapter 2 doesn't appear in Figure 3.8. `String` is absent because it is an example of a `class`, which falls under the category of reference types.

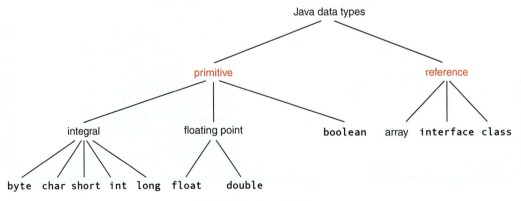

FIGURE 3.8   Java Data Types

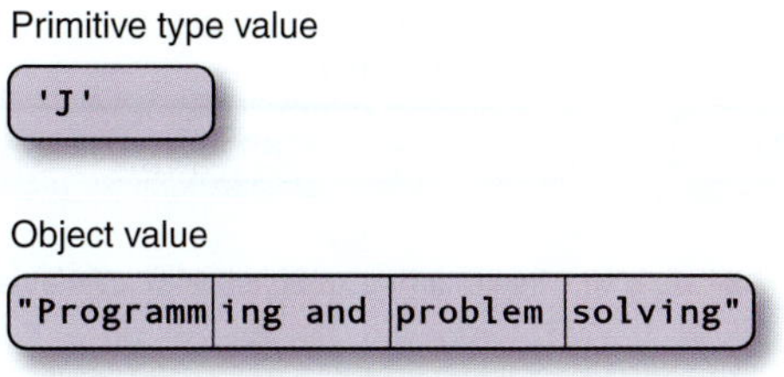

Primitive type value

'J'

Object value

"Programming and problem solving"

FIGURE 3.9 Storage of a Primitive Type Value Versus an Object Value. Note that the quotes are shown only to distinguish `char` from `String`. They are not actually stored in memory.

■ Primitive Versus Reference Types

In Chapter 2, we briefly explained how assignment works with reference types. Now we're ready to take a closer look at the details. The division of Java's data types into primitive and reference types stems from the way that Java stores their values in memory. Each primitive value is stored at the memory location that Java chooses for it. When we assign a value to a variable of a primitive type, Java copies the value into the memory cell at that location. Java can follow this approach because each primitive type takes a small, fixed amount of space.

Reference types can contain different numbers of fields and methods, so naturally they consume different amounts of the computer's memory. Most objects are too large to fit into a single memory location. How, then, are objects stored? They are placed in adjacent memory locations, as shown in Figure 3.9.

Thus there is no single location in memory that holds the entire object. Yet a variable, in Java, always refers to a specific memory location. So how do variables represent objects? The key is to realize that the address of a memory location is a number that can be represented by a primitive type. That is, an address value fits within a single memory location, and we can assign such a value to a variable.

■ Assignment with Reference Types

To represent an object with a variable, Java stores the *address* where the *object* can be found into the variable. That is, the variable contains a binary number that tells the computer where the object is stored in memory. Java knows that the object begins at that address and occupies successive locations in memory. When Java assigns an object to a variable, it copies this starting address into the variable, as Figure 3.10 illustrates.

Let's look at an example that demonstrates the difference between primitive values and reference values in Java.

```
// Some variables for our example
char letter;
String title;
String bookName;
// Some actions applied to these variables
letter = 'J';
title = "Programming and Problem Solving with Java";
bookName = title;
```

Variable that represents an object

Address of start of object:
000011010101

000011010101

"Programm|ing and |problem |solving"

FIGURE 3.10 Representing an Object with a Variable

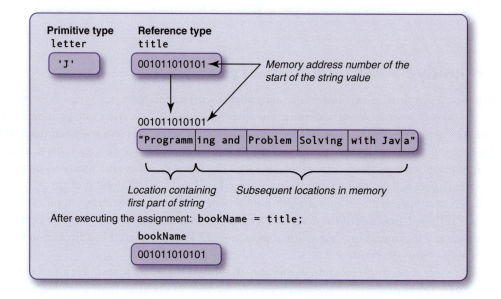

FIGURE 3.11 Primitive Types and Reference Types

When we declare the variables `letter`, `title`, and `bookName`, memory locations are chosen for these variables. Assigning the value `'J'` to the `char` variable `letter` stores the value `'J'` into its memory location. When the program assigns the string `"Programming and Problem Solving with Java"` to the `String` variable `title`, Java chooses a consecutive series of locations into which to store the string, and then stores the address of the first location into `title`. When we assign the value of `title` to the `String` variable `bookName`, Java simply copies the value stored in `title` (the address) to the place it chose for `bookName`.

Figure 3.11 illustrates the relationships in this example. Notice that when assigning one reference variable to another, only the address is copied. Thus only one copy of the actual object exists.

■ Aliases

You can also think of a reference type as being analogous to the call number of a library book. Armed with the call number, you can venture into the library stacks and find the book. If a friend wants to find the same book, you can give a copy of the call number to him or her, which is much easier than giving your friend a copy of the book. There is only one book, but many people can have a copy of the call number. Now consider what happens if someone writes in the book. Everyone who subsequently uses the call number to locate the book will find it altered.

Similarly, if you assign the same object to several variables, each variable stores a reference to the single copy of the object. Then, if you later change the object, the change affects all of the variables that refer to it. With a primitive type, in contrast, a change to the value in one variable doesn't affect any other copies.

For example, `System.out` is an object that is defined by a class called `PrintStream`. We can declare a new `PrintStream` object called `output`, and assign `System.out` to it:

```
PrintStream output;
output = System.out;
```

Both `output` and `System.out` now refer to the same object representing the standard output window on the screen. We say that they are **aliases** of each other. Printing with either one of them causes the output to appear in the same window, as shown in Figure 3.12.

> **Alias** When multiple variables refer to the same object, acting as synonyms of one another

Having variables that are aliases for the same object can occasionally be useful, but more often the result is mystifying behavior. You may spend a long time trying to figure out how an operation could possibly have produced the erroneous value in an object, only to discover that an entirely different operation on an alias for the object caused the problem. Our advice is to avoid the use of aliases wherever possible.

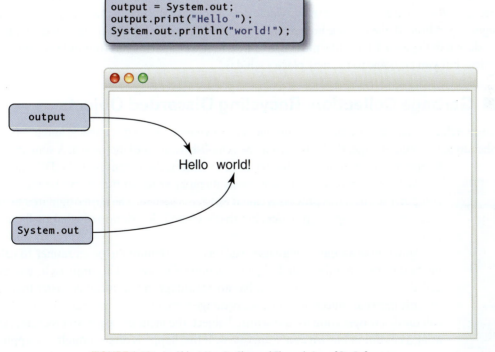

FIGURE 3.12   An Object May Be Changed Through Any of Its References

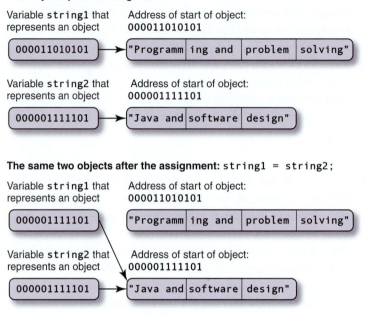

Two objects prior to assignment:

Variable `string1` that   Address of start of object:
represents an object   000011010101

[000011010101] ────▶ ["Programm | ing and | problem | solving"]

Variable `string2` that   Address of start of object:
represents an object   000001111101

[000001111101] ────▶ ["Java and | software | design"]

The same two objects after the assignment: `string1 = string2;`

Variable `string1` that   Address of start of object:
represents an object   000011010101

[000001111101] ──▶ ["Programm | ing and | problem | solving"]

Variable `string2` that   Address of start of object:
represents an object   000001111101

[000001111101] ────▶ ["Java and | software | design"]

FIGURE 3.13   Assigning a New Value to an Object Variable Doesn't Change the Objects

There is another key aspect of the way that reference variables work that you need to appreciate: Assigning a new object to a variable doesn't change the object that was previously assigned to it. Instead, the variable now refers to the new object; the old object remains unchanged, as shown in Figure 3.13. It's like moving to a new house or apartment. Your old residence still exists, but you go home to the new place each day.

■ Garbage Collection: Recycling Discarded Objects

To stretch this analogy a bit further, if no one else is living in your old residence, and it remains abandoned for long enough, the building may be demolished and the land reused. A similar thing happens in Java. If no variable refers to an object, then eventually the JVM detects this lack of a reference and reclaims its memory space so that it can be reused. In computer science, this process is called **garbage collection**. The term originated before recycling was a popular practice, but that's a better description of what really takes place.

Some programming languages, such as C++, require the programmer to call a method to return a discarded object's memory for reuse. This approach, which is called **explicit memory management**, has an advantage in that it can be faster than automatic garbage collection. The disadvantage is that when a programmer forgets to call the delete operation for a discarded object, the memory space isn't recycled, creating a condition known as a **memory leak**. If this happens often enough, the application can run out of memory.

Garbage collection
Recycling of memory when objects are no longer needed

Explicit memory management   Recycling of object memory that must be manually coded

Memory leak   Failure to recycle memory when explicit memory management is being used

Memory leaks are a major source of bugs in modern software. If you have an application written in a language like C++, and it gradually slows down and eventually freezes, it probably has a memory leak. Automatic garbage collection was included in Java to avoid these kinds of problems.

Here's an example that illustrates a case where garbage collection will take place:

```java
String name = "Eleni Kaitlin Proust";
System.out.println(name);
name = "Catherine Kassie Allard";
System.out.println(name);
```

In the first statement, the variable `name` is created and assigned the address of a `String` object containing the letters `"Eleni Kaitlin Proust"`. The second statement prints the value referenced by `name`. The third statement instantiates a new `String` object, containing the letters `"Catherine Kassie Allard"` and assigns its address to `name`, replacing the reference to the original string. At this point, no variable refers to the object containing `"Eleni Kaitlin Proust"`, so its memory space is recycled.

Ethics and Responsibilities in the Computing Profession

Every profession works under a set of ethics that help to define the responsibilities of its practitioners. For example, medical professionals have an ethical responsibility to keep information about their patients confidential. Engineers must protect the public and environment from harm that may result from their work. Writers are ethically bound not to plagiarize.

Computers can affect both people and the environment in dramatic ways. As a consequence, they challenge society to deal with new ethical issues. Some existing ethical practices apply to the computer, whereas other situations require the development of new rules. In some cases, it will be up to you to decide what is ethical.

Software Piracy

Computer software is easy to copy. But just like books, software is usually copyrighted—it is illegal to copy software without the permission of its creator. Such copying is called **software piracy**.

Copyright laws exist to protect the creators of software (and books and art) so that they can make a profit. A major software package can cost millions of dollars to develop, an expense that is reflected in its purchase price. If people make unauthorized copies of the software, then the company loses sales.

Software pirates sometimes rationalize their theft with the excuse that they're just making one copy for their own use. It's not that they're selling a bunch of bootleg copies, after all. Nevertheless, they have failed to compensate the company for the benefit they received. If thousands of people do the same thing, the losses may add up to millions of dollars, which leads to higher prices for everyone.

Background Information

Computing professionals have an ethical obligation to not engage in software piracy and to try to stop it from occurring. You should never copy software without permission. If someone asks to copy some software that you have, you should refuse to supply it. If someone says that he or she just wants to "borrow" the software to "try it out," tell the person that he or she is welcome to try it out on your machine but not to make a copy.

This rule applies to more than just duplication of copyrighted software—it includes plagiarism of all or part of code that belongs to anyone else. If someone gives you permission to copy some of his or her code, then—just like any responsible writer—you should acknowledge that person with a citation in the comments.

Privacy of Data

The computer enables the compilation of databases containing useful information about people, companies, and so on. These databases allow employers to issue payroll checks, banks to cash a customer's check at any branch, the government to collect taxes, and mass merchandisers to send out junk mail. Even though we may not care for every use of databases, they generally have positive benefits. Unfortunately, they can also be used in negative ways.

For example, a car thief who gains access to a state's motor vehicle database could print out a "shopping list" of car models together with their owners' addresses. An industrial spy might steal customer data from a company database and sell it to a competitor. Although these uses are obviously illegal acts, computer professionals face other situations that are not as clearly unethical.

Suppose your job involves managing the company payroll database, which includes the names and salaries of the firm's employees. You might be tempted to poke around the data and see how your salary compares to others–but this act is an unethical invasion of your associates' right to privacy. Any information about a person that is not clearly public should be considered confidential. An example of public information is a phone number listed in a telephone directory. Private information includes any data that has been provided with an understanding that it will be used only for a specific purpose (such as the data on a credit card application).

A computing professional has a responsibility to avoid taking advantage of special access that he or she may have to confidential data. The professional also has a responsibility to guard that data from unauthorized access by others. Protecting data can involve such simple measures as shredding old printouts, keeping backup copies in a locked cabinet, using passwords that are difficult to guess, and implementing more complex safeguards such as file encryption.

Use of Computer Resources

A computer is an unusual resource because there is no significant physical difference between a computer that is working and one that is sitting idle. By contrast, a car is in motion when it is working. To use a car without permission requires taking it physically—stealing it. Conversely, someone can make unauthorized use of a computer without physically taking it, by using its time and resources.

For some people, theft of computer resources is a game. The thief doesn't really want the resources, but likes the challenge of breaking through a computer's security system. Such people may think that their actions are acceptable if they don't do any harm. Whenever real work is displaced by such activities, however, harm is done. If nothing else, the thief is trespassing. By analogy, consider that even though no physical harm may be done by someone who breaks into your bedroom and takes a nap while you are away, that act is certainly disturbing to you because it poses a threat of harm.

Other thieves have malicious intentions and destroy data. Sometimes they leave behind programs that act as time bombs, causing harm later. Another destructive kind of program is a **virus**—a program that replicates itself, with the goal of spreading to other computers, usually via email or shared files. Some viruses are benign, merely using up some resources. Others are more destructive. Incidents have occurred in which viruses have cost millions of dollars in data losses. In contrast to a virus, which is spread by contact between users, a **worm** exploits gaps in a computer's security, hijacking it to search the Internet for other computers with the same gaps. When a computer is taken over and used for some other purpose, such as sending spam email, it is called a **zombie**.

These kinds of harmful programs are collectively known as **malware**. Now that spam accounts for the majority of worldwide email traffic, some viruses attempt to extort money from their victims, and zombies have been used to shut down parts of the Internet, the effects of malware on the computing industry have become very significant.

Computing professionals should never use computer resources without permission. We also have a responsibility to protect computers to which we have access by watching for signs of unusual use, writing applications without introducing security loopholes, installing security updates as soon as they are released, checking files for viruses, and so on.

Software piracy The unauthorized copying of software for either personal use or use by others

Virus Malicious code that replicates and spreads to other computers through email messages and file sharing, without authorization, and possibly with the intent of doing harm

Worm Malicious code that replicates and spreads to other computers through security gaps in the computer's operating system, without authorization, and possibly with the intent of doing harm

Zombie A computer that has been taken over for unauthorized use, such as sending spam email

Malware Software written with malicious purposes in mind

3.3 ⋮ Implementing Responsibilities with Methods

A method consists of a method heading plus a block that can contain executable statements, including local declarations. Here is the syntax diagram for one form of method declaration (the same form that we've been using for `main`):

Method-Declaration

```
Modifiers   void   Identifier  (  Parameter List  )
{
    Statement   ・ ・ ・
}
```

■ Headings and Parameters

The first line in the syntax diagram is the method's heading. Its purpose is to give the method a name, and to specify how the method is called. Chapter 2 drew a distinction between void methods and value-returning methods. As you can no doubt guess, writing the reserved word `void` in the heading indicates a void method. For now, we'll focus on void methods to illustrate other aspects of how methods are declared. Later, we'll look at value-returning methods.

Between the parentheses in a method heading are the method's parameters. A parameter is made up of two parts: a data type or class name, and an identifier (just like a field declaration). For example:

```
public void methodName(String param1)    // A parameter of class String,
                                          // called param1
```

Whereas field declarations end with a semicolon, parameters are listed between the parentheses with commas separating them. For example, here is a method heading with three parameters:

```
public void anotherMethodName(String param1, String param2, char param3)
```

You can think of the parameters as a special kind of local field within the method. Here's an example of a method heading showing a list of three parameters, arranged on separate lines, with comments indicating how each one is used:

```
void prepareTown(String name,    // Name of town
                 String state,   // State name, not abbreviation
                 char type)      // Type is one of (V)illage, (T)own, (C)ity
```

■ Calling a Method with a Given Heading

A call to a method with the preceding heading would contain three arguments: two strings and a character, in that order. For example:

```
myTown.prepareTown("Oconomowoc", "Wisconsin", 'T');
```

The arguments are copied into the parameter variables one-for-one, in the order listed, as shown here:

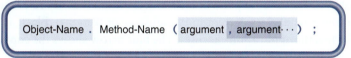

```
void prepareTown(String name, String state, char type)
```

```
myTown.prepareTown("Oconomowoc", "Wisconsin", 'T')
```

Keep in mind that when we say the arguments are copied into the parameters, the same mechanism is used as for assignment to a variable. Values of primitive types are copied directly, whereas copying the value of a reference type means that the reference (memory address value) is copied. Thus, with reference types, a parameter becomes an alias of the argument.

Let's take a closer look at how we call a method and what happens when we do so. Here is the syntax template for a statement that calls an instance method:

Call

```
Object-Name . Method-Name ( argument , argument··· ) ;
```

An instance method call first specifies the name of the object (class instance) that it is being applied to, such as the **myTown** object. The method name then indicates which of the instance methods is being applied. Following the method name is an argument list containing values that correspond in type or class to those of the parameter list in the method heading.

When a call to an instance method is executed, the argument values are copied from the argument list into the parameter variables. Control then jumps to the first statement in the method body. Statements within the body are executed normally and have access to four kinds of fields:

- Instance fields of the specified object
- Class fields
- Parameters
- Local variables or constants

The statements perform operations on these values, doing whatever work is needed. When the last statement in the method has executed, control returns to the statement following the call. Let's illustrate what happens with a small example method declaration and a call statement. Figure 3.14 shows two columns of code. The left column provides a segment of code within an

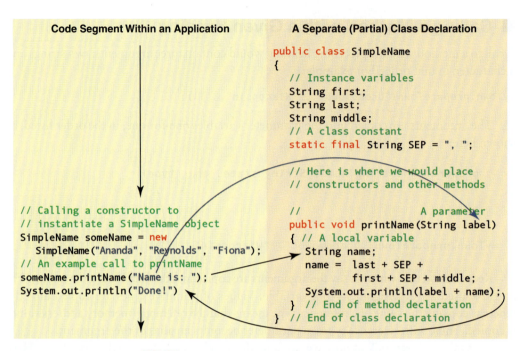

FIGURE 3.14 An Example Method Declaration and Call

application, while the right column shows those parts of a class declaration that are relevant to this example (we'll flesh out this partial class declaration in subsequent sections). Black arrows show the flow of control when the application executes. The blue arrow shows the copying of an argument in a call to a parameter in a method heading.

Control flows down through the statements in the application prior to the segment, as shown by the long black arrow. The first statement in the left column declares a `SimpleName` object called `someName` and uses a constructor to give values to its instance variables. We don't show the declaration of the constructor in the right column. Later in the chapter we will learn how to write a constructor, but for now simply recognize that a constructor assigns the strings in its argument list to the instance variables, and it would appear in the place that the comments indicate.

When the call to `someName.printName` occurs, a reference to the string `"Name is: "` is copied (blue arrow) into the `label` parameter in the method heading. The parameter `label` now contains the address of this string. Control then transfers to the first statement in the method body, which declares the local `String` variable called `name`.

The second statement in the method body concatenates a series of strings consisting of the instance variables `first`, `last`, and `middle` with the class constant `SEP`; it assigns the result to `name`. The last statement in the body concatenates the parameter string `label` with the local variable `name`, before displaying the result on the screen. After the output statement executes, control returns to the statement following the call, which displays "Done!" on the screen. The output on the screen from executing these statements would be

```
Reynolds, Ananda, Fiona
Done!
```

The preceding example happened to use an instance method, but a similar process occurs for a class method. Let's look more formally at the declaration of an instance method and then at class methods.

■ Instance Methods

Most of our methods are instance methods, so their headings are written without the `static` modifier. The appearance of `public` in the method heading indicates that we can use the method outside of its class. That is, client code can call the method. Almost all instance methods are `public`. For example, here is a heading for a `void` method that updates the name stored within a `Town` object:

```
public void updateTownName(String newTownName)
```

If we have an object of class `Town` called `homeTown`, then we could apply this method to that object with the following call:

```
homeTown.updateTownName("Henderson");
```

The body of an instance method is just a block of statements, like the block in `main`. It can include any of the statements we've seen, including local declarations. As we've noted, these statements have access to instance fields, class fields, local fields, and parameters. Here's an example of how we might declare the preceding method:

```
String townName;     // Class declaration of instance variable
 .
 .
 .
public void updateTownName(String newTownName)
{
   townName = newTownName;
}
```

This method simply copies the value in the parameter to the instance variable `townName`.

Because we can have more than one object of a given class, we must indicate to which object a method will be applied, so that the method can access the fields of that particular object. To do so, we write the object name in front of the method name with a dot in between, as we saw in the preceding example (and in Chapter 2):

```
homeTown.updateTownName("Henderson");
```

When `updateTownName` is called this way, it automatically has access to the fields within the `homeTown` object, including the `townName` field. If we called it for a different object,

```
otherTown.updateTownName("Salem");
```

then the method would access the `townName` field within the `otherTown` object instead. In the first case, it updates the name stored in the `homeTown` object; in the latter case, it updates the name stored in `otherTown`.

In Figure 3.14, we introduced the declaration of a `printName` method that has a parameter. We could also have a different version of `printName` that has no parameters:

```
public void printName()
{
  System.out.println(last + SEP + first + SEP + middle);
}
```

We would call it like this:

```
someName.printName();
```

Because there are no parameters in the declaration, there are no arguments in the call. This method can accomplish everything it must do by accessing the instance fields of the `someName` object, so we do not need to supply it with any additional values. In writing this version of the method, we also chose to forego the use of the local variable and simply made the concatenation expression an argument to the `println` method.

Now that we've seen how to declare and use instance methods, let's investigate class methods.

■ Class Methods

Syntactically, the only difference between a class method and an instance method is that a class method heading includes the `static` modifier. Here's an example of a class method heading, with the modifier highlighted:

```
public static void setDefaultTownType(char type)
```

The statements within a class method have access to class fields (fields that are likewise declared `static`), local fields, and parameters. Class methods cannot access the instance fields of individual objects.

As an analogy, consider a classroom (see Figure 3.15). The instructor, writing on the board at the front of the room, is like a class method storing values in class fields. Each student, writ-

FIGURE 3.15 Analogy of Class and Instance with a Classroom

ing in a notebook, is like an instance method accessing values in instance fields. All of the students (instances) and the instructor (class) can see what is on the board. What's written in a particular student's notebook (instance fields) is visible only to the student (instance).

Here's an example of a class method in the context of the `SimpleName` class, from Figure 3.14, that outputs the separator string with a user-supplied label. We again use a local variable, just to show how the method's statements can use local fields, class fields, and parameters:

```
public static void printSep(String label)
{
  String message = label + " \"" + SEP + "\"";
  System.out.println(message);
}
```

Class methods are not associated with any particular object, so we do not call them using an object's name. Rather, we call them using the class name, then a dot, and then the method name. Here is an example call to the preceding method:

```
SimpleName.printSep("The name separator is:");
```

When the call is executed, it outputs

```
The name separator is: ", "
```

Keep in mind that class methods are mainly useful for managing information that pertains to all objects in the class. As another example, suppose we have a `Temperature` class that is designed for general use. Depending on the application, we might want to specify limits on the temperature, so that a warning can be issued if an invalid temperature is input. For a medical application, we might set those limits at 90 and 110 degrees. The class would be written to include class (`static`) fields to hold the maximum and minimum temperatures, and it would have class (`static`) methods for setting and getting the values in those fields. Any object of class `Temperature` could also access those values.

■ Constructors

We use essentially the same syntax for a **constructor** as the syntax for any instance method, but with two special differences: (1) the method name is identical to the class name and (2) we omit the **void** keyword. Like instance methods, constructors have access to both instance and class fields. Constructors are almost always declared as **public**; a **private** constructor would be nearly useless because it could be called only from within the class. Here is an example constructor heading for our `SimpleName` class:

> **Constructor** An operation that creates a new instance of a class

```
public SimpleName(String firstName, String lastName, String middleName)
```

This constructor takes the parts of a name as arguments and stores them in the instance fields of the object that is being instantiated. If we use the field declarations for the `SimpleName` class shown in Figure 3.14 (`first`, `middle`, `last`), then we could write the whole constructor like this:

```
public SimpleName(String firstName, String lastName, String middleName)
{
  first = firstName;              // Assign parameters to fields
  last = lastName;
  middle = middleName;
}
```

As you can see, there's no magic here. It's just a matter of copying the values from the parameters to the fields of the object. Of course, we call a constructor using the **new** operator. Here is an example call to the **Name** constructor:

```
SimpleName myFriend = new SimpleName("Brian", "Smith", "Peter");
```

When the constructor returns, the **myFriend** object's fields will contain those initial values. What about the default constructor for **SimpleName**? Well, it's even easier to write, because it has no parameters and just has to create an empty name. Thus it can merely assign the empty string to the fields.

```
public SimpleName()
{
  first = "";                     // Assign empty string to fields
  last = "";
  middle = "";
}
```

■ An Example Class: SimpleName

Let's put all of the pieces of our **SimpleName** class together into a complete class declaration, and write a short demonstration driver to illustrate its use. We begin with the class declaration:

```
//********************************************
// This is a specialized class representing a
// name, for demonstration purposes only
//********************************************
public class SimpleName
{
  // Instance variables
  String first;
  String last;
  String middle;
  // A class constant
  static final String SEP = ", ";

  // Default constructor
  public SimpleName()
  {
    first = "";                     // Assign empty string to fields
    last = "";
    middle = "";
```

```java
}
// Constructor
public SimpleName(String firstName, String lastName, String middleName)
{
  first = firstName;            // Assign parameters to fields
  last = lastName;
  middle = middleName;
}
// Class method to print the separator
public static void printSep(String label)
{
  String message = label + " \"" + SEP + "\"";
  System.out.println(message);
}
// Instance method to print the name, with a label
public void printName(String label)
{
  String name;
  name = last + SEP + first + SEP + middle;
  System.out.println(label + name);
}
// Instance method to print the name, without a label
public void printName()
{
  System.out.println(last + SEP + first + SEP + middle);
}
}   // End of class declaration
```

Here is the code for a driver that demonstrates the use of this class:

```java
public class DemoSimpleName
{
  public static void main(String[] args)
  {
    // Calling a constructor to instantiate a SimpleName object
    SimpleName someName = new SimpleName("Ananda", "Reynolds", "Fiona");
    // An example call to printName with a label
    someName.printName("Name is: ");
    // An example call to printName without a label
    someName.printName();
    // An example call to class method printSep
    SimpleName.printSep("The separator string is:");
    System.out.println("Done!");
  }
}
```

Here is the output from running the driver:

```
Name is: Reynolds, Ananda, Fiona
Reynolds, Ananda, Fiona
The separator string is: ", "
Done!
```

The code for the class is placed in a file called `SimpleName.java`, and the code for the driver is placed in a file called `DemoSimpleName.java`. Both files are saved in the same directory. When we call the Java compiler to compile `DemoSimpleName.java`, it automatically looks in the same directory for the `SimpleName.java` source file and compiles it as well. The corresponding Bytecode files produced by the compiler are called `DemoSimpleName.class` and `SimpleName.class`, respectively. When we tell the JVM to run the demo, it loads both of these `class` files into memory and starts execution with the first statement in `main`.

■ Helper Methods

In addition to instance methods, class methods, and constructors, sometimes we need a method that just gets a job done within a class. For example, if an application prints a report with a complicated set of column headings, the code will be easier to follow if we place the statements that print the heading within a method. Then, at the point where we want to print the heading, we just call the method:

`printHeading();`

> **Helper method** A method that is private to a class, and called from within other methods of the class. Typically used to simplify code or supply an operation that is used at multiple points in the class.

This isn't a responsibility of the class that we want the user to be able to access. Rather, it's a part of a larger responsibility (printing a page of the report) that we've set aside to make the code easier to read. Such methods are called **helper methods**.

Helper methods are declared privately within a class. They are used in complex classes to help organize the code or to provide operations that are used only internally to the class. These helper methods are called from within other methods of the class. A call to a helper method is not appended to an object or class identifier because it is clear which class it is in, and it is not associated with any specific object. Helper methods therefore use the `private` modifier and are `static`. Here's an example heading:

`private static void printheading()`

Helper methods are not a feature defined by Java. The only thing that distinguishes a helper method from a normal class method is the fact that we use it strictly to help organize our code and simplify the internal implementation of a class.

Overuse of helper methods is often a sign that we have inadequately identified objects and responsibilities in a problem. If you are writing an application and discover that you need many helper methods, you should stop and reconsider your solution to the problem. Most likely you have slipped into the style of programming that was used in procedural languages, in which the focus was on the processing steps, rather than on the coordinated interaction of objects in the problem.

To summarize, instance methods are associated with individual objects. Class (`static`) methods are associated with classes. Constructors are used with the `new` operator to prepare

Method	Use
Instance	Operation associated with a specific object
Class (`static`)	Operation associated with a whole class
Constructor	Used to create a new instance of the class via the `new` operator
Helper (`private static`)	Called only by other methods within a class

TABLE 3.1   Types of Methods

an object for use. Helper (auxiliary) methods are subprograms within a class that help other methods in the class. Table 3.1 lists these four kinds of methods and describes how they are used.

■ A Different Form: Value-Returning Methods

So far we have examined only `void` methods or constructors. Of course, Java also supports value-returning methods. We use value-returning methods to return a single value to the point where the method is called. For example, if we want to get the first name from a `Name` object called `myName`, we would call a value-returning method:

```
myFirstName = myName.getFirstName();
```

Much of what you have learned about `void` methods is valid for value-returning methods. The differences are all related to the process of returning a value:

1. Instead of writing `void` in the heading, we write a data type or a class name that specifies the type of value to be returned.
2. Instead of calling the method as a separate statement, we call it from within an expression so that the returned value can be assigned to a variable or used in another way.
3. The method body includes a *return* statement that specifies the value to be returned.

Value-returning methods can be instance methods, class methods, or helper methods. When we design any of these kinds of methods, we get to choose whether to make them `void` or value-returning. Constructors are neither `void` nor value-returning; they are a special case that is separate from the other kinds of methods.

The same syntax rules apply for writing any method call, whether it is `void` or value-returning. With an instance method, we append the method name to the object name. With a class method, we append the method name to the class name. We call a helper method simply by using its name. The only difference relates to where the call appears—in an expression or as a separate statement. Here are examples that show a call to each type of value-returning method:

```
first = myName.getFirstName();       // Instance call; myName is an object
townType = Town.getDefaultType();    // Class call; Town is the class name
stateAbbrev = getAbbrev(state);      // Helper call; used inside of Town
                                     //   class only
```

Here is an example of a heading for the `getFirstName` value-returning instance method. Note that it takes no parameters and returns a string. The absence of the `static` modifier makes it an instance method.

```
public String getFirstName()  // Public method; returns a string; has no
                              //   parameters
```

The heading of a value-returning method indicates the type or class of the value to be returned. Java uses this information to enforce strong typing. To actually return a value, we use a *return* statement. Its syntax is simple:

Return-Statement

```
return expression ;
```

Whatever value is computed by the expression is returned. The *return* statement also has the effect of causing execution of the method to end. Execution immediately returns to the point where the method was called, and the value from the expression takes the place of the method call in the expression.

The return statement is usually the last statement in a method body. We say "usually" because, as we will see in Chapter 5 when we introduce branching control flow, it is possible to have *return* statements in different branches. Until then, the last statement in a value-returning method body should be a *return*.

Let's look at a complete value-returning method by finishing the definition of `getFirstName`. The following code assumes that `first`, `last`, and `middle` are string variables declared as instance fields in the enclosing `Name` class:

```
public String getFirstName()     // Returns first name
{
  return first;
}
```

Is that it? Yes, it really is just that simple. In fact, many value-returning methods are equally simple. They are often used merely to return a value that is stored in an object. Such methods are known as **observers**.

One characteristic of the object-oriented programming style is that we create many short methods as a means of building up a level of abstraction that simplifies the coding of larger problems. If we hide all of the details within classes and their methods, then the final solution can be coded in a way that is simple and easy to understand and therefore, easy to debug and maintain. We call this kind of hiding *encapsulation*, and we discuss the underlying concepts further in Chapter 8.

Our `Name` class has three such observers, all of which follow this same pattern. Here is the code for the other two:

> **Observer** An operation that returns information from an object without changing the content of the object

```
public String getMiddleName()    // Returns middle name
{
  return middle;
}

public String getLastName()      // Returns Last name
{
  return last;
}
```

■ Constructor-Observer Classes

The `Name` class consists of only constructors and observer methods, and none of its fields are public. Many classes have this simple form. They store some information in an object when it is created and then allow client code to retrieve that information. Some observers operate on the stored data before returning a value. For example, a `Town` object might have an observer that uses the name of the state to look up and return the two-letter postal abbreviation for the state. Observer operations can be quite powerful.

Constructor–observer classes have a special property, called **immutability**. That is, once an object is instantiated with an initial value, it cannot be changed. Immutable classes are immune to aliasing bugs. The Java `String` class, for example, is immutable. To keep our problem solutions simple and avoid these kinds of bugs, we will write only immutable classes until Chapter 8.

> **Immutability** The property of a class that its instances cannot be modified once they are created

Theoretical Foundations

Q.E.D.

Categories of Responsibilities

Class instance responsibilities generally fall into two categories: constructors and observers. Here we consider a third type: **transformer** responsibilities.

Operators that modify the state of an object are called transformers or mutators. Adding a transformer responsibility to a class makes it mutable and opens up the possibility of alias errors. Whenever your design necessitates a transformer to appear in a class, you should watch out for alias-related errors.

A special case of constructor, called a **copy constructor**, takes an object as an argument and returns a new object that holds a copy of the contents of the original object. A copy is not the same as an alias. When you copy an object, you have two objects that hold the same data, stored in different places, and referred to by different variables. If a transformer changes a copy, the original is not affected.

> **Transformer (mutator)** An operation that changes the internal state of an object

> **Copy constructor** An operation that creates a new instance of a class by copying an existing instance, possibly altering some or all of its state in the process

3.4 : Complete Name Class

Now we can create our general class **Name**. This class has the three observers that we just saw and two constructors that are very similar to the constructors for the more specialized **SimpleName** class that we developed previously. We can either leave off the access modifier in the heading for **Name** or we can make it **public**. If we intended to use **Name** in only one application, then omitting the access modifier would be fine. But looking ahead, we know that we will eventually want to put **Name** and some other classes into a separate package for use by multiple applications. Given that anticipated use, we decide to make it **public**.

```
//***************************************************************
//   Class Name
//   Implements a basic class representing a name with three parts.
//***************************************************************
public class Name
{
  String first;                      // Person's first name
  String last;                       // Person's last name
  String middle;                     // Person's middle name

  // Constructors
  public Name()                      // Assign empty strings to fields
  {
```

```
    first = "";
    last = "";
    middle = "";
  }

  public Name(String firstName, String lastName, String middleName)
  {
    first = firstName;              // Assign parameters to fields
    last = lastName;
    middle = middleName;
  }

  // Observer methods
  public String getFirstName()
  {
    return first;
  }

  public String getMiddleName()
  {
    return middle;
  }

  public String getLastName()
  {
    return last;
  }
}
```

Now that we've seen how to write methods and classes, let's go through the process of building an object-oriented application similar to **PrintName**. Because our **Name** class stores the whole middle name, the formats can be changed to use the middle name rather than just the middle initial. We'll do so in the context of a case study.

May We Introduce

Ada Lovelace

On December 10, 1815, a daughter—Augusta Ada Byron—was born to Anna Isabella (Annabella) Byron and George Gordon, Lord Byron. In England at that time, Byron's fame derived not only from his poetry but also from his wild and scandalous behavior. The marriage was strained from the beginning, and Annabella left Byron shortly after Ada's birth. By April 1816, the two had signed separation papers. Byron left England, never to return. Throughout the rest of his life, he regretted that he was unable to see his daughter. At one point he wrote of her,

> I see thee not. I hear thee not.
> But none can be so wrapt in thee.

Before he died in Greece, at age 36, he exclaimed,

> Oh my poor dear child! My dear Ada!
> My God, could I but have seen her!

Meanwhile, Annabella, who eventually became a baroness in her own right, and who was educated as both a mathematician and a poet, carried on with Ada's upbringing and education. Annabella gave Ada her first instruction in mathematics, but it soon became clear that Ada was gifted in the subject and should receive more extensive tutoring. Ada received further training from Augustus DeMorgan, today famous for one of the basic theorems of Boolean algebra. By age eight, Ada had demonstrated an interest in mechanical devices and was building detailed model boats.

When she was 18, Ada visited the Mechanics Institute to hear Dr. Dionysius Lardner's lectures on the Difference Engine, a mechanical calculating machine being built by Charles Babbage. She became so interested in the device that she arranged to be introduced to Babbage. It was said that, upon seeing Babbage's machine, Ada was the only person in the room to understand immediately how it worked and to recognize its significance. Ada and Babbage became lifelong friends. She worked with him, helping to document his designs, translating writings about his work, and developing programs for his machines. In fact, Ada today is recognized as history's first computer programmer.

When Babbage designed his Analytical Engine, Ada foresaw that it could go beyond arithmetic computations and become a general manipulator of symbols, and thus would have far-reaching capabilities. She even suggested that such a device eventually could be programmed with rules of harmony and composition so that it could produce "scientific" music. In effect, Ada foresaw the field of artificial intelligence more than 150 years ago.

In 1842, Babbage gave a series of lectures in Turin, Italy, on his Analytical Engine. One of the attendees was Luigi Menabrea, who was so impressed that he wrote an account of Babbage's lectures. At age 27, Ada decided to translate the account into English, with the intent to add a few of her own notes about the machine. In the end, her notes were twice as long as the original material, and the document, "The Sketch of the Analytical Engine," became the definitive work on the subject.

It is obvious from Ada's letters that her "notes" were entirely her own and that Babbage was acting as a sometimes unappreciated editor. At one point, Ada wrote to him,

> I am much annoyed at your having altered my Note. You know I am always willing to make any required alterations myself, but that I cannot endure another person to meddle with my sentences.

Ada gained the title Countess of Lovelace when she married Lord William Lovelace. The couple had three children, whose upbringing was left to Ada's mother while Ada pursued her work in mathematics. Her husband was supportive of her work, but for a woman of that day, such behavior was considered almost as scandalous as some of her father's exploits.

Ada died in 1852, just one year before a working Difference Engine was built in Sweden from one of Babbage's designs. Like her father, Ada lived only to age 36. Even though they led very different lives, she undoubtedly had admired him and took inspiration from his unconventional and rebellious nature. In the end, Ada asked to be buried beside him at the family's estate.

PROBLEM SOLVING CASE STUDY

Display a Name in Multiple Formats

Problem: You are beginning to work on a problem that needs to output names in several formats. To start, you decide to write a short Java application that inputs a single name and displays it in a variety of formats, so you can be certain that all of your string expressions are correct. From the `PrintName` application in Chapter 2, you are already familiar with much of the work that needs to be done. Now that you have a `Name` class, however, you can take advantage of its capabilities.

Input: The name in three parts, as input from the keyboard via a `Scanner` object:

First

Last

Middle

Output: The input name in two formats:

First Last

Last, First, Middle

Discussion: You could easily type the name in the two formats as string literals in the code, but the purpose of this exercise is to develop and test the string expressions you need for the larger problem. This case study is also a good opportunity to make use of the `Name` class that we've defined previously.

Our application must input the name, create a name object, and output the name in the two formats. Here we list these steps:

Name Driver
Define a Name myName Input the first, middle, and last names, instantiate a Name object, and assign it to myName Print First Last Format Print Last First Middle Format

Let's start with the first step. To do this, we must define a variable of class `Name`.

```
Name myName;
```

Well, that was certainly easy! The second step must input the name using the `nextLine` method in class `Scanner`. To do so, we first instantiate a `Scanner`, then for each of the three parts, we prompt the user to input the part and read it via the `Scanner`. There are quite a few steps here. Let's make this operation a helper method called `getName`. It will return an object of class `Name` that we can assign to `myName`. Here is a list of what it must do:

getName Helper, returns Name
Declare String variables for first, last, and middle names Declare a Scanner called in Instantiate a Scanner using System.in, and assign it to in

```
Prompt for first name on System.out
Get first name from in
Prompt for last name on System.out
Get last name from in
Prompt for middle name on System.out
Get middle name from in
return a Name object, created from the input values
```

The last two steps of the application use straightforward string expressions to output the different formats. The only difference from our prior examples is that the strings must be retrieved from `myName` by calling its observers. Let's use literals in the output strings rather than defining named constants.

Print First Last Format

```
println myName.first() + " " + myName.last()
```

Print Last First Middle Format

```
println myName.last() + ", " + myName.first() + ", " + myName.middle()
```

To each of these output statements, we should add strings that explain what is being output. When a program outputs results without telling the user what they represent, the results may be nearly useless.

We are almost ready to write the code for the application. It consists of an enclosing class, called `PrintName`, that contains the `getName` helper method and the `main` method.

What do we do with the `Name` class? We compile it separately in the same directory as the application. When the JVM begins to execute the application, it also looks for other classes in the same directory and connects them with the application (a process called *linking*).

Many development environments allow you to create a *project* that contains all of the files associated with an application. In such an environment, you may begin by specifying the name of the application. The environment then creates a new directory containing a file that holds the application code. To create an associated class such as `Name`, you ask the environment to create a new Java source file, and it then automatically remembers to compile this file together with your application. In a later chapter, we look at how to enclose a class in a package with other classes and see how to import it from a different directory.

Now we can code the application. We also include comments as necessary.

```java
//*********************************************************************
// PrintName Application
// This application inputs a name and prints it in two different formats
//*********************************************************************
import java.util.Scanner;

public class PrintName
{
  // Helper method: Gets a name from System.in
  private static Name getName()
```

```java
{
  String first;
  String last;
  String middle;
  Scanner in;                                    // Input for strings
  in = new Scanner(System.in);                   // Instantiate Scanner

  System.out.print("Enter first name: ");        // Prompt for first name
  first = in.nextLine();                         // Get first name
  System.out.print("Enter last name: ");         // Prompt for last name
  last = in.nextLine();                          // Get last name
  System.out.print("Enter middle name: ");       // Prompt for middle name
  middle = in.nextLine();                        // Get middle name
  in.close();                                    // Close Scanner object
  return new Name(first, last, middle);          // Create a Name and return
                                                 // it
}

//Driver for application
public static void main(String[] args)
{
  Name myName;                                   // Declare a name
  myName = getName();                            // Instantiate a
                                                 // name
  System.out.println("Name in first-last format is " +
                 myName.getFirstName() + " " +
                 myName.getLastName());          // First format
  System.out.println("Name in last-first-middle format is " +
                 myName.getLastName() + ", " +
                 myName.getFirstName() + ", " +
                 myName.getMiddleName());        // Second format
}
}
```

It's hard to believe that **main** contains just four statements! But the combination of a helper method and the **Name** class has made it possible to write **main** so that it looks just like our initial algorithm.

The output from the program follows:

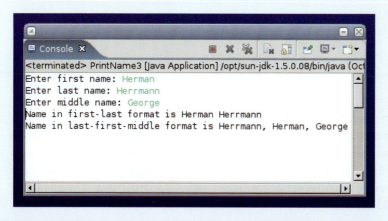

This application is very similar to the `PrintName` application that we wrote in Chapter 2, yet it is longer. In some ways it seems like a waste to make this extra effort. The advantage, however, is that now we have a `Name` class that we can use in other applications. We also have the ability to instantiate multiple names just by adding declarations and constructor calls to the application. The object-oriented version is much easier to reuse, to maintain, and to extend. The original version had fewer lines of code, but was monolithic in its construction and solved one specific problem. The object-oriented version is divided into useful pieces that can be applied to solve many different problems. We've done a little more work now, but have potentially saved much more work in the future.

3.5 : Testing and Debugging

Testing and Debugging Hints

1. Take the time to design a problem solution properly, identifying the classes and responsibilities before you start coding.
2. Be clear about which methods are class methods and which are instance methods. The heading for a class method includes the `static` modifier. The heading for an instance method does not.
3. When you call a class method, be aware that its name is appended to the name of the class. When you call an instance method, its name is appended to an object identifier.
4. Recognize that constructors are neither `void` nor value-returning; they are not `static`. A constructor's name must be identical to the name of the enclosing class.
5. Make sure that the application class and `main` are `public`. Classes should also be `public` if they will be used by client code. If a class will be used with just one application and always compiled together with it, then you can omit the access modifier.
6. If class declarations are to be accessed by a `static` method, they must also be marked `static`.
7. Do not include `void` in the heading of a value-returning method. In its place, write a data type or class name.
8. Remember to include a *return* statement in a value-returning method.

Summary

Every class has a set of attributes and responsibilities, which can be associated with either instances or the class. Each time a new object is created, a new set of instance attributes is created along with it to hold its specific values. Class attributes exist in only one place, and all objects have access to the same ones. Instance responsibilities have access to instance attributes and class attributes, whereas class responsibilities can access only class attributes. The attributes are implemented with field declarations, and the responsibilities are implemented by methods.

Java distinguishes between two major categories of data types: primitive and reference. A value of a primitive type is stored directly in a memory location of a field of that type. A value of a reference type, such as an object, is stored at a different place in memory, and the field contains the address of that place. A reference type field is thus said to refer to its object. Assignment of one reference type variable to another copies the address, rather than the object itself. When multiple fields refer to the same object, they are said to be aliases. Unintentional use of aliases can lead to some hard-to-find bugs.

Four types of methods exist: instance methods, class methods, constructors, and helper methods. Each of these methods is called with its name and an argument list, but is preceded by an object name, a class name, `new`, or nothing, respectively. A constructor is called when an object is instantiated via the `new` operator, and its name is the same as the name of the class. Class methods are associated with the class itself, rather than with a specific object. An instance method must be applied to a specified object when it is called. Helper methods are `private` to a class and can be called only from other methods within the class.

All kinds of methods, except constructors, can be either value-returning or `void`. Value-returning methods are called from within an expression, whereas `void` methods are called as separate statements. A *return* statement is used to pass the value back to the calling point of a value-returning method.

Methods that return information from an object without changing its contents are called observers. Classes whose `public` methods consist only of constructors and observers, and which have no public fields, are said to be immutable.

LEARNING / Portfolio

Quick Check

1. What are attributes and responsibilities? (pp. 108–112)
2. When we assign a string to a variable, what is actually stored in the variable? (pp. 117–118)
3. What do we call the situation in which multiple identifiers refer to the same object? (pp. 118–120)
4. What does a class heading consist of? (pp. 106–107)
5. What does a `void` method heading consist of? (p. 124)
6. Write a call to the default constructor for the class `Name`. (pp. 129–130)
7. What distinguishes an instance method from a class method? (pp. 127–129)
8. Name four types of methods. (p. 133)
9. To what is a class method applied? (pp. 128–129)
10. To what is an instance method applied? (pp. 127–128)
11. What is a property of a constructor–observer class? (p. 135)

LEARNING / Portfolio

Answers

1. The data values and operations associated with a class and its objects. 2. The address where the string can be found in memory. 3. Aliases. 4. A class heading consists of modifiers, the reserved word `class`, and a name. 5. The heading consists of modifiers, the reserved word `void`, a name, and a parameter list. 6. `new Name()` 7. A class method has the word `static` in its heading. 8. instance, class, constructor, helper. 9. The class name. 10. An object. 11. Immutability.

Exam Preparation Exercises

1. Is a field declaration an implementation of an attribute or a responsibility?

2. How does an instance value differ from a class value?

3. Which reserved word does Java use to distinguish class fields?

4. Which reserved word does Java use to distinguish class methods?

5. What kinds of fields can an instance method access?

6. What kinds of fields can a class method access?

7. How do primitive and reference types differ, in terms of what happens when we assign a value to a variable?

8. Class fields can hold only reference types. (True or False?)

9. When you print a reference type variable, you find that it has been modified, yet you don't see any statement that changes the variable. What is the likely source of this error?

10. What happens during garbage collection?

11. How does the heading for a `void` method differ from the heading for a value-returning method?

12. What happens to the flow of control when we call a method?

13. A method has three parameters in its parameter list–A, B, and C, in that order. All three parameters are strings. The method is called with the arguments "cat", "dog", and "bird", in that order. Which parameter receives the reference to "dog"?

14. Which modifiers usually appear in a helper method heading?

15. A value-returning method heading includes a type or class name. How does Java use this information?

16. What does a constructor do?

17. Name three kinds of methods other than a constructor.

18. Do we use a *return* statement with a `void` method?

19. Can a method have more than one *return* statement?

20. Helper methods should be only value-returning. (True or False?)

LEARNING / Portfolio

Programming Warm-Up Exercises

1. What would be the attributes for a business address class?

2. What would be the attributes for a phone number class that includes country and area codes?

3. List the responsibilities for a constructor-observer version of a business address class.

4. List the responsibilities for the phone number class described in Exercise 2, assuming it has only constructors and observers for each attribute.

5. Write the field declarations for a `LongName` class that includes instance attributes for a title, first name, middle name, last name, and suffix. All of the fields are strings.

6. Write a default constructor for the `LongName` class described in Exercise 5 that sets all of the fields to the empty string.

7. Write a constructor for the `LongName` class described in Exercise 5 that takes five strings as arguments and assigns their values to the fields.

8. Write a value-returning instance method for the `LongName` class, called `getTitle`, that returns the title as a string.

9. Write a statement that instantiates a `LongName` object with a given name and assigns it to a variable called `yourName`.

10. Given the statement written in Exercise 9, write a statement that calls the `getTitle` method described in Exercise 8 and prints the value that it returns.

11. Write a helper method that inputs the values needed to construct a `LongName` object. The method should construct the object with the input values and return it.

12. Write a class that represents a user name and a password, each of which is a string. The class should include a default constructor, a constructor that supplies both attribute values, and observers that return each attribute, plus an observer that returns the concatenation of the two, separated by the string contained in a class variable called `sep`. The constructors should initialize `sep` to `"//"`.

13. To the class written in Exercise 12, add class methods that give a new value to `sep` and that return the current value of `sep`.

14. To the class written in Exercise 12, add a `void` method that prints the user name and password on separate lines.

15. Write a class that represents a date, with the month, day, and year represented by strings. The class should have a constructor that takes the three parts of the date as parameters, and value-returning methods that return the date in mm/dd/yyyy format and in yyyy-mm-dd format. (*Hint*: The general structure of this class is very similar to that of `Name`.)

LEARNING / Portfolio

Programming Problems

1. Design and implement a class to represent a product description for a catalog. It should have as attributes the name of the product, the category, and the description, each of which can be represented by a string. The class should provide a default constructor and a direct constructor, and observers for the attributes. Implement a driver that tests the class.

2. Design and implement a class to represent a multiple-choice question on an exam. Each question consists of a section that asks the question, and then four choices of answer, each of which is a letter followed by the answer. For example:

   What type of method is typically declared as private and static?
   a. Constructor
   b. Instance
   c. Class
   d. Helper

   The class should have attributes for the question, the four answers, and the correct response. An example call to a constructor for this class would be

   ```
   ExamQuestion q17 =

       new ExamQuestion(

           "What type of method is typically declared as private and static?",

           "Constructor", "Instance", "Class", "Helper", 'd');
   ```

   The class should supply observers that return each of the attributes as well as supply a method that prints the question on System.out in the format shown above. Develop a driver that tests the class.

3. Design and implement a class that represents an email entry. It should have an attribute for the person's name (which can be of class Name) and attributes for the user name and address portions of the email address. For example:

   ```
   Catherine Mahoney

   cmahoney

   gwebcast.com
   ```

   The class should provide an observer for each attribute, and it should provide a method that returns the email address in the usual form. In the case of the example, this would be

   ```
   cmahoney@gwebcast.com
   ```

   Develop a driver that tests this class.

4. Develop an application that inputs a name and an address, and prints out a form letter. The letter should begin with the address, including the person's full name. Then it should use the salutation "Dear <firstname>," where <firstname> is the person's first name. Within the letter, the text should address the person by his or her first name at least once. You can use the `Name` class to represent the name, and develop your own class to represent the address. You get to make up the content of the form letter, which can be as serious or silly as you like.

Case Study Follow-Up

1. Change the `PrintName` application so that the two formats are shown in the opposite order on the screen.

2. In the `PrintName` application, explain what takes place in the *return* statement in the method `getName`.

3. Change the `PrintName` application so that it also prints the name in the following format:

First-name Middle-name Last-name

4. Change the `PrintName` application so that it inputs two names and displays them in the different formats. You should be able to do this by adding just three statements to `main`.

4 Numeric Types

Goals

Knowledge Goals

To:

- Discover why different numeric types have different ranges of values
- Understand the differences between integral and floating-point types
- See how precedence rules affect the order of evaluation in an expression
- Understand implicit type conversion and explicit type casting
- Be able to use additional operations associated with the `String` class
- Understand how value-returning methods work with numeric types

Skill Goals

To be able to:

- Declare named constants and variables of types `int` and `double`
- Construct simple arithmetic expressions
- Evaluate simple arithmetic expressions
- Construct and evaluate expressions that include multiple arithmetic operations
- Read numeric values using the methods in class `Scanner`
- Use Java math methods in expressions
- Format the statements in a class in a clear and readable fashion

---

1943
The first "Walkie-Talkie" is invented by Dan Nobel. This portable FM two-way radio uses 35 lb. backpacks

1945
J. Presper Eckert and John Mauchly join forces to develop the Electronic Discrete Variable Automatic Computer (EDVAC)

1945
John von Neumann outlines the principles of a stored-program computer

1945
A moth is discovered in a computer being used by Grace Murray Hopper. She later popularizes it as the first computer "bug"

1946
The ENIAC is unveiled at the Moore School of Electrical Engineering at UPENN and is accepted by the U.S. Army Ordnance Corps

1947
Magnetic drum memory is introduced

Introduction

In the preceding chapters, we focused on the `char` type and `String` class, and we saw how to construct expressions using the concatenation operator. In the first part of this chapter, we concentrate on additional built-in data types: `int`, `long`, `float`, and `double`. These numeric types include multiple operators that enable us to construct complex arithmetic expressions. Calls to Java's math methods can make expressions even more powerful. Later in the chapter, we reconsider value-returning methods in the context of numeric types. Finally, we introduce a simple form of graphical user interface (GUI), called a dialog, that lets us ask the user a question and get a response.

1947
The world's first transistor is developed at Bell Labs

1948
Researchers at the University of Manchester develop the Manchester Mark I, a computer with all the main components of today's computers that can store data and user programs in electronic memory

1949
Jay Forrester refines magnetic core memory in his work on the Whirlwind computer

1949
John Mauchly creates the first high-level programming language: Short Order Code

1950
Alan Turing asks "Can Machines Think?" and outlines criteria for the Turing Test of machine intelligence

1951
The UNIVAC (Universal Automatic Computer) I is completed

4.1 ⋮ Numeric Data Types

In Chapter 3, we focused on reference types. In this chapter, we add the integral and floating-point types to our tool kit (see Figure 4.1). The one remaining primitive type is `boolean`, which we cover in Chapter 5.

You are already familiar with the basic concepts of integers and real numbers in mathematics. On a computer, however, the corresponding data types have certain limitations.

■ Integral Types

The data types `byte`, `short`, `int`, and `long` are known as integral (or integer) types because they refer to integer values—whole numbers with no fractional part. In Java, the simplest form of integer value is a sequence of one or more digits:

```
22   16   1   498   0   4600
```

Commas are not allowed.

A minus sign preceding an integer value makes the integer negative:

```
-378   -912
```

Unlike the mathematical definition of the integers, which allows numbers to have an infinite number of digits, integers in the computer are limited in size. The data types `byte`, `short`, `int`, and `long` represent different sizes of integers, as shown in Figure 4.2. The Java language specifies the sizes of the integral types in terms of the number of bits used to store their values. The more bits in the type, the larger the integer value that can be stored.

The `int` type is, by far, the most commonly used choice for manipulating integer data. The `byte` and `short` types are rarely used, but you may need to use `long` if your application re-

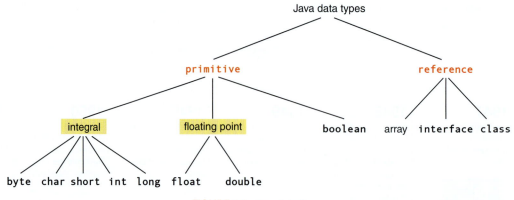

FIGURE 4.1   Java Data Types

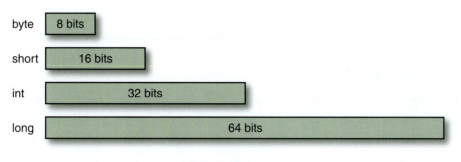

FIGURE 4.2 The Integral Types in Java

quires values larger than the maximum `int` value. The range of `int` values is from −2147483648 through +2147483647. As we noted in Chapter 1, such strange values serve as a reminder that the computer works in the base-2 number system.

A variable of type `int` can hold values such as the cost figures for the production of a movie. For values with more digits, such as the U.S. national debt, the `long` type, which can hold any integer up to 18 digits, would be required.

When you write a literal integer value, Java automatically assumes that it is of type `int`. To write a literal of type `long`, follow the last digit of the number with the letter "`L`". A lowercase "`l`" is acceptable, but it looks so much like the digit "`1`" that it is difficult to recognize the literal as `long` when reading the code. Here are some examples of literals of type `int` and `long`:

Literal	Type
0	`int`
0L	`long`
2007	`int`
18005551212L	`long`
18005551212	invalid (11 digits are too many for the type `int`)

If your code tries to compute a value larger than a type's maximum value, it results in integer overflow. Some programming languages give you an error message when overflow occurs, but Java doesn't. If a computation in Java produces a value that is too large for the type to represent, you simply get an erroneous result.

One caution about integer literals in Java: A literal constant beginning with a zero is assumed to be an octal (base 8) number instead of a decimal (base 10) number. For example, if you write

015

the Java compiler takes it to mean the decimal number 13. If you aren't familiar with the octal number system, don't worry about why an octal 15 is the same as a decimal 13. The important thing to remember is not to start a decimal integer literal with a zero (unless you want the number 0, which is the same in both octal and decimal).

■ Floating-Point Types

We use floating-point types to represent real numbers. Floating-point numbers have an integer part and a fractional part, with a decimal point in between the two parts. Either the integer part or the fractional part—but not both—may be missing. Here are some examples:

18.0   127.54   0.57   4.   193145.8523   .8

Starting 0.57 with a 0 does not make it an octal number. That rule applies only to integer values.

Just as the integral types in Java come in different sizes, so do the floating-point types, which are **float** and **double** (meaning double precision). The **double** type gives us a wider range of values and more precision (the number of significant digits in the number) than the **float** type, albeit at the expense of twice the memory space to hold the number. In Java, **float** values take up 32 bits of memory space, and **double** values take up 64 bits.

Floating-point values also can have an exponent, as in scientific notation. (In scientific notation, a number is written as a value multiplied by 10 to some power.) Instead of writing 3.504 $\times 10^{12}$, in Java we would write 3.504E12. The E (you can also use e) means "exponent of 10." The number preceding the letter E doesn't need to include a decimal point. Here are some examples of floating-point numbers in Java scientific notation, and their equivalent values in traditional scientific notation:

Java Notation	Scientific Notation
1.74536E-12	1.74536×10^{-12}
3.652442E4	3.652442×10^{4}
7E20	7×10^{20}
-8.01994E-23	-8.01994×10^{-23}

A **float** value can represent any 7-digit decimal number with an exponent ranging from -45 through 38. A **double** value can represent any 15-digit decimal number with an exponent in the range of -324 to 308.

In Java, the compiler automatically assumes that floating-point literals are of type **double**. To write a literal of type **float**, end the number with the letter F (or f). Here are some examples of floating-point literals:

Literal	Type
0.0	double
0.0f	float
2.001E3	double
2.001E3F	float
1.8E225F	Invalid (the exponent 225 is too large for the type **float**)

Computers cannot always represent floating-point numbers exactly. In fact, many decimal floating-point values can only be approximated in the binary number system. Don't be surprised if your application prints out the number 4.8 as 4.799998. In most cases, slight inaccuracies in the rightmost fractional digits are to be expected and are not the result of programmer error.

4.2 : Declarations for Numeric Types

Just as with the types `char` and `String`, we can declare fields of type `int`, `long`, `float`, and `double`. Such declarations use the same syntax, but the literals and the names of the data types are changed to the appropriate type.

■ Named Constant Declarations

Here are some constant declarations that define `int`, `long`, `float`, and `double` values. For comparison, declarations of `char` and `String` values are included.

```
final double PI = 3.14159;
final float  E = 2.71828F;
final long   MAX_TEMP = 1000000000L;
final int    MIN_TEMP = -273;
final char   LETTER = 'W';
final String NAME = "Elizabeth";
```

We put character and string literals in quotes to distinguish them from identifiers, but we do not put quotes around literal integers and floating-point numbers. Why? Because there is no confusion—identifiers must start with a letter or underscore, and numbers must start with a digit or sign.

Software Engineering Tip

Using Named Constants Instead of Literals

It's a good idea to use named constants instead of literals in your code. They make your code both more readable and easier to modify. Suppose you wrote an application last year to compute taxes. In several places you used the literal 0.05, which was the sales tax rate at the time. Now the rate has gone up to 0.06. To change your code, you must locate every mention of the literal 0.05 and change it to 0.06. If 0.05 is used for some other reason—to compute deductions, for example—then at each place where it is used, you also need to figure out its purpose, and decide whether to change it.

This process is much simpler if you use a named constant. If you had declared a named constant TAX_RATE with a value of 0.05, you would simply change the declaration,

Software
Engineering Tip

setting `TAX_RATE` equal to `0.06`. This one modification changes all of the tax rate computations without affecting the other places where `0.05` is used.

Java allows us to declare constants with different names but the same value. If a value has different meanings in different parts of an application, it makes sense to declare and use a constant with an appropriate name for each meaning.

Named constants are also reliable—they protect you from mistakes. If you mistype the name PI as PO, for example, the Java compiler will tell you that the name PO has not been declared. On the other hand, even though we may recognize that the number `3.14149` is a mistyped version of pi (`3.14159`), the number is perfectly acceptable to the compiler. It won't warn us that anything is wrong.

■ Variable Declarations

We declare numeric variables the same way that we declare `char` and `String` variables. Here are some example declarations and appropriate assignment statements:

```
int      studentCount;    // Number of students
int      sumOfScores;     // Sum of their scores
long     sumOfSquares;    // Sum of squared scores
double   average;         // Average of the scores
char     grade1;          // Student's letter grade
char     grade2;          // Another student's letter grade
String   stuName;         // Student's name

studentCount = 100;
sumOfSquares = 0L;
grade1 = 'A';
stuName = "Moonlight";
grade2 = grade1;
```

In each of these assignment statements, the data type of the expression matches the data type of the variable to which it is assigned. Later in this chapter, we will see what happens when the data types don't match.

4.3 : Simple Arithmetic Expressions

Now that we have looked at declarations and assignments, we are ready to write arithmetic expressions to perform calculations. We look first at simple expressions with just one operator, and then move on to compound expressions having multiple operations.

■ Arithmetic Operators

Expressions are made up of constants, variables, and operators. The following are all valid expressions:

```
alpha + 2     rate - 6.0     4 - alpha     rate     alpha * num
```

The operators allowed in an expression depend on the data types of the constants and variables being used. The arithmetic operators are

- `+`   Unary plus
- `-`   Unary minus
- `+`   Addition
- `-`   Subtraction
- `*`   Multiplication
- `/`   { Floating-point division (floating-point result) / Integer division (no fractional part) }
- `%`   Modulus (remainder from division)

> **Unary operator** An operator that has just one operand
>
> **Binary operator** An operator that has two operands

The first two operators are **unary operators**—they take just one operand. The last five are **binary operators**—they take two operands.

Unary plus and minus are used as follows:

```
-54     +259.65     -rate
```

Programmers rarely use the unary plus. Without any sign, a numeric constant is assumed to be positive.

You may be less familiar with integer division and modulus (`%`), so let's look at them more closely. The `%` operator can be used with both integers and floating-point numbers. When you divide one integer by another, you get an integer quotient and a remainder. Integer division gives only the integer quotient, and `%` gives only the remainder.

```
  3  ← 6 / 2        3  ← 7 / 2
2)6               2)7
  6                 6
  0  ← 6 % 2        1  ← 7 % 2
```

In Java, the sign of the remainder is the same as the sign of the dividend. For example:

Expression	Value
3 % 2	1
3 % -2	1
-3 % 2	-1
-3 % -2	-1

In contrast to integer division, floating-point division yields a floating-point result. For example, the expression

```
7.2 / 2.0
```

yields the value 3.6.

The floating-point **%** operation returns the remainder after dividing the dividend by the divisor a whole number of times. For example,

`7.2 % 2.1`

yields the value 0.9 because 2.1 goes into 7.2 exactly 3 times (3 × 2.1 = 6.3), with 0.9 remaining.

Here are some expressions using arithmetic operators and their values:

Expression	Value
`3 + 6`	9
`3.4 - 6.1`	–2.7
`2 * 3`	6
`8 / 2`	4
`8.0 / 2.0`	4.0
`8 / 8`	1
`8 / 9`	0
`8 / 7`	1
`8 % 8`	0
`8 % 9`	8
`8 % 7`	1
`0 % 7`	0
`5.0 % 2.3`	0.4

Be careful with division and modulus calculations. For instance, the expressions `7 / 0` and `7 % 0` will produce error messages, because the computer cannot divide an integer by zero. With floating-point values, however, the expressions `7.0 / 0.0` and `7.0 % 0.0` do not result in error messages. The result of the expression `7.0 / 0.0` is a special value representing infinity. The result of `7.0 % 0.0` is another special value called *not a number* (which is shown in output as NaN). Calculations involving these special values produce unusual results. For example, if you execute an application with the following statement in it,

`System.out.println(7.0 / 0.0);`

the output will be

`Infinity`

and the statement

`System.out.println(7.0 % 0.0);`

will display

`NaN`

If you encounter such results, carefully reexamine the expressions in your code to confirm that division and remainder cannot have a zero divisor.

To keep things simple, we've shown only literal values in our example expressions. Here are some examples using variables:

```
alpha = num + 6;
alpha = num / 2;
num = alpha * 2;
num = 6 % alpha;
alpha = alpha + 1;
num = num + alpha;
```

As we saw with assignment statements involving `String` expressions, the same variable can appear on both sides of the assignment operator. In the case of

```
num = num + alpha;
```

the value in `num` and the value in `alpha` are added together, and then the sum of the two values is stored into `num`, replacing the value previously stored there. This example shows the difference between mathematical *equality* and *assignment*. The mathematical equality

```
num = num + alpha
```

is true only when `alpha` equals zero. The assignment statement

```
num = num + alpha;
```

is valid for any value of `alpha`.

Here's a simple application that uses arithmetic expressions:

```java
//****************************************************************
// FreezeBoil application
// This application computes the midpoint between
// the freezing and boiling points of water
//****************************************************************

public class FreezeBoil
{
  public static void main(String[] args)
  {
    final double FREEZE_PT = 32.0;          // Freezing point of water
    final double BOIL_PT = 212.0;           // Boiling point of water
    double avgTemp;                         // Holds the result of averaging
                                            // FREEZE_PT and BOIL_PT

    // Display initial data
    System.out.print("Water freezes at " + FREEZE_PT);
    System.out.println(" and boils at " + BOIL_PT + " degrees.");
    // Calculate and display average
    avgTemp = FREEZE_PT + BOIL_PT;
    avgTemp = avgTemp / 2.0;
    System.out.println("Halfway between is " + avgTemp + " degrees.");
  }
}
```

Inside the `main` method are local declarations of the constants **FREEZE_PT** and **BOIL_PT** and the variable **avgTemp**. They are followed by a sequence of statements that displays the initial data, adds **FREEZE_PT** and **BOIL_PT**, divides the sum by 2, and then shows the result. Here is the output from the application:

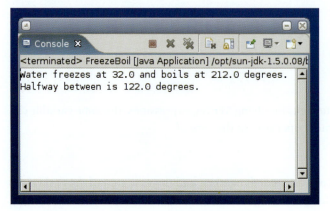

■ Inputting Numeric Types

In Chapter 2, we introduced the `Scanner` class and `nextLine` method. Table 4.1 lists additional `Scanner` input methods for numeric types and an additional `String` input method.

Note that the `Scanner` looks for *tokens* in the input. A token is a series of characters that ends with what Java calls *whitespace*. A whitespace character can be a blank, a tab character, a return character (the character that is entered when you press the return key on your keyboard), or the end of the file (we explore file input in Chapter 6). Thus, if we read a line that contains a series of numbers separated by blanks, the scanner will take each number as a separate token.

Although Table 4.1 shows only four numeric input methods, each numeric data type has a corresponding method that reads values of that type. We'll see shortly what it means for `InputMismatchException` to be thrown. For now, it is enough to know that this exception causes the program to halt with an error message.

Method	Returns
`int nextInt()`	Returns the next token as an `int`. If the next token is not an integer, `InputMismatchException` is thrown.
`long nextLong()`	Returns the next token as a `long`. If the next token is not an integer, `InputMismatchException` is thrown.
`float nextFloat()`	Returns the next token as a `float`. If the next token is not a float or is out of range, `InputMismatchException` is thrown.
`double nextDouble()`	Returns the next token as a `long`. If the next token is not a `float` or is out of range, `InputMismatchException` is thrown.
`String next()`	Finds the next complete token from this `Scanner` and returns it as a string; a token is usually ended by whitespace such as a blank or line break.

TABLE 4.1 `Scanner` Methods

The numeric values may all be on one line with blanks between them or they may appear on separate lines. Blanks and return characters behave the same way in terms of separating tokens. The `next` method returns the next input value as a string, even if it is apparently a numeric value. As an example, suppose we are given the following data:

```
44 23
2222222222
22222.33 End
3.14159
```

If we execute the following statements (where `in` has been declared as a `Scanner`),

```
int number = in.nextInt();
float real = in.nextFloat();
long number2 = in.nextLong();
double real2 = in.nextDouble();
String string = in.next();
String string2 = in.next();
```

then the variables have the values shown here:

```
Number      44
Real        23.0
number2     2222222222
real2       22222.33
string      "End"
string2     "3.14159"
```

Notice that method `nextFloat` read an integer (23) and stored it as a `float` value (23.0). This is legal because an integer value can be stored exactly as a real value; there is no ambiguity.

If we had typed a decimal point after the value 44, however, the system would have thrown an `InputMismatchException`. A real number cannot always be stored exactly as an integer, so Java follows the simple rule that any value with a decimal point cannot be read as an integer. Even though 44.0 is an example of a real number with an exact integer equivalent, Java doesn't check for this special case. In the last example, a real value (3.14159) was read by `next` and stored as a string (`"3.14159"`).

Given that multiple values can be read from a line, we need to redefine `nextLine`. The `nextLine` method actually reads the *rest* of the line and returns it as a string. The return character is not appended to the string, because `nextLine` reads it and then discards it.

Input of a numeric value does not include the whitespace that ends the value, so if a call to `nextLine` is issued after a call to `nextInt`, for example, and the numeric value is at the end of the line, `nextLine` returns the empty string and discards the return character at the end of the line. The `nextLine` method stops at the end of the line. A subsequent call to `nextLine` would then get the next line of input. For example, suppose we are given the following data:

```
44 23
22.5
22222.33 End
```

After executing the code fragment

```
int number = in.nextInt();
String string = in.nextLine();
float real = in.nextFloat();
String string2 = in.nextLine();
```

the variables have the following values:

```
number     44
string     " 23"
real       22.5
string2    ""        (empty string)
```

Notice that the value in `string` includes the blank that separates the two numbers in the input. What happens to the extra data in this example? It would be read by the next input operation that is executed. If the application ends without doing any further input, the data is simply discarded.

Here is a program that demonstrates the use of `nextDouble`, `nextInt`, and `nextLine` to input a series of values from a line entered by the user and output them in a different format.

```java
//******************************************************************
// Class SongTime uses Scanner to input a double, an int, and a String
// representing the price, the seconds that a song plays, and
// its name. It then outputs the name, price, and time in a different form.
//******************************************************************
import java.util.Scanner;
public class SongTime
{
  public static void main(String[] args)
  {
    // Declarations
    int seconds;
    double price;
    String name;
    Scanner in = new Scanner(System.in);
    // Prompt for input
    System.out.println("Enter the price, the time of the song in seconds,");
    System.out.println("and the name of the song, all separated by blanks:");
    // Read values
    price = in.nextDouble();
    seconds = in.nextInt();
    name = in.nextLine();
    // Output song name, cost, and time in minutes and seconds
    System.out.println();
    System.out.println(name + " costs $" + price + " and is " + seconds/60 +
                       " minute(s), and " + seconds % 60 + " second(s) long.");
  }
}
```

The output from a sample run is shown here:

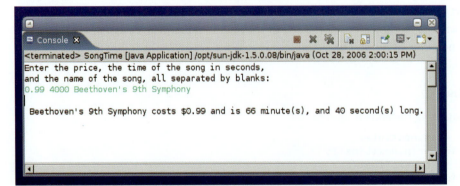

Notice in the last line of the output that there is a blank at the beginning of the line. Where did this blank come from? It is the blank between "4000" and "Beethoven's" in the input. The `nextInt` method stopped reading the number after its last digit. Then `nextLine` started reading at the character following the digit—the blank. Later in the chapter, we learn how to get rid of this extra blank using additional methods associated with the `String` class.

Exceptions with Numeric Input   An **exception** is an unusual condition, often an error. When the system encounters such a condition, it must be handled somehow, or else the application will halt with an error message from the JVM. In Chapter 7, we will see how Java *throws* exceptions—that is, transfers control to a section of code that is designed to handle the unusual condition. We say that the handler code *catches* the exception. The numeric `Scanner` methods throw an exception if the next token is not what the method anticipates.

Java defines two kinds of exceptions: checked and unchecked. **Checked exceptions** require that the programmer provide code to handle them. **Unchecked exceptions** may be either caught or allowed to pass automatically to the JVM. `InputMismatchException` is an unchecked exception, so it does not require us to take any special action; the JVM will simply halt execution and display an error message when this exception is thrown. In Chapter 5, we describe how to keep these mismatches from occurring. In Chapter 6, we encounter a checked exception and describe what should be done.

> **Exception**   An unusual condition in execution of Java code that causes control to be transferred to statements that are designed to handle the condition. The exception is thrown when the condition is detected and is caught by the handling code
>
> **Checked exception**   An exception in Java that must either be caught with a *catch* statement or explicitly thrown to the next level
>
> **Unchecked exception** An exception in Java that can optionally be caught or allowed to propagate automatically to the next level

■ Increment and Decrement Operators

In addition to the familiar arithmetic operators, Java provides increment and decrement operators:

    ++   Increment

    --   Decrement

These unary operators take a single variable name as an operand. For integer and floating-point operands, the effect is to add 1 to (or subtract 1 from) the operand. If `num` currently contains the value 8, for example, the statement

```
num++;
```

causes `num` to contain 9. You can achieve the same effect by writing the assignment statement

```
num = num + 1;
```

Experienced Java programmers, however, typically prefer the increment operator.

The ++ and -- operators can be either prefix operators

```
++num;
```

or postfix operators

```
num++;
```

Both of these statements behave in exactly the same way; that is, they add 1 to whatever is in **num**. The choice between the two is a matter of personal preference, although most Java programmers favor the latter form.

Java allows you to use ++ and -- in the middle of a larger expression:

```
alpha = num++ * 3;
```

In this case, the postfix form of ++ gives a different result from the prefix form. In Chapter 7, we examine the ++ and -- operators in more detail. In the meantime, you should use them only to increment or decrement a variable as a separate, stand-alone statement.

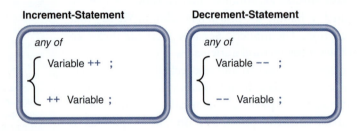

Increment-Statement

any of

Variable ++ ;

++ Variable ;

Decrement-Statement

any of

Variable -- ;

-- Variable ;

Background Information

The Origins of Java

The history of computing is characterized by several distinct families of programming languages. When the idea of high-level languages first arose, it seemed that everyone had his or her own notion of the ideal language. The result has been called the *Tower of Babel* period of programming. As more programs were written, the cost of rewriting them to use the features of a new language increased, so the computing world began to concentrate on a few languages—namely, FORTRAN, Algol, COBOL, Basic, PL/1, Lisp, and BCPL.

As computers were used in more sophisticated ways, it became necessary to create even more powerful languages. In many cases, these new languages were just expanded versions of older languages. Expanding a language allows older code to be used unchanged, but enables programmers to add to applications using the language's new features. This strategy is known as *upward compatibility*. A good example is the FORTRAN series that began with FORTRAN, then FORTRAN II, FORTRAN IV, FORTRAN 77, FORTRAN 90, and High-Performance FORTRAN.

Sometimes, however, extensions to a language result in excess complexity. In such a case, the solution is to redesign the language to eliminate conflicting features while preserving its desirable qualities. Java is a redesign of languages derived from BCPL (Basic Combined Programming Language).

In the 1960s, BCPL had a small but loyal following, primarily in Europe. It spawned another language with the abbreviated name of B. In the early 1970s, Dennis Ritchie, who was working on a new language at AT&T Bell Labs, adopted features from the B language and decided that the successor to B should be named C.

In 1985, Bjarne Stroustrup, also of Bell Labs, added features that supported object-oriented programming to C. Instead of naming the new language D, he named it C++ because ++ is the increment operation in C; thus the name C++ suggests this language is the successor of C.

C includes features that are close to the level of machine code. C++ adds features for writing instructions at a very powerful and abstract level that is far removed from machine language. The combination enables programmers to "shift gears" between programming complex operations and writing instructions that are close to machine code. Many people find it difficult to keep the features separate, however, so the combination has the potential for introducing some truly insidious errors.

In the early 1990s, James Gosling, working at Sun Microsystems, needed a language for programming the microprocessors being used in consumer electronics (for example, digital cameras). Like Stroustrup, he began with C. Gosling, however, decided to eliminate features that would conflict with his extensions. Both the Algol family and several experimental languages inspired some of the new features. Gosling called his language Oak, and he spent several years refining it. When the popularity of the Internet began to grow, Gosling worked with a team at Sun to adapt Oak for writing applications that could operate over the Internet. The revised language was renamed Java and released to the public in May 1996.

Java offers many of the capabilities of C++, but in a less complicated fashion. It supports programming for the Internet and writing applications with graphical user interfaces. In addition, Java applications are highly portable. The combination of these features caused the popularity of Java to skyrocket in the first year after it was released. It is very rare for a new programming language to appear and achieve success so quickly. Because Java is powerful yet simple, it has also become popular as a language for teaching programming.

4.4 : Compound Arithmetic Expressions

The expressions we've used so far have contained at most a single arithmetic operator. We also have been careful to avoid mixing integer and floating-point values in the same expression. Now we look at more complicated expressions—ones with several operators and mixed data types.

■ Precedence Rules

Arithmetic expressions can be made up of many constants, variables, operators, and parentheses. In what order are the operations performed? For example, in the assignment statement

```
avgTemp = FREEZE_PT + BOIL_PT / 2.0;
```

is `FREEZE_PT + BOIL_PT` calculated first or is `BOIL_PT / 2.0` calculated first?

Java performs basic arithmetic operations in the same order that we evaluate mathematical operators. When we include increment and decrement operators, however, we get an expanded set of mathematical precedence rules:

Highest precedence:	( )	(operations within parentheses)
	++ --	(postfix increment and decrement)
	++ --	(prefix increment and decrement)
	+ -	(unary plus and minus)
	* / %	(multiplication, division, and modulus)
Lowest precedence:	+ -	(addition and subtraction)

In the preceding example, we first divide `BOIL_PT` by `2.0` and then add `FREEZE_PT` to the result. Addition and subtraction have the lowest precedence of the operators we have seen thus far, so addition of `FREEZE_PT` occurs after the division.

You can change the order of evaluation by using parentheses. In the statement

`avgTemp = (FREEZE_PT + BOIL_PT) / 2.0;`

`FREEZE_PT` and `BOIL_PT` are added first, and then their sum is divided by `2.0`. We evaluate subexpressions in parentheses first and then follow the precedence of the operators.

When multiple arithmetic operators have the same precedence, their grouping order (or associativity) is from left to right. Thus the expression

`int1 - int2 + int3`

means `(int1 - int2) + int3`, not `int1 - (int2 + int3)`. As another example, we would use the expression

`(double1 + double2) / double1 * 3.0`

to evaluate the expression in parentheses first, then divide the sum by `double1`, and multiply the result by `3.0`. Here are some more examples:

Expression	Value
10 / 2 * 3	15
10 % 3 - 4 / 2	−1
5.0 * 2.0 / 4.0 * 2.0	5.0
5.0 * 2.0 / (4.0 * 2.0)	1.25
5.0 + 2.0 / (4.0 * 2.0)	5.25

Let's look at an example application that involves a compound arithmetic expression. The `SongTime` program required the user to input the duration of the song in seconds. It's more convenient to enter a time in minutes and seconds. The following application accepts a time in this form and displays it in seconds.

```java
//*************************************************************************
// Class TimeConvert uses Scanner to input two integers representing minutes
// and seconds, then computes the time in seconds and displays the result
//*************************************************************************
import java.util.Scanner;
public class TimeConvert
{
  public static void main(String[] args)
  {
    Scanner in = new Scanner(System.in);
    // Prompt for input
    System.out.println("Enter hours, minutes, and seconds separated by " +
                       "blanks:");
    // Declare variables and read values
    int hours = in.nextInt();
    int minutes = in.nextInt();
    int seconds = in.nextInt();
    // Calculate and output time in seconds
    int duration = hours * 3600 + minutes * 60 + seconds;
    System.out.println();
    System.out.println("The time is " + duration + " seconds.");
  }
}
```

The output from a sample run is shown here:

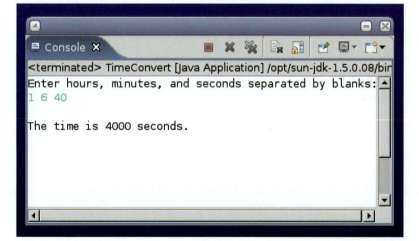

Look carefully at the highlighted line, which computes the value of `duration`. What is the order in which these operations take place? Multiplication is performed before addition. But which multiplication comes first? Because the two * operators have the same precedence, they are evaluated from left to right. Thus `hours` is multiplied by 3600 first. Then `minutes` is multiplied by 60. Next, the products of these multiplications are added. Lastly, `seconds` is added to this sum. The final result is then assigned to `duration`.

Precedence Error

Numerous programming errors result from writing expressions that fail to take the precedence rules into account. For example, take a look at the following application, which is supposed to compute the radius of a circle from its circumference:

```java
import java.util.Scanner;
public class Radius
{
  public static void main (String[] args)
  {
    double circumference;
    double radius;
    Scanner in = new Scanner(System.in);
    System.out.print("Enter the circumference ");
    circumference = in.nextInt();
    radius = circumference / 2 * 3.14159265;
    System.out.println("The radius is " + radius);
  }
}
```

The problem is that, given a circumference of 10, for which the radius is approximately 1.59, the program outputs 15.707963265. What's wrong? If we insert a debug `println` statement that outputs `circumference` immediately after it's input, we see that the data is being read correctly. The source of the error must therefore be the expression that computes the radius.

To get the radius from the circumference, we must divide the circumference by 2 times pi, which is what the statement does. Or does it? Division and multiplication have the same precedence, so they are evaluated from left to right. The expression is really computing

```java
radius = (circumference / 2) * 3.14159265;
```

In our test case, the application divided 10 by 2, giving 5, which it then multiplied by pi to get 15.707963265. What we really want is

```java
radius = circumference / (2 * 3.14159265);
```

Notice how we approached this debugging maintenance task. We first eliminated as many sources of error as possible. In this case, we inserted a debug `println` statement to display the data just before it was used, to ensure that it was read correctly. Having narrowed down the possibilities, we then proceeded to more deeply analyze the semantics of the remaining places where the error could originate. Knowing that incorrect application of the precedence rules is a common source of errors in numeric expressions, we focused on that aspect of the computation.

Whenever you are faced with a debugging task, take the time to narrow down your search for the bug by a process of elimination. Once you isolate the section of code that is most likely to be the source of the error, consider the mistakes commonly associated with those kinds of statements. Efficient debugging is not a hit-or-miss process—it takes careful thought and organization to zero in on the bug.

■ Type Conversion and Type Casting

Integer values and floating-point values are stored differently inside a computer's memory. The pattern of bits that represents the value 2, for example, does not look at all like the pattern for 2.0. What happens if we mix integer and floating-point values in an assignment statement or an arithmetic expression? Let's look first at assignment statements.

Assignment Conversion   Given these declarations

```
int    someInt;
double someDouble;
```

then someInt can hold only int values, and someDouble can hold only double values. The statement

```
someDouble = 12;
```

may seem to store the integer value 12 into someDouble, but Java refuses to store anything other than a double value into someDouble. The compiler inserts extra Bytecode instructions that first convert 12 into 12.0 and then stores 12.0 into someDouble. This implicit (automatic) conversion of a value from one data type to another is known in Java as **type conversion**.

The statement

```
someInt = 4.8;
```

also causes type conversion. When a floating-point value is assigned to an int variable, the fractional part is truncated (cut off). As a result, someInt is assigned the value 4. The code would be less confusing if we avoided mixing data types as follows:

```
someDouble = 12.0;
someInt = 4;
```

> **Type conversion**   The implicit (automatic) conversion of a value from one data type to another
>
> **Widening conversion** A type conversion that does not result in a loss of information
>
> **Narrowing conversion** A type conversion that may result in a loss of some information, as in converting a value of type double to type float

Often entire expressions are involved in type conversions. For example, the assignments

```
someDouble = 3 * someInt + 2;          // Integer expression
someInt = 5.2 / someDouble - anotherDouble;   // Floating-point expression
```

both lead to type conversions. Storing the result of an int expression into a double variable doesn't cause the loss of information because it can be exactly represented in floating-point form. A type conversion that doesn't lose information is known as a **widening conversion**. Assigning int values to long variables and float values to double variables are other examples of widening conversions.

In contrast, assigning a floating-point expression to an int variable can cause a loss of information because the fractional part is truncated. Such a conversion is called a **narrowing conversion**. It is easy to overlook the assignment of a floating-point expression to an int variable, a **double** value to a **float** variable, or a **long** value to an **int** variable when we try to discover why our code is producing the wrong answers.

Type Casting   To make our code as clear (and error-free) as possible, we should use explicit **type casting**.

> **Type casting**   The explicit conversion of a value from one data type to another
>
> **Mixed type (mixed mode) expression**   An expression that contains operands of different data types

A Java cast operation consists of a data type name within parentheses, followed by the expression to be converted:

```
someDouble = (double)(3 * someInt + 2);
someInt = (int)(5.2 / someDouble - anotherDouble);
```

For example, the statements

```
someFloat = someInt + 8;
someFloat = (float)(someInt + 8);
```

produce identical results; the only difference is in their clarity. With the cast operation, it is clear to anyone who reads the code that the mixing of types is intentional, not an oversight. Countless errors have resulted from unintentional mixing of types.

There is a nice way to round off—rather than truncate—a floating-point value before storing it into an **int** variable:

```
someInt = (int)(someDouble + 0.5);
```

With pencil and paper, see for yourself what gets stored into **someInt** when **someDouble** contains 4.7. Now try it again, assuming **someDouble** contains 4.2. (This technique of rounding up by adding 0.5 assumes that **someDouble** is a positive number. Sometimes we want to round negative numbers down, in which case we subtract 0.5. In Chapter 5, we see how to control whether we round up or down.)

Mixed Type Expressions   So far we have discussed mixing data types across the assignment operator (=). It's also possible to mix data types within an expression:

```
someInt * someDouble
4.8 + someInt - 3
```

Such expressions are called **mixed type** (or **mixed mode**) **expressions**.

Whenever an operator joins an integer value and a floating-point value, implicit type conversion occurs as follows:

1. The integer value is temporarily converted to a floating-point value.
2. The operation is performed.
3. The result is a floating-point value.

Let's examine how the computer evaluates the expression

```
4.8 + someInt - 3
```

where `someInt` contains the value 2. First, the operands of the + operator have mixed types, so the value of `someInt` is converted to 2.0. (This conversion is merely temporary; it does not affect the value that is currently stored in `someInt`.) From the computer's perspective, the expression is now

```
4.8 + 2.0 - 3
```

The addition takes place, yielding a value of 6.8. Next, the subtraction (-) operator joins a floating-point value (6.8) and an integer value (3):

```
6.8 - 3
```

The value 3 is converted to 3.0:

```
6.8 - 3.0
```

Subtraction can now take place, and the result is the floating-point value 3.8.

Just as with assignment statements, you can use explicit type casts within expressions to lessen the risk of errors. Writing expressions such as

```
(double)someInt * someDouble
4.8 + (double)(someInt - 3)
```

makes it clear what your intentions are.

Not only are explicit type casts valuable for code clarity, but in some cases they are mandatory for correct programming. To see why this is so, given the declarations

```
int    sum;
int    count;
double average;
```

suppose that `sum` and `count` currently contain 60 and 80, respectively. Assuming that `sum` represents the sum of a group of integer values and `count` represents the number of values, let's find the average value:

```
average = sum / count;     // Gives the wrong answer
```

Unfortunately, this statement stores the value 0.0 into `average`. Here's why: The expression to the right of the assignment operator is not a mixed type expression. Both operands are of type `int`, so integer division is performed. Dividing 60 by 80 yields the integer value 0. Next, the machine implicitly converts 0 to the value 0.0 before storing it into `average`. The correct (and clear) way to find the average is

```
average = (double)sum / (double)count;
```

This statement gives us floating-point division, so that 0.75 is stored into `average`.

As a final remark about type conversion and type casting, you may have noticed that we have concentrated on the `int` and `double` types. It is also possible to stir `byte`, `long`, `short`, and `float` values into the pot. The results can be confusing and unexpected. You should avoid unnecessarily mixing values of these types within an expression. Whenever it becomes necessary to do so, you should use explicit type casting to clarify your intentions.

Type Conversion Example   As a practical example of type conversion, suppose that we want a version of our `SongTime` application that computes the cost per minute for a song. We need to divide `seconds` by 60 to get the minutes, and then divide the time in minutes into `price` to get the cost per minute:

```
costPerMinute = price / (seconds / 60);              // Wrong!
```

Is that all? Of course not! After all, this section is supposed to show an example of type conversion. Looking at the expression, we can see that because `seconds` is an `int` variable and `price` is a `double`, an implicit conversion takes place. The expression first does the integer division `(seconds / 60)`. Then it converts the result to a `double` value before performing the floating-point division into `price`. The `double` result is then assigned to `costPerMinute`. We can eliminate the implicit conversion with a cast:

```
costPerMinute = price / (double)(seconds / 60);      // Still wrong!
```

But there is still a serious problem. To find out why, let's look at an example. Suppose that the value of `seconds` is 119 and the value of `price` is 1.0. The expression thus does integer division of 119 by 60, giving the result of 1. The result is cast to a `double`, 1.0, and divided into `price` to produce a price per minute of $1.00. But that's clearly wrong. The song is almost two minutes long! To get an accurate result, we must convert `seconds` to `double`, and then do floating-point division. Is the following correct?

```
costPerMinute = price / ((double)seconds / 60);      // Almost right
```

Almost. Now we have an implicit conversion of 60 to 60.0 as part of the first division. We should simply make it a `double` constant as follows:

```
costPerMinute = price / ((double)seconds / 60.0);    // Correct at last!
```

Now the entire expression uses floating-point values and the result has the desired accuracy. Here is the modified program, with the changes highlighted.

```java
//*************************************************************************
// Class SongTime uses Scanner to input a double, an int, and a String
// representing the price, the seconds that a song plays, and
// its name. It then outputs the name, price, and time in a different form.
//*************************************************************************
import java.util.Scanner;
public class SongTime
{
  public static void main(String[] args)
```

```
{
    // Declarations
    int seconds;
    double price;
    String name;
    Scanner in = new Scanner(System.in);
    // Prompt for input
    System.out.println("Enter the price, the time of the song in seconds,");
    System.out.println("and the name of the song, all separated by blanks:");
    // Read values
    price = in.nextDouble();
    seconds = in.nextInt();
    name = in.nextLine();
    // Output song name, cost, and time in minutes and seconds
    System.out.println();
    System.out.println(name + " costs $" + price + " and is " + seconds/60 +
                       " minute(s), and " + seconds%60 + " second(s) long.");
    double costPerMinute = price / ((double)seconds / 60.0);
    System.out.println("Cost per minute is $" + costPerMinute);
    in.close();
}
}
```

Here is a sample run:

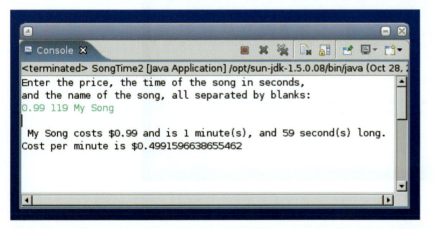

Well, that certainly works, but perhaps we're giving the user just a bit too much accuracy. An answer of $0.50 would be quite sufficient. Let's see how we can use type casting to round this result to dollars and cents.

Casting a floating-point value to an integer truncates the decimal portion. In this case, however, we want two decimal digits to remain. How can we do that? Well, suppose we multiply by 100:

```
0.499159663865542 * 100.0                    // Result is 49.9159663865542
```

Then truncate:

```
(int) (0.499159663865542 * 100.0)            // Result is 49
```

Then divide the result by 100:

```
(int) (0.499159663865542 * 100.0) / 100.0    // Result is 0.49
```

That's pretty close to what we want. All that remains is to round the value up. To do so, we add 0.5 before we truncate, as highlighted here:

```
0.499159663865542 * 100.0 + 0.5                    // Result is 50.4159663865542
```

Then we truncate and divide the result by 100:

```
(int) (0.499159663865542 * 100.0 + 0.5) / 100.0 // Result is 0.5
```

Lastly, we insert this formula into our application, replacing the literal cost per minute with the variable `costPerMinute`. The code for the application remains the same, with the only change being the insertion of one line between the existing formula and the output statement:

```
double costPerMinute = price / ((double)seconds / 60.0);
costPerMinute = (int) (costPerMinute * 100.0 + 0.5) / 100.0;
System.out.println("Cost per minute is $" + costPerMinute);
```

The output from a sample run now gives the desired answer:

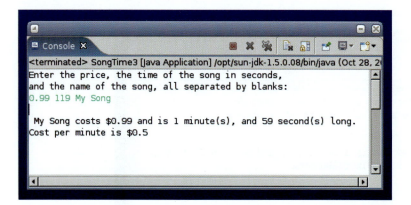

That's better, but a value of $0.5 still looks odd. We would normally expect to see $0.50. Unfortunately, there is no easy way to make Java format the number in this manner. If we were to test the application with other values, we might also find some cases where the final division by 100.0 produces a number with many decimal digits because of the problem mentioned earlier: Binary floating-point numbers can't always represent decimal numbers exactly. To truly solve this problem, we have to convert the result to a string, and then change the string to have the proper format.

Numeric Type to `String` Conversion Just as Java attempts to convert between numeric types when we mix them in expressions, so it also converts numeric values to strings when we mix them into expressions with the string concatenation operator. For instance, if we declare a `String` object called `answer`, we can write an assignment expression of the following form:

```
answer = "The average is: " + average;
```

If `average` contains the value 27.65, then `answer` contains the following string:

```
"The average is: 27.65"
```

When one of the operands of the + operator is a string and the other operand is a numeric type, the numeric type is converted to a string prior to concatenation. The + operator has the same precedence whether it is adding numeric values or concatenating strings. Java's string conversion is a useful feature for formatting output in which we mix numeric values with text that explains their meaning.

You can use a series of concatenation operators to create complex strings. For example,

```
answer = "The results are: " + 27 + 18 + " and " + 9;
```

produces the string

```
"The results are: 2718 and 9"
```

Notice two things about this result. First, the values `27` and `18` were concatenated without any spaces between them. String conversion of numeric values doesn't add any space around the digits of the number. Instead, we must explicitly include any spaces that we need as part of the expression. Second, the values `27` and `18` were concatenated, not added. Why? The answer lies in the precedence rules. All of the operators in the expression have the same precedence and thus are evaluated from left to right. The first operand is a string, so the first + operation is a concatenation, which gives a string as its result. Thus, each successive operation has a string as the left operand, making each + a concatenation operation.

As you can see from the preceding discussion, when an expression mixes strings and numeric types, you must consider the entire expression in light of the precedence rules. Take a look at the following expression and see if you can determine what its result is:

```
answer = 27 + 18 + 9 + " are the results.";
```

If you think it is

```
"27189 are the results."
```

then you are forgetting the effect of the left-to-right evaluation precedence rule. The actual result is

```
"54 are the results."
```

The first two + operators are integer additions because neither of their operands are strings. Only the last + operation is a concatenation; its left operand is the sum of the three numbers, which it converts into a string. The following is an invalid assignment:

```
answer = 27 + 18 + 9;              // Invalid; expression type is int
```

`String` conversion occurs only with the concatenation operator, not with assignment. The result of this expression is an `int` value, which can't be assigned to a string. However, we can use a trick to turn this expression into a series of string concatenations. That is, we can concatenate the values with the empty string:

```
answer = "" + 27 + 18 + 9;         // Valid; expression is a String
```

The value stored in `answer` is then `"27189"`. But what if we want `answer` to contain the string representing the sum of these integers? We use parentheses.

```
answer = "" + (27 + 18 + 9);
```

Now the sum is computed, converted to a string, and concatenated with the empty string. The assignment thus stores `"54"` into `answer`.

To summarize, Java's string conversion is a useful feature for formatting numeric output. But keep in mind that it works only as part of string concatenation. Also, you must consider the precedence rules whenever you write a complex expression containing multiple numeric values.

`String` to Numeric Type Conversion   We've seen how to convert a numeric type to a string, but how do we go the other way? That is, given a string containing a number, how do we convert it into a numeric type? Actually, we've already seen how to do this: We use a `Scanner`.

When we read numeric values from `System.in`, we are really reading them in string form. The job of the `Scanner`'s `nextInt`, `nextDouble`, and similar methods is actually to convert such a string into a numeric type. Thus far, we've worked with the form of `Scanner` that gets its string from `System.in`. There is actually another form that we can instantiate directly with a string. That is, we can write

```
Scanner intString = new Scanner("42");   // Creates Scanner to scan the
                                          // String "42"
int someInt = intString.nextInt();       // Assigns 42 to someInt
```

We could create such a `Scanner` with multiple values in the string, and each successive call to `nextInt` would return the next value.

Suppose you have a `String` variable called `boiling` that has the value `"212.0"`, and you want to convert this string representation of the number into a `double`. We can create a `Scanner` for this string and get the value with `nextDouble`. The following line shows how to do this and demonstrates a shortcut that avoids defining a `Scanner` variable.

```
double someDouble = new Scanner(boiling).nextDouble(); // Assign 212.0 to
                                                       // someDouble
```

May We Introduce

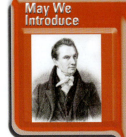

Charles Babbage

The British mathematician Charles Babbage (1791–1871) is generally credited with designing the world's first computer. Unlike the electronic computers of today, however, Babbage's machine was mechanical. It was made of gears and levers, which were the predominant technology of the 1820s and 1830s.

Babbage actually designed two different machines. The first, called the Difference Engine, was intended to be used in computing mathematical tables. For example, it could produce a table of squares. However, it could not be programmed.

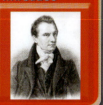

The Difference Engine was meant to improve the accuracy of computing tables, which until then had been produced by hand, resulting in numerous errors. Because much of science and engineering depended on the use of accurate tables, such errors had serious consequences. The Difference Engine could perform the calculations automatically, without error. One of its features was that it would stamp its output directly onto copper plates that could be placed into a printing press, thereby avoiding typographical errors.

By 1833, the project seeking to build the Difference Engine had run into financial trouble and was abandoned. A version of the machine was eventually completed in 1853 by Per Georg and Edvard Scheutz, of Sweden. Babbage himself had lost interest in the Difference Engine because he had developed the idea for a much more powerful machine, which he called the Analytical Engine—that is, a truly programmable computer.

Babbage's new idea originated from the Jacquard automatic loom, in which a series of paper cards with punched holes were fed through the machine to produce a woven cloth pattern. The pattern of holes constituted a program for the loom, making it possible to automatically weave patterns of arbitrary complexity. Its inventor even had a portrait of himself woven by one of his machines.

Babbage realized that such a mechanism could be used to control a computing machine. Instead of calculating just one formula, the device could be programmed to perform arbitrarily complex computations, including the manipulation of algebraic symbols. As Ada Lovelace elegantly put it, "We may say most aptly that the Analytical Engine weaves algebraical patterns." It is clear that Babbage and Lovelace fully understood the power of a programmable computer, and even contemplated the notion of artificial thought.

Babbage never completed construction of the Analytical Engine. Although some historians suggest that the technology of the period couldn't support such complex machinery, most believe that Babbage's failure was his own doing. He was both brilliant and eccentric (he was afraid of Italian organ grinders, for example). As a consequence, he had a tendency to abandon projects midway through so that he could concentrate on newer and better ideas. He always believed that his new approaches would allow him to complete a machine in less time than it would take if the old ideas were continued to completion.

When he died, Babbage had developed numerous pieces of computing machines and partial drawings of designs, but none of them were sufficiently complete to produce a single working computer. Babbage had come upon the idea of the computer a full century before it was eventually developed. We can only imagine how different the world today would be if he had succeeded.

4.5 : Useful Value-Returning Methods

As we said in Chapter 2, value-returning methods are methods that are used *in* expressions and that return a value *for use in* the expression. In the following sections we examine some useful methods provided in the `String` and `Math` classes.

■ String Methods

Now that we have introduced numeric types, we can take advantage of additional features of the `String` data type that take numeric arguments. Here we introduce five useful methods that operate on strings: `length`, `indexOf`, `substring`, `charAt`, and `trim`. All five are value-returning instance methods.

The `length` Method   The `length` method, when applied to a `String`, returns an `int` value that equals the number of characters in the string. Here are two examples of its use (the calls are highlighted, and the comments indicate what is returned from each call):

```
String firstName = "Alexandra";
int len = firstName.length();             // Assigns 9 to len
String fullName = firstName + " Jones";
len = fullName.length();                   // Assigns 15 to len
```

The `indexOf` Method   The `indexOf` method searches a string to find the first occurrence of a particular substring and returns an `int` value indicating the point where the substring was found. The substring, which is passed as an argument to the method, can be a literal string or a `String` expression.

Given the assignment

```
String phrase = "The dog and the cat";
```

the statement

```
int position = phrase.indexOf("the");
```

finds the following match:

Position	0	1	2	3	4	5	6	7	8	9	10	11	12	13	14	15	16	17	18
Character	T	h	e		d	o	g		a	n	d		t	h	e		c	a	t

It therefore assigns the value 12 to `position`. Note that positions within strings are numbered starting at zero. In this example, `"the"` did not match `"The"` at the beginning of the `phrase` string, because their capitalization did not match. The statement

```
position = phrase.indexOf("rat");
```

assigns the value of −1 to `position`, because no match is found.

The argument to the `indexOf` method can also be a `char` value. In this case, `indexOf` searches for the first occurrence of that character within the string and returns its position.

If a string contains multiple copies of the substring, `indexOf` returns only the position of the first copy. Keep in mind that matches can be either separate words or parts of words— `indexOf` merely tries to match the sequence of characters given in the argument list.

The `charAt` Method   The `charAt` method returns the character at a specified position within a string. For example, the statement

```
char letter = phrase.charAt(16);
```

returns the character at position 16 in `phrase`, which has the value `'c'`, as shown here:

Position	0	1	2	3	4	5	6	7	8	9	10	11	12	13	14	15	16	17	18
Character	T	h	e		d	o	g		a	n	d		t	h	e		c	a	t

The `substring` Method   The `substring` method returns a specified section of a string. Here is an example:

```
String newPhrase = phrase.substring(4, 11)
```

The arguments are integers that specify positions within the string. The method returns the piece of the string that starts with the position specified by the first argument and continues to the position given by the second argument minus 1, as shown here:

Position	0	1	2	3	4	5	6	7	8	9	10	11	12	13	14	15	16	17	18
Character	T	h	e		d	o	g		a	n	d		t	h	e		c	a	t

Here the variable `newPhrase` is assigned the value `"dog and"`. The length of the substring returned by the example call is the difference of the arguments, or 11 − 4 = 7 characters. Note that `substring` doesn't change `phrase`; instead, it returns a new `String` that is a copy of part of `phrase`.

   If the two arguments are the same, the result is the empty string. If zero is the starting position and the ending position is the length of the string, `substring` returns the entire string. If either argument specifies a position beyond the end of the string, or the second argument is smaller than the first, the call results in an error message. In Chapter 5, we see how the *if* statement can prevent such errors

The `trim` Method   The `trim` method returns a copy of a string, with all whitespace characters removed from each end. For example, the result of the statements

```
myString = "     Progamming     "; // Includes blanks at beginning and end
trimmedString = myString.trim();    // Returns copy without extra blanks at ends
```

is that `trimmedString` is assigned the string `"Programming"`.
   Do you remember the problem we had in the output of `SongTime`?

```
 My Song costs $0.99 and is 1 minute(s), and 59 second(s) long.
Cost per minute is $0.5
```

An extra blank appears at the beginning of the song name, because `nextLine` includes the separator whitespace as part of the name. We can delete the blank using `trim`, as highlighted here:

```
seconds = in.nextInt();    // Stops reading at the blank following the number
name = in.nextLine();      // Reads the blank as if it is part of the name
name = name.trim();        // Removes leading and trailing blank(s)
```

■ Applying Instance Methods to Return Values

We could shorten the preceding code even more by noticing that `in.nextLine()` returns a `String` object. We can thus apply `trim` directly to that object:

```
seconds = in.nextInt();      // Stops reading at the blank following the number
name = in.nextLine().trim();   // Removes leading and trailing blank(s) from
                               // input
```

Do you see what is happening here? Just as we can apply an instance method to an object that is assigned to an identifier, so we can also apply an instance method to an object that is returned from a method. In both cases, we have an object. The difference is merely that one object has been given a name and the other has no name.

```
name = in.nextLine().trim(); // Removes leading and trailing blank(s) from
                             // input
```

Returns a `String` object   Instance method applied to `String` object

We will use this convenient shortcut in Java frequently. Just as we can compose expressions with multiple arithmetic operators, we can also compose expressions with multiple calls to value-returning methods.

■ A String Method Example

Suppose we have an application in which the user wants to enter a time in the form of minutes and seconds, with a colon as the separator instead of a blank. For example, 23:45.6, means 23 minutes and 45.6 seconds. However, within the application, we want to treat the time as a `double` value.

We can use `indexOf` to find the position of the colon. Then we can get the number of minutes by taking the `substring` starting at the first character position, and continuing up to the character preceding the colon. The number of seconds is the remainder of the string, which can be extracted with another `substring` operation using `length` to get the second argument. These two string values are converted to numeric quantities with `Scanner` and then added after multiplying the minutes by 60.0. To be safe, let's also `trim` any leading or trailing blanks from the original string.

Here is a demonstration application that shows how we can do this. It inputs the time string, and outputs the time as a `double` value.

```
//****************************************************************
// Class TimeDemo reads a time as a string in the format of minutes and
// seconds separated by a colon, then outputs the time in seconds as a
// value of type double
//****************************************************************
import java.util.Scanner;
public class TimeDemo
{
  public static void main(String[] args)
  {
```

```
        Scanner inTime = new Scanner(System.in);
        System.out.print("Enter a time as minutes:seconds: ");
        String in = inTime.nextLine();
        in = in.trim();                                // Delete whitespace
        int colon = in.indexOf(':');                   // Find position of colon
        String minStr = in.substring(0, colon);        // Get minutes string
        String secStr = in.substring(colon+1, in.length()); // Get seconds string
        Scanner minScan = new Scanner(minStr);         // Create minutes Scanner
        Scanner secScan = new Scanner(secStr);         // Create seconds Scanner
        // Convert strings to numbers, and return minutes * 60.0 + seconds
        System.out.println("Time in seconds is " +
        // This formula is in parentheses because the + is concatenation
                          (minScan.nextDouble() * 60.0 + secScan.nextDouble()));
    }
}
```

Here is a sample run:

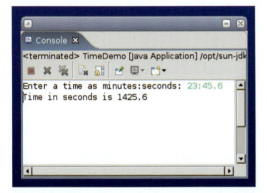

Software
Engineering Tip

Understanding Before Changing

When you are testing an application and come across an error, it's tempting to start changing the code to fix it. *Don't!* You'll nearly always make matters worse. It's essential that you understand exactly what is causing the error and carefully think through the solution. Run the application with different data until you are certain of the pattern of the unexpected behavior.

No magic trick—inserting an extra semicolon or right brace, for example—can automatically fix a coding error. If the compiler tells you that a semicolon or a right brace is missing, you need to examine the code in light of the syntax rules and determine precisely what the problem is. Perhaps you accidentally typed a colon instead of a semicolon. Or maybe you included an extra left brace.

If the source of a problem isn't immediately obvious, it can be helpful to leave the computer and go somewhere where you can quietly look over a printed copy of the code. Studies show that people who do their debugging away from the computer actually get their code to work in less time *and ultimately produce better code* than those who continue to work on the machine—more proof that there is still no mechanical substitute for human thought.

■ Numeric Methods

In this section we examine some methods that return numeric values. Certain computations, such as taking the square root of a number or finding the absolute value of a number, are very common in programming. It would be an enormous waste of time if every programmer had to start from scratch and create methods to perform these tasks. To make our lives easier, the class `java.lang.Math` is automatically imported into every application by the Java compiler. Java's `Math` class provides a collection of useful numerical methods. Table 4.2 lists the most commonly used methods.

The third column in Table 4.2 tells you the type of the value that is returned by each of the `Math` methods. All of these `Math` methods are value-returning *class* methods. For example, the statement

```
rootX = Math.sqrt(x);
```

Method	Argument Type(s)	Result Type	Result
`Math.abs(x)`	int, long, float, or double	same as argument	absolute value of x
`Math.cos(x)`	double	double	cosine of x (x is in radians)
`Math.sin(x)`	double	double	sine of x (x is in radians)
`Math.tan(x)`	double	double	tangent of x (x is in radians)
`Math.acos(x)`	double	double	arc cosine of x (result in radians)
`Math.asin(x)`	double	double	arc sine of x (result in radians)
`Math.atan(x)`	double	double	arc tangent of x (result in radians)
`Math.toRadians(x)`	double	double	converts x from degrees to radians
`Math.toDegrees(x)`	double	double	converts x from radians to degrees
`Math.log(x)`	double	double	natural (base e) logarithm of x
`Math.exp(x)`	double	double	e raised to the power x
`Math.log10(x)`	double	double	base-10 logarithm of x
`Math.pow(x, y)`	double	double	x raised to the power y (if $x = 0.0$, y must be positive; if $x \leq 0.0$, y must be a whole number)
`Math.min(x, y)`	int, long, float, or double	same as argument	smaller of x and y
`Math.max(x, y)`	int, long, float, or double	same as argument	larger of x and y
`Math.random()`	none	double	a random number greater than or equal to 0.0 and less than 1.0
`Math.round(x)`	double	long	x rounded up to the nearest integer
`Math.round(x)`	float	int	x rounded up to the nearest integer
`Math.sqrt(x)`	double	double	square root of x ($x \geq 0.0$)

TABLE 4.2   Math Methods

calls the `sqrt` method associated with the `Math` class, which returns the square root of `x`, which is then assigned to `rootX`. Note that the class name must precede each of these methods with a dot in between.

For applications that make extensive use of the `Math` methods, typing the class name in front of every call can prove very tedious. Java provides a variation on the `import` statement that avoids this step. If we explicitly import the `Math` class using the `static` modifier, then Java makes the public class fields and methods of the `Math` class available without the need to specify the class name. For example, if we write

```
import static java.lang.Math.*;
```

at the top of a class, then we can write the assignment as

```
rootX = sqrt(x);
```

Keep in mind that the effect of `import static` is similar to declaring the identifiers within the class itself. Thus, if you declare an identifier called `round` in your class, it creates a conflict with the `round` method in the `Math` class. Java resolves the conflict by requiring you to refer to the method as `Math.round`.

Matters of Style

Code Formatting

As far as the compiler is concerned, Java statements are *free format:* They can appear anywhere on a line, more than one can appear on a single line, and one statement can span several lines. The compiler needs only blanks (or comments or new lines) to separate important symbols, and it needs semicolons to terminate statements. Of course, it is extremely important that your code be readable, both for your sake and for the sake of anyone else who has to examine it.

When you write an outline for an English paper, you follow certain rules of indentation to make it readable. The same kinds of rules can make your code easier to read. In addition, it is much easier to spot a mistake in a neatly formatted class than in a messy one. For these reasons, you should keep your code formatted neatly while you are working on it. If you've gotten lazy and let your code become sloppy while making a series of changes, take the time to straighten it up. Often the source of an error becomes obvious during the process of formatting the code.

Take a look at the following application for computing the cost per square foot of a house. Although it compiles and runs correctly, it does not conform to any formatting standards.

```
// HouseCost application This application computes the cost per square foot
// of living space for a house, given the dimensions of the house, the
// number of stories, the size of the nonliving space, and the total cost
// less land
```

Matters of Style

```
public class HouseCost { public static void main(String[] arg){final double
WIDTH = 30.0; final double LENGTH = 40.0; //Length of the house
final double STORIES = 2.5; /*Number of full stories*/ final double
NON_LIVING_SPACE = 825.0; /*Garage, closets, etc.*/ final double PRICE =
150000.0; /*Selling price less land*/ double grossFootage;
/*Total square footage*/ double livingFootage;/*Living area*/
double costPerFoot;/*Cost/foot of living area*/ grossFootage = LENGTH *
WIDTH * STORIES; /*Compute gross footage*/ livingFootage = grossFootage -
NON_LIVING_SPACE; /*Compute net footage*/ costPerFoot = PRICE /
livingFootage; /*Compute cost per usable foot*/ System.out.println(
"Cost per square foot is " + costPerFoot);}}
```

Now look at the same class with proper formatting:

```
//******************************************************************
// HouseCost application
// This application computes the cost per square foot of
// living space for a house, given the dimensions of
// the house, the number of stories, the size of the
// nonliving space, and the total cost less land
//******************************************************************
public class HouseCost
{
  public static void main(String[] args)
  {
    final double WIDTH = 30.0;                  // Width of the house
    final double LENGTH = 40.0;                 // Length of the house
    final double STORIES = 2.5;                 // Number of full stories
    final double NON_LIVING_SPACE = 825.0;      // Garage, closets, etc.
    final double PRICE = 150000.0;              // Selling price less land

    double grossFootage;                        // Total square footage
    double livingFootage;                       // Living area
    double costPerFoot;                         // Cost/foot of living area

    grossFootage = LENGTH * WIDTH * STORIES;    // Compute gross footage
    livingFootage = grossFootage - NON_LIVING_SPACE; // Compute net footage
    costPerFoot = PRICE / livingFootage;        // Compute cost per usable
                                                // foot

    System.out.println("Cost per square foot is " +    // Output result
        costPerFoot);
  }
}
```

Need we say more?

Appendix F discusses coding style. We suggest you use it as a guide for writing your own code.

4.6 : An Example Class Using Numeric Types: `Time`

As an example of using numeric types and value-returning methods, let's develop a class to represent elapsed time.

■ Attributes

Elapsed time can be represented by a single attribute that holds the number of seconds. From this value, we can calculate hours, minutes, seconds, and so on. Because we may want to represent fractions of a second, let's use a floating-point type to hold the seconds.

This is certainly one way to represent the data within a `Time` object. Can you think of another? Yes, we could keep the time in separate variables for hours, minutes, and seconds. Such a representation would be more appropriate for representing the time of day, however, rather than the elapsed time.

Either representation can be made to work. The choice depends on factors such as ease of programming and efficiency. For example, if we want the ability to add one time to another, then it is much easier to add two `double` values than to add two sets of values representing hours, minutes, and seconds. By contrast, if we plan to emphasize operations that format time values for output, then it is more convenient to use hours, minutes, and seconds.

How do we know whether `seconds` should be a class attribute or an instance attribute? To make this decision, we ask the following question: Does each object created from the class need to have its own value for the attribute, or is the value the same for every object of the class? If the value may be different for each object, then it should be an instance attribute.

We want to create multiple `Time` objects, each with its own value. Thus we should make `seconds` an instance attribute. We can implement this decision using the following declaration:

```
double seconds;      // Records the total elapsed time
```

Now we turn to the operations that we want our `Time` objects to support.

■ Constructors

We'll need at least one constructor. It can take an argument that directly specifies the elapsed time. Of course, it would also be convenient to have a constructor that takes hours, minutes, and seconds. What about fractions of seconds? As long as both constructors allow the value for `seconds` to be of type `double`, then we already have this capability. For this class, the default constructor can simply set the time to 0.0.

The default constructor looks like this:

```
public Time()
{
  seconds = 0.0;
}
```

The constructor that sets the time directly looks like this:

```
public Time(double newSeconds)
{
  seconds = newSeconds;
}
```

We frequently encounter constructors of this form in designing classes. We'll refer to constructors that directly set the field(s) of a new object with the value(s) in the parameter list as *direct constructors*. Note that this is not a formal term. Nevertheless, many classes have only a default constructor and a direct constructor, and we'll find it convenient to be able to refer to them by name.

Setting `seconds` from parameters for hours, minutes, and seconds takes some additional thought. In `TimeDemo`, we saw the formula for converting minutes and seconds to elapsed time, so we just have to extend it to include hours.

```
hours * 3600 + minutes * 60 + newSeconds
```

However, `newSeconds` is a `double` value, while `hours` and `minutes` are `int` values, so we should explicitly convert the integer result to `double` before adding `newSeconds`. Here is the constructor:

```
public Time(int hours, int minutes, double newSeconds)
{
  seconds = (double)(hours * 3600 + minutes * 60) + newSeconds;
}
```

■ Observers

What sort of actions might we want to apply to `Time` values? At a minimum, we should be able to return the value of the `seconds` field. Because this value is stored in an instance variable of type `double`, this method would be a value-returning `double` instance method:

```
public double getTime()
{
  return seconds;
}
```

Sometimes we want to output the time in hours, minutes, and seconds. For this reason, we'll supply an observer instance method for each of these values. How do we get the hours, minutes, and seconds from the elapsed time? In `SongTime`, we saw how to use integer division and remainder to perform this conversion for minutes and seconds. Now we extend the concept for hours and fractions of a second.

We need to perform integer division of `seconds` by 3600, which is the number of seconds per hour, to get the number of hours. First we convert `seconds` to an integer so that we can use integer division:

```
hours = (int)seconds / 3600;            // Compute whole hours from seconds
```

The remaining seconds, after hours are divided out, is given by the remainder operation. If we divide that number by 60, we get the number of minutes:

```
remainingSeconds = (int)seconds % 3600;    // Seconds after whole hours taken
                                           // out
minutes = remainingSeconds / 60;           // Compute whole minutes from
                                           // remainder
```

The remainder of dividing `seconds` by 60.0 gives us the seconds that are left after hours and minutes have been taken out:

```
secondsOnly = seconds % 60.0;              // Seconds after minutes taken out
```

Do you see why? The floating-point remainder gives us the number of seconds left after dividing by 60.0, the number of seconds in a minute. Because hours are made up of a whole number of minutes, we are effectively taking away all of the whole hours and the whole minutes with this one operation. What remains is the number of seconds that are a portion of a minute, including the fractional part.

The observers for our class look like this:

```
// Observers for class Time
public double getTime()
{
  return seconds;                          // Return elapsed time
}

public int getHours()
{
  return (int)seconds / 3600;              // Compute whole hours from seconds
}

public int getMinutes()
{
  int remainingSeconds = (int)seconds % 3600; // Seconds after whole hours
                                              // taken out
  return remainingSeconds / 60;            // Compute minutes from remainder
}

public double getSeconds()
{
  return seconds % 60.0;                   // Seconds after minutes taken out
}
```

■ Other Operations

What other operations would we like to support? Adding and subtracting `Time` objects would be useful. We should also include a method called `toString`, which returns the content of the object in some format that is convenient to output. Why? When a class has a `toString` method, then its contents can be output directly with `print` or `println`. For example, if `Time` has a `toString` method, and `someTime` is a `Time` variable, then to display it on the screen we can simply write

```
System.out.println(someTime);
```

Let's use the common format of HH:MM:SS.FF. For example, a time of 16 hours, 23 minutes, and 37.43 seconds would appear as 16:23:37.43.

Now, let's consider the methods for these operations. We begin with the operation to add times. We want to add two `Time` values together, returning a new `Time` value and leaving the original values unchanged.

Just from the fact that we refer to returning a value, you know this will be a value-returning method. Because we are starting with the value of a given `Time` object, an instance method is appropriate. Here's an example of how we would call such a method:

```
newTime = someTime.plus(nextTime);    // Adds values of someTime and nextTime
```

The operation itself is trivial—all we need to do is add the `seconds` values from the two objects. Because the method is called with respect to one of the objects (`someTime`), it has direct access to the `seconds` instance field of that object. But how does the method gain access to the `seconds` value stored in the argument object (`nextTime`)?

Once the argument is passed to the parameter, we can simply refer to it using a qualified identifier. Java allows an object to use a qualified identifier to access the fields of another object of the same class, as long as they aren't `private`.[1] For example, if the heading of the `plus` method is

```
public Time plus(Time otherTime)
```

then, within the method, we can get the seconds from parameter `otherTime` like this:

```
otherTime.seconds
```

Next, we add the value of the `seconds` field for this object to the time from the other object:

```
seconds + otherTime.seconds
```

---

1. In Chapter 10, we see that another modifier, `protected`, also prevents access. The ability to access instance fields in another object of the same class doesn't include local declarations.

We use the result to instantiate a new `Time` object, and return it. Here is the complete `plus` method:

```java
public Time plus(Time otherTime)
{
  return new Time(seconds + otherTime.seconds);
}
```

It is important to understand where the value of `seconds` comes from within the method. It is stored in the `seconds` field of the current object. Suppose we instantiate two `Time` objects as follows:

```java
Time someTime = new Time(23.0);
Time nextTime = new Time(10.5);
```

Then, within `someTime` we have a field called `seconds` that contains 23.0, and within `nextTime` we have a field called `seconds` that contains 10.5. Suppose we call `plus` with respect to `someTime`, passing `nextTime` as an argument:

`someTime`.plus(`nextTime`)

We color-code the two objects to make it easier to see them in the illustrations that follow. When the method is called, the value in `nextTime` is copied into the parameter, `otherTime`. Thus the expression operates on the values shown below it here:

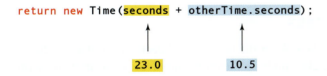

In this case, `seconds` refers to the field within `someTime`. Now, let's reverse the call to `plus` so that it is made with respect to `nextTime`, and `someTime` is the argument:

`nextTime`.plus(`someTime`)

Within the `plus` method, `otherTime` contains a copy of the value of `someTime`, and `seconds` now refers to the field within `nextTime`.

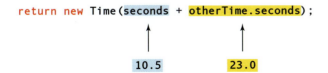

This is a key concept associated with instance methods. The call is always made with respect to an object (which appears to the left of the dot in the call). Inside the method, accesses to instance fields refer to the fields within that particular object.

The subtraction operation is nearly identical. We just change the name of the method and change + to -, as highlighted here:

```java
public Time minus(Time otherTime)
{
  return new Time(seconds - otherTime.seconds);
}
```

Given the formulas that we've already seen for the observer methods, it's easy to write the `toString` method. We merely compute the hours, minutes, and seconds, and then combine them into a string that we return.

```java
public String toString()                        // Returns HH:MM:SS.FF
{
  int hours = (int)seconds / 3600;
  int minutes = (int)seconds % 3600 / 60;
  return  hours + ":" + minutes + ":" + seconds % 60.0;
}
```

Is that it? Well, it is if we don't care about how `toString` formats negative times. If the time is negative, then the hours, minutes, and seconds values will all be negative. For example, given a time of -3675.0 seconds, `toString` will return `"-1:-1:-15.0"`. We'll simply document this fact in the code.

■ The Complete Time Class

We are now ready to write our `Time` class. After the heading and declaration of `seconds`, we gather all the methods together in the class body. In the Problem-Solving Case Study we write an application that uses the class.

```java
//**********************************************************************
// This class implements an object representing elapsed time.
// It supports formats of time that include a decimal representation,
// and hours, minutes, and seconds. It provides operations to add and
// subtract times. Negative times are not formatted properly by toString
//**********************************************************************

public class Time
{
  double seconds;                     // Variable to hold seconds

  // Constructors for class Time

  public Time()
  {
    seconds = 0.0;
  }
```

```
public Time(double newSeconds)
{
  seconds = newSeconds;
}

public Time(int hours, int minutes, double newSeconds)
{
  seconds = (double)(hours * 3600 + minutes * 60) + newSeconds;
}

// Observers for class Time

public double getTime()
{
  return seconds;                              // Return elapsed time
}

public int getHours()
{
  return (int)seconds / 3600;                  // Compute whole hours from
                                               // seconds
}

public int getMinutes()
{
  int remainingSeconds = (int)seconds % 3600; // Seconds after hours taken out
  return remainingSeconds / 60;               // Compute minutes from remainder
}

public double getSeconds()
{
  return seconds % 60.0;                       // Seconds after minutes taken
                                               // out
}

public String toString()                       // Returns HH:MM:SS.FFF
{
  int hours = (int)seconds / 3600;
  int minutes = (int)seconds % 3600 / 60;
  return  hours + ":" + minutes + ":" + seconds % 60.0;
}

// Operations for class Time

public Time plus(Time otherTime)
{
  return new Time(seconds + otherTime.Seconds);
}
```

```
public Time minus(Time otherTime)
{
  return new Time(seconds - otherTime.Seconds);
}
}
```

■ A Class Test Plan and Driver

Before we use a class, we must test it. In many cases, testing merely means calling each method with the necessary arguments and checking that it produces the expected result. For some methods, it takes several calls to ensure correct operation under different conditions. For example, if negative values are allowed, it is a good idea to test with negative, zero, and positive values to ensure that these ranges are handled properly.

It's handy to write the tests as a table, where each row is a test, and the columns contain the test number, method under test, input data, and expected result. From this, we can write a driver that tests the class.

TEST PLAN

Number	Method	Input	Expected Result
1	Time()		Creates object time1 with 0.0 seconds
2	Time(double)	3845.123	Creates object time2 with 3845.123 seconds
3	Time(int, int, double)	8, 2, 5.5	Creates object time3 with 28925.5 seconds
4	time1.getTime()		Returns 0.0
5	time2.getTime()		Returns 3845.123
6	time3.getTime()		Returns 28925.5
7	time3.getHours()		Returns 8
8	time3.getMinutes()		Returns 2
9	time3.getSeconds()		Returns 5.5
10	time2.plus(Time)	time3	Returns Time with value 32770.623
11	time3.minus(Time)	time2	Returns Time with value 25080.377
12	time1.toString()		Returns "0:0:0.0"
13	time2.toString()		Returns "1:4:5.123"
14	time3.toString()		Returns "8:2:5.5"

Here is a driver application that carries out these tests:

```
class TimeDriver
{
  public static void main(String[] args)
  {
    // Tests 1-6
    Time time1 = new Time();
```

```java
        Time time2 = new Time(3845.123);
        Time time3 = new Time(8, 2, 5.5);
        System.out.println("Tests 1 - 6");
        System.out.println("Created time1 = " + time1.getTime() +
                                "  time2 = " + time2.getTime() +
                                "  time3 = " + time3.getTime());
        // Tests 7-9
        System.out.println("Tests 7 - 9");
        System.out.println("time3 = " + time3.getHours() + " hours, " +
                                    time3.getMinutes() + " minutes, " +
                                    time3.getSeconds() + " seconds.");
        // Test 10
        System.out.println("Test 10");
        System.out.println("time2.plus(time3) = " +
                        time2.plus(time3).getTime());
        // Test 11
        System.out.println("Test 11");
        System.out.println("time3.minus(time2) = " +
                        time3.minus(time2).getTime());
        // Tests 12-14
        System.out.println("Tests 12 - 14");
        System.out.println("Using toString, time1 = " + time1 +
                        ", time2 = " + time2 +
                        ", time3 = " + time3);
    }
}
```

Here is a sample run of the driver:

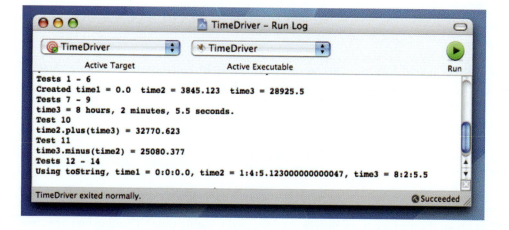

Hold on—that's not right. Test 12 returned 1:4:5.123000000000047 instead of 1:4:5.123. Well, we did say that floating-point numbers cannot always be represented accurately in the computer, and now we've just seen a good example. It's not a bug. However, we might want to change **toString** to round the number of seconds to hundredths. We ask you to complete this task as an exercise.

Race Report

Problem You're volunteering for a local track association, which would like a program that can print out a report for a race. A race has two runners. The program should input the name of each runner and his or her running time. It should then output a report that lists the input for each team, with names formatted as last, first, middle, followed by the average time for the two runners, the difference in time between them, and the minimum (winning) time.

Brainstorming and Filtering Initial Objects To begin, you brainstorm about the objects in the problem by identifying nouns in the problem statement. You come up with *race, report, runner, name, time, average time, difference time, winning time,* and *computer.* A little more thought reveals that *race* and *computer* are really not part of the problem. The race and the report are what the entire application represents, and the computer is just the tool you are using.

Brainstorming List	Filtered List
race	runner
report	runner name
runner	runner time
runner name	average time
runner time	difference time
average time	winning time
difference time	
winning time	
computer	

Looking at the filtered list, you can see an obvious set of collaborations among three of these objects: Each runner has name and time attributes. Thus we can implement a class `Runner` with two fields.

```
public class Runner
{
  Name name;                // Name object
  Time time;                // Time object
  . . .
}
```

What about the average time, difference time, and winning time? Those values are computed from the times of the two runners; they are not attributes of an individual `Runner`. Once we have the `Runner` class, we can calculate these values within the driver.

Initial Responsibilities Now we determine the responsibilities for this class. We need at least a default constructor and a direct constructor to set the fields to a specific name and time. We also need observers that let us get the values from the object. Let's include a `toString` method as well. Here is our initial list of responsibilities:

Runner (Collaborates with Name and Time)
Default constructor
Direct constructor
Get name
Get time
toString

Scenario Walkthrough What other responsibilities does this class have? To answer that question, we walk through a scenario that uses the class. Our scenario calls for us to enter the data for the two runners and output the report. The names are in the format of last, first, middle, with a blank separating each name. The middle name is followed by another blank, and the time appears as a decimal value. Here's an example:

```
Smith Isaiah John 85.74
```

Given this data format, here is how the scenario begins:

> The application asks for input of the first runner's data, and reads it in.

Where in the application does this data request come from? The driver creates a `Runner` object, but does the `Runner` object get its own data? Putting a specific style of input into the class would limit its reusability, so we'll have the driver read the data. Each name string can be input with `next`, and we can use `trim` to get rid of the extra blank. Let's continue with our scenario.

> The application calls `next` and `trim` to get each name, and `nextDouble` to get the time.
> It instantiates `Name` and `Time` objects to create the first `Runner`.
> The application asks for input of the second runner's data.
> The application calls `next` and `trim` to get each name, and `nextDouble` to get the time.
> It instantiates `Name` and `Time` objects to create the second `Runner`.
> The application prints the report.
>> Use the `toString` responsibility of the first runner to output that runner's information.
>> Use the `toString` responsibility of the second runner to output that runner's information.

To compute the average, we can use the `plus` method of our `Time` class to add the times for the runners, but how do we divide the sum by 2.0? We can use `getTime` to get the time as a **double** value, perform the division with normal arithmetic, and use the direct constructor for `Time` to convert the result back into an object.

194

The `minus` method gives us the (possibly negative) difference between the total times, which we convert to a `double` value so that `Math.abs` can take its absolute value. We'll need to take a similar approach with the winning time. We convert the two times to `double` values and use `Math.min` to return the lesser of the two, which we instantiate as a `Time`. Once we have the average, `difference`, and `winning` times, we use their `toString` methods to output them.

> Use the `plus` responsibility of the `Time` class to compute the total time for the runners.
> Use the total time with `getTime` and `toString` to compute and output the average time.
> Use `minus`, `getTime`, `Math.abs`, and `toString` to compute and output the difference in time.
> Use `getTime` with each runner's time and `Math.min` to determine the winning time.
> Use `toString` to output the winning time.

This scenario has given us the complete algorithm for the driver. Because the application is so simple, this is the only scenario we need, and we know we have all of the necessary responsibilities. More complex problems will involve multiple scenarios to identify all of the responsibilities.

Implementation of Runner Class Now we can implement the `Runner` class. We start with the fields and the constructors. What initial values do we assign to the `name` and `time` fields in the default constructor? Each is an object, so we can use the default constructors for `Name` and `Time`, as shown here:

```java
import java.util.Scanner;
public class Runner
{
  Name name;                // Holds the runner's name
  Time time;                // Holds the runner's time
  // Default constructor
  public Runner()
  {
    name = new Name();
    time = new Time();
  }
```

The direct constructor takes `Name` and `Time` objects as parameters and assigns them to the fields:

```java
  // Direct constructor
  public Runner(Name newName, Time newTime)
  {
    name = newName;
    time = newTime;
  }
```

Each get method simply returns a field value. These methods are so simple that we adopt a special way of formatting them. To save space, we write each one on a single line:

```java
public Name getName() { return name; }
public Time getTime() { return time; }
```

The only responsibility that remains is **toString**. We have a runner's name and time to place in the string. We already have a **toString** method for **Time**, and if we had one for **Name**, then this task would be trivial. Let's add such a method to the **Name** class. From our work with formatting names (looking for things that are familiar), we already know how to write the expression. We simply have to wrap it in the necessary value-returning method syntax:

```java
public String toString()                    // New method in class Name
{
  return last + ", " + first + " " + middle;
}
```

A side benefit of adding this method to **Name** is that now we can directly output **Name** objects and use them in string expressions. Returning to the **toString** method for **Runner**, we now write the string expression as shown here:

```java
public String toString()
{
  return name + "   " + time;    // Automatic calls to toString within this
                                 // expression
}
```

That completes the implementation of the **Runner** class. Here we gather all of the code together:

```java
//*************************************************************
// This class implements an object representing a runner in a
// race, and contains the name and time for the runner
//*************************************************************
import java.util.Scanner;
public class Runner
{
  Name name;                    // Holds the runner's name
  Time time;                    // Holds the runner's time
  // Default constructor
  public Runner()
  {
    name = new Name();
    time = new Time();
  }
  // Direct constructor
  public Runner(Name newName, Time newTime)
  {
    name = newName;
    time = newTime;
  }
  // Observers
  public Name getName() { return name; }
  public Time getTime() { return time; }

  public String toString()      // Converts Runner to String
  {
    return name + "   " + time;
  }
}
```

Driver Implementation Now that we have our `Runner` class, we are ready to write the driver. We need a pair of `Runner` variables. In addition, we declare variables to hold the average time, the time difference, and the winning time.

We begin by showing the user the proper format for the data. Then we ask the user to enter the data for each runner.

We can input each part of a name using `next`. After the first call to `next`, however, the next character to input is the blank separating the last and first names. Thus a second call to `next` returns the first name with a leading blank. We can use `trim` to pare away this extra blank. That process is repeated for the middle name, and then we call `nextDouble` to get the time. Having those values, we can instantiate the first runner, and then prompt for the next runner. Here's how we code the reading of data for the first runner:

```java
String last = in.next();
String first = in.next().trim();
String middle = in.next().trim();
double time = in.nextDouble();
runner1 = new Runner(new Name(first, last, middle), new Time(time));
```

Following is the code for the driver. Notice that it follows the same steps we identified in our scenario walkthrough. By storing the data in objects with associated `toString` methods, we can generate the output directly in the application, even though its formatting is fairly sophisticated.

```java
//***************************************************************
// This application gets data for two runners in a race, and
// displays a report of the input and some statistics for the race
//***************************************************************
import java.util.Scanner;
public class RaceReport
{
  public static void main (String[] args)
  {
    Runner runner1;       // Holds first runner
    Runner runner2;       // Holds second runner
    Time time1;           // Holds first runner's time
    Time time2;           // Holds second runner's time
    Time average;         // Holds average time for the runners
    Time difference;      // Holds difference in time between the runners
    Time winning;         // Holds winning time for the race
    Scanner in = new Scanner(System.in);

    // Output general instructions for input
    System.out.println("For each runner, enter the data in the following " +
                       "format:");
    System.out.println("Last First Middle time");
    System.out.println("For example: Smith Jane Louise 87.491");
```

```java
        // Prompt for and input data for the runners
        System.out.println("Enter the name and time for Runner 1");
        String last = in.next();
        String first = in.next().trim();
        String middle = in.next().trim();
        double time = in.nextDouble();
        runner1 = new Runner(new Name(first, last, middle), new Time(time));

        System.out.println("Enter the name and time for Runner 2");
        last = in.next();
        first = in.next().trim();
        middle = in.next().trim();
        time = in.nextDouble();
        runner2 = new Runner(new Name(first, last, middle), new Time(time));

        // Output the report for the race
        System.out.println();
        System.out.println("Race Report ");
        System.out.println();
        System.out.println("Runner 1: " + runner1);
        System.out.println("Runner 2: " + runner2);

        time1 = runner1.getTime();
        time2 = runner2.getTime();
        average = new Time(time1.plus(time2).getTime()/2.0);
        System.out.println();
        System.out.println("Average time: " + average);
        difference = new Time(Math.abs(time1.minus(time2).getTime()));
        System.out.println("Difference: " + difference);
        winning = new Time(Math.min(time1.getTime(), time2.getTime()));
        System.out.println("Winning time: " + winning);
    }
}
```

Testing No application is complete until it has been thoroughly tested. We need a test plan that exercises the application on a range of data values to verify it is working correctly.

Number	Input	Expected Result
1	All times zero	Zero times, average, difference, winning time
2	Runner 1 > Runner 2	Correct times, average, positive difference, second time is winner
3	Runner 1 < Runner 2	Correct times, average, positive difference, first time is winner

Although we could include tests for unusual values such as negative times, badly formatted names, and so on, we know that our application is not designed to handle these cases. In the next chapter we see how to use the branching control structure to validate input data. For now, we simply accept that our program generates invalid results for invalid data. Here we show the result of running the application for test number 2:

```
RaceReport – Run Log

RaceReport          RaceReport              ▶
Active Target       Active Executable      Run

For each runner, enter the data in the following format:
Last First Middle time
For example: Smith Jane Louise 87.49
Enter the name and time for Runner 1
Alvarez Doreeen Maude 505.2
Enter the name and time for Runner 2
Gupta Sarita Jean 501.58

Race Report

Runner 1: Alvarez, Doreeen Maude  0:8:25.19999999999999
Runner 2: Gupta, Sarita Jean   0:8:21.579999999999984

Average time: 0:8:23.389999999999986
Difference: 0:0:3.6200000000000045
Winning time: 0:8:21.579999999999984

RaceReport exited normally.
```

4.7 : Testing and Debugging

■ Class Test Plan

> **Test plan** A document that specifies how a class is to be tested
>
> **Test plan implementation** Writing and running a driver that implements the test cases specified in a test plan to verify that the class methods produce the predicted results

Earlier, we created a driver to test the `Time` class. Now let's look at the testing process in more detail. To test a class thoroughly, you must design and implement a **test plan**—a document that specifies the test cases that should be tried for each method, the expected output, and any other information required to explain the test. **Test plan implementation** involves writing and running a driver, using the data specified by the test cases in the plan, and checking and recording the results.

Let's develop a test plan for class `Runner`. Here are the data fields and method headings in this class:

```
// Data fields
Name name;
Time time;
// Constructors
public Runner()
public Runner(Name newName, Time newTime)
```

Number	Method	Expected Result
1	`Runner().toString();`	`,  0:0:0:0`
2	`ourRunner = new Runner(`	
	`        new Name("Davis", "Desiree", "Mary"),`	
	`        new Time(122.34));`	ourRunner has the specified values
	`ourRunner.getName().toString()`	`Davis, Desiree Mary`
3	`ourRunner().getTime().toString()`	`0:2:2.34`
4	`ourRunner.toString()`	`Davis, Desiree Mary 0:2:2.34`

TABLE 4.3 Test Plan for the Runner Class

```
// Observers
public Name getName()
public Time getTime()
public String toString()
```

We test each constructor by executing it. We then use the observers to access and return values from the objects, and finally print the results. The default constructor needs to be called only once. Given that the direct constructor simply stores the arguments into the data fields, one call to it should be sufficient as well.

To test the observers, we print out the value that each returns. For `Name` and `Time`, we simply use the associated `toString` method. We test the `toString` of `Runner` by printing its result.

In this class, the fields are both user-defined classes. We can choose to assume that these classes have been tested, or we can test them again here. Because we wrote the classes ourselves, we already know that they have been tested. If `Name` and `Time` had come from someone else, without any documentation of their testing, we would want to add further tests to ensure that they work in this context.

Table 4.3 shows the complete test plan for class `Runner`. A driver is written to implement this test plan, and the results are checked against the Expected Result column. Of course, implementing the test plan does not guarantee that your code is completely correct. It means only that a careful, systematic test of the code has not demonstrated any bugs.

Testing and Debugging Hints

1. An `int` literal other than 0 should not start with a zero. If it starts with zero, it is an octal (base 8) number.

2. Watch out for integer division. The expression `47 / 100` yields 0, the integer quotient. This is one of the major sources of wrong output in Java code.

3. When using the `/` and `%` operators with integers, remember that division by zero is not allowed.

4. Double-check every expression according to the precedence rules to confirm that the operations are performed in the desired order, especially with expressions involving string conversion.

5. Avoid mixing integer and floating-point values in expressions. If you must mix them, use explicit type casts to reduce the chance of mistakes.

6. For each assignment statement, verify that the expression result has the same data type as the variable to the left of the assignment operator (=). If it does not, use an explicit type cast for clarity and safety. Also, remember that storing a floating-point value into an `int` variable truncates the fractional part.

7. If an application is producing erroneous results and all of its expressions appear to be correct, check whether any of them might potentially result in integer overflow. Also, check whether they contain any unintentional type conversions.

8. For every library package you use in your application, be sure to include an `import` declaration.

9. Examine each method call to confirm that you have the right number of arguments and that the data types of the arguments are correct.

10. Remember to return an expression from a value-returning method. This expression must produce the same type as the result type specified in the method heading.

11. Keep your code neatly formatted so that it is easier to read.

12. If the cause of an error in your code is not obvious, leave the computer and study a printed listing. Change your code only after you understand the source of the error.

13. Remember to use a class name with a class method, and an object name with an instance method.

14. When inputting a numeric value, remember that the separator following the number is not consumed.

15. Recognize that method `nextLine` returns the *rest* of the line.

16. If a call to `nextLine` is issued after a numeric read, it might return the empty string. You may need to include an extra `nextLine` to get past the end-of-line separator.

Graphical User Interfaces

`JOptionPane` Message Dialog

Thus far, we have used `System.in` for our input. While this approach is easy to code, you are probably more accustomed to seeing input windows with data entry fields. Creating windows to allow arbitrary user input and output is not a simple process in Java.

Most user input dialogs are much simpler than the general case. For example, we might display a message and ask the user to click an OK button once it has been read. In recognition of such common cases, Java provides a class that handles limited types of interactions.

Class **JOptionPane** enables you to perform simple input and output through a normal window. Because it is part of the **javax.swing** package, you must place the following **import** statement at the top of any class that uses it:

```
import javax.swing.*;
```

A single **JOptionPane** method call displays a window according to our specification. Such a window is called a **dialog box**. It is a dialog in the sense that, as in a dialog between actors in a play, an exchange takes place. We provide some information to the user and the user responds in some manner. Here we introduce the simplest **JOptionPane** dialog. In succeeding chapters, we explore additional capabilities of the class.

> **Dialog box**   A small temporary panel that appears on the screen, with which a user can interact

showMessageDialog is a **void** method that displays a message in a dialog box. The simplest form of this method has two parameters. A dialog box can be used in conjunction with other windows, and the first parameter is used to specify the window (which Java calls the **parentComponent**) over which the dialog box should be centered. Because we have not explored the use of other windows, we simply put the special Java value **null** there (**null** represents the absence of an object), so that the dialog box will be centered on the screen. The second parameter is the string that we wish to display as a message. For example:

```
JOptionPane.showMessageDialog(null, "Click OK when ready to begin " +
                                    "entering data.");
```

The following simple driver creates a message dialog:

```
import javax.swing.*;
public class DemoDialog
{
  public static void main(String args[])
  {
    JOptionPane.showMessageDialog(null, "Input plus 10 is 44");
  }
}
```

Here is the dialog box that it displays:

The icon that appears as part of the dialog is called the information icon; the default label for the window is "Message." In later chapters, we will see how to change these aspects of the dialog.

The driver calls `showMessageDialog`, and the message is displayed. When the user clicks OK, the method returns and execution continues with the next statement.

Summary

Java provides several built-in numeric data types, of which the most commonly used are `int` and `double`. The integral types are based on the mathematical integers, and the floating-point types are based on the mathematical notion of real numbers. The computer limits the range of integer and floating-point numbers that can be represented. In addition, it limits the number of digits of precision in floating-point values. We can write literals of type `double` in several forms, including scientific (E) notation. Java provides the standard mathematical operations to go with these data types: addition (+), subtraction (-), multiplication (*), division (/), and remainder (%). Java also provides an increment operation (++) and a decrement operation (--).

Expressions can contain more than one operator. The order in which the operations are performed is determined by precedence rules. In arithmetic expressions, the unary operators (such as negation) are performed first; then type casts; then multiplication, division, and modulus; and finally addition and subtraction. Multiple arithmetic operations of the same precedence are grouped from left to right. You can use parentheses to override these precedence rules.

Class `Scanner` provides a variety of methods with which to input numeric values. Method `nextInt` inputs the next integer value; method `nextFloat` inputs the next `float` value. There is a corresponding method for each of Java's other built-in types. If the next value to be read is not of the matching type, an exception is thrown.

Mixing values of the integer and floating-point types in an expression results in automatic type conversion to achieve compatibility between the operands of all of the operators. If you aren't careful, these conversions can have unintended results. The best approach is to use type cast operations whenever you need to mix types within expressions. String conversion is done when we concatenate a numeric value with a string.

The `Math` class contains static methods that provide standard mathematical operations. The `String` class provides useful instance methods for working with strings.

Not only should the output produced by an application be easy to read, but the format of the code itself should also be clear and readable. A consistent style that uses indentation, blank lines, and spaces within lines will help you (and other programmers) understand and work with your code. Code should be tested with a plan that checks every aspect of its operation, specifying test data and expected results in each distinct case.

LEARNING / Portfolio

Quick Check

1. Which integer and real types take up the same number of bits in the computer's memory? (pp. 150–152)

2. What syntactic parts do floating-point values have that integral types lack? (pp. 152–153)

3. If you want to change the precedence of operations in an expression, which symbols do you use? (pp. 163–165)

4. Add type casts to the following statements to make the type conversions clear and explicit. Your answers should produce the same results as the original statements. (pp. 167–168)

    a. `someDouble = 5 + someInt;`

    b. `someInt = 2.5 * someInt / someDouble;`

5. Write a local Java constant declaration that gives the name PI to the value 3.14159. (p. 153)

6. Declare a local `int` variable named `count` and a local `double` variable named `sum`. (p. 154)

7. You want to divide 9 by 5.

    a. How do you write the expression if you want the result to be the floating-point value 1.8? (pp. 155–157)

    b. How do you write the expression if you want only the integer quotient? (pp. 155–157)

8. What is the value of the following Java expression? (pp. 155–157)

    `5 % 2`

9. What is the result of evaluating the following expression? (pp. 163–165)

    `(1 + 2 * 2) / 2 + 1`

10. How would you write the following formula as a Java expression that produces a floating-point value as a result? (pp. 152–153, 163–165)

    $$\frac{9}{5}C + 32$$

11. Which `Scanner` method do you use to input a value of type `double`? (pp. 158–161)

12. If the `String` variable `str` contains the string `"Now is the time"`, what is the result of the following expression? (pp. 176–177)

```
str.length() + " " + str.substring(1, 3)
```

13. If the `String` variable `str` contains the string `"Quick Check Exercise Thirteen"`, what is the result of the following expression? (pp. 176–177)

```
str.indexOf("Ex") + str.indexOf("Q") + str.length()
```

14. You want to compute the square roots and absolute values of some floating-point numbers. Which Java methods would you use? (pp. 180–181)

15. Who needs to have code formatted in a clear and readable manner—the Java compiler, the human reader, or both? (pp. 181–182)

Answers

1. `int` and `float` are both 32 bits. `long` and `double` are both 64 bits. 2. A decimal point, a fractional part, and an exponent. 3. Parentheses `( )`
4. a. `someDouble = (double)(5 + someInt);`
   b. `someInt = (int)(2.5 * (double)(someInt) / someDouble);`
5. `final double PI = 3.14159;`
6. `int     count;`
   `double sum;`
7. a. `9.0 / 5.0` or `(double) 9 / (double) 5` b. `9 / 5`
8. The value is 1. 9. The result is 3. 10. `9.0 / 5.0 * c + 32.0` 11. `nextDouble` 12. `"15 ow"` 13. 41 14.
`Math.sqrt` and `Math.abs` 15. The human reader. The compiler ignores code formatting.

Exam Preparation Exercises

1. Mark the following constructs either valid or invalid. Assume all variables are of type `int`.

	Valid	Invalid
a. `x * y = c;`	_____	_____
b. `y = con;`	_____	_____
c. `private static final int x : 10;`	_____	_____
d. `int x;`	_____	_____
e. `a = b % c;`	_____	_____

2. If `alpha` and `beta` are `int` variables with `alpha` = 4 and `beta` = 9, what value is stored into `alpha` in each of the following? Answer each part independently of the others.

a. `alpha = 3 * beta;`

b. `alpha = alpha + beta;`

c. `alpha++;`

d. `alpha = alpha / beta;`

e. `alpha--;`

f. `alpha = alpha + alpha;`

g. `alpha = beta % 6;`

3. Compute the value of each legal expression. Indicate whether the value is an integer or a floating-point value. If the expression is not legal, explain why.

	Integer	Floating Point
a. `10.0 / 3.0 + 5 * 2`	_____	_____
b. `10 % 3 + 5 % 2`	_____	_____
c. `10 / 3 + 5 / 2`	_____	_____
d. `12.5 + (2.5 / (6.2 / 3.1))`	_____	_____
e. `-4 * (-5 + 6)`	_____	_____
f. `13 % 5 / 3`	_____	_____
g. `(10.0 / 3.0 % 2) / 3`	_____	_____

4. What value is stored into the `int` variable result in each of the following?

a. `result = 15 % 4;`

b. `result = 7 / 3 + 2;`

c. `result = 2 + 7 * 5;`

d. `result = 45 / 8 * 4 + 2;`

e. `result = 17 + (21 % 6) * 2;`

f. `result = (int)(4.5 + 2.6 * 0.5);`

5. If **a** and **b** are `int` variables with a = 5 and b = 2, what output does each of the following statements produce?

a. `System.out.println("a = " + a + "b = " + b);`

b. `System.out.println("Sum:" + a + b);`

c. `System.out.println("Sum:  " + a + b);`

d. `System.out.println(a / b + " feet");`

6. What does the following application print?

```
public class ExamPrep
{
  public static void main(String[] args)
  {
    final int LBS = 10;
    int  price;
    int  cost;
    char ch;
```

```
        price = 30;
        cost = price * LBS;
        ch = 'A';
        System.out.println("Cost is ");
        System.out.println(cost);
        System.out.println("Price is " + price + "Cost is " + cost);
        System.out.println("Grade " + ch + " costs ");
        System.out.println(cost);
    }
}
```

7. Translate the following Java code into algebraic notation. (All variables are **double** variables.)

```
y = -b + Math.sqrt(b * b - 4.0 * a * c);
```

8. Given the following code fragment:

```
int    i;
int    j;
double z;
i = 4;
j = 17;
z = 2.6;
```

Determine the value of each of the following expressions. If the result is a floating-point value, include a decimal point in your answer.

a. i / (double)j

b. 1.0 / i + 2

c. z * j

d. i + j % i

e. (1 / 2) * i

f. 2 * i + j - i

g. j / 2

h. 2 * 3 - 1 % 3

i. i % j / i

j. (int)(z + 0.5)

9. Evaluate the following expressions. If the result is a floating-point number, include a decimal point in your answer.

a. Math.abs(-9.1)

b. Math.sqrt(49.0)

c. `3 * (int)7.8 + 3`

d. `Math.pow(4.0, 2.0)`

e. `Math.sqrt((double)(3 * 3 + 4 * 4))`

f. `Math.sqrt(Math.abs(-4.0) + Math.sqrt(25.0))`

10. Given the following statements:

```
String heading;
String str;
heading = "Exam Preparation Exercises";
```

What is the output of each of the following code segments?

a. `System.out.println(heading.length());`

b. `System.out.println(heading.substring(6, 16));`

c. `System.out.println(heading.indexOf("Ex"));`

d. `str = heading.substring(2, 26);`
   `System.out.println(str.indexOf("Ex"));`

e. `str = heading.substring(heading.indexOf("Ex") + 2, 24);`
   `System.out.println(str.indexOf("Ex"));`

f. `str = heading.substring(heading.indexOf("Ex")+2, heading.length());`
   `System.out.println(str.indexOf("Ex"));`

11. Incorrectly formatting an application causes an error. (True or False?)

12. Which `Scanner` methods are used to read floating-point values?

13. Which `Scanner` methods are used to read integer values?

Programming Warm-Up Exercises

1. Change the application in Exam Preparation Exercise 6 so that it prints the cost for 15 pounds.

2. Write an assignment statement to calculate the sum of the numbers from 1 through *n* using Gauss's formula:

$$sum = \frac{n(n+1)}{2}$$

Store the result into the `int` variable `sum`.

3. Given the following declarations:

```
int    i;
int    j;
double x;
double y;
```

Write a valid Java expression for each of the following algebraic expressions:

a. $\dfrac{x}{y} - 3$

b. $(x+y)(x-y)$

c. $\dfrac{1}{x+y}$

d. $\dfrac{1}{x} + y$

e. $\dfrac{i}{j}$ (the floating-point result)

f. $\dfrac{i}{j}$ (the integer quotient)

g. $\dfrac{\dfrac{x+y}{3} - \dfrac{x-y}{5}}{4x}$

4. Given the following declarations:

```
int    i;
long   n;
double x;
double y;
```

Write a valid Java expression for each of the following algebraic expressions. Use calls to `Math` methods wherever they are useful.

a. $|i|$

b. $|n|$

c. $|x+y|$

d. $|x| + |y|$

e. $\dfrac{x^3}{x+y}$

f. $\sqrt{x^6 + y^5}$

g. $\left(x + \sqrt{y}\right)^7$

5. Write expressions to compute both solutions for the quadratic formula. The formula is

$$\dfrac{-b \pm \sqrt{b^2 - 4ac}}{2a}$$

LEARNING Portfolio

The ± symbol means "plus or minus" and indicates that the equation has two solutions: one in which the result of the square root is added to 2*a* and one in which the result is subtracted from 2*a*. Assume all variables are `float` variables.

6. Enter the following application into your computer and run it. In the initial comments, replace the items within parentheses with your own information. (Omit the parentheses.)

```java
//**********************************
// Programming Assignment One
// (your name)
// (date application was run)
// (description of the problem)
//**********************************
public class WarmUp
{
  public static void main(String[] args)
  {
    final double DEBT = 300.0;       // Original value owed
    final double PMT = 22.4;         // Payment
    final double INT_RATE = 0.02;    // Interest rate
    double charge;                   // Interest times debt
    double reduc;                    // Amount debt is reduced
    double remaining;                // Remaining balance
    // Compute values for output
    charge = INT_RATE * DEBT;        // Compute interest charge
    reduc = PMT - charge;            // Compute debt reduction
    remaining = DEBT - reduc;        // Compute remaining balance
    // Output result
    System.out.println("Payment: " + PMT + " Charge: " + charge +
                     " Balance owed: " + remaining);
  }
}
```

7. Rewrite the program in Exercise 6 so that the values for `DEBT`, `PMT`, and `INT_RATE` are read rather than set as constants.

8. Enter the following application into your computer and run it. Add comments, using the pattern shown in Exercise 6. (Notice how difficult it is to tell what the code does without the comments.)

```java
public class WarmUp2
{
  public static void main(String[] args)
  {
    final int TOT_COST = 1376;
```

```
      final int POUNDS = 10;
      final int OUNCES = 12;
      int    totOz;
      double uCost;
      totOz = 16 * POUNDS;
      totOz = totOz + OUNCES;
      uCost = TOT_COST / totOz;
      System.out.println("Cost per unit: " + uCost);

   }
}
```

9. Complete the following Java application. The application should find and output the perimeter and area of a rectangle, given the length and the width. Be sure to label the output. Don't forget to use comments.

```
//**********************************************
// Rectangle application
// This application finds the perimeter and the area
// of a rectangle, given the length and width
//**********************************************
public class Rectangle
{
   public static void main(String[] args)
   {
      double length;              // Length of the rectangle
      double width;               // Width of the rectangle
      double perimeter;           // Perimeter of the rectangle
      double area;                // Area of the rectangle
      length = 10.7;
      width = 5.2;
      // Add code here as needed
   }
}
```

10. Write an expression whose result is the position of the first occurrence of the characters "res" in a String variable named sentence. If the variable contains the first sentence of this question, then what is the result? (Look at the sentence carefully!)

11. Write a sequence of Java statements to output the positions of the second and third occurrences of the characters "res" in the String variable named sentence. You may assume that there are always at least three occurrences in the variable. (*Hint:* Use the substring method to create a new string whose contents are the portion of the sentence following an occurrence of "res".)

12. Reformat the following application to make it clear and readable.

```
//*************************************************************
   // This application computes the sum and product of two integers
//*************************************************************
public class SumProd {  public static void main(String[] args){
final int INT2=8;   final int INT1=20; System.out.println(
"The sum of " + INT1 + " and "
+ INT2 + " is " + (INT1+INT2)); System.out.println (
"Their product is " + (INT1*INT2)); }}
```

13. Write a code fragment that reads in two `int` values followed by two `float` values.

14. Write a code fragment that reads in two `int` values followed by a date. Numeric values are on one line with the date (a `String`) on the next line.

15. Change the `toString` method in the `Time` class so that it rounds the seconds to two digits after the decimal point (hundredths of seconds).

Programming Problems

1. Java systems provide a set of user-defined types that duplicate the names of primitive types except that the first letter of the type name is capitalized (for example, `Double` and `Long` instead of `double` and `long`). The one exception is that the type corresponding to `int` is called `Integer`. Each of these types contains declarations of constants related to the corresponding primitive type. Two of these constants are `Integer.MAX_VALUE` and `Integer.MIN_VALUE`, the largest and smallest `int` values that Java allows, respectively. Write an application to display the values of `Integer.MAX_VALUE` and `Integer.MIN_VALUE`. The output should identify which value is `Integer.MAX_VALUE` and which value is `Integer.MIN_VALUE`. Be sure to include appropriate comments in your code, and use indentation as we do in the code in this chapter. Each of these types defines similar constants, so you may want to extend your application to display `Long.MIN_VALUE`, and so on, just to learn what the actual maximum and minimum numbers are for each of the primitive types.

2. Write an application that outputs three lines as follows:

7 / 4 using integer division equals <result>

7 / 4 using floating-point division equals <result>

7 modulo 4 equals <result>

where <result> stands for the result computed by your application. Use named constants for 7 and 4 everywhere in your application (including the output statements) to make the application easy to modify. Be sure to include appropriate comments in your code, choose meaningful identifiers, and use indentation as we do in the code in this chapter.

3. Write a Java application that takes an integral Celsius temperature as input and converts it to its Fahrenheit equivalent. The formula is

$$\text{Fahrenheit} = \frac{9}{5}\text{Celsius} + 32$$

After the Celsius temperature is input, it should be displayed along with the corresponding Fahrenheit equivalent. The application should include appropriate messages identifying each value. Be sure to include appropriate comments in your code, choose meaningful identifiers, and use indentation as we do in the code in this chapter.

4. Write an application to calculate the diameter, circumference, and area of a circle with a radius input by the user. Assign the radius to a `float` variable, and then output the radius with an appropriate message. Declare a named constant `PI` with the value 3.14159. The application should output the diameter, circumference, and area, each on a separate line, with identifying labels. Be sure to include appropriate comments in your code, choose meaningful identifiers, and use indentation as we do in the code in this chapter.

LEARNING / Portfolio

Case Study Follow-Up

1. Modify the `RaceResult` application so that it works for three runners. The new application should output the difference in time between each pair of runners. Which classes require modification?

2. Write a test plan for the modified `RaceResult` application, as specified in Question 1.

3. Change the modified `RaceResult` application so that it outputs the minimum of the three times. (*Hint:* Use a call to `Math.min` within another call to `Math.min`.)

4. Write a test plan for the `Runner` class.

5. Write a driver that implements the test plan in Question 4.

5 Branching and Method Algorithm Design

Goals

Knowledge Goals

To:

- Understand the Boolean operators AND, OR, and NOT
- Understand the concept of control flow with respect to selection statements
- Understand how nested control flow works
- Understand the differences between the *if-else* and *if-else-if* selection structures
- Understand the differences between a nested *if* structure and a series of *if* structures
- Know when each form of selection structure is appropriate
- Understand the functional decomposition process

Skill Goals

To be able to:

- Use the relational operators <, >, <=, >=, ==, and !=
- Construct a simple logical (Boolean) expression to evaluate a given condition
- Construct a complex Boolean expression to evaluate a given condition
- Construct an *if-else* statement to perform a specific task
- Construct an *if* statement to perform a specific task
- Construct a set of nested *if* statements to perform a specific task
- Apply functional decomposition to design a method algorithm
- Apply testing strategies for *if* structures
- Test and debug a Java application

1951
Admiral Grace Murray Hopper invents the first compiler

1952
The EDVAC, the first stored-program computer, is operational

1952
IBM introduces the IBM 701 computer

1953
The IBM 650 Magnetic Drum Calculator is introduced, mass produced, and becomes the best selling computer of the 1950s

1954
Earl Masterson at Univac introduces his Uniprinter, a line printer that prints 600 lines per minute

1954
Texas Instruments develops the world's first silicon transistor

FIRST SILICON TRANSISTOR

Introduction

Until now, all of our applications and methods have been simple sequences of statements. This situation is analogous to driving a car down a highway with no exits. It gets us from point A to point B, but it provides no options for alternate routes. If a section of the highway is flooded, that's the end of our trip. In the Race Report case study in Chapter 4, if the user enters the data in the wrong format, the application throws an exception and quits.

In many problems, there are different ways of getting from start to finish that depend on specific conditions. For example, if the input value is negative, then perhaps it should be handled differently from positive values. If the first runner is the winner, then print his or her report first; otherwise, print the report for the other runner first. We often ask a question about some data (Is it negative? Is it less than some other value?), and then take an action based on the answer.

In the first part of this chapter, we see how the computer can pose questions. In the next part, we use the Java *if* statement to select different courses of action. Once we can respond with different actions for different conditions, we can write classes that perform more complex operations.

1956–1957	**1957**	**1957**	**1957**	**1957**	**1957**
The RAMAC, random-access method of accounting and control, is introduced by IBM for hard disk data storage	The concept of artificial intelligence is developed at Dartmouth College	John Backus debuts the first Fortran compiler	John McCarthy founds MIT's Artificial Intelligence Department	The first computer-controlled launch of the Atlas missile takes place	Russia launches Sputnik I into orbit

5.1 : Boolean Expressions

To ask a question in Java, we don't phrase it as a question; rather, we state it as an assertion. If our assertion is true, the answer to the question is yes. If our assertion is false, the answer to the question is no. We simplify assertions to true-false form because it is easiest for the computer to work with answers that can be represented by the 1s and 0s of the binary number system. For example, to ask, "Are we having spinach for dinner tonight?" we would say, "We are having spinach for dinner tonight." If the assertion is true, the answer to the question is yes. If it is false, the answer is no.

The computer evaluates the assertion, checking it against some internal condition (the value stored in a variable, for instance) to see whether it is true or false. Internally, the computer would use 1 to represent true and 0 to represent false. Actually, we don't need to be aware of this internal representation because Java provides a more natural representation for us to use: the data type `boolean`, which is the last of Java's primitive types.

■ Boolean Data Type

The `boolean` type consists of just two values, the constants `true` and `false`. The reserved word `boolean` is pronounced "bōo̅′-lē-ən." [1] Boolean data is used for testing conditions in code so that the computer can make decisions (as in a selection control structure).

We declare variables of type `boolean` in the same way that we declare variables of other standard types—by writing the name of the data type and then an identifier:

```java
boolean dataOK;      // True if the input data is valid
boolean done;        // True if the process is done
boolean taxable;     // True if the item has sales tax
```

Each variable of type `boolean` can contain one of two values: `true` or `false`. It's important to understand that `true` and `false` are neither variable names nor strings. Rather, they are special constants in Java and, in fact, are reserved words.

■ Logical Expressions

In programming languages, assertions take the form of logical expressions (also called Boolean expressions). Just as an arithmetic expression is made up of numeric values and operations, a

---

1. The name `boolean` is a tribute to George Boole, a nineteenth-century mathematician who described a system of logic using variables with just two possible values, true and false. (See the May We Introduce feature on pages 226–227.)

logical expression is made up of Boolean values and logical operations. Whenever the computer evaluates a logical expression, the result is one of the values `true` or `false`.

Here are the basic forms of logical expressions (we explain each form in the following sections):

- A `boolean` variable or constant
- An arithmetic expression followed by a relational operator followed by an arithmetic expression
- A logical expression followed by a logical operator followed by a logical expression

Let's look at each of these possibilities in detail.

Variables and Constants   As we have seen, a `boolean` variable is a variable declared to be of type `boolean`, which can contain either the value `true` or the value `false`. For example, if `dataOK` is a `boolean` variable, then

```
dataOK = true;
```

is a valid statement that assigns the literal constant `true` to the variable `dataOK`. It is possible to declare named constants of type `boolean`, but we rarely do so because such a constant could have only two possible values.

Relational Operators   Another way of assigning a value to a `boolean` variable is to set it equal to the result of a relational comparison (such as *greater than*). Relational operators test a relationship between two values and give a result of either `true` or `false`. For example, if we test whether 10 is greater than 2, the result is `true`.

Let's look at a Java example. In the following code fragment, `lessThanZero` is a `boolean` variable and `i` is an `int` variable:

```
lessThanZero = i < 0;      // Compare i and 0 with the "less than"
                           // operator, and assign the result to lessThanZero
```

By comparing two values, we assert that a relationship (such as "less than") exists between them. If the relationship does exist, the assertion is true; if not, it is false. We can test for the following relationships in Java:

Operator	Relationship Tested
==	Equal to
!=	Not equal to
>	Greater than
<	Less than
>=	Greater than or equal to
<=	Less than or equal to

An expression followed by a relational operator followed by an expression is called a *relational expression.* The result of a relational expression is of type `boolean`. For example, if x is 5 and y is 10, the following expressions all have the value `true`:

```
x != y
y > x
x < y
y >= x
x <= y
```

If x and y are instead of type `char`, and x contains the character `'M'` and y holds `'R'`, the values of the expressions are still `true` because the relational operator <, when used with letters, means "comes before in the alphabet" or, more properly, "comes before in the collating sequence of the character set." For example, in the ASCII subset of the Unicode character set, all of the uppercase letters are in alphabetical order, as are the lowercase letters, but all of the uppercase letters come before the lowercase letters. So the expressions

```
'M' < 'R'
```

and

```
'm' < 'r'
```

have the value `true`, but

```
'm' < 'R'
```

has the value `false`.

Of course, we have to be careful about the data types of things that we compare. The safest approach is to compare identical types: `int` with `int`, `double` with `double`, `char` with `char`, and so on. If you mix data types in a comparison, implicit type conversion takes place just as it does in arithmetic expressions. If you try to compare an `int` value and a `double` value, for example, the computer temporarily converts the `int` value to its `double` equivalent before making the comparison. As with arithmetic expressions, it's best to use explicit type casting to make your intentions known:

```
someDouble >= (double)someInt
```

If you try to compare a `boolean` value with a numeric value (probably by mistake), the compiler will display an error message.

Values of type `boolean` cannot be converted to any type other than `String`. When a `boolean` variable is concatenated with a string, its value is automatically converted to either `"true"` or `"false"`. No type can be converted automatically to `boolean`. Here is a demonstration application that illustrates output of `boolean` values.

```java
//*********************************************************************
// Application BooleanOutputDemo
// This application indicates whether the response to a quiz question is true
//*********************************************************************
import java.util.Scanner;
class BooleanOutputDemo
{
  public static void main(String[] args)
  {
    boolean answer;
    Scanner in = new Scanner(System.in);
    System.out.println("Enter 1 if you think the sun travels east to west.");
    System.out.println("Enter 2 if you think the sun travels west to east.");
    int response = in.nextInt();
    answer = response == 1;
    System.out.println("Your answer is " + answer);
  }
}
```

Here is a run of the demo:

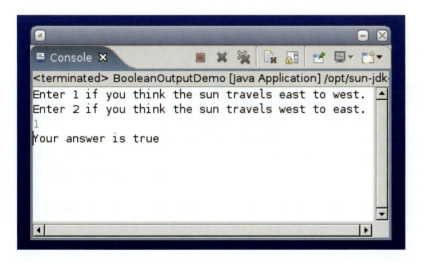

Be careful to compare **char** values only with other **char** values. For example, the comparisons

`'0' < '9'`

and

`0 < 9`

are appropriate, but comparing a digit in quotes (a character) and a digit, such as

`'0' < 9`

generates an implicit type conversion and a result that probably isn't what you expect. The character for the digit `'0'` is converted to its equivalent `int` value in the Unicode character set, which is 48, and the comparison returns `false` because 48 is greater than 9. (If you are curious about why `'0'` has the `int` value 48 in the character set, look at Appendix D to see how a number is assigned to each `char` value.)

To keep our initial examples clear, we have restricted ourselves to expressions consisting of a single variable or literal constant. In fact, we can also apply relational operators to arithmetic expressions. In the following table, we compare the results of adding 3 to x and multiplying y by 10 for different values of x and y:

Value of x	Value of y	Expression	Result
12	2	x + 3 <= y * 10	true
20	2	x + 3 <= y * 10	false
7	1	x + 3 != y * 10	false
17	2	x + 3 == y * 10	true
100	5	x + 3 > y * 10	true

Caution: It's easy to confuse the assignment operator (=) and the equality relational operator (==). These two operators have very different effects in your code. Some people pronounce the relational operator as "equals-equals" to remind themselves of the difference.

Comparing Strings You cannot compare strings using the relational operators. Syntactically, Java lets you write the comparisons for equality (==) and inequality (!=) between values of class `String`, but such a comparison is not what you typically want.

Recall from Chapter 2 that `String` is a reference type. A `String` variable contains the memory address for the beginning of the string object. When you compare two strings, Java therefore checks whether they have the same address; it does not check whether they contain the same sequence of characters.

Mistakenly using the == or != operator to compare strings is a source of some insidious errors. Sometimes the comparison seems to work; at other times it fails. The reason for this inconsistency is that most Java compilers are quite clever about how they store `String` literals. If you type the same literal in two different places in your code, the compiler recognizes their equality and stores the character sequence just once; it then uses the same address in the Bytecode. Thus comparing a `String` literal to a variable that has been assigned an identical literal elsewhere in the program is likely to indicate that they are equal (if the Java compiler is well designed). For example, the following code fragment is likely to assign `true` to the `boolean` variable `same`:

```
String message = "Good Morning";
String newMessage = "Good Morning";
same = (message == newMessage);   // A good Java compiler notes that the
                                  // literal strings are the same, keeps just
                                  // one copy, and stores the same address in
                                  // both variables
```

If you input a string and compare it to a `String` literal, however, the two always compare as unequal, even when they contain the exact same sequence of characters. The string that was input and the `String` literal are stored in different places in memory, which means that their addresses compare as unequal. The following code fragment demonstrates this behavior.

```java
// Declarations for the example
Scanner in = new Scanner(System.in);
final String MESSAGE = "Good morning";        // A string to compare with
// Input a string
System.out.print("Enter the first message: ");
String firstMessage = in.nextLine();
// Input a second string
System.out.print("Enter the second message: ");
String secondMessage = in.nextLine();
// Output some comparisons of the three strings
System.out.println(MESSAGE == firstMessage);
System.out.println(firstMessage == secondMessage);
System.out.println(MESSAGE == secondMessage);
```

Assume that when this code is executed, the user enters `"Good morning"` for both the first and second messages. What is output? In all three cases, `false` is printed because the three strings are stored in different places in memory.

Rather than using the relational operators, we compare strings with a set of value-returning instance methods that Java supplies as part of the `String` class. Because we sometimes want to convert strings to all lowercase or to all uppercase, the `String` class provides methods called `toLowerCase` and `toUpperCase`. The three most useful comparison methods are summarized in Table 5.1, along with `toLowerCase` and `toUpperCase`.

Many of Java's classes provide a useful method called `compareTo`. As we will see later in this chapter, this convention of supplying a `compareTo` method enables us to consistently code a comparison of the contents of two objects, rather than comparing their addresses. With strings, we often combine the use of `compareTo` with the use of either `toLowerCase` or `toUpperCase`, as we show later. Note that `equals` and `equalsIgnoreCase` test only for equality. We must use

Method Name	Argument Type	Returns	Operation Performed
equals	String	boolean	Tests for equality of string contents
equalsIgnoreCase	String	boolean	Returns `true` if the strings are equal, ignoring the case of the letters; returns `false` if they are unequal
compareTo	String	int	Returns 0 if equal, a positive integer if this string comes after the string in the argument, and a negative integer if it comes before the argument string
toLowerCase	none	String	Result is identical except the characters are all lowercase
toUpperCase	none	String	Result is identical except the characters are all uppercase

TABLE 5.1   Java Instance Methods for Comparison and Case-Conversion of Strings

the `compareTo` method to test for relationships such as "greater than" or "less than" between strings.

Let's look at some examples. If `lastName` is a `String` variable, we can write

```
lastName.equals("Olson")          // Tests whether lastName equals "Olson"
```

Because every `String` literal is also a `String` object, Java lets us append the method call to a literal, if we so choose.

```
"Olson".equals(lastName)          // Tests whether lastName equals "Olson"
```

As another example, we might write

```
lastName.compareTo("Olson") > 0   // Tests whether lastName comes after "Olson"
```

When the computer compares two strings, it begins with the first character of each, compares the two characters, and if they are the same, repeats the comparison with the next character of each string. The character-by-character test continues until a mismatch is found, in which case the string with the character that comes before the other is the "lesser" string. Remember that "comes before" means the character has a lesser value in the Unicode character set. If all their characters are equal, then the two strings are equal.

For example, given the statements

```
String word1;
String word2;

word1 = "Tremendous";
word2 = "Small";
```

the following relational expressions have the values shown:

Expression	Value	Reason
`word1.equals(word2)`	false	They are unequal in the first character
`word1.compareTo(word2) > 0`	true	"T" comes after "S" in the collating sequence
`word1.compareTo("Tremble") < 0`	false	The fifth characters don't match, and "e" comes after "b"
`word2.equals("Small")`	true	They are equal
`"cat".compareTo("dog") == 0`	false	They are unequal

Remembering exactly how `compareTo` works can be a bit challenging at first. A convention that helps overcome this confusion is to write the relational expression with zero on the right side of the operator. Then the operator has the same meaning as if we were able to substitute it for the method name. That is, writing

```
word1.compareTo(word2) > 0
```

has the same effect as if Java allowed us to write

```
word1 > word2
```

In most cases, the ordering of strings corresponds to alphabetical ordering. When strings have mixed-case letters, however, we can get nonalphabetical results. For example, in a phone book we would expect to see "Macauley" before "MacPherson." Unicode places all English uppercase letters before the lowercase letters, so the string "MacPherson" compares as less than "Macauley" in Java. To compare strings for strict alphabetical ordering, all of the characters must be in the same case. In the following examples, `toLowerCase` and `toUpperCase` are used to convert strings to a single case:

```
lowerCaseString = mystring.toLowerCase();
upperCaseString = mystring.toUpperCase();
```

We can use these methods directly in a comparison expression. For example, the following expressions convert `word1` and `word2` to the same case before comparing them. It doesn't matter whether the strings are both converted to uppercase or both converted to lowercase, as long as both are converted using the same method.

```
word1.toLowerCase().compareTo(word2.toLowerCase()) > 0

word1.toUpperCase().compareTo(word2.toUpperCase()) > 0
```

If two strings with different lengths are compared and the comparison is equal up to the end of the shorter string, then the shorter string compares as less than the longer string. For example, if `word2` contains `"Small"`, the expression

```
word2.compareTo("Smallness") < 0
```

yields `true`, because the strings are equal up to their fifth character position (the end of the string on the left), and the string on the right is longer.

If you are just interested in testing the equality of strings, ignoring their case, then `equalsIgnoreCase` method is a perfect choice. For example, the following expression returns `true`:

```
"MacPherson".equalsIgnoreCase("macpherson")
```

Logical Operators   Logical operators are used for compound relational expressions—those that have two or more relational operators. In mathematics, the logical (or Boolean) operators AND, OR, and NOT take logical expressions as operands. Java uses special symbols for the logical operators: `&&` (for AND), `||` (for OR), and `!` (for NOT). By combining relational operators with logical operators, we can make more complex assertions. For example, suppose we want to determine whether a student's final score is greater than 90 and his or her midterm score is greater than 70. In Java, we would write the expression this way:

```
finalScore > 90 && midtermScore > 70
```

The AND operation (**&&**) requires both relationships to be true for the overall result to be true. If either or both of the relationships are false, then the entire result is false.

The OR operation (**||**) takes two logical expressions and combines them. If either or both are true, the result is true. Both values must be false for the result to be false. Now we can determine whether the midterm grade is an A or the final grade is an A. If either the midterm grade or the final grade equals A, the assertion is true. In Java, we write the expression like this:

```
midtermGrade == 'A' || finalGrade == 'A'
```

The **&&** and **||** operators always appear between two expressions. The NOT operator (**!**) precedes a single logical expression and gives its opposite as the result. For example, if **(grade == 'A')** is false, then **!(grade == 'A')** is true. NOT gives us a convenient way of reversing the meaning of an assertion. For example,

```
!(hours > 40)
```

is the equivalent of

```
hours <= 40
```

In some contexts, the first form is clearer; in others, the second form makes more sense.

The following pairs of expressions are equivalent:

Expression	**Equivalent Expression**
!(a == b)	a != b
!(a == b || a == c)	a != b && a != c
!(a == b && c > d)	a != b || c <= d

Look closely at these expressions to be sure you understand why they are equivalent. Try evaluating them with some values for **a, b, c,** and **d**. Notice the pattern: The expression on the left is just the one to its right with **!** added and the relational and logical operators reversed (for example, == instead of != and || instead of &&). Remember this pattern. It allows you to rewrite expressions in the simplest form.[2]

You can apply logical operators to the results of comparisons. You can also apply them directly to variables of type **boolean**. For example, instead of writing

```
isElector = (age >= 18 && district == 23);
```

---

2. In Boolean algebra, the pattern is formalized by a theorem called DeMorgan's law.

to assign a value to the `boolean` variable `isElector`, we could use two intermediate `boolean` variables, `isVoter` and `isConstituent`:

```
isVoter = (age >= 18);
isConstituent = (district == 23);
isElector = isVoter && isConstituent;
```

The following tables summarize the results of applying `&&` and `||` to a pair of logical expressions (represented here by the `boolean` variables x and y).

Value of x	Value of y	Value of (x && y)
true	true	true
true	false	false
false	true	false
false	false	false

Value of x	Value of y	Value of (x || y)
true	true	true
true	false	true
false	true	true
false	false	false

The following table summarizes the results of applying the `!` operator to a logical expression (represented by the `boolean` variable x).

Value of x	Value of !x
true	false
false	true

Short-Circuit Evaluation   Consider the logical expression

```
i == 1 && j > 2
```

Some programming languages use full evaluation to parse such a logical expression. With full evaluation, the computer first evaluates both subexpressions (both `i == 1` and `j > 2`) before applying the `&&` operator to produce the final result.

In contrast, Java uses **short-circuit** (or **conditional**) **evaluation** of logical expressions. That is, evaluation proceeds from left to right, and the computer stops evaluating subexpressions as soon as possible—as soon as it knows the Boolean value of the entire expression. How can the computer know whether a lengthy logical expression will yield `true` or `false` if it doesn't examine all of the subexpressions? Let's look first at the AND operation.

An AND operation yields the value `true` only if both of its operands are `true`. In the preceding expression, suppose that the value of `i` is 95. The first subexpression yields `false`, so it

> **Short-circuit (conditional) evaluation** Evaluation of a logical expression in left-to-right order with evaluation stopping as soon as the final Boolean value can be determined

isn't necessary to even look at the second subexpression. The computer stops evaluation and produces the final result of `false`.

With the OR operation, the left-to-right evaluation stops as soon as a subexpression yielding `true` is found. Recall that an OR produces a result of `true` if either one or both of its operands are `true`. Given the expression

```
c <= d || e == f
```

if the first subexpression is `true`, then evaluation stops and the entire result is `true`. The computer doesn't waste time evaluating the second subexpression.

Does it really matter that Java uses conditional evaluation, other than that this approach saves a little time? Yes. Consider the following Boolean expression, which uses division to compute one operand of a relational operator:

```
X > 0 && 10/x > 0        // Another way of asserting x > 0 && X <= 10
```

This expression always gives a valid result when the operands of `&&` are written in this order. But what if we write it with the operands of `&&` reversed?

```
10/x > 0 && x > 0
```

Now, whenever `x` has the value 0, we get an error. Why? In the first version, when `x` is 0, the first operand of `&&` is `false`, so the `10/x` operation is skipped. In the second arrangement of the operands, the `10/x` term is always evaluated, so when `x` is 0, we are trying to divide by 0.

Java provides a second set of logical operators that result in full evaluation of Boolean expressions. The single `&` and `|` perform logical AND and OR operations, respectively, with full evaluation. We don't recommend their use at this stage in your experience with programming. In Java, these operators have another meaning with variables or constants of type `byte`, `short`, `int`, or `long`, which can lead to errors that may prove difficult to find.

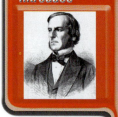

May We Introduce

George Boole

Boolean algebra is named for its inventor, English mathematician George Boole, who was born in 1815 (the same year as Ada Lovelace). Boole's father, a tradesman, began teaching him mathematics at an early age. But Boole initially was more interested in classical literature, languages, and religion—interests that he maintained throughout his life. By the time he was 20, he had taught himself French, German, and Italian. He was well versed in the writings of Aristotle, Spinoza, Cicero, and Dante, and wrote several philosophical papers himself.

At 16, to help support his family, Boole took a position as a teaching assistant in a private school. His work there and a second teaching job left him little time to study. A few years later, he opened his own school and began to study higher mathematics independently. Despite his lack of formal training, his first scholarly paper was published in the *Cambridge Mathematical Journal* when he was just 24. Boole went on to publish more than 50 papers and several major works before he died in 1864, at the peak of his career.

Boole's *The Mathematical Analysis of Logic* was published in 1847. It would eventually form the basis for the development of digital computers. In his book, Boole set forth the formal axioms of logic (much like the axioms of geometry) on which the field of symbolic logic is built.

Boole drew on the symbols and operations of algebra in creating his system of logic. He associated the value 1 with the universal set (the set representing everything in the universe) and the value 0 with the empty set, restricting his system to just these two values. He then defined operations that are analogous to subtraction, addition, and multiplication. Variables in the system have symbolic values. For example, if a Boolean variable P represents the set of all plants, then the expression $1 - P$ refers to the set of all things that are not plants. We can simplify the expression by using $-P$ to mean "not plants." ($0 - P$ is simply 0 because we can't remove elements from the empty set.) The subtraction operator in Boole's system corresponds to the `!` (NOT) operator in Java. In Java code, we might set the value of the Boolean variable `plant` to `true` when the name of a plant is entered, so that `!plant` is `true` when the name of anything else is input.

The expression $0 + P$ is the same as P. However, $0 + P + F$, where F is the set of all foods, is the set of all things that are either plants or foods. So the addition operator in Boole's algebra is the same as the Java `||` (OR) operator.

The analogy can be carried to multiplication as well: $0 \times P$ is 0, and $1 \times P$ is P. But what is $P \times F$? It is the set of things that are both plants and foods. In Boole's system, the multiplication operator is the same as the Java `&&` (AND) operator.

In 1854, Boole published *An Investigation of the Laws of Thought, on Which Are Founded the Mathematical Theories of Logic and Probabilities*. In the book, he described theorems built on his axioms of logic and extended the algebra to show how probabilities could be computed in a logical system. Five years later, Boole published *Treatise on Differential Equations*, then *Treatise on the Calculus of Finite Differences*. The latter is one of the cornerstones of numerical analysis, which deals with the accuracy of computations.

During his lifetime, Boole received recognition and honors for his work on differential equations. But the importance of Boolean algebra for computer and communication technology was not recognized until the early twentieth century. George Boole was truly one of the founders of computer science.

May We Introduce

■ Precedence of Operators

In Chapter 4, we discussed the rules of precedence, which govern the evaluation of complex arithmetic expressions. Java's rules of precedence also apply to relational and logical operators. The following list shows the order of precedence for the arithmetic, relational, and logical operators (with the assignment operator thrown in as well):

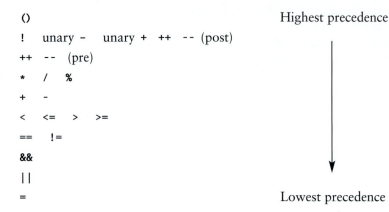

```
()                                              Highest precedence
!   unary -   unary +   ++   -- (post)
++  --  (pre)
*   /   %
+   -
<   <=   >   >=
==   !=
&&
||
=                                               Lowest precedence
```

Operators on the same line in the list have the same precedence. If an expression contains several operators with the same precedence, most of the operators group (or associate) from left to right. For example, the expression

`a / b * c`

means `(a / b) * c`, not `a / (b * c)`. However, the ! operator groups from right to left. Although you'd never have occasion to use the expression

`!!badData`

it means `!(!badData)` rather than the meaningless `(!!)badData`. Appendix B gives the order of precedence for all operators in Java.

You can use parentheses to override the order of evaluation in Boolean expressions. If you're not sure whether parentheses are necessary, use them anyway. The compiler disregards unnecessary parentheses. So, if they clarify an expression, use them.

One final comment about parentheses: Java, like other programming languages, requires that you always use parentheses in pairs. Whenever you write a complicated expression, take a minute to go through and pair up all of the opening parentheses with their closing counterparts.

PEANUTS: © United Feature Syndicate, Inc.

Changing English Statements into Logical Expressions

Many logical expressions cannot be written directly from a mathematical expression or English statement. The expression or statement must be changed so that each operator has the correct number of operands. Recall our example logical expression:

```
midtermGrade == 'A' || finalGrade == 'A'
```

In English, you would be tempted to write this expression: "Midterm grade or final grade equals A." In Java, you can't write the expression as you would in English. That is,

```
midtermGrade || finalGrade == 'A'        // Incorrect
```

won't work because the || operator connects a `char` value (`midtermGrade`) and a logical expression (`finalGrade == 'A'`). Both operands of || must be logical expressions. This example will generate a syntax error.

A variation of this mistake is to express the English assertion "*i* equals either 3 or 4" as

```
i == 3 || 4      // Incorrect
```

This syntax is incorrect. In the second subexpression, 4 is an `int` rather than a `boolean` value. The || operator (and the && operator) can only connect two `boolean` expressions. Here's what we really want:

```
i == 3 || i == 4
```

In math books, you might see notation like this:

$$12 < y < 24$$

It means "*y* is between 12 and 24." If we were to write this expression directly in Java it would be illegal. First, the relation 12 < y is evaluated, giving a `boolean` result. Next, the computer tries to compare it with the literal 24. Because a `boolean` value cannot be converted to any type other than `String`, the expression is invalid. To write this expression correctly in Java, you must use the && operator:

```
12 < y && y < 24
```

■ Relational Operators with Floating-Point Types

So far, we've talked about comparing `int`, `char`, and `String` values. Here we look at `float` and `double` values.

We should never compare floating-point numbers for equality. Because small errors in the rightmost decimal places are likely to arise when calculations are performed on floating-point numbers, two `float` or `double` values rarely are exactly equal. For example, consider the following code, which uses two `double` variables named `oneThird` and `x`:

```
oneThird = 1.0 / 3.0;
x = oneThird + oneThird + oneThird;
```

We would expect `x` to contain the value 1.0, but it probably doesn't. The first assignment statement stores an approximation of 1/3 into `oneThird`, perhaps 0.333333. The second statement stores a value like 0.999999 into `x`. If we now ask the computer to compare `x` with 1.0, the comparison will yield `false`.

Instead of testing for equality, we test for near equality. To do so, we compute the difference between the numbers and see whether the result is less than some maximum allowable difference. For example, we often use comparisons such as the following:

```
Math.abs(r - s) < 0.00001
```

where `Math.abs` is the absolute value method from the Java library. The expression `Math.abs (r - s)` computes the absolute value of the difference between two variables `r` and `s`. In this case, if the difference is less than 0.00001, the two numbers are close enough to call them equal.

5.2 : Branching with the *if* Statement

The order in which statements execute is called the **flow of control**. In a sense, the computer is under the control of one statement at a time. After a statement executes, control turns over to the next statement (like a baton being passed in a relay race).

The flow of control is normally sequential (see Figure 5.1). That is, when one statement is finished executing, control passes to the next statement.

> **Flow of control** The order in which the computer executes statements
>
> **Control structure** A statement used to alter the normally sequential flow of control

■ Controlling the Flow of Execution

Where we want the flow of control to be nonsequential, we use **control structures**—special statements that transfer control to a statement other than the one that physically comes next. As we saw earlier, method calls are control structures that alter the flow of control so that a separate sequence of statements can be executed.

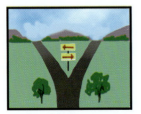

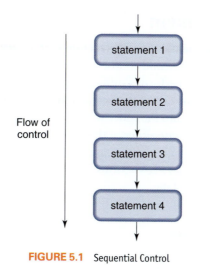

FIGURE 5.1 Sequential Control

We use a selection (or branching) control structure when we want the computer to choose between alternative actions. Given an assertion, if it is true, the computer executes one statement. If it is false, it executes another (see Figure 5.2). The computer's ability to solve practical problems is a product of its ability to make decisions and execute different sequences of instructions.

If an input value represents rainfall in inches, for example, a negative value is clearly incorrect. The computer can respond to erroneous input by testing the assertion that the number is less than zero. If it is true, the computer displays an error message. If the assertion is false, the computer adds the amount to the total rainfall. Now let's look at how to change the flow of control so that one sequence of statements or another is executed.

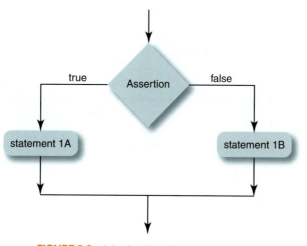

FIGURE 5.2 Selection (Branching) Control Structure

■ The *if-else* Statement

The *if* statement is the fundamental control structure that allows branches in the flow of control. With it, we can ask a question and choose a course of action: If a certain condition exists, perform one action; otherwise, perform a different action.

The computer performs just one of the two actions under any given set of circumstances. Yet we must write both actions into the code. Why? Because, depending on the circumstances, the computer can choose to execute either of them. The *if* statement gives us a way of including both actions in our code and gives the computer a way of selecting which action to take.

In Java, the *if* statement comes in two forms: the *if-else* form and the *if* form. Let's look first at *if-else*. Here is its syntax template:

If-Statement (the *if-else* form)

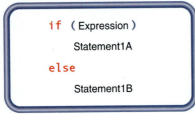

The expression in parentheses must produce a `boolean` result. At run time, the computer evaluates the expression. If the value is `true`, the computer executes Statement1A. If the value of the expression is `false`, it executes Statement1B. Statement1A is often called the *then* clause; Statement1B is the *else* clause. Figure 5.3 illustrates the flow of control of the *if-else* statement. In the figure, Statement2 is the next statement in the code after the entire *if* statement.

Notice that a Java *if* statement uses the reserved words `if` and `else` but the *then* clause does not include the word "then." The following demonstration application shows how to write an

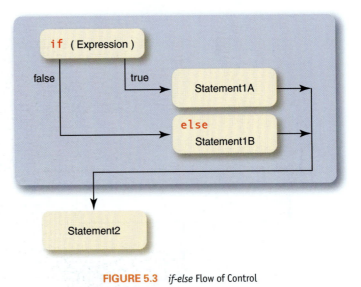

FIGURE 5.3   *if-else* Flow of Control

if statement. Observe the indentation of the *then* clause and the *else* clause, which makes the statement easier to read. Also notice the placement of the statement following the *if* statement.

```
//*******************************************************************
// Application IfDemo
// This application reads hours worked and computes pay
//*******************************************************************
import java.util.Scanner;
public class IfDemo
{
  public static void main(String[] args)
  {
    final double rate = 8.55;
    double pay;
    Scanner in = new Scanner(System.in);
    System.out.print("Enter hours worked: ");
    double hours = in.nextDouble();
    if (hours <= 40.0)
      pay = rate * hours;                       // Regular pay
    else
      pay = rate * (40.0 + (hours - 40.0) * 1.5);   // Regular + overtime pay
    System.out.println("Pay is " + pay);
  }
}
```

In terms of instructions to the computer, this *if* statement says, "If **hours** is less than or equal to 40.0, compute the regular pay and then go on to execute the output statement. But if **hours** is greater than 40, compute the regular pay and the overtime pay, and then go on to execute the output statement." Figure 5.4 shows the flow of control of this *if* statement.

If-else statements are often used to check the validity of input. For example, before we ask the computer to divide by a data value, we should be sure that the value is not zero. (If you try to divide something by zero with int values, the computer will halt the execution of your

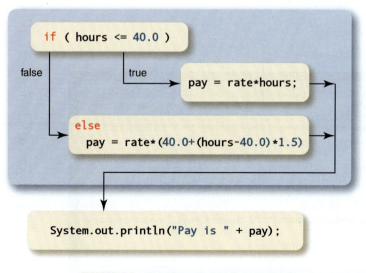

FIGURE 5.4 Flow of Control for Calculating Pay

application. With floating-point types, you get the special infinity value.) If the divisor is zero, our code should display an error message.

```java
if (divisor != 0)
  result = dividend / divisor;
else
  System.out.println("Division by zero is not allowed.");
```

Here's an example program that reads in two numbers, tests the second to be sure it is not zero, and divides the first number by the second.

```java
//***********************************************************************
// Application Divide
// This application reads two integers and divides the first by the
// second if the second is non-zero.
//***********************************************************************

import java.util.Scanner;
public class Divide
{
  public static void main(String[] args)
  {
    int first;
    int second;
    Scanner in = new Scanner(System.in);
    System.out.println
      ("Enter two integer numbers; the second must be non-zero.");
    first = in.nextInt();
    second = in.nextInt();
    if (second != 0)
      System.out.println(first + " divided by " + second + " is " +
                          first/second);
    else
      System.out.println("Second number must be non-zero.");
  }
}
```

Output from three runs:

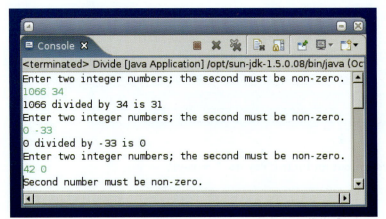

Before we examine *if* statements further, take another look at the syntax template for *if-else*. According to the template, no semicolon appears at the end of an *if* statement. Yet, in all of our examples, a semicolon seems to appear at the end of each *if* statement. In reality, the semicolons belong to the statements in the *then* clause and the *else* clause in those examples; assignment statements end in semicolons, as do method calls. The *if* statement doesn't have its own semicolon at the end.

■ Blocks (Compound Statements)

In our division-by-zero example, suppose that when the divisor is equal to zero, we want to do two things: write the error message and set the variable named `result` equal to a special value such as `Integer.MAX_VALUE`. We would need two statements in the same branch to do so, but the syntax template seems to limit us to one.

What we really want to do is turn the *else* clause into a sequence of statements. This is easy. Recall from Chapter 2 that the compiler treats the block (compound statement)

```
{
   .
   .
   .
}
```

as a single statement. If you put a { } pair around the sequence of statements you want in a branch of the *if* statement, the sequence of statements becomes a single block. For example:

```
if (divisor != 0)
   result = dividend / divisor;
else
{
   System.out.println("Division by zero is not allowed.");
   result = Integer.MAX_VALUE;
}
```

If the value of `divisor` is zero, the computer both displays the error message and sets the value of `result` to `Integer.MAX_VALUE`, before continuing with whatever statement follows the *if* statement.

Blocks can be used in both branches of an *if-else* statement. For example:

```
if (divisor != 0)
{
   result = dividend / divisor;
   System.out.println("Division performed.");
}
else
{
   System.out.println("Division by zero is not allowed.");
   result = Integer.MAX_VALUE;
}
```

When you use blocks in an *if* statement, you must remember a rule of Java syntax: Never use a semicolon after the right brace of a block. Semicolons are used only to terminate simple statements such as assignment statements and method calls.

Matters of Style

Braces and Blocks

Java programmers use different styles when it comes to locating the left brace of a block. The style used in this book puts the left and right braces directly below the words `if` and `else`, with each brace on its own line:

```java
if (n >= 2)
{
    alpha = 5;
    beta = 8;
}
else
{
    alpha = 23;
    beta = 12;
}
```

Another popular style is to place the statements following `if` and `else` on the same line as the left brace; the right braces still line up directly below the left braces.

```java
if (n >= 2)
{ alpha = 5;
  beta = 8;
}
else
{ alpha = 23;
  beta = 12;
}
```

It makes no difference to the Java compiler which style you use (and other styles exist as well, such as placing the left braces at the ends of the lines containing `if` and `else`). It's a matter of personal preference. Whichever style you use, though, you should maintain it throughout the entire application. Inconsistency can confuse a person reading your code and give the impression of carelessness on the programmer's part.

■ The *if* Statement

Sometimes you may run into a situation where you want to say, "If a certain condition exists, perform some action; otherwise, don't do anything." In other words, you want the computer to skip a sequence of instructions if a certain condition isn't met. You could do so by leaving the `else` branch empty, using only the *null* statement:

```java
if (a <= b)
    c = 20;
else
    ;
```

Better yet, you could simply leave off the `else` part. The resulting statement is the *if* form of the *if* statement. Here is its syntax template:

If-Statement (the *if* form)

```
if ( Expression )
    Statement
```

   Here's an example of an *if* form. Notice the indentation and the placement of the statement that follows the *if*.

```
if (age < 18)
  System.out.print("Not an eligible ");  // Skipped if age >= 18
System.out.println("voter.");
```

This statement means that if age is less than 18, first print `"Not an eligible "` and then print `"voter."` If age is not less than 18, skip the first statement and go directly to printing `"voter."` Figure 5.5 shows the flow of control for an *if* form.

   Like the two branches in an *if-else* statement, the one branch in an *if* statement can be a block. For example, suppose you are writing an application to compute income taxes. One of the lines on the tax form says, "Subtract line 23 from line 17 and enter the result on line 24; if the result is less than zero, enter zero and check box 24A." You can use an *if* to perform this task in Java:

```
result = line17 - line23;
if (result < 0.0)
{
  System.out.println("Check box 24A");
  result = 0.0;
}
line24 = result;
```

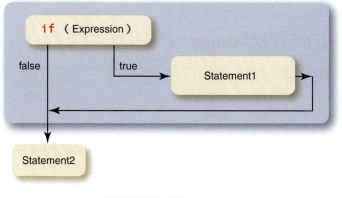

FIGURE 5.5 *if* Flow of Control

This code does exactly what the tax form says it should: First it computes the result of subtracting line 23 from line 17. Then it checks whether **result** is less than zero. If it is, the *then* branch displays a message telling the user to check box 24A and sets **result** to zero. Finally, the calculated result (or zero, if **result** is less than zero) is stored into a variable named line24.

What happens if we leave out the left and right braces from the code fragment? Let's look at it:

```
result = line17 - line23;                 // Incorrect version
if (result < 0.0)
  System.out.println("Check box 24A");
  result = 0.0;
line24 = result;
```

Despite the way we have indented the code, the compiler assumes that the first clause is a single statement—the output statement. If **result** is less than zero, the computer executes the output statement, sets **result** to zero, and then stores result into **line24**. So far, so good. But if **result** is initially greater than or equal to zero, the computer skips the output statement and proceeds to the statement following the *if* statement—the assignment statement that sets **result** to zero. The unhappy outcome is that **result** ends up as zero no matter what its initial value was!

The moral here is not to rely on indentation alone; you can't fool the compiler. If you want a compound statement for either clause, you must include the left and right braces.

To this point, our examples have used the relational operators. In reality, an *if* statement can use any expression that gives a **boolean** result, such as a **boolean** value-returning method. For example, we can use the **boolean** method **equals**, together with the *if* statement to take one action if two strings are equal and another if they are not.

```
if (stringOne.equals(stringTwo))
  System.out.println(stringOne + " and " + stringTwo + " are equal.");
else
  System.out.println(stringOne + " and " + stringTwo + " are not equal.");
```

5.3 : Nested *if* Statements

Java does not place any restrictions on what the statements in an *if* can be. Therefore, an *if* within an *if* is okay. In fact, an *if* within an *if* within an *if* is legal. The only limitation here is that people cannot readily follow a structure that is overly complicated. Of course, readability is one of the hallmarks of a good program.

When we place an *if* within an *if*, we are creating a *nested control structure*. Control structures nest much like mixing bowls do, with smaller ones tucked inside larger ones. Here's an example, written in English, but in the form of nested Java *if* statements:

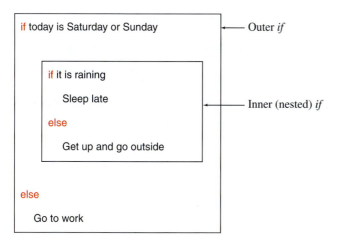

In general, any problem that involves a multiway branch (more than two alternative courses of action) can be coded using nested *if* statements. For example, to store the name of a month into a string variable, given its number, we could use a sequence of *if* statements (unnested):

```
if (month == 1)
  monthName = "January";
if (month == 2)
  monthName = "February";
if (month == 3)
  monthName = "March";
    .
    .
    .
if (month == 12)
  monthName = "December";
```

The equivalent nested *if* structure,

```
if (month == 1)
  monthName = "January";
else
  if (month == 2)                        // Nested if
    monthName = "February";
  else
    if (month == 3)                      // Nested if
      monthName = "March";
      .
      .
          else
            monthName = "December";
```

is actually more efficient because it makes fewer comparisons. The first version—the sequence of independent *if* statements—always tests every condition (all 12 of them), even if the first one is satisfied. In contrast, the nested *if* solution skips all of the remaining comparisons after one alternative has been selected.

Despite the speed of modern computers, many applications require so much computation that an inefficient algorithm can waste hours of computer time. Always be on the lookout for ways to make your code more efficient, as long as doing so doesn't make it difficult for other programmers to understand. It's usually better to sacrifice a little efficiency for the sake of readability.

In the last example, notice how the indentation of the *then* and *else* clauses causes the statements to move continually to the right. Alternatively, we can use a special indentation style with deeply nested *if-else* statements to indicate that we are just choosing one of a set of alternatives. This multiway branch is known as an *if-else-if* control structure:

```
if (month == 1)
  monthName = "January";
else if (month == 2)              // Nested if
  monthName = "February";
else if (month == 3)              // Nested if
  monthName = "March";
    .
    .
    .
else
  monthName = "December";
```

This style prevents the indentation from marching continuously to the right. Even more importantly, it visually conveys the idea that we are using a 12-way branch based on the variable `month`.

Note an important difference between the sequence of *if* statements and the nested *if* structure: More than one alternative can be taken by the sequence of *if* statements, but the nested *if* can select only one choice. To appreciate this difference, consider the analogy of filling out a questionnaire. Some questions are like a sequence of *if* statements, asking you to check all the items in a list that apply to you (such as all of your hobbies). Other questions ask you to select only one item in a list (your age group, for example) and, therefore, are like a nested *if* structure. Both kinds of questions occur in programming problems. Being able to recognize which type of question is being asked permits you to immediately select the appropriate control structure.

■ An Application of Nested *if* Statements: compareTo

Let's see how we can use a nested *if* to write a method that many classes provide: `compareTo`. We've already seen one example of `compareTo`, as provided by the `String` class. For many of our classes, we will automatically include `compareTo` in the design. Here, we see how to implement `compareTo` for two of our existing classes, `Time` and `Name`.

Maintaining the same naming convention as in the `String compareTo` operation, if we have a pair of `Time` objects, `time1` and `time2`, where `time1` = 20.0 seconds and `time2` = 30.0 seconds, then our `Time compareTo` should behave as follows:

`time2.compareTo(time1)` gives a positive integer result (time2 > time1)

`time1.compareTo(time2)` gives a negative integer result (time1 < time2)

`time1.compareTo(time1)` gives zero as the result (time1 = time1)

Recall that the value for a `Time` object is stored in a `double` variable called `seconds`. Thus we simply need to compare the value in the variable with the `seconds` from the object passed as a parameter. If it is greater, we return 1; if it is less, we return −1; and if the two values are equal, we return 0.

Is that it? Not quite! Remember that we cannot compare floating-point values exactly. For example, we would probably like the time 143.000000000 to compare as equal with 143.000000003. Let's compare time to a precision of hundredths of a second. To make this an exact comparison, we multiply the value in `seconds` by 100 and then convert it to an integer. Let's round up, too, because we would also like 142.999999997 to compare as equal to 143.000000000.

We can write the method as follows:

```
public int compareTo(Time other)
{
  int roundSeconds =
      (int)(seconds * 100.0 + 0.5);         // Round up seconds * 100
  int roundOther =
      (int)(other.getTime() * 100.0 + 0.5); // Round up other * 100
  if (roundSeconds > roundOther)            // If this object > other,
    return 1;                               //   then positive result
  else if (roundSeconds < roundOther)       // If this object < other,
    return -1;                              //   then negative result
  else                                      // If this object = other,
    return 0;                               //   then zero result
}
```

Now let's implement `compareTo` for the `Name` class. If we had only the last names, the comparison would be easy. We would just convert both last names to all lowercase and return the result of comparing them with the `compareTo` operation in class `String`:

```
return last.toLowerCase().compareTo(otherLast.toLowerCase());
```

Unfortunately, if the last names are equal, we have to compare the first names. And if the first names are also equal, we must compare the middle names. Only when all of the names are equal do we return zero, indicating that they are equal. Obviously, this is another case for using a nested *if*. Here is the algorithm:

> Apply `String` compareTo to the lowercase last names and assign the result to compare
> if compare isn't 0 (the last names are unequal)
>   return compare
> else
>   Apply `String` compareTo to the lowercase first names and assign the result to compare
>   if compare isn't 0 (the first names are unequal)
>   return compare
>   else
>   return result of applying `String` compareTo to the lowercase middle names

Following is the code that implements the new method for class **Name**. Note that we use an **int** variable called **compare** to hold the result of each comparison both for testing by the *if* statement and to use as a return value.

```
public int compareTo(Name other)
{
  int compare =
       last.toLowerCase().compareTo(other.getLastName().toLowerCase());
  if (compare != 0)
    return compare;
  else
  {
    compare =
      first.toLowerCase().compareTo(other.getFirstName().toLowerCase());
    if (compare != 0)
      return compare;
    else
      return
        middle.toLowerCase().compareTo(other.getMiddleName().toLowerCase());
  }
}
```

■ Comparing Ranges of Values

Another particularly helpful use of the nested *if* becomes apparent when you want to select from a series of consecutive ranges of values. For example, suppose that we want to display a message indicating an appropriate activity for the outdoor temperature, given the following table:

Activity	Temperature
Swimming	Temperature > 85
Tennis	70 < Temperature <= 85
Golf	32 < Temperature <= 70
Skiing	0 < Temperature <= 32
Dancing	Temperature <= 0

At first glance, you might be tempted to write a separate *if* statement for each range of temperatures. On closer examination, however, it becomes clear that these conditions are interdependent. That is, if one of the statements executes, none of the others should execute. We are really selecting just one alternative from a set of possibilities—just the situation for using a nested *if* structure.

With consecutive ranges, we take advantage of that relationship to make our code more efficient, by arranging the branches in range order. Then, if a particular branch is reached, we know that the preceding ranges have been eliminated from consideration. As a consequence, the *if* expressions must compare the temperature to only the lowest value of each range.

```java
message = "The recommended activity is ";
if (temperature > 85)
  message = message + "swimming.";
else if (temperature > 70)
  message = message + "tennis.";
else if (temperature > 32)
  message = message + "golf.";
else if (temperature > 0)
  message = message + "skiing.";
else
  message = message + "dancing.";
System.out.println(message);
```

To see how this *if-else-if* structure works, consider the branch that tests for `temperature` greater than 70. If it has been reached, we know that `temperature` must be less than or equal to 85 because that condition causes this particular *else* branch to be taken. Thus we need to test only whether `temperature` is above the bottom of this range (> 70). If that test fails, then we enter the next *else* clause, knowing that `temperature` must be less than or equal to 70. Each successive branch checks the bottom of its range until we reach the final *else*, which takes care of all the remaining possibilities.

If the ranges aren't consecutive, of course, we must test the data value against both the highest and lowest values of each range. We still use an *if-else-if* because it is the best structure for selecting a single branch from multiple possibilities, and we may arrange the ranges in consecutive order to make them easier for a human reader to follow. Nevertheless, we cannot reduce the number of comparisons when there are gaps between the ranges.

Application `Temperature` prompts for and reads a temperature and prints out the appropriate sport.

```java
//**********************************************************
// Application Temperature reads a temperature and prints an
// appropriate sport
//**********************************************************
import java.util.Scanner
public class Temperature
{
  public static void main(String args[])
  {
    Scanner in = new Scanner(System.in);
    int temperature;                // Holds input temperature
    String message;                 // Output string
    System.out.println("Enter an integer Fahrenheit temperature.");
    temperature = in.nextInt();
    // Determine activity
    message = "The recommended activity for " + temperature + " is ";
    if (temperature > 85)
      message = message + "swimming.";
```

```
    else if (temperature > 70)
      message = message + "tennis.";
    else if (temperature > 32)
      message = message + "golf.";
    else if (temperature > 0)
      message = message + "skiing.";
    else
      message = message + "dancing.";
    System.out.println(message);
  }
}
```

Here is the output from four different runs:

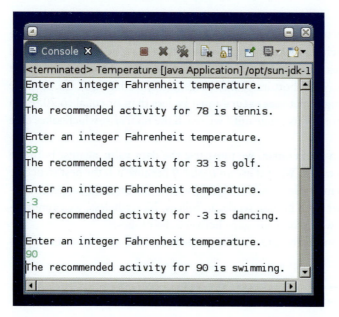

■ The Dangling *else*

When *if* statements are nested, you may find yourself confused about the *if-else* pairings. That is, to which *if* does an *else* belong? For example, suppose that if a student's average is less than 60, we want to display "Failing"; if it is at least 60 but less than 70, we want to display "Passing but marginal"; and if it is 70 or greater, we don't want to display anything.

We code this information with an *if-else* nested within an *if*:

```
if (average < 70.0)
  if (average < 60.0)
    System.out.println("Failing");
  else
    System.out.println("Passing but marginal");
```

But how do we know to which *if* the *else* belongs? Here is the rule that the Java compiler follows: In the absence of braces, an *else* is always paired with the closest preceding *if* that doesn't already have an *else* paired with it. We indented the code to reflect this pairing.

Suppose we write the fragment with the nesting reversed, like this:

```
if (average >= 60.0)                                    // Incorrect version
  if (average < 70.0)
    System.out.println("Passing but marginal");
else
  System.out.println("Failing");
```

Here we want the *else* branch attached to the outer *if* statement, not the inner one, so we indent the code as shown. Indentation does not affect the execution of the code, of course. Even though the *else* aligns with the first *if*, the compiler pairs it with the second *if*. An *else* that follows a nested *if* is called a *dangling else*. It doesn't logically belong with the nested *if* but is attached to it by the compiler.

To attach the *else* to the first *if* (not the second), you can turn the outer *then* clause into a block:

```
if (average >= 60.0)                                    // Correct version
{
  if (average < 70.0)
    System.out.println("Passing but marginal");
}
else
  System.out.println("Failing");
```

The **{ }** pair indicates that the first *if* statement has a compound first clause that contains an *if* statement (with no *else* clause), so the *else* must belong to the outer *if*.

5.4 ┊ Scanner Class Boolean Methods

In Chapter 4, we said that the `Scanner` methods that read numeric data throw an `InputMismatchException` if the next value isn't what the method expects. Now that we know about Boolean methods, we can avoid that problem. Here are three useful Boolean methods that allow us to check to be sure that the next value is what we expect.

Method	Returns
`boolean hasNextLine()`	`true` if the scanner has another line in its input; `false` otherwise
`boolean hasNextInt()`	`true` if the next token in the scanner can be interpreted as an `int` value; `false` otherwise
`boolean hasNextDouble()`	`true` if the next token in the scanner can be interpreted as a `double` value; `false` otherwise

Here's a short demonstration application that reads and prints an integer value only if one is provided for input. If the user types something other than an integer, an error message is printed.

```java
import java.util.Scanner;
public class GuardedInputDemo
{
  public static void main (String[] args)
  {
    int value;
    Scanner in = new Scanner(System.in);
    System.out.print("Enter an integer: "); // Prompt for input
    if (in.hasNextInt())                     // Check if there is an integer to read
    {
      value = in.nextInt();                  // If so, read the value
      System.out.println(value);             // and then print it
    }
    else                                     // Otherwise, print an error message
      System.out.println("Non-integer value entered.");
  }
}
```

By guarding the input with an *if* statement, we avoid the problem of having the application throw an **InputMismatchException**. Methods equivalent to these are available for each of the Java built-in types (for example, **hasNextFloat**, **hasNextLong**, and **hasNextBoolean**). There is also a **hasNext** method that tests whether a token of any type is available to be input. We will see the value of this method when we look at file input.

SOFTWARE MAINTENANCE CASE STUDY

Incorrect Output

Maintenance Task When you were buying your motorcycle, you wrote a program to determine the monthly payments given the cost, the interest rate, and the number of years. You gave it to a friend to use when she was buying a car. According to your friend, the program gives very strange results. You ask for an example of the erroneous output. She reports that the program gave a ridiculously high rate for a loan of $3000 for 2 years at an interest rate of 6.8%.

Verifying the Behavior Whenever a user reports a bug, you should begin by making sure that you can generate the reported behavior yourself. This step sets up the necessary conditions for isolating the problem and testing your modifications. You run the program using the data your friend supplied and the answers seem reasonable.

```
Input loan amount: 3000
Input yearly interest rate: .068
Input number of years: 2

Your monthly payment is 134.04589708614688
```

Because you can't get the program to exhibit the bug, you go back to your friend to ask more questions. (Remember, that's one of our problem-solving strategies—they apply just as much to debugging as to writing new applications.) "What sort of ridiculously high rate did you get?" you ask her. Your friend says that she got 1700.0355647311262 as the payment amount. Clearly, $1700.03 per month for 2 years is not correct. What could have gone wrong?

Just as a mechanic may have to go for a drive with a car's owner to understand what's wrong, sometimes you have to sit and watch a user run your application. You ask your friend to show you what happened. Here's what she did:

```
Input loan amount: 3000
Input yearly interest rate: 6.8
Input number of years: 2

Your monthly payment is 1700.0355647311262
```

Aha! You wrote the code to read the percentage as a decimal fraction, and your friend is entering it as a percentage! There's an easy solution to this problem. You can tell her to enter the value as a decimal fraction, and you won't have to change the code at all. Such a "fix" is known as a *workaround*.

Your friend can do this, but says, "It's annoying to have to do the math in my head. Why can't you fix the program so that it takes the percentage the way that people normally write it?" She has a good point. As a programmer, you wrote the code in a way that made it easier for you. But a good application should be designed to make it easier for the user, which is what we mean by *user friendly*. If other people will be using your application, you must think in those terms.

Clearly, you have to change the program to first divide the input percentage by 100. But then you remember that you've given the same program to another friend who is a math major and who prefers to enter percentages as decimal fractions. The program could ask the user for his or her preference, but again, that's more work for the user. What should you do? How can you accommodate both kinds of users with the least amount of hassle?

Obviously, the application needs a branch somewhere that chooses between dividing the percentage by 100 or using the value as entered. Interest rates on loans are generally no more than about 25% and no less than one quarter of 1%. So we could simply say that any number greater than or equal to 0.25 is assumed to be a percentage, and any number less than that is a decimal fraction. The necessary *if* statement would be written as follows:

```
if (yearlyInterest >= 0.25)                    // Assume percent entered
  yearlyInterest = yearlyInterest / 100.0;
```

Is that the only change? That's all that's required to make the program do the proper calculations. But we should include our assumption in the instructions, and just to be sure that the user understands the basis for the calculation, let's also print out the data.

Modified Code You call up the file with your source code so that you can modify it. You also re-familiarize yourself with the compound interest formula:

$$\frac{\text{Amount} \times (1 + \text{Monthly Interest})^{\text{number of payments}} \times \text{Monthly Interest}}{(1 + \text{Monthly Interest})^{\text{number of payments}} - 1}$$

248

You then insert the *if* statement and make the necessary changes to the prompt and the output. The changes are highlighted in the following code.

```java
//***********************************************************************
// Loan Payment Calculator application
//
// This application determines the monthly payments on a loan given
// the loan amount, the yearly interest rate, and the number of years
//***********************************************************************

import java.util.Scanner;
public class LoanCalc
{
  public static void main(String[] args)
  {
    // Declarations
    double loanAmount;          // Loan amount
    double yearlyInterest;      // Yearly interest rate
    int numberOfYears;          // Number of years
    double monthlyInterest;     // Monthly interest rate
    int numberOfPayments;       // Number of payments
    double payment;             // Monthly payment

    Scanner in = new Scanner(System.in);

    // Prompt for and read input values
    System.out.print("Input loan amount: ");
    loanAmount = in.nextDouble();
    System.out.println
      ("Input yearly interest rate (an amount less than 0.25 is");
    System.out.print
      ("assumed to be a decimal fraction rather than a percent): ");
    yearlyInterest = in.nextDouble();
    if (yearlyInterest >= 0.25)              // Assume percent entered
      yearlyInterest = yearlyInterest / 100.0;
    System.out.print("Input number of years: ");
    numberOfYears = in.nextInt();

    // Calculate values
    monthlyInterest = yearlyInterest / 12;
    numberOfPayments = numberOfYears * 12;
    payment = (loanAmount *
              Math.pow(monthlyInterest + 1, numberOfPayments)
              * monthlyInterest)/(Math.pow(monthlyInterest + 1,
              numberOfPayments) - 1 );

    // Output results
    System.out.println();
    System.out.println("For an initial amount of $" + loanAmount);
    System.out.println("An annual percentage rate of " +
                       yearlyInterest * 100.0 + "%");
    System.out.println("And " + numberOfPayments + " payments:");
    System.out.println("Your monthly payment is " + payment);
  }
}
```

Here is a test run of the application, with data entered as a percentage:

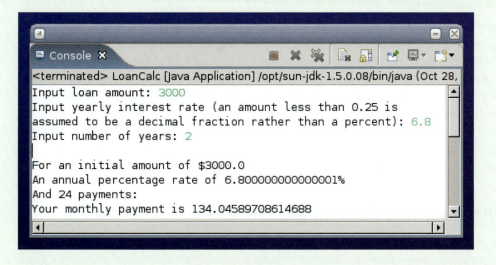

Here is another test run, this time with data entered as a decimal fraction:

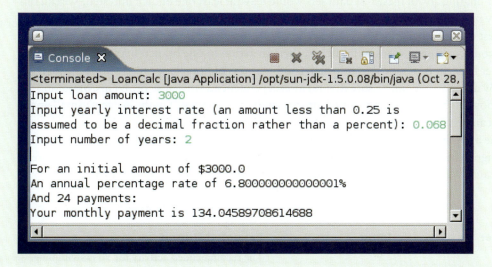

The application now works for either style of input and is much more user friendly.

5.5 : Testing with Branches

In Chapter 1, we discussed the problem-solving and implementation phases of computer programming. Testing is an integral part of both phases. Testing in the problem-solving phase occurs after the solution is developed but before it is implemented. In the implementation phase, we test the code. Compilation automatically checks the syntax of our code, but after the code has compiled successfully we must test its operation. In Chapter 4, we saw an example of a test plan for this last stage of testing.

Until now, our testing has been very straightforward because our programs have been just sequences of instructions. With the inclusion of branching, testing is no longer so simple, and we must apply it more consciously at each phase of development.

■ Choosing Test Data for Branches

To test an application or method with branches, we need to execute each branch at least once. For example, our `Temperature` application includes a nested *if* statement that selects among five possible activities. We therefore need at least five data sets to test the different branches. Table 5.2 shows sample values for the variable that causes all of the branches to be executed.

Eliminating any of these test data sets would leave at least one branch untested. We call this strategy *minimum complete coverage* of the application's branching structure. You should always test every branch.

If code contains a series of branches, then an action in one branch may affect processing in a later branch. It is critical to test such combinations of branches, called *paths*, through the code. By doing so, we can be sure that no interdependencies will cause problems. Shouldn't we try all possible paths? Yes, in theory. Unfortunately, the number of paths in even a small application can be very large.

The approach to testing that we've used here is called *code coverage* because the test data are designed by looking at the code. Code coverage is also called white-box (or clear-box) testing because we are allowed to see the application code while designing the tests.

Number	Input	Expected Output
1	90	The recommended activity for 90 is swimming.
2	75	The recommended activity for 75 is tennis.
3	40	The recommended activity for 40 is golf.
4	20	The recommended activity for 20 is skiing.
5	−10	The recommended activity for −10 is dancing.

TABLE 5.2 Data Sets to Test the `Temperature` Application

An alternative approach to testing, called *data coverage*, attempts to test without seeing the code; hence it is also called black-box testing. Complete data coverage is as impractical as complete code coverage for many applications. For example, the `Temperature` application takes an `int` value and thus has about 4 billion possible input values!

Often, testing combines these two strategies. Instead of trying every possible data value (data coverage), we examine the code (code coverage) and look for ranges of values for which processing is identical. Then we test the values at the boundaries and, sometimes, a value in the middle of each range. For example, a condition such as

```
alpha >= 0 && alpha <= 100
```

divides the integers into three ranges:

1. `Integer.MIN_VALUE` through -1
2. 0 through 100
3. 101 through `Integer.MAX_VALUE`

Now we have six values to test. In addition, to verify that the relational operators are correct, we should test for values of 1 (> 0) and 99 (< 100).

Conditional branches are merely one factor in developing a testing strategy. We consider more of these factors in later chapters.

■ Syntactic Errors and Semantic Errors

Once a design is coded and test data have been prepared, the class is ready for compiling. The compiler has two responsibilities: to report any errors it finds and, if it finds no errors, to translate the source code into Bytecode or object code.

Errors can be either syntactic or semantic. The compiler finds syntactic errors. For example, the compiler warns you when a reserved word is misspelled. It won't find all of your typing errors, however. If you type > instead of >= within an *if* expression, you won't receive an error message; instead, you will get erroneous results. This particular error will be caught by a properly designed test plan that checks for both the greater than condition and the equality condition. It's your responsibility to inspect and test the code to detect these sorts of errors.

Semantic errors (also called logic errors) are mistakes that give wrong answers. They can be more difficult to locate and usually surface when code is executing. Java detects only the most obvious semantic errors—those that result in an invalid operation (dividing by zero, for example). Semantic errors are usually a product of a faulty algorithm design, but they may also result from coding errors. By walking through the algorithm and the code, tracing the execution of methods and applications, and developing a thorough test strategy, you should be able to avoid—or at least quickly locate—semantic errors in your code.

5.6 : Method Algorithm Design: Functional Decomposition

As we have stressed throughout this book, programming begins with the problem-solving phase. We've used object-oriented design (OOD) in the Case Studies to identify objects and their responsibilities, which we implement with classes and methods. Here we describe functional decomposition, a methodology that is useful when designing the algorithm for a method.

OOD focuses on the entities (objects) in a problem. In contrast, **functional decomposition** views the solution to a problem as a task to be accomplished. It focuses on the sequence of operations that are required to complete the task. When the series of steps is long or complex, we divide it into easier-to-solve subproblems. This technique is an application of the divide-and-conquer approach, which we saw in Chapter 1.

When a responsibility clearly involves a series of major steps, we break it down (decompose it) into pieces. In the process, we move to a lower level of abstraction—that is, some of the implementation details (but not too many) are now specified. Each of the major steps then becomes an independent subproblem that we can tackle separately. The process continues until all of the subproblems have obvious solutions.

By subdividing the problem, you create a hierarchical structure called a *tree*. Each level of the tree is a complete solution to the problem that is more detailed than the level above it. Figure 5.6 shows a generic solution tree for a problem. Steps shown in black type have enough implementation details to be translated directly into Java statements; they are **concrete steps**. Those shown in colored type are **abstract steps**; they reappear as subproblems in the next level down. Each box in the figure represents a **module**. The diagram in Figure 5.6 is, therefore, also called a module structure chart. Notice that the lowest-level module in each branch contains only concrete steps.

To produce the final algorithm for the responsibility, we take all of the concrete steps and arrange them in the proper order. These concrete steps can then be translated directly into corresponding Java statements within the method's body. Sometimes, when the responsibility algorithm is lengthy, we may implement parts of it as helper methods that correspond to subproblems in the module structure chart. Breaking up the method body in this way helps to make the design easier to understand, just as breaking up the problem helps make it easier to solve.

> **Functional decomposition** A technique for developing software in which the problem is divided into more easily handled subproblems, whose solutions are combined to create a solution to the overall problem
>
> **Concrete step** A step for which the implementation details are fully specified
>
> **Abstract step** A step for which some implementation details remain unspecified
>
> **Module** A self-contained collection of steps that solves a problem or subproblem; it can contain both concrete and abstract steps

■ Determining Modules

Here's one approach to writing modules:

1. Think about how you would solve the subproblem by hand.
2. Write down the major steps.
3. If a step is simple enough that you can see how to implement it directly in Java, it is at the concrete level; it doesn't need any further refinement.

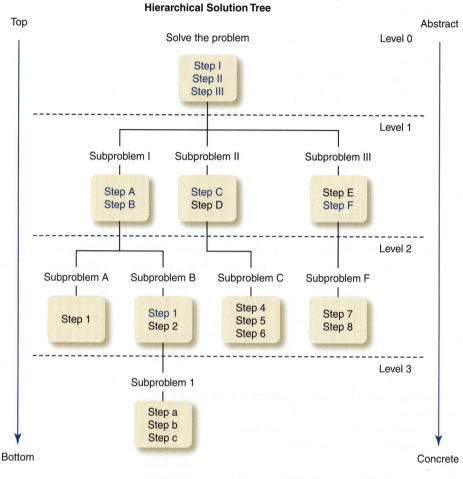

Hierarchical Solution Tree

FIGURE 5.6 Hierarchical Solution Tree

4. If you have to think about implementing a step as a series of smaller steps or as several Java statements, it is still at an abstract level.

5. If you are trying to write a series of steps and start to feel overwhelmed by details, you are probably bypassing one or more levels of abstraction. Stand back and look for pieces that you can write as more abstract steps.

We could call this approach the "procrastinator's technique." If a step is cumbersome or difficult, put it off to a lower level; don't think about it today, think about it tomorrow. Of course, tomorrow does come eventually, but the whole process can be applied again to the subproblem. A trouble spot often seems much simpler when you can focus on it more narrowly. Ultimately, the entire problem is broken up into manageable units. In the following case study, we see how to develop an application that involves branching, and we take the opportunity to demonstrate functional decomposition on one method.

PROBLEM SOLVING CASE STUDY

Comparing Race Results

Problem In Chapter 4, we created an application that computed some statistics for a pair of runners. That first application was well received by the track association, and now its members would like you to extend the application to print out the name and time of the winning runner first. If the runners are tied, then their data should be printed in the order it was entered, with a message indicating a tie.

Discussion We have already written most of this application, and we merely need to change part of the output. We can reuse the **Runner** class from Chapter 3. First, let's analyze what we've already done in the **RaceReport** driver by casting it as a module structure chart, as shown in Figure 5.7.

All we have to do is change the step that prints the runner data so that it prints the runners in order by their time. However, that operation is now an abstract step that needs to be expanded in a level-2 module. Also, it has become redundant to print the winning time, so we can delete that step.

Next, we expand the module that prints the runners in order. How do we do that? We can use our **Time** comparison operation. Based on the result of the comparison, we use a nested *if* statement to output the runners in the proper order or to output them in the original order with a message indicating a tie.

```
if (runner1.getTime().compareTo(runner2.getTime()) < 0)
    Output runner1 and then runner2
else if (runner1.getTime().compareTo(runner2.getTime()) > 0)
    Output runner2 and then runner1
else
    Output message indicating a tie
```

There's one more aspect of the driver that the module structure chart makes clear: Input of the runners is essentially the same set of statements repeated for each race participant. As programmers, we tend to look for ways to avoid this kind of repetition. This is actually a perfect opportunity to create a helper method. We simply wrap these statements with a method header and return the result instead of assigning it to a variable.

```java
// Helper method that reads a Runner from a Scanner
private static Runner nextRunner(Scanner in)
{
  String last = in.next();
  String first = in.next().trim();
  String middle = in.next().trim();
  double time = in.nextDouble();
  return new Runner(new Name(first, last, middle), new Time(time));
}
```

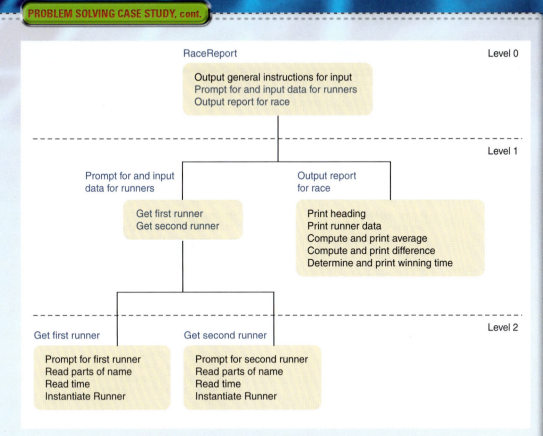

FIGURE 5.7   Module Structure Chart for **RaceReport** Application

Figure 5.8 shows the revised module structure chart.

Driver Implementation We're ready to implement the new driver, which we call `RaceReport2`.

```
//***************************************************************
// This application gets data for two runners in a race and
// displays a report indicating the winner and race statistics
//***************************************************************
import java.util.Scanner;
public class RaceReport2
{
  // Helper method that reads a Runner from a Scanner
  private static Runner nextRunner(Scanner in)
  {
    String last = in.next();
    String first = in.next().trim();
```

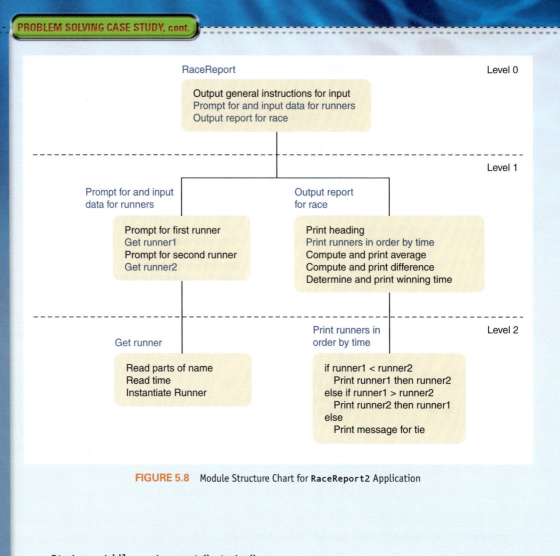

FIGURE 5.8 Module Structure Chart for `RaceReport2` Application

```
    String middle = in.next().trim();
    double time = in.nextDouble();
    return new Runner(new Name(first, last, middle), new Time(time));
}

public static void main (String[] args)
{
    Runner runner1;     // Holds first runner
    Runner runner2;     // Holds second runner
    Time time1;         // Holds first runner's time
    Time time2;         // Holds second runner's time
    Time average;       // Holds average time for the runners
    Time difference;    // Holds difference in time between the runners
    Scanner in = new Scanner(System.in);
```

```java
// Output general instructions for input
System.out.println
  ("For each runner, enter the data in the following format:");
System.out.println("Last First Middle time");
System.out.println("For example: Smith Jane Louise 87.491");

// Prompt for and input data for the runners
System.out.println("Enter the name and time for Runner 1");
runner1 = nextRunner(in);
System.out.println("Enter the name and time for Runner 2");
runner2 = nextRunner(in);

// Output the report for the race
System.out.println();
System.out.println("Race Report ");
System.out.println();
time1 = runner1.getTime();
time2 = runner2.getTime();
if (time1.compareTo(time2) < 0)
{
  System.out.println("Runner 1 is the winner.");
  System.out.println(runner1 + "\n" + runner2);
}
else if (time1.compareTo(time2) > 0)
{
  System.out.println("Runner 2 is the winner.");
  System.out.println(runner2 + "\n" + runner1);
}
else
{
  System.out.println("The race is a tie.");
  System.out.println(runner1 + "\n" + runner2);
}
average = new Time(time1.plus(time2).getTime()/2.0);
System.out.println();
System.out.println("Average time: " + average);
difference = new Time(Math.abs(time1.minus(time2).getTime()));
System.out.println("Difference: " + difference);
  }
}
```

Application Testing Which cases must we test for application `RaceReport2`? We must test all three possible branches in the application—that is, a case where the first runner's time is less, a case where the second runner's time is less, and the case where the times are the same. Let's summarize these observations in a test plan.

TEST PLAN

Number	Input	Expected Output
1	Allen Hannah Rachel 42.5 Ginsburg Nadine Anastasia 41.11	Race Report Runner 2 is the winner. Ginsburg, Nadine Anastasia 0:0:41.11 Allen, Hannah Rachel 0:0:42:5 Average time: 0:0:41:805 Difference: 0:0:1.39
2	Allen Hannah Rachel 41.11 Ginsburg Nadine Anastasia 42.5	Race Report Runner 1 is the winner. Allen, Hannah Rachel 0:0:41.11 Ginsburg, Nadine Anastasia 0:0:42:5 Average time: 0:0:41:805 Difference: 0:0:1.39
3	Allen Hannah Rachel 42.5 Ginsburg Nadine Anastasia 42.5	Race Report The race is a tie. Allen Hannah Rachel 0:0:42:5 Ginsburg Nadine Anastasia 0:0:42:5 Average time: 0:0:42:5 Difference: 0:0:0:0

Here are the results of implementing test case number 1. We leave the running of the other cases as a Case Study Follow-Up exercise.

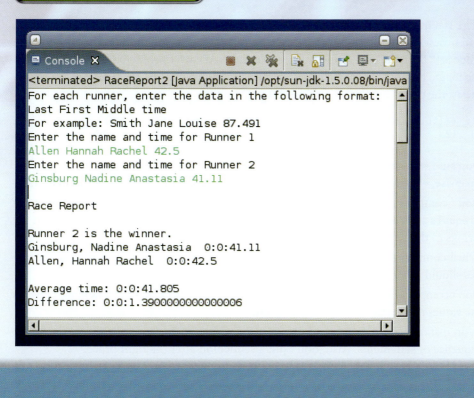

```
Console ✕
<terminated> RaceReport2 [Java Application] /opt/sun-jdk-1.5.0.08/bin/java
For each runner, enter the data in the following format:
Last First Middle time
For example: Smith Jane Louise 87.491
Enter the name and time for Runner 1
Allen Hannah Rachel 42.5
Enter the name and time for Runner 2
Ginsburg Nadine Anastasia 41.11

Race Report

Runner 2 is the winner.
Ginsburg, Nadine Anastasia  0:0:41.11
Allen, Hannah Rachel  0:0:42.5

Average time: 0:0:41.805
Difference: 0:0:1.3900000000000006
```

Testing and Debugging Hints

1. Java has three pairs of operators that are similar in appearance but different in effect: == and =, && and &, and || and |. Double-check all of your logical expressions to make sure you're using the "equals-equals," "and-and," and "or-or" operators. Then check them again to confirm that you didn't double-type the < or > operators.

2. If you use extra parentheses for clarity, make sure that the opening and closing parentheses match up. To verify that parentheses are properly paired, start with the innermost pair and draw a line connecting them. Do the same for the other pairs, working your way out to the outermost pair. For example:

```
if (((total/scores) > 50) && ((total/(scores - 1)) < 100))
```

3. Here is a quick way to tell whether you have an equal number of opening and closing parentheses. The scheme uses a single number (the "magic number"), whose initial value is 0. Scan the expression from left to right. At each opening parenthesis, add 1 to the magic number; at each closing parenthesis, subtract 1. At the final closing parenthesis, the magic number should be 0. For example,

```
if (((total/scores) > 50) && ((total/(scores - 1)) < 100))
   0   123            2    1    23       4          32      10
```

4. Don't use =< to mean "less than or equal to"; only the symbol <= works for this operation. Likewise, => is invalid for "greater than or equal to"; you must use >= for this operation.

5. Don't compare strings with the == operator. Use the associated instance methods such as **equals** and **compareTo**. When testing for alphabetical order, remember to convert the strings to the same case before making the comparison.

6. When comparing values of different types, use explicit casting to clarify how the values should be converted before comparison.

7. Don't compare floating-point types for exact equality. Check that the difference between the values is less than some small amount.

8. In an *if* statement, remember to use a { } pair if the *then* clause or the *else* clause is a sequence of statements. Also, don't put a semicolon after the right brace.

9. Test for bad data. If a data value must be positive, use an *if* statement to test the value. If the value is negative or zero, an error message should be displayed; otherwise, processing should continue.

10. Take some sample values and try following their progress by hand. Develop a test plan before you start testing your code.

11. If your application produces an answer that does not agree with a value you've calculated by hand, try these suggestions:

   ■ Redo your arithmetic.
   ■ Recheck your input data.
   ■ Carefully review the section of code that performs the calculation. If you're in doubt about the order in which the operations are performed, insert clarifying parentheses.

12. Check for integer overflow. The value of an **int** variable may have exceeded **Integer.MAX_VALUE** in the middle of a calculation. Java doesn't display an error message when this problem occurs.

13. Check the conditions in branching statements to confirm that the correct branch is taken under all circumstances.

Graphical User Interfaces

Customizing Message Dialog Boxes

In Chapter 3, we saw how to use the `showMessageDialog` method in the `JOptionPane` class to display a dialog box on the screen. Recall that `showMessageDialog` has two arguments: the `parentComponent` (the window containing the dialog, which we specify as `null`) and a `String` message to be written in the box. For example:

```
JOptionPane.showMessageDialog
   (null, "Today is a great day for a dialog!");
```

When this call executes, a box is displayed with a default label (the word "Message") at the top of the dialog and a default icon. To make our output look more professional, we should label the dialog window in a way that is relevant to its contents. Also, it would be better to have an appropriate icon. Let's see how we can do this.

A second version of the `showMessageDialog` method has four arguments. The first two are the same as the ones we saw before. The two new arguments are a `String` that is used to label the box and the `messageType`, which indicates the style of icon to display in the box. `JOptionPane` supplies a set of predefined constants that can be passed as `messageType` arguments. Because the constants are `static`, we must precede them with the name of the class.

```
JOptionPane.ERROR_MESSAGE
JOptionPane.INFORMATION_MESSAGE
JOptionPane.WARNING_MESSAGE
JOptionPane.QUESTION_MESSAGE
JOptionPane.PLAIN_MESSAGE
```

The default message type is `INFORMATION_MESSAGE`. As you might expect, specifying `QUESTION_MESSAGE` displays a question mark icon. A `PLAIN_MESSAGE` doesn't display an icon, and an `ERROR_MESSAGE` shows a symbol resembling a stop sign. A `WARNING_MESSAGE` shows an exclamation point in a yellow triangle.

To demonstrate the use of this version of `showMessageDialog`, let's reimplement the output section of the Problem-Solving Case Study so that the report appears in a series of dialog boxes. Each branch is now just a single statement (a method call), so we no longer need to use braces as we did in the original version. Other than the changes to the output section shown here, we just need to import `javax.swing.*` at the top of the application.

```
// Output the report for the race
time1 = runner1.getTime();
time2 = runner2.getTime();
```

```java
if (time1.compareTo(time2) < 0)
  JOptionPane.showMessageDialog(null, runner1 + "\n" + runner2,
    "Runner 1 is the Winner", JOptionPane.INFORMATION_MESSAGE );
else if (time1.compareTo(time2) > 0)
  JOptionPane.showMessageDialog(null, runner2 + "\n" + runner1,
    "Runner 2 is the Winner", JOptionPane.INFORMATION_MESSAGE);
else
  JOptionPane.showMessageDialog(null, runner1 + "\n" + runner2,
    "The Race is a Tie", JOptionPane.INFORMATION_MESSAGE );
average = new Time(time1.plus(time2).getTime()/2.0);
JOptionPane.showMessageDialog(null, "" + average, "Average Time",
    JOptionPane.INFORMATION_MESSAGE );
difference = new Time(Math.abs(time1.minus(time2).getTime()));
JOptionPane.showMessageDialog(null, "" + difference, "Difference",
    JOptionPane.INFORMATION_MESSAGE );
```

In the last two calls to `showMessageDialog`, we had to concatenate `average` and `difference` with the empty string to cause string conversion to occur. Unlike `println`, which can directly output numbers, `showMessageDialog` can accept only a string as its second argument. Here are the dialog boxes displayed by the application once the data has been input via `System.in`. We use the same test data as we did with the original version of the application.

Summary

Using logical expressions is a way of asking questions while code is executing. The computer evaluates each logical expression, producing the value `true` if the expression is true or the value `false` if the expression is not true.

The *if* statement allows you to take different paths through the code based on the value of a logical expression. The *if-else* statement is used to choose between two courses of action; the *if* statement is used to choose whether to take a particular course of action. The branches of an *if* and *if-else* can be any statement, either simple or compound. They can even be another *if* statement.

The `Scanner` class provides methods to test the data type of the next value to be read. `hasNextInt` returns `true` if the next value is an integer within the range of type `int`. `hasNextFloat` returns `true` if the next value is a real value within the range of type `float`. `hasNextLine` returns `true` if another line is waiting to be read.

A test plan is a document that outlines the cases that must be tested, the input data, and the expected results. A driver implements the test plan by executing each of the cases and documenting the results. The actual results are then compared to the expected results to determine whether the code is correct. Testing branches involves combining code coverage and data coverage in designing a test plan.

Functional decomposition begins with an abstract solution that is then divided into major steps. Each step becomes a subproblem that is analyzed and subdivided further if necessary. A concrete step is one that can be translated directly into Java; an abstract step is one that needs more refining. A module is a collection of concrete and abstract steps that solves a subproblem. We can use functional decomposition as an aid in designing the algorithm for a complex class responsibility, a driver, or an implementation of a test plan. However, functional decomposition is not generally appropriate for designing whole systems. For that, we use object-oriented design.

LEARNING / Portfolio

Quick Check

1. If x is 10 and y is 5, what is the result of x <= y? (pp. 217–220)
2. Write the expression that compares two `String` variables x and y. (pp. 220–223)
3. Which `String` method compares two strings without regard to case? (pp. 220–223)
4. Write a Java expression that compares the variable `letter` to the constant `'Z'` and yields `true` if `letter` is less than `'Z'`. (pp. 217–220)

5. Write a Java expression that yields `true` if `letter` is between `'A'` and `'Z'`, inclusive. (pp. 223–225)

6. Given that A holds `true` and B holds `false`, what are the values of `A && B`, `A || B`, and `!A`? (pp. 223–225)

7. How does an *if* statement let us affect the flow of control? (pp. 230–231)

8. If an *if-else* structure contains a nested *if-else* in each of its branches, as shown below, how many different paths can be taken through the whole structure? (pp. 238–240)

```
if
  if
  else
else
  if
  else
```

9. What is the difference between the *if* and the *if-else* control structures? (pp. 236–238)

10. Which actions below are more like a sequence of *if* statements, and which are more like nested *if* statements (mark the questions with *S* or *N*) (pp. 238–240)

   a. Indicating your age in a list of ranges

   b. Marking all of your hobbies in a list

   c. Checking off in a list all of the magazines you receive

   d. Marking the items you want to order on a menu

   e. Checking the box that indicates your marital status on a tax form

11. In a problem where you are determining the grade for a test score, given a series of score ranges and corresponding grades, would it be more appropriate to use a nested *if* structure or a sequence of *if* statements? (pp. 238–240)

12. Write a Java statement that sets the variable `value` to its negative if it is greater than zero. (pp. 236–238)

13. Extend the statement in Question 12 so that it sets `value` to 1 if it is less than or equal to 0. (pp. 232–235)

14. On a telephone, each of the digits 2 through 9 has a segment of the alphabet associated with it. What kind of control structure would you use to decide which segment a given letter falls into and to display the corresponding digit? (pp. 242–244)

15. You've written an application that displays the corresponding digit on a phone, given a letter of the alphabet. Everything seems to work right except that you can't get the digit 5 to display; you keep getting the digit 6. What steps would you take to find and fix this bug? (pp. 250–251)

16. What is the method that returns `true` if there is another line to be read? (pp. 245–246)

17. A functional decomposition design is based on a hierarchy of tasks. (True or False?) (pp. 252–253)

18. What are the building blocks of a functional decomposition? (pp. 252–253)

19. Steps that need no further decomposition are called _____ steps. (pp. 252–253)

20. Steps that require further decomposition are called _____ steps. (pp. 252–253)

Answers

1. `false` 2. `x.equals(y)` 3. `equalsIgnoreCase` 4. `letter < 'Z'` 5. `letter >= 'A' && letter <= 'Z'`
6. `false`, `true`, `false` 7. It enables us to choose one course of action (control flow path) or another. 8. Four paths. 9. The *if* lets us choose whether to perform an action; the *if-else* allows us to choose between two courses of action. 10. a. *N*, b. *S*, c. *S*, d. *S*, e. *N* 11. A nested *if* structure. 12. `if (value > 0) value = -value;`
13. `if (value > 0) value = -value; else value = 1;` 14. A nested *if* statement. 15. Carefully review the section of code that should display 5. Check the branching condition and the output statement there. Try some sample values by hand. 16. `hasNextLine` 17. True. 18. Modules. 19. concrete 20. abstract

Exam Preparation Exercises

1. What is the purpose of a control structure?

2. What is a logical expression?

3. Given the following relational expressions, state in English what they say.

Expression	Meaning in English
`one == two`	_____
`one != two`	_____
`one > two`	_____
`one < two`	_____
`one >= two`	_____
`one <= two`	_____

4. Given these values for the `boolean` variables x, y, and z:

```
x = true
y = false
z = true
```

Evaluate the following logical expressions. In the blank next to each expression, write a T if the result is `true` or an F if the result is `false`.

_____ **a.** x && y || x && z

_____ **b.** (x || !y) && (!x || z)

_____ **c.** x || y && z

_____ **d.** !(x || y) && z

5. Given these values for variables i, j, p, and q:

```
i = 10
j = 19
p = true
q = false
```

Add parentheses (if necessary) to the expressions below so that they evaluate to **true**.

a. i == j || p

b. i >= j || i <= j && p

c. !p || p

d. !q && q

6. Given these values for the **int** variables i, j, m, and n:

```
i = 6
j = 7
m = 11
n = 11
```

What is the output of the following code?

```
System.out.print("Madam");
if (i < j)
  if (m != n)
    System.out.print("How");
  else
    System.out.print("I'm");
if (i >= m)
  System.out.print("Cow");
else
  System.out.print("Adam");
```

7. Given the **int** variables x, y, and z, where x contains 3, y contains 7, and z contains 6, what is the output of each of the following code fragments?

a.
```
if (x <= 3)
  System.out.print ("x" + "y");
System.out.print("x" + "y");
```

b.
```
if (x != -1)
  System.out.print("The value of x is " + x);
else
  System.out.print("The value of y is " + y);
```

c.
```
if (x != -1)
{
    System.out.print(x);
    System.out.print(y);
    System.out.print(z);
}
else
    System.out.print("y");
    System.out.print("z");
```

8. Given this code fragment:

```
if (height >= minHeight)
    if (weight >= minWeight)
        System.out.print("Eligible to serve.");
    else
        System.out.print("Too light to serve.");
else
    if (weight >= minWeight)
        System.out.print("Too short to serve.");
    else
        System.out.print("Too short and too light to serve.");
```

   a. What is the output when `height` exceeds `minHeight` and `weight` exceeds `minWeight`?

   b. What is the output when `height` is less than `minHeight` and `weight` is less than `minWeight`?

9. Match each logical expression in the left column with the logical expression in the right column that tests for the same condition.

_____	**a.** `x < y && y < z`	(1) `!(x != y) && y == z`
_____	**b.** `x > y && y >= z`	(2) `!(x <= y || y < z)`
_____	**c.** `x != y || y == z`	(3) `(y < z || y == z) || x == y`
_____	**d.** `x == y || y <= z`	(4) `!(x >= y) && !(y >= z)`
_____	**e.** `x == y && y == z`	(5) `!(x == y && y != z)`

10. The following expressions make sense but are invalid according to Java's rules of syntax. Rewrite them so that they are valid logical expressions. (All the variables are of type `int`.)

   a. `x < y <= z`

   b. `x`, `y`, and `z` are greater than 0

   c. `x` is equal to neither `y` nor `z`

   d. `x` is equal to `y` and `z`

11. Given these values for the **boolean** variables x, y, and z,

    ```
    x = true
    y = true
    z = false
    ```

    Indicate whether each expression is **true** (T) or **false** (F).

    _____ **a.** `!(y || z) || x`

    _____ **b.** `z && x && y`

    _____ **c.** `!y || (z || !x)`

    _____ **d.** `z || (x && (y || z))`

    _____ **e.** `x || x && z`

12. For each of the following problems, decide which is more appropriate, an *if-else* or an *if*. Explain your answers.

    a. Students who are candidates for admission to a college submit their SAT scores. If a student's score is equal to or greater than a certain value, print a letter of acceptance for the student. Otherwise, print a rejection notice.

    b. For employees who work more than 40 hours per week, calculate overtime pay and add it to their regular pay.

    c. In solving a quadratic equation, whenever the value of the discriminant (the quantity under the square root sign) is negative, print out a message noting that the roots are complex (imaginary) numbers.

    d. In a computer-controlled sawmill, if a cross section of a log is greater than certain dimensions, adjust the saw to cut 4-inch by 8-inch beams; otherwise, adjust the saw to cut 2-inch by 4-inch studs.

13. What causes the error message "UNEXPECTED ELSE" to appear when this code fragment is compiled?

    ```
    if (mileage < 24.0)
    {
      System.out.print("Gas ");
      System.out.print("guzzler.");
    };
    else
      System.out.print("Fuel efficient.");
    ```

14. The following code fragment is supposed to print `"Type AB"` when **boolean** variables typeA and typeB are both **true**, and to print `"Type 0"` when both variables are **false**. Instead, it prints `"Type 0"` whenever just one of the variables is **false**. Insert a `{ }` pair to make the code segment work the way it should.

```
if (typeA || typeB)
  if (typeA && typeB)
    System.out.print("Type AB");
else
  System.out.print("Type 0");
```

15. The nested *if* structure below has five possible branches depending on the values read into **char** variables **ch1**, **ch2**, and **ch3**. To test the structure, you need five sets of data, each set using a different branch. Create the five test data sets.

```
if (ch1 == ch2)
  if (ch2 == ch3)
    System.out.print("All initials are the same.");
  else
    System.out.print("First two are the same.");
else if (ch2 == ch3)
  System.out.print("Last two are the same.");
else if (ch1 == ch3)
  System.out.print("First and last are the same.");
else
  System.out.print("All initials are different.");
```

a. Test data set 1:   ch1 = _____   ch2 = _____   ch3 = _____

b. Test data set 2:   ch1 = _____   ch2 = _____   ch3 = _____

c. Test data set 3:   ch1 = _____   ch2 = _____   ch3 = _____

d. Test data set 4:   ch1 = _____   ch2 = _____   ch3 = _____

e. Test data set 5:   ch1 = _____   ch2 = _____   ch3 = _____

16. If **x** and **y** are **boolean** variables, do the following two expressions test the same condition?

```
x != y
(x || y) && !(x && y)
```

17. The following *if* condition is made up of three relational expressions:

```
if (i >= 10 && i <= 20 && i != 16)
  j = 4;
```

If **i** contains the value 25 when this *if* statement is executed, which relational expression(s) does the computer evaluate? (Remember that Java uses short-circuit evaluation.)

18. **a.** If strings cannot be compared using the relational operators in Java, how can you compare two strings?

b. Fill in the following table that describes methods that can be applied to string objects.

Method Name	Argument	Returns	English Description
equals	_____	_____	_____
equalsIgnoreCase	_____	_____	_____
compareTo	_____	_____	_____
toUpperCase	_____	_____	_____
toLowerCase	_____	_____	_____

19. Name the methods that test whether the next data value is an integer of some sort.

20. Name the methods that test whether the next data value is a real value.

Programming Warm-Up Exercises

1. Declare `eligible` to be a `boolean` variable, and assign it the value `true`.

2. Write a statement that sets the `boolean` variable `available` to `true` if `numberOrdered` is less than or equal to `numberOnHand` minus `numberReserved`.

3. Write a statement containing a logical expression that assigns `true` to the `boolean` variable `isCandidate` if `satScore` is greater than or equal to 1100, `gpa` is not less than 2.5, and `age` is greater than 15. Otherwise, `isCandidate` should be `false`.

4. Given the declarations

```
boolean leftPage;
int    pageNumber:
```

write a statement that sets `leftPage` to `true` if `pageNumber` is even. (*Hint:* Consider what the remainders are when you divide different integers by 2.)

5. Write an *if* statement (or a series of *if* statements) that assigns to the variable `biggest` the greatest value contained in variables `i`, `j`, and `k`. Assume the three values are distinct.

6. Rewrite the following sequence of *if* statements as a single *if-else*.

```
if (year % 4 == 0)
  System.out.print(year + " is a leap year.");
if (year % 4 != 0)
{
  year = year + 4 - year % 4;
  System.out.print(year + " is the next leap year.");
}
```

7. Simplify the following code segment, taking out unnecessary comparisons. Assume that `age` is an `int` variable.

```
if (age > 64)
  System.out.print("Senior voter");
```

```
if (age < 18)
  System.out.print("Under age");
if (age >= 18 && age < 65)
  System.out.print("Regular voter");
```

8. The following code fragment is supposed to print out the values 25, 60, and 8, in that order. Instead, it prints out 50, 60, and 4. Why?

```
length = 25;
width = 60;
if (length = 50)
  height = 4;
else
  height = 8;
System.out.print("" + length + " " + width + " " + height);
```

9. The following Java code segment is almost unreadable because of the inconsistent indentation and the random placement of left and right braces. Fix the indentation and align the braces properly.

```
// This is a nonsense program segment
if (a > 0)
if (a < 20)
        {
 System.out.print("A is in range.");
b = 5;
    }
        else
                    {
    System.out.print("A is too large.");
    b = 3;
}
     else
System.out.print("A is too small.");
System.out.print("All done.")
```

10. Given the **float** variables **x1, x2, y1, y2,** and **m,** write a code segment to find the slope of a line through the two points (**x1, y1**) and (**x2, y2**). Use the formula

$$m = \frac{y2 - y1}{x2 - x1}$$

to determine the slope of the line. If **x1** equals **x2,** the line is vertical and the slope is undefined. The segment should display the slope with an appropriate label. If the slope is undefined, it should display the message "Slope undefined."

11. Given the `float` variables `a`, `b`, `c`, `root1`, `root2`, and `discriminant`, write a code segment to determine whether the roots of a quadratic polynomial are real or complex (imaginary). If the roots are real, find them and assign them to `root1` and `root2`. If they are complex, write the message "No real roots."

    The formula for the solution to the quadratic equation is

    $$\frac{-b \pm \sqrt{b^2 - 4ac}}{2a}$$

    The $\pm$ means "plus or minus" and indicates that the equation has two solutions: one in which the result of the square root is added to $-b$ and one in which the result is subtracted from $-b$. The roots are real if the discriminant (the quantity under the square root sign) is not negative.

12. Write an expression that tests whether the next value on `Scanner in` is an `int`.

Programming Problems

1. Design and write a Java application that takes as input a single letter and displays the corresponding digit on a telephone. The letters and digits on a telephone are grouped this way:

2 = ABC	4 = GHI	6 = MNO	8 = TUV
3 = DEF	5 = JKL	7 = PQRS	9 = WXYZ

   The screen dialog might look like this:

   ```
   Enter a single letter, and I will tell you what the corresponding
   digit is on the telephone.
   R
   The digit 7 corresponds to the letter R on the telephone.
   ```

   Here's another example:

   ```
   Enter a single letter, and I will tell you what the corresponding
   digit is on the telephone.
   G
   The digit 4 corresponds to the letter G on the telephone.
   ```

   Your code should display a message indicating that there is no matching digit for any nonalphabetic character entered by the user. Also, the application should recognize only uppercase letters. Include the lowercase letters with the invalid characters.

LEARNING Portfolio

Prompt the user with an informative message for the input value, as shown on the preceding page. The application should include the input letter as part of the output.

Use proper indentation, appropriate comments, and meaningful identifiers throughout the code.

2. People who deal with historical dates use a number called the Julian day to calculate the number of days between two events. The Julian day is the number of days that have elapsed since January 1, 4713 B.C. For example, the Julian day for October 16, 1956, is 2435763.

There are formulas for computing the Julian day from a given date, and vice versa. One very simple formula computes the day of the week from a given Julian day:

```
Day of the week = (Julian day + 1) % 7
```

where **%** is the Java modulus operator. This formula gives a result of 0 for Sunday, 1 for Monday, and so on, up to 6 for Saturday. For Julian day 2435763, the result is 2 (Tuesday). Your job is to write a Java application that requests and inputs a Julian day, computes the day of the week using the formula, and then displays the name of the day that corresponds to that number.

Your output might look like this:

```
Enter a Julian day number and press Enter.
2451545
Julian day number 2451545 is a Saturday.
Enter a Julian day number and press Enter.
2451547
Julian day number 2451547 is a Monday.
```

3. You can compute the date for any Easter Sunday from 1982 to 2048 as follows (all variables are of type `int`):

a is year % 19
b is year % 4
c is year % 7
d is (19 * a + 24) % 30
e is (2 * b + 4 * c + 6 * d + 5) % 7

Easter Sunday is March (22 + d + e)

For example, Easter Sunday in 1985 is April 7.

Write an application that inputs the year and outputs the date (month and day) of Easter Sunday for that year. Note that when the formula gives a value greater than 30, the month is April.

4. The algorithm for computing the date of Easter can be extended easily to work with any year from 1900 to 2099. There are four years—1954, 1981, 2049, and 2076—for which the algorithm gives a date that is seven days later than it should be. Modify the application from Programming Problem 3 to check for these years and subtract 7 from the day

of the month. This correction does not cause the month to change. Be sure to change the documentation for the code to reflect its broadened capabilities.

5. Write a Java application that calculates and prints the diameter, the circumference, or the area of a circle, given the radius. The application should input a character corresponding to one of three actions: D for diameter, C for circumference, and A for area. The user should be prompted to enter the radius in floating-point form and then the appropriate letter. The output should be labeled appropriately. For example, if the input is 6.75 and A, your application should print something like this:

The area of a circle with radius 6.75 is 143.14.

Here are the formulas you need:

Diameter = $2r$

Circumference = $2\pi r$

Area of a circle = πr^2

where r is the radius. Use 3.14159265 for π.

6. The factorial of a number n is $n * (n - 1) * (n - 2) * \cdots * 2 * 1$. Stirling's formula approximates the factorial for large values of n:

$$\frac{n^n \sqrt{2\pi n}}{e^n}$$

where $\pi = 3.14159265$ and $e = 2.718282$.

Write a Java application that inputs an integer value (but stores it into a `double` variable n), calculates the factorial of n using Stirling's formula, assigns the (rounded) result to a `long` integer variable, and then displays the result appropriately labeled.

Depending on the value of n, you should obtain one of these results:

- A numerical result.
- If n equals 0, the factorial is defined to be 1.
- If n is less than 0, the factorial is undefined.
- If n is too large, the result exceeds `Long.MAX_VALUE`.

Because Stirling's formula is used to calculate the factorial of very large numbers, the factorial approaches `Long.MAX_VALUE` quickly. If the factorial exceeds `Long.MAX_VALUE`, it causes an arithmetic overflow in the computer, in which case the program continues with a strange-looking integer result, perhaps a negative value. Before you write the application, then, you first must write a small application that lets you determine, by trial and error, the largest value of n for which Java can compute a factorial using Stirling's formula. After you've determined this value, you can write the application using nested *if* statements that display different messages depending on the value of n. If n is within the acceptable range, output the number and the result with an appropriate message. If n is 0, write the message, "The number is 0. The factorial is 1." If **n** is less than 0, write "The number is less than 0. The factorial is undefined." If the number is greater than the largest value of **n** for which Java can compute a factorial, write "The number is too large."

Hint: Don't compute Stirling's formula directly. The values of n^n and e^n can be huge, even in floating-point form. Take the natural logarithm of the formula and manipulate it algebraically to work with more reasonable floating-point values. If r is the result of these intermediate calculations, the final result is e^r. Make use of the standard library methods **Math.log** and **Math.exp**. These methods compute the natural logarithm and natural exponent, respectively.

Case Study Follow-Up

1. Write a test plan for method **compareTo** in class **Time**.
2. Write a driver to implement your test plan written in Exercise 1.
3. Implement test cases 2 and 3 from the test plan for **RaceReport2**.
4. The **Math.min** method returns the least of its two operands. Internally, it uses an *if* statement to do so. Write a new helper method called **triMin** that returns the least of its three **double** arguments, using a nested *if* statement.
5. Change the **RaceReport2** application so that it works for three runners. The reported differences should be the difference between the winning time and each of the other times. The **triMin** method written for Exercise 4 could be useful here.

6 Loops and Files

Goals

Knowledge Goals

To:

- Understand the semantics of a *while* loop
- Understand when a count-controlled loop is appropriate
- Understand when an event-controlled loop is appropriate
- Know the difference between an iteration counter and an event counter
- Know where nested loops are needed in a problem solution
- Understand the principles of testing programs that contain loops
- Recognize when file input/output is appropriate and how it differs from interactive input/output

Skill Goals

To be able to:

- Construct syntactically correct *while* loops
- Construct count-controlled loops with a *while* statement
- Construct event-controlled loops with a *while* statement
- Use the end-of-file condition to control the input of data
- Use flags to control the execution of a *while* statement
- Construct counting loops with a *while* statement
- Construct summing loops with a *while* statement
- Write statements to read from a text file
- Write statements to write to a text file
- Write applications that use data files for input and output

1958
Kenneth Olsen, Stan Olsen, and Harlan Anderson form Digital Equipment Corp.

1958
Jack Kilby at Texas Instruments invents the integrated circuit

1958
Bell Labs' modem data phone makes possible the transmission of binary data through phone lines

1959
The language Cobol, Common Business Oriented Language, is developed

1959
John McCarthy at M.I.T. develops the language Lisp on the IBM 704 for artificial intelligence applications

1959
Japan introduces its first commercial transistor computer

Introduction

In Chapter 5, we saw how the flow of control in an application can be altered to select among different actions with the *if* statement. In this chapter, we examine another algorithmic control structure, the *loop*, which allows us to repeat actions. We explore looping in algorithms using a Java construct called the *while* statement. Once we have seen how any loop can be expressed with this statement, we will expand our repertoire of Java looping statements in Chapter 7 to include forms that simplify the coding of specific kinds of loops.

With the ability to repeat processing steps comes the potential to work with larger sets of data. Entering more than a few data values interactively becomes tedious and is prone to error. Thus, using files for input and output has a natural synergism with looping, so after introducing the basics of looping we move quickly to writing loops that perform I/O with files.

1959
Xerox debuts the first commercial copy machine

1959
General Electric develops the GE ERMA, the first machine that can process checks encoded with magnetic ink

1960
Digital Equipment Corporation debuts the PDP-1, which has a monitor and keyboard input

1961
The first robot patent is obtained by Georg Devol whose "Unimates" are the first modern industrial robots

1961
Computer capabilities launch forward with the IBM 7030, which runs 30 times faster than the 704

1962
The first computer science departments are established at Stanford University and Purdue University

6.1 ⋮ Looping Control Flow

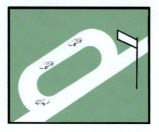

In Chapter 5, we developed an application that input data for two runners and output a report for the race with the winner listed first. Now the track association wants to do the same thing for a track meet in which as many as 40 runners may compete. Oh my! Will we have to write 20 times as much code to handle all of those runners? In this chapter, we see that we can get all of that work done with just a few more lines of code. How? By having the computer repeat the same set of actions for each team. The general algorithm for solving this new problem then becomes the following, where the steps being repeated are highlighted.

While there is data left to input, do the following highlighted steps for each runner:
  Get the data for a runner
  If the time for the runner is less than the time for the best runner so far
    Replace the best runner so far with this runner
After the last runner has been processed, report that the best runner so far is the winner

Loop A control structure that causes a statement or group of statements to be executed repeatedly

Count-controlled loop A loop that executes a specified number of times

Event-controlled loop A loop that terminates when something happens inside the loop body to signal that the loop should be exited

In the computer, this form of repetition is called a **loop**. Like the *if* statement, the loop alters the flow of control so that statements are executed in an order that differs from their physical order in the code. Whereas a branch lets us *choose different statements* to execute, a loop *repeats the same statement(s)* over and over, as long as a condition or a set of conditions remains satisfied.

In solving problems, you will encounter two major types of loops: **count-controlled loops**, which repeat a specified number of times, and **event-controlled loops**, which repeat until something happens within the loop. In the context of a loop, we use the word *event* to mean a specific condition that we expect to occur during some repetition of the loop and that can be tested by a Boolean expression.

If you are making an angel food cake and the recipe reads, "Beat the mixture 300 strokes," you are executing a count-controlled loop. If you are making a pie crust and the recipe reads, "Cut with a pastry blender until the mixture resembles coarse meal," you are executing an *event-controlled loop*—you don't know ahead of time the exact number of loop repetitions.

■ Implementing Looping with the *while* Statement

The *while* statement is a Java looping control structure, and its syntax template is shown here:

While-Statement

```
while ( Expression )
   Statement
```

Like the *if* statement, the *while* statement tests a conditional expression. In the syntax template, the *Statement*, which is the part that is executed repeatedly, is called the body of the loop. Here is an example *while* loop:

```
int count = 1;            // Declare count with initial value of 1
while (count <= 25)       // While statement
  count++;                // Loop body
```

The body of this loop adds 1 to the value of `count`. The *while* condition says to execute the statement as long as `count` is less than or equal to 25. When `count` is greater than 25, the loop exits and control proceeds to whatever statement follows it. The effect of this loop, then, is to count through the `int` values from 1 to 25.

The condition in a *while* statement must be a `boolean` expression. The *while* statement says, "If the value of the expression is `true`, execute the body and then go back and test the expression again. If the value of the expression is `false`, skip the body." Thus the loop body is executed over and over as long as the expression remains `true` when it is tested. When the expression is `false`, control jumps from the *while* directly to the statement immediately following the loop. Of course, if the expression is `false` initially, the body never executes. Figure 6.1 shows the flow of control of the *while* statement, where Statement1 is the body of the loop and Statement2 is the statement following the loop.

The body of a loop can consist of a block of statements, which allows us to execute any group of statements repeatedly. Typically, we use *while* loops in the following form:

```
while (Expression)
{
   .
   .
   .
}
```

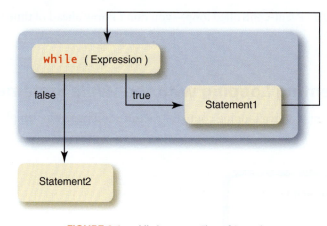

FIGURE 6.1   *while* Statement Flow of Control

In this structure, if the expression is `true`, the statements in the block are executed, and then the expression is checked again. If it is still `true`, the statements are executed again. The cycle continues until the expression becomes `false`.

Although the *if* and *while* statements are alike in some ways, there are fundamental differences between the two (see Figure 6.2). In the *if* structure, Statement1 is either skipped or executed exactly once. In the *while* structure, Statement1 can be skipped, executed once, or executed over and over. It bears repeating: The *if* is used to choose a course of action; the *while* is used to repeat a course of action.

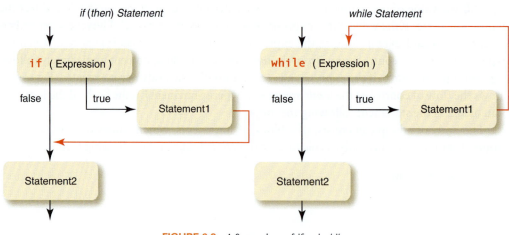

FIGURE 6.2   A Comparison of *if* and *while*

■ Phases of Loop Execution

The body of a loop is executed in several phases:

- The moment that the flow of control reaches the first statement inside the loop body is the **loop entry**.
- Each time the body of a loop is executed, a pass is made through the loop. This pass is called an **iteration**.
- Before each iteration, control is transferred to the **loop test** at the beginning of the loop.
- When the last iteration is complete and the flow of control has passed to the first statement following the loop, control has **exited the loop**. The condition that causes a loop to be exited is the **termination condition**. In the case of a *while* loop, the termination condition is that the expression becomes `false`.

Notice that the loop can exit at only one point: when the loop test is performed. Even though the termination condition may become satisfied midway through the execution of the loop, the current iteration is completed before the computer checks the *while* expression again.

The concept of looping is fundamental to programming. Next we look at typical kinds of loops and ways of implementing them with the *while* statement. These looping situations come up again and again when you are analyzing problems and designing algorithms.

> **Loop entry** The point at which the flow of control reaches the first statement inside a loop
>
> **Iteration** An individual pass through, or repetition of, the body of a loop
>
> **Loop test** The point at which the *while* expression is evaluated and the decision is made either to begin a new iteration or to skip to the statement immediately following the loop
>
> **Loop exit** The point at which the repetition of the loop body ends and control passes to the first statement following the loop
>
> **Termination condition** The condition that causes a loop to be exited

■ Implementing Count-Controlled Loops

A count-controlled loop uses a variable called the *loop control variable* as part of the loop test. Before we enter a count-controlled loop, we must initialize (set the initial value of) the loop control variable and then test it. Then, as part of each iteration of the loop, we must increment (increase by 1) the loop control variable. Let's look at a demonstration application that prints "Hello world!" ten times.

```java
public class HelloWorldX10
{
  public static void main(String[] args)
  {
    int loopCount = 1;                      // Initialization
    while (loopCount <= 10)                 // Test
    {
      System.out.println("Hello world!");   // Process being repeated
      loopCount++;                          // Incrementation
    }
  }
}
```

Here `loopCount` is the loop control variable. It is set to 1 before loop entry. The *while* statement tests the expression

```
loopCount <= 10
```

and executes the loop body as long as the expression is `true`—printing "Hello world!" in this case. Look at the last statement in the body:

```
loopCount++;
```

In our example, `loopCount` is incremented for each iteration of the loop—we use it to count the iterations. Variables that are used this way are called **counters**. The loop control variable of a count-controlled loop is always a counter.

> **Counter**   A variable that is incremented repeatedly

When designing a count-controlled loop, the programmer is responsible for ensuring that the condition to be tested is set correctly (initialized) before the *while* statement begins. The programmer must also ensure that the loop control variable is incremented so that the *while* expression eventually becomes `false`; otherwise, the loop never exits. We call this situation an infinite loop because, in theory, the loop executes forever. In the preceding code, omitting the incrementing of `loopCount` at the bottom of the loop leads to an infinite loop:

```
loopCount = 1;                        // Initialization
while (loopCount <= 10)               // loopCount remains 1 for every
                                      // iteration
{
  System.out.println("Hello world!"); // Outputs "Hello world!" endlessly
                                      // if loopCount++ is omitted at this
                                      // point
}
```

This *while* expression is always `true` because the value of `loopCount` is forever 1. If your application runs for much longer than expected, chances are that you've created an infinite loop. In such a case, you may have to use an operating system command to stop the application.

How many times does the loop in the following example execute?

```
loopCount = 0;                        // Initialization
while (loopCount <= 10)               // Test
{
  System.out.println("Hello world!");
  loopCount = loopCount++;            // Incrementation
}
```

To answer this question, we look at the initial value of the loop control variable and then at the test to see its final value. Here we've initialized `loopCount` to 0, and the test indicates that the loop body is executed for each value of `loopCount` up through 10. If `loopCount` starts at 0 and runs up to 10, the loop body is executed 11 times. If we want the loop to execute 10 times, we must either initialize `loopCount` to 1 (as in our original example) or change the test to

```
loopCount < 10    // Change relation from <= to <
```

or

```
loopCount <= 9    // Change test value from 10 to 9
```

Here is a loop that reads seven integer values from `System.in` and prints them on `System.out`:

```
//***********************************************************
// Application ReadInts reads and prints seven integer
// numbers using a count-controlled loop
//***********************************************************
import java.util.Scanner;
public class ReadInts
{
  public static void main(String args[])
  {
    Scanner in = new Scanner(System.in);
    int number;                       // Holds input value
    int counter = 0;                  // Loop control variable

    System.out.println("Enter seven integers separated by blanks.");
    while (counter < 7)
    {
      number = in.nextInt();
      System.out.print(number + " ");
      counter++;
    }
    System.out.println();
  }
}
```

Output:

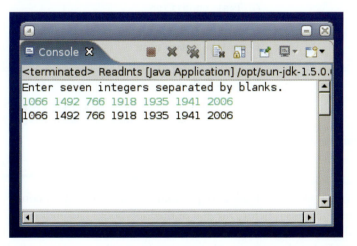

■ Implementing Event-Controlled Loops

Count-controlled loops are appropriate for solving problems that involve a predictable number of repetitions of some task. Of course, many problems aren't nearly so predictable. For example, if we are to process data until a negative value is encountered or we should perform a computation until some value exceeds a threshold, then we don't know the number of loop iterations in advance. These problems are examples of cases in which an event-controlled loop is needed. Here's how we would solve these problems algorithmically:

Process data until negative input

Get a value
While value is not negative
   Process value
   Get a value

Perform computation until threshold is reached

Set threshold
Initialize value
While value is less than the threshold
   Do computation
   Update value

In each case we initialize some condition before the loop. The body does some processing and then updates the condition before returning to the loop test. This is similar to what is done in a count-controlled loop, in which we initialize the counter and then increment it in the loop body. Because the termination condition is now more general, however, the initialization and update steps take more thought. Once we have worked out the algorithmic solution, implementation is basically the same as for any *while* loop. Here are implementations of the two earlier examples:

```
int value = in.nextInt();            // Initialize condition
while (value >= 0)                   // Test condition
{
  // Process value
  value = in.nextInt();              // Update condition
}

double threshold = 100.0;            // Initialize condition
double value = 0.0;
while (value < threshold)            // Test condition
{
  // Do computation, producing result
  value = value + result;            // Test condition
}
```

As the comments indicate, each event-controlled loop initializes the termination condition, tests the condition, and then updates it before the end of the loop body. The update can occur anywhere within the body, depending on where the event actually occurs. But remember—the condition will not be checked again until control returns to the test. An event-controlled loop doesn't exit when the event occurs; it exits when the *while* statement tests the condition and discovers that the event occurred somewhere in the last iteration.

As an example of an event-controlled loop in which computation produces a result that indicates an event, let's develop a method that computes the square root of a value given in a parameter called **square**. The algorithm begins by guessing an initial value for the square root (any value works). It then divides **square** by **guess**, and the average of this quotient and **guess** becomes the new **guess**. That is:

$$guess = \frac{\dfrac{square}{guess} + guess}{2.0}$$

With each iteration, **guess** is replaced by a value that is closer to the square root of **square**. An expression computes the difference between **square** and **guess** squared. The process stops when **guess** squared is close enough to **square**. Here is the method, followed by a simple driver application:

```java
//****************************************************
// Class NewMath supplies a Square Root operation as a
// demonstration of a loop that repeats until calculation
// converges on a solution
//****************************************************
public class NewMath
{
  static double squareRoot(double square)
  {
    double guess = square/4.0;              // Initial guess
    boolean goodEnough = false;             // Initialize while expression
    while (!goodEnough)
    {
      guess = ((square / guess) + guess)/2.0;   // Calculate next guess
      // Recalculate boolean value for while expression
      goodEnough = Math.abs(square - guess*guess) < 0.001;
    }
    return guess;
  }
}


//****************************************************
// Application SqRoot takes the square root of an integer
//****************************************************
public class SqRoot
{
  public static void main(String[] args)
  {
    // Call the method and display the result
    System.out.println("" + NewMath.squareRoot(64.0));
  }
}
```

> **Flag** A Boolean variable that is used as a loop control variable

The *while* expression is the logical NOT operator (!) applied to the `boolean` variable `goodEnough`. If the difference between `square` and `guess` squared is smaller than 0.001, `goodEnough` is set to `true` and the loop exits because `!true` is `false`. The method then returns `guess`. The variable `goodEnough` is a **flag** that controls the loop. Reasonably enough, this type of loop is called a *flag-controlled loop*. By the way, the value of `guess` that was printed was `8.000000371689179`.

One common use of loops is in processing data from files. Let's take a break from our exploration of loops to see how we work with files in Java. Then we'll see how to use loops with files.

6.2 : File Input and Output

In everything we've done so far, we've assumed that input occurs via the keyboard and output goes to the screen. This approach is fine for input/output (I/O) of a few values, but beyond that we need to consider I/O using files, which simplify the processing of larger quantities of data. The information in a file usually is stored on an auxiliary storage device, such as those shown in Figure 6.3.

■ Reading and Writing Files

Reading and writing data on files is similar to input and output on the screen. The main difference is that file data is essentially permanent, whereas screen I/O is transient. You can appreciate this distinction when you debug a program that requires entry of several data values.

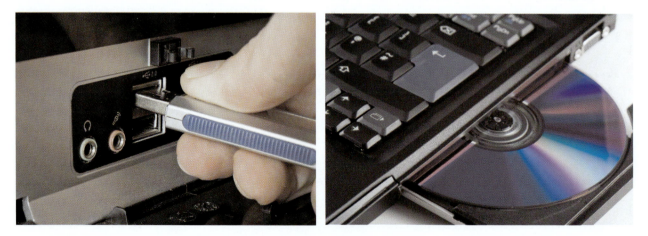

FIGURE 6.3 Devices Used for File Storage

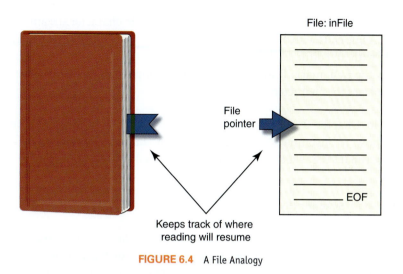

FIGURE 6.4 A File Analogy

With screen I/O, you type in the data every time the program is run, which grows quite tedious after a few trials. With file I/O, the program gets the data from the disk each time, and you merely check the results.

A file contains a sequence of values, and it has a distinct beginning and end—that is, a first value and a last value. Reading a file is analogous to reading a book, in that both are read from the front to the back. Just as you use a bookmark to keep track of your place in a book, Java uses a *file pointer* to remember its place in a file (see Figure 6.4). Each time data are read, the file pointer advances to where reading should resume. Eventually the pointer passes the last value in the file; it is then said to be at end-of-file (EOF).

Writing data on a file is like writing in an empty notebook. At the beginning, the file is empty. Then data are written onto it from front to back. The file pointer always indicates the end of the last value written so that writing can resume at that point. In effect, the file pointer is always at EOF when a file is being written. The size of the file increases with each write operation.

■ File Classes

Many Java library classes relate to files. For example, Java has classes that read and write images, sound files, and so on. We cover three of Java's character stream file classes here: `FileReader`, `FileWriter`, and `PrintWriter`. These classes are part of the package `java.io`, so we must write

```
import java.io.*;
```

at the beginning of any program that does file I/O. **Character stream files** allow us to read and write data as characters, much as we have been doing with `System.in` and `System.out`. For example, we can prepare an input file and save it as text with an editor, read it with `FileReader`, output results to another file using `PrintWriter`, and view the output with the editor.

> **Character stream file**
> A file that is stored as a sequence of characters

Just like the data we enter from the keyboard, the data in character stream files are organized into lines. A line ends with a special character called an end-of-line (EOL) mark. When you examine a file with an editor, each line in the file appears as a line on the screen. The editor doesn't display the EOL mark. Rather, the EOL mark simply tells the editor when to go to the next line as it places the characters on the screen.

FileReader   In Chapter 2, we introduced the `Scanner` class as a way of reading data, and we saw how to instantiate it using `System.in`. Because `System.in` is a predefined object of class `InputStreamReader`, we can simply pass it as an argument to the `Scanner` constructor:

```
Scanner in = new Scanner(System.in);
```

`Scanner` also has a constructor that accepts an object of class `FileReader`, which represents a character stream file for input. Once we have constructed such a `Scanner`, we can use all of our familiar methods, such as `nextLine` and `nextInt`, to read from the file. Unlike with `System.in`, there are no predefined `FileReader` objects, so we must instantiate one with `new` before we call the constructor for `Scanner`. For example, we can write the following statements to construct a `FileReader` object representing a disk file called `inFile.dat`, and then instantiate a `Scanner` that uses it:

```
FileReader inFileReader = new FileReader("inFile.dat"); // Make a FileReader
                                                        // object
Scanner inFile = new Scanner(inFileReader);             // Instantiate the
                                                        // Scanner
```

Of course, we can use the following shortcut to accomplish the same thing in one statement, thereby avoiding the need for the variable `inFileReader`:

```
Scanner inFile = new Scanner(new FileReader("inData.dat"));
```

Once we've created this `Scanner`, we use it much like a `Scanner` for `System.in`. Here are some examples:

```
int someInt = inFile.nextInt();
double someDouble;
if (inFile.hasNextDouble())
  someDouble = inFile.nextDouble();
else
  someDouble = 0.0;
String someString = inFile.nextLine();
```

Keep in mind that the parameter for the `Scanner` constructor is a `FileReader` object. The parameter for the `FileReader` constructor is a string representing the name of a file on the disk. A file always has two names: the variable that you use to refer to it in your program (inFile) and the name under which the file is stored on the disk (inData.dat). These two names are bound together (associated) when the constructor is called—a step referred to as *opening* the file.

When your code uses inFile, the JVM knows that you are referring to file inData.dat on the disk. If inData.dat cannot be located on the disk, an IOException is thrown. Recall that two types of exceptions exist: checked and unchecked. IOException is a checked exception, which means that either it must be caught (which we see how to do in Chapter 7) or it must be thrown again by the method in which it occurs.

If a method doesn't explicitly catch an exception, Java automatically throws it again from that method. Thus we don't have to write any code at all to handle the exception! Nevertheless, to ensure that we didn't just forget to catch the exception, Java does require us to specify that the method may throw it.

To indicate that the method throws the exception, we add the clause throws IOException at the end of its heading. For example, if the method throwing the exception is main, then we write

```
public static void main(String args[]) throws IOException
```

The throws clause should be included in any method that instantiates a Scanner with a file.

Some Scanner methods are especially useful with files. These methods ask if there are more values in the file. For example,

```
inFile.hasNext()
```

returns true if inFile has another token (a number or string) in the file, and

```
inFile.hasNextLine()
```

returns true if there is another line in the file. We can always get more data from the keyboard; once the file pointer reaches EOF, however, we can't get any more data from a file. If we try to read when the file pointer is at EOF, an IOException is thrown. Thus we should use an *if* statement to test for more data before reading from a file.

Scanner also has a close method that breaks the connection between the variable and the disk file, and releases the file to the operating system so that another application can use it. You should always close a file as soon as you are done using it.

The close operation has another side effect: It returns the file pointer to the beginning of the file. Thus, if you want the application to again read the data from the file, starting over at the beginning, you can simply close it and then reopen it as follows:

```
inFile.close();
Scanner inFile = new Scanner(new FileReader("inData.dat"));
```

Now that we've seen how file input works, we turn to file output.

PrintWriter We use class `PrintWriter`, found in package `java.io`, to write to a file. Analogous to the way that the `Scanner` constructor takes a `FileReader` as its argument, the constructor for `PrintWriter` takes a `FileWriter` object as its parameter. Within the call to the `PrintWriter` constructor, we must therefore nest a call to the `FileWriter` constructor, which takes a file name given by a string argument. Here is an example:

```
PrintWriter outFile = new PrintWriter(new FileWriter("outFile.dat"));
```

Notice the similarity to the statement we use to create a `Scanner` for file input:

```
Scanner inFile = new Scanner(new FileReader("inFile.dat"));
```

Be sure that you understand the difference between these two operations, because it is a common mistake to get them mixed up. To instantiate an output file, we use `PrintWriter` and `FileWriter`. To instantiate an input file, we use `Scanner` and `FileReader`. Otherwise, the statements have the same form. Note that any method that instantiates a `PrintWriter` must also include the `throws IOException` clause in its heading.

The `FileWriter` constructor checks whether the file already exists. If the file doesn't exist, it creates a new empty file. If the file does exist, it deletes the old file before creating the new empty file. Then the file pointer is placed at the beginning of the empty file. Figure 6.5 shows the difference between instantiating an input file and an output file.

Obviously, you must call the constructor to open the file before you use any methods that output data to it. We didn't have to do this with `System.out`, because it is predefined by Java.

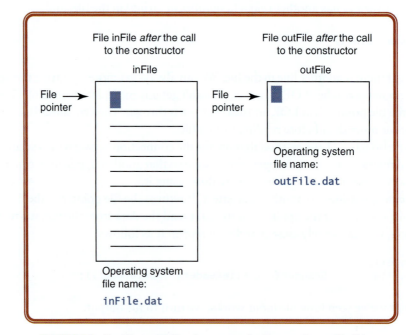

FIGURE 6.5 The Effects of Calling Constructors for Character Stream File Objects

What methods are supported by `PrintWriter`? The same ones that we've been using with `System.out`: `print` and `println`. As an example, here is a demo application that opens files for output and input, prints some messages on the output file, and then copies a line from the input file to the output file if the input file isn't empty. If the input file is empty, it prints an error message on the output file.

```java
import java.io.*;                           // Import file I/O classes
import java.util.Scanner;                   // Import Scanner class
public class FileIOExample
{
  public static void main(String args[]) throws IOException
  {
    String inString;
    // Open files for output and input, printing success messages on out
    PrintWriter out = new PrintWriter(new FileWriter("outFile.dat"));
    out.println("Successfully opened outFile.dat");
    Scanner in = new Scanner(new FileReader("inFile.dat"));
    out.println("Successfully opened inFile.dat");
    out.println();
    out.print("String from Scanner object: ");
    // Check whether inFile has a line to be input
    if (in.hasNextLine())
      inString = in.nextLine();             // If a line is available, read it
    else
      inString = "*** infile.dat is empty ***"; // Else substitute error message
    out.println(inString);                      // Print line or message on out
    // Close files
    in.close();
    out.close();
  }
}
```

Once a file is closed, it can again be assigned to a file object using `new`. For example, we can close a file that we have just written and open it for reading as follows:

```java
PrintWriter dataFile = new PrintWriter(new FileWriter("dataFile.dat"));
dataFile.println("Let's write a line of data on this file!");
dataFile.close();
// Now let's read the line back in and print it on System.out
dataFile = new Scanner(new FileReader("dataFile.dat"));
System.out.println(dataFile.nextLine());
```

6.3 : Looping and Files

`Scanner` has methods ideally suited for setting up event-controlled file-processing loops. Let's use `hasNext` and `nextInt` to write a loop that prints the integer values on a file associated with a `Scanner` called `inFile`. Recall that `hasNext` returns `true` if the `Scanner` has another token to be input.

```java
while (inFile.hasNext())                    // Checks if inFile has another int
  System.out.println(inFile.nextInt());     // Gets next int from inFile and
                                            //  displays it on System.out
```

If `hasNext` returns `true`, the loop body is executed. Method `nextInt` is applied to `inFile`, returning the next integer, which is printed. The *while* expression is then reevaluted. This process continues until there are no more data values on the file, at which time `hasNext` returns `false` and the statement following the loop body is executed.

■ EOF-Controlled Loops

Here is a demo application that uses an event-controlled loop to print all of the integers on a file:

```java
//*********************************************************
// Application ReadFile reads and prints all integer numbers
// from file "myDataFile.dat" using an event-controlled loop
//*********************************************************
import java.util.Scanner;
import java.io.*;
public class ReadFile
{
  public static void main(String args[]) throws IOException
  {
    Scanner in = new Scanner(new FileReader("myDataFile.dat"));
    int number;                              // Holds input value

    System.out.println("Numbers on file myDataFile.dat: ");
    while (in.hasNextInt())
    {
      number = in.nextInt();
      System.out.print(number + " ");
    }
    System.out.println();
    in.close();
  }
}
```

Output:

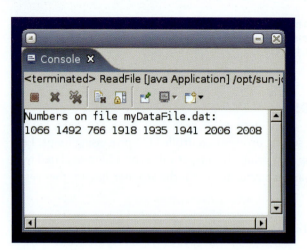

Loops that read until all data have been input are called *end-of-file (EOF) loops*. We can use **hasNextInt, hasNextFloat, hasNext,** and so forth to test for the end of the data, but technically they do not check for EOF. Recall that numeric reads do not consume (move the file pointer beyond) the separating blank or end-of-line mark. After the last numeric value is input, the separator is still waiting to be read before the pointer reaches EOF. Because most of the **hasNext** methods look ahead for the next token, they return **false** when there are no more data to read, even though the file pointer never reaches EOF. (For convenience, we still refer to them as EOF loops.)

For example, if we apply **nextInt** to the file shown below, the file pointer is left on the end-of-line mark (**<EOLN>**), as highlighted:

Contents of file in (file pointer is highlighted)

```
in.nextInt()              42<EOLN>
                          <EOF>
in.hasNextInt()
```

The subsequent call to **hasNextInt** returns **false** because there is no valid integer remaining to be input, even though the file pointer never reached EOF.

With a **Scanner**, we encounter EOF only when using **nextLine**. Recall that **nextLine** reads past the current end-of-line mark. After it inputs the last line on a file, it leaves the file pointer at EOF. If we then call one of the **hasNext** methods such as **hasNextInt**, it detects the EOF mark and returns **false**.

Contents of file in (file pointer is highlighted)

```
in.nextLine()             42<EOLN>
                          <EOF>
in.hasNextInt()
```

In most cases, this technicality doesn't matter. If you use **hasNextLine** to test for the end of the data after reading a numeric value, however, it will return **true** even though the last value has been input. That's because **hasNextLine** sees the trailing separator as representing a line that hasn't been completely input. Remember, you should use **hasNextLine** to test for the end of data only if you precede it with a call to **nextLine**.

Now we take a look at another form of event-controlled loop in which a special value on a file indicates the end of the data.

■ Sentinel-Controlled Loops

Suppose that you are working for a stockbroker and must write an application that copies stock prices from one file to another. The input file contains a series of numbers representing prices for different stocks, recorded every minute of the trading day. Your application will create a new file that has just the opening price of each stock. That is, you want the stock prices during the first minute. The input file is structured so that a negative number is inserted at the end of each minute. Your task is to copy the first part of the input file up to (but not including) the negative number, onto the output file. For example, if the input file is

```
283.45 166.07 451.85 98.06 110.44 -1 284.55 165.38 450.80 102.37 111.02 -1
```

then the output file would contain

```
283.45 166.07 451.85 98.06 110.44
```

This seems easy enough. Let's just write the loop in the obvious manner (we assume for now that we don't have to test for EOF, although we should do so in a real application):

```
while (price >= 0)                           // This doesn't work
{
  price = inFile.nextDouble();
  outFile.print(price + " ");
}
```

Do you see the problem here? The *while* expression tests whether `price` is nonnegative before a value has been read into `price`! We could initialize `price` to some nonnegative value to force entry into the loop. But then what happens if the first data value is negative? It is read and output to `outFile`. What we really want to do is get the first data value prior to entering the loop.

```
price = inFile.nextDouble();                 // This still doesn't work
while (price >= 0)
{
  price = inFile.nextDouble();
  outFile.print(price + " ");
}
```

Now we have a new problem. The first value is input, and then as soon as execution enters the loop, a second value is input, which replaces the first value. Thus the first value is never output to `outFile`. What we need to do is move the input statement to the end of the loop, after the first value has been output:

```
price = inFile.nextDouble();                 // Finally, this does work!
while (price >= 0)
{
  outFile.print(price + " ");
  price = inFile.nextDouble();
}
```

> **Priming read** An input operation preceding an event-controlled loop that gets an initial value to be tested as part of the termination condition of the loop

Once the first value has been output, the second value is input. Then the loop returns to the test and checks whether the new value is negative. If it is not, the body is executed again so that the value is output and another value is then input. This arrangement works correctly for all cases.

Reading before the loop to get an initial value is called a **priming read**. (The idea is similar to priming a pump by pouring a bucket of water into the mecha-

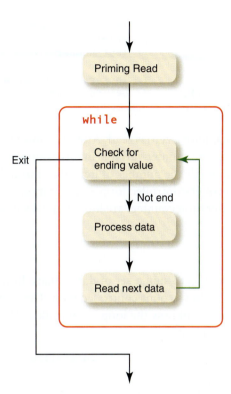

FIGURE 6.6 Operation of an Event-Controlled Loop with a Priming Read

nism before starting it.) Figure 6.6 diagrams the operation of a priming-read loop.

6.4 : Looping Subtasks

The loop body must perform a useful task for the loop to accomplish something. In this section, we look at two tasks—counting and summing—that often are used in both count-controlled and event-controlled loops.

■ Counting

A common task in a loop is to keep track of the number of times the loop has been executed. For example, the following code fragment reads and counts integer input values until it comes to a zero. (Both `number` and `count` are of type `int`.) The loop in the following example has a counter variable, but it is not a count-controlled loop because the variable is not used as a loop control variable. We highlight the parts of the loop that perform the counting operation.

```
count = 0;                          // Initialize counter before loop
number = inFile.nextInt();          // Priming read
while (number != 0)                 // Test number
{
  counter++;                        // Increment counter with each iteration
  number = inFile.nextInt());       // Get next number
}
```

Iteration counter   A counter variable that is incremented in each iteration of a loop

The loop continues until a zero is read. After it is finished, `count` contains the number of values read. The counter variable in this example is called an **iteration counter** because its value equals the number of iterations through the loop. The loop control variable of a count-controlled loop is an iteration counter. However, as you've just seen, not all iteration counters are loop-control variables.

■ Summing

Another common looping task is to sum a set of data values. In the following example, we show a summing operation within a count-controlled loop. The summing operation is always written the same way, regardless of how the loop is controlled. The parts of the loop that do the summing are highlighted in blue.

```
sum = 0;                            // Initialize sum before loop
count = 1;
while (count <= 10)
{
  number = inFile.nextInt();        // Input a value
  sum = sum + number;               // Add value to sum
  count++;
}
```

A priming read isn't necessary here because the loop condition doesn't depend on the input value. We initialize `sum` to 0 before the loop starts so that the first time the loop body executes, the statement

```
sum = sum + number;
```

adds the current value of `sum` to `number` to form the new value of `sum`. After the entire code fragment has executed, `sum` contains the total of the ten values read, `count` contains 11, and `number` contains the last value read.

Let's look at another example. This time, let's also check for the end of the data using method `hasNextInt`. We want to count and sum the first ten odd numbers in a data set. To do so, we need to test each number to see whether it is even or odd. (We can use the modulus operator to find out. If `number % 2` equals 1, `number` is odd; otherwise, it's even.) If the input value is even, we do nothing. If it is odd, we increment the counter and add the value to `sum`. We use a `boolean` flag variable to control the loop because this is not a normal count-controlled loop.

We again highlight the parts of the code that perform the counting (yellow) and summing (blue) tasks. We also highlight the parts that initialize and update the flag (green).

```
int count = 0;                      // Initialize event counter before loop
int sum = 0;                        // Initialize sum before loop
boolean notDone = true;             // Initialize loop control flag
while (notDone)
{
  if (dataFile.hasNextInt())        // If not end of data
  {
    number = dataFile.nextInt();    // Get an int
    if (number % 2 == 1)            // Is the int value odd?
    {
      count++;                      // Yes--increment counter
      sum = sum + number;           // Add value to sum
      notDone = (count < 10);       // Update loop control flag
    }
  }
  else                              // Hit EOF unexpectedly
  {
    System.out.println("End of data reached before ten odd values read.");
    notDone = false;                // Update loop control flag
  }
}
System.out.println("Sum contains " + sum);
```

We control the loop with the flag `notDone`, because the loop exits when either of two events occur: reading and processing ten odd values or reaching EOF.

In this example, no relationship exists between the value of the counter variable and the number of times that the loop is executed. Note that `count` is incremented only when an odd number is read; for this reason, it is called an **event counter**. We initialize an event counter to 0 and increment it only when a certain event occurs. The counter in the previous counting example was an iteration counter; it was initialized to 1 and incremented with each iteration of the loop.

> **Event counter** A variable that is incremented each time a particular event occurs

6.5 : How to Design Loops

It's one thing to understand how a loop works when you look at it and something else again to design a loop that solves a given problem. In this section, we consider how to design loops. We can divide the design process into two tasks: designing the flow of control and designing the processing that takes place in the loop. Each task consists of three parts: the task itself, initialization, and updating. It's also important to specify the state of the code when it exits the loop, because a loop that leaves variables and files in a mess is not well designed.

Here are seven points to consider in designing any loop:

1. What condition ends the loop?
2. How should the condition be initialized?
3. How should the condition be updated?
4. What is the process being repeated?
5. How should the process be initialized?
6. How should the process be updated?
7. What is the state of the code on exiting the loop?

We can use these questions as a checklist. The first three help us design the parts of the loop that control its execution. The next three help us design the processing within the loop. The last question reminds us to make sure that the loop exits in an appropriate manner.

■ Designing the Flow of Control

The most important step in loop design is deciding what should make the loop stop. If the termination condition isn't well thought out, infinite loops and other mistakes could potentially occur. Here is our first question:

- What condition ends the loop?

We can usually answer this question by closely examining the problem statement. For example:

Key Phrase in Problem Statement	Termination Condition
"Sum 365 temperatures"	The loop ends when a counter reaches 365 (count-controlled loop).
"Process all the data in the file"	The loop ends when EOF occurs (EOF-controlled loop).
"Process until 10 odd integers have been read"	The loop ends when 10 odd numbers have been input (event counter).

Now we need statements that make sure the loop starts correctly and statements that allow the loop to reach the termination condition. We ask the next two questions:

- How should the condition be initialized?
- How should the condition be updated?

The answers to these questions depend on the type of termination condition.

Count-Controlled Loops   For a count-controlled loop, we initialize the condition by giving an initial value to the loop control variable. For count-controlled loops in which the loop control variable is also an iteration counter, the initial value is usually 1.

We update the condition by increasing the value of the counter by 1 for each iteration. (Occasionally, you may come across a problem that requires a counter to count from some value down to a lower value. In this case, the initial value is the greater value, and the counter is decremented by 1 for each iteration.) For count-controlled loops that use an iteration counter, these are the answers to the two questions:

- Initialize the iteration counter to 1.
- Increment the iteration counter at the end of each iteration.

Here's an example with the counting operations highlighted:

```
count = 1;
while (count <= limit)
{
   // Do some processing that we don't show here
   count++;
}
```

If the loop is controlled by an event counter, the control variable usually is initialized to 0 and incremented each time the event occurs. In such a case, these are the answers to the two questions:

■ Initialize the event counter to 0.
■ Increment the event counter each time the event occurs.

Here's an example, highlighting the event counting:

```
count = 0;
while (count <= limit)
{
  // Do some processing that we don't show here
  if (result == 0)            // Test for an event, such as a value being zero
    count++;                  // Increment event counter if the event occurs
}
```

Event-Controlled Loops   In EOF loops, a priming read—if required—may be the only initialization necessary. It also may be necessary to open the file in preparation for reading (if it isn't already open). To update the condition, a new value is read either at the beginning (if using a method such as **hasNext**) or at the end (if using a sentinel and a priming read) of each iteration. For EOF loops, we answer our questions this way:

■ Open the file, and input a value before entering the loop if necessary.
■ Input a new value for processing.

Here's an example:

```
Scanner inFile = new Scanner(new FileReader("datafile.dat"));
while (inFile.hasNextInt())
{
  someInt = inFile.nextInt();
  // Do some processing of the input value that we don't show here
}
```

Updating the loop condition happens implicitly; the loop must read data or it won't reach EOF. Thus updating the loop condition means that the loop must keep reading data.

For other types of event-controlled loops, the event must be initialized outside the loop, tested in the *while* expression, and updated within the loop.

■ Initialize the event.
■ Update the event.

For example, the following loop advances the file pointer to the end of the first odd integer in the input file:

```
Scanner inFile = new Scanner(new FileReader("dataFile.dat"));
if (inFile.hasNextInt())
  someInt = inFile.nextInt();                      // Initialize the event
while (someInt % 2 == 0 && inFile.hasNextInt())
  someInt = inFile.nextInt();
// Loop exits when first odd value has been input or at EOF
```

■ Designing the Process Within the Loop

Once we've decided on the appropriate looping structure, we can fill in the details of the process. In designing this process, we must first decide what a single iteration should do. Assume for a moment that the process will execute only once. What tasks must it perform?

- What is the process being repeated?

To answer this question, we return to the problem statement. The definition of the problem may require the process to sum data values or to keep a count of data values that satisfy some test. For example:

"Count the number of integers in the file `howMany`.*"*

This statement tells us that the process to be repeated is a counting operation.

Here's another example:

"Read a stock price for each business day in a week and compute the average price."

In this case, part of the process involves reading a data value. We conclude from our knowledge of how an average is computed that the process also involves summing the data values.

In addition to counting and summing, another common loop process is reading data, performing a calculation, and writing out the result. Many other operations can also appear in looping processes.

After we've determined the operations to be performed if the process is executed only once, we can design the parts of the process that are necessary for it to be repeated correctly. We often have to add some steps to account for the fact that the loop executes more than once. This part of the design typically involves initializing certain variables before the loop begins and then reinitializing or updating them before each subsequent iteration.

- How should the process be initialized?
- How should the process be updated?

For example, if the process within a loop requires several different counts and sums to be performed, each must have its own statements to initialize variables, increment counters, or add values to sums. Just deal with each counting or summing operation by itself—that is, first write the initialization statement, and then write the incrementing or summing statement. After you've handled this task for one operation, go on to the next operation.

■ Designing the Loop Exit

When the termination condition occurs and the flow of control passes to the statement following the loop, the variables used in the loop still contain values. Also, if an input file has been used, the reading marker has been left at some position in the file. Or maybe an output file has new contents. If these variables or files are used later in the application, the loop must leave them in an appropriate state. For this reason, the final step in designing a loop is answering this question:

- What is the state of the code on exiting the loop?

Now we have to consider the consequences of our design and double-check its validity. Suppose we've used an event counter and later processing depends on the number of events. It's important to confirm (with an algorithm walkthrough) that the value left in the counter is the exact number of events—that it is not off by 1.

Look at this code segment:

```
lineCount = 1;                    // This code is incorrect
while (inFile.hasNextLine())
{
  lineCount++;
  someString = inFile.nextLine();
}
System.out.println("There are " + lineCount + " lines in the file.");
```

This loop reads lines from an input file and counts the number of lines in the file. However, when the loop terminates, `lineCount` equals the actual number of lines plus 1 because the loop initializes the event counter to 1 before any events take place. By determining the state of `lineCount` at loop exit, we've detected a flaw in the initialization: `lineCount` should be initialized to zero.

Designing correct loops depends as much on experience as it does on the application of design methodology. At this point, you may want to read through the Problem-Solving Case Study at the end of this chapter to see how the loop design process is applied to a real problem. The next section considers how to read and modify an application that contains a loop.

SOFTWARE MAINTENANCE CASE STUDY

Appending a Date at the End of Copying a File

Maintenance Task Application `ReadFile` (shown earlier in the chapter) copies integer values from a file to `System.out`. Unfortunately, the requirements for the application changed while we were writing it. (This kind of change often happens in real-world development projects and is known as *requirements creep*, because small changes seem to keep coming in a manner that perpetually delays completion.) The new requirements specify that a date should appear on the last line of the file to keep track of which version of the data is being processed. Application `ReadFile2` needs to be updated to print the date. Oh, and one more thing: The customer wants the application to print the number of integers on the file at the end of the output.

Existing Code The existing code is reprinted here.

```java
//*************************************************************
// Application ReadFile reads and prints all integer numbers
// from file myDataFile.dat using an event-controlled loop
//*************************************************************
import java.util.Scanner;
import java.io.*;
public class ReadFile
{
  public static void main(String args[]) throws IOException
  {
    Scanner in = new Scanner(new FileReader("myDataFile.dat"));
    int number;                          // Holds input value

    System.out.println("Numbers on file myDataFile.dat: ");
    while (in.hasNextInt())
    {
      number = in.nextInt();
      System.out.print(number + " ");
    }
    System.out.println();
    in.close();
  }
}
```

The structure of the application is simple: The `Scanner` is instantiated, a variable to hold an input value is declared, and a heading is written. The loop is an end-of-data event-controlled loop. Following the loop, an end-of-line is written and the file is closed.

Modifications Two modifications are necessary: read and print the date, which is the last item in the file, and print the number of integers in the file. The reading of the date must occur after the loop. The `hasNextInt` method looks ahead at the date, recognizes that it is not an integer, and returns `false`. Should the end-of-line be written before or after the date? When we go back to the customer for clarification, we are told that the date should start on a new line. Thus the processing of the date comes after the `println`. The following code fragment takes care of reading and printing the date:

```java
String date =  in.nextLine();
System.out.println("Date of file: " + date);
```

The second task is to insert an iteration counter within the count-controlled loop. We know how to do this: We initialize a counter to zero and increment it within the loop. Here is the revised application, with the changes highlighted.

SOFTWARE MAINTENANCE CASE STUDY, cont.

```java
//*************************************************************
// Application ReadFile2 reads and prints all integer numbers
// from file myDataFile.dat using an event-controlled loop,
// then prints the data from the last line of the file and a
// count of the values that were read
//*************************************************************
import java.util.Scanner;
import java.io.*;
public class ReadFile2
{
  public static void main(String args[]) throws IOException
  {
    Scanner in = new Scanner(new FileReader("myDataFile.dat"));
    int number;                          // Holds input value
    int counter = 0;                     // Iteration counter
    String date;                         // Holds date of file
    System.out.println("Numbers on file myDataFile.dat: ");
    while (in.hasNextInt())
    {
      number = in.nextInt();
      System.out.print(number + " ");
      counter++;
    }
    System.out.println();
    date = in.nextLine();
    System.out.println("Date of file: " + date);
    System.out.println("Number of values: " + counter);
    in.close();
  }
}
```

Output:

```
[ Console ]
<terminated> ReadFile2 [Java Application] /o|

Numbers on file myDataFile.dat:
1066 1492 766 1918 1935 1941 2006 2008
Date of file:
Number of values: 8
```

What happened to the date? We read it and printed it—why isn't it there? Well, actually it is there. We forgot that method `nextLine`, following a numeric read, returns the separator. We need to insert an extra call to `nextLine` to move the pointer past the separator to the start of the next line.

```
date = in.nextLine();    // Just advances past EOL. Doesn't actually get a date
date = in.nextLine();    // Now it reads the date from the last line
```

With this change, the output is correct.

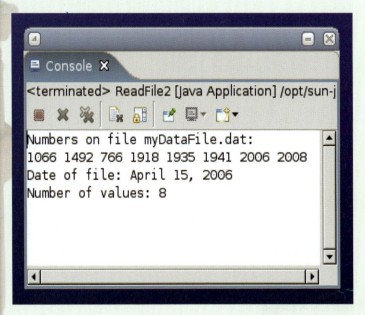

6.6 : Nested Loops

In Chapter 5, we described nested *if* statements. It's also possible to nest *while* statements. Both *while* and *if* statements contain statements and are themselves statements. So the body of a *while* statement or the branch of an *if* statement can contain other *while* and *if* statements. By nesting, we can create control structures that solve more complex problems.

Suppose we have a file with seven integer values per line and an unknown number of lines. We want to print the average of each line of values. The outer loop is an EOF-controlled loop that reads each line. If we use a `Scanner` for input, we can use `hasNextLine` to test for EOF. Within each iteration of this loop, we need to read seven `int` values. A count-controlled loop that runs from 1 to 7, reading values and summing them, will get the job done. Thus the EOF-controlled loop contains a second (count-controlled) loop within its body. We highlight this inner loop.

```
while (inFile.hasNextLine())          // Repeat until no more data
{
  loopCount = 1;                      // Initialize inner loop counter
  sum = 0;                            // Initialize sum for each iteration
  while (loopCount <= 7)
  {
    sum = sum + inFile.nextInt();     // Input and sum value
    count++;                          // Increment loop counter
  }
  System.out.println(average / 7.0);  // Print average
  separator = inFile.nextLine();      // Skip over the separator
}
```

The EOF-controlled outer loop continues until the last line of data has been read. The count-controlled inner loop processes individual lines of data. Note that the inner loop control variable and the sum must be initialized before each execution of the inner loop. The average is calculated and printed as the last task in the outer loop.

■ General Pattern

Let's examine the general pattern of a simple nested loop. Here the dots represent places where the processing and updating may take place in the outer loop:

```
Initialize outer loop
while ( Outer loop condition )
{

  ⋮

    Initialize inner loop
    while ( Inner loop condition )
    {
      Inner loop processing and update
    }

  ⋮

}
```

Notice that each loop has its own initialization, test, and update steps. An outer loop could potentially do no processing other than to execute the inner loop repeatedly. Conversely, the inner loop might be just a small part of the processing done by the outer loop; many statements could precede or follow the inner loop.

Let's look at another example. For nested count-controlled loops, the pattern looks like this (where `outCount` is the counter for the outer loop, `inCount` is the counter for the inner loop, and `limit1` and `limit2` are the number of times each loop should be executed). We highlight the inner loop to distinguish it from the outer loop.

```
outCount = 1;                   // Initialize outer loop counter
while (outCount <= limit1)
{
       .
       .
       .
   inCount = 1;                 // Initialize inner loop counter
   while (inCount <= limit2)
   {
       .
       .
       .
     inCount++;                 // Increment inner loop counter
   }
       .
       .
       .
   outCount++;                  // Increment outer loop counter
}
```

Here, both the inner and outer loops are count-controlled loops, but the pattern can be used with any combination of loops.

The following code fragment is another example of a count-controlled loop nested within an EOF-controlled loop. The outer loop inputs an integer value telling how many asterisks to print on each line of an output file. (We'll use the numbers to the right of the code to trace its execution below.) The inner loop is highlighted.

```
while (infile.hasNextInt())                 1
{
  starCount = infile.nextInt();             2
  loopCount = 1;                            3
  while (loopCount <= starCount)            4
  {
    outFile.print('*');                     5
    loopCount++;                            6
  }
  outFile.println();                        7
}
outFile.println("End");                     8
```

To see how this code works, let's execute it by hand with these data values (`<EOF>` denotes end-of-file):

```
2
1
<EOF>
```

We'll keep track of the variables `starCount` and `loopCount`, as well as the logical expressions. To do so, we've numbered each line (except lines containing only a brace). As we execute the code, we indicate the first execution of line 3 by 3.1, the second by 3.2, and so on. Each loop iteration is enclosed by a brace, and `true` and `false` are abbreviated as T and F (see Table 6.1). We refer to execution by hand, keeping track of relevant variable values, as *tracing* the code.

Here's the output on `outFile` from the code given the input used for our trace:

```
**
*
End
```

Because `starCount` and `loopCount` are variables, their values remain the same until they are explicitly changed, as indicated by the repeating values in Table 6.1. The values of the logical expressions `infile.hasNextInt()` and `loopCount <= starCount` exist only when the test is made. We indicate this fact with dashes in those columns at all other times.

Statement	starCount	loopCount	infile.hasNextInt	loopCount <= starCount	Output
1.1	—	—	T	—	—
2.1	2	—	—	—	—
3.1	2	1	—	—	—
4.1	2	1	—	T	—
5.1	2	1	—	—	*
6.1	2	2	—	—	—
4.2	2	2	—	T	—
5.2	2	2	—	—	*
6.2	2	3	—	—	—
4.3	2	3	—	F	—
7.1	2	3	—	—	\n
1.2	2	3	T	T	—
2.2	1	3	—	—	—
3.2	1	1	—	—	—
4.4	1	1	—	T	—
5.3	1	1	—	—	*
6.3	1	2	—	—	—
4.5	1	2	—	F	—
7.2	1	2	—	—	\n
1.3	1	2	F	—	—
8.1	1	2	—	—	End

TABLE 6.1   Code Trace

■ Designing Nested Loops

To design a nested loop, we begin with the outer loop. The process being repeated includes the nested loop as one of its steps. Because that step is complex, we defer designing it; we will come back to this task later. Then we can design the nested loop just as we would any other loop.

As an example, here's the design process for the outer loop in the preceding code segment:

1. What condition ends the loop? EOF is reached in the input as recorded by the `hasNext` method.
2. How should the condition be initialized? It is automatically initialized.
3. How should the condition be updated? The condition is automatically updated as part of reading data.
4. What is the process being repeated? Using the value of the current input integer, the code should print that many asterisks across one output line.
5. How should the process be initialized? No initialization is necessary (initialization of the inner loop will take care of this).
6. How should the process be updated? A sequence of asterisks is output and then a new-line character is output. There are no counter variables or sums to update.
7. What is the state of the code on exiting the loop? The file `inFile` is at EOF, `starCount` contains the last integer read from the input stream, and the rows of asterisks have been printed along with a concluding message.

From the answers to these questions, we can write this much of the algorithm:

```
Outer Loop

while NOT EOF
    Read int from dataFile into starCount
    Print starCount asterisks
    Output newline on outFile
Print "End"
```

After designing the outer loop, it's obvious that the step that prints a sequence of asterisks (highlighted in the algorithm) requires us to design an inner loop. So we repeat the checklist for the inner loop:

1. What condition ends the loop? An iteration counter exceeds the value of `starCount`.
2. How should the condition be initialized? The iteration counter should be initialized to 1.
3. How should the condition be updated? The iteration counter is incremented at the end of each iteration.
4. What is the process being repeated? The code should print a single asterisk on the output file.
5. How should the process be initialized? No initialization is needed.
6. How should the process be updated? No update is needed.
7. What is the state of the code on exiting the loop? A single row of asterisks has been printed, the writing marker is at the end of the current output line, and `loopCount` contains a value one greater than the current value of `starCount`.

Now we can write the full algorithm. The steps that resulted from this last design stage are highlighted.

```
Complete Algorithm
while NOT EOF
    Read int from dataFile into starCount
    Set loopCount = 1
    while loopCount <= starCount
       Print "*" on outFile
       Increment loopCount
    Output newline on outFile
Print "End"
```

Of course, nested loops themselves can contain nested loops (called doubly nested loops), which can contain nested loops (triply nested loops), and so on. You can use this design process to handle any number of levels of nesting. The trick is to defer details—that is, focus on the outermost loop first, and treat each new level of nested loop as a single step within the loop that contains it.

It's also possible for the process within a loop to include more than one loop. As an example, here's an algorithm that reads students' test scores and homework scores from a file (homework scores follow test scores on the file) and prints their average on another file. It contains two steps (highlighted below) that will each be implemented by a nested loop.

```
Two Loops Nested Within Another
while NOT EOF
    Input line with name
    Print name
    Read and average test scores until a negative score is input
    Print average test score
    Read and average homework scores until a negative score is input
    Print average homework score
    Output newline
```

The steps for reading and averaging the test and homework scores require us to design two separate loops. All of these loops are event-controlled.

This kind of complex control structure would be difficult to read if written out in full. It contains too many variables, conditions, and steps to remember at one time. When an algorithm becomes so complex, it is an indication that we failed to identify objects that would naturally hide some of this complexity via abstraction. In this case, we could create a new class with a method that gets the scores for a student and returns their average. We might call the new class `ScoreFileReader`. The individual loops would then be hidden in the class, and the application would look essentially like the algorithm shown above.

Sometimes the inner loop is hidden within a method call. As an example, here is our application that finds a square root, modified to input a value from the keyboard and calculate the square root until the value entered is 0. We know that the `NewMath.squareRoot` method contains a loop because we wrote it. But to the casual reader of this code, it isn't obvious that this application involves a nested loop

```java
//*********************************************************
// Application SqRoot takes the square root of an integer
//*********************************************************
import java.util.Scanner;
import java.io.*;
public class SqRoot
{
  public static void main(String[] args)
  {
    int number;                              // Number to process
    Scanner in = new Scanner(System.in);     // Instantiate Scanner
    // Prompt for and input a value
    System.out.println("Enter an integer, 0 stops the processing");
    number = in.nextInt();
    while (number != 0)
    {
      // Call the method and display the result
      System.out.println("Square root of " + number + " is " +
                        NewMath.squareRoot(number));
      // Prompt for and input a value
      System.out.println("Enter an integer, 0 stops the processing");
      number = in.nextInt();
    }
  }
}
```

Output:

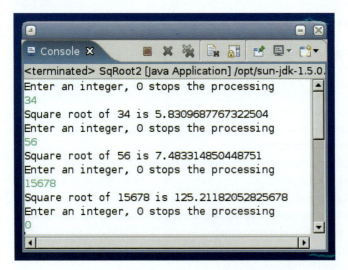

Lawn Care Company Billing

Problem A lawn care company has hired you to write a program to help with its monthly billing. The company works for each client several times a month. Customers are billed based on the number of hours spent on each job. Thus the monthly record for a client is a sheet with the client's name, address, and a series of times in hours and minutes. Your program should read this information from a file, print a bill for each client, and output the monthly total and average of the time and charges for the company, as well as the average time and total charge per client.

More specifically, the file contains a series of client records. Each client record begins with the client's name and address. The next line holds a number indicating how many jobs were done for the client that month. Following that number are a series of times, one on each line, made up of a pair of integer values (hours and minutes). The name is written in last, first, middle form, with blanks separating the three parts. An address consists of a street address, a city, a state, and a ZIP code. The street address is on one line, and the city, state, and ZIP code are on the next line, separated by blanks. Here's an example of a client record:

```
Llewelynn Francis Gene
518034 West Elm Street
Cypressville SD 58234
3
1 30
2 15
1 50
```

Discussion As usual, we begin by brainstorming the list of objects in this problem from the nouns in the statement. To save space, we arrange the list in columns.

Client	Bills	Record sheet	Name
Address	Street address	City	State
ZIP code	Time	Hours	Minutes
Input file	Totals and averages		

Filtering Bills are generated from the input data, so they are not really objects—but that realization reminds us that we do need an output file object on which to write them. The record sheet is represented by the data on the input file. We already have a `Name` class and a `Time` class that includes hours and minutes, but not an Address class. The street address, city, and state are parts of an address object. They can be represented by strings, and the

ZIP code can be stored as an integer. The totals and averages are values computed as part of processing all of the clients. Here is the filtered and annotated list:

Class	Implementation
Client	New class
Name	Class `Name`
Address	New class
Time	Class `Time`
Input File	`Scanner` and `FileReader`
Output File	`PrintWriter` and `FileWriter`

Representation and Initial Responsibilities In solving this problem, we need to define two new classes. Let's begin with `Address`, because we already know how it will be represented (three strings and an integer). What responsibilities does it need? A default constructor, of course. For this problem, all we really need in addition is to create an `Address` and retrieve it with `toString`. But, as we will see in later chapters, an `Address` is a more generally useful object, so let's take the time now to define a class that can be reused in other problems.

Our direct constructor should let us instantiate an address with three strings and an integer. It would also be convenient to provide a constructor that allows us to read the values from a `Scanner`. Let's also provide a set of responsibilities that get the individual fields. Thus the representation and responsibilities for an `Address` are as follows:

Representation		Responsibilities	
Street address	`String`	Default constructor	`getStreet`
City	`String`	Direct constructor	`getCity`
State	`String`	Constructor from Scanner	`getState`
ZIP code	`int`	toString	`getZipCode`

Now we turn to the `Client` class. Does it need a direct constructor? What is its representation? Obviously, it has a name and an address, but how do we represent the series of times and amounts? It looks like we need to explore a scenario to answer these questions.

Scenario Walkthrough Our scenario is to get two client records, print their bills, and then output the final statistics. The driver gets the input and output file names, and opens the two files. We then need to read a client's data.

Let's assume the `Client` class has a constructor that extracts its data from a `Scanner`. We then have the `Client` object output the bill and give us its total time and total charges. The totals are added to the totals for the month, and we increment the count of clients. Then the process repeats for the next client, until we reach the end of the file. (You make a note to yourself here for later: The driver contains an EOF-controlled loop.) Hence, we can see that the `Client` class has at least the following responsibilities:

Responsibilities
Default constructor
Constructor from Scanner
printBill
getTotalTime
getTotalCharges

We still need to walk through the scenario that takes place within the `Client` constructor to determine its representation. The constructor first reads the three parts of the name from the `Scanner` and then instantiates a `Name` field. Next, it passes the `Scanner` to the constructor for `Address` and creates an `Address` field. The next item to read is the number of jobs for the client. We can use that data with a count-controlled loop to read the series of times for the different jobs.

For each job, we multiply the time by the rate to get the charge. Where does the rate come from? It's a value that is common to all clients but is set seasonally by the company. Let's make it a class field that is set by a class method—that's a new responsibility to add to the list.

We output the hours and minutes to the bill, along with the computed charge. We add the time to a total time and add the charge to a total charge amount; these data will be retrieved later by `getTotalTime` and `getTotalCharges`.

But wait! We can't have the constructor output the times and charges to the bill. That's a separate responsibility! We need a way to save the job time and charge information for printing when the `printBill` responsibility is called.

Once we've added the time and charge to the totals, we no longer need to perform any calculation with them. Thus we could append them in string form to a string that represents that section of the bill. The time and charge for each job appear on a separate line of the bill, so we have to insert a newline character (`\n`) after each job. When `printBill` is called, it outputs the name and address, all of the times and charges, and the totals.

The representation for a `Client` object is as follows:

Representation

Name	`Name` class
Address	`Address` class
Billing	`String`
Total time	`Time` class
Total charges	`double`
Rate	`static double`

To the list of responsibilities, we must also add a class method to set the rate.

314

Implementation of Address Class We are now ready to implement our new classes. First we look at the **Address** class, which is straightforward for the most part. Only the constructor that takes a **Scanner** requires some thought. Here are the default constructor, the **get** methods, and **toString**:

```java
//*******************************************************************
// This class represents an address
//*******************************************************************
import java.util.Scanner;
import java.io.*;
public class Address
{
  String street;        // Street address
  String city;          // City part of the address
  String state;         // The state (two-letter abbreviation)
  int zipCode;

  public Address()      // Default constructor
  {
    street = "";
    city = "";
    state = "";
    zipCode = 0;
  }

  // Field get methods
  public String getStreet() {return street;}
  public String getCity() {return city;}
  public String getState() {return state;}
  public int getZipCode() {return zipCode;}

  public String toString()
  {
    return street + '\n' + city + ", " + state + "  " + zipCode;
  }
```

To instantiate an **Address** object from a **Scanner**, we put the entire first line into **street** using **nextLine**. Then we get the **city** and **state** using **next**. After that, we read the **zipCode** using **nextInt**. To force the **Scanner** to go past the EOL mark that ends the second line of the address, we call **nextLine** one last time.

```java
  public Address(Scanner in)              // Scanner constructor
  {
    street = in.nextLine();
    city = in.next();
    state = in.next();
    zipCode = in.nextInt();
    String separator = in.nextLine();  // Read past end-of-line mark
  }
```

Before we use it, we should test the `Address` class according to a well-designed test plan. We ask you to develop such a plan in the exercises.

Implementation of `Client` Class Next we look at `Client`. Let's begin by writing the declarations. It's a good idea to initialize class variables such as `rate`, just in case the user forgets to call the `setRate` method. Let's make the initial value 0, so it will be obvious if the user fails to give it a value. Here are the declarations:

```java
//*********************************************************************
// This class represents a lawncare client for billing purposes
//*********************************************************************
import java.util.Scanner;
import java.io.*;
public class Client
{
  Name name;                    // Client name
  Address address;              // Client address
  String billing;               // Time and charge string
  Time totalTime;               // Total time for this client
  double totalCharges;          // Total charges for this client
  static double rate = 0.0;     // Billing rate for all clients
```

Now we can write the default constructor, which initializes the instance fields to default values. As long as we're developing the obvious parts of the implementation, let's go ahead and write the `get` methods for `totalTime` and `totalCharges`. The method that sets the `rate` for all clients is equally simple.

```java
public Client()        // Default constructor
{
  name = new Name();
  address = new Address();
  billing = "";
  totalTime = new Time();
  totalCharges = 0.0;
}

// Field get methods
public Time getTotalTime() {return totalTime;}
public double getTotalCharges() {return totalCharges;}
// Field set method
public static void setRate(double newRate) {rate = newRate;}
```

With all of the usual parts taken care of, we can now focus on the two responsibilities that are unique to this class. Let's begin with the constructor that builds an object from a `Scanner`. Here is its heading:

```java
public Client(Scanner in)  // Scanner constructor
```

We use functional decomposition to design this algorithm. The top-level steps are

> **Client (Scanner)**
>
> Read name
> Read address
> Read number of jobs
> Read and process jobs to create billing string and totals

We can input the three parts of the name with **next**. To go past the EOL separator, however, we need to call **nextLine**. We input **address** with the **Address** constructor that takes a **Scanner** as an argument. Reading the number of jobs is done with **nextInt**.

The last step requires expansion. So let's look at our loop-design checklist:

1. What condition ends the loop? **count** is greater than the number of jobs.

2. How should the condition be initialized? **count** is set to 1.

3. How should the condition be updated? **count** is incremented.

4. What is the process being repeated? Input **hours** and **minutes**, and create a **Time** object. Compute **charge**. Keep a sum of **totalTime** and **totalCharges**. Append a line to the **billing** string. Go to the next line of input.

5. How should the process be initialized? Set totals to zero. Set **billing** string to empty.

6. How should the process be updated? Add **time** and **charge** values to the totals, and append **hours**, **minutes**, and **charge** to the **billing** string.

7. What is the state of the code on exiting the loop? The input file pointer is on the line that begins the next client or EOF. The totals contain the proper sums of **time** and **charge** values for the client. The **billing** string is ready for output. **count** is equal to the number of jobs plus 1.

The loop body inputs the **hours** and **minutes**, and then instantiates a **Time** object. We use **getTime** to get the **time** as a *double* value; however, it is in seconds, and we bill by hours. We therefore divide the time by 3600 before multiplying by **rate** to get the **charge**. Here is the algorithm:

> **Read and process jobs to create billing string and totals**
>
> Set count to 1
> Set billing to ""
> Set totalTime to 0.0
> Set totalCharges to 0.0
> while count <= number of jobs
>   Read hours and minutes with nextInt
>   Instantiate time with hours and minutes
>   Set charge to time/3600.0 * rate
>   Set billing to billing + hours + ':' + minutes + '$' + charge + newline
>   Set totalTime to totalTime plus time
>   Set totalCharges to totalCharges plus charges
>   Increment count
> Go to next line

We have now refined the algorithm to the point that each step can be directly translated into Java. Here is the implementation of this constructor:

```java
public Client(Scanner in) throws IOException   // Scanner constructor
{
  Time time;                                   // Declare local variables
  int hours;
  int minutes;
  double charge;

  String last = in.next();                     // Read name
  String first = in.next();
  String middle = in.next();
  name = new Name(first, last, middle);
  String separator = in.nextLine();
  address = new Address(in);                    // Read address
  int numberOfJobs = in.nextInt();              // Loop termination value

  // Read and process jobs to create billing string and totals
  int count = 1;                                // Initialize loop
  billing = "";
  totalTime = new Time();
  totalCharges = 0.0;
  while (count <= numberOfJobs)
  {
    hours = in.nextInt();                       // Read time
    minutes = in.nextInt();
    time = new Time(hours, minutes, 0);
    charge = time.getTime()/3600.0 * rate;      // Compute charge
    // Add time and charge to billing string
    billing = billing + "   " + hours + ":" + minutes + "      $" + charge + '\n';
    totalTime = totalTime.plus(time);           // Update totals
    totalCharges = totalCharges + charge;
    count++;                                    // Increment loop control variable
  }
  separator = in.nextLine();
}
```

The one remaining responsibility is to print the bill. All we need to do is output the name, address, billing string, and totals to the file. A heading for the time and charge columns would be a nice touch. The method can be written as follows:

```java
public void printBill(PrintWriter out)
{
  out.println(name);
  out.println(address);
  out.println();
  out.println("Job Time    Charge");
  out.println(billing);
  out.println("Total time: " + totalTime.getHours() + ":" +
              totalTime.getMinutes());
  out.println("Total charges: $" + totalCharges);
  out.println();
}
```

We leave the testing of the `Client` class as an exercise for you. Be certain that you read the Testing section that follows the case study to see how we go about testing methods that contain loops.

Implementation of the Driver Having completed the implementation of the `Address` and `Client` classes, we are ready to design the driver. From our scenario, we know that the algorithm has an EOF-controlled loop. Once again we use our checklist:

1. What condition ends the loop? `hasNextLine` returns `false`.
2. How should the condition be initialized? `inFile` is opened for a given file name.
3. How should the condition be updated? The file pointer has advanced to the following line.
4. What is the process being repeated? Read a client, print the bill, sum the monthly totals for time and charges, and keep a count of clients for averaging.
5. How should the process be initialized? Open the output file. Set the hourly rate. Set the monthly totals to zero. Set the client count to zero.
6. How should the process be updated? Add `totalTime` and `totalCharges` values to the monthly totals. Increment the client count.
7. What is the state of the code on exiting the loop? The input file pointer is at EOF. The monthly totals contain the proper sums of `totalTime` and `totalCharges` for all clients. The client count equals the number of clients processed. All of the bills have been printed.

In addition to carrying out the main loop, the driver must finish up by computing the averages and output them with the totals. And let's not forget to close the files! The algorithm consists of the following steps:

Lawncare Billing

Initialize monthly time, monthly charges, and client count
Get input file name and instantiate input `Scanner`
Get output file name and instantiate `PrintWriter`
Get the hourly rate and set it for all clients
while hasNextLine
    Read client
    Print client bill
    Add total time to monthly time
    Add total charges to monthly charges
    Increment client count
Output monthly time and monthly time / client count
Output monthly charges and monthly charges / client count
Close files

From the preceding algorithm, we can translate each line into one or two Java statements as shown here:

```java
//**********************************************************************
// Application LawncareBilling reads client job records from a file
// and prints bills on another file. At the end, totals and averages are
// output on System.out
//**********************************************************************
import java.util.Scanner;
import java.io.*;
public class LawncareBilling
{
  public static void main(String[] args) throws IOException
  {
    // Declare and initialize variables
    String inputFileName;
    String outputFileName;
    Scanner in = new Scanner(System.in);
    Client client;
    int clientCount = 0;
    Time monthlyTime = new Time();
    double monthlyCharges = 0.0;
    // Get input file name and instantiate input Scanner
    System.out.print("Enter input file name: ");
    inputFileName = in.nextLine();
    Scanner inFile = new Scanner(new FileReader(inputFileName));
    // Get output file name and instantiate PrintWriter
    System.out.print("Enter output file name: ");
    outputFileName = in.nextLine();
    PrintWriter outFile = new PrintWriter(new FileWriter(outputFileName));
    // Ask user for hourly rate
    System.out.print("Enter hourly rate: ");
    Client.setRate(in.nextDouble());
    while (inFile.hasNextLine())
    {
      client = new Client(inFile);
      client.printBill(outFile);
      monthlyTime = monthlyTime.plus(client.getTotalTime());
      monthlyCharges = monthlyCharges + client.getTotalCharges();
      clientCount++;
    }
    System.out.println("Total time for month:      " + monthlyTime.getHours() +
      ":" + monthlyTime.getMinutes());
    Time avgTime = new Time(monthlyTime.getTime()/(double)clientCount);
    System.out.println("Average time for month:    " + avgTime.getHours() +
      ":" + avgTime.getMinutes());
    System.out.println("Total charges for month:  $" + monthlyCharges);
    System.out.println("Average charge for month: $" +
      monthlyCharges/(double)clientCount);
    inFile.close();
    outFile.close();
  }
}
```

Testing In an application involving loops, our testing should check that each loop works properly with no iterations, one iteration, and multiple iterations. With such a test plan, we would discover that the application crashes with a `NoSuchElement-Exception` when the input file is empty, as a result of trying to input a client name when there are no tokens to be read. In the next section, we see how to design test plans for looping code, and then we develop a test plan for the `LawncareBilling` application.

6.7 : Testing and Debugging

■ Loop-Testing Strategy

Even if a loop has been properly designed, it is still important to test it, because there is always the chance of an error creeping in during the implementation phase. Recall that a loop has seven parts (corresponding to the seven questions in our checklist). Although all seven may not be distinct in every loop, the checklist reminds us that some loop operations serve multiple purposes, each of which should be tested. For example, the incrementing statement in a count-controlled loop may update both the process and the ending condition. It's important to verify that it performs both actions properly.

Consider what the acceptable ranges of variables are and what sorts of I/O operations you expect to see in the loop. Try to devise data sets that could cause the variables to go out of range or leave the files in unexpected states.

It's also good practice to test a loop for four special cases:

1. When the loop is skipped entirely
2. When the loop body executes just once
3. When the loop executes some normal number of times
4. When the loop fails to exit

Statements following a loop often depend on its processing. If a loop can be skipped, those statements may not execute correctly. By executing a single iteration of a loop, we see whether the body performs correctly in the absence of the effects of previous iterations. Obviously, it's important to test a loop under normal conditions, with a variety of inputs. If possible, you should test it with real data in addition to made-up data. Check that count-controlled loops execute exactly the right number of times. Finally, if there is any chance that a loop might never exit, your test data should try to make that happen.

Testing an application can be as challenging as writing it. To test an application, you need to step back, take a fresh look at what you've written, and then attack it in every way possible to make it fail. This isn't always easy to do, but it's necessary to make your applications be reliable. (A reliable application works consistently and without errors regardless of whether the input data is valid or invalid.)

■ Test Plans Involving Loops

Now let's look at some test cases that are specific to the types of loops that we've examined in this chapter.

Count-Controlled Loops   For a count-controlled loop, you should include a test case that specifies the output for all the iterations. It may help to add an extra column to the test plan that lists the iteration number. If the loop reads data and outputs a result, then each input value should produce a different output to make it easier to spot errors. For example, in a loop that is supposed to read and print 100 data values, it is easier to tell that the loop executes the correct number of iterations when the values are 1, 2, 3, . . . , 100 than if they are all the same.

If the application inputs the iteration count for the loop, you need to test the cases in which the count is invalid. For example, when a negative number is input, the application should output an error message and skip the loop. You should also test various valid cases. When a count of 0 is input, the loop should be skipped; when a count of 1 is input, the loop should execute once; and when some typical number of iterations is input, the loop should execute the specified number of times.

Event-Controlled Loops   For an event-controlled loop, you should test the situation in which the event occurs before the loop, in the first iteration, and in a typical number of iterations. For example, if the event is that EOF occurs, then try an empty file, a file containing one data set, and another file containing several data sets. If you are reading from test files, you should attach copies of the files to the test plan and identify each so that the plan can refer to them. It also helps to identify where each iteration begins in the Input and Expected Result columns of the test plan.

Let's look at how we would test the `LawncareBilling` application. We assume that the classes have already been tested. Now we focus on testing the EOF-controlled loop in `main`. In a full test plan, we would also test the code outside the loop to see what happens when an invalid file name is entered, when the number of clients is zero, and so on.

With an EOF-controlled loop, we need to test the case when there is no data on the file, one set of data values on the file, and several sets of data values on the file. Here is a plan for the loop in question. Notice that, because it is a test plan for `main`, we do not include a column with the method name, as in class testing.

Number	Input	Expected Result
1	Empty file	Throws **NoSuchElementException**
2	File with one client record	Correct bill; monthly total time and charges equal the totals for the one bill
3	File with multiple client records as below	Correct bills; total time for month is 23:20, Hourly rate of $35; average time is 5:50, total charges are $816.67, and average charge is $204.17

In the exercises, we ask you to create test files for the first two cases and run the tests. The following test data was prepared for case number 3, on file **July.txt**. To save space, we list it in three columns.

```
Marengoni Christina        8 45                      Davis Allan James
Louise                     Castor Julia Maude        223 Red Wing Terrace
25 Pomegranate Loop        18472 East Main Street    Altamont WY 67606
Egremont WY 67624          Egremont WY 67624         5
0                          4                         1 45
Soucy Steven Carl          1 30                      2 0
12 Wildblossom Court       1 30                      0 30
Englebrook WY 67628        1 30                      1 30
1                          1 30                      2 50
```

Given the following session with the user:

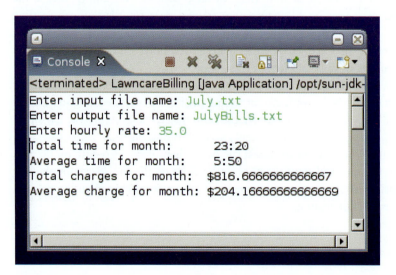

```
<terminated> LawncareBilling [Java Application] /opt/sun-jdk-
Enter input file name: July.txt
Enter output file name: JulyBills.txt
Enter hourly rate: 35.0
Total time for month:       23:20
Average time for month:     5:50
Total charges for month:  $816.6666666666667
Average charge for month: $204.16666666666669
```

The following bills were output on file **JulyBills.txt** (shown here in two columns to save space):

```
Marengoni, Christina Louise
25 Pomegranate Loop
Egremont, WY  67624

Job Time    Charge

Total time: 0:0
Total charges: $0.0

Soucy, Steven, Carl
12 Wildblossom Court
Englebrook, WY  67628

Job Time    Charge
  8:45      $306.25

Total time: 8:45
Total charges: $306.25

Castor, Julia, Maude
18472 East Main Street
Egremont, WY  67624
```

```
Job Time    Charge
  1:30      $52.5
  1:30      $52.5
  1:30      $52.5
  1:30      $52.5

Total time: 6:0
Total charges: $210.0

Davis, Allan, James
223 Red Wing Terrace
Altamont, WY  67606

Job Time    Charge
  1:45      $61.25
  2:0       $70.0
  0:30      $17.5
  1:30      $52.5
  2:50      $99.16666666666667

Total time: 8:35
Total charges: $300.4166666666667
```

The last case produces bills with amounts that include fractions of cents. The Case Study Follow-up Exercises ask you to fix this problem.

Testing and Debugging Hints

1. Plan your test data carefully to test all sections of an application.

2. Beware of infinite loops, where the expression in the *while* statement never becomes **false**. The symptom: The application doesn't stop.

3. If you have created an infinite loop, check your logic and the syntax of your loops. Be sure no semicolon follows immediately after the right parenthesis of the *while* condition:

```
while (Expression);        // Wrong
   Statement
```

This semicolon causes an infinite loop in most cases; the compiler thinks that the loop body is the *null* statement. In a count-controlled loop, make sure the loop control variable is incremented within the loop. In a flag-controlled loop, make sure the flag eventually changes.

4. Check the loop termination condition carefully, and verify that something in the loop causes it to be met. Watch closely for values that cause one iteration too many or too few (the "off-by-one" syndrome).

5. Write out the consistent, predictable part of a loop's behavior in each iteration. Look for patterns that it establishes. Are they just what you want? Perform an algorithm walkthrough to verify that all of the appropriate conditions occur in the right places.

6. Trace the execution of the loop by hand with a code walkthrough. Simulate the first few passes and the last few passes carefully to see how the loop really behaves.

7. Use a debugger if your system provides this kind of application. A debugger runs your application in "slow motion," allowing you to execute one instruction at a time and to examine the contents of variables as they change. If you haven't already done so, find out whether a debugger is available on your system.

8. If all else fails, use debug output statements—output statements inserted into an application to help debug it. They output a message to a separate file that indicates the flow of execution or reports the values of variables.

     For example, if you want to know the value of variable `beta` at a certain point in an application, you could insert this statement:

```
logFile.println("beta = " + beta);
```

     If this output statement appears in a loop, as many values of `beta` will appear on `logFile` as there are loop iterations. Later, you can remove the statements or just precede them with `//` so that they'll be treated as comments. (This practice is referred to as commenting out a piece of code.) You can remove the slashes if you need to use the statements again.

9. An ounce of prevention is worth a pound of debugging. Use the checklist questions, and design your loop correctly at the outset. It may seem like extra work, but it pays off in the long run.

10. For each file that a class or an application uses, check that all five required steps are performed: import the necessary packages (`java.io.*` and `java.util.Scanner`), declare a variable of the given file class, instantiate the file object, use the methods associated with the file object to perform input or output operations, and close the file when you are done.

11. Remember that the constructor for `Scanner` (with files) takes a `FileReader` object, instantiated with the name of the file on disk.

12. Remember that the constructor for `PrintWriter` takes a `FileWriter` object, instantiated with the name of the file on disk.

13. If you use file I/O, remember to include the **throws** `IOException` clause if needed.

14. All files have two names: the name you call the file in the code and the name of the file on disk. These may be the same or different; it makes no difference.

Graphical User Interfaces

showConfirmDialog

Thus far we have been looking at a style of dialog box that just shows a message. We can also get input values from a dialog, however. In this chapter we look at a type of dialog box that asks a question to be answered by clicking one of a small set of buttons. The following statement creates this type of box:

```
int reply = JOptionPane.showConfirmDialog(null, "Time to Quit?");
```

As before, the first argument of `null` specifies that the box should appear centered on the screen, rather than within another window. The string `"Time to Quit?"` is displayed over a set of buttons labeled Yes, No, and Cancel.

When the user clicks one of the buttons, the `showConfirmDialog` method returns the value associated with that button. This version of the method defaults to these three buttons, although we will later see how to create a dialog with different buttons. `JOptionPane` provides five kinds of buttons and a set of named, `static int` constants that we can use to refer to them. Here are the names of the constants:

```
JOptionPane.YES_OPTION
JOptionPane.NO_OPTION
JOptionPane.CANCEL_OPTION
JOptionPane.OK_OPTION
JOptionPane.CLOSED_OPTION
```

These are also the values returned by the `showConfirmDialog` method to indicate the button that was pressed by the user. By comparing the return value with one of these values, we can control a loop as shown in the following code segment:

```
int keepGoing = JOptionPane.YES_OPTION;
while (keepGoing == JOptionPane.YES_OPTION)
{
  . . .
  keepGoing = JOptionPane.showConfirmDialog(null, "Keep going?");
}
```

A variation of this method allows you to name the dialog and choose a different arrangement of the built-in buttons. The first two parameters are the same, the third is a string used as the label for the dialog, and the fourth is `optionType`, which is defined as one of the following named constants:

```
JOptionPane.DEFAULT_OPTION
JOptionPane.YES_NO_OPTION
JOptionPane.YES_NO_CANCEL_OPTION
JOptionPane.OK_CANCEL_OPTION
```

Here is an example of this variation:

```
int reply = JOptionPane.showConfirmDialog(null,
  "Time to Quit?",                        // Prompt displayed in box
  "My Confirm Pane",                      // Label at top of box
  JOptionPane.OK_CANCEL_OPTION);          // Option type for OK and
                                          // Cancel buttons
```

As you can see, the dialog displays only OK and Cancel buttons, so these are the only two constants that the dialog may return. The `DEFAULT_OPTION` is the same as `YES_NO_CANCEL_OPTION`. Using the `YES_NO_OPTION` constant causes a dialog to be displayed with just the Yes and No buttons.

The `showConfirmDialog` method is a handy way to control an interactive input loop. Unlike reading a string and comparing it to `"Yes"` or `"No"` to control the loop, we avoid the potential problem of having the user type something other than one of the acceptable inputs. Button input constrains the user to entering valid data, which simplifies our handling of the user's reply. In Chapter 7, we see how to use dialog boxes to input arbitrary data values.

As an example of using `showConfirmDialog`, here we reimplement the driver for the square root application that we saw earlier. Instead of using a value of zero to terminate the input of values, the application now displays a dialog that asks if the user wants to enter another number. The response is compared to `YES_OPTION`, and the **boolean** result is used as the loop control flag.

```java
//**********************************************************
// Application GUISqRoot takes the square root of an integer
//**********************************************************
import java.util.Scanner;
import javax.swing.*;
public class GUISqRoot
{
  public static void main(String[] args)
  {
    int number;                           // Number to process
    Scanner in = new Scanner(System.in);  // Instantiate Scanner
    boolean more = true;                  // Loop control flag
    while (more)
    {
      System.out.print("Enter an integer: ");
      number = in.nextInt();
      // Call the method and display the result
      System.out.println("Square root of " + number + " is "+
                         NewMath.squareRoot(number));
      // Display dialog and compare result to YES_OPTION
      more = JOptionPane.YES_OPTION ==
               JOptionPane.showConfirmDialog(null,
               "Would you like to enter another number?", "Square Root",
               JOptionPane.YES_NO_OPTION);
    }
  }
}
```

After asking for a number and displaying the result on `System.out`, the application displays the following dialog:

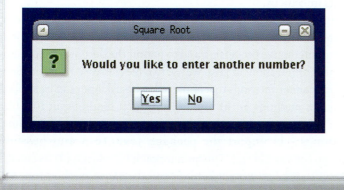

Summary

The *while* statement is a looping construct that allows the application to repeat a statement as long as the value of an expression remains true. When the value of the expression becomes false, the statement is skipped, and execution continues with the first statement following the loop.

With the *while* statement, you can construct several types of loops that are used in many different situations. These types of loops are classified into two categories: count-controlled loops and event-controlled loops.

In a count-controlled loop, the loop body is repeated a specified number of times. You initialize a counter variable immediately before the *while* statement. This loop control variable is then tested against the limit in the *while* expression. The last statement in the loop body increments the control variable.

Event-controlled loops continue executing until something inside the body signals that the looping process should stop. Event-controlled loops include those that test for end-of-file or a change in a variable used within the *while* expression.

Counting is a looping operation that keeps track of how many times a loop is repeated or how many times some event occurs. This count can be used in computations or to control the loop. A counter is a variable that is used for counting. It may be the loop control variable in a count-controlled loop, an iteration counter in a counting loop, or an event counter that counts the number of times a particular condition occurs in a loop.

Summing is a looping operation that keeps a running total of certain values. It resembles counting in that the variable that holds the sum is initialized outside the loop. The summing operation, however, adds up unknown values; the counting operation adds a constant to the counter (or decrements it by a constant) each time.

When you design a loop, you must consider seven points: how the termination condition is initialized, tested, and updated; how the process in the loop is initialized, performed, and updated; and what the state of the code is upon loop exit. By answering the checklist questions, you can bring each of these points into focus.

To design a nested loop structure, begin with the outermost loop. When you reach the point where the inner loop must appear, make it a separate module and come back to its design later.

Data files are often used for noninteractive processing and to permit the output from one application to be used as input to another application. In Java, we use two file classes to read text data: `Scanner` and `FileReader`. All of the `Scanner` methods that apply to keyboard input can be applied to a file. Class `PrintWriter` provides methods `print` and `println` that send output to a file. `PrintWriter` is instantiated with a `FileWriter` object that has been instantiated with a file name.

To use files, we do five things: (1) import the package `java.io.*` and possibly `java.util.Scanner`; (2) declare the file variables; (3) instantiate each file object; (4) use methods associated with each file object to read or write it; and (5) call the `close` method for each file. When using files, we must forward exceptions to the JVM by adding a `throws IOException` clause to the heading of any method that performs file I/O.

LEARNING / Portfolio

Quick Check

1. Write the first line of a *while* statement that loops until the value of the `boolean` variable **done** becomes `true`. (pp. 279–281)

2. What are the four parts of a count-controlled loop? (pp. 281–283)

3. Should you use a priming read with an EOF-controlled loop that is reading data from a `Scanner`? (pp. 292–293)

4. What is the difference between a counting operation in a loop and a summing operation in a loop? (pp. 295–297)

5. What is the difference between a loop control variable and an event counter? (pp. 295–297)

6. What kind of loop would you use in an application that reads the closing price of a stock for each day of the week? (pp. 281–283)

7. How would you extend the loop in Question 6 to make it read prices for 52 weeks? (pp. 305–307)

8. Describe the data sets you would use to test an EOF-controlled loop that averages test scores. (pp. 321–323)

9. If an application will have input consisting of 100 integer numbers, is interactive input appropriate? (pp. 286–287)

10. What does a constructor for an input file do? (pp. 287–289)

11. What does the following series of statements write on the `PrintWriter` file `fileOut`? (pp. 290–291)

```
fileOut.print('W');
fileOut.print(88);
fileOut.print(" What comes next?");
```

12. Write a statement that reads in a line and stores it into a string called **sentence**, using a `Scanner` called `in` (pp. 288–289)

13. Write a statement that reads in an integer value, using a `Scanner` called `inFile`. (pp. 288–289)

14. Write an expression that tests whether there is another integer in the `Scanner inFile`. (pp. 291–293)

Answers

1. `while(!done)` 2. The process being repeated, plus initializing, testing, and incrementing the loop control variable 3. No. 4. A counting operation increments by a fixed value with each iteration of the loop; a summing operation adds unknown values to the total. 5. A loop control variable controls the loop; an event counter simply counts certain events during execution of the loop. 6. Because there are five days in a business week, you would use a count-controlled loop that runs from 1 to 5. 7. Nest the original loop inside a count-controlled loop that runs from 1 to 52. 8. Normal data, data with erroneous values such as negative test scores, a set with a single input value, and an empty file. 9. No. File input is more appropriate for applications that input large amounts of data. 10. The constructor associates the name of the disk file with the file variable used in the code, and places the file pointer at the first piece of data in the file. 11. `W88  What comes next?` 12. `sentence = in.nextLine();` 13. `number = inFile.nextInt();` 14. `inFile.hasNextInt()`

Exam Preparation Exercises

1. Explain the difference between a loop and a branch.

2. What does the following loop print out? (`number` is of type `int`.)

```
number = 1;
while (number < 11)
{
  number++;
  out.println(number);
}
```

3. By rearranging the order of the statements (don't change the way they are written), make the loop in Exercise 2 print the numbers from 1 through 10.

4. When the following code is executed, how many iterations of the loop are performed?

```
number = 2;
done = false;
while (!done)
{
  number = number * 2;
  if (number > 64)
    done = true;
}
```

5. What is the output of the following nested loop structure?

```
i = 4;
while (i >= 1)
{
  j = 2;
  while (j >= 1)
  {
    out.print(j + " ");
    j--;
  }
  out.println(i);
  i--;
}
```

6. The following code segment is supposed to write out the even numbers between 1 and 15 (n is an `int` variable.) It has two flaws in it.

```
n = 2;
while (n != 15)
```

```
{
    n = n + 2;
    out.print(n + " ");
}
```

a. What is the output of the code as written?

b. Correct the code so that it works as intended.

7. The following code segment is supposed to copy one line from the file `inFile` to the file `outFile`. (A call to `aString.charAt(i)` returns the character at the ith position of `aString`.)

```
inLine = inFile.readLine();
count = 1;
while (count < inLine.length())
{
    outFile.print(inLine.charAt(count));
    count++;
}
outFile.println();
```

a. What is the output if the input line consists of the characters ABCDE?

b. Rewrite the code so that it works properly.

8. Does the following code segment need any priming reads? If not, explain why. If so, add the input statement(s) in the proper place. (`letter` is of type `char`.) See Exercise 7 for the definition of `charAt`.

```
while (!datum.equals("endofdata"))
{
    letter = datum.charAt(0);
    count = 0;
    while (count < datum.length())
    {
        outFile.print(letter);
        count++;
        letter = datum.charAt(count);
    }
    outFile.println();
    datum = inFile.next();
    outFile.println("Another token read . . . ");
}
```

9. Consider the following code segment:

```
sum = 0;
i = 1;
limit = 8;
```

```
finished = false;
while (i <= limit && !finished)
{
  number = dataFile.nextInt();
  if (number > 0)
    sum = sum + number;
  else if (number == 0)
    finished = true;
  i++;
}
out.print("End of test. " + sum + " " + number);
```

and these data values:

```
5  6  -3  7  -4  0  5  8  9
```

  a. What are the contents of `sum` and `number` after exit from the loop?

  b. Does the data fully test the code? Explain your answer.

10. What is the output of the following code segment? (All variables are of type `int`.)

```
i = 1;
while (i <= 5)
{
  sum = 0;
  j = 1;
  while (j <= i)
  {
    sum = sum + j;
    j++;
  }
  System.out.print(sum + " ");
  i++;
}
```

11. The physical order of the statements in an application is the order in which the statements are _____ (written, executed).

12. The logical order of the statements in an application is the order in which the statements are _____ (written, executed).

13. **a.** When do we need to use a priming read?

  b. Distinguish between a count-controlled loop and an event-controlled loop.

  c. What happens if you forget to increment the loop control variable in a count-controlled loop?

  d. What happens if you forget to change the event within the body of an event-controlled loop?

14. Distinguish between an iteration counter and an event counter.

15. What does the following code fragment do? (Look carefully!)

```
sum = 0;
j = 1;
while (j <= 10);
{
    sum = sum + j;
    j++;
}
System.out.print(sum + " ");
```

16. What are the five steps in using file input?

17. What is the meaning of the argument to the constructor for file types `FileReader` and `FileWriter`?

18. Where should the file declarations and the calls to the appropriate constructors be placed in an application? Why?

19. What does the following statement do? (`moreData` is a `boolean` variable and `inFile` is a `Scanner`.)

```
moreData = inFile.hasNextLine();
```

20. What does the `nextDouble` method for the class `Scanner` return?

21. What value does the `hasNext` method return at end-of-file?

22. What does the `next` method for class `Scanner` return?

Programming Warm-Up Exercises

1. Write an expression that checks whether a `Scanner` object `in` contains more data.

2. Write an application segment that sets a `boolean` variable `dangerous` to `true` and stops reading data if `pressure` (a `float` variable being read in) exceeds 510.0. Use `dangerous` as a flag to control the loop.

3. Here is a simple count-controlled loop:

```
count = 1;
while (count < 20)
    count++;
```

   a. List three ways of changing the loop so that it executes 20 times instead of 19.

   b. Which of those changes makes the value of `count` range from 1 through 21?

4. Write a code segment that counts the number of times the integer 28 occurs in a file of 100 integers. Assume the file is a `Scanner` called `inFile`.

5. Write a nested loop code segment that produces this output:

```
1
1 2
1 2 3
1 2 3 4
```

6. Write a code segment that reads a file of student scores for a class (any size) and finds the class average. Assume the file is a `Scanner` called `scoreFile`.

7. Write a code segment that reads in integers and then counts and prints the number of positive integers and the number of negative integers. If a value is zero, it should not be counted. The process should continue until end-of-data occurs. You do not know how many numbers are on a line. Assume the file is a `Scanner` called `numFile`.

8. Write a code segment that sums the even integers from 16 through 26, inclusive.

9. Write a statement that increments `count` by 1 and sets it back to 0 when it reaches 13.

10. Write a code segment that prints out the sequence of all the hour and minute combinations in a day, starting with 1:00 A.M. and ending with 12:59 A.M.

11. Rewrite the code segment for Exercise 10 so that it prints the times in 10-minute intervals.

12. Write a loop or loops to count the number of not-equal operators (`!=`) in a file that contains a Java application. Your algorithm should count the number of times an exclamation mark (`!`) followed by an equals sign (`=`) appears in the input. Process the input file one character at a time, keeping track of the two most recent characters (the current value and the previous value). In each iteration of the loop, a new current value is extracted from the input line with `charAt` and the old current value becomes the previous value. (A call to `aString.charAt(i)` returns the character at the `i`th position of `aString`.) When EOF is reached, the loop is finished. Use functional decomposition to aid in the design of this code segment.

13. Write statements that print a floating-point number on the file `outFile`, with four digits after the decimal point. Use the `String.valueOf` method to convert the floating-point value to a string. (It is a value-returning class method that takes the floating-point value as an argument.) Then use `indexOf('.')` to locate the decimal point within the string. After the decimal point, select the next four digits using the `substring` method. Note that fewer than four digits may follow the decimal point. You can check this by comparing the result of `indexOf` with the length of the string. When fewer than four digits appear to the right of the decimal point, you should concatenate `"0"` characters to the string to fill it out to the correct number of places. Use functional decomposition to aid in the design of this code segment.

14. Write an expression that returns `true` if there is another line of data.

15. Write the constructor call that associates an object of the class `FileReader` with the file `inFile.dat`.

16. Write the constructor call that associates an object of the class `Scanner` with the file `inFile.dat`.

17. Write the constructor call that associates an object of the class `PrintWriter` with the file `outFile.dat`.

18. What does the following series of statements write on the `PrintWriter` file `fileOut`?

```
fileOut.print('W');
fileOut.print('\n');
fileOut.print(88);
fileOut.print('\n');
fileOut.println(" This is a string.");
```

19. What is printed on the `PrintWriter` file `fileOut` by the following series of statements?

```
fileOut.println('W');
fileOut.println(88);
fileOut.println(" This is a string");
```

20. Write a code fragment that reads a line from `fileIn` and stores the first two characters into two `char` variables `first` and `second`. (`fileIn` is of the class `Scanner` and has been declared and assigned.)

21. Write a code fragment that reads a line from `Scanner fileIn` and prints it on `fileOut` with blank lines before and after it.

22. Write the statements that close `fileOut` and then associate it with the file `dataOut.dat`.

23. Write a statement that reads a `float` value from a `Scanner` object `in` if the next data value is a `float`.

24. Write an expression that checks whether a `Scanner` object `in` contains more data.

Programming Problems

1. Design and write a Java application that takes as input an integer and a character from the screen. The output should be a diamond on the screen composed of the character and extending for the width specified by the integer. For example, if the integer is 11 and the character is an asterisk (*), the diamond would look like this:

```
     *
    ***
   *****
  *******
 *********
***********
 *********
  *******
   *****
    ***
     *
```

If the input integer is an even number, it should be increased to the next odd number. Use meaningful variable names, proper indentation, appropriate comments, and good prompting messages. Use `Scanner` for input and a `PrintWriter` object for output.

2. Design and write a Java application that takes as input an integer larger than 1 and calculates the sum of the squares from 1 to that integer. For example, if the integer equals 4, the sum of the squares is 30 (1 + 4 + 9 + 16). The output should be the value of the integer and the sum, properly labeled on the screen. The application should repeat this process for several input values. Use a sentinel value to end processing, and use screen input and output.

3. You are burning some music CDs for a party. You've arranged a list of songs in the order in which you want to play them. You would like to maximize your use of space on the CD, which holds 80 minutes of music. To do so, you want to figure out the total time for a group of songs and see how well they fit. Design and write a Java application to help you complete this task. The data is on the file `songs.dat`. The time is entered as seconds. For example, if a song takes 7 minutes and 42 seconds to play, the data entered for that song would be

   462

   After all the data has been read, the application should print a message indicating the time remaining on the CD. The output should be in the form of a table with columns and headings written on a file. For example:

Song Number	Song Time Minutes	Seconds	Total Time Minutes	Seconds
-----	-------	-------	-------	-------
1	5	10	5	10
2	7	42	12	52
5	4	19	17	11
3	4	33	21	44
4	10	27	32	11
6	8	55	41	6

   There are 38 minutes and 54 seconds of space left on the 80 minute CD.

   Note that the output converts the input from seconds to minutes and seconds. (You can use the `Time` class to help with this conversion.)

4. Design and write an application that prints out the approximate number of words in a file of text. For our purposes, this number is the same as the number of gaps following words. A gap is defined as one or more spaces in a row, so a sequence of spaces counts as just one gap. The newline character also counts as a gap. Anything other than a space or newline is considered to be part of a word. For example, there are 13 words in this sentence, according to our definition. The application should echo-print the data. Use meaningful variable names, proper indentation, and appropriate comments. Thoroughly test the application with your own data sets.

LEARNING Portfolio

Case Study Follow-Up

1. Test the `LawncareBilling` application on files with zero, one, and five clients. Note what happens in the case of the empty file.

2. Design and implement a test plan (write a dedicated driver) for class `Address`.

3. Design and implement a test plan (write a dedicated driver) for class `Client`.

4. Modify the `Client` class so that it rounds charges up to dollars and cents.

5. How would you change the test plan for `Client` to check that the modification in Exercise 4 is working correctly?

6. What happens when the value given in the client record for the number of jobs doesn't match the actual number of jobs in the record? There are two cases to consider here: the number is greater than the actual number of time entries, or the number is less than the number of time entries. Did you think to include this possibility in your test plan for `Client`?

7. Modify the loop in the `Client` constructor so that it checks whether there is an integer token to read before attempting to input a time.

8. Modify the `Address` class so that it allows two lines of street address. When one of the lines is empty, `toString` should omit the line from the value it returns.

7 Additional Control Structures

Goals

Knowledge Goals

To:

- Understand the role of the *switch* statement
- Understand the purpose of the *break* statement
- Understand the distinctions among the alternative looping statements
- Understand what is and what is not an exception
- Know when throwing an exception is appropriate
- Know how an exception should be handled
- Be aware of Java's additional operators and their place in the precedence hierarchy with respect to one another

Skill Goals

To be able to:

- Write a *switch* statement for a multiway branching problem
- Write a *do* statement and contrast it with a *while* statement
- Write a *for* statement as an alternative to a *while* statement
- Choose the most appropriate looping statement for a given problem
- Use the Java exception-handling facilities *try*, *catch*, and *throw*
- Use a *throw* statement to throw a predefined exception

1962
MIT grad student Steve Russell uses the DEC computer PDP-1 to create Spacewar, the first video game

1962
The Bell Labs Telstar communications satellite makes possible the first transatlantic television pictures

1963
Joseph Weizenbaum develops "Eliza," a program that acts like a psychotherapist by following a script, but appears to have intelligence

1963
The ASCII character code, largely the work of Bob Bemer, is accepted by the American National Standards Institute

1963
The Semi-Automatic Ground Environment (SAGE) system, a real-time computer-based command and control defense system, is fully deployed

1964
John Kemeny and Thomas Kurtz develop the programming language BASIC

Introduction

In Chapters 5 and 6, we introduced the Java *if* statement for selection and the *while* statement for looping. With these statements, we can write any algorithm. So why do we have a chapter entitled "Additional Control Structures"? Experience has shown that many algorithms use particular patterns of branching and looping. For example, count-controlled loops are quite common. If a programming language includes a statement that simplifies the writing of such loops, then the programmer's job becomes easier. Java provides several of these convenience-oriented structures, which are the subject of this chapter.

The *switch* statement makes it easier to write selection structures that have many branches. Two new looping statements, *for* and *do*, simplify the construction of certain types of loops. The *break* and *continue* statements are control statements that are used as part of larger looping and selection structures. There is nothing that you can do with these new structures that you could not do with the *if* and *while* statements, but in some contexts you will find them more convenient.

Exceptions are another convenience-oriented control structure. We could, of course, do all of our error checking using *if* statements. In many problems, however, the number of error tests grows so large that the *if* statements completely obscure the main algorithm. Even worse, the programmer may get tired of writing code to check for errors and produce an application that is susceptible to many more bugs. Exceptions provide a very convenient way to check for errors without cluttering up the algorithm with additional *if* statements.

1964
Control Data Corporation presents Seymour Cray's CDC 6600, the first commercial supercomputer

1964
IBM develops a computer-aided design (CAD) system

1964
Douglas Engelbart invents the computer mouse

1965
J.A. Robinson sets the stage for logic programming with the development of unification

1967
Ole-Johan Dahl and Kristen Nygaard create Simula, the first object-oriented programming language

1967
The first hand-held electronic calculator that can add, subtract, multiply, and divide is created by Jack Kilby, Jerry Merryman, and James Van Tassel at Texas Instruments

Until now, we have handled exceptions by forwarding them to "someone else." In this chapter, we stop passing the buck and handle exceptions within our code by using the *try-catch* statement. We also show how to generate exceptions of our own.

The control structures covered here are like the dessert that follows a good meal: nice but not essential. But in each case, the construct may also make the code easier to read.

7.1 ⋮ The *switch* Statement

> **switch expression** The expression whose value determines which *switch* label is selected

The *switch* statement is a selection control structure for multiway branches. It is similar to nested *if* statements—that is, it is an alternative construct for processing a choice of options. The value of a **switch expression** determines which of the branches executes.

Look at the following example *switch* statement, in which `digit` is the *switch* expression:

```
switch (digit)              // The switch expression is (digit)
{
  case 1 : Statement1;      // Statement1 executes if digit is 1
           break;           // Go to Statement5
  case 2 :
  case 3 : Statement2;      // Statement 2 executes if digit is 2 or 3
           break;           // Go to Statement5
  case 4 : Statement3;      // Statement3 executes if digit is 4
           break;           // Go to Statement5
  default: Statement4;      // Execute Statement4 and go to Statement5
}
Statement5;                 // Always executes
```

The highlighted parts represent any valid Java statement. This *switch* statement means, "If `digit` is 1, execute Statement1 and then break out of the *switch*, continuing with Statement5. If `digit` is 2 or 3, execute Statement2 and go to Statement5. If `digit` is 4, execute Statement3 and jump to Statement5. If `digit` is none of the values previously mentioned, execute Statement4 and go on to Statement5." Figure 7.1 shows the flow of control through this statement.

The *break* statement causes control to immediately jump to the statement following the *switch* statement. We will see shortly what happens if we omit the *break* statements.

Let's look at the syntax template for the *switch* statement and then consider what actually happens when it executes:

Switch-Statement

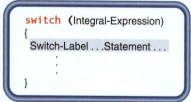

```
switch (Integral-Expression)
{
   Switch-Label . . .Statement . . .
        ⋮
        ⋮
}
```

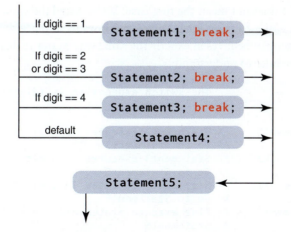

FIGURE 7.1 Flow of Control in the Example *switch* Statement

Here Integral-Expression is an expression of type `char`, `byte`, `short`, `int` (or `enum`, which we cover in Chapter 8). The Switch-Label in front of a statement is either a case label or a default label:

Switch-Label

```
case Constant-Expression :
default :
```

In a case label, Constant-Expression is an expression of type `char`, `byte`, `short`, `int` (or `enum`), whose operands must be literal or named constants. Following are examples of constant expressions (where `CLASS_SIZE` is a constant of type `int`):

```
3
CLASS_SIZE
'A'
```

The data type of Constant-Expression is converted, if necessary, to match the type of the *switch* expression.

In our earlier example that tests the value of `digit`, the following are the case labels:

```
case 1 :
case 2 :
case 3 :
case 4 :
```

As that example shows, multiple case labels may precede a single branch.

The value resulting from each Constant-Expression within a *switch* statement must be unique. If a value appears more than once among the case labels, a syntax error results because the compiler cannot determine which of the identical cases to use. Also, only one `default` label can appear in a *switch* statement. Remember: If a construct is ambiguous, it is illegal.

Be careful: `case 1` does not mean the first case. We've listed the values in order because it makes the statement easier to read. Java, however, allows us to place them in any order. The following *switch* statement behaves in exactly the same way as our earlier example, but is not as easy for a human reader to understand:

```
switch (digit)              // The switch expression is (digit)
{
  case 3  :
  case 2  : Statement2;     // Statement2 executes if digit is 2 or 3
            break;          // Go to Statement5
  case 4  : Statement3;     // Statement3 executes if digit is 4
            break;          // Go to Statement5
  case 1  : Statement1;     // Statement1 executes if digit is 1
            break;          // Go to Statement5
  default : Statement4;     // Else execute Statement4 and go to
                            // Statement5
}
Statement5;                 // Always executes
```

The flow of control through a *switch* statement goes like this: First, the *switch* expression is evaluated. Next, each expression beside the reserved word `case` is tested to see whether it matches the *switch* expression. If the values match, control branches to the statement associated with that case label (the statement on the other side of the colon). From there, control continues sequentially until it encounters either a *break* statement or the end of the *switch* statement. If the value of the *switch* expression doesn't match any case value, then one of two things happens. If there is a `default` label, control branches to the associated statement. If there is no `default` label, the statements in the *switch* are skipped and control proceeds to the statement following the entire *switch* statement.

The following *switch* statement prints an appropriate comment based on a student's `grade` (`grade` is of type `char`). The *switch* expression can be a `char`, as Java considers `char` to be an integral type because it can be converted to `int`.

```
switch (grade)
{
  case 'A' :
  case 'B' : outFile.print("Good Work");
             break;
  case 'C' : outFile.print("Average Work");
             break;
  case 'D' :
  case 'F' : outFile.print("Poor Work");
             numberInTrouble++;
             break;            // Unnecessary, but a good habit
}
```

Note that the final *break* statement is unnecessary, but programmers often include it anyway. One reason is that it's easier to insert another case label at the end if a *break* statement is already present.

If `grade` does not contain one of the specified characters, none of the statements within the *switch* executes. It would be wise to add a `default` label to account for an invalid `grade`:

```
switch (grade)
{
  case 'A' :
  case 'B' : outFile.print("Good Work");
             break;
  case 'C' : outFile.print("Average Work");
             break;
  case 'D' :
  case 'F' : outFile.print("Poor Work");
             numberInTrouble++;
             break;
  default  : outFile.print(grade + " is not a valid letter grade.");
}
```

A *switch* statement with a *break* statement after each case alternative behaves exactly like an *if-else-if* control structure. For example, the preceding *switch* statement is equivalent to the following code:

```
if (grade == 'A' || grade == 'B')
  outFile.print("Good Work");
else if (grade == 'C')
  outFile.print("Average Work");
else if (grade == 'D' || grade == 'F')
{
  outFile.print("Poor Work");
  numberInTrouble++;
}
else
  outFile.print(grade + "is not a valid letter grade.");
```

Is one of these two versions better than the other? There is no absolute answer to this question. In this particular example, the *switch* statement is easier to understand because of its table-like form. When implementing a multiway branching structure, our advice is to use the structure that you feel is easiest to read. Keep in mind that Java provides the *switch* statement as a matter of convenience. Don't feel obligated to use a *switch* for every multiway branch.

Finally, let's consider what happens if we omit the *break* statements inside a *switch* statement. We'll rewrite the preceding code segment as if we forgot to include the *break* statements and see how it behaves:

```
switch (grade)     // Wrong version
{
  case 'A' :
  case 'B' : outFile.print("Good Work");
  case 'C' : outFile.print("Average Work");
  case 'D' :
  case 'F' : outFile.print("Poor Work");
             numberInTrouble++;
  default  : outFile.print(grade + " is not a valid letter grade.");
}
```

If `grade` happens to be 'H', control branches to the statement at the `default` label and the output to the file is

```
H is not a valid letter grade.
```

Unfortunately, this case alternative is the only one that works correctly. If `grade` is 'A', all of the branches execute and the resulting output is

```
Good WorkAverage WorkPoor WorkA is not a valid letter grade.
```

Remember that after a branch is taken to a specific case label, control continues sequentially until it encounters either a *break* statement or the end of the *switch* statement. Forgetting a *break* statement in a case alternative is a very common source of errors in Java code.

7.2 : The *do* Statement

The *do* statement is a looping control structure in which the loop condition is tested at the end (bottom) of the loop. This format guarantees that the loop body executes at least once. The syntax template for the *do* statement follows:

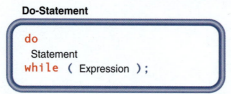

Do-Statement

```
do
  Statement
while ( Expression );
```

As usual in Java, Statement is either a single statement or a block. Also, note that the *do* statement ends with a semicolon.

The *do* statement

```
do
{
   Statement1;
   Statement2;
     .
     .
     .
   StatementN;
} while (Expression);
```

means "Execute the statements between `do` and `while` as long as Expression has the value `true` at the end of the loop." In other words, you execute the statements before you test the expression. Because `while` appears at the end of the block, this statement is sometimes called the *do-while* statement.

Let's compare a *while* loop and a *do* loop that perform the same task: They find the first line that contains just a period in a file of data. We assume that the file contains at least one such line.

while Solution
```
inputStr = dataFile.nextLine();
while (!inputStr.equals("."))
   inputStr  = dataFile.nextLine();
```

do Solution
```
do
   inputStr = dataFile.nextLine();
while (!inputStr.equals("."));
```

The *while* solution requires a priming read so that `inputStr` has a value before the loop is entered. This preliminary activity isn't required for the *do* solution because the input statement within the loop executes before the loop condition is evaluated.

We can also use the *do* statement to implement a count-controlled loop if we know in advance that the loop body should always execute at least once. Following are two versions of a loop to sum the integers from 1 through n:

while Solution
```
sum = 0;
counter = 1;
while (counter <= n)
{
   sum = sum + counter;
   counter++;
}
```

do Solution
```
sum = 0;
counter = 1;
do
{
   sum = sum + counter;
   counter++;
} while (counter <= n);
```

If n is a positive number, both of these versions are equivalent. If n is 0 or negative, however, the two loops give different results. In the *while* version, the final value of `sum` is 0 because the loop body is never entered. In the *do* version, the final value of `sum` is 1 because the body executes once and then the loop test occurs.

Because the *while* statement tests the condition before executing the body of the loop, it is called a *pretest loop*. The *do* statement does the opposite, so it is known as a *posttest loop*. Figure 7.2 compares the flow of control in the *while* and *do* loops.

When we finish introducing all of the new looping constructs, we will offer some guidelines to help you decide when to use each type of loop.

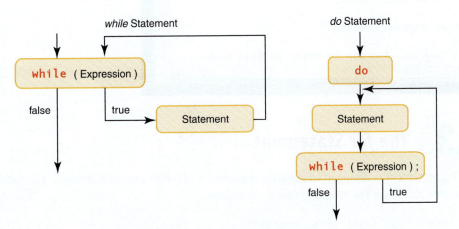

FIGURE 7.2 Flow of Control: *while* and *do*

We often use *do* statements when checking whether input data is correct. For example, the following application uses a *do* loop to continue asking the user to enter an even number:

```java
//**************************************************************
// This application demonstrates the use of the do statement
// ensuring correct input.
//**************************************************************

import java.util.Scanner;
public class loopTest
{
  public static void main(String args[])
  {
    Scanner in = new Scanner(System.in);
    int number;
    int howManyTries = 0;
    do
    {
      howManyTries++;
      System.out.println("Enter an even number.");
      number = in.nextInt();
    } while (number/2 * 2 != number);
    System.out.println("It took you " + howManyTries +
                        " tries to enter an even number.");
  }
}
```

Output:

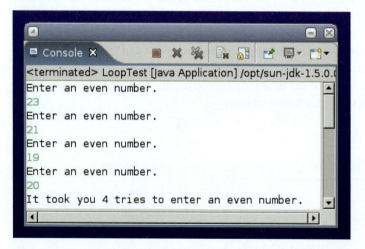

7.3 : The *for* Statement

The *for* statement is designed to simplify the writing of count-controlled loops. The following statement prints out the integers from 1 through n:

```java
for (count = 1; count <= n; count++)
  outFile.println("" + count);
```

This *for* statement says, "Initialize the loop control variable `count` to 1. While `count` is less than or equal to `n`, execute the output statement and increment `count` by 1. Stop the loop after `count` has been incremented to n + 1."

The syntax template for a *for* statement follows:

For-Statement

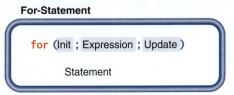

Here Expression is the condition that continues the loop; it must be of type `boolean`. Init can be any of the following:

- Nothing
- A local variable declaration
- An expression
- A series of local variable declarations and expressions separated by commas

Update can be

- Omitted
- An expression
- A series of expressions separated by commas

Most often, a *for* statement is written such that Init initializes a loop control variable and Update increments or decrements the loop control variable. Here are two loops that execute the same number of times (50) but count in opposite directions:

```
for (loopCount = 1; loopCount <= 50; loopCount++)
   .
   .
   .
for (loopCount = 50; loopCount >= 1; loopCount--)
   .
   .
   .
```

Just like *while* loops, *do* and *for* loops may be nested. For example, the nested *for* structure

```
for (lastNum = 1; lastNum <= 7; lastNum++)
{
  for (numToPrint = 1; numToPrint <= lastNum; numToPrint++)
    outFile.print("" + numToPrint);
  outFile.println();
}
```

prints a triangle of numbers:

```
1
12
123
1234
12345
123456
1234567
```

The *for* statement is designed primarily for use in count-controlled loops. Although Java allows you to write any *while* loop by using a *for* statement, it is not considered good style to do so. To use *for* loops intelligently, you should know the following facts:

1. In the syntax template, Init and Update are optional. If you omit Update, the termination condition is not automatically updated.

2. According to the syntax template, Expression—the continuation condition—is also optional. Thus you can write a *for* statement as shown here:

   ```
   for ( ; ; )
     outFile.println("Hi");
   ```

   If you omit the continuation condition, it is assumed to be `true`, creating an infinite loop.

3. As highlighted here, Init can be a declaration with initialization:

   ```
   for (int count = 1; count <= 20; count++)
     outFile.println("Hi");
   ```

In the last example, the variable `count` is defined only for the duration of the *for* statement. That is, `count` is inaccessible outside the *for* statement. Therefore, it's possible to write code like this:

```
for (int count = 1; count <= 20; count++)
  outFile.println("Hi");
for (int count = 1; count <= 100; count++)
  outFile.println("Ed");
```

As the highlights show, `count` is declared twice in this code segment. Yet this doesn't generate a compile-time error (such as "Multiply defined identifier"). Instead, we have declared two distinct variables named `count`, each of which is defined only within its own *for* statement.

As noted earlier, Init and Update can have multiple parts, which must be separated by commas. All of the parts execute as if they form a block of statements. For example, it is sometimes useful to have a second variable in a loop that is a multiple of the iteration counter. The following loop declares two variables: one variable that counts by 1 and is used as the loop control variable, and a second variable that counts by 5. In the Init and Update we highlight the different parts to emphasize that there are two of them.

```
for (int count = 1, int byFives = 5; count <= n; count++, byFives = count * 5)
  outFile.println("Count = " + count + " * 5 = " + byFives);
```

If n is 7, this loop produces the following output:

```
Count = 1 * 5 = 5
Count = 2 * 5 = 10
Count = 3 * 5 = 15
Count = 4 * 5 = 20
Count = 5 * 5 = 25
Count = 6 * 5 = 30
Count = 7 * 5 = 35
```

7.4 : Guidelines for Choosing a Looping Statement

Here are some guidelines to help you decide when to use each of the three looping statements (*while*, *do*, and *for*):

1. If the loop is a simple count-controlled loop, the *for* statement is a natural choice. Gathering the three loop control actions—initialize, test, and increment/decrement—into one location (the heading of the *for* statement) reduces the chances that you will forget to include one of them.

2. If the loop is an event-controlled loop whose body should execute an unknown number of times but at least once, a *do* statement is appropriate.

3. If the loop is an event-controlled loop and nothing is known about the first execution or the number of executions, use a *while* statement.

4. When in doubt, use a *while* statement.

Theoretical Foundations

Analysis of Algorithms

If you were given the choice of cleaning a room with a toothbrush or a broom, you probably would choose the broom. Using a broom sounds like less work than using a toothbrush. True, if the room is located in a doll house, it may be easier to use the toothbrush, but in general a broom is the faster way to clean. If you are given the choice of adding numbers together with a pencil and paper or a calculator, you would probably choose the calculator because it is usually less work. If you are given the choice of walking or driving to a meeting, you would probably choose to drive; it sounds like less work.

What do these examples have in common? And how do they relate to computer science? In each of the settings mentioned, one of the choices seems to involve significantly less work. Measuring the amount of work precisely is difficult in each case, however, because there are unknowns. How large is the room? How many numbers must be added? How far away is the meeting? In each case, the unknown information relates to the size of the problem. With an especially small problem (for example, adding 2 + 2), our original guess at which approach to take (using the calculator) might be wrong. Of course, our intuition is usually correct, because most problems are reasonably large.

In computer science, we need a way to measure the amount of work done by an algorithm relative to the size of a problem, because usually more than one algorithm is available to solve any given problem. We often must choose the most efficient algorithm—that is, the algorithm that does the least work for a problem of a given size.

Theoretical Foundations

Q.E.D.

The amount of work involved in executing an algorithm relative to the size of the problem is the algorithm's **complexity**. We would like to be able to look at an algorithm and determine its complexity. Then we could take two algorithms that perform the same task and determine which completes the task faster (requires less work).

How do we measure the amount of work required to execute an algorithm? We use the total number of steps executed as a measure of work. One statement, such as an assignment, may require only one step; another statement, such as a loop, may require many steps. We define a step as any operation roughly equivalent in complexity to a comparison, an I/O operation, or an assignment.

Given an algorithm with just a sequence of simple statements (no branches or loops), the number of steps performed is directly related to the number of statements. When we introduce branches, however, it becomes possible to skip some statements in the algorithm. Branches allow us to subtract steps without physically removing them from the algorithm because only one branch executes at a time. Because we usually want to express work in terms of the worst-case scenario, we use the number of steps in the longest branch.

Now consider the effect of a loop. If a loop repeats a sequence of 15 simple statements 10 times, it performs 150 steps. Loops allow us to multiply the work done in an algorithm without physically adding statements.

Now that we have a measure for the work done in an algorithm, we can compare algorithms. Suppose that Algorithm A always executes 3124 steps and Algorithm B always does the same task in 1321 steps. In this example, Algorithm B is more efficient—that is, it takes fewer steps to accomplish the same task.

If an algorithm, from run to run, always takes the same number of steps or fewer, we say that it executes in an amount of time bounded by a constant. Such algorithms are said to have constant time complexity. Be careful: Constant time doesn't mean small; it just means that the amount of work done does not exceed some amount from one run to another regardless of the size of the problem.

If a loop executes a fixed number of times, the work done is greater than the physical number of statements but is still constant. But what happens if the number of loop iterations can change from one run to the next? Suppose a data file contains N data values to be processed in a loop. If the loop reads and processes one value during each iteration, then the loop executes N iterations. The amount of work done therefore depends on a variable—the number of data values. In this example, the variable N determines the size of the problem.

> **Complexity** A measure of the effort expended by the computer in performing a computation, relative to the size of the computation

Q.E.D.

If we have a loop that executes N times, the number of steps to be executed is some factor times N. This factor is the number of steps performed within a single iteration of the loop. Specifically, the work done by an algorithm with a data-dependent loop is given by the expression

$$\overbrace{S_1 \times N}^{\text{Steps performed by the loop}} + \underbrace{S_0}_{\text{Steps performed outside the loop}}$$

where S_1 is the number of steps in the loop body (a constant for a given simple loop), N is the number of iterations (a variable representing the size of the problem), and S_0 is the number of steps outside the loop. Mathematicians call expressions of this form linear; hence, algorithms such as this one are said to have linear time complexity. Notice that if N grows very large, the term $S_1 \times N$ dominates the execution time. That is, S_0 becomes an insignificant part of the total execution time. For example, if S_0 and S_1 are each 20 steps, and N is 1,000,000, then the total number of steps is 20,000,020. The 20 steps contributed by S_0 represent only a tiny fraction of the total in this case.

What about a data-dependent loop that contains a nested loop? The number of steps in the inner loop, S_2, and the number of iterations performed by the inner loop, L, must be multiplied by the number of iterations in the outer loop:

$$\overbrace{(S_2 \times L \times N)}^{\substack{\text{Steps performed} \\ \text{by the nested loop}}} + \overbrace{(S_1 \times N)}^{\substack{\text{Steps performed} \\ \text{by the outer loop}}} + \overbrace{S_0}^{\substack{\text{Steps performed outside} \\ \text{the outer loop}}}$$

By itself, the inner loop performs $(S_2 \times L)$ steps. Because it is repeated N times by the outer loop, however, it accounts for a total of $(S_2 \times L \times N)$ steps. If L is a constant, then the algorithm still executes in linear time.

Now suppose that for each of the N outer loop iterations the inner loop performs N steps ($L = N$). Here the formula for the total steps is

$$(S_2 \times N \times N) + (S_1 \times N) + S_0$$

or

$$(S_2 \times N^2) + (S_1 \times N) + S_0$$

Because N^2 grows much faster than N (for large values of N), the inner loop term $(S_2 \times N^2)$ accounts for the majority of steps executed and the work done. The corresponding execution time is essentially proportional to N^2. Mathematicians call this type of formula quadratic.

Theoretical Foundations

If we have a doubly nested loop, where each loop depends on N, then the complexity expression is

$$(S_3 \times N^3) + (S_2 \times N^2) + (S_1 \times N) + S_0$$

and the work and time are proportional to N^3 whenever N is reasonably large. Such a formula is called cubic.

The following table shows the number of steps required for each increase in the exponent of N, where N is a size factor for the problem, such as the number of input values.

N	N^0 (Constant)	N^1 (Linear)	N^2 (Quadratic)	N^3 (Cubic)
1	1	1	1	1
10	1	10	100	1000
100	1	100	10,000	1,000,000
1000	1	1000	1,000,000	1,000,000,000
10,000	1	10,000	100,000,000	1,000,000,000,000
100,000	1	100,000	10,000,000,000	1,000,000,000,000,000

As you can see, each time the exponent increases by 1, the number of steps is multiplied by an additional order of magnitude (factor of 10). That is, if N is made 10 times greater, the work involved in an N^2 algorithm increases by a factor of 100, and the work involved in an N^3 algorithm increases by a factor of 1000. To put this idea in more concrete terms, an algorithm with a doubly nested loop, in which each loop depends on the number of data values, takes 1000 steps for 10 input values and 1 quadrillion steps for 100,000 values. On a computer that executes 1 billion instructions per second, the latter case would take more than 10 days to run.

The table also shows that the steps outside the innermost loop account for an insignificant portion of the total number of steps as N gets bigger. Because the innermost loop dominates the total time, we classify the complexity of an algorithm according to the highest order of N that appears in its complexity expression, called the *order of magnitude*, or simply the order of that expression. Thus we talk about algorithms having "order N squared complexity" (or "cubed" or so on) or we describe them with what is called Big-O notation. In Big-O notation, we express the complexity by putting the highest-order term in parentheses with a capital "O" in front. For example, $O(1)$ is constant time, $O(N)$ is linear time, $O(N^2)$ is quadratic time, and $O(N^3)$ is cubic time.

Determining the complexities of different algorithms allows us to compare the work they require without having to program and execute them. For example, if you had an $O(N^2)$ algorithm and a linear algorithm that performed the same task, you would probably choose the linear algorithm. We say "probably" because an $O(N^2)$ algorithm actually may

Theoretical Foundations

Q.E.D.

execute fewer steps than an $O(N)$ algorithm for small values of N. Recall that if the size factor N is small, the constants and lower-order terms in the complexity expression may be significant.

To see how this idea works, let's look at an example. Suppose that Algorithm A is $O(N^2)$ and Algorithm B is $O(N)$. For large values of N, we would normally choose Algorithm B because it requires less work than Algorithm A. But suppose that in Algorithm B, $S_0 = 1000$ and $S_1 = 1000$. If $N = 1$, then Algorithm B takes 2000 steps to execute. Now suppose that for Algorithm A, $S_0 = 10$, $S_1 = 10$, and $S_2 = 10$. If $N = 1$, then Algorithm A takes only 30 steps to execute. The following table compares the number of steps taken by these two algorithms for different values of N.

N	Algorithm A	Algorithm B
1	30	2000
2	70	3000
3	130	4000
10	1110	11,000
20	4210	21,000
30	9310	31,000
50	25,510	51,000
100	101,010	101,000
1000	10,010,010	1,001,000
10,000	1,000,100,010	10,001,000

From this table we can see that the $O(N^2)$ Algorithm A is actually faster than the $O(N)$ Algorithm B, up to the point where N equals 100. Beyond that point, Algorithm B becomes more efficient. Thus, if we know that N is always less than 100 in a particular problem, we would choose Algorithm A. For example, if the size factor N is the number of test scores on an exam and the class size is limited to 30 students, Algorithm A would be more efficient. If N is the number of scores at a university with 25,000 students, however, we would choose Algorithm B.

Constant, linear, quadratic, and cubic expressions are all examples of polynomial expressions. Algorithms whose complexity is characterized by such expressions are said to execute in polynomial time and form a broad class of algorithms that encompasses everything we've discussed so far.

In addition to polynomial-time algorithms, we will encounter a logarithmic-time algorithm in Chapter 11. There are also factorial [$O(N!)$], exponential [$O(N^N)$], and hyperexponential [$O(N^{NN})$] class algorithms, which can require vast amounts of time to execute and are beyond the scope of this book. For now, the important point to remember is that different algorithms that solve the same problem can vary significantly in the amount of work they do.

Reimplementing the `Client` Constructor

Problem Now that you know about *for* loops, you decide to reimplement the constructor for the `Client` class, previously developed in the case study for Chapter 5, so that it uses a *for* loop.

Discussion Recall that the `Client` constructor reads the data for a client from a `Scanner`. The input data includes the number of jobs for the client, which we used in a count-controlled loop to read the job data. The first step in converting any method to use a *for* in place of a *while* is to identify the parts of the loop that relate to its control.

> Identify the loop control variable (LCV)
> Determine where the LCV is declared
> Determine where the LCV is initialized
> Determine where and how the LCV is updated
> Identify the loop termination condition

Here is the existing code, with highlighting indicating those parts:

```java
public Client(Scanner in) throws IOException   // Scanner constructor
{
  Time time;                                    // Declare local variables
  int hours;
  int minutes;
  double charge;
  String last = in.next();                      // Read name
  String first = in.next();
  String middle = in.next();
  name = new Name(first, last, middle);
  String separator = in.nextLine();
  address = new Address(in);                     // Read address
  int numberOfJobs = in.nextInt();               // Loop termination value
  // Read and process jobs to create billing string and totals
  int count = 1;                                 // Initialize loop
  billing = "";
  totalTime = new Time();
  totalCharges = 0.0;
  while (count <= numberOfJobs)
  {
    hours = in.nextInt();                        // Read time
    minutes = in.nextInt();
    time = new Time(hours, minutes, 0);
    charge = time.getTime()/3600.0 * rate;       // Compute charge
    // Add time and charge to billing string
    billing = billing + "   " + hours + ":" + minutes + "      $" + charge + '\n';
    totalTime = totalTime.plus(time);            // Update totals
    totalCharges = totalCharges + charge;
    count++;                                      // Increment loop control variable
  }
  separator = in.nextLine();
}
```

We can see from the code that the LCV is **count**. It is declared and initialized in a single statement prior to the loop. The LCV update is simply an increment operation at the end of the loop. The termination condition compares the LCV to a variable that is set prior to entry into the loop.

It is important to check that the update of the LCV is an expression that we can write within the *for* loop. For example, if the LCV is an event counter that is incremented in an *if* statement, rather than an iteration counter, then the *for* loop isn't appropriate. Also, if the LCV is used outside the loop for other purposes, then we must likewise declare it outside the *for* statement.

We should also check if the termination condition is only testing whether a counter reaches a limit. For example, if it also tests for EOF, then a *while* statement is more appropriate. Remember—the reason that we use a *for* statement is to succinctly implement a count-controlled loop.

Now we are ready to perform the conversion. The control elements of the *while* form of the loop can be summarized by the following lines of code:

```
int count = 1;                       // Initialize loop
while (count <= numberOfJobs)
  count++;                           // Increment loop control variable
```

Taken in isolation, it is clear that we can rewrite this *while* as a *for* loop. Notice that **count** is used only within the loop, so we can declare it within the *for* loop:

```
for (int count = 1; count <= numberOfJobs; count++)
```

Finally, we delete the existing code from the method and replace the *while* statement with the new *for* statement, as highlighted here:

```
public Client(Scanner in) throws IOException  // Scanner constructor
{
  Time time;                         // Declare local variables
  int hours;
  int minutes;
  double charge;
  String last = in.next();           // Read name
  String first = in.next();
  String middle = in.next();
  name = new Name(first, last, middle);
  String separator = in.nextLine();
  address = new Address(in);         // Read address
  int numberOfJobs = in.nextInt();   // Loop termination value
  // Read and process jobs to create billing string and totals
  billing = "";
  totalTime = new Time();
  totalCharges = 0.0;
  for (int count = 1; count <= numberOfJobs; count++)
```

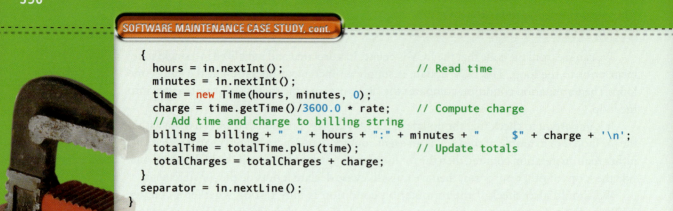

```
  {
    hours = in.nextInt();                    // Read time
    minutes = in.nextInt();
    time = new Time(hours, minutes, 0);
    charge = time.getTime()/3600.0 * rate;   // Compute charge
    // Add time and charge to billing string
    billing = billing + "   " + hours + ":" + minutes + "      $" + charge + '\n';
    totalTime = totalTime.plus(time);        // Update totals
    totalCharges = totalCharges + charge;
  }
  separator = in.nextLine();
}
```

7.5 : The *break* Statement

Haven't we already seen how *break* works? Well, yes, but only within a *switch* statement. In reality, Java lets us insert a *break* within any looping statement. The effect is to immediately exit the loop. Any remaining statements in the loop body are skipped, and execution continues with the statement following the loop body. For example, the following loop reads and prints ten lines from file `infile` to `System.out`. If `infile` reaches EOF before ten lines have been read, the *break* statement is executed, which causes the loop to exit immediately.

```
for (int count = 1; count <= 10; count++)
{
  if (infile.hasNext())
    System.out.println(infile.nextLine());
  else
    break;
}
```

We typically use a *break* in cases where we would otherwise create a `boolean` flag that we test in the loop termination expression. For example, the preceding loop could replace the following, longer implementation (we highlight the code that provides the effect of the *break*):

```
boolean eof = false;
int count = 1;
while (count <= 10 && !eof)
{
  if (infile.hasNext())
  {
    System.out.println(infile.nextLine());
    count++
  }
  else
    eof = true;
}
```

7.6 : The *continue* Statement

The *continue* statement can appear only within a looping statement. It causes the flow of control to go directly to the start of the next loop iteration, skipping any remaining statements in the loop body. In the case of a *while* statement, execution jumps to the conditional test at the top of the loop. With a *do* statement, execution skips to the test at the bottom of the loop. A *continue* within a *for* causes the Update to be done, and then the Expression is checked. Here's an example that reads ten integers and sums the even values:

```java
int someInt;
int total = 0;
for (int count = 1; count <= 10; count++)
{
  System.out.println("Enter an integer: ");
  someInt = in.nextInt();
  if (someInt / 2 * 2 != someInt)          // If odd, skip to next iteration
    continue;
  total = total + someInt;
  System.out.println(someInt + " is even.");
}
System.out.println("Total of even numbers entered is: " + total);
```

This task could have been accomplished just as easily by replacing the last four lines of the loop body with

```java
if (someInt / 2 * 2 == someInt)          // If even, then sum and print
{
  total = total + someInt;
  System.out.println(someInt + " is even.");
}
```

This latter form is actually clearer. It's easy to use the *continue* statement inappropriately and produce code that's more difficult to read. Where would it be appropriate? When a loop contains a complex nested selection structure and there are multiple cases in which processing should skip to the next iteration, using *continue* can eliminate some of the branches and simplify the structure. Such cases are rare, however, so we won't see any further examples of *continue* in this text.

7.7 : Java Operators Revisited

Java offers a rich—but sometimes bewildering—array of operators that allow you to manipulate values of the primitive data types. Appendix B lists all of the Java operators, many of which we do not discuss further because they are beyond the scope of this text. Some of them are included because of Java's historical connection to C and C++.

Operators you have learned about so far include the assignment operator (=), the arithmetic operators (+, -, *, /, %), the increment and decrement operators (++, --), the relational operators (==, !=, <, <=, >, >=), the string concatenation operator (+), and the conditional (short-circuit evaluation) logical operators (**!**, **&&**, **||**). In certain cases, a pair of parentheses is also considered to be an operator—namely, the type cast operator:

```
y = (float)someInt;
```

Until now, we've used the assignment, increment, and decrement operators in specific ways and cautioned you to avoid other uses. In this section we see how they actually operate and why caution is needed.

■ Assignment Expressions

> **Assignment expression**
> A Java expression with (1) a value and (2) the side effect of storing the expression value into a memory location
>
> **Expression statement**
> A statement formed by appending a semicolon to an assignment expression, an increment expression, or a decrement expression

The equals sign (=) is the assignment operator. When combined with its two operands, it forms an **assignment expression** (not an assignment statement). Every assignment expression has a value and a side effect—namely, the value is stored into the variable denoted by the left side of the expression. For example, the expression

```
delta = 2 * 12
```

has the value 24 and the side effect of storing this value into `delta`.

Because an assignment is an expression and not a statement, you can use it anywhere that an expression is allowed. The following statement stores the value 20 into `firstInt`, the value 30 into `secondInt`, and the value 35 into `thirdInt`:

```
thirdInt = (secondInt = (firstInt = 20) + 10) + 5;
```

Although some Java programmers use this style of coding, we do not recommend it. It is hard to read and error-prone.

In Chapter 5, we cautioned against the mistake of using the = operator in place of the == operator:

```
if (alpha = 12)   // Wrong
    .
    .
    .
```

The condition in this *if* statement is an assignment expression, not a relational expression. The value of the expression is 12, which is not a **boolean** value, so a compiler error results.

When an assignment expression is terminated by a semicolon, it becomes a form of what Java calls an **expression statement**. Specifically, it is an assignment statement.

■ Increment and Decrement Operators

The increment and decrement operators (++ and --) operate only on variables, not on constants or arbitrary expressions. In Java, an expression consisting of a variable and an increment or decrement expression also becomes an expression statement when it is terminated by a semicolon.

All four of the following are valid Java statements:

```
alpha++;
beta--;
--gamma;
++delta;
```

Each of these statements either increments or decrements the given variable.

Suppose a variable `someInt` contains the value 3. The expression `++someInt` denotes pre-incrementation. The side effect of incrementing `someInt` occurs first, so the expression has the value 4. In contrast, the expression `someInt++` denotes post-incrementation. The value of the expression is 3, and then the side effect of incrementing `someInt` takes place. The following code illustrates the difference between pre- and post-incrementation:

```
int1 = 14;
int2 = ++int1;
// At this point, int1 == 15  and  int2 == 15
int1 = 14;
int2 = int1++;
// At this point int1 == 15  and  int2 == 14
```

Some people make a game of seeing how much they can accomplish in the fewest key-strokes possible by using side effects in the middle of larger expressions. Professional software development, however, requires writing code that other programmers can read and under-stand. Use of side effects within larger expressions reduces readability and clarity.

By far, the most common use of `++` and `--` is to perform the incrementation or decremen-tation as a separate expression statement:

```
count++;
```

Here, the value of the expression is not used, but we get the desired side effect of incrementing `count`.

■ Operator Precedence

Table 7.1 summarizes the rules of operator precedence for the Java operators we have encoun-tered so far. (Appendix B contains the complete list.) In the table, the operators are grouped by precedence level, and a horizontal line separates each precedence level from the next-lower level.

The column labeled "Associativity" describes the grouping order. Within a precedence level, most operators are grouped from left to right. For example,

```
a - b + c
```

means

```
(a - b) + c
```

and not

```
a - (b + c)
```

Operator	Associativity	Remarks
++ --	Right to left	++ and -- as postfix operators
++ --	Right to left	++ and -- as prefix operators
Unary + Unary −	Right to left	
!	Right to left	
(cast)	Right to left	
* / %	Left to right	
+ −	Left to right	
+	Left to right	String concatenation
< <= > >=	Left to right	
instanceof	Left to right	
== !=	Left to right	
&	Left to right	Boolean operands
^	Left to right	Boolean operands
|	Left to right	Boolean operands
&&	Left to right	
||	Left to right	
? :	Right to left	
= += −= *= /= %=	Right to left	Assignment operators

TABLE 7.1   Precedence (Highest to Lowest)

Certain operators, however, are grouped from right to left—specifically, the unary operators, the assignment operators, and the ?: operator. Look at the unary - operator, for example. The expression

```
sum = - -1
```

means

```
sum = -(-1)
```

instead of the meaningless

```
sum = (- -)1
```

This associativity makes sense because the unary - operation is naturally a right-to-left operation.

A word of caution: Although operator precedence and associativity dictate the grouping of operators with their operands, the precedence rules do not define the order in which subexpressions are evaluated. Java further requires that the left-side operand of a two-operand operator be evaluated first. For example, if `i` currently contains 5, the statement

```
j = ++i + i;
```

stores 12 into `j`. Let's see why. The expression statement contains three operators: `=`, `++`, and `+`. The `++` operator has the highest precedence, so it operates just on `i`, not on the expression `i + i`. The addition operator has higher precedence than the assignment operator, giving implicit parentheses as follows:

```
j = (++i + i);
```

So far, so good. But now we ask this question: In the addition operation, is the left operand or the right operand evaluated first? As we just saw, the Java language tells us that the left-side operand is evaluated first. Therefore, the result is 6 + 6, or 12. If Java had instead specified that the right-side operand comes first, the expression would have yielded 6 + 5, or 11.

In most expressions, Java's left-side rule doesn't have any surprising effects. But when side-effect operators such as increment and assignment are involved, you need to remember that the left-side operand is evaluated first. To make the code clear and unambiguous, it's better to write the preceding example with two separate statements:

```
i++;
j = i + i;
```

The moral here is that it's best to avoid unnecessary side effects altogether.

May We Introduce

Augustus de Morgan

The English mathematician Augustus de Morgan was born in June 1806 on the island of Madura off the northeast coast of Java, where his father was working at the time. When de Morgan was about 7 months old, the family returned to London. By the time he turned 14, Augustus had learned Latin, Greek, and some Hebrew. He received his bachelor's degree from Trinity College but was prevented from going for his master's degree because he believed strongly in freedom of religion and refused to take the required theology exams.

Although de Morgan's family encouraged him to become a lawyer, when a new school, University College, opened in London, he became a professor of mathematics there at the age of 22. He quickly earned a reputation as an excellent teacher. de Morgan lectured with hardly any notes, graded his students' work personally with lengthy written explanations, and handed out many supplementary papers that he wrote for his classes.

de Morgan's work in symbolic logic strongly influenced Charles Babbage in the design of the Analytical Engine. He was also one of the few people of his day to recognize the importance of George Boole's work, helping Boole to get a college professorship.

In addition to his full-time teaching duties, de Morgan tutored private students (including Ada Lovelace), consulted for businesses, served actively in the Royal Astronomical

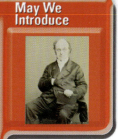

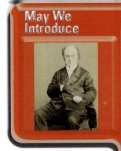

Society, and wrote numerous scientific papers. He wrote on a wide range of subjects for popular magazines and newspapers. In one project, he provided more than 850 articles for a new encyclopedia that was meant to be affordable for the average worker.

Both Boole and de Morgan recognized that the principles of logic handed down from Aristotle were too restricted in their scope. By introducing symbolic notation, however, it became possible to manipulate mathematical formulas in an abstract manner. This idea forms the basis of modern algebra and is a key element of computer programming.

Although de Morgan's development of symbolic logic was extensive, it was poorly organized. Boole's clear and careful approach is today recognized as the turning point in the history of the subject. Nonetheless, de Morgan is credited with one of the fundamental laws of Boolean logic. de Morgan's law is stated in two parts:

$$\text{NOT}(P \text{ OR } Q) = \text{NOT } P \text{ AND NOT } Q$$
$$\text{NOT}(P \text{ AND } Q) = \text{NOT } P \text{ OR NOT } Q$$

He also introduced the modern notation of using the slash (/) for fractions—the same notation that we use for division in Java.

Augustus de Morgan loved unusual and rare books, often spending all of his spare money on a new volume. Another of his loves was music, and he was an accomplished flutist.

He married Sophia Elizabeth Frend, and together they had seven children. It was Sophia who escorted Ada Lovelace to see Charles Babbage. de Morgan was so devoted to his family that he refused invitations to give lectures requiring travel, because he could not bear to be away from his wife and children.

In 1866, at the age of 60, he resigned from University College over another dispute involving freedom of religion. Shortly thereafter, one of his sons died and de Morgan entered a period of depression during which his health steadily declined.

Augustus de Morgan died in 1871, the same year as Charles Babbage, seven years after the death of George Boole, and twenty years after the death of Ada Lovelace. That year truly marks the end of an important age in the history of computer science.

7.8 : Exceptions

In Chapter 2, we defined an exception as an unusual situation that is detected while an application is running. An exception halts the normal execution of a method. Now, we have passed predefined exceptions such as `IOException` to the JVM, where they simply caused the application to crash. However, Java also allows us to detect and respond to an exception with code of our own. Java even lets us define our own exceptions. We can then include code in our methods to throw those exceptions when necessary.

Java's exception-handling mechanism has three parts: defining the exception, raising (or throwing) the exception, and handling the exception. We look first at handling exceptions and then at defining and raising them.

■ The *try* Statement

In Chapter 6, when we introduced files, we found it necessary to forward an `IOException` to the JVM because it is a checked exception. We noted there that the alternative to forwarding an exception is to catch it.

When an error occurs in a method call, it isn't always possible for the method itself to take care of it. For example, suppose we ask the user to enter a file name and then we attempt to open the file by calling the `FileReader` constructor. The constructor discovers that the file doesn't exist and, therefore, cannot be opened. Perhaps the file has been deleted, or maybe the user just mistyped the name. The constructor has no way of knowing that the proper response to the error is to ask the user to reenter the name. Because the constructor can't deal with this error appropriately, it doesn't even try. It passes the problem back to the method that called it.

> **Exception handler** A section of code that is executed when a particular exception occurs; in Java, an exception handler appears within the *catch* clause of a *try* control structure

When a call returns with an exception, rather than resuming execution with the statement that follows the call, the JVM determines whether code is available to take care of the problem. That code is called an **exception handler** and is part of a *try* statement.

The syntax template for a *try* statement follows:

any of

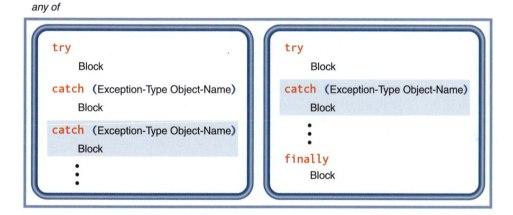

As the diagram shows, similar to the *if* statement, the *try* statement has two forms: *try-catch* and *try-catch-finally*. With *try-catch*, the statement is required to have at least one *catch* section. With *try-catch-finally*, it is possible to omit the *catch* section, but then a *finally* section must be present.

The first part of either form is the reserved word `try` and a block (a `{ }` pair enclosing any number of statements). The second part is a series of *catch* clauses, each consisting of the reserved word `catch`, a single parameter declaration enclosed in parentheses, and a block. The last part, which is present only in the *try-catch-finally* form, consists of the reserved word `finally` and a block.

When a statement or a series of statements in an application may result in an exception, we enclose it in the block following `try`. For each type of exception that can be produced by the statements, we write a *catch* clause. Here's an example of a *try-catch-finally* with one *catch* clause:

```
try
{
    . . .              // Statements that try to open a file
}
catch (FileNotFoundException ioErr)
{
    . . .              // Statements that execute if the file can't be opened
}
finally
{
    . . .              // Statements that are always executed
}
```

The *try* statement is meant to sound something like the coach telling the gymnast, "Go ahead and try this move that you're unsure of, and I'll catch you if you fall." We are telling the computer to try executing some operations that might fail, and then providing code to catch the potential exceptions. The *finally* clause provides an opportunity to clean up, regardless of what happens in the *try* and *catch* blocks. We focus on the execution of the *try-catch* form and briefly describe at the end of this section what happens when we add the *finally* clause.

■ Execution of *try-catch*

If none of the statements in the *try* block throws an exception, then control transfers to the statement following the entire *try-catch* statement. That is, we try some statements and, if everything goes according to plan, we continue with the succeeding statements.

When an exception occurs, control immediately transfers to the block associated with the appropriate *catch* statement. Note that control jumps directly from whatever statement caused the exception to the *catch* block. If statements appear in the *try* block following the one that caused the exception, they are skipped. If the *catch* block executes without causing any new exceptions, then control transfers to the statement following the *try-catch* structure.

How does the computer know which *catch* clause is appropriate? In Java, each kind of exception is an object of a different class. The JVM looks at the class of the parameter declared in each *catch* clause and selects the first clause with a class that matches the class of the thrown exception. For example, the following code tries to read an `int` from a file that has been opened with a `Scanner` called `in`. Two errors could potentially occur: the file is at EOF or the next token isn't an `int`. For each of these cases, `Scanner` throws a different class of exception. Thus the code has two *catch* clauses.

```
try
{
    someInt = in.nextInt();                     // Try to read an int
}
catch (NoSuchElementException ioErr)
{
    System.out.println("File is at EOF");       // Executed if at EOF
    someInt = 0;
}
catch (InputMismatchException numErr)
```

```
{
  System.out.println("No integer to read");  // Executed if next token
                                             // isn't an int
  someInt = 0;
}
System.out.println(someInt);                 // Executed after try-catch
```

If the file is at EOF, a `NoSuchElementException` is thrown, so the *catch* clause with the `NoSuchElementException` parameter is executed. If the file isn't at EOF but the `Scanner` finds something other than an `int`, an `InputMismatchException` is thrown and execution jumps to the second *catch* clause. In both cases, a default value is assigned to `someInt` so that the statement following the *try-catch* has a value to output.

Java defines many exception classes. For example, a class called `ArithmeticException` is used when we attempt to execute an invalid arithmetic operation (such as integer division by zero). The most general class of exception is simply called `Exception`. A *catch* clause with a parameter of the class `Exception` will catch any exception that is thrown. Conceptually, adding such a clause to a *try-catch* is similar to including the `default` case in a *switch* statement. Such a catch clause would look like this:

```
catch (Exception except)
{
            // Statements to handle all other exceptions
}
```

Because we don't know the specific kind of exception that is being caught by such a clause, the statements to handle it can only do something general, such as printing an error message.

What happens if we fail to provide a *catch* clause for a class of exception that is thrown from within the *try* clause? In that case, the *try-catch* statement fails to catch the error, and its enclosing method throws the exception to its caller. If the caller doesn't have a handler for the error, it throws the exception to its caller, and so on, until the exception is either caught or ends up at the JVM. In the latter case, the JVM halts the application and displays an error message.

Every exception object has an associated value-returning method called `getMessage`, which returns a string containing a message. For example, it might contain the name of the file that could not be opened. Because an exception object is passed as a parameter to the corresponding *catch* clause, we have access to its `getMessage` method within the clause.

Let's look at an actual example. The following code tries to instantiate a `Scanner` object for a file:

```
try
{
  outFile = new Scanner(new FileReader("notfound.dat"));
}
catch (FileNotFoundException ioErr)
{
  System.out.println("Unable to open file " + ioErr.getMessage());
}
```

When this code executes, if file `notfound.dat` doesn't exist, then the following message is displayed on the screen:

```
Unable to open file notfound.dat
```

■ Execution of the *finally* Clause

When a *finally* clause appears in a *try* statement, the block following *finally* is always executed, no matter what happens in the *try* and *catch* blocks. Thus, even when a *catch* throws a new exception, the *finally* block executes. The *finally* block gives us an opportunity to clean up after a failed *catch*. In writing the algorithm for the *finally* block, however, we must recognize that this block always executes, even if the *try* succeeds.

In this book we use only *try-catch* statements, and we keep our exception handlers simple so that they won't produce additional exceptions. The *finally* clause is really needed only when a *catch* contains statements that might generate a new exception, and we need to undo some of its processing before throwing the exception.

■ Generating an Exception with *throw*

Thus far, all of our examples have shown exceptions being thrown from methods associated with Java library classes. Here we introduce the *throw* statement, which allows us to throw an exception from within our own methods. Its syntax is quite simple:

Throw-Statement

```
throw Object-Expression ;
```

The Object-Expression must be an object of one of the Java exception classes. We will see how to define our own exception classes in Chapter 10. For now, we will use only the exception classes that are predefined by Java. All exception classes have a constructor that takes a string as an argument; this string is then returned by the `getMessage` method. For example, if `someproblem` is `true` in the code fragment

```java
try
{
  if (someproblem)
    throw new Exception("Some problem occurred.");
. . .
}
catch(Exception except)
{
  System.out.println("Exception thrown: " + except.getMessage());
}
```

then an object of class `Exception` is instantiated and thrown. The object contains the message `"Some problem occurred."` The object is passed to the parameter (`except`) of the *catch* clause,

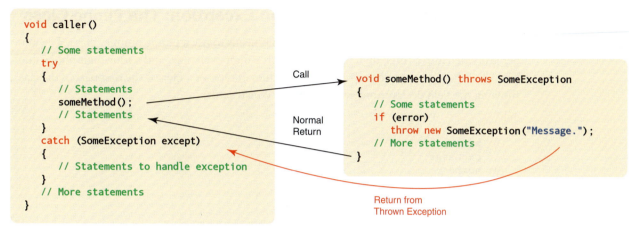

```
void caller()
{
    // Some statements
    try
    {
        // Statements
        someMethod();
        // Statements
    }
    catch (SomeException except)
    {
        // Statements to handle exception
    }
    // More statements
}
```

Call

Normal
Return

```
void someMethod() throws SomeException
{
    // Some statements
    if (error)
        throw new SomeException("Message.");
    // More statements
}
```

Return from
Thrown Exception

FIGURE 7.3   Throwing an Exception to Be Caught in a Calling Method

which is then executed. By calling the `getMessage` method associated with `except`, the *catch* clause is able to retrieve the message. It then displays `Exception thrown: Some problem occurred.`

The *throw* statement may be written within a *try* statement that is intended to catch it. In that case, control is transferred to the *catch* clause with the corresponding class.

More often, the *throw* occurs inside a method that is called from within a *try* statement, as shown in Figure 7.3. The JVM first looks for a *catch* within the method. If it fails to find one, it causes the method to return. The JVM then looks around the point where the method was called and finds an appropriate *catch* clause. The *catch* executes, and control transfers to the statement following the *try-catch*.

As we've seen previously, we must handle each class of exception either by catching it or explicitly forwarding it with a *throws* clause in the method heading. Thus an exception can cause a chain of returns that reaches the JVM only when our code is written to allow it to do so. We can't generate an exception that is accidentally uncaught.

We can throw any of the standard exceptions that Java provides. For example:

```
throw new FileNotFoundException(filename + " (No such file or directory)");
```

It's actually quite rare to write code that throws one of the standard exceptions. Instead, we typically throw exception classes that we have defined. Before we can define such an exception class, however, we must learn how to use a feature of Java called *inheritance*, which we cover in Chapter 10. Until then, we will throw objects of the `Exception` class to illustrate the use of exceptions.

Note that the use of `Exception` isn't normally recommended because a *catch* clause that has a parameter of class `Exception` catches all kinds of exceptions. As a consequence, we run the risk that in trying to catch the exception we've thrown, we might catch other exceptions that we haven't designed the *catch* clause to handle. Keep in mind that here we are illustrating the workings of the *throw-catch* mechanism, but not good programming style! With that caveat, we turn to an example.

■ An Example of Throwing an Exception: The Phone Class

Suppose that we are writing an application that needs to use a phone number class. The number is divided into a three-digit area code, a three-digit exchange, and a four-digit phone number. All of these parts can be represented by values of type `int`. Here is the first part of the class, showing the field declarations, with a default constructor:

```java
public class Phone
{
  int area;
  int exchange;
  int number;

  public Phone()
  {
    area = 999;
    exchange = 999;
    number = 9999;
  }
```

Now we consider the direct constructor. Notice that we did not assign zeroes to the fields in the default constructor. That's because a phone number with all zeroes isn't valid. Specific rules govern the values that are assigned as phone numbers. For example, the area code and exchange must both be greater than 199 and less than 1000, and 911 is not allowed. The phone number cannot be greater than 9999 or less than zero. What should the constructor do if it is passed invalid data? We don't know! And when we don't know how to handle an error, we throw it back to the caller as an exception. Thus the direct constructor looks like this:

```java
public Phone(int newArea, int newExch, int newNum) throws Exception
{
  if ( newArea < 200 || newArea > 999 || newArea == 911 ||
       newExch < 200 || newExch > 999 || newExch == 911 ||
       newNum < 0 || newNum > 9999)
    throw new Exception("Invalid phone number: (" + newArea + ")" +
                        newExch + "-" + newNum);
  else
  {
    area = newArea;
    exchange = newExch;
    number = newNum;
  }
}
```

Note that the constructor includes a *throws* clause in the heading, in addition to the *throw* statement in the body. Whenever we write a method that throws an exception, we have to include a corresponding *throws* clause in the heading.

The remainder of the Phone class is straightforward, with observers for each of the fields, and a `toString` method that does a little formatting of the number:

```java
public int getArea() { return area; }
public int getExchange() { return exchange; }
public int getNumber() { return number; }
public String toString()
  { return "(" + area + ")" + exchange + "-" + number; }
}
```

The following code might appear in a test driver for this class:

```
try
{
    Phone testPhone = new Phone(0, 555, 1212);
}
catch (Exception except)
{
    System.out.println(except.getMessage());
}
```

When it executes, it produces the following output:

```
Invalid phone number: (0)555-1212
```

In the exercises, you are asked to design and implement a test plan for the `Phone` class. Note that the plan must test values that are both within and outside the valid ranges for each of the arguments to the constructor. In Chapter 10, we will see how to define an `InvalidPhoneException` class that we can throw from `Phone` instead of throwing `Exception`.

PROBLEM SOLVING CASE STUDY

Address Book Lookup

Problem You have been given a file of data (`addressbook.txt`) representing an address book. Each entry on the file consists of a name, address, and phone number. You are to write an application to search this file and find particular entries. The desired searches are to find an entry with a matching name, to find all entries with a matching ZIP code, and to find all entries with a matching area code.

An entry consists of four lines of data. The first line contains the name in first, last, middle order, separated by blanks. The next line contains the street address. The third line has the city, state, and ZIP code, also separated by blanks. The last line contains the phone number as three integers (area, exchange, number), separated by blanks.

The first line of the file holds an integer representing the number of entries on the file, and the first entry begins on the second line. Each group of four lines after the first line is an entry.

Discussion As always, we start by brainstorming the classes we need for the problem. Here is a list of the objects that are mentioned in the problem statement:

> File of data
> Address book
> Entry
> Name

Address
Phone number
Number of entries

Filtering The address book is clearly an object in the problem. We don't have an entry class, so that will be new, but we already have the classes `Name`, `Address`, and `Phone`. The number of entries is just an integer, so we can use an `int` to hold it. Here is the filtered and annotated list:

Class	Implementation
Address book	New class
Entry	New class
Name	Class `Name`
Address	Class `Address`
Phone number	Class `Phone`
Input file	`Scanner` and `FileReader`

Attributes and Initial Responsibilities The classes that we must develop, other than the driver, are `AddressBook` and `Entry`. Let's begin with `AddressBook`. Internally, `AddressBook` is represented by the file. A default constructor will initialize the `Scanner` for file name `addressbook.txt`. Because we may want to specify a different file in the future, let's also provide a constructor that takes a file name.

The operations on the address book are the three searches. Thus we have the following attribute and responsibilities:

Attribute	
AddressBook	`Scanner`

Responsibilities

Default constructor
Parameterized constructor
printEntryWithName
printEntriesWithZip
printEntriesWithArea

Next we turn our attention to `Entry`. We know that it contains `Name`, `Address`, and `Phone` objects. We'll want a default constructor, an observer for each attribute, and a `toString` operation. What other responsibilities should it have? Because we'll be reading entries from a file, it would be helpful to have a constructor that takes its data from a `Scanner`. In the future, a direct constructor may also be helpful. Here are the attributes and responsibilities for `Entry`:

Attributes

Name	`Name`
Address:	`Address`
Phone Number:	`Phone`

Responsibilities

```
Default constructor
Scanner-based constructor
Direct constructor
getName
getAddress
getPhone
toString
```

To see if there are any additional responsibilities, we have to walk through some scenarios.

Scenario Walkthrough   Let's look at a pair of scenarios. The first is a search by name, and the second is a search by ZIP code.

First Scenario   The driver first instantiates the `AddressBook`. It then asks the user for the search type. How does the user choose? Let's display a menu that tells the user to enter a corresponding number:

```
Enter the number of the type of search you would like to perform:
1: First entry with matching name
2: All entries with matching ZIP code
3: All entries with matching area codes
```

We input this number and use a *switch* statement to select the search. In this scenario, the user enters a choice of 1. We ask the user to enter the name, and we then instantiate a `Name` object. Next we call `printEntryWithName` for the `AddressBook` object, passing it the `Name` object as its argument.

Now what does that operation do? Consider how you would do this task by hand with a pile of index cards. You would take each card and compare the name on it to the given name. If they match, then the search ends and you copy down the information from the card. If they don't match, you take the next card and repeat the process. Clearly, we need a loop for this task.

Because the file contains at least one entry, we can use a *do-while* loop to read until we find a match. What if the file is empty, or we get to EOF before a match is found? We can handle those exceptional cases by catching the `NoSuchElementException` that `Scanner` throws. How do we detect a match? We use the `getName` observer for the entry, and compare the two names using `compareTo`. When the match is found, we exit the loop and output the entry. No additional responsibilities are required for this scenario.

Second Scenario   Now we turn to the ZIP code search. The scenario begins the same way, but the user enters 2 for the type of search. We input the ZIP code and call `printEntriesWithZip`. How do we search for all matching entries in our pile of index cards? We begin as before, but when we find a match, we write down the information from the card and continue searching. In this case, the search ends when we read the last card.

We could use an EOF-controlled loop for this search, but given that we know the number of entries in the file, we can also use a *for* loop. We choose to use a *for* loop here, partly because it provides an instructive example. After each entry is read, we use `getAddress` and then `getZipCode` to retrieve the ZIP code for the entry. An equality comparison tells us if we have a match, in which case we output the entry.

What if the number of entries at the start of the file is wrong? If it is too small, then some entries won't be checked; otherwise, the application executes normally (we ask you to solve this problem in the exercises). If the number is too large, then we get a `NoSuchElementException`, which we must catch. Like the first scenario, this scenario doesn't add any more responsibilities.

A scenario with the area code search reveals that it is nearly identical to the ZIP code search and doesn't need any new responsibilities. Normally, we would implement such a similar responsibility by replicating the code from the ZIP code search, merely changing it to use area code. But because we'd like you to see an alternative algorithm, we'll actually write this code using an EOF-controlled *while* loop.

Now we have all of the responsibilities required for the application, and we can move into the implementation phase. We begin with the `Entry` class, because `AddressBook` uses it.

Implementation of `Entry` Class   All of the `Entry` responsibilities are very simple and straightforward, with the exception of the constructor that reads from a `Scanner`. Let's just review the steps involved.

Entry Constructor (Scanner)

Read first, last, and middle names
Instantiate a Name and assign it to the name field
Instantiate an Address object with the Address constructor that reads from a Scanner
Assign the address to the address field
Read area code, exchange, and number
try
    Instantiate a Phone object from area code, exchange, and number
    Assign Phone object to phone field
catch Exception (invalid phone number)
    Assign default Phone object to phone field

We're now ready to implement the `Entry` class:

```java
import java.util.*;
public class Entry
{
  Name name;
  Address address;
  Phone phone;
```

```java
  // Default constructor
  public Entry ()
  {
    name = new Name();
    address = new Address();
    phone = new Phone();
  }
  // Direct constructor
  public Entry (Name newName, Address newAddr, Phone newPhone)
  {
    name = newName;
    address = newAddr;
    phone = newPhone;
  }
  // Scanner-based constructor
  public Entry (Scanner in)
  {
    String first = in.next();
    // Get name
    String last = in.next();
    String middle = in.next();
    String separator = in.nextLine();
    name = new Name(first, last, middle);
    // Get address
    address = new Address(in);
    // Get phone number
    int area = in.nextInt();
    int exch = in.nextInt();
    int numb = in.nextInt();
    try { phone = new Phone(area, exch, numb); }
    catch (Exception ex) { phone = new Phone(); }
  }
  // Observers
  public Name getName () { return name; }
  public Address getAddress () { return address; }
  public Phone getPhone () { return phone; }
  public String toString ()
  {
    return name.toString() + '\n' +
           address.toString() + '\n' +
           phone.toString();
  }
}
```

To test this class, we would instantiate an `Entry` object using each of the constructors, and then output the contents of those objects using the observers and `toString`. We would also try to instantiate an `Entry` object with an invalid phone number to ensure that this error is caught correctly. We ask you to write and implement this test plan in the exercises.

It's worth taking a moment to appreciate what a simple matter it is to implement `Entry`, given all of the effort that has previously gone into developing the `Name`, `Address`, and `Phone` classes. This layering up of classes (called *composition*) is a basic aspect of object-oriented design that enables us to write very sophisticated applications with comparatively little new code.

Implementation of AddressBook The two constructors for **AddressBook** are simple and very similar. However, a little thought reveals that we don't actually want to instantiate the **Scanner** from the file name when we construct the object. Instead, we want each search operation to handle that task, so that it can also close the file when it is done. That way, if we decide to extend the application to allow the user to perform a series of searches, each search will automatically start from the beginning of the file. Thus the constructor just records the file name, which we declare as an instance field in the class declarations.

Note that this is a change in the representation that we first specified. Instead of representing the **AddressBook** with a file, we're using a file name. Here is the first part of the class:

```java
import java.util.*;
import java.io.*;
public class AddressBook
{
  String filename;
  public AddressBook()
  {
    filename = "addressbook.txt";
  }
  public AddressBook(String newFilename)
  {
    filename = newFilename;
  }
```

Now we can turn to the search operations. In each case, we begin by opening the file. The first line on the file is the number of entries. If the search uses this value, we read it into an **int** variable. In all cases, we need to call **nextLine** to go to the first line of the first entry.

Each search contains a loop that runs through the entries in the file. Within the loop, an *if* statement checks the entry and outputs it when it matches the value. We use a *do-while* loop to search for a matching name. So that we can show two other ways of implementing a similar search, we use a *for* loop to search for ZIP codes and an EOF-controlled *while* loop to search for area codes. We place the loops for the first two searches in *try-catch* statements that check for a **NoSuchElementException**. Because the area code search includes a check for EOF, it doesn't have to catch the exception.

Here is the implementation of the name search:

```java
public void printEntryWithName(Name name) throws IOException
{
  Entry entry;
  Scanner in = new Scanner(new FileReader(filename));
  try
  {
    in.nextLine();                        // Go to next line
    boolean done = false;
    do                                    // Scan file for a match
    {
      entry = new Entry(in);
      if (entry.getName().compareTo(name) == 0)
      {
        System.out.println(entry);        // Output matching entry
```

```
          done = true;
        }
      }
    while (!done);
  }
  catch (NoSuchElementException ex)
  {
    System.out.println("No match found.");
  }
  in.close();
}
```

Should we catch the `IOException` that occurs if the file doesn't exist? We could, but what would we do with it? At best, we could output an error message and throw the exception again. It's better to just let the client code handle the exception.

Here is the search for matching ZIP codes:

```
public void printEntriesWithZip(int zipCode) throws IOException
{
  Entry entry;
  Scanner in = new Scanner(new FileReader(filename));
  try
  {
    int numEntries = in.nextInt();        // Get number of entries on file
    in.nextLine();                        // Go to next line
    for (int entryNum = 1; entryNum <= numEntries; entryNum++)
    {                                     // Scan file for all matches
      entry = new Entry(in);
      if (entry.getAddress().getZipCode() == zipCode)
        System.out.println(entry);        // Output matching entry
    }
  }
  catch (NoSuchElementException ex)
  {
    System.out.println("File has fewer entries than indicated.");
  }
  in.close();
}
```

Searching for area codes is essentially the same operation, except that we instead retrieve the area code from the `Phone` field of the entry. In this case, we see how it can be done with an EOF-controlled *while*:

```
public void printEntriesWithArea(int areaCode) throws IOException
{
  Entry entry;
  Scanner in = new Scanner(new FileReader(filename));
  if (in.hasNextLine())
    in.nextLine();                        // Go to next line
  else
    System.out.println("File is empty.");
  while (in.hasNext())
  {                                       // Scan file for all matches
    entry = new Entry(in);
    if (entry.getPhone().getArea() == areaCode)
```

```
        System.out.println(entry);            // Output matching entry
    }
    in.close();
}
```

Implementation of the Driver Now that we have our new classes, we create the driver. From our scenarios, we know what most of the steps will be. Basically, we get the type of search from the user and then use a *switch* to call the appropriate search after reading the value to match. We'll include a **default** *switch*, in case the user enters an invalid search number. Here is the code for the driver class:

```
//***************************************************************************
// Application AddressBookLookup searches for entries in an address book on
// file addressbook.txt. It supports three kinds of queries:
//    1: first entry with matching name
//    2: all entries with matching ZIP code
//    3: all entries with matching area code
// It catches errors in which an invalid entry is specified or when the
// number of entries specified is greater than the number on the file
//***************************************************************************
import java.util.*;
import java.io.*;
public class AddressBookLookup
{
  public static void main (String[] args) throws IOException
  {
    AddressBook book = new AddressBook();
    System.out.println("Enter the number of the type of search " +
                       "you would like to perform:");
    System.out.println("1: First entry with matching name");
    System.out.println("2: All entries with matching ZIP code");
    System.out.println("3: All entries with matching area codes");
    Scanner in = new Scanner(System.in);
    int type = in.nextInt();                  // Get search type
    switch (type)
    {
      case 1 :                                // First entry with matching name
        System.out.print("Enter name (first last middle): ");
        String first = in.next();             // Get name to match
        String last = in.next();
        String middle = in.next();
        Name name = new Name(first, last, middle);
        System.out.println();                 // Output a blank line
        book.printEntryWithName(name);        // Output the matching entry
        break;
      case 2 :                                // All entries with matching ZIP
        System.out.print("Enter ZIP code: ");
        int zipCode = in.nextInt();           // Get ZIP code to match
        System.out.println();                 // Output a blank line
        book.printEntriesWithZip(zipCode);    // Output the matching entries
        break;
      case 3 :                                // All entries with matching
                                              // area code
        System.out.print("Enter area code: ");
        int areaCode = in.nextInt();          // Get area code to match
```

```
        System.out.println();                    // Output a blank line
        book.printEntriesWithArea(areaCode);     // Output the matching entries
        break;
      default : System.out.println("Invalid search selected.");
    }
  }
}
```

For testing purposes, we have created a data file with five entries:

```
5
Sylva Santana Marie
128 Binoway St.
Leafton MA 11048
617 222 1111
Evan Parsival Sunny
32 East Pleasant St.
Arbuelo AZ 73421
480 444 9999
William Herrold Michael
31415 Pieman Lane
Leafton MA 11048
617 888 3333
Madeline Corby Jenelle
2048 Earlham St.
Clarkson AZ 73438
480 555 6666
Laurens Gruman Franke
1024 Ibiem Road
Leafton MA 11048
781 777 7777
```

Here is a test run of the application with this file. We will have more to say about testing this application in the following section.

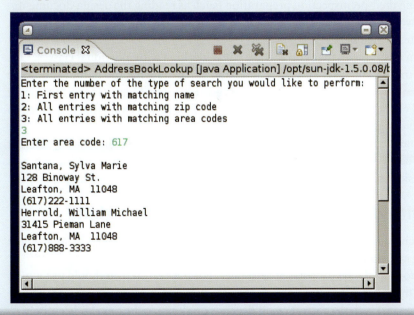

7.9 : Testing and Debugging

■ General Testing Strategies

> **Desk checking**   Tracing the execution of a design on paper
>
> **Walkthrough**   A verification method in which a team performs a manual simulation of the code or design
>
> **Inspection**   A verification method in which one member of a team reads the code or design line by line and the other team members point out errors
>
> **Execution trace**   Going through the code with actual values, recording the state of the variables

When an individual programmer is designing a class or application, he or she can find many errors with pencil and paper. **Desk checking** is a very common method of manually verifying a design. The programmer writes down essential data (variables, input values, parameters of methods, and so on) and walks through the design, manually simulating the actions and recording changes. Portions of the design that are complex or a source of concern should be double-checked.

Desk checking can be performed by an individual, but most larger applications are developed by teams of programmers. Two extensions of desk checking that are used effectively by programming teams are the design or code **walkthrough** and the code **inspection**. These formal team activities are intended to transfer the responsibility for uncovering bugs from the individual programmer to the group. Because testing is time-consuming and errors cost more the later they are discovered, the goal is to identify errors before testing begins.

In a walkthrough, the team conducts a manual simulation of the design or code with sample test inputs, keeping track of the variable's values by hand. Unlike thorough testing, the walkthrough is not intended to simulate all possible test cases. Instead, its purpose is to stimulate discussion about the way the programmer chose to design or implement the code's requirements.

At an inspection, a reader (typically not the code's author) goes through the design or code line by line. Inspection participants point out errors, which are recorded on an inspection report. Some errors are uncovered just by the process of reading aloud; others are uncovered by team members during their preinspection preparation (such as reading the design documentation). As with the walkthrough, the chief benefit of the team meeting is the discussion that takes place among team members.

Now let's return to strategies that you can use when working with individual classes. One useful technique is to take some actual values and hand-calculate what the output should be by doing an **execution trace** (or hand trace). When the code is executed, you can use these same values as input and check the results. Hand tracing is merely desk checking that is applied to code—rather than a design—in a more formal manner.

When code contains control structures, it's a good idea to retrace its execution using different input data so that broader code coverage is achieved. In the next section, we note specific test cases to be taken into consideration with each of the new control structures introduced in this chapter.

■ Testing with *do-while, for, switch,* and Exceptions

The same testing techniques we used with *while* loops apply to *do* and *for* loops as well. There are, however, a few additional considerations with the latter loops.

The body of a *do* loop always executes at least once. For this reason, you should test it with data sets that show the result of executing the *do* loop the minimal number of times. Make sure that there are no cases in which the correct result depends on skipping the loop body entirely.

With a data-dependent *for* loop, it is important to test for proper results when the loop executes zero times. This situation arises when the starting value is greater than the ending value (or less than the ending value if the loop is counting down).

When an application contains a *switch* statement, you should test it with enough different data sets to ensure that each branch is selected and executed correctly. You should also test it with a *switch* expression value that is not in any of the case labels.

An application that handles exceptions must be tested to ensure that the exceptions are generated appropriately and then handled properly. Test cases must be included that cause exceptions to occur, and the expected results from handling those exceptions must be specified.

■ Testing with Nested Control Structures

When we nest control structures, the number of test cases can grow quite large. For example, when we test a branch, our test cases must exercise each side of the branch. That requires a minimum of two test cases, and even more if the conditional test is complex. If each side of the branch contains a nested branch, then at least four cases are required, assuming that each one also tests the enclosing branch.

Let's use the `printEntryWithName` method as an example, to see how many test cases we would need to cover the paths through a set of nested control structures. Figure 7.4 shows a diagram of the control flow paths in the method.

In this method, a *try-catch* encloses a *do* loop that contains an *if*. We can organize the test plan for this method according to the following outline:

1. *try*
2. *do*
3.   *if* true
4.   *if* false
5. *catch*

Enumerating the paths would seem to indicate that at least five test cases are required. This scheme ignores the relationships between the structures, however. If we are testing the *if*

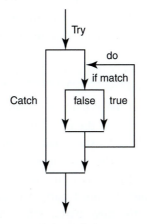

FIGURE 7.4   Control Flow Paths in `printEntryWithName`

within the *do*, then we have already exercised the steps that cause the *do* to be entered. One carefully designed test case, therefore, can cover both.

With each independent entry in the list, we apply our testing strategy for that kind of structure. For example, we should test a *for* loop with different numbers of iterations (including zero). An *if* may also have a compound condition that requires multiple test cases. When a *catch* is handling an exception that could be generated at more than one point in the *try*, then we should verify that all of those cases are properly caught.

Thus the outline is merely a way of organizing our testing. It helps us identify overlapping cases, and it serves as a checklist to ensure that we are achieving full code coverage. As we identify additional cases associated with particular structures, it provides a place to insert them in the plan.

Here is the revised outline, with comments indicating the purpose of each test case:

1. *try*, *do* (1 iteration), *if* true/false: Name matches first entry on file
2. *try*, *do* (*n* iterations), *if* true/false: Name matches entry in middle of file
3. *try*, *do* (all), *if* true/false: Name matches last entry on file
4. *catch:* Name is not on file
5. *catch:* File is empty

Notice how the *try*, *do*, and *if* paths have been transformed into a trio of combined tests, whereas the *catch* has been expanded to multiple tests (4 and 5). Given such a commented outline, we can devise an input data set for each test case. An execution trace on each data set will help us determine the expected output. We are then ready to specify and implement our test plan for the method (which we ask you to do in the exercises).

Testing and Debugging Hints

1. Make sure that all exceptions are either caught or forwarded as appropriate.
2. In a *switch* statement, make sure that a *break* statement appears at the end of each case alternative. Otherwise, control "falls through" to the code in the next case alternative.
3. Case labels in a *switch* statement consist of values, not variables. They may, however, include named constants and expressions involving only constants.
4. A *switch* expression must be one of the types `char`, `byte`, `short`, `int`, or `enum`. It cannot be of type `long` or a floating-point or string expression.
5. The case constants of a *switch* statement cannot be of type `long` or be floating-point or string constants.
6. If the possibility exists that the value of the *switch* expression might not match one of the case constants, you should provide a `default` alternative.
7. Double-check long *switch* statements to make sure that you haven't omitted any branches.
8. The *do* loop is a posttest loop. If the possibility exists that the loop body might be skipped entirely, use a *while* or *for* statement instead.
9. The *for* statement heading (the first line) always has three parts within the parentheses. Typically, the first part initializes a loop control variable, the second part tests the variable, and the third part increments or decrements the variable. Semicolons must separate the three parts. Any of the parts can be omitted, but the semicolons must still be present.

Graphical User Interfaces

showInputDialog

In Chapter 6, we saw how a dialog can be used to input a value indicating a button clicked by the user. Here we introduce a dialog that allows the user to enter arbitrary data values. The effect is similar to entering values via `System.in`, except that the dialog appears as a new window that disappears after the data is entered. In addition, the prompt and the input operations are combined in a single method call, rather than prompting via `System.out` and then reading from `System.in`.

The `showInputDialog` method creates a dialog box that asks the user to input information and click an OK button. This value-returning method then returns the string that the user has input. We look at two versions of the method, which are distinguished based on their argument lists. The first version just takes a `String` argument:

```
String inputValue =
        JOptionPane.showInputDialog("Please input an integer value");
```

It creates the following window:

The dialog box is labeled Input, which is a default value. The argument string appears above an input field. Two buttons are found below the field, and the default icon for a question-message dialog is to the left. When the user types a value in the field and clicks OK, the value is returned. If the user clicks the Cancel button, `null` is returned. If the user enters the value "44", the string `"44"` is stored in `inputValue`.

A second version of method `showInputDialog` has four arguments:

```
JOptionPane.showInputDialog(parentComponent, prompt, label, messageType)
```

Just as we saw with `showConfirmDialog`, the first argument applies to a parent window, which we have been specifying as `null`, and indicates that the dialog should be centered on the screen. The second argument is the prompt to be written above the input field. The third argument is the string that should appear as the label at the top of the window. The fourth argument is similar to the fourth argument to `showMessageDialog`, which specifies the type of icon to display. As a reminder, here are the possible values for this final argument:

```
JOptionPane.ERROR_MESSAGE
JOptionPane.INFORMATION_MESSAGE
JOptionPane.WARNING_MESSAGE
JOptionPane.QUESTION_MESSAGE
JOptionPane.PLAIN_MESSAGE
```

Here is an example of this method call and the dialog box it produces:

```
String inputValue =
  JOptionPane.showInputDialog(null,          // Parent component (null =
                                              //   the screen)
        "Please input an integer value",     // Prompt message
        "My Input Pane",                      // Label for top of dialog
        JOptionPane.QUESTION_MESSAGE);        // Message type
```

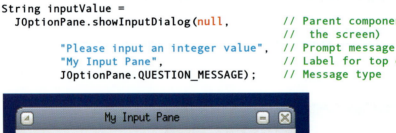

The third parameter now labels the dialog box, but the icon is still the same. Didn't the fourth parameter change it? Yes, but the message type that we chose (QUESTION_MESSAGE) is the same as the default, so the icon remains the same.

Using Scanner with showInputDialog

The `showInputDialog` method returns whatever string the user types in the input field. But what if we want to read either a single number or a series of numbers that the user has entered? This is the same problem that we encountered when reading directly from `System.in`, which returns only string data. We solved that problem using a `Scanner`, and we'll solve it the same way in this context.

Recall that a `Scanner` can read from a string as well as `System.in`. Thus we can apply a `Scanner` to the value returned from `showInputDialog`. As an example, let's see how we could have used `showInputDialog` to read the ZIP code in our case study. In the driver, this operation was implemented as follows:

```java
Scanner in = new Scanner(System.in);
.
.
.
case 2 :                                        // All entries with
                                                // matching ZIP code

  System.out.print("Enter ZIP code: ");
  int zipCode = in.nextInt();                   // Get ZIP code to match
```

We can replace these statements with the following (assuming `inString` is declared as a `String` variable):

```java
case 2 :                                        // All entries with
                                                // matching ZIP code
  inString = JOptionPane.showInputDialog("Enter ZIP code:");
  Scanner inDialog = new Scanner(inString);
  int zipCode = inDialog.nextInt();             // Get ZIP code to match
```

To be on the safe side, we should check that the user didn't click cancel (`inString != null`):

```java
case 2 :                                        // All entries with
                                                // matching ZIP code
  inString = JOptionPane.showInputDialog("Enter ZIP code:");
  if (inString != null)                         // Checks whether user
                                                // clicked Cancel
  {
    Scanner inDialog = new Scanner(inString);
    int zipCode = inDialog.nextInt();           // Get ZIP code to match
    book.printEntriesWithZip(zipCode);          // Output the
                                                // matching entries
  }
  else
    System.out.println("Search cancelled.");
  break;
```

If we don't perform this check, then the code throws an exception when the user clicks Cancel. Changing the case study to read the area code from a dialog would be done in essentially the same way. Here's how we can use `showInputDialog` to read the name in the case study:

```java
case 1 :                                        // First entry with
                                                // matching name
  inString =
    JOptionPane.showInputDialog("Enter name (first last middle): ");
```

```java
if (inString != null)                              // Checks whether user
                                                   // clicked Cancel
{
  Scanner inDialog = new Scanner(inString);
  String first = inDialog.next();                  // Get name to match
  String last = inDialog.next();
  String middle = inDialog.next();
  Name name = new Name(first, last, middle);
  book.printEntryWithName(name);                   // Output the
                                                   // matching entry
}
else
  System.out.println("Search cancelled.");
break;
```

As you can see, once the `Scanner` is instantiated, it is possible to read multiple values from it. Of course, if the user doesn't enter enough values, a `NoSuchElementException` will be thrown. Even so, it's clear that input from `showInputDialog` can be as flexible as reading from `System.in`.

Here is the dialog that is displayed when the GUI version of `AddressBookLookup` is run, with the user choosing to search by area code:

There is one other point that we should note. Until now, we have always imported `java.util.Scanner`. The `NoSuchElementException` class is also part of the `java.util` package. Thus, if we plan to catch such errors, we should import `java.util.*`, so that both the `Scanner` class and the `NoSuchElementException` class are available to us.

Summary

The *switch* statement is a multiway selection statement. It allows the code to choose among a set of branches. A *switch* statement containing *break* statements can always be simulated by an *if-else-if* structure. If a *switch* statement can be used, however, it often makes the code easier to read and understand. It cannot be used with floating-point or string values in the case labels.

The *do* loop is a general-purpose looping statement. It works like the *while* loop, except that its test occurs at the end of the loop, guaranteeing at least one execution of the loop body. Like a *while* loop, a *do* loop continues as long as the loop condition remains `true`. A *do* loop is a convenient choice for loops that test input values and then repeat if the input is not correct.

The *for* statement is a looping statement that is commonly used to implement count-controlled loops. The initialization, testing, and incrementation (or decrementation) of the loop control variable are centralized in one location, the first line of the *for* statement.

An exception occurs when an error condition is encountered. The source of the error is said to "throw an exception," which we can catch using a *try-catch* statement. Catching an exception and handling it properly enable the application to continue executing, rather than allowing the error to be passed to the JVM, which halts the application with an error message. Typical exceptions include `IOException`, `NumberFormatException`, and `NoSuchElementException`. The *throw* statement gives us the ability to throw exceptions when we detect them.

The increment and assignment operators produce both a result and a side effect, which enables them to be used in clever ways that aren't always easy to understand. We recommend that you use these operators only in their simple forms so that the meaning is always clear. Even so, you must be able to interpret such usage when you encounter it in code written by a programmer who values compact syntax over clarity.

The *for*, *do*, *switch*, *try-catch*, and *throw* statements are the "ice cream and cake" of Java. We can live without them if we absolutely must, but they are very nice to have.

LEARNING Portfolio

Quick Check

1. Given a *switch* expression that is the `int` variable `nameVal`, write a *switch* statement that writes the following to the `PrintWriter` file called `outData`: your first name if `nameVal = 1`, your middle name if `nameVal = 2`, and your last name if `nameVal = 3`. (pp. 340–344)

2. How would you change the code you wrote for Question 1 so that it writes an error message if the value is not 1, 2, or 3? (pp. 340–344)

3. What happens if you forget to include a *break* statement at the end of a *switch* case? (pp. 340–344)

4. What is the primary difference between a *while* loop and a *do* loop? (pp. 344–346)

5. A certain problem requires a count-controlled loop that starts at 10 and counts down to 1. Write the heading (the first line) of a *for* statement that controls this loop. (pp. 346–348)

6. Which Java looping statement would you choose for a loop that is both count-controlled and event-controlled and whose body might not execute even once? (p. 349)

7. What is the difference between an expression and an expression statement in Java? (pp. 357–361)

8. Write a statement that inputs an integer from `Scanner in` and writes out the exception message string if a `NumberFormatError` occurs. (pp. 362–366)

9. Which exception class includes all exceptions? (pp. 368–369)

10. Name the three parts of an exception-handling mechanism. (pp. 366–368)

11. When an exception is thrown, we instantiate an exception object with a constructor that takes a string as its argument. What is the string used for? (pp. 366–368)

Answers

```
1.  switch (nameVal)
    {
      case 1 : outData.println("Mary");
               break;
      case 2 : outData.println("Lynn");
               break;
      case 3 : outData.println("Smith");
               break;   // Not required
    }
2.  switch (nameVal)
    {
      case 1  : outData.println("Mary");
                break;
      case 2  : outData.println("Lynn");
                break;
      case 3  : outData.println("Smith");
                break;
      default : outData.println("Invalid name value.");
    }
```

3. Execution proceeds to the statements in the next *case* clause. 4. The body of a *do* loop always executes at least once; the body of a *while* loop may not execute at all. 5. `for (count = 10; count >= 1; count--)` 6. A *while* (or perhaps a *for*) statement. 7. An expression becomes an expression statement when it is terminated by a semicolon.

```
8.  try
    {
      intValue = in.nextInt();
    }
    catch(NumberFormatException except)
    {
      System.out.println(except.getMessage());
    }
```

9. `Exception`

10. Defining the exception, raising the exception, and handling the exception.

11. It provides an error message that can be retrieved in the *catch* with the `getMessage` method.

LEARNING Portfolio

Exam Preparation Exercises

1. Define the following terms: *switch* expression, pretest loop, posttest loop.

2. A *switch* expression may be an expression that results in a value of type `int`, `float`, `boolean`, or `char`. (True or False?)

3. The values in *case* labels may appear in any order, but duplicate *case* labels are not allowed within a given *switch* statement. (True or False?)

4. All possible values for the *switch* expression must be included among the *case* labels for a given *switch* statement. (True or False?)

5. Rewrite the following code fragment using a *switch* statement:

```
if (n == 3)
   alpha++;
else if (n == 7)
   beta++;
else if (n == 10)
   gamma++;
```

6. If n equals 3, what is printed by the following code fragment? (Be careful here.)

```
switch (n + 1)
{
   case 2  : outData.println("Bill");
   case 4  : outData.println("Mary");
   case 7  : outData.println("Joe");
   case 9  : outData.println("Anne");
   default : outData.println("Whoops!");
}
```

7. If a *while* loop whose condition is `delta <= alpha` is converted to a *do* loop, the loop condition of the *do* loop is `delta > alpha`. (True or False?)

8. A *do* statement always ends in a semicolon. (True or False?)

9. What is printed by the following code fragment? (All variables are of type `int`.)

```
n = 0;
i = 1;
do
{
   outData.print(i);
   i++;
} while (i <= n);
```

10. What is printed by the following code fragment? (All variables are of type `int`.)

```
n = 0;
for (i = 1; i <= n; i++)
   outData.print(i);
```

11. What is printed by the following code fragment? (All variables are of type `int`.)

```
for (i = 4; i >= 1; i--)
{
  for (j = i; j >= 1; j--)
    outData.print(j + " ");
  outData.println(i);
}
```

12. What is printed by the following code fragment? (All variables are of type `int`.)

```
for (row = 1; row <= 10; row++)
{
  for (col = 1; col <= 10 - row; col++)
    outData.print("*");
  for (col = 1; col <= 2 * row - 1; col++)
    outData.print(" ");
  for (col = 1; col <= 10 - row; col++)
    outData.print("*");
  outData.println();
}
```

13. A *break* statement located inside a *switch* statement that is located within a *while* loop causes control to exit the loop immediately. (True or False?)

14. Classify each of the following as either an expression or an expression statement.
    a. `sum = 0`
    b. `sqrt(x)`
    c. `y = 17;`
    d. `count++`

15. Rewrite each statement as described.
    a. Rewrite the following statement using the ++ operator.
       `count = count + 1;`
    b. Rewrite the following statement without using the decrement operator.
       `count = --count;`
    c. Rewrite the following as three separate assignment statements.
       `a = (b = (c = 10) + 20) + 30;`

16. Which control structure should you use if you think an operation might throw an exception?

17. Which statement raises an exception?

18. What part of the *try-catch-finally* structure must have a parameter consisting of an exception object?

19. Our code can catch exceptions it throws, but not exceptions that library methods throw. (True or False?)

20. Mark the following statements as true or false. If a statement is false, explain why.

  a. There can be only one *catch* clause for each *try* statement.

  b. The exception handler is located within the *catch* clause.

  c. The *finally* clause is optional.

  d. The *finally* clause is rarely used.

Programming Warm-Up Exercises

1. Write a *switch* statement that does the following:

If the value of **grade** (a variable of type **char**) is

'A', add 4 to **sum**

'B', add 3 to **sum**

'C', add 2 to **sum**

'D', add 1 to **sum**

'F', print **"Student is on probation"** on the **PrintWriter** file **outData**

2. Modify the code you wrote for Exercise 1 so that it prints an error message if **grade** does not equal one of the five possible grades.

3. Write a code segment that reads and sums values until it has summed ten data values or until a negative value is read, whichever comes first. Use a *do* loop for your solution.

4. Rewrite the following code segment using a *do* loop instead of a *while* loop.

```
response = inData.nextInt();
while (response >= 0 && response <= 127)
{
   response = inData.nextInt();
}
```

5. Rewrite the following code segment using a *while* loop.

```
inInt = inData.nextInt();
if (inInt >= 0)
   do
   {
      System.out.println("" + inInt);
      inInt = inData.nextInt();
   } while (inInt >= 0);
```

6. Rewrite the following code segment using a *for* loop.

```
sum = 0;
count = 1;
while (count <= 1000)
{
  sum = sum + count;
  count++;
}
```

7. Rewrite the following *for* loop as a *while* loop.

```
for (m = 93; m >= 5; m--)
  outData.println( m + " " + m * m);
```

8. Rewrite the following *for* loop as a *do* loop.

```
for (k = 9; k <= 21; k++)
  outData.println( k + " " + 3 * k);
```

9. Write a value-returning method that accepts two `int` parameters, `base` and `exponent`, and returns the value of `base` raised to the `exponent` power. Use a *for* loop in your solution.

10. Write a statement that throws an `ArithmeticException` if there is an attempt to divide by zero.

11. Write a *try-catch* statement that attempts to open the file `data.in` for reading and writes an error message if an exception is thrown.

12. Write a *try-catch* statement that attempts to read an integer from `System.in` using a `Scanner`, and outputs an error message if something other than an integer is entered.

13. Extend the code you wrote for Exercise 12 so that it uses a *do* loop to keep asking for input until the user enters an integer.

14. Write a statement that throws an exception of class `Exception`, with the message `"Data out of range."`

15. Design and implement a test plan for the `Phone` class developed in this chapter. Remember that you must check for instantiation of `Phone` objects with area and exchange numbers that are both within and outside the valid ranges. The `Phone` constructor throws an exception of class `Exception` if any of its arguments are invalid.

Programming Problems

1. Develop a Java application that inputs a two-letter abbreviation for one of the 50 states and displays the full name of the state. If the abbreviation isn't valid, the application

LEARNING Portfolio

should display an error message and ask for an abbreviation again. The names of the 50 states and their abbreviations are given in the following table.

State	Abbreviation	State	Abbreviation
Alabama	AL	Montana	MT
Alaska	AK	Nebraska	NE
Arizona	AZ	Nevada	NV
Arkansas	AR	New Hampshire	NH
California	CA	New Jersey	NJ
Colorado	CO	New Mexico	NM
Connecticut	CT	New York	NY
Delaware	DE	North Carolina	NC
Florida	FL	North Dakota	ND
Georgia	GA	Ohio	OH
Hawaii	HI	Oklahoma	OK
Idaho	ID	Oregon	OR
Illinois	IL	Pennsylvania	PA
Indiana	IN	Rhode Island	RI
Iowa	IA	South Carolina	SC
Kansas	KS	South Dakota	SD
Kentucky	KY	Tennessee	TN
Louisiana	LA	Texas	TX
Maine	ME	Utah	UT
Maryland	MD	Vermont	VT
Massachusetts	MA	Virginia	VA
Michigan	MI	Washington	WA
Minnesota	MN	West Virginia	WV
Mississippi	MS	Wisconsin	WI
Missouri	MO	Wyoming	WY

(*Hint:* Use nested *switch* statements, where the outer statement uses the first letter of the abbreviation as its *switch* expression.)

2. Design and write a Java application that reads a date in numeric form using three integers and displays it in English. For example, given the date

6   6   1944

the application displays:

```
June sixth, nineteen hundred forty-four.
```

Given the date

```
12  10  2010
```

the application displays:

```
December tenth, two thousand ten.
```

The application should display an error message for any invalid date, such as 2 29 1883 (1883 wasn't a leap year).

3. Write a Java application that reads full names from an input file and writes the initials for the names to an output file named `initials`. For example, the input

```
John James Henry
```

should produce the output

```
JJH
```

The names are stored in the input file as first name, middle name, last name, with each name separated by an arbitrary number of blanks. Only one name appears per line. The first name or the middle name could be just an initial, or there may not be a middle name.

4. Write a Java application that converts letters of the alphabet into their corresponding digits on the telephone. The application should let the user enter letters repeatedly until the user responds "No" when asked if he or she would like to enter another letter. It should print an error message when any nonalphabetic character is entered.

The letters and digits on the telephone have the following correspondence:

```
ABC = 2    DEF   = 3    GHI  = 4
JKL = 5    MNO   = 6    PQRS = 7
TUV = 8    WXYZ  = 9
```

Here is an example:

When the user enters P, the application displays

```
The letter P corresponds to 7 on the telephone.
```

When the user enters A, the application displays

```
The letter A corresponds to 2 on the telephone.
```

When the user enters D, the application displays

```
The letter D corresponds to 3 on the telephone.
```

When the user enters 2, the application displays

```
Invalid letter.
```

Case Study Follow-Up

1. Change the `AddressBookLookup` application so that, when it searches for all matches, it detects the situation in which the number of entries specified by the file is smaller than the actual number of entries. To do so, after exiting the *for* loop, use `hasNextLine` to determine whether the file is at EOF. If not, then there may be more entries, and a warning message should be output.

2. Specify the test data and expected results needed to implement the test plan for the `printEntryWithName` method, as outlined in the "Testing and Debugging" section.

3. Develop a test plan for the `AddressBook` class that extends the plan in Exercise 2 to include the remaining methods.

4. Develop a test plan for the `AddressBookLookup` application.

5. The `AddressBookLookup` application assumes that the data file exists. Add exception handling to the application for the case in which the file can't be found.

6. Write and implement a test plan for the `Entry` class developed in this chapter.

7. Extend the `AddressBookLookup` application so that it searches for all entries with matching last names. You will need to extend the `AddressBook` class with another search method.

8. Extend the class and application test plans to include the extension developed in Exercise 7.

9. Extend the `AddressBookLookup` application so that it allows the user to search repeatedly, ending the process by entering a value for the type of search, which indicates that the application should stop.

10. Extend the application test plan to include the extension developed in Exercise 9.

8 Object-Oriented Software Engineering

Goals

Knowledge Goals

To:

- Understand the concepts of encapsulation and abstraction
- Know how control and data abstraction facilitate modifiability and reuse
- Understand the basic principles of object-oriented design
- Know how packages support encapsulation
- Appreciate the abstraction provided by the **enum** type
- Understand how objects collaborate
- Know how to interpret a UML class diagram

Skill Goals

To be able to:

- Declare and use an **enum** type
- Develop a transformer (mutator) method
- Create a package with multiple compilation units
- Write a CRC card for an object
- Conduct scenarios using CRC cards
- Identify collaborations between objects
- Convert a CRC card into a Java class
- Draw a UML class diagram
- Write and read objects

1968
A NATO Science Committee introduces the term "software engineering"

1968
Edsger Dijkstra advocates for reliable software with a letter citing the weaknesses of the Go To statement

1968
Integrated circuits debut in computers

1968
The Federal Information Processing Standard promotes the YYMMDD standard for the date, setting the stage for the Y2K problem

1968
Intel Corporation is established by Andy Grove, Robert Noyce, and Gordon Moore

1969
ARPANET, the precursor to the Internet, is commissioned by the US Department of Defense

Introduction

In Chapter 1, we introduced some general techniques for solving problems. In the real world, many programming efforts involve solving multiple problems in a coordinated manner. Consequently, we need to learn how to organize our problem solving to achieve success in the face of greater complexity. The organizational methods used for this purpose are known as software engineering.

Entire courses can be devoted to the discipline of software engineering. In this chapter, we touch upon some key aspects that relate to object-oriented programming, and we introduce some formal notation that is useful in managing larger projects.

In the first part of this chapter, we look at two concepts that guide us in developing classes that are a part of larger problem solutions: encapsulation and abstraction. Then we see how the Java `package` construct helps us group related classes together so that others can conveniently import them, while preserving encapsulation and abstraction. Next we present Java's object I/O classes and the `enum` type as examples that both illustrate and support encapsulation and abstraction.

At the end of the chapter, we reexamine the programming process and formalize the software engineering strategy that we have been using. The first formalism we'll introduce is the CRC card, which is a notation that helps us manage the exploration of scenarios involving many classes. A second notation, called a UML diagram, allows us to document designs for the implementation and maintenance phases.

1970
The mobile robot Shakey uses artificial intelligence in its navigation

1970
Dennis Ritchie and Kenneth Thompson at Bell Labs develop the UNIX operating system for which they later received the U.S. National Medal of Technology

1970
IBM introduces the 8-inch floppy disk

1971
A team at Intel creates the first microprocessor, the Intel 4004

1971
Ray Tomlinson uses the @ sign, and sends the first electronic-mail message through ARPANET

1971
The programming language Pascal is developed by Niklaus Wirth

8.1 : Class Design Principles

■ Encapsulation

We begin this chapter by considering the principles that result in a well-designed class that can be used in the context of larger projects. Primary among these class design principles is the concept of **encapsulation**. The dictionary tells us that a capsule is a sealed container that protects its contents from outside contaminants or harsh conditions so as to keep them intact. To encapsulate something is to place it into a capsule. In object-oriented programming, the capsule is a class, and its attributes are the contents we want to protect. By itself, the class construct doesn't protect its attributes. We must consciously provide that protection by defining a formal class interface that limits access from other classes.

> **Encapsulation** Designing a class so that its attributes are isolated from the actions of external code except through the formal interface
>
> **Formal interface** The components of a class that are externally accessible, which consist of its nonprivate fields and methods
>
> **Reliable** A property of a unit of software such that it always operates consistently, according to the specification of its interface

What is the **formal interface**? In terms of class design, it is a written description of all the ways that the class may interact with other classes. The collection of methods and fields that are not `private` defines the formal interface syntactically.

If the contents of an object can be changed only through a well-designed interface, then we don't have to worry about bugs in the rest of the application affecting it in unintended ways. As long as we design the class so that its objects can handle any data that are consistent with the interface, we know that it is a **reliable** unit of software.

Here's an analogy that illustrates the difference between a class that is encapsulated and one that is not. Suppose you are a builder, constructing a house in a new development. Other builders are working in the same development. If each builder keeps all of his or her equipment and materials within the property lines of the house that he or she is building, and enters and leaves the site only via its driveway, then construction proceeds smoothly. The property lines encapsulate the individual construction sites, and the driveway is the only interface by which people, equipment, and materials can enter or leave a site.

Imagine the chaos that would ensue if builders started putting their materials and equipment in other sites without telling one another. And what would happen if they began driving through other sites with heavy equipment to reach their own sites? The materials might be used in the wrong houses, tools would be lost or run over by stray vehicles, and the whole process would break down. Figure 8.1 illustrates this situation.

Let's make this analogy concrete in Java by looking at two different interface designs for the same `Date` class, one that is encapsulated and one that is not.

```
// Encapsulated interface --         // Unencapsulated interface --
// avoids errors due to misuse       // potential source of bugs
private int month;                   public int month;
private int day;                     public int day;
private int year;                    public int year;

public void setDate (int newMonth,
                     int newDay,
                     int newYear)
// Checks that the new date is valid;
// otherwise, it leaves the current
// value unchanged
```

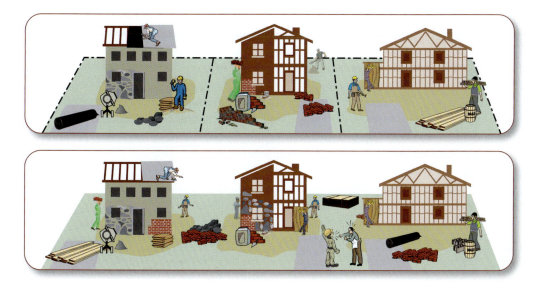

FIGURE 8.1   Encapsulation Draws Clear Boundaries Around Classes. Failing to Encapsulate Classes Can Lead to Chaos.

The interface on the right allows client code to directly change the fields of a `Date`. Thus, if the client code assigns the values 14, 206, and 83629 to these fields, you end up with a nonsense date of the 206th day of the 14th month of the year 83,629. The encapsulated implementation on the left makes these fields `private`. It then provides a `public` method that takes date values as arguments, and it checks that the date is valid before changing the fields within the object.

This example shows that Java does not provide any special syntax for encapsulation. Rather, we achieve encapsulation by carefully designing the class interface to ensure that its objects have complete control over what information enters and leaves them.

Encapsulation greatly simplifies the work of a programming team, because a different team member can develop each class without worrying how other classes are being implemented. In other words, in a large project, encapsulation permits each programmer to work independently on a different part. As long as each class meets its **specification**, then the separate classes can interact safely.

> **Specification**   The written description of the behavior of a class with respect to its interface
>
> **Abstraction**   The separation of the logical properties (interface and specification) of an object from its implementation

What do we mean by "specification"? Given a formal interface to a class, the specification is additional written documentation that describes how a class will behave for each possible interaction through the interface. For example, the formal interface defines how we call a method, and the specification describes what the method will do. You can think of the formal interface as the syntax of a class, and the specification as its semantics. By definition, the specification includes the formal interface.

■ Abstraction

Encapsulation is the basis for **abstraction** in programming. Consider, for example, that abstraction lets us use a `Scanner` without having to know the details of its operation.

Abstraction is how we simplify the design of a large application. As long as the interface and specification of a class are complete, the programmer who implements the class doesn't have to understand how the client code uses it. Conversely, as long as the programmer implements the interface and specification correctly, the programmer who uses the class doesn't have to think about how it is implemented.

Even when you are the programmer in both cases, abstraction simplifies your job because it allows you to focus on different parts of the implementation in isolation from each other. What might initially seem like a huge programming problem becomes much more manageable when you break it into little pieces. Solving each piece separately is an example of the divide-and-conquer strategy introduced in Chapter 1.

> **Data abstraction** The separation of the logical representation of an object's attributes from its implementation

There are basically two types of abstraction: data abstraction and control abstraction. **Data abstraction** is the separation of the external representation of an object's attributes from its internal implementation. For example, the external representation of a date might be integer values for the day and year, plus a string that specifies the name of the month. Within the class, however, we might implement the date using a standard value that calendar makers call the Julian day, which is the number of days since January 1, 4713 BC.

The advantage of using the Julian day is that it simplifies arithmetic involving dates, such as computing the number of days between dates. All of the complexity of dealing with leap years and the different number of days in the months is captured in formulas that make conversions between the conventional representation of a date and the Julian day. From the user's perspective, however, the methods of a **Date** object receive and return a date as two integers and a string. Figure 8.2 shows the two implementations, which have the same external abstraction.

In many cases, the external and internal representations are identical. However, we don't tell the user that, because we may want to change the implementation in the future. For example, we might initially develop a **Date** class using three fields for the month, day, and year. Later on, if we decide that a Julian day representation is more efficient, we can rewrite the implemen-

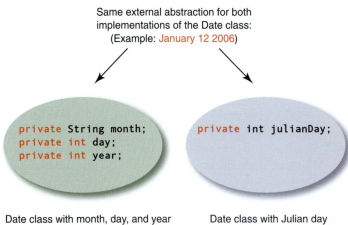

Same external abstraction for both implementations of the Date class: (Example: January 12 2006)

```
private String month;
private int day;
private int year;
```

```
private int julianDay;
```

Date class with month, day, and year internal representation

Date class with Julian day internal representation

FIGURE 8.2 Data Abstraction Permits Different Internal Representations for the Same External Abstraction

tation of the class. Because encapsulation has provided data abstraction, the change doesn't affect the client code.

Control abstraction is the separation of the specification of the behavior of a class from the implementation of that behavior. For example, suppose that the specification for the `Date` class says that it takes into account all of the special leap-year rules. In the Julian day implementation, only the Julian day conversion formulas handle those rules; the other responsibilities merely perform integer arithmetic on the Julian day number. A user may assume that every `Date` responsibility separately deals with leap years. Control abstraction lets us program a more efficient implementation and then hide those details from the user.

> **Control abstraction** The separation of an object's behavioral specification from the implementation of the specification
>
> **Modifiability** The property of an encapsulated class definition that allows the implementation to be changed without having an effect on code that uses it (except in terms of speed or memory space)
>
> **Reuse** The ability to import a class into code that uses it, without additional modification to either the class or the user code; the ability to extend the definition of a class

■ Designing for Modifiability and Reuse

Applying the principle of abstraction has two additional benefits: **modifiability** and **reuse**.

Encapsulation enables us to modify the implementation of a class after its initial development. Perhaps we are rushing to meet a deadline, so we create a simple but inefficient implementation. In the maintenance phase, we replace the existing implementation with a more efficient version. The modification is undetectable with the exception that applications using the class run faster and require less memory.

An encapsulated class is self-contained, which means we can import and use it in other applications. Whether we want to do so depends on whether it provides a useful abstraction. For example, a `Date` class that assumes all years are in the range of 1900 to 1999 is not very useful today, even though that was a common approach used by twentieth-century programmers.

As we will see in Chapter 10, reuse also means that a class can be extended to form new related classes. As an example, suppose a utility company has software to manage its fleet of vehicles. As shown in Figure 8.3, a class that describes a Vehicle can be used in multiple applications. Each application extends the Vehicle class in unique ways to suit its particular requirements. Reuse is a way to save programming effort. It also ensures that objects have the same behavior wherever that they are used. Consistent behavior helps us avoid programming errors.

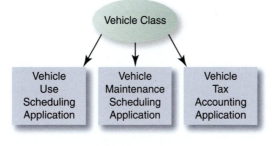

FIGURE 8.3   Reuse

Of course, preparing a class that is suitable for wider reuse requires us to think beyond the immediate situation. The class should provide certain basic services that enable it to be used more generally. For example, it should have a full set of observers that enable client code to retrieve any necessary information from an object.

Not every class needs to be designed for general reuse. In some cases, we merely need a class that has specific properties for the problem at hand and that won't be used elsewhere. But if you are designing a class that may be used in other situations, then it is a good idea to make it more general.

Keep in mind that even though Java's `class` construct provides a mechanism to *support* encapsulation, the programmer has the responsibility of using it in a way that results in actual encapsulation. There is no keyword or construct that specifically identifies a class as being encapsulated. The programmer must draw the boundaries around the class in a manner that keeps other code out.

We can draw two types of boundaries: physical and visual. We can physically keep a user from accessing fields in a class by using an access modifier such as `private`. We can make the class implementation invisible to a user by using the `package` construct (discussed later in this chapter).

■ Mutable Objects

Since Chapter 2 we have been creating immutable constructor–observer classes. Immutable objects cannot be changed after they are instantiated. While many objects can be represented in this manner, some require the ability to change their internal contents (**mutate**) after instantiation. Mutability is a key characteristic of the interface of an object. While immutable objects are naturally encapsulated, because they are immune to change, we must take special care to ensure that mutable objects remain encapsulated.

Mutate Changing the value(s) of an object's attribute(s) after it is created

Let's look at an example of a mutable object. Suppose we are creating a database of birth records for a hospital. A Birth Record is an object that contains the following information:

Birth Record

Date of Birth
Time of Birth
Mother's Name
Father's Name
Baby's Name
Baby's Weight
Baby's Length
Baby's Gender

A nurse enters all of this information into the database shortly after the baby is born. However, in some cases, the parents have not yet chosen a name for the baby. Rather than keep the nurse waiting for the parents to make up their minds, the database allows all of the other information to be entered and creates a Birth Record object with an empty string for the name of the baby. Later, when the name is chosen, the nurse changes the name in the database.

There are two ways to change this database record. The first strategy is to call a method that directly changes the value in the Baby's Name field. For example, we could write the method as follows:

```
public void setBabyName (Name newName)
{
  babysName = newName;
}
```

Given an instance of the `BirthRecord` class, called `newBaby`, we can now call this method with the following statement:

```
newBaby.setBabyName(new Name(first, last, middle));   // Changes the baby
                                                       // name field
```

Such a method is called a **transformer** or a **mutator**. Having a transformer makes `BirthRecord` a mutable class. Java does not define any special syntax to denote that `setBabyName` is a transformer. Rather, a method is a transformer simply by virtue of what it does: It changes the information stored in an existing object.

> **Transformer (mutator)**
> A method that changes the information contained in an object

Wouldn't it be easier to just make the `babysName` field `public` and assign a new value to it without calling a method? Yes, but that approach would destroy the encapsulation of the `BirthRecord` class. Making all changes through transformers preserves encapsulation because it permits us to employ data and control abstraction. For example, we could later enhance this transformer to check that the new name contains only alphabetic characters.

The second way to change the name assumes that `BirthRecord` is an immutable class. We create a new record, copy into it all of the information except the name from the old record, and insert the new name at that point. Then the old record is deleted. For example, the following constructor takes another `BirthRecord` object as an argument and automatically does the copying:

```
public BirthRecord (BirthRecord oldRecord,   // Constructor
                    Name newName)
{
  dateOfBirth = oldRecord.dateOfBirth;
  timeOfBirth = oldRecord.timeOfBirth;
  mothersName = oldRecord.mothersName;
  fathersName = oldRecord.fathersName;
  babysName = newName;                        // Change name to new name
  babysWeight = oldRecord.babysWeight;
  babysLength = oldRecord.babysLength;
  babysGender = oldRecord.babysGender;
}
```

We would update the birth record as follows:

```
newBaby = new BirthRecord(newBaby, new Name(first, last, middle));
```

Note that this statement doesn't change the old object. Instead, it creates a new object, copies the required information from the old object, and then assigns the new object to the old variable. If no other variable refers to the old object, then it is deleted (its storage is garbage-collected).

As you can see, using the transformer is simpler than the second approach. The computer can call a method that assigns a new value to a field more quickly than it can create a whole

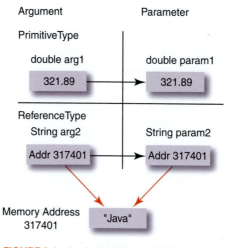

Argument   Parameter

PrimitiveType

double arg1   double param1

321.89   321.89

ReferenceType
String arg2   String param2

Addr 317401   Addr 317401

Memory Address   "Java"
317401

FIGURE 8.4 Passing Primitive and Reference Types

new object and delete an old one. Is there any reason why we shouldn't always use mutable objects? Yes, there is, and it has to do with how objects are used when they are passed as arguments to methods.

Recall from Chapter 3 that an object variable contains the address where the object's fields are stored in memory. This address is copied from the argument to the parameter inside the method. Only one copy of the object's fields exists, which both the calling code and the method use. Figure 8.4 serves as a visual reminder of this difference.

Just from looking at Figure 8.4, you might assume that changes to `param2` also change the original argument value. But `String` is an immutable class. Because it doesn't have any transformers, there aren't any operations that allow the user to change `param2`.

The only way to "change" an immutable object is to create a new object and assign it to the same variable. Figure 8.5 illustrates what happens when we call a method with a string argument and then assign a new string to the parameter. After the assignment, the parameter just refers to the new string; the argument string is not changed.

In contrast, with a mutable class, transformers can change the original argument. For example, in addition to the immutable `String` class, Java provides a mutable class called `StringBuffer` that is very similar to `String`, except that it can be directly modified. Suppose we want to add a method to the `Name` class that takes a title (such as Dr.) as an argument and returns a string containing the name with the title. With a `String` parameter, the method looks like this:

```
public String titleName(String title)
{
   return title + " " + firstName + " " + lastName;
}
```

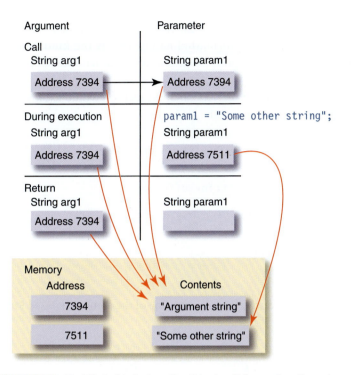

FIGURE 8.5   The Effect of Assigning a New Value to a Reference Type Parameter

Because **String** is immutable, the expression in the *return* statement actually creates four **String** objects and deletes three of them. Each concatenation operation in Java creates a new **String** object that consists of the contents of the **String** to the left of the plus joined with the contents of the **String** to its right. That's rather inefficient. Here's how we might be tempted to use a **StringBuffer** parameter to write the same method and avoid the inefficiency:

```java
public String titleName(StringBuffer title)  // A really BAD idea
{
  title.append(" ");
  title.append(firstName);
  title.append(" ");
  title.append(lastName);
  return title.toString();
}
```

In each call to **append**, the argument string is attached to the end of the current contents of **title**. Thus there is just one object whose contents change. The result is that we avoid creating and deleting intermediate objects, and the method executes faster. Unfortunately, it's fast but wrong. Not only does the method return the formatted name, but it also changes the contents of `title`. Upon returning from the method, the argument variable no longer contains just the title, but the entire formatted name. This is the kind of side effect error we warned of in Chapter 3. It is very poor programming practice and can produce bugs that are difficult to identify.

A properly written `StringBuffer` version of the method would use a `String` parameter and keep the `StringBuffer` strictly internal:

```
public String titleName(String title)   // This avoids side effects and is
                                         // efficient
{
  StringBuffer outName = new StringBuffer(title);
  outName.append(" ");
  outName.append(firstName);
  outName.append(" ");
  outName.append(lastName);
  return outName.toString();
}
```

Before we move on, we briefly summarize some of the commonly used `StringBuffer` methods for your reference.

Method	Argument Types	Effect
append	boolean, char, int, long, float, double, String, or StringBuffer	Appends a string representation of the argument to the current contents of the `StringBuffer`
delete	int start, int end	Deletes the characters in the specified range of positions from the `StringBuffer`
indexOf	String	Like `indexOf` in class `String`
insert	int offset, String string	Inserts the given string at the position specified.
length		Returns the number of characters in `StringBuffer`
replace	int start, int end, String string	Replaces the characters in the specified range with the given string
substring	int start, int end	Like `substring` from class `String`

Mutability is an abstract property of an object. When you design the interface to a new class, you should always consciously decide whether it is mutable or immutable. The danger occurs when a programmer uses a mutable class under the assumption that it is immutable, and passes an object of that class to a method that unexpectedly changes the argument.

Software Engineering

Humans have come to depend greatly on computers in many aspects of their lives. That reliance is fostered by the perception that computers function reliably; that is, they work correctly most of the time. In reality, the reliability of a computer depends on the care that is taken in writing its software.

Errors in code can have serious consequences. Here are a few examples of real incidents involving software errors:

- An error in the control software of the F-18 jet fighter caused it to flip upside down the first time it flew across the equator.
- A rocket launch went out of control and had to be blown up because a comma was typed in place of a period in its control software.
- A radiation therapy machine killed several patients because a software error caused the machine to operate at full power when the operator typed certain commands too quickly.

Even when software is used in less critical situations, errors can have significant effects. Examples of such errors include the following:

- An error in your word processor that causes your term paper to be lost just hours before it is due.
- An error in a statistical package that causes a scientist to draw a wrong conclusion and publish a paper that must later be retracted.
- An error in a tax preparation application that produces an incorrect return, leading to a fine.

Programmers have a responsibility to develop software that is free from errors and easy to maintain. The process that is used to develop correct software is known as **software engineering**.

Software engineering has many aspects. The software life cycle described in Chapter 1 outlines the stages in the development of software. Different techniques are used at each of these stages. We address many of these techniques in this text. In this chapter we introduce methodologies for developing object-oriented designs. We discuss strategies for testing and validating programs in every chapter. We use a modern programming language that enables us to write readable, well-organized code. Other aspects of software engineering, such as the development of a formal, mathematical specification for an application, are beyond the scope of this text.

> **Software engineering**
> The application of traditional engineering methodologies and techniques to the development of software

8.2 : Encapsulation and Abstraction in Java

Now that we've seen how to design individual classes that achieve data and control abstraction through physical encapsulation, in this section we turn to the issues of organizing groups of classes and hiding the implementation details that support encapsulation. We also examine ways to perform file I/O with whole objects in binary form, which helps to visually hide the implementation of the attributes of a class from curious users. We close the section by introducing another Java type, enum, which is a good example of abstraction at work.

As we noted previously, Java lets us group related classes together into a unit called a package. Classes within a package can access one another's nonprivate members, which can save us programming effort and make it more efficient to access their data.

Packages provide additional support for encapsulation because they distinguish between member and nonmember classes. We are thus able to restrict access by nonmember classes to the fields and methods of member classes. Another advantage of packages is that they can be compiled separately and imported into our code. Because it is hard to extract information about the implementation of a class from looking at its Bytecode, we say that separate compilation of the classes in a package provides visual hiding of the implementation.

■ Package Syntax

The syntax for a package is extremely simple: We merely have to specify the package name at the start of each class that belongs to the package. The first line of a class that belongs to a package consists of the keyword package followed by an identifier and a semicolon. By convention, Java programmers start a package identifier with a lowercase letter to distinguish it from class identifiers.

```
package someName;
```

We declare class someClass to be a member of the package someName as follows:

```
package someName;
// Class Documentation
public class someClass
{...}
```

> **Compilation unit** A file containing Java code that can be compiled

Java calls the file containing a class a compilation unit. The file may contain a package declaration, import declarations, and zero or more class declarations. Many Java systems also impose the restrictions that a compilation unit can have only one public class and that the name of the file must match the name of the class. For example, if we have a public class called RegistrationData, then its source code would be stored in a file called RegistrationData.java.

You may be wondering what has been happening with the classes we've developed previously, because they haven't included package declarations. They are actually part of an unnamed package associated with the application. Their files are stored by most Java systems in the same directory as the application, and this directory becomes a default package for the project. Using the unnamed package is acceptable for small projects, but in most cases it is better to organize classes into named packages to provide better encapsulation.

All of the classes declared within a package have access to one another's nonprivate members. We say "nonprivate" because, in addition to using the keywords `public` or `private` with fields and methods, we can write member declarations without any modifiers. When we do so, then the field or method is neither `public` nor `private`, but rather something in between—it can be accessed by any member of the package.

When we use `public`, then a field or method can be used by other package members and by any class that imports the package. When we use `private`, then the field or method can be accessed only within the class itself. When we use neither, the field or method can be used by class members, but not by classes outside the package. As an analogy, you can think of packages as being like a family. Some things are yours alone (`private`), some things you share with your family (package), and some things anyone can use (`public`).

Classes that are imported into a package can be used by any classes declared in the package, but the imported classes can access only the `public` members of the importing package. That is, imported classes are not members of the package. You can think of an imported package as a guest in your house. Your guest may share some things (`public`) with your family, but the things that you share only with your family are not shared with the guest, and the things that the guest shares only with his or her family aren't shared with you.

If a Java system specifies that a compilation unit can hold at most one `public` class, how do we create packages with multiple `public` classes? We use multiple compilation units, as we describe next.

■ Packages with Multiple Compilation Units

Each Java compilation unit is stored in its own file,[1] which is named to match the one `public` class in the file. All of the compilation units of a package are stored in a single directory, which is named after the package itself. Suppose we want to create a package that contains some of our existing classes, such as Name and Phone. We would have to make the following changes in classes Name and Phone:

```
package utility;
// Class documentation
public class Name
{ . . . }

package utility;
// Class documentation
public class Phone
{ . . . }
```

---

[1]Some Java systems keep compilation units in a database. In that case, the restriction of one public class per compilation unit doesn't apply. In this text, we assume you are using the more common approach of storing compilation units in files and directories.

Is that it? Well, that's the only change to the code. We also need to create a file directory called `utility` and place the files into that directory:

```
directory: utility
    file: Name.java
    file: Phone.java
```

The Java compiler uses the combination of the name of the class and the package that contains it to locate the source file within the appropriate directory on the disk. For example, suppose you have the following `import` statement in a class declaration:

```
import utility.Name;
```

This statement tells the Java compiler to look in the `utility` directory for a file called `Name` that provides the `Name` class. The compiler first looks for a file called `Name.class` that contains the Bytecode version of the class. In many development environments, if `Name.class` is not present but `Name.java` is, then the source is compiled to produce `Name.class`.

The Java philosophy is to use packages to support encapsulation by making it possible to distribute Bytecode rather than source code for others to use. This approach is an example of *visibility encapsulation* because the source code isn't visible to other programmers who are using it. Because they don't see how the interface is implemented, the programmers can't write code that depends on the specific implementation.

Many programmers simply place every class in its own compilation unit. Others gather the nonpublic classes into one unit, separate from the `public` classes. How you organize your packages is up to you, but you should use a consistent approach to make it easy to find the members of the package among all of its files.

Splitting a package among multiple files has one other benefit: Each compilation unit can have its own set of `import` declarations. Thus, if the classes in a package need to use different sets of imported classes, you can place them in separate compilation units, each with just the `import` declarations that are required.

Keep in mind that your files are stored within a larger directory structure. Most Java development environments create a new directory for each project, and then use the previously described naming scheme within that directory. They also know how to access packages in the Java library directories. If you need to import a class or package from another project, however, you may need to specify its place within the larger directory structure (some environments require that you issue a command that tells them where to look; others simply let you drag and drop `.class` or `.java` files into the project).

■ Output and Input of Objects

The title of this section looks a bit strange, because we usually talk about "input and output," not "output and input." But objects cannot be created outside the application and read in. Rather, they must be created in an application and then written to a file. Once they are on a file, we can read the data values back in and re-create the object.

Until now, if we wanted to write an object to a file, we would convert each data field into a string and then output it. Any user could then read the file to see how we implemented the attributes of the class. That practice clearly violates encapsulation.

To input an object with this approach, we read in each string, convert it to the proper form, and store it in the corresponding field of the object. That's a lot of work for the programmer. Fortunately, Java provides a way to directly save objects and read them back again, which both preserves encapsulation and makes object I/O easier.

Java provides two file classes for which the object is the basic unit of data: `ObjectOutputStream` and `ObjectInputStream`. To write an object to a file, we use the `writeObject` method of the `ObjectOutputStream` class, which converts an object into binary bytes for storage on a file. To read objects from a file, we use the `readObject` method of the `ObjectInputStream` class.

How can this be? Untold numbers of objects exist, whose structures vary in size and shape. Writing would seem to be easy, but how do we figure out how to convert the bytes back into the form of an object when we input it? Fortunately, we don't have to know.

One of the most important features in the `java.io` package is the ability to convert an object into a stream of bytes that can later be converted back into a copy of the original object. This translation from object to bytes is called **serializing**. The reverse translation is called **deserializing**. We do not need to understand how Java performs this conversion—we just have to know how to use this feature. It is another example of abstraction at work.

> **Serializing** Translating an object into a stream of bytes
>
> **Deserializing** Translating a serialized stream of bytes back into an object

Let's see how this technique works through the use of a pair of application programs. The first creates an object and writes it out; the second reads the object back in and writes it to the screen. We'll use the class `Name` for this example. Recall that `Name` has three data fields: `first`, `middle`, and `last`. To serialize objects of the class `Name`, we need to add the words `implements Serializable` beside the class name. Because `Serializable` is defined in the package `java.io`, we must import it into `Name`. Here is the documentation of the interface for `Name`, with these modifications highlighted:

```java
import java.io.*;
public class Name implements Serializable
// This class defines a name consisting of three parts
{
    // Constructor headings
    public Name()
    public Name(String firstName, String lastName, String middleName)

    // Observer method headings
    public String getFirstName()
    public String getMiddleName()
    public String getLastName()
    public String toString()
    public int compareTo(Name other)
}
```

Our first application instantiates a `Name` object and then writes the `Name` object onto a file. The second application reads the `Name` object and prints it.

```java
import java.io.*;
public class ObjectFileWrite
{
  public static void main(String[] args) throws IOException
  {
    // Prepare file
    ObjectOutputStream outObject;        // Output data file
    outObject =
      new ObjectOutputStream(new FileOutputStream("outObject.dat"));
    // Instantiate a Name
    Name person = new Name("Callisto", "Mooney", "Europa");
    // Write out person
    outObject.writeObject(person);
    // Close file
    outObject.close();
  }
}
```

The application that reads the object back in and prints it is very straightforward. We apply **readObject** to the file of type **ObjectInputStream**, which returns an object of the class **Object**. We must mention one other detail: **readObject** can throw a **ClassNotFoundException**. Rather than handle the exception, we just add it to the *throws* clause of the **main** method to keep the example simple. This detail is highlighted below.

```java
import java.io.*;
public class ObjectFileRead
{
  public static void main(String[] args) throws IOException,
    ClassNotFoundException
  {
    // Prepare file
    ObjectInputStream inObject;          //Input file
    inObject = new ObjectInputStream(new FileInputStream("outObject.dat"));
    //Read Name object and display it
    Name person = (Name)inObject.readObject();
    System.out.println(person);
    inObject.close();
  }
}
```

Here is the output from the application **ObjectFileRead**:

Callisto Europa Mooney

You should note two additional points of syntax. The first is how the object files are instantiated:

```java
inObject = new ObjectInputStream(new FileInputStream("outObject.dat"));
outObject = new ObjectOutputStream(new FileOutputStream("outObject.dat"));
```

This follows the familiar pattern that we used with text files. We must instantiate a simpler form of file object as an argument to the more specialized file constructor: **FileInputStream** and

`FileOutputStream` objects are instantiated as arguments to the `ObjectInputStream` and `ObjectOutputStream` constructors, respectively.

The second thing to notice is that the input object has to be cast into a `Name` object. The object that is input is just a sequence of bytes. We must indicate how to break up this sequence of bytes into the proper fields by using the appropriate class name as a type cast.

```
Name person = (Name)inObject.readObject();
```

We've seen how to output and input a single object. But what if an input file contains multiple objects? Then, as with any other kind of file input, we use a loop to read the objects until we reach EOF. However, there is no simple way for an `ObjectInputStream` to indicate EOF, so instead it throws an exception, called `EOFException`. Here's an example application that copies one object file to another, showing how we use this exception to test for EOF on a file containing `Name` objects:

```java
import java.io.*;
public class DemoObjectFileCopy
{
  public static void main (String[] args)
    throws IOException, ClassNotFoundException
  {
    ObjectInputStream in =
      new ObjectInputStream(new FileInputStream("in.dat"));
    ObjectOutputStream out =
      new ObjectOutputStream(new FileOutputStream("out.dat"));
    try
    {
      while (true)                          // Copy until exception thrown
        out.writeObject((Name) in.readObject());
    }
    catch (EOFException ex)                 // Reached EOF, close files
    {
      in.close();
      out.close();
      System.out.println("Copy completed.");
    }
  }
}
```

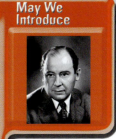

May We Introduce

John von Neumann

John von Neumann was a brilliant mathematician, physicist, logician, and computer scientist. His astonishing memory and the phenomenal speed at which he solved problems are legendary. He used his talents not only for furthering his mathematical theories, but also for memorizing entire books and reciting them years after he had read them.

John von Neumann was born in Hungary in 1903, the oldest son of a wealthy Jewish banker. He was able to divide 8-digit numbers in his head by the age of 6. He entered high

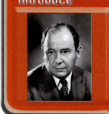

school by the time he was 11, and it wasn't long before his math teachers recommended that he be tutored by university professors. In spite of his interest in mathematics, he enrolled at the University of Berlin in 1921 to study chemistry. This path was a compromise with his father, who wanted him to have a career that would allow him to make money. Five years later, von Neumann received his diploma in chemical engineering from the Technische Hochschule in Zürich. In the same year, however, he also received his doctorate in mathematics from the University of Budapest, with a thesis on set theory! During the period from 1926 to 1929, von Neumann lectured in Berlin and Hamburg while holding a Rockefeller fellowship for postdoctoral studies at the University of Göttingen.

von Neumann came to the United States in the early 1930s to teach at Princeton, while still keeping his academic posts in Germany. He resigned the German posts when the Nazis came to power. While at Princeton, he worked with the talented British student Alan Turing, who would become an important figure in computing theory. During World War II, von Neumann was hired as a consultant for the U.S. Armed Forces because of his knowledge of hydrodynamics. He was also called upon to participate in the construction of the atomic bomb in 1943.

Even though bombs and their performance fascinated von Neumann for many years, a fortuitous meeting in 1944 with Herbert Goldstine, a developer of one of the first electronic digital computers, introduced the mathematician to this new field. von Neumann's chance conversation with Goldstine in a train station sparked a new fascination for him. He started working on the stored program concept and concluded that internally storing a program eliminated the hours of tedious labor required to reprogram computers (in those days). He also developed a new computer architecture to perform this storage task. In fact, today's computers are often referred to as von Neumann machines because the principles he described have proven so successful. Changes in computers over the past 40 years have been primarily in terms of the speed and composition of the circuits, but the basic concept developed by von Neumann has persisted.

During the 1950s, von Neumann was a consultant for IBM, where he reviewed advanced technology projects. One such project was John Backus's FORTRAN, one of the first high-level programming languages, which von Neumann reportedly questioned, asking why anyone would want more than one machine language. von Neumann died in Washington, D.C., at the age of 54. We can only imagine the contributions that his brilliant mind might have made to computer science, had he lived longer.

■ Java's enum Type

Beginning with version 5 of the language, Java provides a new data type that is an excellent example of data abstraction. The type is called **enum**, which is an abbreviation of enumeration. In a programming language, an enumeration type is one that consists of an ordered set of identifiers. The set has a first value and a last value; between these terminal values, each element has a unique value that precedes it and another unique value that follows it.

An **enumeration** is said to be **atomic**, **scalar**, and **ordinal**. The type `boolean` is atomic but not scalar because Java doesn't define an ordering between `true` and `false`. Real numbers (in the mathematical sense) are scalar but not ordinal—given a real number such as 1.0, there is no unique next value.[2] The type `int` is scalar and ordinal. An enumeration is also ordinal, but the values are not numbers. They are identifiers. For example, the names of the colors of the spectrum are an enumeration, and are usually listed in the following order:

Red, Orange, Yellow, Green, Blue, Indigo, Violet

A Java `enum` type consists of ordered identifiers, where the ordering is the sequence in which the identifiers are listed. An `enum` type is a form of class declaration that can be defined in its own compilation unit. For example, the following compilation unit in package `colorManagement` declares an `enum` type called `Spectrum` that is publicly accessible. The source code for this unit would be saved in a file called `Spectrum.java` in the `colorManagement` directory.

```
package colorManagement;
public enum Spectrum
{
  RED, ORANGE, YELLOW, GREEN, BLUE, INDIGO, VIOLET
}
```

> **Enumeration** A data type in which the elements are a set of identifiers that are ordered so that each element (except the first) has a unique predecessor in the ordering and each (except the last) has a unique successor
>
> **Atomic** A property of a data type that its values have no component parts
>
> **Scalar** A property of a data type in which the values are ordered and each value is atomic (indivisible)
>
> **Ordinal** A property of a data type in which each value (except the first) has a unique predecessor and each value (except the last) has a unique successor

In this case we used the capitalization convention of making constants all uppercase, but this is not a requirement of Java. We can declare an `enum` in a package-level compilation unit whenever we want the classes in a package to be able to use it directly. We use a `public enum` type, if we want classes outside the package to have access to it.

Sometimes, we just want to declare an `enum` for use within a single class. In that situation, we place its declaration among the field declarations of that class. For example, within a class we could declare a `Spectrum` `enum` type and a class variable of that type as follows:

```
enum Spectrum {RED, ORANGE, YELLOW, GREEN, BLUE, INDIGO, VIOLET}
static Spectrum defaultColor;
```

Notice that the declaration does not need a semicolon after it. Technically, Java considers such a declaration to be a class nested within a class, and class declarations do not end in semicolons. An `enum` type cannot be declared locally within a method.

Note that `enum` values are not variables, nor are they constants defined elsewhere and set equal to some value. They are actual values. `RED` comes before `ORANGE`; `ORANGE` comes after `RED` and before `YELLOW`; and so on. Thus you can declare a variable of type `Spectrum` and assign it one of these values:

```
Spectrum color = Spectrum.GREEN;
```

---

[2]You might think 1.1 would be next, but then how about 1.01? Or 1.001? With real numbers we can play this "which comes next game" for an infinite number of digits of precision. So there really isn't a unique next value.

Each enum type that we define automatically has a `compareTo` method that can be applied to values of that type. Given the preceding declaration, you can compare `color` to a `Spectrum` value with an expression such as

```
color.compareTo(Spectrum.GREEN)
```

As you can see, the enum type provides a layer of data abstraction that lets us create lists of common values. We don't need to know how Java actually represents the values of `Spectrum` to be able to use them. What can we do with enum values? Plenty! We can print them out, we can convert a string to its matching enum value, we can use them in *switch* expressions, and we can iterate through the values using a *for* loop. For example, the following statement prints out the letters `"GREEN"`, given the preceding assignment statement:

```
System.out.println(color);
```

Here's a statement that converts the string `"YELLOW"` into the `Spectrum` value `YELLOW`:

```
color = Spectrum.valueOf("YELLOW");   // Assigns YELLOW to color
```

If you call `valueOf` with a string that doesn't match any of the enum values, an unchecked `IllegalArgumentException` is thrown.

Suppose we want to print out all of the `Spectrum` values, one per line. Java provides a special version of the *for* loop that iterates through the values of an enum type, called the *for-each* loop. In it, we declare a loop control variable of the enum type, and then specify that it should iterate over all of the values in the type, using a special method (called `values`) that is automatically associated with every enum type. Here's an example:

```
for (Spectrum color : Spectrum.values())
  System.out.println(color);
```

The preceding loop prints the following:

```
RED
ORANGE
YELLOW
GREEN
BLUE
INDIGO
VIOLET
```

Here's a demo program that shows how we can use an enum type in a *switch* statement:

```
import java.util.*;
public class ColorDemo
{
  enum Spectrum {RED, ORANGE, YELLOW, GREEN, BLUE, INDIGO, VIOLET}
  public static void main(String[] args)
  {
    Spectrum color;
    Scanner in = new Scanner(System.in);
    System.out.print("Enter RED, YELLOW, or GREEN: ");
    color = Spectrum.valueOf(in.nextLine());
    switch (color)
    {
```

```
        case RED   : System.out.println("High forest fire danger"); break;
        case YELLOW: System.out.println("Moderate forest fire danger"); break;
        case GREEN : System.out.println("Low forest fire danger"); break;
        default    : System.out.println("No forest fire rating");
      }
    }
}
```

Clearly, the enum type has many valuable features. You can use it wherever you need a set of named values that have an ordering. The advantage of using enum rather than named int constants is that the values are meaningful.[3]

As further examples, here are definitions of some commonly used enumerations:

```
enum Gender {FEMALE, MALE}
enum NoYes {NO, YES}
enum Day {SUNDAY, MONDAY, TUESDAY, WEDNESDAY, THURSDAY, FRIDAY, SATURDAY}
enum Month {JANUARY, FEBRUARY, MARCH, APRIL, MAY, JUNE,
            JULY, AUGUST, SEPTEMBER, OCTOBER, NOVEMBER, DECEMBER}
enum AMPM {AM, PM}
```

----

[3]Java actually supports many more features for enum types than we cover here, such as associating fields with enum values and declaring methods that access field values. In many ways, enum types are as powerful as classes in Java. In this text, we focus on object-oriented design using the class construct, and we leave exploration of the advanced features of enum types for future study. Our use of Java's enum type will be in a manner that is more consistent with how other languages implement enumerations.

SOFTWARE MAINTENANCE CASE STUDY

Improving Internal Data Representation

Maintenance Task You're maintaining an application that was written in an earlier version of Java. A user has complained that the program gives an erroneous cost estimate when the starting month and the ending month of a contract are both in July.

Preliminary Analysis The program computes the cost estimate by determining the length of the contract and then applies a formula that takes into account the personnel and materials that will be used. Because the problem is associated with a specific month, one obvious place to look is in the part of the code that computes the difference between the two months.

Existing Code Here is the code for the method that computes the difference between the start and end months:

```
public int monthDif(String month1, String month2)
// Returns the difference between two months
// that are given as strings
{
  int month1Number;
  int month2Number;
  if (month1.equals("January")) month1Number = 1;
    else if (month1.equals("February")) month1Number = 2;
    else if (month1.equals("March")) month1Number = 3;
    else if (month1.equals("April")) month1Number = 4;
    else if (month1.equals("May")) month1Number = 5;
    else if (month1.equals("June")) month1Number = 6;
    else if (month1.equals("July")) month1Number = 7;
    else if (month1.equals("August")) month1Number = 8;
    else if (month1.equals("September")) month1Number = 9;
    else if (month1.equals("October")) month1Number = 10;
    else if (month1.equals("November")) month1Number = 11;
    else if (month1.equals("December")) month1Number = 12;
  if (month2.equals("January")) month2Number = 1;
    else if (month2.equals("February")) month2Number = 2;
    else if (month2.equals("March")) month2Number = 3;
    else if (month2.equals("April")) month2Number = 4;
    else if (month2.equals("May")) month2Number = 5;
    else if (month2.equals("June")) month2Number = 6;
    else if (month2.equals("July")) month2Number = 6;
    else if (month2.equals("August")) month2Number = 8;
    else if (month2.equals("September")) month2Number = 9;
    else if (month2.equals("October")) month2Number = 10;
    else if (month2.equals("November")) month2Number = 11;
    else if (month2.equals("December")) month2Number = 12;
  return Math.abs(month1Number - month2Number);
}
```

Code Analysis Knowing that the problem is for a specific month, you examine the code and see that it is basically two blocks of an *if-else-if* structure with a branch for each month. The first block handles the first parameter, and the second block handles the second parameter. You can immediately zero in on the two branches for the month of July. In the second block, the number 6 is assigned for July, when it should be 7.

Clearly, this bug will produce an erroneous value whenever the ending month is July. The user noticed the problem only when she happened to enter a yearlong contract that began in July, for a single employee, and the estimated cost was less than what she knew was the annual cost for that person. The company may have been losing money because of this bug for some time, but it took this special case to make it obvious. You change the 6 to 7, and make a note to ask for a raise!

Now the method works, but you are still troubled by how bulky the code is. There has to be a better way to solve this problem. You could define another method that converts a string to a month, and then call it for each of the parameters. The new code will be roughly half as long. But you realize you can do even more.

Instead of converting the parameters to `int` values, you can convert them to an `enum` type using the `valueOf` method. Then you can use the `enum` type's `ordinal` method, which returns an integer representing the position of the particular value in the ordering, to get the number of the month. The values in an `enum` type are numbered starting at zero, so the ordinal number for January is 0, the ordinal number for February is 1, and so on. For example, if we have

```
enum Months {JANUARY, FEBRUARY, MARCH, APRIL, MAY, JUNE,
             JULY, AUGUST, SEPTEMBER, OCTOBER, NOVEMBER, DECEMBER}
Months someMonth = Months.MAY;
System.out.println(someMonth + " is month number " + someMonth.ordinal());
```

then the output will be

```
MAY is month number 4
```

Revised Code You have been able to rewrite the method much more compactly. To be safe, you apply `toUpperCase` to each of the arguments, so that lowercase month names are converted to the same form as the values in `Months`. Recall that `enum` types cannot be declared locally within a method; instead, they must be declared as part of a class or in a separate compilation unit.

```
enum Months {JANUARY, FEBRUARY, MARCH, APRIL, MAY, JUNE,
             JULY, AUGUST, SEPTEMBER, OCTOBER, NOVEMBER, DECEMBER}
public int monthDif(String month1, String month2)
// Returns the difference between two months
// that are given as strings
{
  Months firstMonth = Months.valueOf(month1.toUpperCase());
  Months secondMonth = Months.valueOf(month2.toUpperCase());
  return Math.abs(firstMonth.ordinal() - secondMonth.ordinal());
}
```

By changing the internal representation and taking advantage of the power of the `enum` type, you have greatly simplified the method. As a result, it will be easier to maintain in the future. And because the numbers are generated automatically, this kind of bug cannot recur. It's definitely a good time to ask for that raise!

8.3 : Formal Notation for Object-Oriented Design

Given a complex problem—one that results in a 10,000-line program, for example—it's simply not reasonable to skip the design process and go directly to writing Java code. What we need is a systematic way of designing a solution to a problem.

We've used the term **object-oriented design** (**OOD**) frequently throughout this book, and we have employed OOD in an intuitive manner in the Case Studies. In this part of the chapter, we formalize and extend the technique that we've been using all along. This methodology helps you create applications that are readable, understandable, and encapsulated. Java was developed in part to facilitate the use of the OOD methodology.

> **Object-oriented design (OOD)** A technique for developing software in which the solution is expressed in terms of objects that interact with one another
>
> **Responsibility** An action that an implementation of an object must be capable of performing
>
> **Collaboration** An interaction between objects in which one object requests that another object carry out one of its responsibilities

■ Classes, Responsibilities, and Collaborations

As we've seen in our case studies, we begin by brainstorming a set of object classes that are present in a problem. Next we filter out duplicate or unnecessary classes, and define initial responsibilities for those classes that remain. We then consider some scenarios in which the objects interact to accomplish a task. In the process of envisioning how a scenario happens, we identify additional classes and interactions. We keep creating new scenarios until we find that our set of classes and their interactions is sufficient to accomplish any task required by the problem.

In the problem-solving phase, we say that each class has a set of **responsibilities**, which are the actions that its objects support. Objects **collaborate** with each other: One object may ask another object to carry out one of its responsibilities. The collection of classes, responsibilities, and collaborations (CRC) works together to solve a problem. As we've seen, in the implementation phase, responsibilities become methods and collaborations become method calls.

Until now, our problems have involved fairly simple collaborations. In more complex settings, when you call a method, it may in turn make other calls. Indeed, a wide range of collaborations may take place in the background before the method finally returns. In the next section, we see how to use a notation, called a CRC card, to keep track of classes, responsibilities, and collaborations.

Background Information

What's the Best Solution?

As we discuss OOD, keep in mind that many different correct solutions are possible for most problems. The techniques we use may seem imprecise, especially when contrasted with the precision required by the computer. In fact, the computer merely demands that we express (code) a solution precisely. The process of deciding which particular solution to use involves the skills of judgment and reasoning. It is our human ability to make choices without having complete information that enables us to solve problems.

For example, in developing a simulation of an air traffic control system, we might decide that airplanes and control towers are objects that communicate with each other. Or we might decide that pilots and controllers are the objects that communicate, as shown in Figure 8.6. This choice affects how we subsequently view the collaborations and hence the responsibilities that we assign to the objects. Either choice can lead to a working application. We may simply prefer the one with which we are most familiar (recall the "look for things that are familiar" strategy from Chapter 1).

Some of our choices lead to designs that are more or less efficient than others. For example, keeping a list of names in alphabetical order rather than in random order enables the computer to find a particular name much faster. Choosing to leave the list randomly ordered produces an equally valid (but slower) solution.

The point is this: Don't hesitate to begin solving a problem because you are waiting for some flash of inspiration that leads to the perfect solution. There is no such thing. It is better to jump in and try something, step back and see if you like the result, and then either proceed in the same direction or make changes. The CRC card technique that we examine next allows you to easily explore different design choices and keep track of them.

FIGURE 8.6 Alternative Choices of Objects in an Air Traffic Control Application

■ The CRC Card Notation for Design

In our case study problems, we have simply needed to walk through a few scenarios to check whether our list of classes and responsibilities is complete. In a larger problem, we must define a set of processing scenarios that covers the essential tasks that the application will perform. Many classes may be involved, and it often becomes difficult to keep track of how they are being used during a long scenario. The CRC card is a notation that helps us keep track of classes, responsibilities, and collaborations during a scenario walkthrough.

Now we look at how CRC cards are developed and used. We'll do this in the context of developing a problem solution.

Identifying the Initial Classes Suppose we have the following problem statement: Create an application that allows a user to edit entries on a file representing an address book. The file is accessed via an `ObjectInputStream` that contains `Entry` objects like those used in the Chapter 7 case study. The user enters a name, and the application displays the entry for that name. The user then chooses which field to change and enters a new value, and the updated entry is saved in the file.

Here is the list of potential objects, based on the nouns in the problem statement and some brainstorming:

Address Book

User

Entry

Name

Address

Phone

Input File

Output File

Format

Field

Some of these items are clearly not a part of our solution, such as the User. The purpose of brainstorming, however, is to generate ideas without any inhibitions.

Filtering Once we've run out of ideas, we move on to filtering the classes. The discussion about filtering may reveal some classes that were overlooked. Here is our filtered list, indented to show objects that are contained within other objects:

Address Book

User Interface

Entry

   Name

   Address

   Phone

Output File

Field

For each class that survives the filtering stage, we create a CRC card, which is just an index card with a line drawn down the middle. The name of the class is written at the top, and the two columns have the headings Responsibilities and Collaborations. Figure 8.7 shows a blank CRC card.

We have provided spaces at the top of the CRC card for naming the superclass and subclasses of the class. These items are discussed in Chapter 10.

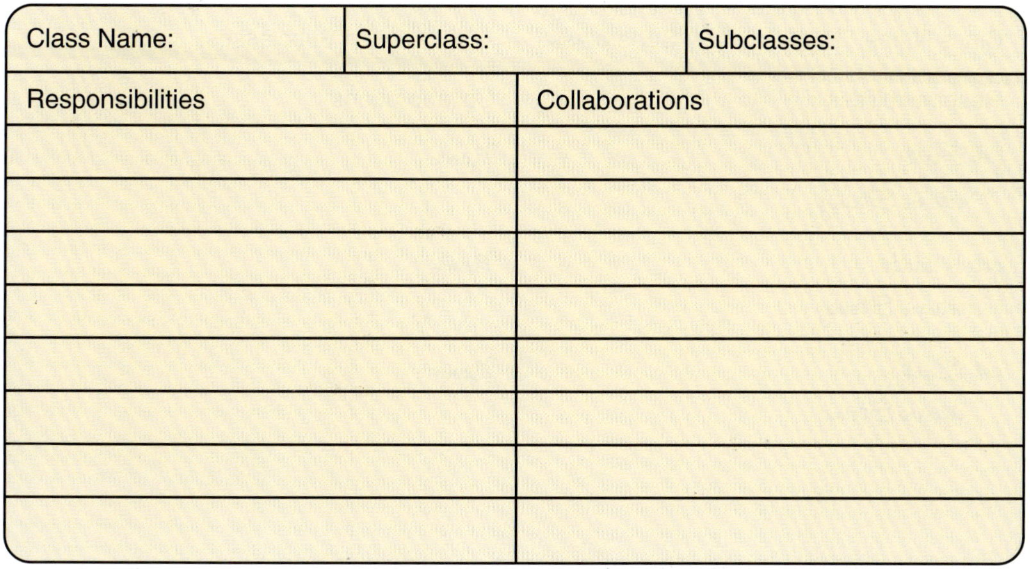

Class Name:	Superclass:	Subclasses:
Responsibilities		Collaborations

FIGURE 8.7   A Blank CRC Card

To begin filling in a CRC card, we simply put the name of the class at the top. The next step is to define the initial responsibilities for each class.

Initial Responsibilities   Once you have created CRC cards for the classes, go over each card and write down any responsibilities that are obvious. For example, you know that a `Name` class has responsibilities to get its first name, its middle name, and its last name, as shown in Figure 8.8. It may have additional responsibilities in this problem, but if you aren't certain about what they are, then don't include them at this stage. They will be added as you walk through scenarios.

Scenario Walkthrough   To further expand the responsibilities of the classes and see how they collaborate, we carry out processing scenarios by hand. We ask a question such as "What happens when the user wants to change the phone number?" We then answer this question by observing how each object is involved in accomplishing this task. In a team setting, the CRC cards are distributed among the team members. When an object of a class is doing something, its card is held in the air to visually signify that it is active. If you're walking through the scenario by yourself, you may set the card off to one side or put it on a bulletin board. Figure 8.9 shows a team in the middle of a walkthrough.

To answer the question that began the scenario we need to make a decision. What are the responsibilities of `UserInterface` and `AddressBook` for getting the `Entry` and displaying it? The team decides that `UserInterface` has a responsibility to get the `Entry` corresponding to a name that the user enters. It will input the name as text, instantiate a `Name` object, collaborate with

Class Name: *Name*	Superclass:		Subclasses:
Responsibilities		Collaborations	
get First *return String*		*None*	
get Middle *return String*		*None*	
get Last *return String*		*None*	
. . .			

FIGURE 8.8 A CRC Card with Initial Responsibilities

FIGURE 8.9 A Scenario Walkthrough in Progress

Class Name: *UserInterface*	Superclass:	Subclasses:
Responsibilities		**Collaborations**
GetEntry		*Scanner, Name, AddressBook*

FIGURE 8.10   A Partial CRC Card for `UserInterface`

`AddressBook` to get the `Entry`, and then return it. That responsibility and its collaborations are written down on the card. Figure 8.10 shows the state of the `UserInterface` CRC card at this point in the scenario.

This scenario proceeds with selection of the field to change, input of the new field value, and writing the updated entry to the output file along with all of the unmodified entries. When the last CRC card is lowered because all of the work is done, the scenario ends.

To keep a scenario moving, it is important to avoid becoming bogged down with implementation details. Remember that abstraction allows us to specify responsibilities without indicating how they will be implemented. If you can say to yourself, "I know how to implement this responsibility," then it probably needs no further exploration. If you're unsure of how to implement the responsibility, then it becomes part of the walkthrough, and the entire team turns its attention to solving this part of the problem.

Subsequent Scenarios   The preceding was an example of using CRC cards in a single scenario. The particular scenario was selected from a list that was developed in a scenario brainstorming session. Here's a list of initial scenarios for our address book example:

What happens when the user
Wants to change the phone number? (*done*)
Wants to change the name?
Wants to change the address?
Decides to not make any changes?
Wants to change more than one field?
Wants to change only one part of a field (such as the ZIP code)?

We walk through each additional scenario, adding responsibilities and collaborations to the CRC cards as necessary, and possibly extending the list of scenarios as we discover new requirements (such as identifying unanticipated error situations). When every scenario we can envision seems to be feasible with the existing classes, responsibilities, and collaborations, then the design is finished.

■ Attributes and Their Internal Representation

The CRC card describes the formal interface to a class. The information recorded on the CRC card, together with a description of what each responsibility does, forms the basis for a formal specification of the class. A specification (which adds the types of the arguments to the CRC card information) is what enables another programmer to use the class.

Before we can begin developing algorithms for the methods, we must determine the attributes of the class. Notice that the following CRC card shows the responsibilities of the `Phone` class that we developed in Chapter 7, but not its attributes.

Class Name: *Phone*	Superclass:		Subclasses:
Responsibilities		**Collaborations**	
Create itself (area code, exchange, number)		*None*	
Get area code *return int*		*None*	
Get exchange *return int*		*None*	
Get number *return int*		*None*	
toString *return String*		*None*	

Some attributes may emerge during the design phase, and these may be noted on the back of the CRC card. When we start implementing the responsibility algorithms, we may realize that we need additional attributes, which can also be written on the back of the CRC card. Alternatively, as we see in the next section, we may switch to a different notation that specifically includes space for documenting attributes.

Once the attributes have been established, the next step is to decide on their internal representation and to note that decision next to the attribute. Our goal in selecting an internal representation should be to simplify the implementation of the responsibilities and to make the object efficient in terms of storage space and execution time. These goals sometimes conflict, and we must balance simplicity against efficiency.

Rarely will you have to invent an entirely new data representation. That's because most programs are written to solve problems with which people have dealt in the past. Consider who would normally use such data, and consult with those people or look in books that they would use (Figure 8.11). For example, astronomers use dates in computing the positions of planets over the centuries. You can find the formulas for computing the Julian day in some astronomy texts.

Julian Day Formula

```
intRes1 = 2-year/100+year/400
intRes2 = (int) (365.25*year)
intRes3 = (int) (30.6001*(month+1))
julianDay = intRes1+intRes2+intRes3+day+1720994.5
```

FIGURE 8.11   Who Would Use Similar Data?

It should be clear that we can't provide a set of rules that will automatically lead you to an internal data representation for a class. Each situation you encounter is different. Be prepared to devote some careful thought to this part of your design, to go to a library and do some research, to consult with other people, and to trade off issues of efficiency and complexity.

The CRC card provides a way to keep track of class design decisions that are made in the problem-solving phase and in the early stages of implementation. The front of the card can be used to produce documentation for users of the class. The back holds information that the programmer uses when implementing the class. This convenient and easy-to-use convention offers the flexibility we need during the most dynamic stages of problem solving and implementation. However, once the design is reasonably stable, it should be rewritten in a more formal industry-standard notation. For that, we use UML class diagrams, as described in the next section.

Documentation

As you create your object-oriented design, you are simultaneously developing documentation for your code. Documentation includes the written problem specifications, design, development history, and actual code.

Good documentation helps other programmers read and understand your code and can prove invaluable when software is being debugged and modified (maintained). If you haven't looked at your code for six months and need to change it, you'll be happy that you documented it well. Of course, if someone else has to use and modify your program, good documentation is indispensable.

Documentation is both external and internal to the code. External documentation includes the specifications, the development history, the design documents (such as CRC cards and UML diagrams), and the interface specification. Internal documentation includes code formatting and **self-documenting code**—code that contains meaningful identifiers and comments. You can use the pseudocode from your design as comments in your code.

This kind of documentation may be sufficient for someone reading or maintaining your applications. However, if an application will be used by people who are not programmers, you must provide a user's manual as well.

Be sure to keep your documentation up-to-date. Indicate any changes you make in the code in all of the pertinent documentation. Also use self-documenting code to make your programs more readable.

Many Java programmers use a tool called `javadoc` to generate the interface documentation as web pages. To use `javadoc`, you must write a set of specially formatted comments in your code and then run the code through the `javadoc` tool, much as you run it through the compiler. Instead of outputting Bytecode, `javadoc` outputs web page code called HTML. Learning to write `javadoc` comments is like learning another programming language, so we do not explore this issue further in this text.

> **Self-documenting code**
> Program code that contains meaningful identifiers as well as judiciously used clarifying comments

■ UML Class Diagrams

It can be difficult to understand the operation of an application just by looking at the written documentation. When many classes are collaborating, keeping track of their relationships involves building a mental picture. Before long, we start drawing diagrams, just to keep everything straight. Perhaps we use boxes to represent classes, and lines between them to represent collaborations. Inside the boxes, we make notes about the classes. Then we start using solid and dashed lines to indicate different kinds of collaboration. Eventually, we have a diagram that captures all of the important structural information about the application. The trouble is, no one else knows what our diagram means! If programmers used a common set of symbols, then they could read one another's diagrams.

The Unified Modeling Language (UML) is just such a collection of symbols. It was developed specifically for diagramming object-oriented applications. Even though it has the word *language* in its name, UML is not a programming language; it is a collection of graphical symbols. It is *unified* in the sense that it was created from a combination of three sets of symbols that were in use prior to its development. Each of those earlier conventions had different strengths and weaknesses, and UML was developed to provide a single set of symbols incorporating all of their best features.

The UML symbols are divided into subsets that are used for different purposes. For example, the Use-Case symbols could be used to identify scenarios for the CRC card process: Stick figures of people represent users and what they want to do with the application. A UML Collaboration diagram charts the collaborations that take place during a scenario walkthrough. Activity diagrams show the steps that carry out a responsibility. UML diagrams are available for documenting just about every aspect of programming, from analyzing the problem to deploying the code on customer's computers. You could take an entire course in drawing UML diagrams!

In this text we use the simpler CRC card notation for the early stages of development. Once a design is nearly done, we shift to using one specific part of UML to document an implementation: the Class diagram.

Diagramming a Class   A class is represented in UML by a box that's divided into three sections. The top section has the name of the class; the middle section lists its attributes; and the bottom section lists responsibilities. Here's a UML diagram of the **Phone** class:

```
                          Phone
-----------------------------------------------------------
-areaCode: int
-exchange: int
-number: int
-----------------------------------------------------------
+Phone(area: int, exchange: int, number: int)
+getAreaCode(): int
+getExchange(): int
+getNumber(): int
+toString(): String
```

As you can see, the diagram lists the attributes and their types in the middle section. The minus sign in front of each attribute is shorthand for `private`. UML uses + to mean `public`, and ~ to mean package-level visibility. All of **Phone**'s responsibilities are listed in the bottom section, showing parameters and return types for value-returning methods. As the plus signs indicate, **Phone**'s responsibilities are all `public`.

To convert a CRC card into a UML Class diagram, you copy the class name from the top of the card to the top section of a class box. The responsibilities from the CRC card go into the bottom section, using the appropriate notation. The attributes on the back of the CRC card go into the middle section. Next we see how UML represents collaborations.

Diagramming Collaborations   The Class diagram gives us a compact summary of the class interface. We can put several of these diagrams on a page and draw lines between them to indicate their relationships. For example, a collaboration is indicated by a line with an arrow. The arrow shows that one class uses a responsibility of another class. You can also add a note next to the arrow to indicate how the calling class uses the collaborating class. For example, the following diagram shows a `UserInterface` class that collaborates with `System` to read a file name. To keep the diagram simple, here we just show the name of each class and the relevant operation.

Diagramming Composition of Classes   When a class contains an instance of another class, such as the `Name` class field contained in the `Entry` class for the Address Book Lookup application, we draw a solid diamond at the end of the line next to the containing class. (Again, we just show the constructor as an example responsibility—in a proper UML diagram, all of the responsibilities would be listed.)

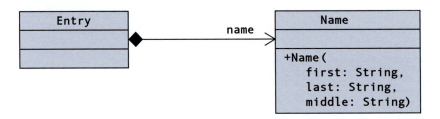

In UML, we refer to this kind of relationship as *composition*. The class with the solid diamond is composed of (among other things) an instance of the class at the other end of the arrow. Notice that the name of the instance (`name`) is indicated beside the arrow. All of the attributes that are listed on the back of a CRC card are listed in the middle section of the corresponding UML class box, but those that are classes also appear as separate classes in the diagram, with composition arrows connecting them.

UML provides graphical conventions for representing other kinds of relationships between classes, but these are sufficient for our immediate purposes. Before we leave this section, look at the UML representation of the `AddressBookLookup` objects in the case study in Chapter 7. Notice how the relationships become clearer using this graphical technique.

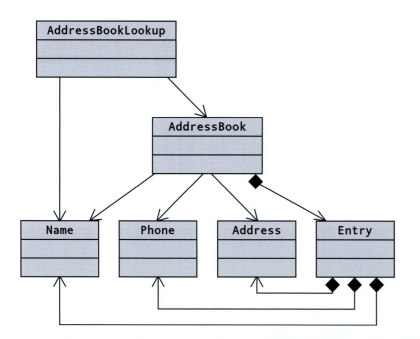

Address Book Update

Problem Develop the application for updating the address book that was used as the example in our discussion of CRC cards, providing just the operation of changing the phone number. Other update operations are left to the exercises.

Brainstorming and Filtering We've already started this process, having brainstormed the initial set of classes and filtered them. After the initial scenario walkthrough, we have the following list:

    Address Book
    User Interface
    Entry
       Name
       Address
       Phone
    Output File
    Field

Determining Responsibilities In developing the CRC card for the user interface, we decided that it would be responsible for getting the name from the user and returning the entry. We also know that this `AddressBook` class isn't the same as the one from Chapter 7, because one of its responsibilities is to search an `ObjectInputStream` file for an entry by name and then return that entry. The Chapter 7 class was designed to display entries from a text file; our new `AddressBook` class also needs the ability to replace an entry on the file.

We can assume that the `Entry` class from Chapter 7 will need to be augmented with transformers that update the different fields. As we'll see shortly, their implementation is trivial.

Scenario Walkthrough Let's continue the walkthrough of the scenario that we began in the section on CRC cards. The `UserInterface` has returned the entry that matches the name. Algorithmically, here is the process that the `getEntryByName` responsibility went through:

```
getEntryByName(Name name) returns Entry

Open input file
try
  Set done to false
  Initialize index to 0
  do
    Read entry
    Increment index
    if entry matches name
      Set done to true
      Set place to index
  while not done
catch EOFException when EOF occurs before a match is found
  Close input file
  Set place to invalid (-1)
  return null
Close input file
return the entry that was found
```

Notice that the input loop doesn't test for EOF directly. Because an `ObjectInputStream` doesn't provide an EOF test method, like `hasNext`, we must place the loop inside a *try* statement and catch the exception that occurs when we attempt to read past the end of the file.

Next, the driver tells the `UserInterface` to ask the user which field of the entry should be changed. The only field that is initially supported is the `Phone` field, but let's write the design as if the user could change any field. That decision will simplify extension to include those options.

We can represent the field names with an `enum` type, and convert the string that the user enters to this type. The `enum` should be in its own compilation unit, because both `UserInterface` and the driver use it. `UserInterface` returns the `enum` value entered. (This attribute information is written on the back of the CRC cards for `UserInterface` and the driver.)

Now the driver tells the `UserInterface` to input the new value for the appropriate type of field. `UserInterface` gets the data from the user and collaborates with the appropriate class to construct an instance of that field type, which it then returns. The driver calls the appropriate `Entry` transformer to update the entry; it then calls on `AddressBook` to update the file.

How does `AddressBook` update the file? It needs to copy the contents of the old file to a new file, replacing the updated entry. In the `getEntryByName` method, we had an instance variable, `place`, save the count of the entries read prior to finding the match. In `updateEntry`, we can use a *for* loop to copy that many entries, write the new entry, read and discard the old entry, and then copy the remainder of the input file to the output file. Keep in mind that an `ObjectInputStream` doesn't have a method equivalent to `hasNext`, so we simply read until it throws an `IOException`, which we catch.

After the new file has been completely written, let's delete the old file and rename the new file to have the old file's name. That way, the user can run the application repeatedly without having to manually rename the files. Here are these steps as a responsibility algorithm:

```
updateEntry(Entry entry)

  Open input and output files
  for index running from 0 to place - 1
      Copy object from input file to output file
  Write entry on output file
  Read old entry from input file (will just be discarded)
  try
      while true
          Copy object from input file to output file
  catch EOFException
      Close files
      Delete input file
      Rename output file to input file name
```

Subsequent Scenarios We've now seen how the most common case works. Let's look at a couple of exceptional cases. What if the user enters a name that's not on the file? What if the user enters an invalid field to change?

The first scenario is actually quite easy. `AddressBook` should return `null` for the entry, and then the driver can check for this special case and output a warning message.

The second scenario requires some thought. The user might have simply mistyped the field name and might like another chance to enter it correctly. Conversely, perhaps the user doesn't want to make any changes. We should provide an option for the user to select "none" for the field to change. In that case, we're done. If an invalid field has been entered, `UserInterface` should again ask for the name of a field after displaying an error message.

Here are the CRC cards for the new classes, following the walkthrough of the scenarios:

Class Name: UserInterface	Superclass:		Subclasses:
Responsibilities		**Collaborations**	
Constructor		Scanner	

GetEntry(AddressBook)
    return Entry
		System.out, Scanner, Name,
		    Addressbook, Entry	

InputField return Field		System.out, Scanner, Field	
InputPhone return Phone		System.out, Scanner, Phone	

Class Name: AddressBook	Superclass:		Subclasses:
Responsibilities		**Collaborations**	
Constructor		File	
Constructor(String)		File	
GetEntryByName(Name) return Entry		ObjectInputStream, Entry, Name	
UpdateEntry(Entry)		ObjectInputStream, ObjectOutputStream	

Class Attributes Now that we have classes and responsibilities, it is time to consider the internal representation for their attributes. For the `UserInterface` class, the only attribute will be a `Scanner` that handles user input via `System.in`. In the `AddressBook` class, only the input and output files are attributes. What about the driver? It has only local variables, but it is worth noting that among them is an `AddressBook` object, a `UserInterface` object, and an `Entry` object.

The UML diagram for this application, shown in Figure 8.12, reveals how much of its work is done by the collaborating classes.

Implementation Now we are ready to code these classes. We begin with the extensions to `Entry`, then turn to the implementation of `AddressBook` and `UserInterface`, and finally create the driver for the application, which we call `UpdateAddressBook`.

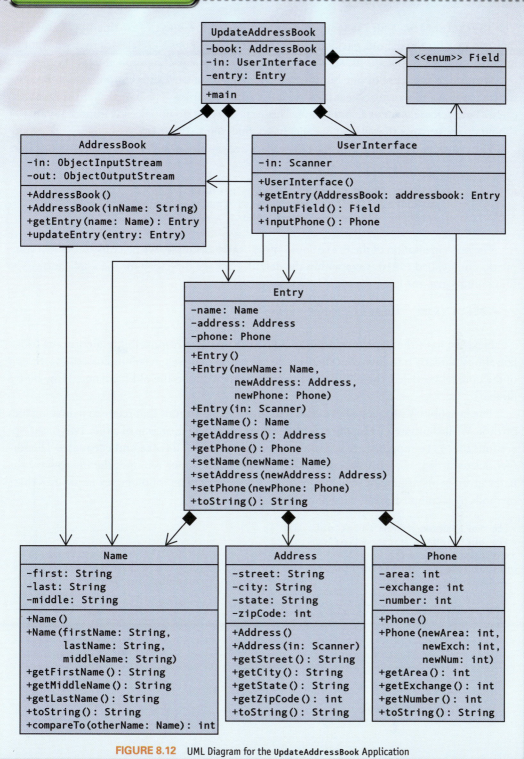

FIGURE 8.12 UML Diagram for the `UpdateAddressBook` Application

The `UserInterface`, `AddressBook`, and `Entry` classes are specific to this application, so they can go into the default package. `Name`, `Address`, and `Phone` are classes that we want to import into other applications, so we bundle them into our package called `utility`.

We need to take care of one bit of housekeeping before we write the application. Because we are reading and writing object files, we must add the phrase `implements Serializable` to classes `Entry`, `Name`, `Address`, and `Phone`. Those classes that do not already import `java.io.*` should do so, because that is the package that defines `Serializable`.

The transformer methods for the `Entry` class are simple enough to code each on one line:

```
// Transformers
public void setName (Name newName) {name = newName;}
public void setAddress (Address newAddress) {address = newAddress;}
public void setPhone (Phone newPhone) {phone = newPhone;}
```

The implementation of the `Field` `enum` type is nearly as simple. We place its source in a compilation unit called `Field.java` within the default package directory for the application. The file contains just one line:

```
enum Field {NAME, ADDRESS, PHONE, NONE}
```

Next we have the implementation of `AddressBook`. The responsibility algorithms translate almost directly into Java. But there is one operation that we haven't discussed—at the end of the update, we delete the old file and rename the new file to the old file name. How do we do that?

The Java library supplies a `File` class that provides operations that relate to managing files on disk. We instantiate a `File` object with a string containing the name of a file. Two of the operations that `File` supports are `void` instance methods called `delete` and `renameTo`. The former deletes a disk file with the corresponding name. The latter renames the file to have the name given by its argument, which is another `File` object. The following example uses these methods to accomplish what we want in this application:

```
File inFileName = new File("data.dat");
File outFileName = new File("new.dat");
inFileName.delete();                    // Delete file data.dat from disk
outFileName.renameTo(inFileName);       // Rename file new.dat to
                                        //   data.dat on disk
```

We are now ready to code `AddressBook`:

```
//*****************************************************************************
// Class AddressBook supplies operations to search and update an address book
//*****************************************************************************
import java.io.*;
import utility.*;
public class AddressBook
```

```java
{
  String inName = "addressbook.dat";
  final String outName = "TempAddrBook.dat";
  File inFile;
  File outFile = new File(outName);
  int place = -1;
  // Default constructor
  public AddressBook()
  {
    inFile = new File(inName);              // Save file name for update
  }
  // Parameterized constructor
  public AddressBook(String inFileName)
  {
    inName = inFileName;                    // Save file name for search
    inFile = new File(inFileName);          // and for update
  }
  // Search address book for entry with matching name
  public Entry getEntryByName(Name name)
    throws IOException, ClassNotFoundException
  {
    Entry entry;
    ObjectInputStream in =
      new ObjectInputStream(new FileInputStream(inName));
    try
    {
      boolean done = false;
      int index = 0;
      do                                    // Search file for a match
      {
        entry = (Entry)in.readObject();
        index++;
        if (entry.getName().compareTo(name) == 0)
        {
          done = true;                      // Found a match
          place = index;                    // Save index for update operation
        }
      }                                     // Can't check for EOF, so
      while (!done);                        //    exit loop if match found
    }                                       //    or else catch the exception if
    catch (EOFException ex)                 //    we hit EOF before match found
    {
      in.close();                           // Loop exited on EOF exception
      place = -1;                           // Set place to invalid
      return null;                          // Return empty entry
    }
    in.close();                             // Loop exited normally
    return entry;                           // Return matching entry
  }
  // Copy input file to output file, replacing matching entry
  public void updateEntry(Entry entry)
    throws IOException, ClassNotFoundException
```

```java
    {
      ObjectInputStream in =
        new ObjectInputStream(new FileInputStream(inName));
      ObjectOutputStream out =
        new ObjectOutputStream(new FileOutputStream(outName));
      // Copy file up to place before where entry was found
      for (int index = 0; index < place-1; index++)
        out.writeObject((Entry) in.readObject());
      out.writeObject(entry);                   // Output new entry
      Entry old = (Entry)in.readObject();       // Skip old entry in input
      try
      {                                         // Copy rest of file to end
        while (true)                            // Loop "forever" until EOF
                                                //    exception

          out.writeObject((Entry)in.readObject());
      }
      catch (EOFException ex)                   // Reached EOF on file in
      {
        in.close();                             // Close files
        out.close();
        inFile.delete();                        // Delete old file
        outFile.renameTo(inFile);               // Rename new file to original
      }
    }
  }
}
```

Here is the implementation of the `UserInterface` class:

```java
//**************************************************************************
// Class UserInterface provides operations to interact via System.in.
// Note: initially implements changing only the Phone field
//**************************************************************************
import java.util.*;
import java.io.*;
import utility.*;
public class UserInterface
{
  Scanner in;
  // Default constructor
  public UserInterface()
  {
    in = new Scanner(System.in);
  }
  // Get name from user and return matching entry from address book
  public Entry getEntry (AddressBook addressBook)
    throws IOException, ClassNotFoundException
  {
    System.out.println("Enter the name you wish to search for.");
    System.out.print("(Format: first middle last):");
    String first = in.next();
    String middle = in.next();
    String last = in.next();
```

```java
    String eol = in.nextLine();              // Discard rest of line
    Name name = new Name(first, last, middle);
    return addressBook.getEntryByName(name);
  }
  // Get field name from user and return matching enum
  public Field inputField ()
  {
    boolean invalidField;
    Field inField = Field.NONE;
    do
    {
      System.out.println
        ("Enter the field you wish to change from the following:");
      for (Field type : Field.values()) System.out.println(type);
      try                                    // Read string and convert to enum
      {
        inField = Field.valueOf(in.nextLine().toUpperCase());
        invalidField = false;
      }
      catch (IllegalArgumentException ex)   // User entered invalid field
      {
        invalidField = true;
        System.out.println("Invalid field name entered.");
      }
    }
    while (invalidField);                    // Try again until field is valid
    return inField;
  }
  // Get phone number from user and return Phone object
  public Phone inputPhone() throws Exception
  {
    System.out.println("Enter the phone number. Example: 800 555 1212");
    int area = in.nextInt();
    int exch = in.nextInt();
    int numb = in.nextInt();
    String eol = in.nextLine();              // Discard rest of line
    return new Phone(area, exch, numb);
  }
}
```

Next we can turn to the driver implementation. Its algorithm follows the scenario walk-through. We instantiate an **AddressBook** and a **UserInterface**, and then we get the entry from the user. If the entry is in the address book, then we display it and ask which field to change. The only options currently implemented are to change the phone field or to make no change. For unimplemented types of changes, we simply display a warning message. We do the same when no change is selected. For a change in phone number, we have **UserInterface** get the new **Phone** from the user, we change the entry, and then we update **AddressBook**.

Given a name that's not in the book, we know that **AddressBook** has already closed the file, so all we need to do is report the error.

Now we are ready to implement the driver:

```java
//**************************************************************************
// Application UpdateAddressBook enables a user to select an entry in an
// address book by name, and then update the value in a field of the entry.
// The address book is stored on an object stream file, and the application
// creates a new temporary file with the update before deleting the old file
// and renaming the temporary file to the original name.
//**************************************************************************
import java.io.*;
import utility.*;
public class UpdateAddressBook
{
  public static void main (String[] args)
    throws IOException, ClassNotFoundException, Exception
  {
    AddressBook book = new AddressBook("addressbook.dat");
    UserInterface in = new UserInterface();
    Entry entry = in.getEntry(book);    // Get the entry to change
    if (entry != null)                  // If it's on the file, display it
    {
      System.out.println("You selected the following entry: \n" + entry + "\n");
      Field field = in.inputField(); // Ask which field to change
      switch (field)                  // Process request according to field
      {
        case NAME:    System.out.println("Name change not yet implemented.");
                      break;
        case ADDRESS: System.out.println
                         ("Address change not yet implemented.");
                      break;
        case PHONE:   Phone phone = in.inputPhone();  // Get the phone number
                      entry.setPhone(phone);          // Change the entry
                      book.updateEntry(entry);        // Update the address book
                      System.out.println("Phone number updated.");
                      break;
        case NONE:    System.out.println("No change to address book.");
                      break;
      }
    }
    else                                              // Invalid name
      System.out.println("Name not found in address book. No change made.");
  }
}
```

Testing To test the application, it is necessary to write a separate application that converts the address book from text into an object file. Once this conversion has been done, the book can be kept in that format.

Test cases should involve valid input (entry on the file, choosing to update the **Phone** field, entering a valid phone number). The valid data test should be tried for the first and last address book entries to be certain that the entire file is processed properly. Then the application should be tested with a valid name, but selecting each of the unimplemented fields in turn, and then the choice of NONE. Finally, a test should be tried with a name that's not in the book. These test cases came directly from our scenarios.

Given the following data file, we summarize this discussion in a test plan.

```
5
Sylva Santana Marie
128 Binoway St.
Leafton MA 11048
617 222 1111
Evan Parsival Sunny
32 East Pleasant St.
Arbuelo AZ 73421
480 444 9999
William Herrold Michael
31415 Pieman Lane
Leafton MA 11048
617 888 3333
Madeline Corby Jenelle
2048 Earlham St.
Clarkson AZ 73438
480 555 6666
Laurens Gruman Franke
1024 Ibiem Road
Leafton MA 11048
781 777 7777
```

TEST PLAN

Number	Input	Expected Output
1	Sylva Marie Santana PHONE 512 222 1066	Phone number updated.
2	Laurens Franke Gruman PHONE 713 444 1492	Phone number updated.
3	Madeline Jenelle Corby ADDRESS	Address change not yet implemented.
4	Evan Sunny Parsival NAME	Name change not yet implemented.
5	William Michael Herrold NONE	No change to address book.
6	Sony Silver Strand	Name not found in address book. No change made.

The exercises ask you to implement this test plan. As the application is extended to include changing the other fields, the test plan should be amended to test those operations.

8.4 : Testing and Debugging

In addition to providing a design that is easy to implement, using CRC cards makes it easy to create an initial test plan. The scenario walkthroughs naturally correspond to test cases in our plan. We simply need to note an example of the data and expected results from each walkthrough. For example, in the walkthrough for updating an entry, we could write down a set of typical values that the user might enter for a name, and we could specify that the address book must contain the corresponding entry. We could also indicate which field the user will select and what the update value will be.

The scenarios produce a plan that combines aspects of both code and data coverage. At the level of collaborations, we cover the structure of the code. That is, our test plan naturally covers the pattern of method calls corresponding to the collaborations that implement each responsibility.

If we think a little bit about the range of values that could appear as arguments in each call during a scenario walkthrough, then we can also include data coverage in our plan. As you go through a scenario, each time a collaboration invokes a responsibility of another class, record the range of values that could appear in the arguments as well as an example value and its expected result.

Remember, however, that CRC cards are notational devices to help us keep track of classes, their responsibilities, and their collaborations. They do not include the algorithms for the individual responsibilities. For this reason, we must extend the test plan with cases that exercise the paths found within each responsibility. Once the responsibility algorithms are written, review the test cases that were recorded during the scenario walkthroughs. In each case, consider whether your knowledge of the algorithm indicates control-flow paths that should be tested specifically.

It may be easiest to test individual classes with a separate driver application class, as we have been doing all along. This driver provides a very simple environment that allows us to directly test the methods of a class, explicitly controlling the argument values that are passed to them. When a class is part of a complex design that involves many different collaborations, it can be difficult to constrain the testing to just that class and to ensure that errors in other classes do not affect its arguments.

Testing and Debugging Hints

1. If you use any file I/O, remember that `main` may need to have the `throws` `IOException` clause appended to its heading.

2. The constructors for arguments to the `ObjectInputStream` and `ObjectOutputStream` are instances of `FileInputStream` and `FileOutputStream`, respectively.

3. For instances of a class to be written on a file, the class must implement the `Serializable` interface.

4. When an instance of a class is read from a file, the object must be type cast back to its original class. For this reason, a method that uses the method `readObject` must include `ClassNotFoundException` in its *throws* clause.

5. Use the methodologies presented in this chapter to carefully design a complete OOD solution to a problem before you start writing any Java code. The design should be sufficiently detailed that converting it to Java becomes almost a mechanical process.

6. During brainstorming, don't try to filter ideas while they are being generated. It is the free flow of ideas that often produces the most innovative approaches.

7. If you are developing a design by yourself, wait to start filtering until the next day, or at least after a few hours of doing something different. It takes some mental distance to gain the necessary perspective for successful filtering.

8. Pick a simple initial scenario, and then work your way into the more complex scenarios. Otherwise, the number of new responsibilities that you have to create initially can seem overwhelming.

9. Don't hesitate to write down additional useful information that is identified during the scenario walkthroughs. At the same time, don't get bogged down in writing responsibility algorithms during the walkthrough process.

10. Use package-level access for each data field unless your design specifically calls for it to be `public` or `private`.

Graphical User Interfaces
The `JFileChooser` Class

Until now, when we opened a file for input, we have asked the user to enter a file name; we then used this input as an argument to the constructor for a `FileReader`. For example:

```java
Scanner in = new Scanner(System.in);
System.out.print("Enter the name of the input file: ");
String filename = in.nextLine();
Scanner infile = new Scanner(new FileReader(filename));
```

Although this approach works, it has some drawbacks. First, if the user mistypes the file name, then the call to `FileReader` throws an exception. Second, this code assumes that the file is located in the current working directory. If the file is actually in another directory, the user must type a string that gives the full path to the file through the directory structure. For example, the user might have to type

/users/smith/documents/mydata/todaysdata.txt

This strategy is not only inconvenient, but also error prone.

Most users are used to seeing applications pop up a window that allows them to navigate through the file system and select a file. As you might expect, the Java library provides a class (called `JFileChooser`) for precisely that purpose. It is a wonderful example of abstraction, because the complexity of showing this information and allowing the user to make a choice is completely hidden. We simply make a method call, and the method returns not just the name of the file, but an actual `File` object that can be passed to the `Scanner` constructor. For example:

```
Scanner infile = new Scanner(fileChooser.getSelectedFile());
```

Of course, this assumes that we've already instantiated a `JFileChooser` object and assigned it to `fileChooser`. Let's see how that task is accomplished. As is often the case with Java library classes, many options are available for `JFileChooser` objects, so we begin with the simplest case and then show a few of the additional possibilities. To instantiate a `JFileChooser`, we simply call its default constructor and assign its result to a variable:

```
JFileChooser fileChooser = new JFileChooser();
```

Once we have instantiated the object, we can cause it to display a dialog window that allows the user to select which file to open. The method takes an argument that specifies the parent window, which we specify as `null`, just as we did for `JOptionPane`. It returns an `int` value, indicating whether the user clicked the Open button, clicked the Cancel button, or closed the window. Here is an example call:

```
int action = fileChooser.showOpenDialog(null);
```

And here is the window it displays:

The actual style of the window and how it allows you to navigate through the file system depends on the operating system you are using.

After this call, the value in `action` corresponds to one of these constants:

```
JFileChooser.CANCEL_OPTION
JFileChooser.APPROVE_OPTION
JFileChooser.ERROR_OPTION
```

For example, we most commonly call `showOpenDialog` within an *if* statement as follows:

```
if (fileChooser.showOpenDialog(null) == JFileChooser.APPROVE_OPTION)
  Scanner infile = new Scanner(fileChooser.getSelectedFile());
else
  System.out.println("No file selected");
```

We've seen how to use `JFileChooser` to open a file for input, but what if we want to open a file for output? In such a case, the user should be able to enter a new file name, in addition to being able to select an existing file. If we instead call the `showSaveDialog` method, then the window that appears also includes a field where the user can enter a file name. Here's an example of opening an output file:

```
if (fileChooser.showSaveDialog(null) == JFileChooser.APPROVE_OPTION)
  PrintWriter outfile = new PrintWriter(fileChooser.getSelectedFile());
else
  System.out.println("No file selected");
```

The button in this window displays the word "Save" instead of "Open." What if neither label describes the action that the application will perform on the file? There is a third method that is identical to `showSaveDialog`, except that its second argument lets us specify the string to appear in the button. The following call to `showDialog` displays the window with the word "Select" in the button:

```
fileChooser.showDialog(null, "Select")
```

Lastly, we mention one more method associated with each `JFileChooser` object: `setDialogTitle`. As you can probably guess, this method specifies the string to appear at the top of the dialog. This `void` method takes a string as its argument.

Here's a complete example application demonstrating the use of `JFileChooser`. Notice that we import `javax.swing.*`, just as we did for `JOptionPane`, because that package contains `JFileChooser`.

```
import javax.swing.*;
import java.io.*;
public class DemoJFileChooser
{
  public static void main(String[] args) throws IOException
  {
    JFileChooser fileChooser = new JFileChooser();
```

```
        fileChooser.setDialogTitle("Select a File for Output");
        if (fileChooser.showDialog(null, "Select") ==
            JFileChooser.APPROVE_OPTION)
        {
          PrintWriter out = new PrintWriter(fileChooser.getSelectedFile());
          out.println("Hello file system!");
          out.close();
        }
        else
          System.out.println("No file selected.");
    }
}
```

Here is the dialog that it displays, where the user has just entered `"TestFile.txt"`:

As another example, in the **UpdateAddressBook** application, we used a literal to specify the name of the input file. Now we can use **JFileChooser** to allow the user to select a file by inserting the following code just after the declaration of **outName** in the application:

```
JFileChooser fileChooser = new JFileChooser();
fileChooser.setDialogTitle("Select an Address Book file");
if (fileChooser.showOpenDialog(null) == JFileChooser.APPROVE_OPTION)
  inName = fileChooser.getSelectedFile().toString();
else
  System.out.println("Using default file.");
```

Of course, we also must remember to import the `javax.swing` package. But those are really the only changes needed to provide the user with a convenient way to select an address book file.

Summary

Encapsulation is an approach to implementing a class that should be reusable in other contexts. By starting with an abstraction of an object and then designing an interface that documents how client code can interact with the object, we create a design that is logically complete yet hides its implementation details from the user. For a class to be truly encapsulated, it must be physically safe from user changes, be invisible to the user, and have a formal specification that describes its behavior.

A package collects a set of related classes into a common structure that can be imported by other classes. Java systems that store compilation units within files allow just one `public` class per compilation unit. A package with multiple `public` classes therefore consists of multiple files, all of which begin with identical `package` statements.

Objects can be written to and read from a file. They can be written on a file of the class `ObjectOutputStream` and read from a file of the class `ObjectInputStream`. Only objects of classes that implement the `Serializable` interface can be written on object files. Object files are used when the output from one application is used as input into another application.

The `enum` data type is a Java syntactic feature that allows the programmer to declare a collection of ordered identifiers. The `enum` values can be assigned to an `enum` variable, can be used to iterate through the collection of values, and can be used with a *switch* statement.

Object-oriented design leads the way to a problem solution by focusing on objects, their associated operations, and their interactions. The use of CRC cards helps us keep track of classes, responsibilities, and collaborations as we explore scenarios. The information on the front of the CRC card is easily translated into an interface specification for users of the class. Designs developed using CRC cards naturally facilitate the development of test plans.

The Unified Modeling Language is a collection of symbols that was developed specifically for diagramming object-oriented applications. In a UML Class diagram, classes are represented in boxes with three parts: one for the name, one for the attributes, and one for the method signatures. Collaborative relationships between classes are represented by arrows. The Class diagram is especially suited for documenting class implementations.

LEARNING Portfolio

Quick Check

1. Name two types of abstraction. (p. 398)
2. Name two benefits of encapsulating a class. (pp. 399–400)
3. What makes a class mutable? (pp. 400–404)
4. Write the statement that says that class `Address` is in package `utility`. (pp. 406–407)

5. If there are multiple compilation unit files in a package, where are they all stored? (pp. 407–408)

6. The members of a package can access one another's `private` fields. (True or false?) (pp. 406–407)

7. If no access modifier is specified for a field, package access is assumed. (True or false?) (pp. 406–407)

8. How many `public` classes may a compilation unit file contain? (pp. 407–408)

9. What is the name of the file class that inputs objects? (pp. 408–411)

10. Declare an enumerated type containing the names of the members of your family. (pp. 412–415)

11. Object-oriented design focuses on the _____ (nouns, verbs) when identifying potential objects in a problem statement. (p. 420)

12. What do we write on a CRC card? (pp. 419–423)

13. Does each CRC card result in the creation of a new class? (pp. 419–423)

14. What symbol does UML use to represent public access? (pp. 426–429)

15. What type of relationship between two classes does an arrow that begins with a solid diamond shape represent in UML? (pp. 426–429)

Answers

1. Data and control. 2. Modifiability and reuse. 3. A class is mutable if it has a transformer method. 4. `package utility;` `// at the beginning of class Address` 5. In a directory with the same name as the package. 6. False. 7. True. 8. 1 9. `ObjectInputStream` 10. `enum` `Family {SUSAN, HENRY, JOHN, MARK}` 11. Nouns. 12. The name of the class, its responsibilities, and its collaborators. 13. No. A CRC card may refer to an existing class that can be used directly. 14. The plus sign. 15. Composition: The class adjacent to the diamond contains a field of the class pointed to by the arrow.

Exam Preparation Exercises

1. Encapsulation has two benefits: modifiability and reuse.

   a. Define these terms.

   b. Distinguish between them.

2. What do we mean by physical hiding of a class?

3. What do we mean by visual hiding of a class?

4. Explain the following statement: "Encapsulation is not a Java language construct."

5. Distinguish between data abstraction and control abstraction.

6. Why is abstraction an important concept in computing?

7. **a.** What is a compilation unit file?

   b. Can one compilation unit file include multiple `public` classes?

   c. Where is each compilation unit file in a package stored?

   d. How is the file containing a compilation unit named?

   e. Can multiple `public` classes appear in the same package?

   f. Define package access.

8. Name the steps in the OOD methodology presented in this chapter.

9. What is the goal of the brainstorming in the design process?

10. Do we need to identify all of the classes for solving a problem in the brainstorming stage? Explain.

11. Is there a CRC card for every class identified during brainstorming? Explain.

12. At what point do you add initial responsibilities to the CRC cards?

13. During a scenario walkthrough, how do you indicate that a class is active?

14. When does a class become inactive in a scenario?

15. What happens when the need for a new class is identified in the middle of a scenario?

16. What is the role of a CRC card in the design process?

17. Name the three parts to the UML diagram of a class.

18. Draw the UML diagram for classes `Time`, `RaceReport`, and `Runner` that were developed in previous chapters.

19. What is self-documenting code?

20. Name four responsibilities that might be associated with a class that represents a calendar date.

21. Name two responsibilities that might be associated with a class that represents an exam score.

22. Which method is associated with each `enum` type that allows us to iterate through its values in a *for* loop?

23. The same identifier can appear more than once in the list of identifiers used to declare an `enum` type. (True or False?)

24. When the `valueOf` method for an `enum` type is passed a `String`, it converts the `String` to the matching value in the `enum` type, ignoring whether the letters in the `String` are uppercase or lowercase. (True or False?)

25. Can an object file be written with a text editor? Explain.

26. Why does an object read from an object file have to be type cast back to its original class?

Programming Warm-Up Exercises

1. Write a CRC card for a class, `Car`, representing an automobile with its make, model, color, and license plate number. Provide constructors, get and set responsibilities for each attribute, and a `toString` responsibility.

2. Write a CRC card for a class, `Book`, representing a library book. It should support creating a book with a title, author, and call number, and observing each of these values.

3. Write a CRC card for a class, `Cow`, representing a cow in a dairy herd. The class should include a name, an ID number, a date of birth, and the date of most recent calving.

4. Brainstorm a set of classes for the following problem statement: You are creating an application that records progress in a fitness program. For each participant in the program, you should keep track of the person's initial weight, quarter-mile jog time, standing long-jump distance, and bench-press weight. After each training session, new values are entered for each of these measurements, and the differences from the original values are displayed. The total number of sessions should also be counted.

5. Filter the classes that were brainstormed in Exercise 4.

6. Write CRC cards for the classes that remain after the filtering in Exercise 5. Include the initial responsibilities.

7. Conduct a first scenario walkthrough of the CRC cards from Exercise 6 for recording a training session, and indicate any additional classes or responsibilities that you find.

8. Brainstorm a list of additional scenarios for the problem given in Exercises 4–7.

9. Use the scenario in Exercise 7 as the basis for the first test case in a test plan for the application.

10. Write the package declarations and headings for the public classes `AddressLabel` and `PrintLabel` that are contained in a package named `somePackage`.

11. How does Java manage to put all the pieces of a package together?

12. Write the declaration of an `enum` type that represents the four seasons. Then write a *for* loop that prints out the names of the seasons as defined in this enumeration.

13. Show the declaration of an enumeration that contains the names of the twelve signs of the zodiac. Then write a *switch* statement that prints out the range of dates associated with a given sign. You can find this information in the horoscope that is printed each day in most newspapers.

14. Declare an `enum` type that consists of the abbreviations of the compass points (N, NE, E, SE, S, SW, W, NW). Write a method that takes a value of this type as its argument and returns a string containing the full name for the compass point. For example, given SW, it would return "Southwest."

15. a. Write the statement that declares a variable `outFile`, instantiates an object of the class `ObjectOutputStream`, and assigns its address to `outFile`.

  b. Write the statement that writes `myName`, an instance of the class `Name`, on `outFile`.

  c. Write the statement that declares a variable `inFile`, instantiates an object of class `ObjectInputStream`, and assigns its address to `inFile`.

  d. Write the statement that reads `myName`, an instance of the class `Name` from `inFile`.

Programming Problems

1. Use the design process described in this chapter to design a game application that simulates a roulette table. The roulette table has 36 numbers (1–36) that are arranged in three columns of 12 rows. The first row has the numbers 1 through 3, the second row contains 4 through 6, and so on. The number 0 is outside the table of numbers. The numbers in the table are colored red and black (0 is green). The red numbers are 1, 3, 5, 7, 9, 12, 14, 16, 18, 19, 21, 23, 25, 27, 30, 32, 34, and 36. The other half of the numbers are black. In a simplified set of rules, players can bet on an individual number (including 0), the red numbers, the black numbers, the even numbers, the odd numbers, the numbers 1–18, the numbers 19–36, and any of the columns or rows in the table.

The user should be allowed to enter one of the bets, and the application should use the `Math.random` method as the basis for computing the number that would be rolled on the wheel. It should then compare this number to the bet, and report whether it won or lost. The process repeats until the user closes the application window. Note that there are several opportunities to make use of enumeration types in this problem.

2. Develop the responsibility algorithms for the CRC cards designed in Problem 1 and code the application. Use the scenarios to design the test plan.

3. Use the design process described in this chapter to design an extension to the application of Problem 1. The new application should allow the user to enter an initial amount of money into an account. In addition to placing a bet, the user should be able to specify an amount to go with the bet; this amount should be deducted from the account. Any winnings should be added to the account. The current winnings or losses (difference from the original amount) should be displayed as well as the value of the account. Winnings are computed as follows:

> Single-number bets pay 36 times the amount placed.
>
> Row bets pay 12 times.
>
> Column bets pay 3 times.
>
> Odd/even, red/black, and high/low half-bets pay 2 times the amount.

The user should not be allowed to bet more than the total in the account.

4. Develop the responsibility algorithms for the CRC cards designed in Problem 3 and code the application. Use the scenarios to design the test plan.

5. Use the design process described in this chapter to design a game application that plays the children's game of rock, paper, scissors. The user enters a letter, indicating a choice. The `Math.random` method is then used to pick a value in the range of 1 through 3, with 1 corresponding to rock, 2 corresponding to paper, and 3 corresponding to scissors. The computer's choice is compared to the user's choice according to the rules: rock breaks scissors, scissors cut paper, paper covers rock. Choices that match are ties. Display a count of the wins by the user and the computer, and the number of ties. The application ends when the user enters an invalid choice.

6. Develop the responsibility algorithms for the CRC cards designed in Problem 5 and code the application. Use the scenarios to design the test plan. Note that an enumeration type is well suited to representing the three moves in this game.

Case Study Follow-Up

1. Implement the test plan for the `UpdateAddressBook` case study. You will need to develop an application that allows you to create input test files.

2. Implement the operations for changing the name and address fields of an entry in the case study.

3. Extend the `UpdateAddressBook` application so that the user is given the choice of changing an existing entry or adding a new entry to the book.

4. To the list of choices for changing the fields of an address book entry, add the option to delete the entry. (*Hint:* The `updateEntry` method should not write out the entry if it is `null`.)

5. Change the `UpdateAddressBook` application so that it allows the user to make multiple changes in one run. (*Hint:* Surround the main section of the application with a loop.)

6. The `Phone` constructor can throw an `Exception` if the number isn't valid. Change the `inputPhone` method to handle this case.

9 Arrays

Goals

Knowledge Goals

To:

- Understand the difference between atomic and composite data types
- Understand the difference between unstructured and structured composite data types
- Know how Java implements arrays
- Know how an array is passed as an argument
- Understand the difference between an array and the information stored or referenced within the array
- Understand the role of an array in structuring data within a problem
- Understand the role of a two-dimensional array in representing a table with rows and columns
- Know how a two-dimensional array is constructed as an array of arrays

Skill Goals

To be able to:

- Declare and instantiate a one-dimensional array
- Access and manipulate the individual components in a one-dimensional array where the elements are
  - Atomic types
  - Composite types
- Use an initializer list to instantiate a one-dimensional array
- Declare a two-dimensional array
- Perform fundamental operations on a two-dimensional array:
  - Access a component of the array
  - Process the array by rows
  - Process the array by columns
- Declare a two-dimensional array as a parameter
- Declare and process a multidimensional array

1972
HP introduces the hand-held scientific calculator; hand-held calculators replace the slide rule

1972
Nolan Bushnell takes his video game Pong and founds Atari, launching the computer-entertainment industry

1972
Alan Kay's ideas fuel the development of the computer language Smalltalk

1972
Dennis Ritchie develops the programming language C

1972
Alain Colmerauer develops the programming language Prolog

1972
The first programmable word processor is introduced in Canada

Introduction

Java's data types are classified into primitive and reference types. In previous chapters, we have explored all of the primitive types and the class type. In this chapter, we extend the discussion of the Java data types by examining the array type, which is highlighted in Figure 9.1. (Notice that we've also included the **enum** type in this familiar diagram, now that we've covered it.) As you can see from the way that "array" is shown in black in the figure, it is the only type that doesn't have a reserved word associated with it.

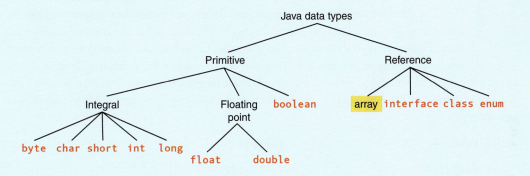

FIGURE 9.1   Java Data Types

1972
Steve Wozniak makes free phone calls using his invention, the "blue box"

1973
Xerox PARC's experimental Alto personal computer, featuring a mouse, a graphical user interface, and connection to a local area network, becomes operational

1973
Ten thousand components are placed on a 1-square-cm chip through large-scale integration

1973
Eckert and Mauchley's ENIAC patent is invalidated, and John Vincent Atanasoff is federally recognized as the inventor of the modern computer

1974
Charles Simonyi writes the first WYSIWYG ("What You See Is What You Get") program entitled Bravo

1974
The first World Computer Chess Tournament takes place in Stockholm; the winner is the program Kaissa

453

9.1 : Review of Java Data Types

Before we define the array data type, we should first step back and look more broadly at data types to see where arrays fit in the overall picture. Recall that a data type is a set of data values, along with a set of operations on those values. As we saw in Chapter 8, integer, real, character, Boolean, and enumerated types are said to be *atomic* because they have no component parts that can be accessed separately. For example, a single character is atomic, but the string `"Good Morning"` is not atomic because it is composed of 12 characters.

> **Composite data type**
> A data type that allows a collection of values to be associated with an identifier of that type
>
> **Unstructured data type**
> A collection of components that are not organized with respect to one another
>
> **Structured data type**
> An organized collection of components; the organization determines the means used to access individual components

Sometimes we may need to show a relationship among variables or to store and reference collections of variables as a group. For this reason, we need a way to associate an identifier with a collection of values. A data type made up of a collection of values is called a **composite data type**.

Composite data types come in two forms: unstructured and structured. In an **unstructured data type**, no relationship exists among the values in the data type other than their membership in the collection. A **structured data type**, by contrast, is an organized collection of components in which a relationship exists among the items in the collection. We use this relationship to access individual items within the collection as well as to manipulate the collection as a whole.

In a composite data type, each value is a collection of component items. The entire collection is given a single name, yet each component can still be accessed individually.

The class is an example of a composite data type. A class has a name and can be composed of named data fields and methods. The data fields and methods can be accessed individually by name. A class is unstructured because access does not depend on an ordering relationship among the data fields or the methods. That is, if we change the order in which the members of the class are listed, this change has no effect on how we access them. For example, here is the same class, declared with its data fields in two different orders:

```
class Example              class Example
{                          {
  int field1;                double field3;
  int field2;                int field2;
  double field3;             int field1;
}                          }
```

Regardless of which order we use, the fields are accessed the same way: by name.

A string is another example of a composite object in Java. When you declare a variable `myString` to be of class `String`, `myString` does not reference an atomic data value; rather, it references a collection of characters. You can access each component in the string individually by using an expression such as `myString.charAt(3)`, which accesses the `char` value at position 3. Because the characters within the string are organized by position, the string is structured.

Atomic data types, which we defined in Chapter 8, serve as the building blocks for composite types. A composite type gathers together a set of component values and usually imposes

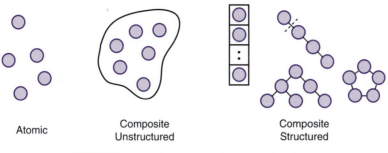

FIGURE 9.2 Atomic (Simple) and Composite Data Types

a specific arrangement on them (see Figure 9.2). If the composite type is a built-in type, the syntax of the language provides the accessing mechanism. If the composite type is user-defined, the accessing mechanism is defined by the methods provided with the class.

9.2 : One-Dimensional Arrays

How we organize our data plays an important role in the design process. If the internal data representation for a class is a composite type (that is, if it contains more than a single atomic field), we call the internal representation a **data structure**. We need to be careful with terminology here. The term *data structure* refers to any composite type. The term *structured data type* refers to a composite type whose internal organization affects its behavior. The choice of data structure directly affects the design because it determines the algorithms used to process the data.

> **Data structure** The implementation of a composite data type

Many problems have so many components that it is difficult to process them if each one must have a unique name. For example, to read and print a file in reverse order, all of the values must be read and saved before the last one can be printed. If we use individually named values, and there are 1000 values on the file, then we must define 1000 individual variables to hold the values and input and output each value separately—an incredibly tedious task! An array—one of Java's built-in reference types—is a data type that allows us to program operations of this kind with ease.

Let's look at how we would have to solve this problem with simple variables.

```java
// Read 1000 numbers and print them in reverse order
import java.io.*;
public class ArrayExample
{
  public static void main(String[] args) throws IOException
  {
    Scanner inFile;
    PrintWriter outFile;
    inFile = new Scanner(new FileReader("infile.dat"));
    outFile = new Scanner(new FileWriter("outfile.dat"));
```

```
// Declare 1000 integer variables
int value0;
int value1;
int value2;
      .
      .
      .
int value999;

// Read 1000 integer values
value0 = inFile.nextInt();
value1 = inFile.nextInt();
value2 = inFile.nextInt();
      .
      .
      .
value999 = inFile.nextInt();
// Write 1000 values
outFile.println(value999);
outFile.println(value998);
outFile.println(value997);
      .
      .
      .
outFile.println(value0);
inFile.close();
outFile.close();
   }
}
```

This application is more than 3000 lines long, and we have to use 1000 separate variables. Note that all of the variables have the same name except for an appended number that distinguishes each one. Wouldn't it be more convenient if we could put the number into a counter variable and use it to go from 0 through 999, and then from 999 back down to 0? For example, if the counter variable is **number**, we can replace the 2000 original input/output statements with the following four lines of code (as you can see in the highlighted areas, we enclose **number** in brackets to set it apart from **value**):

```
for (number = 0; number < 1000; number++)
  value[number] = inFile.nextInt();
for (number = 999; number >= 0; number--)
  outFile.println(value[number]);
```

This code fragment is correct in Java, *if* we declare **value** to be a one-dimensional array. Such an array is a collection of variables—all of the same type—for which the first part of each variable name is the same and the last part is an index value.

The declaration of a one-dimensional array is similar to the declaration of a simple variable (a variable of a simple data type), with one exception: You must indicate that it is an array by putting square brackets next to the type. As we noted earlier, there is no reserved word associated with the array type.

```
int[] value;
```

Because an array is a reference type, it must be instantiated. At that time, we must specify the size of the array.

```
value = new int[1000];
```

Here `value` represents an array with 1000 components, all of type `int`. The first component has index value 0, the second component has index value 1, and the last component has index value 999.

The following application prints out numbers in reverse order using an array. It is certainly much shorter than our first version!

```
// Read 1000 numbers and print them in reverse order
import java.io.*;
public class ArrayExample
{
  public static void main(String[] args) throws IOException
  {
    Scanner inFile;
    PrintWriter outFile;
    inFile = new Scanner(new File("infile.dat"));
    outFile = new PrintWriter(new FileWriter("outfile.dat"));

    // Declare and instantiate an array
    int[] value = new int[1000];
    // Read and print in reverse
    for (int number = 0; number < 1000; number++)
      value[number] = inFile.nextInt();
    for (int number = 999; number >= 0; number--)
      outFile.println(value[number]);

    inFile.close();
    outFile.close();
  }
}
```

```
infile outfile
10     9999
20     9998
30     9997
40     .
.      .
.      40
9997   30
9998   20
9999   10
```

In general terminology, an array differs from a class in three fundamental ways:

1. An array is a homogeneous data structure (all components in the structure are of the same data type), whereas classes are heterogeneous types (their components may be of different types).
2. A component of an array is accessed by its position in the structure, whereas a data component of a class is accessed by an identifier (the field name).
3. Because array components are accessed by position, an array is a structured data type.

Let's define Java arrays formally and look at the rules for accessing individual components.

■ Declaring an Array

> **One-dimensional array**
> A structured collection of components, all of the same type, that is given a single name; each component (array element) is accessed by an index that indicates the component's position within the collection

A **one-dimensional array** is a structured collection of components (often called array *elements*) that can be accessed individually by specifying the position of a component with a single index value.

Let's examine several declarations:

```java
int[] numbers;          // Declares an int array variable
float[] realNumbers;    // Declares a float array variable
char[] letters;         // Declares a char array variable
double[] money;         // Declares a double array variable
```

The `numbers`, `realNumbers`, `letters`, and `money` variables can all contain the address of an array (remember, arrays are reference types, so an array variable holds a memory address just as an object variable holds the address of an object). The variable `numbers` can contain the address of an array of integers; `realNumbers` can contain the address of an array of `float` values; `letters` can contain the address of an array of characters; and `money` can contain the address of an array of `double` values.

Notice the syntax: The type of the values in the array comes first, followed by a pair of brackets that signifies that this structure is an array, and finally the name of the variable that can hold the address of the array.

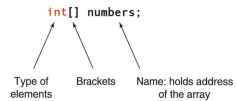

```java
int[] numbers;
```

Type of elements   Brackets   Name: holds address of the array

■ Instantiating an Array

You instantiate an array with the same operator that you use to instantiate an object: `new`. The following code fragment instantiates the arrays declared in the previous section:

```java
numbers = new int[4];           // Instantiates the array object
realNumbers = new float[10];    // Instantiates the array object
letters = new char[26];         // Instantiates the array object
money = new double[100];        // Instantiates the array object
```

Notice how the syntax differs from object instantiation. We don't use a constructor name with a list of arguments. Instead, we write the type of the array, and then we put the number of elements the array will hold in brackets.

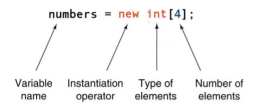

The number of elements is an expression that must have a value greater than or equal to 0. If the value is n, the range of index values is 0 through $n - 1$, not 1 through n. For example, two of the preceding examples instantiate the arrays shown in Figure 9.3. The `numbers` array has four components, each capable of holding one `int` value. The `realNumbers` array has a total of ten components, all of type `float`.

An array can be declared and instantiated in separate statements, or the declaration and creation can be combined into one step, as shown here:

```java
// Declared and instantiated in one statement
int[] numbers = new int[4];
// Declared and instantiated in one statement
float[] realNumbers = new float[10];
```

Because arrays are reference types in Java, they are instantiated at run time, not at compile time. Therefore, the expression used to instantiate an array object does not have to be a constant. It can also be a value that has been input. For example, if you have read the value of `dataSize` from a file, the following declaration is legal:

```java
int[] data = new int[dataSize];
```

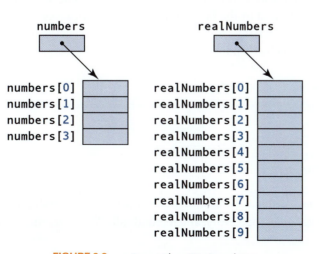

FIGURE 9.3   `numbers` and `realNumbers` Arrays

Once instantiated, the array always has the specified number of components. For example, if `dataSize` is 10 when the array is instantiated but `dataSize` is later changed to 15, the array `data` still has only 10 components.

■ Array Initializers

Java provides an alternative way to instantiate an array. You learned previously that Java allows you to initialize a variable in its declaration:

```
int delta = 25;
```

The value 25 is called an initializer. You can also initialize an array in its declaration, by using a special syntax for the initializer. In this case, you specify a list of initial values for the array elements, separate them with commas, and enclose the list within braces:

```
int[] age = {23, 10, 16, 37, 12};
```

In this declaration, `age[0]` is initialized to 23, `age[1]` is initialized to 10, and so on. Notice two interesting things about this syntax. First, it does not use the `new` operator. Second, it does not specify the number of components. When the compiler sees an initializer list, it determines the size by finding the number of items in the list, instantiates an array of that size, and stores the values into their proper places. Of course, the types of the values in the initializer list must match the type of the array.

What values are stored in an array when it is instantiated by using `new`? If the array components are primitive types, they are set to their default values: 0 for integral types, 0.0 for floating-point types, character code zero in Unicode for `char`, and `false` for the `boolean` type. If the array components are a reference type, they are set to `null`.

■ Accessing Individual Components

To access an individual field of a class, we use dot notation—the name of the class object, followed by a period, followed by the field name. In contrast, to access an individual array component, we write the array name, followed by an expression enclosed in square brackets. The expression specifies which component to access.

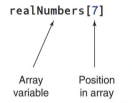

```
realNumbers[7]
```

Array
variable

Position
in array

This *index expression* may be as simple as a constant or a variable name or as complex as a combination of variables, operators, and method calls. Whatever the form of the expression,

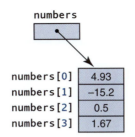

numbers

FIGURE 9.4 numbers Array with Values

it must give an integer value as a result. Index expressions can be of type **byte**, **char**, **short**, or **int**.[1] Using an index expression of type **long** produces a compile-time error. Mathematically, **realNumbers[7]** is known as a *subscripted variable*.

The simplest form of index expression is a constant. For example, using our **numbers** array, the sequence of assignment statements

```
numbers[0] = 1066;
numbers[1] = -32;
numbers[2] = 1492;
numbers[3] = 2003;
```

fills the array with the components one at a time (see Figure 9.4).

Each array component—**numbers[2]**, for instance—can be treated exactly the same as any simple variable of type **int**. For example, we can perform the following operations on the individual component **numbers[2]**:

```
// Assign it a value
numbers[2] = 1945;

// Read a value into it
numbers[2] = inFile.nextInt();

// Write its contents
outFile.println(numbers[2]);

// Pass it as an argument
y = Math.sqrt(numbers[2]);

// Use it in an expression
x = 6.8 * (double)(numbers[2] + 103);
```

[1]Java inherits the notion that **char** is a numeric type from C. The Java language specifications say that arrays must be indexed by **int** values but that values of type **short**, **byte**, or **char** may also be used because they are automatically cast to **int** values. For clarity, we explicitly cast **char** values to **int** when using them as indexes.

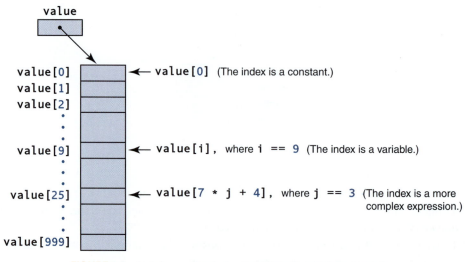

FIGURE 9.5 An Index as a Constant, a Variable, and an Arbitrary Expression

Now let's look at a more complicated index expression. Suppose we declare a 1000-element array of `int` values with the statement

```
int[] value = new int[1000];
```

and execute the following statement:

```
value[counter] = 5;
```

In this statement, 5 is stored into an array component. If `counter` is 0, then 5 is stored into the first component of the array; if `counter` is 1, then 5 is stored into the second place in the array; and so forth. If we execute the statement

```
if (value[number+1] % 10 != 0)
```

then the expression `number + 1` selects an array component. The specific array component accessed is divided by 10 and checked to see whether the remainder is nonzero. If `number + 1` is 0, we are testing the value in the first component; if `number + 1` is 1, we are testing the second place; and so on. Figure 9.5 shows the index expression as a constant, a variable, and a more complex expression.

■ Out-of-Bounds Array Indexes

Given the declaration

```
float[] alpha = new float[100];
```

the valid range of index values is 0 through 99. Starting at 0 seems awkward, because we are used to numbering things beginning with 1. However, you should not be surprised; the positions in a string begin with 0. What happens if we try to execute the statement

```java
alpha[i] = 62.4;
```

when i is less than 0 or when i is greater than 99? A memory location outside the array would be accessed, which causes an out-of-bounds error. Some languages—C++, for instance—do not check for this kind of error, but Java does. If your code attempts to use an **out-of-bounds array index**, Java throws an `ArrayIndexOutOfBoundsException`.

> **Out-of-bounds array index** An index value that is either less than 0 or greater than the array size minus 1

The most common error in processing arrays is an out-of-bounds array index. Rather than attempt to catch this error, you should write your code so as to prevent it.

In Java, each array that is instantiated has a `public` instance variable, called `length`, associated with it that contains the number of components in the array. We can use `length` when processing the components in the array to avoid having an out-of-bounds error. How? Array-processing algorithms often use *for* loops to step through the array elements one at a time. The following loop zeroes out the 100-element `alpha` array:

```java
for (int index = 0; index < alpha.length; index++)
  alpha[index] = 0.0;
```

If you use this pattern—initialize the counter to zero, and then use a "less than" test against the size of the array as recorded in `length`—then you can be sure that your counter is within the bounds of the array. If your code crashes with an `ArrayIndexOutOfBoundsException`, immediately verify that your relational operator is the "less than" operator, not the "less than or equal to" operator.

■ Aggregate Array Operations

We can assign one array to another and we can compare two arrays for equality—but keep in mind that arrays are reference types. As a consequence, assignment produces an alias of the array, and the equality test is `true` when two array variables refer to the same place in memory. Let's see what happens when we test two arrays for equality (yellow highlight), and then assign one array to another (red highlight) before again testing them for equality (green highlight):

```java
int[] numbers = {2, 4, 6};
int[] values = new int[3];
values[0] = 2;
values[1] = 4;
values[2] = 6;

if (numbers == values)
  ...
numbers = values;
if (numbers == values)
  ...
```

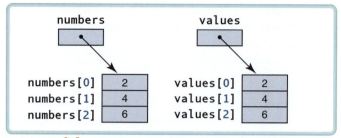

a. Result is `false`; these are two different arrays.

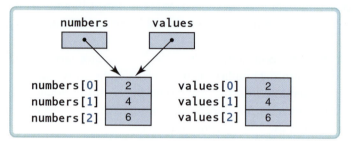

b. Result is `true` after a shallow copy.

FIGURE 9.6 Comparison of Array Variables

The first *if* expression is `false`, because the variables `numbers` and `values` hold different memory addresses. (See Figure 9.6a.) The next statement takes the contents of `values` (the address where the array is stored) and stores it into `numbers`. The next *if* expression is `true`, because the two variables now hold the same memory address. (See Figure 9.6b.)

You should not be surprised at this example. An assignment for a reference type copies the address; an equality test for a reference type compares addresses. If you want to compare arrays by their contents, you must write a method to perform an element-by-element comparison, as follows:

```
// Compare arrays component by component
boolean compareArrays(int[] one, int[] two)
{
  if (one.length != two.length)
    return false;

  boolean result = true;
  int index = 0;
  while (index < one.length && result)
  {
    if (one[index] == two[index])
      index++;
    else
      result = false;
  }
  return result;
}
```

Given the preceding comparison operation, what would be the result of each of the following expressions, given that `numbers` and `sameNumbers` are different arrays that contain the same values in their elements?

```
numbers == sameNumbers
   . . .
compareArrays(numbers, sameNumbers)
   . . .
```

The first expression is `false`. The arrays might contain the same values, but the equality test is for addresses, not values. We call this a *shallow* comparison. The second expression is `true`, because `compareArrays` is a method that performs what we call a *deep* comparison.

Method `Arrays.equals`   The Java library contains a class called `Arrays` in the `java.util` package that holds static `equals` methods to test for deep equality of arrays whose elements are any of the primitive types. For example, instead of using the preceding `compareArrays` method, we could write the following:

```
import java.util.Arrays;
.
.
.
System.out.println(Arrays.equals(numbers, sameNumbers));
```

If `numbers` and `sameNumbers` are the same length and have the same element values, then this code fragment outputs `true`. But be careful: Use `equals` only to compare arrays whose elements are primitive types. Applying `equals` to an array of reference types will produce `true` when the elements of the two arrays contain the same memory addresses.

Method `clone`   Each Java array has an instance method, called `clone`, associated with it that copies its element values. This method is automatically supplied by Java (it is not part of the `Arrays` package). For example, we can write

```
sameNumbers = numbers.clone();
```

This assignment creates a new array that is the same length as `numbers`, and all of the element values are copied from `numbers` to this new array before its address is assigned to `sameNumbers`. Thus, if we execute the statements

```
sameNumbers = numbers.clone();
System.out.println(numbers == sameNumbers);
System.out.println(Arrays.equals(numbers, sameNumbers));
```

the output is

```
false
true
```

The first comparison is `false` because the arrays are stored in different places. The second comparison is `true` because the `clone` operation ensures that they contain the same element values.

9.3 : Examples of Processing One-Dimensional Arrays

We now look in detail at two specific examples of processing arrays. These examples demonstrate different uses of arrays in applications.

■ Occupancy Rates

An application might use the following declarations to analyze occupancy rates in an apartment building:

```
final int BUILDING_SIZE = 350;  // Number of apartments

int[] occupants = new int[BUILDING_SIZE];
// occupants[aptNo] is the number of occupants in apartment aptNo
int totalOccupants;             // Total number of occupants
```

Here `occupants` is a 350-element array of integers (see Figure 9.7). If the first apartment has three occupants, `occupants[0] == 3`; if the second apartment has five occupants, `occupants[1] == 5`; and so on.

If values have been stored into the array, then the following code totals the number of `occupants` in the building:

```
totalOccupants = 0;
for (int aptNo = 0; aptNo < occupants.length; aptNo++)
  totalOccupants = totalOccupants + occupants[aptNo];
```

The first time through the loop, `counter` is 0. We add the contents of `totalOccupants` (that is, 0) and the contents of `occupants[0]`, storing the result into `totalOccupants`. Next, `counter` becomes 1 and the loop test occurs. The second loop iteration adds the contents of `totalOccupants`

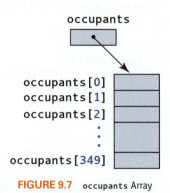

FIGURE 9.7 `occupants` Array

and the contents of `occupants[1]`, storing the result into `totalOccupants`. Now `counter` becomes 2 and the loop test is made. Eventually, the loop adds the contents of `occupants[349]` to the sum and increments `counter` to 350. At this point, the loop condition is `false`, and control exits the loop.

Note how we used the named constant `BUILDING_SIZE` in the array declaration and `occupants.length` in the *for* loop. When we use a constant in this manner, it is easy to make changes. If the number of apartments changes from 350 to 400, for example, we just need to alter the declaration of `BUILDING_SIZE`. We could also have written

```
for (int aptNo = 0; aptNo < BUILDING_SIZE; aptNo++)
```

but we prefer to use the `length` field because it is specifically associated with the array. In the future, we might modify the application to use a different constant to set the size of `occupants`. Then `BUILDING_SIZE` would no longer be the correct value to terminate the loop, but `occupants.length` would remain valid.

■ Character Counts

As a second example, let's use an array to count the number of times that each letter in the English alphabet is used in text, either in uppercase or in lowercase. We declare an array of 26 integers, one for each letter. We do not need to set the contents of the array slots to 0, because they are automatically initialized to 0 when we instantiate the array. See Figure 9.8.

```
int[] letterCount = new int[26];
```

Here `letterCount[0]` is the counter for the number of times we see `'A'` or `'a'`, `letterCount[1]` is the counter for the number of times we see `'B'` or `'b'`, and `letterCount[25]` is the counter for the number of times we see `'Z'` or a `'z'`. How do we convert a letter to its position in the array? We read a character and see if it is a letter. If so, we convert it to uppercase

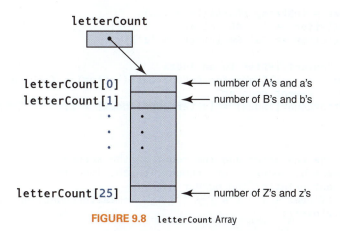

FIGURE 9.8 `letterCount` Array

using a method called **toUpperCase** that is a class method in a Java library class called **Character**. The uppercase letter (cast to **int**) minus **'A'** (also cast to **int**) gives us the letter's place in the array. The following code fragment accomplishes this conversion and increments the counter for the character:

```
if ((letter >= 'A' && letter <= 'Z') || (letter >= 'a' && letter <= 'z'))
{
  index = (int)Character.toUpperCase(letter) - (int)'A';
  letterCount [index] = letterCount [index] + 1;
}
```

All of the pieces are tied together in the following application:

```
//****************************************************************************
// Class CountLetters reads in a sample of text line by line and counts the
// frequency of occurrence of each alphabetic character.
//****************************************************************************
import java.io.*;
import java.util.*;
public class CountLetters
{
  public static void main(String[] args) throws IOException
  {
    Scanner dataFile;
    char letter;
    int index;
    int location;
    String inString;
    int[] letterCount = new int[26];
    dataFile = new Scanner(new FileReader("Words.in"));

    while (dataFile.hasNextLine())
    {
      inString = dataFile.nextLine();

      for (location = 0; location < inString.length(); location++)
      {
        letter = inString.charAt(location);
        if ((letter >= 'A' && letter <= 'Z') ||
            (letter >= 'a' && letter <= 'z'))
        {
          // Convert letter to an index
          index = (int)Character.toUpperCase(letter) - (int)'A';
          // Increment counter
          letterCount[index] = letterCount[index] + 1;
        }
      }
    }
    // Write the character and the count on the screen
    for (index = 0; index < letterCount.length; index++)
      System.out.println("The number of " +
        (char)(index + (int)'A') + "'s is " + letterCount[index]);
    dataFile.close();
  }
}
```

Here are the first and last paragraphs of the input, followed by the output:

○ ○ ○ 📄 Words.in

The Abacus (which appeared in the sixteenth century) was the first calculator. In the middle of the seventeenth century Blaise Pascal, a French mathematician, built and sold gear-driven mechanical machines which performed whole number addition and subtraction. (Yes, the language Pascal is named for him.)

○ ○ ○ 📄 Words.in

The general organization of a computer has remained constant over the last 40 years. This organization or architecture is based on the ideas of von Neumann and bears his name. The essence of this architecture is sequentiality. That is, instructions (a program) are stored in sequential memory locations in binary form and are executed in sequence, one after the other.

○ ○ ○ 📄 screen.out

```
The number of A's is 305
The number of B's is 54
The number of C's is 142
The number of D's is 150
The number of E's is 421
The number of F's is 59
The number of G's is 49
The number of H's is 192
The number of I's is 254
The number of J's is 6
The number of K's is 9
The number of L's is 114
The number of M's is 109
The number of N's is 258
The number of O's is 204
The number of P's is 60
The number of Q's is 6
The number of R's is 195
The number of S's is 184
The number of T's is 327
The number of U's is 96
The number of V's is 32
The number of W's is 48
The number of X's is 5
The number of Y's is 41
The number of Z's is 5
```

This example, in which the index is a function of the letter being counted, is an example of a type of problem in which the index has *semantic content*. That is, the index has meaning within the problem itself. An index having semantic content is an important property of many problems in which an array is the appropriate data structure. This property is used in the first Problem-Solving Case Study.

May We Introduce

Admiral Grace Murray Hopper

From 1943 until her death on New Year's Day in 1992, Admiral Grace Murray Hopper was intimately involved with computing. In 1991, she was awarded the National Medal of Technology "for her pioneering accomplishments in the development of computer programming languages that simplified computer technology and opened the door to a significantly larger universe of users."

Admiral Hopper was born Grace Brewster Murray in New York City on December 9, 1906. She attended Vassar and received a Ph.D. in mathematics from Yale. For the next ten years, she taught mathematics at Vassar.

In 1943, Hopper joined the U.S. Navy and was assigned to the Bureau of Ordnance Computation Project at Harvard University as a programmer on the Mark I. The machine was a room-sized electro-mechanical automated calculator that was programmed with a punched-paper tape. It was the first large-scale digital computer in the United States and a precursor to the stored-program von Neumann design. After World War II ended, she remained at Harvard as a faculty member and continued work on the Navy's Mark II and Mark III computers. She loved to tell the story of how, while she was working on the Mark II, one of the operators discovered the first computer "bug"—a moth caught in one of the relays. In 1949, she joined Eckert-Mauchly Computer Corporation and worked on the UNIVAC I, which was the first computer to be commercially produced in the United States.

Hopper had a working compiler in 1952, a time when the conventional wisdom was that computers could do only arithmetic. Although not on the committee that designed the computer language COBOL, she was active in its design, implementation, and use. COBOL (Common Business-Oriented Language) was developed in the early 1960s and is still widely used in data processing.

In 1966, Hopper retired from the Navy, only to be recalled within a year to full-time active duty. Her mission was to oversee the Navy's efforts to maintain uniformity in programming languages. It has been said that just as Admiral Hyman Rickover was the father of the nuclear navy, Admiral Hopper was the mother of computerized data automation in the Navy. She served with the Naval Data Automation Command until she retired again in 1986 with the rank of Rear Admiral. At the time of her death, she was a senior consultant at Digital Equipment Corporation.

During her lifetime, Hopper received honorary degrees from more than 40 colleges and universities. She was honored by her peers on several occasions, including the first Computer Sciences Man of the Year award given by the Data Processing Management

> Association, and the Contributions to Computer Science Education Award given by the Special Interest Group for Computer Science Education, which is part of the Association for Computing Machinery (ACM).
>
> Hopper loved young people and enjoyed giving talks on college and university campuses. She often handed out colored wires, which she called nanoseconds because they were cut to a length of about one foot—the distance that light travels in a nanosecond (billionth of a second). Her advice to the young: "You manage things, you lead people. We went overboard on management and forgot about the leadership."
>
> When asked of which of her many accomplishments she was most proud, she answered, "All the young people I have trained over the years."

May We Introduce

9.4 : Arrays of Objects

Although arrays with atomic components are very common, many applications require a collection of composite objects. For example, a business may need a list of parts records, and a teacher may need a list of students in a class. Arrays are ideal for these applications. We simply define an array whose components are references to objects.

■ Arrays of Strings

Let's define an array of strings, each of which is a grocery item. Declaring and creating an array of objects is exactly like declaring and creating an array where the components are atomic types.

```
String[] groceryItems = new String[10];  // Array of references to strings
```

Here `groceryItems` is an array of 10 strings. How many characters appear in each string? We don't know yet. The array of strings has been instantiated, but the string objects themselves have not been created. In other words, `groceryItems` is an array of references to string objects, which are set to `null` when the array is instantiated. We must instantiate the string objects separately. The following code segment reads 10 strings and stores references to them into `groceryItems`:

```
inFile = new Scanner(new FileReader("infile.dat"));
outFile = new PrintWriter(new FileWriter("outfile.dat"));
...
int index;                                // Index into groceryItems
String[] groceryItems = new String[10];  // Provides places for 10 references

// Read strings from file inFile and store references
for (index = 0; index < groceryItems.length; index++)
{
  groceryItems[index] = inFile.nextLine();
}
```

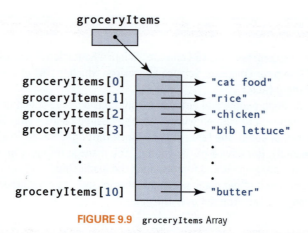

FIGURE 9.9 groceryItems Array

The `nextLine` method returns a reference to an input string that is stored into `groceryItems`. Figure 9.9 shows what the array looks like with values in it.

An array name with no brackets is an array variable. An array name with brackets is a component. We can manipulate the component just like any other variable of that type or class.

Expression	Class/Type
`groceryItems`	Reference to an array
`groceryItems[0]`	Reference to a string
`groceryItems[0].charAt(0)`	A character

How would you read in grocery items if you know that there are no more than 10 items, but you don't know exactly how many? You could use a *while* loop that starts by reading in a grocery item and storing it into the first place. If there is another item, it is stored into the second place, and so on. As a consequence, you must keep a counter of how many items are read in. The following code fragment reads and stores grocery items until 10 have been read or the file is empty:

```
// Read and store strings from file inFile
int numItems = 0;
while (numItems < groceryItems.length && inFile.hasNextLine())
{
  anItem = inFile.nextLine();
  groceryItems[numItems] = anItem;
  numItems++;
}
System.out.println(numItems + " grocery items were read and stored.");
```

Look carefully at Figures 9.9 and 9.10. In Figure 9.9, every slot in the array is filled with grocery items. In Figure 9.10, `numItems` items have been read in and stored. If `numItems` equaled 10, then the two figures would be the same. To process the items in Figure 9.10, you use a loop that goes from 0 through `numItems - 1`. This type of processing is known as *subarray process-ing*. As we put values into the array, we keep a count of how many components are filled. We then use this count to process only those components that contain valid values. The remaining places are not processed. Subarray processing is examined in detail in Chapter 11.

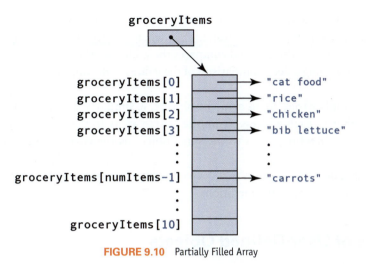

FIGURE 9.10   Partially Filled Array

You first saw a reference to an array of strings in Chapter 1. In the class `HelloWorld`, the following statement appears:

```
public static void main(String[] args)
```

The parameter for the method `main` is an array of strings, called `args` by convention. You can run Java applications in ways that allow you to pass string arguments to `main`. Although we do not use this feature in our applications, we still have to list the parameter in the heading.

In the figures throughout this chapter, we have drawn array variables with an arrow pointing to the array's collection of objects because an array is a reference type. The address that is stored in an array variable is called the **base address** of the array. Java adds the index value to the base address to compute the location in memory where a given element is stored.

> **Base address**   The memory address of the first element of an array

If the component type is a primitive type, the values are actually stored in the memory locations beginning at the base address. If the component type is a reference type, a reference to the first component is stored at the base address. The location following the base address has a reference to the second component, and so on. We have used arrows in our drawings as a visual reminder that a reference variable contains the address indicating where the actual object can be found.

Clearly, strings and arrays are related. You can visualize a string as an array of characters. Conversely, you can visualize an array as a string of values. Because of this similarity, the `String` class has methods that transform a string into an array of `char` and an array of `char` (`char[]`) into a string. The method `toCharArray` in the class `String` converts a string value into a `char[]`. The method `valueOf` takes a `char[]` and converts it into a string.

`Arrays.equals` and `clone` with Arrays of Objects   Earlier, we explored Java's `Arrays.equals` and `clone` methods, which allow us to do comparison and copying of an array whose elements are any of the primitive types. The same methods can be applied to arrays of objects, but the effects aren't usually what you want.

`Arrays.equals` uses the == operator to compare two arrays, element by element. When it is applied to an array of objects, the result is `true` when the elements of the two arrays refer to the same objects. That is, this method compares the addresses that are stored in the array elements, rather than doing a deep comparison of the values of the objects that the array elements refer to.

When you apply `clone` to an array of objects, it similarly uses the = operator to copy each element (that is, each address) from the source array to the copy array. Each element of the copy array therefore refers to the same object as the corresponding element in the source array.

To perform a deep comparison or a deep copy of an array of objects, you must still write your own comparison and copy operations.

■ Arrays of User-Defined Objects

In the last example, the components of the array were strings. Now let's look at an array of user-defined objects. The following code declares and instantiates an array of elements of the class `Entry` introduced in the Problem-Solving Case Study in Chapter 7:

```
Entry[] friends = new Entry[10];
```

The following table shows some of the types involved and indicates how to access some of the components:

Expression	Class/Type
`friends`	Reference to an array
`friends[0]`	Reference to an `Entry` object
`friends[0].getName()`	Reference to a `Name` object
`friends[0].getName().getLastName()`	Reference to a `String` object
`friends[0].getName().getLastName().charAt(1)`	A character
`friends[0].getAddress()`	Reference to an `Address` object
`friends[0].getAddress().getZipCode()`	An integer

■ Arrays and Methods

We can pass an array as an argument to a method. Recall that a copy of each argument is sent to a method. Because an array, like a class, is a reference type, the method receives a copy of the address indicating where the array is stored.

In the application that counts the characters in text, we had the following output loop:

```
// Write the character and the count on the screen
for (index = 0; index < letterCount.length; index++)
  System.out.println("The number of " +
    (char)(index + (int)'A') + "'s is " + letterCount[index]);
```

We can define a helper method that takes the `letterCount` array and prints the output. Let's also add a helper method that returns the total number of characters in the array (letters in the text).

```
static void output(int[] letterCount)
{
  // Write the character and the count on the screen
  for (int index = 0; index < letterCount.length; index++)
    System.out.println("The number of " +
      (char)(index + (int)'A') + "'s is " + letterCount[index]);
}

static int sumLetters(int[] letterCount)
{
  int sum = 0;
  for (int index = 0; index < letterCount.length; index++)
    sum = sum + letterCount[index];
  return sum;
}
```

The following code uses these methods:

```
output(letterCount);
System.out.println("There are " + sumLetters(letterCount) + " in the text.";
```

What do these methods receive as an argument? The base address of `letterCount`.

What about passing array components as arguments? We must consider two cases when passing array components as arguments to a method: (1) the component is of a primitive type or (2) the component is of a reference type. If the component is of a primitive type, the method cannot change the value of its argument. If the component is of a reference type and the method changes its parameter, there are two possible outcomes. Assigning a new value to the parameter causes it to refer to a different object and doesn't affect the argument. Changing the parameter with a transformer method has the side effect of changing the argument and is considered poor programming style.

Although we have shown how to pass arrays as parameters, this approach is rarely employed in object-oriented programming. An array is typically a field in a class and is therefore accessible to all of the methods of the class. Some exceptions are the case of passing an array to a helper method, as in the preceding example, and constructors with array parameters that are used to instantiate objects having array fields.

■ The `Vector` Class

We cannot end our discussion of declaring, instantiating, and processing one-dimensional arrays without mentioning a class that is available in the `java.util` package: the `Vector` class. The `Vector` class offers functionality similar to that of a one-dimensional array of objects. In fact, the array is the underlying implementation structure used in this class. In contrast to an array, however, a vector can grow and shrink; its size is not fixed for its lifetime. The disadvantage of the `Vector` class is that changing the size of the underlying array is time-consuming. To grow beyond the initial size requires the system to create a larger array and move the existing elements into it.

The following list includes some of the useful methods in the `Vector` class and the corresponding array operations.

Vector **Methods**	**Array Equivalent**
`Vector myVector;`	`Object[] myVector;`
`MyVector = new Vector(10);`	`myVector = new Object[10];`
`MyVector.set(item, 9);`	`myVector[9] = item;`
`item = myVector.get(5);`	`item = myVector[5];`
`MyVector.add(item);`	`myVector[numItems] = item;` `numItems++;`
`MyVector.add(item, index)`	`myVector[index] = item;`
`MyVector.size()`	`numItems`
`MyVector.capacity()`	`myVector.length`

An `ArrayList` class that is very similar to `Vector` is examined in some detail in Chapter 11.

PROBLEM SOLVING CASE STUDY

Exam Statistics

Problem You are working as the grader for a Government class. The teacher has asked you to prepare the following statistics for the last exam: average grade, maximum grade, minimum grade, number of grades above the average, and number of grades below the average. Because this is the first exam, you decide to calculate these statistics by writing an application that you can use for the remaining exams as well.

Brainstorming As usual, we begin by brainstorming the list of objects in the problem:

> Grader
> Teacher
> Statistics
> Exam
> Average grade
> Maximum grade
> Minimum grade
> Number above the average
> Number below the average

Filtering The Grader and Teacher set the scene but are not objects in the solution. Statistics is a collective noun, which in this case includes the average, maximum, minimum, number above, and number below. Thus Statistics is an object that includes the specific statistical measures as responsibilities.

Exam is a set of data that is used to instantiate a Statistics object. The grades are objects that need to be in the solution; they are the input to the Statistics class constructor. Our filtered list therefore contains only one class: `Statistics`. Do we need a default constructor? The responsibilities of the class are all based on the array containing valid data, so we don't really need one. As always, though, we include a default constructor as a matter of good style. It can be a single line that instantiates the object with zero grades. Here is the CRC card for this class:

Class Name: Statistics	Superclass:	Subclasses:
Responsibilities	**Collaborations**	
Create	Scanner	
Create(file of grades)		
Get average		
Get maximum grade		
Get minimum grade		
Get number above average		
Get number below average		

Representation Let's abstract this problem from the given context and look at the tasks in isolation. Three separate things must be done to solve this problem: compute an average of values, find the minimum value and maximum value, and compare each value to the average. Several approaches to the solution to this problem are possible, of course. Here we base our solution on the fact that the teacher always writes exams where the scores range between 0 and 100. We use an array where the indexes have semantic content: Each index represents a grade.

The by-hand analogy is to mark off 101 lines on a sheet of paper and number (or label) the lines from 0 to 100. Each line number represents a possible grade. As you read a grade, make a hash mark on the line whose number is the same as the grade. When you have finished recording each grade in this fashion, you compute the sum of the grades by summing the products of each grade (line number) multiplied by the number of hash marks on that line. The number of grades can be calculated when they are read.

To calculate the lowest grade, start at line number 0 and then look forward; the line number of the first line with a hash mark is the lowest grade. To calculate the highest grade, look down from line number 100; the line number of the first line with a hash mark is the highest grade. To determine how many grades are above the average, start at the line whose number is the rounded average grade and count the hash marks on the lines from there through line 100. To determine how many grades are below the average, sum the hash marks from the line whose number is the truncated average through line 0.

The data structure equivalent of your sheet of paper is an integer array declared to be of size 101. The index is the line number; the component is where you make hash marks each time the grade corresponding to the index occurs.

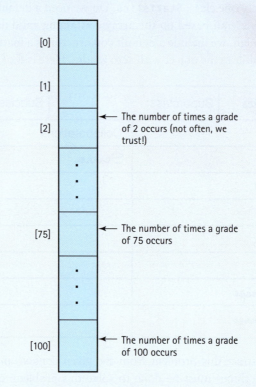

Class Attributes The array of grade counters forms the main attribute for class `Statistics`. However, the average is needed to carry out two other responsibilities, so we must record the average when it is calculated. Should it be a `float` or an `int`? The calculations use the rounded integer version, so let's store the value as an `int`. We also need to know the number of grades to calculate the average. We can have the constructor count them as they are processed. What about the other calculated values? Should they be saved? No—there is no reason to save them as they can be recalculated so easily.

Responsibility Algorithms The constructor must instantiate the array, read in each value, use each value as an index, and add 1 to that slot in the array. We will also have the constructor compute the index corresponding to the average grade, for use in the methods that determine the number of grades above and below the average. We use functional decomposition to design this algorithm.

```
Statistics(Scanner gradeFile)

Instantiate array of grades
Set numGrades to zero
while gradeFile.hasNextInt()
    Read grade from gradeFile
    Increment grades[grade]
    Increment numGrades
    Add grade to sum
Compute intAverage from (int) ((float)sum / (float)numGrades + 0.5)
```

We didn't set each slot in the array to zero; should we have? No. Recall that when instantiating an array, the default value for that type is stored in each slot. Because this is an array of integer values, each slot is set to zero automatically. Each of these steps can be directly coded into Java, so we turn to the other responsibilities.

To calculate the average, we must recreate and sum the scores. Because each slot in the array holds the number of times the index to that slot was a grade, we multiply the index times the value and add that to the sum for each slot in the array.

```
Get average

Set sum to 0
for index going from 0 through 100
    Set sum to sum + grades[index] * index;
return (float)sum / (float)numGrades;
```

Getting the maximum and the minimum are mirror images of one another. For the maximum grade, we examine each slot beginning at index 100. The index of the first nonzero value is the maximum value. For the minimum grade, we examine each slot beginning at index 0. The index of the first nonzero value is the minimum.

```
Get maximum grade

Set highGrade to 100;
while grades[highGrade] equal to 0
    Decrement highGrade
return highGrade;
```

Get minimum grade

Set lowGrade to 0
while grades[lowGrade] equal to 0
    Increment lowGrade
return lowGrade

To find the number of grades above the average, we sum the values in the array from index 100 through index intAverage. The number of grades from index intAverage − 1 through index 0 is the number of grades below the average. Note that we are counting average grades as part of the set of grades that are above average.

Get number above average

Set number to zero
for index going intAverage to 100
    Set number to number + grades[index]
return number

Get number below average

Set number to zero
for index going from 0 to intAverage - 1
    Set number to number + grades[index]
return number

As we look back over this design, we realize that there is an alternative: We could have calculated all of the statistics in the constructor and stored the values in fields of the class. The knowledge responsibilities would then just return the stored values. Is this a better design? For the original problem, it probably is. The original problem stated that all of the statistics would be needed. If the application allowed the teacher to choose which statistics she wants, then our present design is better because we only calculate each statistic as it is needed. We'll implement this design and ask you to explore the alternative in the Case Study Follow-Up exercises.

Before we code the class, let's draw the UML diagram for this class, which should be included in the documentation. Notice the difference between the CRC card and the Class diagram. The CRC card contains no information about the internal representation of the class and its attributes; the UML diagram displays the internal details. The CRC card is a way of collecting our thoughts during the design phase; the UML class diagram documents the class for a prospective maintainer.

```
              Statistics

-grades: int[101]
-numGrades: int
-intAverage: int

+Statistics(gradeFile: Scanner)
+getAverage(): float
+getMinGrade(): int
+getMaxGrade(): int
+getAboveAverage(): int
+getBelowAverage(): int
```

```java
//****************************************************************
// Class Statistics provides methods to calculate statistics
// on a file of integers whose values range between 0 and 100.
// The constructor takes the instantiated file as a parameter.
// The statistics are the average, the minimum value, the
// maximum value, the number of values above the average, and
// the number of values below the average.
//****************************************************************
import java.util.Scanner;
public class Statistics
{
  int[] grades = new int[101];
  int numGrades = 0;
  int intAverage;

  public Statistics() { }                 // Default constructor

  public Statistics(Scanner gradeFile)    // Scanner-based constructor
  {
    int grade;
    int sum = 0;
    while (gradeFile.hasNextInt())
    {
      grade = gradeFile.nextInt();
      grades[grade]++;
      numGrades++;
      sum = sum + grade;
    }
    intAverage = (int)((float) sum / (float) numGrades + 0.5);
  }

  public float getAverage()                    // Returns average grade
  {
    int sum = 0;
    for (int index = 0; index <= 100; index++)
      sum = sum + grades[index] * index;
```

```java
    return (float) sum / (float) numGrades;
  }

  public int getMaxGrade()                    // Returns maximum grade
  {
    int highGrade = 100;
    while (grades[highGrade] == 0)
      highGrade--;
    return highGrade;
  }

  public int getMinGrade()                    // Returns minimum grade
  {
    int lowGrade = 0;
    while (grades[lowGrade] == 0)
      lowGrade++;
    return lowGrade;
  }

  public int getAboveAverage()                // Number of grades above average
  {
    int number = 0;
    for (int index = intAverage; index <= 100; index++)
      number = number + grades[index];
    return number;
  }

  public int getBelowAverage()                // Number of grades below average
  {
    int number = 0;
    for (int index = 0; index < intAverage; index++)
      number = number + grades[index];
    return number;
  }
}
```

Class Testing Although this class was written to solve a particular problem, it is very general and can be used to calculate these statistics for any set of integer values that range between 0 and 100. Therefore the class must be tested very thoroughly. The constructor and the average do not require any special cases, but `getMinGrade` and `getMaxGrade` do because the loops do not cover the entire array. The same is true for `getAboveAverage` and `getBelowAverage`. Here are some of the situations that should be tested:

- A file that contains 0, 100, and values in between
- A file that does not contain 0 and 100
- A file that contains duplicates
- A file that does not contain duplicates (could be combined with another)
- A file of all the same values

Here are files that meet these requirements, along with the expected output of the tests:

Number	File	Expected Output
1	0 100 7 9 78 99 67 44	getAverage 50.5 getMinGrade 0 getMaxGrade 100 getAboveAverage 4 getBelowAverage 4
2	95 75 88 66	getAverage 81.0 getMinGrade 66 getMaxGrade 95 getAboveAverage 2 getBelowAverage 2
3	95 95 44 66 66	getAverage 73.2 getMinGrade 44 getMaxGrade 95 getAboveAverage 2 getBelowAverage 3
4	75 75 75 75	getAverage 75 getMinGrade 75 getMaxGrade 75 getAboveAverage 4 getBelowAverage 0 *Note:* If they are all the same, they are considered "above" the average.

Driver Now we must write a driver that will instantiate the `Statistics` object, call each of the methods, and print the result. Because more than one file of data will be tested, we have the user input the file name. The algorithm for the driver follows:

```
Driver

  Statistics statistics
  Prompt for and input the file name
  Scanner gradeFile = new Scanner(fileName)
  statistics = new Statistics(gradeFile)
  System.out.println("average ", statistics.getAverage())
  System.out.println("minimum grade " , statistics.getMinGrade())
  System.out.println("maximum grade ", statistics.getMaxGrade())
  System.out.println("number above average ", statistics.getAboveAverage())
  System.out.println("number below average ", statistics.getBelowAverage())
```

There are no abstract statements, so this module can be coded directly.

```java
//**************************************************************
// This application reads a file of integer grades and outputs
// a set of statistics for that data
//**************************************************************
import java.io.*;
import java.util.Scanner;
public class StatisticsDriver
{
  public static void main(String[] args) throws IOException
  {
    Statistics statistics;
    Scanner in = new Scanner(System.in);
    System.out.println("Enter the file name.");
    String fileName = in.next();
    Scanner gradeFile = new Scanner(new FileReader(fileName));
    statistics = new Statistics(gradeFile);
    System.out.println("average " + statistics.getAverage());
    System.out.println("minimum grade " + statistics.getMinGrade());
    System.out.println("maximum grade " + statistics.getMaxGrade());
    System.out.println("number above average " +
                       statistics.getAboveAverage());
    System.out.println("number below average " +
                       statistics.getBelowAverage());
  }
}
```

Here are the observed results from our test plan:

File	Observed Output
0 100 7 9 78 99 67 44	average 50.5
	minimum grade 0
	maximum grade 100
	number above average 4
	number below average 4
95 75 88 66	average 81.0
	minimum grade 66
	maximum grade 95
	number above average 2
	number below average 2
95 95 44 66 66	average 73.2
	minimum grade 44
	maximum grade 95
	number above average 2
	number below average 3
75 75 75 75	average 75.0
	minimum grade 75
	maximum grade 75
	number above average 4
	number below average 0

9.5 : Two-Dimensional Arrays

A one-dimensional array is used to represent items as a sequence of values or in a list (explored in Chapter 11). A two-dimensional array is used to represent items in a table with rows and columns, provided each item in the table is of the same type.

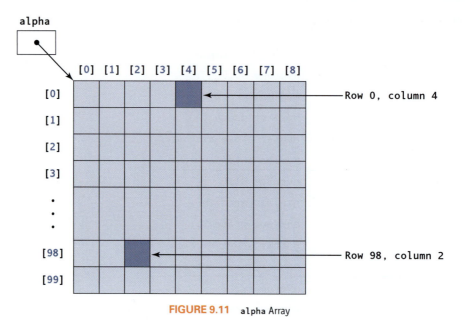

FIGURE 9.11 alpha Array

Two-dimensional array
A collection of components, all of the same type, structured in two dimensions; each component is accessed by a pair of indexes that represent the component's position in each dimension

Formally, we say that a **two-dimensional array** is a named collection of homogeneous components structured in two dimensions. Just like in a one-dimensional array, all of the elements are of the same type, and they are arranged in memory so that we can access them using index values. But with two dimensions, we use two index values to find particular elements. Why would we want two indexes? Because we often encounter data that is conveniently arranged and accessed in tabular form.

We access a component in a two-dimensional array by specifying the row and column indexes of the item in the array. This task is a familiar one. For example, if you want to find a street on a map, you look up the street name on the back of the map to find the coordinates of the street, usually a number and a letter. The number specifies a row, and the letter specifies a column. You find the street where the row and the column intersect.

Figure 9.11 shows a two-dimensional array with 100 rows and 9 columns. The rows are accessed by an integer ranging from 0 through 99; the columns are accessed by an integer ranging from 0 through 8. Each component is accessed by a row–column pair—for example, (0, 4 or 98, 2).

■ Array Declaration and Instantiation

We declare a two-dimensional array variable in exactly the same way that we declare a one-dimensional array variable, except that we use two pairs of brackets. Likewise, we instantiate a two-dimensional array object in exactly the same way, except that we must specify sizes for two dimensions. The following code fragment would create the two-dimensional array shown in Figure 9.11, where the data in the table are floating-point numbers:

```
double[][] alpha;
alpha = new double[100][9];
```

Declaration:

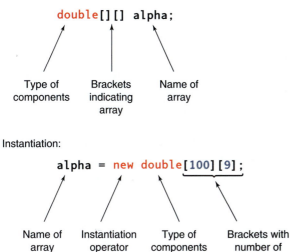

Instantiation:

The first dimension specifies the number of rows, and the second dimension specifies the number of columns. Once the two-dimensional array has been created, `alpha.length` gives the number of rows in the array. We will see shortly how to obtain the number of columns in a row.

■ Accessing Individual Components

To access an individual component of the `alpha` array, we use two expressions (one for each dimension) to specify its position. We place each expression in its own pair of brackets next to the name of the array. If the array access is on the left side of the equals sign, a value is being stored into that cell. If the array access is on the right side of the equals sign, a value is being retrieved from that cell.

```
alpha[0][4] = 36.4;
```

Access:

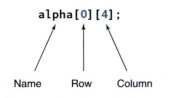

As with one-dimensional arrays, each index expression must result in an integer value between 0 and the number of slots in that dimension minus one.

Let's look now at some examples. Here is the declaration of a two-dimensional array with 364 integer components ($52 \times 7 = 364$):

```
int[][] hiTemp;
hiTemp = new int[52][7];
```

Here `hiTemp` is an array with 52 rows and 7 columns. Each place in the array (each component) can contain an `int` value. Our intention is that the array hold high temperatures for each day in a year. Each row represents one of the 52 weeks in a year, and each column represents one of the 7 days in a week. (To keep the example simple, we ignore the fact that there are 365—and sometimes 366—days in a year.) The expression `hiTemp[2][6]` refers to the `int` value in the third row (row 2) and the seventh column (column 6). Semantically, `hiTemp[2][6]` is the temperature for the seventh day of the third week. The code fragment shown in Figure 9.12 would print the temperature values for the third week.

To obtain the number of columns in a row of an array, we access the `length` field for the specific row. For example, the statement

```
midYear = hiTemp[26].length;
```

stores the `length` of row 26 of the array `hiTemp`, which is 7, into the `int` variable `midYear`.

■ Using Initializer Lists

Just as we can create a one-dimensional array with a list of values, so we can create a two-dimensional array with a list of lists of values. For example, the following statement instantiates

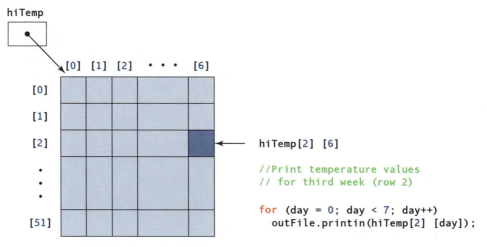

FIGURE 9.12 `hiTemp` Array

a two-dimensional array of baseball hits. This array represents the hits for a five-day period for your four favorite baseball players.

```java
int[][] hits = {{2, 1, 0, 3, 2},
                {1, 1, 2, 3, 4},
                {1, 0, 0, 0, 0},
                {0, 1, 2, 1, 1}};
```

As in the case of a one-dimensional array, you do not use new with an initializer list. Now what would happen if one of your favorite players went into a slump, and the manager gave him a rest for a few days? Suppose that the third player sat out three games. Here is how you would represent that scenario in your array:

```java
int[][] hits = {{2, 1, 0, 3, 2},
                {1, 1, 2, 3, 4},
                {1, 0},
                {0, 1, 2, 1, 1}};
```

The third row in the table would have only two columns, not five like the others. In such a ragged array, the lengths of the rows are not all the same. In fact, we could instantiate the same ragged array as follows:

```java
int[][] hits;
hits = new int[4][];        // Note that second index is left unspecified
hits[0] = new int[5];
hits[1] = new int[5];
hits[2] = new int[2];
hits[3] = new int[5];
```

If we then access the lengths of rows 1 and 2 with the code

```java
one = hits[1].length;
two = hits[2].length;
```

we would find that variable one has been assigned a value of 5 and variable two contains 2.

The moral of the story: In Java, each row of a two-dimensional array is itself a one-dimensional array. Many programming languages directly support two-dimensional arrays; Java doesn't. In Java, a two-dimensional array is an array of references to array objects. Because of the way that Java handles two-dimensional arrays, the drawings in Figures 9.11 and 9.12 are not quite accurate. Figure 9.13 shows how Java actually implements the array hiTemp.

From the Java programmer's perspective, however, the two views are synonymous in the majority of applications. We typically instantiate arrays with the same number of columns in every row, rarely creating a ragged array.

Earlier we saw that the methods Arrays.equals and clone, when applied to an array of objects, do not perform a deep comparison or copy. Because a two-dimensional array is really a one-dimensional array of references to array objects, the same situation applies with two-dimensional arrays. For example, if you were to call hiTemp.clone(), the result of the method

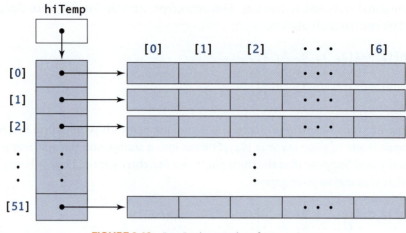

FIGURE 9.13   Java Implementation of `hiTemp` Array

would be a new array containing alias references to the same 52 arrays that `hiTemp` refers to. To use `clone` to perform a deep copy of a two-dimensional array, you must enclose it in a loop that copies each of the rows. For example:

```
int[][] hiTempCopy = new int[52][];
for (int row = 0; row < 52; row++)
  hiTempCopy[row] = hiTemp[row].clone();
```

9.6 : Processing Two-Dimensional Arrays

Processing data in a two-dimensional array generally means accessing the array in one of four patterns: randomly, along rows, along columns, or throughout the entire array. Each of these strategies may also involve subarray processing.

The simplest way to access a component is to look directly in a given location. For example, a user might enter map coordinates that we use as indexes into an array of street names to access the desired name at those coordinates. This process is referred to as random access because the user may enter any set of coordinates at random.

Let's take a closer look at these patterns of access by considering three common examples of array processing:

1. Sum the rows.
2. Sum the columns.
3. Initialize the array to all zeros (or some special value).

In the following discussion, we use the generic identifiers `row` and `col`, rather than problem-dependent identifiers, and look at each algorithm in terms of generalized two-dimensional array processing. The array that we use is declared and instantiated by the following statement:

```
int[][] data = new int[50][30];    // A two-dimensional array
```

In the following discussion, we assume that `data` contains valid information.

■ Sum the Rows

Suppose we want to sum row number 3 (the fourth row) in the array and print the result. We can do this easily with a *for* loop:

```
int total = 0;
for (int col = 0; col < data[3].length; col++)
  total = total + data[3][col];
outFile.println("Row sum: " + total);
```

This *for* loop runs through each column of `data`, while keeping the row index fixed at 3. Every value in row 3 is added to `total`.

Now suppose we want to sum two rows—row 2 and row 3—and print the sum. We can use a nested loop and make the row index be a variable:

```
for (int row = 2; row <= 3; row++)
{
  int total = 0;
  for (int col = 0; col < data[row].length; col++)
    total = total + data[row][col];
  outFile.println("Row sum: " + total);
}
```

The outer loop controls the rows, and the inner loop controls the columns. For each value of `row`, every column is processed; then the outer loop moves to the next `row`. In the first iteration of the outer loop, `row` is held at 2 and `col` goes from 0 through `data[2].length`. Therefore, the array is accessed in the following order:

```
data[2][0]    [2][1]    [2][2]    [2][3]    . . .    [2][29]
```

In the second iteration of the outer loop, `row` is incremented to 3, and the array is accessed as follows:

```
data[3][0]    [3][1]    [3][2]    [3][3]    . . .    [3][29]
```

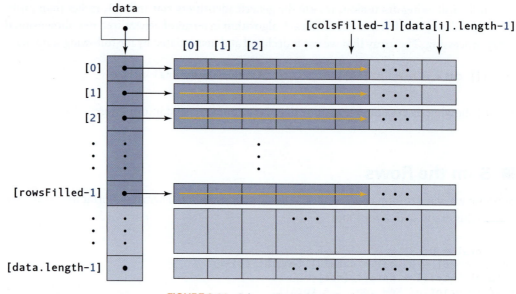

FIGURE 9.14 Subarray Processing by Row

We can generalize this row processing to run through every row of the array by having the outer loop run from 0 through `data.length - 1`. However, if we want to access only part of the array (subarray processing), given variables declared as

```
int rowsFilled;    // Data is in 0..rowsFilled - 1
int colsFilled;    // Data is in 0..colsFilled - 1
```

then we write the code fragment as follows:

```
for (int row = 0; row < rowsFilled; row++)
{
  // Array is not ragged
  total = 0;
  for (int col = 0; col < colsFilled; col++)
    total = total + data[row][col];
  outFile.println("Row sum: " + total);
}
```

This is an example of subarray processing by row, which Figure 9.14 illustrates.

■ Sum the Columns

Suppose we want to sum and print each column. The code to perform this task follows. Again, we have generalized the code to sum only the portion of the array that contains valid data.

```
for (int col = 0; col < colsFilled; col++)
{
  // Array is not ragged
  total = 0;
```

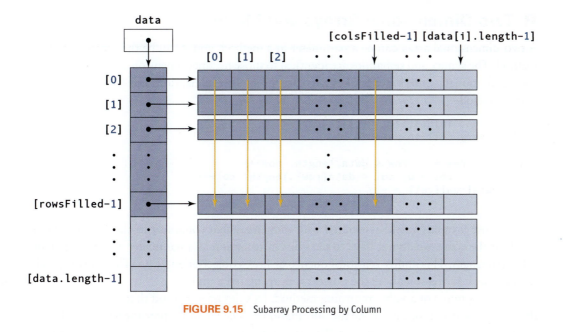

FIGURE 9.15 Subarray Processing by Column

```
for (int row = 0; row < rowsFilled; row++)
    total = total + data[row][col];
  outFile.println("Column sum: " + total);
}
```

In this case, the outer loop controls the column, and the inner loop controls the row. All the components in the first column are accessed and summed before the outer loop index changes and the components in the second column are accessed. Figure 9.15 illustrates subarray processing by column.

■ Initialize the Array

Instantiating an array with initializer lists is impractical if the array is large. For a 100-row by 100-column array, for example, you don't want to list 10,000 values. If the values are all different, you should store them into a file and input them into the array at run time. If the values are all the same, the usual approach employs nested *for* loops and an assignment statement. Here is a general-purpose code segment that sets every item in the array to −1:

```
for (int row = 0; row < data.length; row++)
  for (int col = 0; col < data[row].length; col++)
    data[row][col] = -1;
```

In this case, we initialized the array one row at a time, but we could just as easily have run through each column instead. The order doesn't matter as long as we access every element.

■ Two-Dimensional Arrays and Methods

A two-dimensional array can be a parameter in a method, and it can be the return type for a method. The syntax and semantics are identical to those for one-dimensional arrays except we use an additional pair of brackets. Let's enclose the array initialization code fragment within a helper method:

```java
private void initialize(int[][] data)
// Set every cell in data to -1
{
  for (int row = 0; row < data.length; row++)
    for (int col = 0; col < data[row].length; col++)
      data[row][col] = -1;
}
```

Because Java has a field associated with each array that contains the number of slots defined for the array, we do not have to pass this information as a parameter as we do in many other languages. This ability is a consequence of Java's object orientation. The array is an object and the information about the object is encapsulated with it.

As an example of a value-returning method, let's design a method that returns a copy of the array passed as a parameter. All the information we need to instantiate the new array is present in the array passed as a parameter. We just instantiate it and copy it row by row using `clone`:

```java
public int[][] clone2DInt(int[][] data)
// Returns a deep copy of data. Handles ragged arrays.
{
  int[][] copyData = new int[data.length][];
  for (int row = 0; row < data.length; row++)
    copyData[row] = data[row].clone();
  return copyData;
}
```

9.7 : Multidimensional Arrays

> **Array** A collection of components, all of the same type, ordered on *N* dimensions (*N* ≥ 1). Each component is accessed by *N* indexes, each of which represents the component's position within that dimension

Java does not place a limit on the number of dimensions that an array can have. We can generalize our definition of an **array** to cover all cases.

You might have guessed that you can have as many dimensions as you want. How many should you use in a particular case? As many as there are features that describe the components in the array.

Take, for example, a chain of department stores. Monthly sales figures must be kept for each item by store. There are three important pieces of information for each item: the month in which it was sold, the store from which it was purchased, and the item number. We can declare an array to summarize this data as follows:

```java
int[][][] sales;            // Declare array of sales figures
                            //   first dimension represents store number
                            //   second dimension represents months;
                            //   third dimension represents items
sales = new int[10][12][100]; // Instantiate array
```

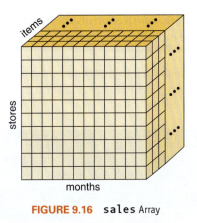

stores

items

months

FIGURE 9.16 `sales` Array

Figure 9.16 provides a graphic representation of the `sales` array.

The number of components in `sales` is 12,000 (10 × 12 × 100). If sales figures are available only for January through June, then half of the array is empty. If we want to process the data in the array, we must use subarray processing. The following code fragment sums and prints the total number of each item sold this year to date by all stores:

```
int currentMonth = 6;     // Range: 1..12

for (int item = 0; item < sales[0][0].length; item++)
{
  numberSold = 0;
  for (int store = 0; store < sales.length; store++)
    for (int month = 0; month < currentMonth; month++)
      numberSold = numberSold + sales[store][month][item];
  outFile.println("Item # " + item + " Sales to date = " + numberSold);
}
```

Because `item` controls the outer *for* loop, we are summing each item's sales by month and store. If we want to find the total sales for each store, we use `store` to control the outer *for* loop and sum that location's `sales` by `month` and `item` with the inner loops.

```
int currentMonth = 6;

for (int store = 0; store < sales.length; store++)
{
  numberSold = 0;
  for (int item = 0; item < sales[0][0].length; item++)
    for (int month = 0; month < currentMonth; month++)
      numberSold = numberSold + sales[store][month][item];
  outFile.println("Store # " + store + " Sales to date = " + numberSold);
}
```

It takes two loops to access each component in a two-dimensional array; it takes three loops to access each component in a three-dimensional array. The task to be accomplished determines which index controls the outer loop, the middle loop, and the inner loop. If we want to calculate monthly sales by store, `month` controls the outer loop and `store` controls the middle loop. If we want to calculate monthly sales by item, `month` controls the outer loop and `item` controls the middle loop.

A multidimensional array can be a parameter and can serve as the return type of a method. Just be sure that you have as many pairs of brackets as you have dimensions following the type or class name.

PROBLEM SOLVING CASE STUDY

Favorite Rock Group

Problem As a fund raising project, a small college is holding a battle of the bands, in which four student rock groups plan to compete. Each student gets to vote for his or her favorite. Two prizes will be given out: for the best group and for the class with the highest participation rate. You are going to write an application to tally the votes and select the winners.

The ballots are scanned to a file called `RockGroupVotes.txt`. The data consists of an arbitrary number of votes, with each vote represented as a pair of numbers on one line: a class number (1 through 4) and a rock group number (1 through 4).

Before we start solving the problem, let's be sure we understand it by doing the analysis by hand. Our first task would be to go through the data, counting how many people in each class voted for each group. We would probably create a table with classes down the side and rock groups across the top. Each vote would be recorded as a hash mark in the appropriate row and column (see Figure 9.17).

When all of the votes had been tallied, a sum of each column would tell us how many votes each group received. A sum of each row would tell us how many people voted in each class.

As is so often the case, our by-hand solution gives us insights into the computer solution. A two-dimensional array in which each component is a counter for the number of votes for a particular group in each class can represent our table. For example, the votes from class 2 (sophomore) for group 1 would be stored in the array at the location indexed by `[1][0]` (keeping in mind that Java arrays are indexed beginning at 0). When we input a class number and group number, we must remember to subtract 1 from each before indexing into the array.

Brainstorming and Filtering Clearly, the table is the data structure and all the processing revolves around it. Thus there is only one class in this problem; let's call it `Table`.

	Group 1	Group 2	Group 3	Group 4
Class 1	### //	//	### ### //	###
Class 2	### ###	//	###	///
Class 3	//	### ///	### ### ###	///
Class 4	###	### ///	### ###	//

FIGURE 9.17   Table for Tallying Votes

Although the problem is stated in terms of classes and rock groups, this is a classic table-processing problem, where the row and column indexes have semantic content. Rows are processed to get the totals for whatever the row represents (a class in this case); columns are processed to get the totals for whatever the column represents (a rock group in this case).

To make class `Table` more general, we don't refer to classes and rock groups in its design. We'll keep all of the application-specific aspects in the driver. The user can input the band name for each column. Because the row names (the classes) don't change, the driver can supply them as constants. These names are passed to the `Table` constructor and used in the output.

Responsibilities The constructor can read in the data from a `Scanner` passed as a parameter and create the array of tallies. It must accept the names for each row and column to be used in converting the table to a string for output (for which we'll define a `toString` method). These names can be passed to the constructor as arrays of strings. In addition to the default constructor, parameterized constructor, and `toString`, we need methods that return the row and column totals as strings, with each total appropriately labeled. Here is the CRC card for the `Table` class.

Class Name: Table	Superclass:	Subclasses:
Responsibilities	**Collaborations**	
Create		
Create(row labels, col labels, file of grades)	Scanner	
toString returns String		
row totals returns String		
col totals returns String		

Parameterized Constructor   The table in the original problem is 4 × 4. But `Table` will be more general if we can instantiate a table as a two-dimensional array of any size. We can determine the number of rows and columns from the `length` fields of the arrays that specify the row and column labels. That way, the table size automatically matches the number of labels for each dimension.

```
Table(String[] rowLabels, String[] colLabels, Scanner inData)

    Set rowNames to rowLabels
    Set colNames to colLabels
    table = new array[rowNames.length][colNames.length]
    int row
    int col
    while inData.hasNext
        Set row to inData.nextInt() − 1
        Set column to inData.nextInt() − 1
        Increment table[row][column]
```

toString   First we generate a line consisting of the column names. Then we generate a series of lines, each of which contains a row name and the data for that row of the table.

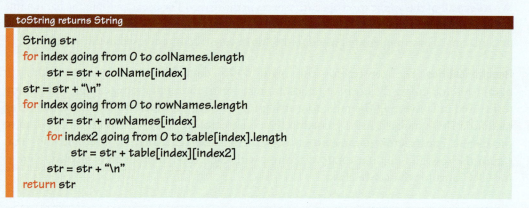

```
toString returns String

    String str
    for index going from 0 to colNames.length
        str = str + colName[index]
    str = str + "\n"
    for index going from 0 to rowNames.length
        str = str + rowNames[index]
        for index2 going from 0 to table[index].length
            str = str + table[index][index2]
        str = str + "\n"
    return str
```

rowTotals   We sum the values in a row, then add the row name and the sum to the output string before going to a newline. This process is repeated for each row in the table. Because we are processing by rows, the inner loop variable (`index2`) controls the second array index (the column number).

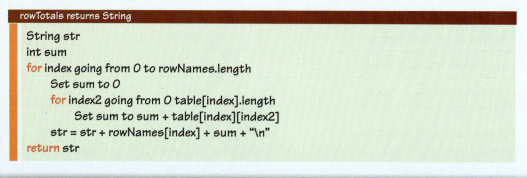

```
rowTotals returns String

    String str
    int sum
    for index going from 0 to rowNames.length
        Set sum to 0
        for index2 going from 0 table[index].length
            Set sum to sum + table[index][index2]
        str = str + rowNames[index] + sum + "\n"
    return str
```

colTotals   The process is the same as for **rowTotals**, except that each line of the output string contains the name and sum for a column in the table. Note how the inner loop variable (**index2**) controls the first array index rather than the second index.

```
colTotals returns String

for index going from 0 to colNames.length
    Set sum to 0
    for index2 going from 0 to table.length
        Set sum to sum + table[index2][index]
    str = str + colNames[index] + sum + "\n"
return str
```

These algorithms contain a number of *for* loops going "from 0 to **rowNames.length** (or **colNames.length**)". The easiest way to code these loops is as follows:

```
for (int index = 0; index < rowNames.length; numOfRows++)
```

We need to be careful: If we code them from **0** to **index < rowNames.length - 1**, we lose one of the values. Here is the UML Class diagram for the **Table** class:

```
              Table

-table: int[][]
-rowNames: String[]
-colNames: String[]

+Table()
+Table (String[], String[], Scanner)
+toString(): String
+rowTotals(): String
+colTotals(): String
```

We are now ready to code the **Table** class:

```
//*************************************************************
// Class Table creates a table made up of the number of times a
// [row][column] pair appears in a data file.  This information may
// be printed along with row and column totals
//*************************************************************
import java.util.Scanner;
public class Table
{
  int[][] table;
  String[] rowNames;
  String[] colNames;

  public Table()                              // Default constructor
```

```java
{
  table = new int[0][0];
  rowNames = new String[0];
  colNames = new String[0];
}

public Table(String[] rowLabels,          // Scanner-based constructor
             String[] colLabels,
             Scanner inData)
{
  rowNames = rowLabels;
  colNames = colLabels;
  table = new int[rowNames.length][colNames.length];
  int row;
  int column;
  while (inData.hasNext())
  {
    row = inData.nextInt() - 1;
    column = inData.nextInt() - 1;
    table[row][column]++;
  }
}

public String toString()                  // Convert table to string
{
  // Generate column headings
  String str = "        ";
  for (int index  = 0; index < colNames.length; index++)
    str = str + "    " + colNames[index];
  str = str + "\n";
  // Generate rows and columns
  for (int index = 0; index < table.length; index++)
  {
    str = str + rowNames[index] + " ";
    for (int index2 = 0; index2 < table[index].length; index2++)
      str = str + "          " + table[index][index2];
    str = str + "\n";
  }
  return str;
}

public String rowTotals()                  // Row totals as strings with labels
{
  String str = "";
  int sum;
  for (int index = 0; index < rowNames.length; index++)
  {
    sum = 0;
    for (int index2 = 0; index2 < table[index].length; index2++)
      sum = sum + table[index][index2];
    str = str + rowNames[index] + "     " + sum + "\n";
  }
  return str;
}
```

501

```
public String colTotals()                    // Col totals as strings with labels
{
  String str = "";
  int sum;
  for (int index = 0; index < colNames.length; index++)
  {
    sum = 0;
    for (int index2 = 0; index2 < table.length; index2++)
      sum = sum + table[index2][index];
    str = str + colNames[index] + "     " + sum + "\n";
  }
  return str;
}
}
```

The driver merely gets the name of the file and the names of the bands. The names of the rows can be specified with an array of strings built from an initializer list. Given this information, the **Table** constructor can be called; its observer methods then generate the output, with some labels supplied by the driver. Here is the code for the driver:

```
//**********************************************************************
// This application reads a file of votes for a battle of the bands,
// tallies the votes, and prints the results
//**********************************************************************
import java.util.Scanner;
import java.io.*;
public class BattleOfTheBands
{
  public static void main(String[] args) throws IOException
  {
    Scanner in = new Scanner(System.in);
    System.out.print("Enter the name of the vote file: ");
    String fileName = in.nextLine();
    Scanner inFile = new Scanner(new FileReader(fileName));
    String[] rowLabels = {"freshman", "sophomore", "junior", "senior"};
    System.out.print("Enter the number of bands: ");
    int bands = in.nextInt();
    String[] colLabels = new String[bands];
    System.out.println("Enter the names of the bands, one per line:");
    String eoln = in.nextLine();
    for (int index = 0; index < bands; index++)
    {
      System.out.print("Band " + (index + 1) + ": ");
      colLabels[index] = in.nextLine();
    }
    Table votes = new Table(rowLabels, colLabels, inFile);
    System.out.println("\nResults for the Battle of the Bands\n\n" + votes);
    System.out.println("\nVotes by class:\n\n" + votes.rowTotals());
    System.out.println("\nVotes by group:\n\n" + votes.colTotals());
    inFile.close();
  }
}
```

Testing This program was executed with the data below. (We show the data in five columns to save space.)

1 1	1 2	1 2	1 3	1 4
2 2	2 2	2 3	2 1	3 1
4 3	3 4	3 2	3 3	2 1
2 3	4 3	4 4	3 2	3 3
4 4	4 4	4 3	4 4	4 4
4 1	4 2	2 4	4 4	

Here is the run log. Input values are in green.

```
Problems  Javadoc  Declaration    Console  ✕
<terminated> BattleOfTheBands [Java Applica

Enter the name of the vote file: battle.txt
Enter the number of bands: 4
Enter the names of the bands, one per line:
Band 1: Chas B Abbage
Band 2: Boole's Brothers
Band 3: Ada Love
Band 4: Augie DeM

Results for the Battle of the Bands

          Chas B Abbage    Boole's Brothers   Ada Love    Augie DeM
freshman           1              2              1            1
sophomore            2              2              2             1
junior           1            2            2          1
senior           1            1            3          6


Votes by class:

freshman    5
sophomore   7
junior    6
senior    11


Votes by group:

Chas B Abbage    5
Boole's Brothers   7
Ada Love     8
Augie DeM    9
```

Well, the answers are correct, but the table is a mess. We didn't think about lining up the columns. How do we accomplish that task? We must find the length of the largest row name and print that many blanks plus a couple of extra spaces before listing the column names. Then we determine the longest column name and pad the other column names so that they are the same length. When we know the width of the columns, we can use the `toString` method to change the values in the table to strings and pad the strings with the necessary blanks to make the numbers line up. This is a tedious—but not difficult—task, which we leave as an exercise.

9.8 : Testing and Debugging

We said earlier that the most common error in processing arrays is an out-of-bounds array index. That is, the application attempts to access a component by using an index that is either less than zero or greater than the array size minus 1. For example, given the declarations

```
String[] line = new String[100];
int   counter;
```

the following *for* statement would print the 100 elements of the `line` array and then try to print a 101st value—the value that resides in memory immediately beyond the end of the array:

```
for (counter = 0; counter <= line.length; counter++)
  outfile.println(line[counter]);
```

This error is easy to detect, because your application will halt with an `ArrayIndexOutOfBoundsException`. The loop test should be `counter < line.length`. You won't always use a simple *for* statement when accessing arrays, however. If you are using a *while* loop to fill the array from a file, and the file contains more data than the array can hold, the same exception can be thrown. The loop termination condition must check both for EOF and for reaching the maximum size of the array.

The moral is this: When processing arrays, pay special attention to the design of loop termination conditions. Always ask yourself if the loop could possibly keep running after the last array component has been processed.

Suppose we are reading data into an array, with the data values themselves specifying the array indexes. The *while* statement in the `Table` constructor is a good example:

```
while (inData.hasNext())
{
  row = inData.nextInt() - 1;
  column = inData.nextInt() - 1;
  table[row][column]++;
}
```

This code seems reasonable enough, but what if the input contains a row number or a column number that's greater than the maximum index for that dimension? The `ArrayIndexOutOfBoundsException` is thrown, which causes the application to crash.

Whenever an array index goes out of bounds, your first suspicion should be that a loop has failed to terminate properly. The second thing to check for is array access involving an index that is based on an input value or a calculation. When an array index is input as data, a data validation check is an absolute necessity.

An additional problem exists with multidimensional arrays: Index expressions can be out of order. Remember our example of the three-dimensional `sales` array?

```
int[][][] sales;              // Declare array of sales figures
                              // First dimension represents store number;
                              //    second dimension represents months;
                              //    third dimension represents items
sales = new int[10][12][100]; // Instantiate array
```

The following code fragment sums and prints the total number of each item sold this year to date by all stores. Or does it? Look at the expression that accesses `sales`. The `item` and `month` indexes are reversed (we highlight the indexes in the loops and the expression to make this behavior easier to see). When `month` reaches 11, an `ArrayIndexOutOfBoundsException` is thrown.

```
int currentMonth = 6;      // Range: 1..12
for (int item = 0; item < sales[0][0].length; item++)
{
  numberSold = 0;
  for (int store = 0; store < sales.length; store++)
    for (int month = 0; month < currentMonth; month++)
      numberSold = numberSold + sales[store][item][month];
  outFile.println("Item # " + item + " Sales to date = " + numberSold);
}
```

How can you avoid such errors? This question has no simple answer. You just have to be careful and thoroughly test your code.

Testing and Debugging Hints

1. When an individual component of a one-dimensional array is accessed, the index must be within the range 0 through the array size minus 1. Attempting to use an index value outside this range will cause your application to crash.

2. The individual components of an array are themselves variables of the component type. When values are stored into an array, they should either be of the component type or be explicitly converted to the component type; otherwise, implicit type conversion occurs.

3. As with all of Java's composite data types, declaring an array variable and instantiating the array object are separate steps. We omit the size of a one-dimensional array in its declaration but must specify it when the array object is instantiated.

4. When an array is an argument, the reference to the array object is passed to the method. The method cannot change the reference, but it can change the elements in the array.

5. An individual array component can be passed as an argument. If the component is of a reference type, the method can change the referenced object if it is a mutable object. If the component is of an atomic type, the method cannot change it.

6. Although an object of a reference type passed as an argument can be changed if the type is mutable, it is poor programming style to do so.

7. We use subarray processing to process array components when the actual number of data items is not known until the application begins executing. The `length` field of the array object contains the number of slots in the array; the number of data values stored into the array may differ.

8. When methods perform subarray processing on a one-dimensional array, the array name and the number of data items actually stored in the array should be encapsulated together into a class.

9. When a one-dimensional array is instantiated without an initializer list, each of the values is automatically initialized to its default value.

10. A one-dimensional array is an object, so a reference to it may be set to `null`.

11. When processing the components in a one-dimensional array, we use a loop that begins at zero and stops when the counter is equal to the `length` field associated with the array object.

12. With multidimensional arrays, use the proper number of indexes when referencing an array component, and make sure those indexes are in the correct order.

13. In loops that process multidimensional arrays, double-check the upper and lower bounds on each index variable to verify that they are correct for that dimension of the array.

14. When declaring a multidimensional array as a parameter, confirm that you have the proper number of brackets beside the type on the parameter list.

15. When passing an array object as an argument, be sure that it has the same number of dimensions as the parameter of the method to which it is being passed.

Graphical User Interfaces

Frames and Fields

In earlier chapters, we used `JOptionPane` and `JFileChooser` to conveniently accomplish common I/O tasks. Now it's time to see how to build more general user interfaces. Keep in mind, however, that generality comes at a price. The Java library includes dozens of predefined classes for creating user interfaces. We can present only a very small subset of these classes, with the goal of conveying the essential concepts of GUI construction. Once you understand the basics, you can delve into the library documentation to learn about the many options available. However, even with the basic classes, working with a general user interface requires considerable programming effort to control features that `JOptionPane` handles automatically.

The type of window that we'll use is called a *frame*, and it is implemented in Java by a class called `JFrame`. A frame has all of the features that you are used to seeing in a window: the ability to change size, the ability to be closed, and so on. Like `JOptionPane`, `JFrame` is part of the `javax.swing` package, so we must import that package into any program that uses it. Along with our `JFrame` objects, we'll use some interface components

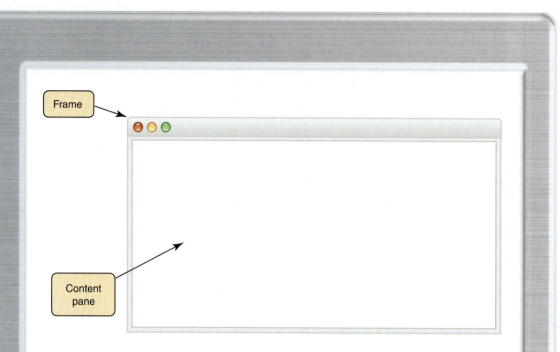

FIGURE 9.18 The Frame and Content Pane of a `JFrame` Window

from another Java package called **java.awt**. So, in every GUI application that we write, we begin with the following import statements:

```
import java.awt.*;
import javax.swing.*;
```

Declaring a `JFrame` is easy:

```
JFrame outFrame = new JFrame();
```

Every `JFrame` consists of two parts. Around the outside is the window frame, which holds controls for the window, such as the Close button. Within the frame is the area that shows the window's contents, called the *content pane*. Figure 9.18 shows these parts of a typical window.

The content pane is an object of class `Container` and, as you might expect from the class name, we put things into it. Whatever we put into the content pane will appear in the window.

The content pane is kept in a nonpublic field[2] within the `JFrame` object. Before we can refer directly to the content pane, we need to get it from the `JFrame` with a call to an

---

[2]The content pane is actually a field within an object that is a field within another object that is a field within the `JFrame`. Thus, when we get the content pane from the `JFrame`, a series of collaborations happens before it is returned. This is another good example of abstraction at work!

observer method. The following statement declares a `Container` variable called `outPane` and then gets the content pane from the `JFrame` called `outFrame`:

```
Container outPane = outFrame.getContentPane();
```

Now that we have access to the content pane, we simply apply `outPane.add` methods to put things into it. But what can we put in? All sorts of things—from buttons to images. We'll start with something simple that allows us to display an area containing text: `JTextArea`. Suppose we want to write a GUI version of the `HelloWorld` application. We can add the following text area containing `"Hello World!"` to `outPane`:

```
outPane.add(new JTextArea("Hello World!"));
```

Is that all it takes to create a window with some text in it? Of course not! As we said, it takes more work to control the available features. We haven't specified the size of the window (and the default size is probably not what we want). Nor have we indicated how the `JTextArea` should be arranged within the window. To specify the size, we apply a `setSize` method to the frame itself:

```
outFrame.setSize(200, 100);       // Sets size to 200 pixels wide by
                                  // 100 pixels high
```

The arguments to `setSize` are integers indicating the width and height of the window (including the frame) in pixels. The word "pixels" is an abbreviation of "picture elements," which are the individual dots displayed on a screen. A typical laptop screen is 1024 by 768 pixels in size, and a common size for a desktop screen is 1280 by 1024 pixels. You should envision a GUI window in terms of what fraction of the screen you want it to occupy, and calculate the size accordingly.[3]

Next we specify how the layout of objects within the content pane is managed. Java provides a variety of layout manager classes from which we can choose. One of the simplest is called `FlowLayout`. To make our content pane use this layout manager, we instantiate a `FlowLayout` object and pass it as an argument to the `setLayout` method for `outPane`:

```
outPane.setLayout(new FlowLayout());
```

---

[3]If you want your program to compute a window size relative to the screen size, here is the code that gets the size of the screen. We leave it to the interested reader to explore the Java library documentation to find out what each piece of these lengthy incantations does.

```
int wide = Toolkit.getDefaultToolkit().getScreenSize().width;
int high = Toolkit.getDefaultToolkit().getScreenSize().height;
```

Well, that wasn't so hard. It took only two lines of code to control those features. Here's what we've seen so far:

```java
JFrame outFrame = new JFrame();
outFrame.setSize(200, 100);
Container outPane = outFrame.getContentPane();
outPane.setLayout(new FlowLayout());
outPane.add(new JTextArea("Hello World!"));
```

Are we done? Not quite. Unlike a `JOptionPane` object, which automatically appears on the screen, a `JFrame` object is kept invisible until we specify that it should appear. That's because we often add multiple objects to a content pane, and we may not want the user to see them until all of them have been added. To make `JFrame outFrame` visible on the screen, we write

```java
outFrame.setVisible(true);
```

Let's put this all together into a demo application that provides a GUI version of `HelloWorld`:

```java
import java.awt.*;
import javax.swing.*;
public class GUIHelloWorld
{
  public static void main(String[] args)
  {
    JFrame outFrame = new JFrame();
    outFrame.setSize(200, 100);
    Container outPane = outFrame.getContentPane();
    outPane.setLayout(new FlowLayout());
    outPane.add(new JTextArea("Hello World!"));
    outFrame.setVisible(true);
  }
}
```

Here is what the application displays:

That certainly took more code than writing

```
System.out.println("Hello World!");
```

or

```
JOptionPane.showMessageDialog(null, "Hello World!");
```

Of course, now that we have the basic mechanism for creating frames, we'll find that we can do quite a bit more with only a little additional effort. For example, suppose we want to reimplement `BattleOfTheBands` using a GUI. There's more output than is appropriate for a `JOptionPane`, so we use a frame. But when we display the vote table in a `JTextArea`, we'll see that its formatting is even more of a mess than before. That's because a `JTextArea` uses a nicer-looking character font than `System.out`. Unfortunately, the characters in that pretty font aren't evenly spaced, so the columns become more misaligned. Fixing this problem is easy, however.

We can choose the font for a `JTextArea` with a single method call. In this case, we use a uniformly spaced font, such as Courier, and we specify that it should be in plain style (rather than italic or bold). We also get to specify its size in printer's units called points (normal sizes for text fonts are 10 or 12 points). If our `JTextArea` is called `summary`, then the call looks like this:

```
summary.setFont(new Font("Courier", Font.PLAIN, 10));
```

Here is the GUI version of `BattleOfTheBands`. Notice that it combines use of a `JFileChooser`, a `JOptionPane`, and a `JFrame` and eliminates use of `System.out` and `System.in`. We are able to reuse the `Table` class without any changes.

```
//**********************************************************
// This application reads a file of votes for a battle of the bands,
// tallies the votes, and prints the results
//**********************************************************
import java.util.Scanner;
import java.io.*;
import java.awt.*;
import javax.swing.*;
public class GUIBattleOfTheBands
{
  public static void main(String[] args) throws IOException
  {
    Scanner inFile;
    JFileChooser fileChooser = new JFileChooser();
    // Get the current working directory
    String workDir = System.getProperty("user.dir");
```

```java
      // Set the chooser to open in our current directory
      fileChooser.setCurrentDirectory(new File(workDir));
      // Get the file from the user
      fileChooser.setDialogTitle("Select the vote file");
      if (fileChooser.showOpenDialog(null) ==
         JFileChooser.APPROVE_OPTION)
      {
        inFile = new Scanner(fileChooser.getSelectedFile());
        String[] rowLabels = {"freshman", "sophomore", "junior",
                              "senior"};
        // Get number of bands from the user
        String inString = JOptionPane.showInputDialog
                          ("Enter the number of bands: ");
        int bands = new Scanner(inString).nextInt();
        String[] colLabels = new String[bands];
        // Get each band name from the user
        for (int index = 0; index < bands; index++)
          colLabels[index] =
            JOptionPane.showInputDialog("Enter the name of band " +
                                        (index + 1));
        // Create the vote table
        Table votes = new Table(rowLabels, colLabels, inFile);
        // Prepare to output results in a frame
        JFrame out = new JFrame();                 // Create a frame
        out.setSize(400, 300);                      // Set its size
        Container outPane = out.getContentPane();   // Get the content
                                                    // pane
        outPane.setLayout(new FlowLayout());        // Use FlowLayout
        // Create the main text area
        JTextArea summary =
          new JTextArea("\nResults for the Battle of the Bands\n\n" +
                        votes);
        // Set it to use a monospaced font, so the table is easier to read
        summary.setFont(new Font("Courier", Font.PLAIN, 10));
        // Add the main text area and the row and column totals to the
        // content pane
        outPane.add(summary);
        outPane.add(new JTextArea("\nVotes by class:\n\n" +
                                  votes.rowTotals()));
        outPane.add(new JTextArea("\nVotes by group:\n\n" +
                                  votes.colTotals()));
        // Make the frame visible
        out.setVisible(true);
        inFile.close();
      }
    }
  }
```

The output shows that the main text area uses Courier font, while the text areas for the row and column totals use the default font. Notice how the **FlowLayout** manager arranged these three areas.

```
Results for the Battle of the Bands

           Chas B Abbage    Boole's Brothers    Ada Love    Augie DeM
freshman          1                2               1            1
sophomore              2                2               2           1
junior            1                2               2            1
senior            1                1               3            6



                   Votes by class:  Votes by group:

                   freshman    5    Chas B Abbage    5
                   sophomore   7    Boole's Brothers  7
                   junior   6       Ada Love    8
                   senior    11     Augie DeM    9
```

If you look closely at this application, you'll see another useful bit of code. When you use a basic **JFileChooser**, it opens with your default directory. That directory may be someplace completely different in the file system, such as the top of the file hierarchy. Usually, it's more convenient to open the **JFileChooser** with a view of the directory in which you are working. As the comments near the beginning of **main** indicate, you can get the current working directory with a method called **System.getProperty**, and the **JFileChooser** can then be set to open with that directory.

Summary

The one-dimensional array is a homogeneous data structure that gives a name to a sequential group of components. Each component is accessed by its relative position within the group (rather than by its name, as in a class), and each component is a variable of the component type. To access a particular component, we give the name of the array and an index that specifies which component of the group we want. The index can be an expression of any integral type except `long`, and it must evaluate to an integer ranging from 0 through the array size minus 1. Array components can be accessed directly in random order, or they can be accessed sequentially by stepping through the index values one at a time. Associated with each one-dimensional array variable is a `final` instance variable `length` that contains the number of slots in the array.

Two-dimensional arrays are useful for processing information that is represented naturally in tabular form. Processing data in two-dimensional arrays typically involves accessing by rows or by columns. Java implements a two-dimensional array as an array of references to one-dimensional arrays. Associated with each two-dimensional array is a `final` instance variable `length` that contains the number of rows. Associated with each row of the table is a `final` instance variable `length` that contains the number of items in the row (the column length). The number of items in a row is usually the same for each row, but does not need to be. If the rows are uneven, the array is called a ragged array.

A multidimensional array is a collection of like components that are ordered on more than two dimensions. Each component is accessed by a set of indexes, one for each dimension that represents the component's position on the various dimensions. Each index may be thought of as describing a feature of a given array component.

LEARNING Portfolio

Quick Check

1. Declare and instantiate a one-dimensional array named `quizAnswer` that contains 12 components indexed by the integers 0 through 11. The component type is `boolean`. (pp. 455–460)

2. Given the declarations

```
final int SIZE = 30;
int[] numbers = new in[SIZE];
```

   a. Write an assignment statement that stores 10 into the first component of the array `numbers`. (pp. 460–462)

   b. Write an output statement that prints the value of the fourteenth component of the array `numbers`. (pp. 460–462)

   c. Write a *for* statement that fills the array `numbers` with zeros. (pp. 466–469)

3. Declare and instantiate a five-element one-dimensional `int` array named `oddNums`, using an initializer list that contains the first five odd integers, starting with 1. (p. 460)

4. Give the heading for a public `void` method named `someFunc`, where `someFunc` has a single parameter: a one-dimensional `float` array called `values`. (pp. 474–475)

5. Given the declarations in Question 2 and the following code fragment, which reads values into the array `numbers` until EOF, write a *for* statement that prints out the portion of the array that is filled with input data. (pp. 471–473)

```
int howMany = 0;
while (inFile.hasNextInt())
{
   numbers[howMany] = inFile.nextInt();
   howMany++;
}
```

6. Declare a two-dimensional array named `plan`, and create an array object with 30 rows and 10 columns. The component type of the array is `float`. (pp. 485–487)

7. Use the array created in Question 6 to answer the following questions.

   a. Assign the value 27.3 to the component in row 13, column 7, of the array `plan`. (pp. 487–488)

   b. We can use nested *for* loops to sum the values in each row of the array `plan`. What range of values would the outer *for* loop count through to do this? (pp. 491–492)

   c. We can use nested *for* loops to sum the values in each column of the array `plan`. What range of values would the outer *for* loop count through to do this? (pp. 492–493)

   d. Write a code fragment that initializes all elements in the array `plan` to 1.0. (p. 493)

   e. Write a code fragment that prints the contents of the array `plan`, one row per line of output. (pp. 491–492)

8. Suppose the array `plan` is passed as an argument to a method in which the corresponding parameter is named `someArray`. What would the declaration of `someArray` look like in the parameter list? (p. 494)

9. Given the declarations

```
final int SIZE = 10;
char[][][][] quick = new char[SIZE][SIZE][SIZE][SIZE-1];
```

   a. How many components does the array `quick` contain? (pp. 494–496)

   b. Write a code fragment that fills the array `quick` with blanks. (pp. 494–496)

LEARNING / Portfolio

Answers

1. `boolean[] quizAnswer = new boolean[12];`
2. a. `numbers[0] = 10;` b. `outFile.println(numbers[13]);`
   c. `for (int index = 0; index < numbers.length; index++)`
       `numbers[index] = 0;`
3. `int[] oddNums = {1, 3, 5, 7, 9};`
4. `public void someFunc(float[] values)`
5. `for (int index = 0; index < howMany; index++)`
     `outFile.print(numbers[index]);`
6. `float[][] plan;`
   `plan = new float[30][10];`
7. a. `plan[13][7] = 27.3;`
   b. `for (row = 0; row < 30; row++)`
   c. `for (col = 0; col < 10; col++)`
   d. `for (row = 0; row < 30; row++)`
       `for (col = 0; col < 10; col++)`
         `plan[row][col] = 1.0;`
   e. `for (row = 0; row < 30; row++)`
       `{`
         `for (col = 0; col < 10; col++)`
           `outFile.print(plan[row][col]);`
         `outFile.println();`
       `}`
8. `float[][] someArray`
9. a. Nine thousand ($10 \times 10 \times 10 \times 9$)
   b. `for (dim1 = 0; dim1 < SIZE; dim1++)`
       `for (dim2 = 0; dim2 < SIZE; dim2++)`
         `for (dim3 = 0; dim3 < SIZE; dim3++)`
           `for (dim4 = 0; dim4 < SIZE - 1; dim4++)`
             `quick[dim1][dim2][dim3][dim4] = ' ';`

Exam Preparation Exercises

1. Every component in an array must have the same type, and the number of components is fixed at creation time. (True or False?)

2. The components of an array must be of a primitive type. (True or False?)

3. Declare and instantiate one-dimensional arrays according to the following descriptions:

   a. A 24-element `float` array

   b. A 500-element `int` array

   c. A 50-element double-precision floating-point array

   d. A 10-element `char` array

4. Write a code fragment to perform the following tasks:

   a. Declare a constant named `CLASS_SIZE` representing the number of students in a class.

b. Declare a one-dimensional array `quizAvg` whose components will contain floating-point quiz score averages.

c. Instantiate the array with size `CLASS_SIZE`.

5. Write a code fragment to do the following tasks:

a. Declare a one-dimensional `int` array named `birdSightings`.

b. Instantiate the array with 20 components.

6. Given the declarations

```
final int SIZE = 100;
int[] count = new int[SIZE];
```

write code fragments to perform the following tasks:

a. Set `count` to all zeros.

b. Read values into the array.

c. Sum the values in the array.

7. What is the output of the following code fragment? The input data are on the next page.

```
int[] a = new int[100];
int[] b = new int[100];
int j;
int m;
int sumA = 0;
int sumB = 0;
int sumDiff = 0;
m = inFile.nextInt();
for (j = 0; j < m; j++)
{
   a[j] = inFile.nextInt();
   b[j] = inFile.nextInt();
   sumA = sumA + a[j];
   sumB = sumB + b[j];
   sumDiff = sumDiff + (a[j] - b[j]);
}
for (j = m - 1; j >= 0; j--)
   outFile.println(a[j] + " " + b[j] + " " + (a[j] - b[j]));
outFile.println();
outFile.println(sumA + " " + sumB + " " + sumDiff);
```

Data

5
11
15
19
14
4
2
17
6
1
3

8. A person wrote the following code fragment, intending to print 10 20 30 40:

```
int[] arr = {10, 20, 30, 40};
int index;
for (index = 1; index <= 4; index++)
  outFile.println(" " + arr[index]);
```

Instead, the application halted with an exception. Explain the reason for this output.

9. What are the two basic differences between a class and an array?

10. If an array is passed as an argument, can the method change the array?

11. For each of the following descriptions of data, determine which general type of data structure (array of primitive values, class, array of class objects, class containing class objects) is appropriate.

  a. A payroll entry with a name, address, and pay rate

  b. A person's address

  c. An inventory entry for a part

  d. A list of addresses

  e. A list of hourly temperatures

  f. A list of passengers on an airliner, including names, addresses, fare classes, and seat assignments

  g. A departmental telephone directory with last name and extension number

12. What happens in Java if you try to access an element that is outside the bounds of the array?

13. To what are the array components initialized when you instantiate an array using new?

14. Given the declarations

```
final int NUM_SCHOOLS = 10;
final int NUM_SPORTS = 3;
int[][]  kidsInSports = new int[NUM_SCHOOLS][NUM_SPORTS];
double[][] costOfSports = new double[NUM_SPORTS][NUM_SCHOOLS];
```

answer the following questions:

a. What is the number of rows in `kidsInSports`?

b. What is the number of columns in `kidsInSports`?

c. What is the number of rows in `costOfSports`?

d. What is the number of columns in `costOfSports`?

e. How many components does `kidsInSports` have?

f. How many components does `costOfSports` have?

g. What kind of processing (row or column) would be needed to total the amount of money spent on each sport?

h. What kind of processing (row or column) would be needed to total the number of children participating in sports at a particular school?

15. Declare and instantiate the following two-dimensional arrays:

a. An array with five rows and six columns that contains `boolean` values

b. An array, indexed from 0 through 39 and from 0 through 199, that contains `double` values

c. An array, indexed from 0 through 3 and from 0 through 2, that contains `char` values

16. Declare and instantiate the following `double` arrays:

a. A three-dimensional array in which the first dimension is indexed from 0 through 9, the second dimension is indexed from 0 through 6 representing the days of the week, and the third dimension is indexed from 0 through 20

b. A four-dimensional array in which the first two dimensions are indexed from 0 through 49, and the third and fourth dimensions have 20 and 30 slots, respectively

Programming Warm-Up Exercises

Use the following declarations in Exercises 1–3. You may declare any other variables that you need.

```
public class Grades
{
  final int NUM_STUDENTS = 100;   // Number of students

  boolean[] failing = new boolean[NUM_STUDENTS];
  boolean[] passing = new boolean[NUM_STUDENTS];
  int[] score = new int[NUM_STUDENTS];
}
```

1. Write a Java instance method that initializes all components of `failing` to `false`.

2. Write a Java instance method that sets the components of `failing` to `true` wherever the corresponding value in `score` is less than 60.

3. Write a Java instance method that reverses the order of the components in `score`; that is, `score[0]` goes into `score[score.length - 1]`, `score[1]` goes into `score[score.length - 2]`, and so on.

4. Write a code segment to read in a set of part numbers and associated unit costs, separated by blanks. Use an array of class objects with two members, `number` and `cost`, to represent each pair of input values. Assume the end-of-file condition terminates the input.

5. Examine the following documentation of a class:

```java
public class TwoDimensions
{
  // Private data
  private int[][] data;
  private int rowsUsed;        // Number of rows that contain data
  private int columnsUsed;     // Number of columns that contain data
  // Methods
  public TwoDimensions(int maxRows, int maxColumns)
  // Constructor: creates a maxRows x maxColumns array
  public void inputData(Scanner inFile)
  // Reads data into the array
  // Data are on the file as follows:
  // First line: number of rows (rowsUsed)
  // Second line: number of columns (columnsUsed)
  // Data are stored one value per line in row order.
  // That is, the first columnsUsed values go into row 0; the
  // next columnsUsed values go into row 1; etc.
  public void print(PrintWriter outFile)
  // Prints the values in the array on outFile, one row per line
  public int maxInRow(int row)
  // Returns the maximum value in the specified row
  public int maxInCol(int column)
  // Returns the maximum value in the specified column
  public int maxInArray()
  // Returns the maximum value in the entire array
}
```

a. Write the code for the constructor `TwoDimensions`.

b. Write the code for the method `inputData`.

c. Write the code for the method `print`.

d. Write the code for the method `maxInRow`.

e. Write the code for the method `maxInCol`.

f. Write the code for the method `maxInArray`.

6. Write a code segment that finds the largest value in a two-dimensional `double` array of 50 rows and 50 columns.

7. Given the following declarations

```
final int NUM_DEPTS = 100;
final int NUM_STORES = 10;
final int NUM_MONTHS = 12;
```

a. Declare an array variable `sales` that will be indexed by the number of departments, number of stores, and number of months and that contains `double` values.

b. Instantiate an array object for the variable `sales`.

c. What values do the components in the array have after it is created?

d. Write a code segment to calculate the sum of the sales for January.

e. Write a code segment to calculate the sum of the sales for store 2.

f. Write a code segment to calculate the sum of the sales for department 33.

8. The `Vector` class in `java.util` provides functionality very similar to that offered by an array. The following questions ask you to explore some aspects of its operation.

a. Run an experiment to determine how many slots are added to a `Vector` object when you add one more `item` than you originally stated should be in the `Vector`.

b. Look up the documentation for the `Vector` class and make a table like the one shown in the chapter, showing five other useful methods in the class.

Programming Problems

1. The local baseball team is computerizing its records. The team has 20 players, identified by the numbers 1 through 20. Their batting records are coded in a file. Each line in the file contains four numbers: the player's identification number and the number of hits, walks, and outs he or she made in a particular game. Here is a sample:

3 2 1 1

This example indicates that during a game, player number 3 was at bat four times and had two hits, one walk, and one out. For each player, there are several lines in the file. To compute each player's batting average, you add the player's total number of hits and divide by the total number of times at bat. A walk does not count as either a hit or an at bat when the batting average is being calculated.

Design and implement an application that prints a table showing each player's identification number, batting average, and number of walks. (Be careful: The players' identification numbers are 1 through 20, but Java array indexes start at 0.)

2. A local bank is gearing up for a big advertising campaign and would like to see how long its customers are waiting for service at its drive-up windows. Several employees have been asked to keep accurate records for the 24-hour drive-up service. The collected information, which is read from a file, consists of the time the customer arrived in hours, minutes, and seconds; the time the customer actually was served; and the teller's ID number. Design and implement a class with the following responsibilities:

a. Reads in the wait data.

b. Computes the wait time in seconds.

c. Calculates the mean, standard deviation, and range.

d. Prints a single-page summary showing the values calculated in part (c).

Input

The first data line contains a title.

The remaining lines each contain a teller ID, an arrival time, and a service time. The times are broken up into integer hours, minutes, and seconds according to a 24-hour clock.

Processing

Calculate the mean and the standard deviation.

Locate the shortest wait time and the longest wait time for any number of records up to 100.

The formula for calculating the mean of a series of integers is to add all the numbers, then divide by the number of integers. Expressed in mathematical terms, the mean $\overline{X}$ of N numbers $X_1, X_2, \ldots, X_N$ is

$$\overline{X} = \frac{\sum_{i=1}^{N} X_i}{N}$$

To calculate the standard deviation of a series of integers, subtract the mean from each integer (you may get a negative number) and square the result, add the squared differ-

LEARNING **Portfolio**

ences, divide by the number of integers minus 1, and then take the square root of the result. Expressed in mathematical terms, the standard deviation S is

$$S = \sqrt{\frac{\sum_{i=1}^{N}\left(X_i - \bar{X}\right)^2}{N-1}}$$

Output

The input data (echo print)

The title

The following values, all properly labeled: number of records, mean, standard deviation, and range (minimum and maximum)

3. Write an application that reads an apartment number and the number of **occupants** in the apartment. The apartment number serves as an index into an array of apartments. The components in the array represent the number of people who live in the apartment. Print the number of people in the building, the average number of people per apartment, the number of apartments with above-average occupancy, and the number with below-average occupancy.

4. Write an application that plays Tic-Tac-Toe. Represent the board as a 3 × 3 character array. The array is initialized to blanks, and each player is asked in turn to input a position. The first player's position is marked on the board with an O, and the second player's position is marked with an X. Continue the process until a player wins or the game is a draw. To win, a player must have three marks in a row, in a column, or on a diagonal. A draw occurs when the board is full and no one has won.

   Each player's position should be input as indexes into the Tic-Tac-Toe board—that is, a row number, a space, and a column number. Make the application user friendly.

   After each game, print out a diagram of the board showing the ending positions. Keep a count of the number of games each player has won and the number of draws. Before the beginning of each game, ask each player if he or she wishes to continue. If either player wishes to quit, print out the statistics and stop. Use buttons as appropriate.

5. The following diagram represents an island surrounded by water (shaded area):

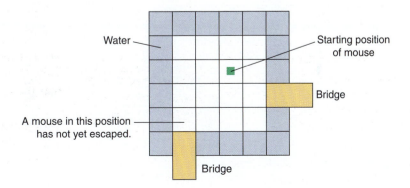

Two bridges lead out of the island. A mouse is placed on the green square. Write an application to make the mouse take a walk across the island. The mouse is allowed to travel one square at a time, either horizontally or vertically. A random number from 1 through 4 should be used to decide which direction the mouse is to take. The mouse drowns when it hits the water; the mouse escapes when it enters a bridge.

You may generate a random number up to 100 times. If the mouse does not find its way by the hundredth try, it will die of starvation. In that case, restart the mouse in a reinitialized array and repeat the whole process. Count the number of times the mouse escapes, drowns, and starves.

Input

First input line—the size of the array, including border of water and bridges (not larger than 20 × 20)

Next N input lines—the rows of the two-dimensional array, where the positions containing negative numbers represent the water, the positions in the edge containing a 0 represent the bridges, the position containing a 1 represents the starting position of the mouse, and all other positions contain 0s

Output

A line stating whether the mouse escaped, drowned, or starved

A line showing the mouse's starting position and the position of the two bridges

A map showing the frequency of the mouse's visits to each position

You should print these items (double-spaced between trips) for each trip by the mouse.

Case Study Follow-Up

1. There is no error checking in class **Statistics**. List at least two errors that you could easily check for.

2. The **Statistics** application makes use of a technique called indexes with semantic content. Explain what this term means in relation to this problem.

3. The **Statistics** application makes the assumption that the grades are between 0 and 100. Could this technique be used with grades in a different range? If so, how would you do it?

4. Code the alternative design discussed in the chapter in which the constructor calculates all the statistics.

5. Rewrite the output from class **Table** so that the columns line up properly.

6. Develop a complete test plan for class **Table**.

10 Inheritance, Polymorphism, and Scope

Goals

Knowledge Goals

To:

- Understand the hierarchical nature of classes in object-oriented programming
- Understand the concept of inheritance in a class hierarchy
- Recognize the distinction between overriding and hiding in Java
- Understand the concept of polymorphism
- Know and understand the access rules for Java classes
- Understand the concept of overloading in Java
- Understand the distinction between an abstract class and an interface
- Explain the difference between static and dynamic binding
- Understand the role of interfaces
- Understand the role of the `Comparable` interface

Skill Goals

To be able to:

- Identify the interface components of a class in a hierarchy
- Draw a UML diagram representing a class hierarchy
- Design a derived class to extend an existing class hierarchy
- Implement a derived class using inheritance
- Use the keywords `super` and `this` to disambiguate references
- Derive a class from an abstract class
- Implement an interface
- Determine the class of an object

1975
IBM introduces the first laser printer

1976
The first commercial e-mail service, OnTyme, struggles to find a market for its product because of the installation requirements for its use

1976
Steve Jobs and Steve Wozniak create the "Apple I" computer

1977
Steve Jobs and Steve Wozniak found Apple Computer Inc.; the Apple II computer sets the standard for personal computers

1977
Bill Gates and Paul Allen form a partnership and create Microsoft

1977
Commodore introduces the PET, a PC with a built-in monitor

Introduction

In Chapter 8, we considered how to use the encapsulation and abstraction of the class and package constructs to organize solutions to larger problems. In this chapter, we introduce new design techniques and Java constructs for solving even larger problems by organizing closely related classes into a hierarchy.

In Chapter 8, we mentioned that classes can be related to each other as subclasses and superclasses. Subclasses acquire properties from their superclasses and add new capabilities. A subclass defines objects that are instances of both the subclass and the superclass. Creating a hierarchy of classes provides more flexibility when managing abstraction. It also makes it easier to code a set of similar classes because we can reuse the capabilities of a common superclass. The key concept behind class hierarchies and reuse is called *inheritance*.

1978
Epson introduces the first successful dot matrix printer, the TX-80

1978
The VAX 11/780 and the VMS operating system developed at DEC popularize the 32-bit architecture

1978
The WordStar program for word processing debuts

1978
Ron Rivest, Adi Shamir, and Leonard Adleman introduce RSA, a strong encryption algorithm for public-key cryptosystems

1979
Bob Frankston and Dan Bricklin develop VisiCalc, the first electronic spreadsheet

1979
Motorola introduces the 32-bit 68000 chip, which is later used for the Macintosh computer

10.1 : Inheritance

Let's look at an analogy between the work of an architect and the work of a programmer. The way that an architect handles the complexity of a large building design sheds some light on how we can organize our own programming work. This analogy lets us consider the same concepts but without the distraction of Java syntax.

■ An Analogy

The architect begins by considering the overall requirements for a building: square footage, number of occupants, usage, and so on. The architect faces a basic aspect of any design: The building is composed of floors. In many buildings, all of the floors have common characteristics: the same size and shape; the same locations for elevator shafts, stairways, and utility trunks; and so on. The architect begins by designing a basic empty floor with these common elements. Once she installs this plan in the library of her computer-aided design (CAD) program, she can use it as the starting point for designing each floor of the building.

The architect may further decide that the building has two main types of floors: office floors and mechanical equipment floors. The office floors might be of two types: executive office space and standard office space. Starting from the basic empty floor design, the architect adds components such as lavatories and hallways to make an empty office floor. She can then add offices and conference rooms to the empty space. In this way, each of the four types of floor is derived from the basic empty floor and added to the library (see Figure 10.1). Drawing the entire building then becomes simply a matter of creating an instance of one of these four floor plans for each story.

The architect uses the same process to design the components that make up the floors. She might design a basic type of office, and then derive several types of offices from that one design. From a given type of office, such as a secretarial office, she might further refine the design into subtypes such as general secretarial, secretary/receptionist, and executive secretary.

Creating hierarchies of designs simplifies the architect's job. She begins each hierarchy with the most general form of a building component, such as the basic empty floor, and then derives new designs by adding details to the more general forms. The new designs inherit all of the characteristics of the general form, saving the architect from having to redraw the common pieces. In some cases, she replaces existing parts of a design, such as when she substitutes a wider door for a reception area than appears in the basic secretarial office. The replacement part overrides what was originally specified in the more general form.

In addition to the components of individual floors, the architect can specify characteristics that are common to all floors, such as a color scheme. Each floor will then inherit these general properties. Sometimes the architect hides or deletes portions of the general properties, such as when she customizes the color scheme for a particular floor that has been rented in advance by a company with its own corporate colors. We will see later how inheritance, overriding, and hiding are formally defined mechanisms in Java.

■ Inheritance and the Object-Oriented Design Process

Now let's consider how a class hierarchy originates in the object-oriented design process. During the problem-solving phase, we sometimes discover that we need a class that is a variation of an existing one. For example, in the `AddressBookUpdate` case study of Chapter 8, we discovered that the `Entry` class from Chapter 7 was appropriate, except that it lacked transformers for its fields.

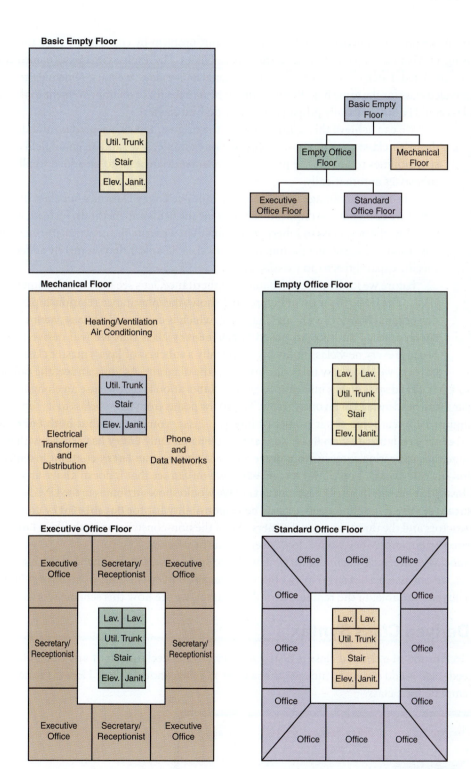

FIGURE 10.1 A Hierarchy of Floor Types

With our present knowledge of Java, we solve this problem by copying the code for `Entry` and using it to create a new class with the extra responsibilities. The result is two classes named `Entry` that are unrelated. Later, if we find a bug in the original `Entry` class, we must remember to check the extended class for the same bug. But wouldn't it be nice if a fix or an improvement to the original class could be automatically propagated to any derived classes?

We can achieve this feat by making the original `Entry` a **superclass** and defining the other classes as **subclasses** of `Entry`. For example, if we add an email field and responsibilities to `Entry`, the property of **inheritance** causes it to be added to all of the subclasses automatically.

The other advantage to defining the mutable `Entry` class as a subclass of `Entry` is that we don't have to duplicate the code for the fields and methods. Instead, we simply allow the new class to inherit them, and then we write the new transformer methods. To someone reading the mutable `Entry` class, it is clear that we merely added these specific capabilities to an existing class.

Before we look at the mechanics of inheritance, let's see how it is documented in UML. The UML diagram in Figure 10.2 shows the inheritance relationship between our original `Entry` class from Chapter 7, which is composed of `Name`, `Address`, and `Phone` objects, and the proposed `MutableEntry` class that we will derive from it. Because every new class in Java is technically a subclass of Java's master class, called `Object`, we also show this relationship in the diagram. As you can see, the only feature of UML that distinguishes inheritance from collaboration is that we use an elongated, triangular arrowhead instead of an open arrow. The arrow points from the subclass to its superclass.

Figure 10.2 has some other points of interest. First, you can see that both `Entry` and `MutableEntry` collaborate with `Name`, `Address`, and `Phone`. Only `Entry` has arrows with black diamond tails indicating composition, however. That's because an `Entry` contains instance attributes of these classes. Looking at `MutableEntry`, you can see that it doesn't have any attributes. Instead, it inherits its attributes from `Entry`. We would show attributes in the UML diagram for `MutableEntry` if it defined new ones. The responsibility list for `MutableEntry` consists of constructors and the three new transformers. All of the non-constructor methods in `Entry` are inherited by `MutableEntry`, so we don't need to list them again.

Subclasses are assignment compatible with the superclasses above them in the hierarchy. That is, we can assign a `MutableEntry` object to a `MutableEntry` variable, or an `Entry` variable, or an `Object` variable. In the remainder of this chapter, we see how this scheme works.

> **Superclass** A class that is extended by one or more derived classes (its subclasses)
>
> **Subclass** A class that is derived from another class (its superclass)
>
> **Inheritance** A mechanism by which one class (a subclass) acquires the properties—the data fields and methods—of another class (its superclass)

■ Derived Class Syntax

The declaration of a derived class is nearly identical to the declaration of any other class. All we need to do is add syntax to indicate that a class **extends** another class. Here is the new syntax template for a class:

```
Class-Modifiers  · · ·  class Identifier  extends Classname
{
    Class-Declaration  · · ·
}
```

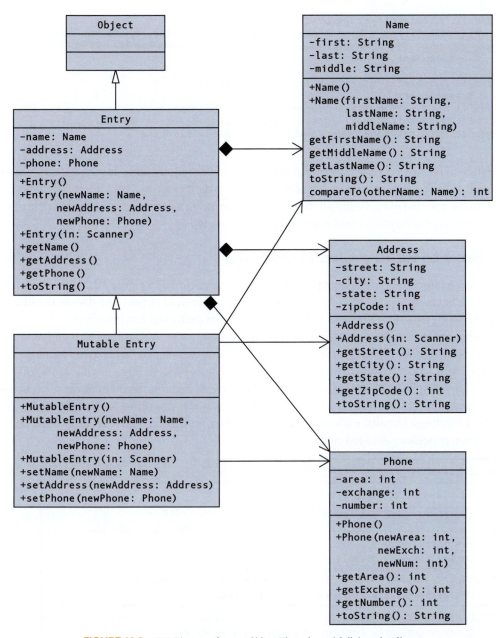

FIGURE 10.2 UML Diagram of `Entry` Object Hierarchy and Collaborating Classes

The only difference between this template and the one in Chapter 2 is that we've added the optional **extends** clause. Here's an example, showing the declaration of the `MutableEntry` class, with the **extends** clause highlighted (we explain the reserved word **super** later in the chapter):

```
public class MutableEntry extends Entry
{
  // Constructors
```

```
public MutableEntry() {super();}
public MutableEntry(Name newName, Address newAddress, Phone newPhone)
{
   super(newName, newAddress, newPhone);
}
public MutableEntry(Scanner in) {super(in);}
// Transformers
public void setName(Name newName) {name = newName;}
public void setAddress(Address newAddress) {address = newAddress;}
public void setPhone(Phone newPhone) {phone = newPhone;}
}
```

This new class inherits all of the fields and methods of `Entry` (including anything `Entry` has inherited) and then adds three methods of its own. It also defines its own constructors, corresponding to the ones in `Entry`. Is that all there is to implementing a derived class? In terms of syntax, yes; in terms of semantics, there is more we need to know.

■ How to Read a Class Hierarchy

Let's take a closer look at the `Entry` hierarchy of classes defined in Figure 10.2. As you can see from the figure, a hierarchy of classes can be multiple levels in depth. The deeper the hierarchy, the more difficult it becomes to keep track of what each class has inherited.

When we look at the documentation for a Java class, we see only those fields and methods that are added by that specific class, along with the name of its superclass. To really understand what a class can do, we must work our way up the hierarchy, determining what it inherits.

As an example, let's look at a summary of the methods in the `MutableEntry` class. Java class summaries (documentation) are typically written as a class heading, field definitions, and method headings. Usually, each entry has a brief description, and a later section of the documentation provides a detailed explanation.

Class Mutable Entry	
`public class MutableEntry extends Entry`	
Constructor Summary	
`MutableEntry()` 　　Constructs an empty `Mutable Entry`.	
`MutableEntry(Name newName, Address newAddress, Phone newPhone)` 　　Constructs a `Mutable Entry` with the given parameters.	
`MutableEntry(Scanner in)` 　　Constructs a `Mutable Entry` by reading from the given Scanner.	
Method Summary	
`public void`	`SetName(Name newName)` 　　Sets the `Name` attribute.
`public void`	`SetAddress(Address newAddress)` 　　Sets the `Address` attribute.
`public void`	`SetPhone(Phone newPhone)` 　　Sets the `Phone` attribute.

A first glance at the class is somewhat disappointing. If we want to display an entry, how do we print the data? None of these methods returns any of the relevant values. But wait! The class header says that `MutableEntry` `extends` `Entry`. That little bit of code reveals that this definition is just part of the story. We have to look at the documentation for `Entry` to determine which attributes `MutableEntry` inherits from it. In fact, `Entry` defines four additional methods that are inherited by `MutableEntry`.

Class Entry	
`public class` `Entry`	
Field Summary	
Name	`name`
Address	`address`
Phone	`phone`
Constructor Summary	
`Entry()` 　　Constructs an empty `Entry`.	
`Entry(Name newName, Address newAddress, Phone newPhone)` 　　Constructs an `Entry` with the given parameters.	
`Entry(Scanner in)` 　　Constructs an `Entry` by reading from the given `Scanner`.	
Method Summary	
`public Name`	`getName()` 　　Returns the **name** attribute.
`public Address`	`getAddress()` 　　Returns the **address** attribute.
`public Phone`	`getPhone()` 　　Returns the **phone** attribute.
`public String`	`toString()` 　　Returns a string representation of the object.

Note that constructors aren't inherited because a constructor's name must match the name of the class in which it is defined. As a consequence, we cannot inherit constructors from `Entry` to act as constructors for `MutableEntry` objects. (As we see later, we can easily reimplement constructors from the superclass by using Java's `super` reserved word.)

By default, `Entry` extends `Object`, which appears at the top of the entire hierarchy. `Object` supplies another 11 methods. Several of these methods are related to features of Java that are beyond the scope of this text. Here we summarize just the ones that are familiar:

Class Object	
`public class Object`	
Constructor Summary	
`Object()`	
Method Summary	
`public Object`	`clone()` Creates and returns a copy of this object.
`protected boolean`	`equals(Object obj)` Indicates whether some other object is equal to this one.
`public String`	`toString()` Returns a string representation of the object.
.	
.	
.	

Now that we have the specification for every class that is an ancestor of `MutableEntry`, we can determine the methods that it has available. `MutableEntry` inherits methods and defines three other methods. We begin at the bottom of the hierarchy (`MutableEntry`) and write a list of all of its methods (plus its constructors) as a column on one side of a page. In the next column, we write the members of `Entry` (excluding its constructors). The process continues until we write the methods of `Object`.

MutableEntry	**Entry**	**Object**
`MutableEntry()`	`getName()`	`clone()`
`MutableEntry(Name, Address, Phone)`	`getAddress()`	`equals(Object)`
`MutableEntry(Scanner)`	`getPhone()`	`finalize()`
`setName(Name)`	`toString()`	`getClass()`
`setAddress(Address)`		`hashCode()`
`setPhone(Phone)`		`notify()`
		`notifyAll()`
		~~toString()~~
		`wait()`
		`wait(long)`
		`wait(long, int)`

> **Override** To provide an instance method in a derived class that has the same form of heading as an instance method in its superclass. The method in the derived class redefines (overrides) the method in its superclass. We cannot override class methods.

■ Overriding

As we know, `Entry` defines a method called `toString`. That definition redefines (**overrides**) the version of `toString` supplied by `Object`. Thus, in our table of methods, we have crossed off `toString` in the `Object` column to indicate that it is redefined by `Entry`.

Taken together, the columns in the complete table tell us every member that is available in the class `MutableEntry`. When we first looked at the documentation for `MutableEntry`, it appeared that the class had just three methods. Now, however, we can identify 17 methods. This example illustrates the power of using inheritance in a hierarchy of classes. Just as the architect can save effort by defining a hierarchy of building parts, we can save ourselves a lot of work by using inheritance.

■ Hiding

Thus far, we have focused on inheritance of methods. Fields can also be inherited through the hierarchy. A `MutableEntry` object contains all of the fields that are defined in its superclasses. Thus it automatically contains fields for `name, address`, and `phone`.

When a derived class defines a field with the same name as one in its superclass, however, the field in the derived class **hides** the one in the superclass. Java also classifies the case where a subclass redefines a `static` (class) method of a superclass as a form of hiding. The term *overriding* technically applies only to instance methods.

Figure 10.3 illustrates hiding. The top-level class, called `Top`, defines two fields, `spin` and `wobble`. A subclass, called `Sub`, is derived from `Top` and changes the internal representation of `spin` from `int` to `long`. The new definition of `spin` hides the inherited definition from the superclass. Within `Sub`, an access to `spin` accesses the value of type `long`. By contrast, an access to `wobble`, which is not hidden, uses the `int wobble` field inherited from the superclass.

If you look at the `Entry` hierarchy carefully, you can see that nothing is deleted as a result of inheritance (except constructors). Java does not provide any way to remove a member that is inherited. We can cover over a member with a replacement member, but we can't delete it.

> **Hide** To provide a field in a derived class that has the same name as a field in its superclass; to provide a class method that has the same form of heading as a class method in its superclass. The field or class method is said to hide the corresponding component of the superclass.

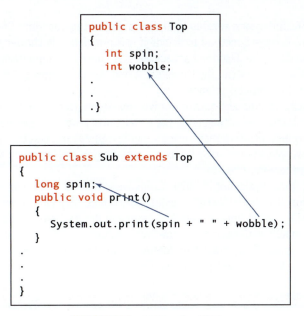

FIGURE 10.3   An Example of Hiding

This restriction is one aspect of the philosophy of object-oriented design: As we go deeper in the hierarchy, we add or change functionality, but we do not lose functionality. In object-oriented design, a derived class is always an extension of its superclass.

For example, we would say that a `MutableEntry` is an `Entry`. In object-oriented design, a fundamental concept is the "is a" relationship between a derived class and its superclass. A derived class is a form of its superclass.

Alan Turing

Although there is no Nobel Prize for computing, the equivalent is the Turing Award, given annually by the Association for Computing Machinery (ACM). The award is named for Alan Turing, a British mathematician who made fundamental contributions to the foundations of computing theory and development of early computers.

Turing was born in England on June 23, 1912, to Julius and Ethel Turing. His parents had met in India, where his father worked. After his birth, his parents continued to live in India until 1926, while Alan and his older brother, John, were left in various foster homes in England.

From an early age, Turing showed a gift for highly original thinking in mathematics and science. But his mother wanted him to have a classical education, so Turing was enrolled in the Sherborne School at age 13, even though the headmaster wrote that it was a waste of time for such a "scientific specialist" to study there.

In 1931, Turing entered King's College, Cambridge, where the open atmosphere provided him with an intellectual home for the first time. He graduated in 1934 and was elected a fellow of the college for a dissertation that proved fundamental results in probability theory.

In early 1936, Turing was seeking to answer a perplexing question: Given any mathematical assertion, is there a method to decide if it is provable? He showed that no such method exists. To do so, he described a machine that could be programmed to carry out any algorithm. What we now call the Universal Turing Machine forms the foundation for research in theoretical computer science.

Alonzo Church, working at Princeton University, announced a similar result at the same time, so he is credited with solving the decidability problem. However, his logic-based approach is less intuitive than Turing's highly original and practical solution. Turing spent the next two years studying at Princeton with Church and John von Neumann, obtaining his Ph.D. there in 1938.

When World War II broke out in 1939, Turing went to work in a secret British code-breaking operation at a former Victorian estate called Bletchley Park. Within weeks he had designed a machine, called Bombe, based on an earlier design from Poland, to decrypt the German Enigma code. The German Navy, however, was using a different system, and it took Turing several more months to crack this "unbreakable" code. Turing was awarded the Order of the British Empire (OBE) for these efforts.

In 1942, the German Navy changed its coding system, and Turing went to the United States to collaborate on a solution. In his absence, colleagues at Bletchley Park discovered a weakness in the new code and were able to break it. When Turing returned, he became a general consultant for code breaking. In this capacity, he observed construction of the huge Colossus machines for decrypting the "Fish" code that was used for Hitler's strategic communications.

His experience with large-scale digital systems led Turing to propose post-war construction of a general-purpose computer called the Automatic Computing Engine (ACE). Turing went to the National Physical Laboratory to build ACE, but became frustrated with the lack of progress. In 1948, he took a position at Manchester University to work on its Mark I computer.

As part of his work in designing ACE, Turing developed the basic concepts of high-level programming languages and use of a central server with remote terminals. He also wrote a pioneering paper in the field of machine learning. During this period he became a marathon runner, achieving a personal best time of 2:46:03.

Turing's work in machine learning resulted in a 1950 paper, "Computing Machinery and Intelligence," which introduced the now-famous *Turing Test* for artificial intelligence. He then sought to explain how biological systems develop their unique forms by simulating chemical reactions on a computer. Turing thus became the first significant user of scientific computing.

Although Turing's homosexuality had never been especially secret, he was arrested for it in 1952, was ordered to undergo hormone therapy, lost his security clearance, and was barred from working as a consultant for the British code-breaking agency. His contacts with foreigners also came under intense government scrutiny. On June 7, 1954, Turing died of cyanide poisoning. His mother believed his death to be an accident related to a chemistry experiment, but the coroner's verdict was suicide.

■ Implementing a Derived Class Design

A CRC card or UML diagram for a subclass and its superclass specifies the responsibilities of the subclass. After you have designed a subclass, you implement it by writing the necessary declarations within a class that `extends` the superclass. Here are the steps in the form of a checklist:

1. Study the design of the superclass and the subclass, identifying which members are inherited.
2. Determine whether any attributes must change in the subclass.
3. Provide constructors as needed.
4. Add fields and methods to those that are inherited, as necessary.
5. Hide any inherited fields or class methods that you wish to replace.
6. Override any instance methods that you wish to replace.

Unless we have a good reason for changing the inherited attributes, they should remain the same. Typically, we just add fields to what we've inherited. However, sometimes an inherited field is inappropriate for the subclass. Perhaps the superclass uses an `int` field, and the purpose of the subclass is to extend its range by using `long`. Then the subclass must hide the inherited field.

Once we have the interface and attributes, we can begin to implement the constructors. Java has some special rules that apply to constructors in derived classes; we examine them next.

■ Constructors in Derived Classes

Java requires every constructor in a derived class to call a constructor in its superclass. That call must be the first statement appearing in the constructor—even preceding any declarations. If it isn't the first statement, Java automatically inserts a call to the default constructor for the superclass. This is why we recommend including a user-defined default constructor in every class.

Java requires us to call a superclass constructor to ensure that the inherited fields of the derived-class object are initialized consistently with how the superclass would prepare them. Of course, the superclass constructor must call a constructor for its superclass, and so on, until the constructor for `Object` is called. Thus the process of instantiating an object calls a chain of constructors that provides initialization all the way up the class hierarchy.

Next, we examine how Java identifies methods, and we explore the Java syntax for calling a superclass constructor from within a subclass.

> **Signature** The distinguishing features of a method heading; the combination of the method name with the number and types(s) of its parameters in their given order
>
> **Overloading** The repeated use of a method name with a different signature

■ Method Signatures and Overloading

As we've noted previously, Java allows us to have methods with the same name, as long as their parameter lists distinguish them. Formally, a method's name, the number and types of parameters that are passed to it, and their arrangement combine into what Java calls the **signature** of the method.

When we use a method name more than once in a class, we are **overloading** its identifier. The following method headings have different signatures and thus overload each other (the parts of the signature are highlighted):

```
public void someName(int formal1, double formal2, int formal3)   // First
                                                                  // version
public void someName(double formal1, int formal2, int formal3)   // Second
                                                                  // version
```

Even though all of these parameters have the same names, the differences in their types enable Java to distinguish calls to the different versions. For example:

```
someName(1, 2.0, 3);    // int, double, int argument pattern indicates first
                        // version
someName(1.0, 2, 3);    // double, int, int argument pattern indicates second
                        // version
```

The following method headings have the same signature (highlighted) and cannot be declared together in a class. The names of the parameters are not part of the signature.

```
public void aName(int param1, double param2, String param3)
public void aName(int thing1, double thing2, String hatCat)
```

Keep in mind that the return type and the modifiers of a method are not part of its signature. In spite of how different they appear, the following headings have the same signature, as the highlighting emphasizes:

```
public static void aName(int param1, double param2, String param3)
private String aName(int thing1, double thing2, String hatCat)
```

Overloading is related to, but different from, hiding and overriding. Hiding and overriding are mechanisms whereby a name is *replaced* in a new context. For example, in a derived class, an instance method may override a superclass method. When you override a method, you are replacing its definition with a new one. If you declare a method with the same name and a different signature, then you are overloading the inherited method. That is, overloading supplies an *additional* definition, and both definitions can be used within the derived class.

■ Using super to Access Overridden and Hidden Methods and Fields

Using the keyword super followed by a parameter list refers to the constructor in the superclass with the same signature. Using the keyword super, followed by a field or method identifier, refers to an overridden or hidden method or field. The word super or the name of the superclass can be used in only two cases:

- When you are accessing a method or field that has been overridden or hidden
- When you are accessing a superclass constructor

Outside of these two cases, the name is inherited, so you can refer to it directly. Here are some examples of using super:

```
super();                       // Call to the default constructor of the
                               // superclass
super(Scanner in);             // Call to superclass constructor with same
                               // signature
someInt = super.someInt;       // Reference to a hidden field in the
                               // superclass
super.instanceMethod();        // Calls to overridden instance method in the
                               // superclass
super.classMethod();           // Call to a hidden class method in the
                               // superclass
SuperClassName.classMethod();  // Another way to call the method, without
                               // using super
```

Extending the Phone Class

In Chapter 7, we developed a class to represent a phone number. Here's the existing code:

```java
package utility;
public class Phone
{
  int area;
  int exchange;
  int number;
  // Default constructor
  public Phone()
  {
    area = 999;
    exchange = 999;
    number = 9999;
  }
  // Direct constructor
  public Phone(int newArea, int newExch, int newNum) throws Exception
  {
    if ( newArea < 200 || newArea > 999 || newArea == 911 ||
         newExch < 200 || newExch > 999 || newExch == 911 ||
         newNum < 0 || newNum > 9999)
      throw new Exception("Invalid phone number: (" + newArea + ")" +
                          newExch + "-" + newNum);
    else
    {
      area = newArea;
      exchange = newExch;
      number = newNum;
    }
  }
  // Observers
  public int getArea() { return area; }
  public int getExchange() { return exchange; }
  public int getNumber() { return number; }
  public String toString()
                { return "(" + area + ")" + exchange + "-" + number; }
}
```

Let's extend the Phone class to include an extension number and call the derived class BusinessPhone. We need to add a field in BusinessPhone to hold the extension. We should also change toString to include the extension. Here, then, is the CRC card for BusinessPhone:

Class Name: *BusinessPhone*	Superclass: *Phone*	Subclasses:
Responsibilities	**Collaborations**	
Create itself (area code, exch, number, extension)	*Phone*	
Get extension *return int*	*None*	
toString *return String*	*Phone*	

The constructor can call its superclass constructor and then store the extension. The `getExtension` method just returns the value of `extension`. The `toString` method can call on its superclass to do most of the work.

```
//*****************************************************************
// Class BusinesssPhone extends class Phone and adds an extension
//*****************************************************************
package utility;
public class BusinessPhone extends Phone
{
  private int extension;       // This is the new field

  public BusinessPhone()
  {
    super();                   // Superclass constructor sets inherited fields
    extension = 9999;          // Here we set the new field
  }
  public BusinessPhone(int area, int exch, int number, int exten)
                                                        throws Exception
  {
    super(area, exch, number);    // Superclass constructor sets inherited
                                  // fields
    extension = exten;            // Here we set the new field
  }
  // Observer method to return the new field
  public int getExtension() { return extension; }
  // New toString method that overrides superclass toString
  public String toString()
  {
    String str = super.toString();    // Superclass toString does the hard
                                      // work
    return (str + "x" + extension);   // Then we append the new field
  }
}
```

Notice that the `toString` method of `BusinessPhone` overrides the instance method of the same name in `Phone`. The new class inherits all of the fields and methods of `Phone` and then adds some of its own.

The following program is a test driver that creates a `Phone` object and a `BusinessPhone` object, and applies the methods from both classes to them:

```java
//*************************************************************
// TestBusPhone is a driver that tests class BusinessPhone,
// a class derived from Phone
//*************************************************************
import java.io.*;
import utility.*;
public class TestBusPhone
{
  public static void main(String[] args) throws Exception
  {
    Phone firstPhone;
    BusinessPhone secondPhone;
    System.out.println("Test results for class BusinessPhone");
    firstPhone = new Phone(523, 373, 3344);
    secondPhone = new BusinessPhone(713, 223, 3121, 1234);
    System.out.println("getArea: " + firstPhone.getArea());
    System.out.println("getExchange: " + firstPhone.getExchange());
    System.out.println("getNumber: " + firstPhone.getNumber());
    System.out.println("toString: " + firstPhone.toString());
    System.out.println("getArea business: " + secondPhone.getArea());
    System.out.println("getExchange business: " + secondPhone.getExchange());
    System.out.println("getNumber business: " + secondPhone.getNumber());
    System.out.println("getExtension business: " +
                      secondPhone.getExtension());
    System.out.println("toString business: " + secondPhone.toString());
  }
}
```

The driver shows that methods `getArea`, `getExchange`, and `getNumber`, as defined in `Phone`, can be applied to objects of both `Phone` and `BusinessPhone`. The overridden method `toString` is applied to objects of both `Phone` and `BusinessPhone`, with the type of the object determining which method is appropriate. Here is the output:

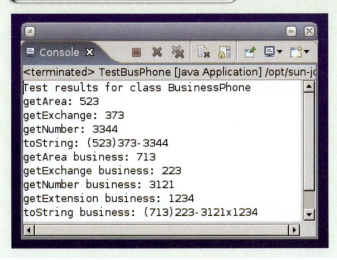

```
□ Console ✕
<terminated> TestBusPhone [Java Application] /opt/sun-jc
Test results for class BusinessPhone
getArea: 523
getExchange: 373
getNumber: 3344
toString: (523)373-3344
getArea business: 713
getExchange business: 223
getNumber business: 3121
getExtension business: 1234
toString business: (713)223-3121x1234
```

10.2 : Scope of Access

In writing a Java class, we declare variables, constants, and methods that are given identifiers. Java defines a set of rules that specify where those identifiers can then be used, both inside and outside the class. These rules determine the **scope of access** of an identifier. This term is usually shortened to scope, so the rules are called the **scope rules** of the language.

Internal access scope rules, the scope rules for access within a class, are straightforward and do not depend on the access modifiers attached to an identifier. External access scope rules determine where an identifier can be used outside a class and depend on both the access modifiers and the location where the access takes place. We look first at internal scope and then at external scope.

> **Scope of access (scope)** The region of program code where it is legal to reference (use) an identifier
>
> **Scope rules** The rules that determine where in a program an identifier may be referenced, given the point where the identifier is declared and its specific access modifiers

■ Internal Scope

Any identifier declared as a `static` or instance member of a class can be used anywhere within the class, with two exceptions:

1. You can't use one class variable to initialize another before the first one has been defined.
2. Within its block, a local identifier hides a class member of the same name.

Let's take a closer look at each of these exceptions.

Order of Definition   Suppose you are defining a `Circle` class and you want to provide class variables that are initially set to pi and pi $\times$ 2, respectively. The first of the following declarations is illegal because its initializer uses `pi` before it has been given a value:

```
public static double twoPi = pi * 2;              // pi isn't defined yet
public static double pi = 3.14159265358979323846;
```

Reversing the order of the statements makes them both legal:

```
public static double pi = 3.14159265358979323846;
public static double twoPi = pi * 2;              // pi now has a value
```

This rule applies only to initializer expressions for class variables. Otherwise, it's legal to refer to class variables before they are defined. For example, the following declarations are legal:

```
public static int circumference(Circle anyCircle)
{
   return anyCircle.radius * pi * 2;              // Okay to refer to pi here
}
static double pi = 3.14159265358979323846;        // even though it's
                                                  // defined here
```

Why is this case different? Before it starts executing the statements in `main`, the JVM evaluates all `static` initializer expressions in the order in which they appear in the code. Thus an initializer can use a class variable only if it already has a value. The method `circumference` isn't executed until after `main` starts executing, which follows evaluation of all of the `static` initializers.

Keep in mind that regular assignment statements that initialize variables in methods are distinct from declaration initializer expressions. They are executed in the normal flow of control, which starts after all of the declaration initializations take place.

Constant declarations do not follow this rule because the compiler computes constant values at compile time. That is, the compiler searches through the code to find all of the constant declarations before it computes their values. As a consequence, it doesn't require us to define a constant before referring to it. The JVM isn't able to search through Bytecode in the same way, so it requires variables to have values before they are used in initializer expressions.

To make life easier for human readers of your code, it's good form to define constants ahead of any references to them. Some programmers even make a point of writing all constant declarations before the variable declarations, just as a reminder that constants are given their values first.

> **Shadowing**   A scope rule specifying that a local identifier declaration blocks access to an identifier declared with the same name outside the block containing the local declaration

Shadowing   Local identifiers block access to class identifiers with the same name. As a reminder, a local identifier is one that is declared within a method. With regard to their scope, formal parameters are treated as if they are local identifiers that are declared at the beginning of the method body. When a local identifier has the same name as a member of its class, it is said to be shadowing the class member.

In Java, the scope of a local identifier is the remainder of the block following the point at which it is declared. The block includes all of the statements between the **{** and **}** that contain the declaration. For example:

```java
public class SomeClass
{
    static int var;                    // Class member var
    static final int CONST = 5;        // Class member CONST
    public static void someMethod(int param)
    {
        int var = CONST;               // Local var
        final int CONST = 10;          // Local CONST
        var = param * CONST;
        System.out.print("" + var);
    }
}
```

Scope of local constant CONST that shadows the same identifier declared as a class member — (brace pointing to the local CONST declarations)

Scope of local variable var that shadows the same identifier declared as a class member — (brace pointing to the local var statements)

In this example, the scope of the local declarations (highlighted in green) extends from the point that each one appears to the end of the block. Thus, in the first use of **CONST**, to initialize **var** as part of its declaration, the initialization refers to the class version of **CONST** (highlighted in yellow). The second use of **CONST**, in the expression assigned to **var**, refers to the local declaration of **CONST**.

What if we want to refer to a class member from within a method that shadows that member? Then we use the qualified name of the member. That is, we write its name preceded by the name of the class and a period. For example, suppose that we want to access the class variable **var** from within **someMethod**, in the preceding example. We can do so simply by writing **SomeClass.var**.

But what if we want to access a shadowed instance member of an object, rather than a class member? How would we qualify the name? When we write a method, we don't yet know the name of the object. We need a way to refer to the object from within itself.

Using this to Refer to an Object from Within Itself   Java provides a keyword, **this**, which can be used within an object to refer to the object itself. That is, we can use **this** to refer explicitly to members of the object.

The following example shows the use of **this** to access instance fields from within a method that defines local names that shadow access to those fields. For comparison, we also show access to a class field that has been shadowed by a local declaration. The instance fields are highlighted in yellow, the class field is in blue, and the local identifiers are in green:

```java
public class SomeClass
{
    static final int CONST = 5;        // Class member CONST
    int var = -1;                      // Instance member var
    int param = 0;                     // Instance member param
    public int someMethod(int param)   // Defines local param
    {
        int var;                       // Defines local var
```

```
final int CONST = SomeClass.CONST*2;   // Define and set local CONST to
                                       //   class CONST * 2
if (param > this.param)                // Compare local and instance
                                       // params
    var = param * CONST;               // Use local values
else
    var = this.param * SomeClass.CONST;  // Use instance and class values
return var;
    }
}
```

You can also use `this` to refer to the object as a whole from within itself. However, Java specifies that the reference represented by `this` is `final`, so you cannot assign a value to `this`.

```
anotherObject = this;    // Legal. Makes anotherObject refer to this object
this = anotherObject;    // Not legal. Cannot change this object to be
                         // anotherObject
```

Understanding the internal scope rules helps us avoid or locate errors when we are implementing the internal representation of the class. For example, a scope-related error occurs when you declare a local identifier that shadows a class member, but you misspell the name in the local declaration. The compiler does not complain, but merely directs all of the references to the local identifier to its correctly spelled class member equivalent, as shown here:

```
public class SomeClass
{
  static int var;                          // Class member var
  public static void someMethod(int param)
  {
    int ver;                               // Misspelling of var
    var = param * param;                   // Accidentally refers to class
                                           // member var
    System.out.print("" + var);            // Accidentally refers to class
                                           // member var
  }
}
```

This program exhibits erroneous behavior—that is, a class member is changed and displayed as a side effect of calling a method. Knowing the scope rules leads us to look for references to the class member within the method, and then to check the local declarations.

■ External Scope

The external access scope rules control access by code that is outside a class. Java allows class members to be accessed from three external places: derived classes, members of the same package, and code external to the package. We have covered access modifiers several times before, especially as they apply to packages. In this section, we repeat and generalize the information on access modifiers. Failure to understand exactly how they operate can lead to obscure errors.

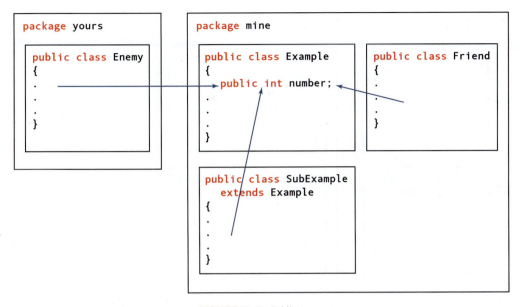

FIGURE 10.4 Public Access

Java defines four levels of access for class members, three of which enable direct access by other package members. The four levels of access are **public**, **protected**, default (package), and **private**. We use keywords as access modifiers for each of these levels except the package level, which is the default level. If you omit an access modifier from the declaration of a class member, it is automatically considered to be at the package level of access.

public Access   A **public** member can be accessed from anywhere outside the class. Figure 10.4 shows a package containing three classes, one of which (**Example**) defines a **public** field (**number**). The derived class (**SubExample**) and an unrelated class (**Friend**) within the package are both able to access this field. A class (**Enemy**) in another package (**yours**) also has access to the field.

A **public** member may still be hidden by a declaration of the same name in another class. Within that class, references to the hidden member must be qualified (i.e., it is written with the name of its class or instance and a dot preceding it).

protected Access   A **protected** member is accessible to classes in the same package and can be inherited by derived classes outside the package. Code that is outside the package can only inherit **protected** members of a class; it cannot access them directly.

Class **Example** in Figure 10.5 is the same as in Figure 10.4, but now with the **number** field **protected**. The classes in package **mine** can access the field in any **Example** object. However, the classes in package **yours** cannot. Within the **SubEx** class in package **yours**, statements can refer to an inherited field called **number** within a **SubEx** object, but they cannot refer to the **number** field of an **Example** object. We use the UML-style triangular arrowhead to indicate this inheritance relationship.

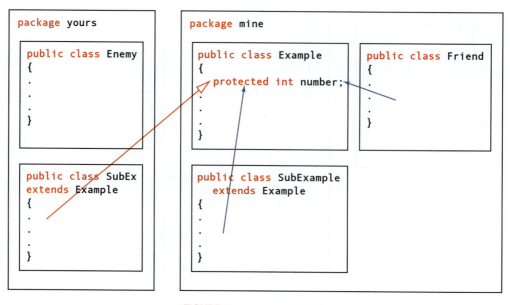

FIGURE 10.5   Protected Access

In the following code segment, we define two packages. Package **two** has a class (**DerivedClass**) that is derived from the **SomeClass** class in package **one**. **DerivedClass** inherits the **protected** field **someInt** from **SomeClass**. Notice that **DerivedClass** doesn't include a declaration of **someInt**. **DerivedClass** defines **demoMethod** with two parameters, one of class **SomeClass** and the other of **DerivedClass**. It then tries to access the **someInt** field in both parameters.

```
package one;
public class SomeClass
{
  protected int someInt;
}

package two;
import one.*;
public class DerivedClass extends SomeClass
{
  void demoMethod(SomeClass param1, DerivedClass param2)
  {
    param1.someInt = 1;    // Generates a compiler error
                           // Can't access member of instance of SomeClass
    param2.someInt = 1;    // This access is legal
                           // It refers to the inherited member
  }
}
```

The compiler issues an error message for the first assignment statement because it is illegal to access the **protected** field of a superclass in a different package. The second assignment is valid because it refers to the inherited field within a **DerivedClass** object.

The **protected** modifier provides the least restrictive level of access that isn't **public**. We use **protected** to enable users to extend our class with a subclass in a different package. The subclass inherits its own version of the **protected** members, but cannot access the original versions in superclass objects.

It is unusual to see `protected` in an application designed using CRC card notation because all of the responsibilities and collaborations are known in advance. If a package of classes exists independently of an application (such as the `java.util` package), however, it may be desirable to let users derive subclasses.

Package Access   As we saw in Chapter 7, the absence of an access modifier indicates package-level access. A package contains related classes, and sometimes we want to make members of those classes accessible to each other, even if they aren't `public`. For example, Figure 10.6 illustrates the case where the `number` field has package access. Note that this field is not inherited by the derived class `SubEx` in package `yours`.

All `public` and `protected` members of a class are inherited by a subclass, regardless of whether it is in the same package. The package level of access lets us restrict the members that are inherited by classes in other packages.

A derived class in the same package retains access to the members of its superclass that are at the package level of access. All classes within the same package have access to each other's `public`, `protected`, and package members.

`private` Access   The `private` modifier cuts off all external access, even by classes in the same package. A `private` member of a class can be referred to only by other members of the class, and only the internal scope rules apply to it. It isn't even permissible for a derived class in the same package to access a `private` member of its superclass.

In Figure 10.7, the `number` field is now `private`, and you can see that it is not accessible from any of the other classes. It can be accessed only within `Example`.

Instances of a class can refer to one another's `private` members. A member is `private` to its class, which includes all instances of the class. Thus two objects, `someObj` and `otherObj`, that

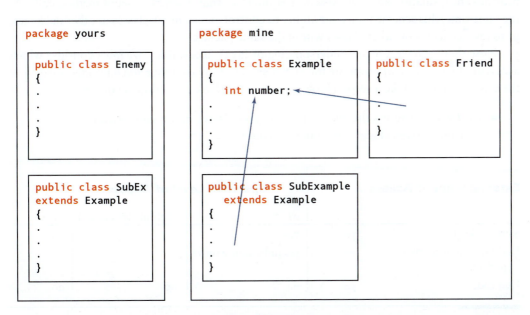

FIGURE 10.6   Package Access Within and Between Packages

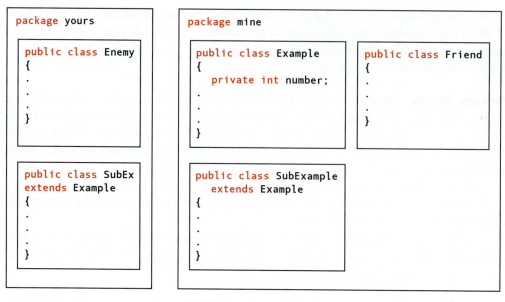

FIGURE 10.7   Private Access

have `private int` fields called `someInt` can refer to each other's fields. That is, `someObj` can refer to `otherObj.someInt` and `otherObj` can refer to `someObj.someInt`. Table 10.1 summarizes the external scope rules.

So far, we have primarily used the `public` and package levels of access, keeping data members at the package level and making most methods and classes `public`. This simple approach provides encapsulation and a consistent user interface that is strictly a set of method calls. At the same time, this scheme limits our ability to control extension by classes in other packages, or to restrict access by other classes within the same package.

Now that we have a better understanding of Java's access rules, we must consider which access modifier is most appropriate for each member of a class. Once you have identified all of the class's members, take a second look at each one and ask the following question:

- Do I want to access this member from other classes in the same package, from derived classes, or from user code?

External Point of Access	Specified Level of Access			
	public	protected	Default (package)	private
Same package	yes	yes	yes	no
Derived class in another package	yes	yes (inheritance only)	no	no
User code	yes	no	no	no

TABLE 10.1   Java's External Scope Rules

Based on your answer to each part of this question, use Table 10.1 to decide which access modifier is most appropriate.

CRC card scenarios help us determine which responsibilities are `public`, `private`, `protected`, or package level in their access requirements; this fact should be written on the cards. As we determine the attributes of a class, we may also notice that certain fields need an access level other than package. For example, we might define some `public` class constants. Armed with this information, we can list the members that a subclass inherits.

`final` Classes and Methods   Among the modifiers that Java allows us to use with a class is `final`:

```
final public class NoSubclasses
```

Although this feature of Java isn't part of the scope rules, it has a related effect. A `final` class cannot be extended with a subclass, even within the same package. Using the `final` modifier indicates that a class is intentionally at the bottom of a hierarchy and will never have a subclass. This modifier is rarely used.

Java also lets us use `final` as a modifier for individual methods, with the result that a `final` method cannot be overridden or hidden. Whether a method is `final` is independent of its scope. For example, a `public final` method can be used by classes in other packages, but cannot be overridden or hidden by methods in subclasses. This behavior contrasts with that of a `protected` method, which can be overridden or hidden (but not used directly) in subclasses external to the package.

Whenever a design requires that a method's implementation remain the same in all subclasses, then it should be `final`. In this way, the `final` modifier for classes and methods provides us with yet another dimension of control for inheritance.

SOFTWARE MAINTENANCE CASE STUDY

Throwing a User-Defined Exception

In Chapter 7, we threw a generic `Exception` in class `Phone` when the arguments of the constructor would generate an invalid phone number.

```java
// Direct constructor
public Phone(int newArea, int newExch, int newNum) throws Exception
{
  if ( newArea < 200 || newArea > 999 || newArea == 911 ||
       newExch < 200 || newExch > 999 || newExch == 911 ||
       newNum < 0 || newNum > 9999)
```

```java
            throw new Exception("Invalid phone number: (" + newArea + ")" +
                                newExch + "-" + newNum);
        else
        {
            area = newArea;
            exchange = newExch;
            number = newNum;
        }
    }
```

At that time, we promised to show you how to implement a user-defined exception class for Phone. Now that we know how to implement a subclass, it's an easy task to create a user-defined exception class. We simply extend Exception with a subclass and supply a pair of constructors that call super. The name that we pick for the subclass identifies the class of exception being thrown. Here is how we define class PhoneException, within our utility package that also contains Phone:

```java
package utility;
public class PhoneException extends Exception
{
    public PhoneException()
    {
        super();
    }
    public PhoneException(String message)
    {
        super(message);
    }
}
```

In the constructor for Phone, we replace Exception with PhoneException, as highlighted here:

```java
public Phone(int newArea, int newExch, int newNum) throws PhoneException
{
    if ( newArea < 200 || newArea > 999 || newArea == 911 ||
         newExch < 200 || newExch > 999 || newExch == 911 ||
         newNum < 0 || newNum > 9999)
        throw new PhoneException("Invalid phone number: (" + newArea + ")" +
                                 newExch + "-" + newNum);
    else
    {
        area = newArea;
        exchange = newExch;
        number = newNum;
    }
}
```

Now, when we call this constructor within a *try-catch* statement, we catch `PhoneException` instead of `Exception`. Here is the updated code from the test driver in Chapter 7, with the change highlighted:

```
try
{
   Phone testPhone = new Phone(0, 555, 1212);
}
catch (PhoneException except)
{
   System.out.println(except.getMessage());
}
```

Before we made this change, the *catch* clause would actually catch any form of checked exception, as all of Java's checked exceptions are subclasses of `Exception`. Now, when we catch a `PhoneException`, we know it originates from the `Phone` constructor.

As a final note, recall that our `BusinessPhone` class calls its superclass constructors. For that reason, its parameterized constructor includes a `throws Exception` clause. Because `PhoneException` is a subclass of `Exception`, technically we do not need to change the *throws* clause. If we want users of `BusinessPhone` to also be able to distinguish between a general exception and one thrown by the class, however, then we should update this code to be `throws PhoneException`. An alternative approach would be to define a `BusinessPhoneException` class, have the constructor catch the `PhoneException` from its `superclass` constructor, and then throw the new exception.

10.3 : Polymorphism

In our `Phone` hierarchy, the `toString` method has two different implementations. When applied to a `Phone` object, it returns a string in one format; when applied to a `BusinessPhone` object, it returns a string in another format. In object-oriented terms, we say that `toString` is **polymorphic**—that is, it has multiple forms. Java decides which form to use depending on the class of the object.

Together with inheritance and encapsulation, polymorphism gives us the ability to flexibly implement a hierarchy of objects. We use polymorphism to substitute different implementations of a responsibility as required by variations in the internal representations of classes at different levels of the hierarchy. In this case, `toString` contains the statements that are necessary to output the values from the fields that are defined by each of the different classes.

For example, a `Phone` variable called `yourPhone` can hold either a `Phone` or a `BusinessPhone` object. Depending on the class of the object to which the variable refers, Java's ability to han-

> **Polymorphic** An operation that has multiple meanings depending on the class of object to which it is bound

dle the polymorphism of `toString` ensures that the appropriate version of the method is called for that object when we write

```
System.out.println(yourPhone.toString());
```

Polymorphism and the assignment compatibility of subclasses make it possible to write statements that handle many different situations. For example, we could have a wide range of `Phone` subclasses with different features, such as international country codes, local numbers without area codes, and so on, each of which has its own `toString` method. The preceding statement would output an object of any of those classes, automatically selecting the appropriate version of `toString`. Without polymorphism, we would need a *switch* statement to choose the proper method to use, as is done in languages that aren't object oriented.

When we create a hierarchy of classes, the class at the top (the one that doesn't have an `extends` clause) defines the basic attributes and responsibilities that are common to all of its subclasses. But what if that class is so general that it isn't useful for anything? We don't want to allow a user to instantiate a useless base class. In another situation, we may want the base class merely to enforce the presence of certain methods in all subclasses. The actual implementation of those methods may then depend entirely on the data types used in each subclass.

In both cases, the problem is that the top of the hierarchy isn't a functional class. It really just outlines the capabilities that its functional subclasses should all support. That is, it is an abstraction of a class.

■ `abstract` **Classes**

Returning to our analogy, the architect would never put the basic empty floor in a building because it isn't usable by itself. Instead, she uses it to ensure that usable floors have certain essential properties in common. The equivalent construct in Java is an **abstract** class. We cannot instantiate an object of an abstract class. Instead, we use an abstract class as a superclass for defining subclasses that are complete.

> **Abstract** A modifier of a class or field that indicates it is incomplete and must be fully defined in a derived class

When a class contains one or more abstract methods, then it must also be declared as `abstract`. An abstract method consists of a heading with the reserved word `abstract` as one of its modifiers; it does not have a body.

Abstract methods are placeholders. A class derived from an abstract class is expected to override the abstract method with an implementation of the method body. If a subclass doesn't define an implementation of an inherited abstract method, then the subclass is also abstract.

Even though we cannot instantiate an abstract class, it can have constructors. Why would we include constructors in an abstract class? So that we can call them from subclasses, using `super`. For example, if the abstract class has instance fields, we can initialize them in its default constructor. By calling that constructor in each subclass, we ensure that the initialization is done consistently throughout the hierarchy.

Let's look at an example of an abstract class called `Worker` that has an abstract method, called `pay`, which serves as a placeholder for a method that calculates pay in a subclass. If class `ContractEmployee` extends `Worker`, it must have a method `pay` that fills in the body of the method with a relevant calculation.

```
abstract public class Worker
{
  float hours;
  float rate;
  abstract public float pay();
  .
  .
  .
}

public class ContractEmployee extends Worker
{
  public float pay()
  {
    if (hours > 40.0F)
      return 40.0F * rate + (hours - 40.0F) * rate * 1.5F;
    else
      return hours * rate;
  }
  .
  .
  .
}
```

The application might further define a class called `NonContractEmployee` that provides a **pay** method with a different formula.

```
public class NonContractEmployee extends Worker
{
  public float pay()
  {
    return hours * rate;
  }
  .
  .
  .
}
```

Both classes are subclasses of `Worker` and, therefore, are assignment compatible with `Worker`. That is, given a variable `someWorker` of class `Worker`, we can assign either a `ContractEmployee` object or a `NonContractEmployee` object to it. If we then call the **pay** method,

```
float someWorkersPay = someWorker.pay();
```

the version of **pay** that executes depends on the class of the object assigned to `someWorker`. Thus **pay** is polymorphic.

The power gained from having a common abstract superclass is further illustrated by the following example. Suppose that an application reads the data for some workers into a `Worker[]` array, as defined here:

```
Worker[] workers;
```

We can't instantiate `Worker` objects to assign to the elements of this array, but we can assign objects of its concrete (non-abstract) subclasses to the elements. Let's assume the application has filled `workers` with a mix of `ContractEmployee` and `NonContractEmployee` objects. We then use the following loop to compute the total pay of all workers:

```
float totalPay = 0.0F;
for (int index = 0, index < workers.length, index++)
  totalPay = totalPay + workers[index].pay();
```

As the loop runs through the array elements, it automatically calls the appropriate **pay** method for the class of worker stored in that slot of the array. The fact that the **pay** method was declared in the abstract `Worker` class ensures that all concrete subclasses of `Worker` have a compatible definition of **pay**.

We have just seen how abstract classes support polymorphism in a hierarchy of subclasses. Defining an abstract method at the top of a hierarchy ensures that every concrete class in the hierarchy provides a compatible method. But what if a problem involves multiple class hierarchies, and we want the same responsibility to appear in several of them?

In our building analogy, there may be certain building-code requirements that apply to office buildings and others that apply to schools. The architect's CAD program may enforce these rules for all projects of a given type. How can we get Java to ensure that a method is included in different hierarchies? The solution is found in the use of another construct, called an interface.

■ The `interface` Type

Suppose that we have three hierarchies that descend from the abstract classes `LandVehicle`, `Watercraft`, and `Aircraft`. We want classes derived from `LandVehicle` and `Aircraft` to support a `numberOfWheels` responsibility, and we want `Watercraft` and `Aircraft` concrete derived classes to have a `homePort` responsibility. We could manually insert matching abstract methods into the different base classes, but that strategy doesn't ensure that Java knows they are related, so it won't check that they are compatible.

What we need is something like a class that can hold the abstract declarations of these methods, and a way to tell Java which of our regular classes are required to implement them. A Java `interface` is a reference type that resembles a class, but contains no implementation. It is made up of method headings and can contain only `static` and `final` fields. Each method in an interface is `abstract`, whether the keyword appears in its heading or not.

We tell Java that a class is compatible with an interface by using an `implements` clause. We've used this clause before. For example, all of the classes in our `utility` package implement the library interface called `Serializable`.

Before we get into the mechanics of using an interface, we should clarify a potential source of confusion. We have used the word *interface* many times in this book, always in the general sense. In Java, an **interface** is part of the language; it is a way of specifying which fields and methods must be present in a class that is an **implementation** of the interface.

> **Interface (in Java)** A model for a class that specifies the fields and methods that must be present in a class that implements the interface
>
> **Implementation (in Java)** A class containing the definitions of the methods specified in an interface

To see how interfaces work, let's look at a Java library interface. `Comparable` is an interface with one method, `compareTo`, which returns a negative integer if the instance comes before its parameter, a positive integer if the instance comes after its parameter, and 0 otherwise. Here is its definition:

```java
public interface Comparable
{
  public abstract int compareTo(Object obj);
  // This object is compared to obj and returns
  // a negative integer if it comes before Object,
  // a positive integer if Object comes before it, and
  // 0 if they are equivalent
}
```

We have used `String`'s method `compareTo` and written a `compareTo` method in class `Name`. If we add `Comparable` to the `implements` clause in the heading for `Name`, then we are specifying that `Name` must supply a concrete method that implements the abstract `compareTo` method defined in `Comparable`.

```java
public class Name implements Serializable, Comparable
```

Is that all we need to do? Not quite. The `Comparable` interface specifies that the `compareTo` parameter be of class `Object`, not class `Name`. Thus we must change the parameter to `Object`. The method then casts the parameter to a variable of class `Name` as highlighted here:

```java
package utility;
//****************************************************************
//  Class Name
//  Implements a basic class representing a name with three parts.
//****************************************************************
import java.io.Serializable;
public class Name implements Serializable, Comparable
{
  String first;                    // Person's first name
  String last;                     // Person's last name
  String middle;                   // Person's middle name
  .
  .  // Constructors and observers not shown
  .
  public int compareTo(Object otherObj)
  {
    Name other = (Name)otherObj;
    int compare =
        last.toLowerCase().compareTo(other.getLastName().toLowerCase());
    if ( compare != 0)
      return compare;
    else
    {
      compare =
        first.toLowerCase().compareTo(other.getFirstName().toLowerCase());
```

```
      if (compare != 0)
        return compare;
      else
        return
          middle.toLowerCase().compareTo(other.getMiddleName().toLowerCase());
    }
  }
}
```

The `Serializable` interface has no methods in its definition, so to use it, we simply include it in the `implements` clause. The `Serializable` interface signals the JVM that it must do some work behind the scenes to ensure that the implementing class is compatible with `ObjectOutputStream` and `ObjectInputStream`.

We've seen how to use an existing interface, but we must keep some special semantic rules in mind when writing our own interfaces. First, an interface can declare only `public` constants and `public` abstract instance methods. Because of these restrictions, you can omit the modifiers and Java will automatically assume that they are implied. Second, unlike abstract classes, interfaces cannot have constructors.

These restrictions stem from the fact that an interface is not a form of class. Interfaces are a notation for specifying method signatures that objects of an implementing class must support. As a consequence, they do not provide any of the implementation, other than `public` class constants.

Because interfaces result in the definition of compatible methods across multiple classes, they also contribute to polymorphism. Whereas abstract classes create methods that are polymorphic across assignment-compatible objects, interfaces lead to the implementation of methods that are polymorphic across unrelated hierarchies of classes.

■ Binding

Given a polymorphic method, Java must determine which version to use in any given situation. The compiler does its best to identify an appropriate method for each call. When it is able to do so, the call is translated directly into Bytecode that invokes the proper version of the method. We say that the call has a **static binding**, where we use the term *static* to mean "fixed at compile time."

Static binding The situation in which Java resolves a polymorphic method call to a specific version of the method at compile time

Dynamic binding The situation in which Java resolves a polymorphic method call to a specific version of a method at run time

In some cases, the compiler can't determine a particular method for a call. For example, if a `Worker` variable can be randomly assigned either a `ContractEmployee` object or a `NonContractEmployee` object prior to a call to `pay`, then the compiler cannot bind the call to a specific version of the method. Instead, it generates Bytecode that determines the class of the object at run time, and chooses the method accordingly. When the version of the method must be decided while the code is running, the situation is termed **dynamic binding**.

If either case works, why do we care about the distinction? Because static binding is much more efficient than dynamic binding. Thus, when the performance of an application is an important consideration, it may not be appropriate to develop a design that relies excessively on polymorphism that can only be resolved dynamically. Polymorphism can save us quite a bit of work in programming, but it can come with a cost of lower performance—and you should be aware of that potential drawback.

■ Determining the Class of an Object

A variable `myPhone` of class `Phone` can hold either a value of class `Phone` or a value of its subclass, `BusinessPhone`. Suppose that we are extending our `UpdateAddressBook` application to handle entries with either kind of phone number, and `myPhone` contains the number from the entry that the user wants to update. The entries in the address book are a mix of personal and business contacts, so we don't know which kind of object has been assigned to `myPhone`.

If `myPhone` contains a `Phone` value, then we have to ask the user to input a simple phone number. If it contains a `BusinessPhone` value, then the user must also input the extension. How do we know which kind of phone number to input? This is one of the complications of polymorphism: Given a superclass variable, we don't know the class of the object to which it refers. Only the object knows the class to which it belongs.

Wouldn't it be handy if we could ask an object for the name of its class? Java supports two ways in which we can accomplish this task. The first approach is to use an operator called `instanceof` that returns `true` if the object to its left is an instance of the class name to its right. Thus, to input the appropriate kind of phone number, we can write

```java
if (myPhone instanceof BusinessPhone)
   newPhone = in.inputBusinessPhone();      // Call method to input business
                                            // phone
else
   newPhone = in.inputPhone();              // Call method to input standard
                                            // phone
```

Keep in mind that a subclass is always an instance of its superclass. For this reason, you must be careful to compare the object to the subclass name. If we use the expression

```java
myPhone instanceof Phone
```

then the result is always `true` because both `Phone` and `BusinessPhone` objects are instances of class `Phone`. (Actually, the result will be `false` if `myPhone` is `null`.)

The second way is to get the name of the class as a string. Java provides a method called `getClass` that can be applied to any object and that returns an object of class `Class`. To get the name from the `Class` object, we use the `getSimpleName` method. Thus we can write

```java
myPhone.getClass().getSimpleName()
```

If `myPhone` refers to a `Phone` object, then the call returns `"Phone"`. If it refers to a `BusinessPhone` object, then the call returns `"BusinessPhone"`. Unlike with `instanceof`, it doesn't matter which class is the subclass. With this information, we can choose which type of phone number to input as follows:

```java
if (myPhone.getClass().getSimpleName().equals("Phone"))
   newPhone = in.inputPhone();              // Call method to input standard
                                            // phone
else
   newPhone = in.inputBusinessPhone();      // Call method to input business
                                            // phone
```

You may be wondering why the method is called `getSimpleName`. There is, indeed, a method called `getName` in class `Class`, but it returns the qualified name of the class, including the package that it resides in. In most cases, we don't need this amount of detail to make a decision about how to treat a polymorphic variable. When the polymorphism extends across multiple packages, however, we should use `getName`.

The following case study provides a perfect opportunity to use our new knowledge of polymorphism, including the use of abstract classes, the implementation of interfaces, and the determination of the class of an object.

PROBLEM SOLVING CASE STUDY

Adding Business Entries to the Address Book

Problem The `AddressBookUpdate` application from Chapter 8 was a big success. But whenever software succeeds, users ask for more features. We've been asked to add support for a mix of business and personal address book entries. To explore the implications of this upgrade, you'll develop a second kind of entry that uses a business phone number. Later, you can add support for a business address.

Some users have complained that with larger data files there is a delay in searching and updating. Now that we know how to use arrays, we can store the data in an array to improve performance. We'll start from the application in Chapter 8, which performed only a single update. We leave it as an exercise for you to enhance the application to process multiple entries in a session.

Brainstorming We already have most of the classes that we need. The driver and user interface will remain almost the same, with the exception of reading business phone numbers. As part of our solution, we plan to reimplement the `AddressBook` class using an array to hold the entries in memory. We already have an `Entry` class; the only new class is the `BusinessEntry`.

Filtering With just one new class, what's to filter? Well, this stage also happens to be where we make decisions about how classes are related. We have several options for our `BusinessEntry` class. We could write it as an independent class, but that ignores its connection to `Entry`. We could write it as a subclass of `Entry`, overriding the existing methods that use the `phone` field. Unfortunately, both of those solutions fail to consider the future. If the application's success continues, we may need to add other kinds of entries. Let's design an `Entry` class hierarchy that provides flexibility for continued expansion.

We place the most general kind of entry at the top of the hierarchy. It only needs to hold a name, because that's how we identify an entry when we search through the address book. We want every entry to also have an address and phone number. The problem is that we don't know how those attributes will be represented in different kinds of `Entry` subclasses. The solution is to make `Entry` abstract, with concrete support for a `name` field, and abstract observers and transformers for the other fields. Then we provide concrete implementations for `PersonalEntry` and `BusinessEntry` objects.

Determining Responsibilities As long as we're redesigning `Entry` to be more general, let's delete the `Scanner`-based constructor. We can always add that specialized capability in a subclass. Let's also have `Entry` implement the `Comparable` interface. And because we want every subclass of `Entry` to use the `Name` for comparison, let's make the `compareTo` method for `Entry` final.

The two subclasses of `Entry` don't need to add any methods. They simply provide concrete methods that override the abstract ones in specific ways, and they inherit the concrete methods provided by `Entry`. Here are the responsibilities:

Entry	PersonalEntry	BusinessEntry

Entry()
Entry(Name)
	PersonalEntry()
	PersonalEntry
	  (Name, Address, Phone)
		BusinessEntry()
		BusinessEntry
		  (Name, Address, Phone)

getName() abstract getAddress() abstract getPhone() setName(Name) abstract setAddress(Address) abstract setPhone(Phone) abstract toString() final compareTo(Name)	getAddress() getPhone() setAddress(Address) setPhone(Phone) toString()	getAddress() getPhone() setAddress(Address) setPhone(Phone) toString()

The responsibilities for `AddressBook` remain the same: default and parameterized constructors, `getEntryByName`, and `upDateEntry`. With `UserInterface`, we need to add one method: `inputBusinessPhone`.

Responsibility Algorithms The responsibilities for `Entry` are mostly abstract. Abstract responsibilities have no algorithms. The default constructor merely calls the default `Name` constructor to initialize `name`, and the parameterized constructor sets the `name` field to the given `Name` parameter. The `getName` and `setName` methods are the same as before. Method `compareTo` merely returns the result of the `compareTo` operation applied to the `name` field and its parameter. But remember that the `Comparable` interface requires that the parameter be of class `Object`, which we then cast to `Name`. Because the responsibility algorithms are all trivial, we are ready to code this class:

```
//****************************************************************
// Abstract class Entry is the base class for various types of address
// book entry classes. Only the Name operations are implemented here
//****************************************************************
```

```java
import java.io.Serializable;
import utility.*;
abstract public class Entry implements Serializable, Comparable
{
  Name name;
  // Default constructor
  public Entry () { name = new Name(); }
  // Direct constructor
  public Entry (Name newName) { name = newName; }
  // Observers
  public Name getName () { return name; }
  abstract public Address getAddress();
  abstract public Phone getPhone();
  abstract public String toString ();
  final public int compareTo(Object obj)
  {
    return name.compareTo((Name) obj);
  }
  // Transformers
  public void setName (Name newName) {name = newName;}
  abstract public void setAddress(Address newAddress);
  abstract public void setPhone(Phone newPhone);
}
```

PersonalEntry has two constructors. Each calls its corresponding super constructor in Entry before initializing the address and phone fields. The observers and transformers simply return and set the field values, respectively. We can reuse the toString operation from the Chapter 8 version of Entry, because the fields of PersonalEntry are likewise a Name, an Address, and a Phone. Because we are reusing so much from our previous case study, we can directly code the class:

```java
//*********************************************************************
// Class PersonalEntry implements Entry using a standard Phone number
//*********************************************************************
import java.io.Serializable;
import utility.*;
public class PersonalEntry extends Entry implements Serializable
{
  Address address;
  Phone phone;
  // Default constructor
  public PersonalEntry ()
  {
    super();
    address = new Address();
    phone = new Phone();
  }
  // Direct constructor
  public PersonalEntry (Name newName, Address newAddr, Phone newPhone)
  {
    super(newName);
    address = newAddr;
```

```
      phone = newPhone;
   }
   // Observers
   public Address getAddress () { return address; }
   public Phone getPhone () { return phone; }
   public String toString ()
   {
      return name + "\n" + address + "\n" + phone;
   }
   // Transformers
   public void setAddress (Address newAddress) {address = newAddress;}
   public void setPhone (Phone newPhone) {phone = newPhone;}
}
```

Class BusinessEntry is identical to class PersonalEntry with the exception that its phone field is of class BusinessPhone. Thus we substitute that class for Phone in several places in the code. In particular, because the abstract setPhone method specifies that the parameter is of class Phone, we need to cast its value to BusinessPhone before assigning it to the phone field. Here is the code for BusinessEntry with the differences from class PersonalEntry highlighted:

```
//***********************************************************************
// Class BusinessEntry implements Entry using a BusinessPhone number
//***********************************************************************
import java.io.Serializable;
import utility.*;
public class BusinessEntry extends Entry implements Serializable
{
   Address address;
   BusinessPhone phone;
   // Default constructor
   public BusinessEntry ()
   {
      super();
      address = new Address();
      phone = new BusinessPhone();
   }
   // Direct constructor
   public BusinessEntry (Name newName, Address newAddr, BusinessPhone
                         newPhone)
   {
      super(newName);
      address = newAddr;
      phone = newPhone;
   }
   // Observers
   public Address getAddress () { return address; }
   public BusinessPhone getPhone () { return phone; }
   public String toString ()
   {
      return name + "\n" + address + "\n" + phone;
   }
   // Transformers
```

```
  public void setAddress (Address newAddress) {address = newAddress;}
  public void setPhone (Phone newPhone)
  {
    phone = (BusinessPhone)newPhone;              // Note cast from Phone
  }
}
```

It's worth noting that we were able to code `toString` exactly as we did for `PersonalEntry`. The `phone` field is of class `BusinessPhone`, so the implicit call to `phone.toString` invokes the version of `toString` that formats this kind of object.

Because we've been reusing so much of the earlier code, we haven't had to dwell on algorithmic issues to this point. Now, however, we turn to `AddressBook`, which requires new algorithms.

`AddressBook` has two constructors and two methods. The constructors are the same, except that the default constructor opens a file with a default name. Because we know how to use `this` to refer to an object from within itself, we can have the default constructor call the parameterized constructor using `this`:

```
this("addressbook.dat");  // Calls parameterized AddressBook constructor
                          // passing default file name as the argument
```

Now we can focus on the parameterized constructor and the two methods. Recall that our plan is to read all of the data from the file into an array, allow the client code to perform any number of searches and updates, and then save the data back to the file when we're done. In our current version of the application, we're performing only one search and update, but we need to think in terms of enabling multiple operations.

When we create the `AddressBook` object, we should get the data from the file. Thus the constructor should be responsible for reading in the data. To read an entire text file, we would use a *while* loop controlled by `hasNext`. But `ObjectInputStream` doesn't have a `hasNext` method. Thus, rather than test this condition in the *while* expression, we *catch* the `EOFException` that is thrown when it runs out of data. We must also stop the loop before we run past the end of the array. We can use a *for* loop to run through the whole array, allowing the exception to force an early exit if we reach EOF before the array is full.

We need to record the number of entries input, so that we can apply subarray processing in the other methods. Here is the algorithm, assuming the array is called `book`:

AddressBook(String inFileName)

Save inFileName so we know where to write the updated address book
Open the input file
int index
try
  for index running from 0 to book.length - 1
    Set book[index] to (Entry)in.readObject()
  The array is full so set the number of entries to book.length
catch EOFException
  We encountered EOF before the array was filled, so set the number of entries to index
Close the input file

Now we turn to **getEntryByName**. Given that the data is organized into an array, we can search it with a loop that runs through the elements from **book[0]** to **book[numEntries-1]**. Either we find a match and return the entry, or we get to the end of the subarray without a match and return **null**. Normally, when a loop is controlled by an event (a match is found) and by a count (**index < numEntries**), we would use a *while* or *do* statement. In this case, however, the loop contains an *if* that includes a *return* from the method. Thus we can use a *for* loop and have the *return* exit the loop early. If the *for* loop exits normally, then no match was found. We record the place where the entry is found for use by **updateEntry**. Here is the algorithm:

```
getEntryByName(Name name) returns Entry

for index running from 0 to numEntries - 1
  if book[index]getName() is the same as name
    Set place to index to record the spot
    return book[place]
Set place to -1 (invalid place—no matching entry)
return null
```

Updating an entry is trivial. If **place** is valid, we assign the new entry to **book[place]**:

```
updateEntry(Entry entry)

if place >= 0
  Set book[place] to entry
```

Client code can now create an address book object (which reads in the data), search for entries, and update them. There's just one problem: We have to save the data back on a file when the user is done. How do we know when to perform that task? We'll have to change the design of **AddressBook** to include a **close** responsibility. The algorithm is simple. We open the file for output, use a *for* loop to write the **numEntries** elements in the array out to the file, and then close the file:

```
close()

Open the input file for output
for index running from 0 to numEntries - 1
  Output book[index]
Close the file
```

Here is the code for **AddressBook**:

```java
//***********************************************************
// Class AddressBook supplies operations to search and update an address book
//***********************************************************
import java.io.*;
import utility.*;
```

```java
public class AddressBook
{
  String inName;
  Entry[] book = new Entry[100];
  int numEntries = 0;
  int place = -1;
  // Default constructor
  public AddressBook() throws IOException, ClassNotFoundException
  {
    this("addressbook.dat");  // Call parameterized constructor for default
                              // file
  }
  // Parameterized constructor
  public AddressBook(String inFileName)
    throws IOException, ClassNotFoundException
  {
    inName = inFileName;        // Save input file name
    ObjectInputStream in =
      new ObjectInputStream(new FileInputStream(inName));
    int index = 0;
    try
    {                           // Copy file into array until array is full
      for (index = 0; index < book.length; index++)
        book[index] = (Entry)in.readObject();
      numEntries = book.length;
    }
    catch (EOFException ex)    // If EOF encountered before array filled
    {
      numEntries = index;      // record actual number of entries
    }
    in.close();
  }
  // Search address book for entry with matching name
  public Entry getEntryByName(Name name)
  {
    for (int index = 0; index < numEntries; index++)    // Search array for
                                                        // match
      if (book[index].getName().compareTo(name) == 0)
      {
        place = index;                                  // Save entry
                                                        //   index
        return book[place];                             // Return
                                                        //   matching entry
      }
    // If not found
    place = -1;                                         // Set place to
                                                        //   invalid
    return null;                                        // Return null
                                                        //   entry
  }
```

```java
// Change current entry
public void updateEntry(Entry entry)
{
  if (place >= 0)                                    // If current is
                                                     //   valid
    book[place] = entry;                             //   replace entry
}
// Write book to file
public void close() throws IOException
{
  ObjectOutputStream out =
    new ObjectOutputStream(new FileOutputStream(inName));
  for (int index = 0; index < numEntries; index ++)
    out.writeObject(book[index]);
  out.close();
}
}
```

Let's consider the `UserInterface` class next. Because we've used `Entry` as the superclass for both types of concrete entries, there's no change to `getEntry`. The field names remain the same, so `inputField` doesn't change either. We can still use `inputPhone` to get a normal phone number. The only change is to add a method that inputs a business phone number. That method is identical to `inputPhone`, with the exception that it has to get the extension number. (We should also update it to use `PhoneException` instead of `Exception`.) Here is the code for this new method, with the differences from `inputPhone` highlighted:

```java
// Get business phone number from user and return BusinessPhone object
public BusinessPhone inputBusinessPhone() throws PhoneException
{
  System.out.println(
    "Enter the phone number and extension. Example: 800 555 1212 0100");
  int area = in.nextInt();
  int exch = in.nextInt();
  int numb = in.nextInt();
  int extn = in.nextInt();
  String eol = in.nextLine();              // Discard rest of line
  return new BusinessPhone(area, exch, numb, extn);
}
```

Before we move on to the driver, we show the UML diagram for the classes in our application. Rather than show the `utility` classes separately, we use the UML notation that indicates a package is being used.

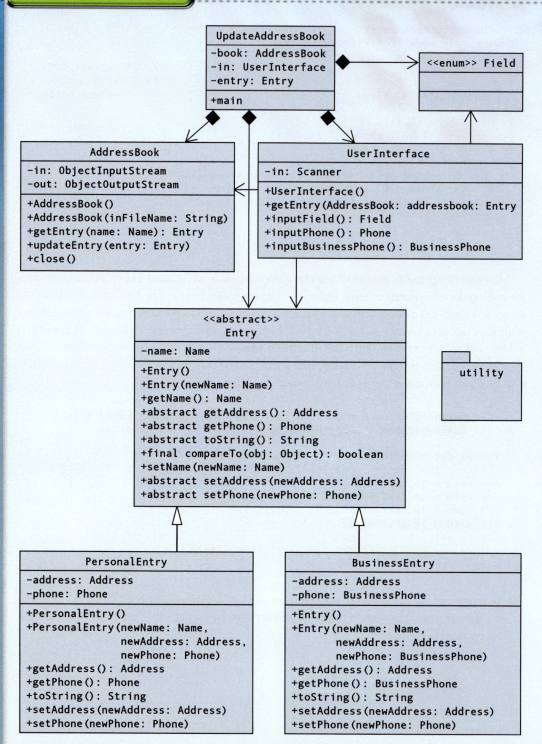

We've tried to preserve the interfaces to the `UserInterface` and `AddressBook` classes so that we can reuse much of the earlier version of `UpdateAddressBook`. Our only changes here are to selectively call `inputPhone` or `inputBusinessPhone`, depending on the class of the entry, and to close the address book at the end. Here is the code, with highlighting showing where it differs from the application in Chapter 8:

```java
//**********************************************************************
// Application UpdateAddressBook2 extends UpdateAddressBook to include a
// business entry and improve performance
//**********************************************************************
import java.io.*;
import utility.*;
public class UpdateAddressBook2
{
  public static void main (String[] args)
    throws IOException, ClassNotFoundException, PhoneException
  {
    AddressBook book = new AddressBook("addressbook.dat");
    UserInterface in = new UserInterface();
    Entry entry = in.getEntry(book);    // Get the entry to change
    if (entry != null)                  // If it's on the file, display it
    {
      System.out.println("You selected the following entry: \n" + entry +
                    "\n");
      Field field = in.inputField();    // Ask which field to change
      switch (field)                    // Process request according to field
                                        //    type
      {
        case NAME:    System.out.println("Name change not yet implemented.");
                    break;
        case ADDRESS: System.out.println("Address change not yet
                                        implemented.");
                    break;
        case PHONE:   Phone phone;
                    if (entry.getPhone().getClass().getSimpleName().equals
                                                ("Phone"))
                        phone = in.inputPhone();    // Get the phone number
                    else
                        phone = in.inputBusinessPhone();
                    entry.setPhone(phone);          // Change the entry
                    book.updateEntry(entry);        // Update the address
                                                    //    book
                    System.out.println("Phone number updated.");
                    break;
        case NONE:    System.out.println("No change to address book.");
                    break;
      }
    }
    else                                            // Invalid name
      System.out.println("Name not found in address book. No change made.");
    book.close();
  }
}
```

The fact that we made so few changes to add the new capability to the earlier driver is a testament to the value of abstraction, inheritance, and polymorphism—the three fundamental concepts of object-oriented programming. Here is the output from the application, showing how it handles a business entry:

```
Console ⊠                                    ■  ✖  ✖  ▤ ▥   ▱ ▱▾ ▱▾
<terminated> UpdateAddressBook2 [Java Application] /opt/sun-jdk-1.5.0.08
Enter the name you wish to search for.
(Format: first middle last):William Michael Herrold
You selected the following entry:
Herrold, William Michael
31415 Pieman Lane
Leafton, MA  11048
(617)888-3333x101

Enter the field you wish to change from the following:
NAME
ADDRESS
PHONE
NONE
phone
Enter the phone number and extension. Example: 800 555 1212 0100
617 888 3333 1001
Phone number updated.
```

10.4 : Testing and Debugging

Testing an application that uses polymorphic methods requires that you consider all possible combinations of classes that may be in use. For example, if a method is supposed to output a **Phone** object, and **Phone** has a subclass, then your test plan needs to include cases for output of both kinds of objects.

In effect, whenever a polymorphic method is applied to a variable that could contain objects of various classes, you should think of that call as being in a *switch* statement, where the *case* branches are the different classes. Just as you would test each branch of the switch, so you should test each class that could be referenced by the variable.

The scope rules don't explicitly affect the test plan. Indeed, it would be impossible to check the accessibility of every class member from every location in the application. However, you should construct the test data so that you can verify that the correct values are used in each location. For example, if all of the test cases use the same data values, then you might not discover that a local variable is unintentionally shadowing an instance variable. If you choose values that are all different, such an error is more likely to become visible.

Testing and Debugging Hints

1. Study the entire hierarchy for a class before you try to use or extend it. Look for cases of overriding and hiding that change the semantics of a class member.

2. An `abstract` class cannot be instantiated as an object; instead, a subclass must be written to extend it.

3. Overriding applies to instance methods; hiding applies to class methods. You cannot hide an instance method with a class method or override a class method with an instance method. However, Java does allow `static` and instance fields to hide each other.

4. When you write a class that extends a superclass in another package, make sure that you import the superclass package.

5. The access modifiers for a method that overrides or hides a method in a superclass must grant the same level of access or greater. The most restrictive form of access is `private`, then package, then `protected`, and finally `public`. You can override a `private` method with a `public` one, but you can't use `private` to override a `public` method.

6. Make sure that the first statement of every constructor is a call to one of the superclass constructors. If you omit the call, Java automatically inserts a call to `super()`.

7. Overloading a method requires that the two methods have different signatures. The signature is the name of the method plus the types of its parameters in their specific order. The return type and modifiers are not part of the signature.

8. Use `super` to access fields or methods of a superclass that have been hidden or overridden by a derived class.

9. Use `this` to access instance fields that have been hidden by a local declaration.

10. Thoroughly document the interface of a class to facilitate its proper use, ensure its correct design, and simplify testing.

Graphical User Interfaces

Frames, Fields, and Buttons

In Chapter 9, we introduced the `JFrame`, `Container`, `JTextArea`, and `FlowLayout` classes, which allow us to display multiple blocks of text within a window. In this chapter, we will add the capability to input values and respond to the user clicking a button. In the following discussion, we assume that these operations have already taken place:

```java
JFrame userFrame = new JFrame();
userFrame.setSize(200, 100);
Container userPane = userFrame.getContentPane();
userPane.setLayout(new FlowLayout());
```

One of the easiest ways to enter data is through a `JTextField`, which is an area into which the user can type information. Before we see how to create a `JTextField`, however, we explore how to make a prompting label for it.

A label is a line of text that is placed into the content pane of a `JFrame`. Its appearance makes it appropriate for labeling other components in a window. We add the label to the pane using the **add** method. Here is an example:

```
JLabel newLabel;
newLabel = new JLabel("This is the text in the label.");
userPane.add(newLabel);
```

We can also take the shortcut of instantiating an anonymous `JLabel` directly within the call to **add**:

```
userPane.add(new JLabel("This is the text in the label."));
```

By default, the text within a label begins at the left edge of the label. Sometimes, however, we want to center the text or have it appear shifted to the right. A second argument to the `JLabel` constructor can specify this alignment, using one of three predefined constants: `JLabel.LEFT`, `JLabel.CENTER`, or `JLabel.RIGHT`. For example, if we want `"Format"` to be centered in a label, we would write

```
userPane.add(new JLabel("Format", JLabel.CENTER));
```

Now we are ready to create a field. The following code creates a `JTextField` that has space for typing six characters within it:

```
JTextField inputField = new JTextField(6);
```

We can give a default value to the field by including a string as the first argument to the constructor. For example,

```
inputField = new JTextField("Replace Me", 10);
```

would cause the `JTextField` object to provide space for ten characters, and initially the words `"Replace Me"` would appear within the field. The user can then replace these words with input data.

The last step is to add the field to a content pane:

```
userPane.add(inputField);
```

In Chapter 9, we introduced `FlowLayout` as the simplest of Java's layout managers. Unfortunately, it limits our ability to control the appearance of output on the screen. For example, we do not have the option of telling `FlowLayout` to place a `JLabel` adjacent to its corresponding `JTextField`. The `GridLayout` manager, however, does provide this capability.

`GridLayout` works much like `FlowLayout` in that we simply **add** objects to the pane, and it places those objects consecutively into the available space. The difference is that `GridLayout` partitions the pane into rows and columns. The columns are all the same size, as are the rows. Values are placed into these spaces in reading order—left to right within a row until it is full, and then moving to the beginning of the next row.

The `GridLayout` constructor takes a pair of `int` arguments. The first argument is the number of rows, and the second is the number of columns. If the first argument is zero, then the grid has an unlimited number of rows and expands as objects are added.[1] Let's look at a demonstration application that has two columns and three rows. The top row contains column headings, and the next row contains a labeled input field for entering an area code. We'll use the third row later.

```java
import java.awt.*;
import javax.swing.*;
public class GUILabelDemo
{
  static JFrame userFrame = new JFrame();          // Create a frame
  static Container userPane = userFrame.getContentPane();
  static JLabel head1 = new JLabel("Prompt", JLabel.CENTER);
  static JLabel head2 = new JLabel("Input Field", JLabel.CENTER);
  static JLabel area = new JLabel("Area Code:");
  static JTextField inputField = new JTextField("999", 3);
  public static void main(String[] args)
  {
    userFrame.setSize(175, 125);                    // 175 wide, 125 long
    userFrame.setLocation(250, 150);                // 250 right, 150 down
    userPane.setLayout(new GridLayout(3, 2));       // Grid layout manager
    userPane.add(head1);                            // Left column heading
    userPane.add(head2);                            // Right column heading
    userPane.add(area);                             // Field label
    userPane.add(inputField);                       // Input field
    userFrame.setVisible(true);                     // Show on screen
  }
}
```

---

[1]If you use zero for the second argument, then the grid has an indeterminate number of columns that depends on the size of the content pane and the sizes of the objects that are added. We recommend against doing this.

We'll see shortly why all of the fields are `static`. Here's the output from the demo:

Once presented with this window, the user can edit the value in the input field. But how do we place this value back into the application? We use the `getText` method associated with the field. For example, the following line retrieves the value within the field of our demo window:

```
String fieldText = inputField.getText();
```

As you can see, the method returns the field contents as a string. We can convert this string to an `int` using a `Scanner` and `nextInt`:

```
int areacode = new Scanner(fieldText).nextInt();
```

Alternatively, we can apply the `parseInt` method from the `Integer` class:

```
int areacode = Integer.parseInt(fieldText);
```

Auto-unboxing
Automatic conversion of an object of one of the primitive type wrapper classes to the corresponding primitive type value

Wrapper class A class that provides additional operations for a primitive type by enclosing a primitive type value in an object

Java provides a set of classes corresponding to the primitive types (called `Float`, `Double`, `Byte`, `Short`, `Integer`, `Long`, and `Boolean`), each of which has a corresponding `parse` method (`parseFloat`, `parseDouble`, `parseByte`, `parseShort`, `parseInt`, `parseLong`, and `parseBoolean`) that converts a string into an object of that class. Prior to Java version 1.5, the primitive value had to be retrieved from the object with a `getValue` method. Since then, Java has supported **auto-unboxing** of these **wrapper classes**—a fancy way of saying that when we assign, for example, an `Integer` value to an `int` variable, Java automatically applies the `getValue` method for us.

Java also supports **auto-boxing** of primitive types. Auto-boxing allows us to assign a primitive value to a variable of the corresponding class:

```
Double piObject = 3.14159265;
```

> **Auto-boxing**
> Automatic instantiation of a primitive type wrapper class object from a primitive type value

In this statement, Java automatically calls the constructor for a `Double` object with the `double` value as an argument. Until now, we've used `Scanner` for all of our numeric conversions. But with a `JTextField` typically holding just a single value, it is a bit more convenient—and somewhat faster—to use the `parse` methods.

We now know how to put properly labeled and arranged text fields in a window, and how to read their values. Just one problem remains: How do we know when to read these values? `JOptionPane` provides a predefined set of buttons that allow the user to signal that a value is ready for input. By contrast, our `JFrame` just places labels and fields on the screen. Displaying a button is easy. If we add the following statements to our demo program

```
static JButton done = new JButton("Done");   // A button showing the
                                              //   word Done
    .
    .
    .
userPane.add(done);                           // Put the button in the
                                              //   content pane
```

now it displays

Responding to the user clicking a button takes us into new Java territory. Recall that in Chapter 1, we listed the control structures of Java as sequence, selection, loop, subprogram, and event. When the user clicks a button, it generates an event, and Java responds to this event. To handle this scenario, we write an event handler.

The Java library defines several **interface** types that specify the responsibilities each different event handler class must support. For example, to respond to a button event, we define a class that `implements` the `ActionListener` interface. A class that implements `ActionListener` must have a method called `actionPerformed`. Events from a `JFrame`, such as closing the window, are defined by the `WindowListener` interface; mouse events are defined by a `MouseListener` interface; and so on.

When the user clicks a button, the JVM invokes the `actionPerformed` method in the corresponding event handler. What can we do within this method? Anything! For example, we can get the value from a field, place it in another label, and show the change on the screen:

```java
import java.awt.event.*;       // Remember to import the event subpackage
                              //   of java.awt
import javax.swing.*;
class ButtonHandler implements ActionListener
{
  public void actionPerformed(ActionEvent event) // Event handler
                                                  //   method
  {
    JLabel outputLabel =                          // Make label from
                                                  //   field value
      new JLabel(GUILabelDemo.inputField.getText());
    GUILabelDemo.userPane.add(outputLabel);       // Put label in pane
    GUILabelDemo.userFrame.setVisible(true);      // Show change on
                                                  //   screen
  }
}                                                 // End of
                                                  //   ButtonHandler
```

There's just one more step. We have a button object and a handler class, but no handler object. We need to instantiate an object of the handler class, and connect it to the button. Java calls this process **registering a listener**. Given a button, we call its `addActionListener` method, passing it an object of our `ButtonHandler` class:

> **Registering a listener**
> Connecting an event handler object to an event source object by calling a method associated with the event source. The method adds the handler to the event source's list of listeners, which are called whenever the event happens

```java
done.addActionListener(new ButtonHandler());
```

When the user clicks the button, the contents of the field are copied to the new label and displayed:

In fact, the user can keep changing the value and clicking the Done button as many times as desired, because we have unintentionally created an **event loop**. In some cases, where we want to input a series of values, an event loop is just what we need. But if we want the user to enter only one value, then we must do something to terminate the loop.

> **Event loop** A situation in which an event handler can be called repeatedly

For example, we can remove the button from the content pane after it has been clicked. We simply place a call to the content pane's `remove` method in our event handler:

```
GUILabelDemo.userPane.remove(GUILabelDemo.done);   // Removes the done
                                                   // button
```

In this case, when the new label appears, the button disappears so that it cannot be clicked again. As an alternative, we can end the loop by simply hiding the frame. To do so, we call `setVisible` with an argument of `false`.

We have now seen the basics of event-driven input and output. However, there are several points to note about our example. The first is that our event handler is designed for just one button. What if we have multiple buttons? As we see in Chapter 11, the `ActionEvent` parameter of our event handler carries information that lets us determine the source of an event. We can use that information with a branch in the event handler to select the appropriate action.

Also notice that we declared all of the GUI components as `static` in the driver because we wanted to access them directly from the event handler. We arranged the scopes of the variables this way so that we could continue to use our demo's driver and write the simplest event handler possible. Of course, this is generally a poor approach to designing an event-driven application.

A more popular technique is to place the creation of the frame and components into the constructor for a class that represents the user interface. This class may also implement `ActionListener` and contain the `actionPerformed` method to handle its own events. Here is a version of our program using this approach:

```java
import java.awt.*;
import java.awt.event.*;
import javax.swing.*;
class GUI implements ActionListener
{
   JFrame userFrame = new JFrame();                        // Create a frame
   Container userPane = userFrame.getContentPane();
   JLabel head1 = new JLabel("Prompt", JLabel.CENTER);
   JLabel head2 = new JLabel("Input Field", JLabel.CENTER);
   JLabel area = new JLabel("Area Code:");
   JTextField inputField = new JTextField("999", 3);
```

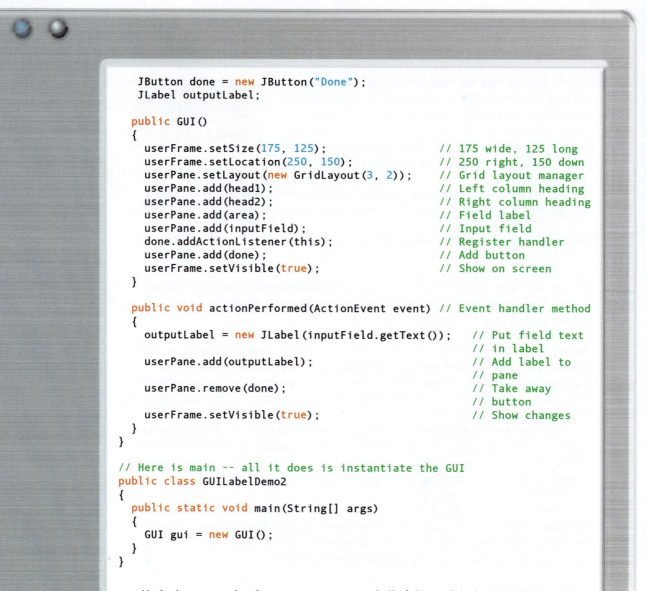

```
    JButton done = new JButton("Done");
    JLabel outputLabel;

  public GUI()
  {
    userFrame.setSize(175, 125);                 // 175 wide, 125 long
    userFrame.setLocation(250, 150);             // 250 right, 150 down
    userPane.setLayout(new GridLayout(3, 2));    // Grid layout manager
    userPane.add(head1);                         // Left column heading
    userPane.add(head2);                         // Right column heading
    userPane.add(area);                          // Field label
    userPane.add(inputField);                    // Input field
    done.addActionListener(this);                // Register handler
    userPane.add(done);                          // Add button
    userFrame.setVisible(true);                  // Show on screen
  }

  public void actionPerformed(ActionEvent event) // Event handler method
  {
    outputLabel = new JLabel(inputField.getText());  // Put field text
                                                     // in label
    userPane.add(outputLabel);                       // Add label to
                                                     // pane
    userPane.remove(done);                           // Take away
                                                     // button
    userFrame.setVisible(true);                      // Show changes
  }
}

// Here is main -- all it does is instantiate the GUI
public class GUILabelDemo2
{
  public static void main(String[] args)
  {
    GUI gui = new GUI();
  }
}
```

Method **main** now has just one statement, and all of the work is done in the **GUI** class. Although we are used to having operations take place in a single flow of control, event-based programming introduces multiple threads of control. In this example, **main** executes its one statement and then terminates; the **GUI** object takes on a life (control thread) of its own and continues to operate. If **main** had created two **GUI** objects, then both would be left running at the same time. As we see in Chapter 11, dealing with these different threads gives us a new perspective on problem solving.

Summary

Object-oriented languages such as Java organize class data types into a hierarchy. At the top of Java's hierarchy is a class called `Object` that provides a few basic operations. Using inheritance, other classes extend `Object` and are said to be derived from it. Derived classes inherit the non-`private` members of their superclass, except for its constructors. We must explore the entire inheritance hierarchy for a class to determine its full interface.

Instance methods can override superclass instance methods, and class methods and fields can hide superclass class methods and fields. Overriding and hiding enable us to change the meaning of a method or field when extending a superclass with a derived class. In this way, the derived class can retain the same form of interface, but operate in a different manner. Any `final` methods cannot be overridden or hidden.

Constructors are not inherited by derived classes. The first statement in a constructor must be a call to a constructor for the superclass. Otherwise, Java will automatically insert such a call to the default constructor for the superclass.

Java allows us to declare multiple methods with the same name as long as they have different signatures. The method is then said to be overloaded. The signature consists of the method name plus the types of its parameters in their given order. The return type and modifiers are not part of the signature. Java determines which version of an overloaded method to call by examining the types in the argument list and selecting the method with the matching parameter list.

Sometimes we need to access a method or field in a superclass that has been overridden or hidden. We can use the `super` keyword to refer to the superclass version of a field or method instead of the local version. Similarly, a method can define a local variable or parameter with the same name as a field in the class; we can then use `this` to refer to the instance version instead of the local version.

Scope rules determine the range of code that has access to an identifier. Internal scope rules specify where class members can be accessed within a class. In Java, class members can be used anywhere within a class, with two exceptions: Class variables must be defined before they are used to initialize other variables, and local variables can shadow class variables (name precedence).

External scope rules specify where a member can be accessed outside a class. Java provides four levels of external access. The default level is package, which extends access to all classes in the same package. With `protected` access, a derived class in another package can inherit members from its superclass. A member with `public` access can be used by any code that imports the class. The `private` access level restricts access to only the class containing the member.

A variable of a superclass can refer to an object of any of its subclasses, a capability called polymorphism. When a method is applied to a polymorphic variable, Java automatically determines the class of the referenced object and calls the corresponding version of the method. When we want the top level of a class hierarchy to specify attributes or responsibilities for subclasses but not implement them, we can make them `abstract`, which also makes the class `abstract`. If we want to define methods that should be implemented with the same interface across different class hierarchies, we put them in an `interface`. Abstract classes and interfaces provide greater flexibility in controlling polymorphism.

When the compiler can determine the appropriate method to apply to a polymorphic variable, it statically binds the call to the method. If the determination cannot be made until run time, the binding is said to be dynamic. We can use a call to `getClass().getSimpleName()` to determine the class of the object to which a polymorphic variable refers.

Now that you know how to design and implement both derived classes and top-level classes, you are prepared to explore a wide range of useful and general abstractions that computer scientists have identified as fundamental to the development of more advanced algorithms. The remainder of this text primarily examines some of these abstractions and their implementation.

LEARNING / Portfolio

Quick Check

1. Which class is at the top of every hierarchy in Java? (pp. 528–529)

2. What is the mechanism that allows one class to extend another class? (pp. 528–530)

3. What do you call a class that is an extension of another class in the hierarchy? (pp. 528–530)

4. Overriding refers to _____ methods; hiding refers to fields and _____ methods. (pp. 532–534)

5. What kinds of members are not inherited by a derived class? (pp. 530–532)

6. What is an operation that has multiple meanings depending on the object to which it is applied? (pp. 551–552)

7. Are constructors inherited? (pp. 530–532)

8. A reference to an instance of a _____ class can be assigned to a variable of its _____ class. (pp. 551–552)

9. Explain the meaning of the keyword `extends`. (pp. 529–530)

10. What do we call the rules that determine where in a program an identifier can be recognized? (p. 541)

11. Which keyword refers to a class's superclass? (p. 537)

12. Which keyword allows an object to refer to itself? (pp. 533–534)

13. In a UML diagram, in which direction does the triangular arrow point to indicate inheritance? (pp. 528–529)

14. Can an abstract class be instantiated? (pp. 552–554)

15. An `interface` can contain variable declarations. (True or False?) (pp. 554–556)

16. When does dynamic binding occur? (p. 556)

Answers

1. `Object` 2. Inheritance 3. Derived class or subclass 4. instance; class 5. `private` 6. Polymorphic operation 7. Constructors are not inherited. 8. derived; super 9. `extends` tells the compiler the class from which this class is being derived. 10. Scope rules 11. `super` 12. `this` 13. From the subclass to its superclass 14. No 15. False 16. At run time

Exam Preparation Exercises

1. **a.** Which kind of scope rules (internal or external) determine accessibility between classes?

   b. Do both internal and external scope depend on the access modifiers of an identifier?

   c. Define internal scope.

   d. What are the two exceptions that apply to internal access of members?

   e. What is shadowing?

   f. Is it legal to define local variables with the same identifier in the same block?

2. Name the three external places from which Java allows class members to be accessed.

3. **a.** List the names of the four levels of external access for class members.

   b. Which of the four levels is the default access?

   c. From where can a `public` member be accessed?

   d. From where can a member with no access modifier be accessed?

   e. From where can a `private` member be accessed?

   f. From where can a `protected` member be accessed?

4. **a.** Which non-`public` members are inherited by a subclass within the same package?

   b. Which non-`public` members are inherited by a subclass in a different package?

5. What happens if you forget to include a constructor in a new class?

6. **a.** If a class contains an abstract method, is it automatically an abstract class?

   b. What does a subclass of an abstract method have to do to avoid also being abstract?

7. To which class can all Java objects trace themselves back?

8. Which modifier of a class or field indicates that it is incomplete and that its details must be filled in by a derived class?

9. What does the inheritance mechanism allow one class to acquire from another?

10. What do you call the class that is extended by a derived class?

11. When we examine a subclass class, we have access to more than just the methods and fields defined in the class. Explain.

12. What happens if a derived class defines an instance method with the same form of heading as a method in its superclass?

13. What happens if a derived class defines a field with the same name as a field in the superclass?

14. Distinguish between overriding and hiding.

15. Is it possible to remove a member that is inherited?

16. Overloading, overriding, and hiding are similar, yet different. Fill in the following table showing whether the sentence describes overloading, overriding, or hiding.

Situation	Hiding	Overriding	Overloading	Shadowing
a. A class method has the same name and signature as a superclass method				
b. An instance method has the same name and signature as a superclass instance method				
c. A class has two methods with the same name but different signatures				
d. A field in a derived class has the same name as a field in its superclass				
e. An instance method has the same name but a different signature than a superclass instance method				
f. A method declares a variable with the same name as a field in the class				
g. A method has a parameter with the same name as a field in the class				

17. Which parts of a superclass cannot be inherited?

18. Why can't you assign a value directly to `this`?

19. What does a method call to `this()` do?

20. Explain the difference between static binding and dynamic binding.

Programming Warm-Up Exercises

1. Declare three constructors with different signatures for a class called `MyClass`.

2. Fill in the blanks in the documentation in the following code segment.

```
public class MyName extends YourName
{
  int myField;                  // myField is an _____field
  public MyName(int myField)    // _____ with a parameter
                                // that shadows the _____ _____

  {
    this.myField = myField;     // Assign the _____ to
                                // the _____ field

  }
}
```

3. **a.** What is the signature of a method?

   b. What happens if a class does not have a constructor?

   c. What must be the first statement in every constructor?

4. **a.** Write the heading for an integer class method **someMethod** that should be accessible to the classes in its own package but not to derived classes in other packages.

   b. Write the heading for an integer class method **someMethod** that should be accessible only to other methods in the class.

   c. Write the heading for a character class method **someMethod** that should be accessible to classes in the package and any derived classes in other packages.

5. **a.** Write the heading for a **void** instance method **someMethod** that can be accessed from anywhere.

   b. Write the heading for an integer instance method **someMethod** that should be accessible to the classes in the same package, but that prohibits overriding by subclasses.

   c. Write the heading for an integer instance method **someMethod** that can be used anywhere, but cannot be overridden by subclasses.

6. Is the following code segment correct? If so, to what does each reference to **var** refer?

```
public class SomeClass
{
  int var;                      // Class member var
  final int CONST = 3;          // Class member CONST
  public void someMethod(int param)
  {
    int var;
    var = param * CONST;
    final int CONST = 10;
    var = 5;
    System.out.println("" + this.var);
  }
}
```

7. Examine the following constructor headings and give the signature for each.

```
public someClass()
public someClass(int a)
public someClass(double a)
public someClass(String a, int b, double c)
```

8. Examine the following method headings and give the signature for each. Could methods with these signatures all be declared within one class?

```
public int someMethod()
public void someMethod()
public double someMethod()
public double someMethod(int a)
public double someMethod(String a)
public double someMethod(int a, int b)
```

9. Are these code segments correct? If not, why not?

a.
```
public double taxRate = 29.3;
public double myRate = taxRate*1.1;
```

b.
```
public double myRate = taxRate*1.1;
public double taxRate = 29.3;
```

10. Write a statement that calls the default constructor for the superclass from within a derived class.

11. Write a statement that calls the constructor with the signature `MyClass(int, int, int)` from within the default constructor for the class, passing it the arguments 1, 2, 3.

12. Write an abstract class, called `Simple`, that has a default constructor and an abstract `toString` method.

13. Write an interface that has one method, `equals`, which performs an equality comparison between two objects and returns a `boolean` result.

14. Write a statement that displays the name of the class of the object to which the variable `myObject` refers.

Programming Problems

1. Extend the `Address` class from our `utility` package with a `BusinessAddress` class that adds a company name attribute and a department attribute. Like the existing `Address` class, the new class will be immutable and merely provide constructors, observers for its attributes, and `toString`. Write a driver that tests the new class.

2. Write an application that allows the user to enter a series of regular or business addresses, which are written as objects (using the `Address` class and the subclass defined in

Problem 1) onto a file. Write a second application that reads in the addresses from the file and prints properly formatted mailing labels on a `PrintWriter` file.

3. Write an application that takes a series of name and phone number pairs from the user and stores them as objects on a file. Define an `Entry` class that contains a name–number pair for this purpose. Use the `Name` and `Phone` classes from our `utility` package. You must decide whether to add `Entry` to the `utility` package or to keep it in the default package. Write a second application that allows a user to enter a last name, a first name, both, or neither, and then displays all of the entries on the file that match the entered values. To facilitate the comparison, you should extend the `Name` class with a subclass containing a Boolean method that tests whether a partial name matches a complete name.

4. Create a class derived from the `Name` class that includes attributes for title (such as Dr. or Ms.), a suffix (such as M.D. or Jr.), a second middle name, and a nickname, and add the new class to the `utility` package. Write an application that allows the user to enter this information for a series of people, storing the extended `Name` objects on a file. Write a second application that reads the values from the file and prints out a form letter that uses the full name and the nickname. You can make up the subject and content of the letter. Be sure that your class properly handles the cases where the name does not include a title or suffix.

Case Study Follow-Up

1. Write a test plan for `UpdateAddressBook2` and implement it.

2. Add support to `UpdateAddressBook2` and `UserInterface` to enable the user to update the name and address.

3. Change `UpdateAddressBook2` so that the user can examine and update any number of entries before quitting the application.

4. Extend the `Address` class with a `BusinessAddress` subclass as described in Programming Problem 1. Change the `BusinessEntry` class of the case study so that it uses the new class instead of `Address`.

5. Given the changes in Exercise 4, add support to `UpdateAddressBook` for updating a `BusinessAddress`.

6. Extend `Phone` with an `InternationalPhone` subclass that has a country code, and extend `Address` with a subclass called `InternationalAddress` that provides a country attribute. Create a concrete subclass of `Entry`, called `InternationalEntry`, that uses these two new subclasses.

7. Given the new classes developed in Exercise 6, add support to `UpdateAddressBook2` and `UserInterface` to support the third kind of entry.

Array-Based Lists

Goals

Knowledge Goals

To:
- Understand the list abstraction and basic list operations
- Recognize the difference between an array and a list
- Understand how to use an array to represent a list
- Know how to use a key to establish the order of a sorted list
- Understand the principle of "divide and conquer" as expressed in the binary search algorithm

Skill Goals

To be able to:
- Add an item to a list
- Remove an item from a list
- Search for an item in a list
- Sort the items in a list into ascending or descending order
- Build a list in sorted order
- Search for an item in a sorted list using a linear search
- Search for an item using a binary search
- Define a class that extends a Java `interface`
- Use Java's `Comparable` interface
- Use `ArrayList` from the Java library

1979
Cellular phone systems are developed and tested in Tokyo and Chicago

1980
IBM chooses to use PC-DOS, an operating system created by the little-known company Microsoft, for its new PC

1980
Jean Ichbiah is instrumental in the development of the programming language Ada, released on December 10, 1980, the anniversary of Ada Lovelace's birthday

1980
Based on his program Vulcan, Wayne Ratliff develops dBase II, the original PC database program

1981
IBM creates a PC and does not patent the architecture, leaving the door open for competition

1982
Columbia Data Products develops its own PC, modeled after IBM's

Introduction

Chapter 9 introduced the array, a structured reference type that holds a collection of components of the same type or class. Typically, a one-dimensional array holds a list of items. We all know intuitively what a "list" is. Indeed, in our everyday lives, we use lists all the time—grocery lists, lists of things to do, lists of addresses, lists of party guests. In computer applications, lists are very useful and popular ways to organize the data. In this chapter, we examine algorithms that build and manipulate a list implemented using a one-dimensional array to hold the items.

1982
AutoCAD, a computer-assisted design software package, is released by Autodesk

1982
John Warnock and Charles Geschke found Adobe Systems Inc., and develop software to improve the relationship between the PC and the printer

1982
Time magazine selects the computer as its "Man of the Year" signifying the incredible growing impact of computer technology on society

1982
Commercial e-mail service is up and running in 25 cities

1983
Lotus 1-2-3, one of the most important early applications for the IBM PC, integrates graphics with the spreadsheet, like VisiCalc did for the Apple II.

1983
DARPA (Defense Advanced Research Projects Agency) makes TCP/IP the primary Internet protocol, setting the framework for a globally connected network

11.1 : What Is a List?

From a logical point of view, a list is a homogeneous collection of elements, where a **linear relationship** exists between elements. Here "linear" means that, at the logical level, every element in the list except the first one has a unique predecessor, and every element except the last one has a unique successor.[1] The number of items in the list, which we call the **length** of the list, is a property of a list. That is, every list has a length. Java calls this value `size`, rather than length.

Lists can be **unsorted**—their elements may be placed into the list in no particular order—or they can be **sorted** in a variety of ways. For instance, a list of numbers can be sorted by value, a list of strings can be sorted alphabetically, and a list of addresses could be sorted by ZIP code. When the elements in a sorted list are of composite types, one of the members of the structure, called the **key** member, determines their logical (and often physical) order. For example, a list of students on a class roll may be sorted alphabetically by name or numerically by student identification number. In the first case, the name is the key; in the second case, the identification number is the key. (See Figure 11.1.)

If a list cannot contain items with duplicate keys, we say that it has unique keys. (See Figure 11.2.) This chapter deals with both unsorted lists and lists of elements with unique keys, sorted from smallest to largest key value. The items on the list can be of any type, atomic or composite. In the following discussion, "item," "element," and "component" are synonyms; they refer to what is stored in the list. As we see in Chapter 12, Java provides several list classes in its library. To be consistent with those classes, in this chapter we'll sometimes use method names that are different from the more general terminology. For example, Java uses `size` as the name of the method that returns the length of a list.

Linear relationship Every element except the first has a unique predecessor, and every element except the last has a unique successor

Length (size in Java) The number of items in a list; it can vary over time

Unsorted list A list in which data items are placed in no particular order with respect to their content; the only relationships between data elements consist of the list predecessor and successor relationships

Sorted list A list whose predecessor and successor relationships are determined by the content of the keys of the items in the list; a semantic relationship exists among the keys of the items in the list

Key A member of a class whose value is used to determine the logical and/or physical order of the items in a list

Client Software that declares and manipulates objects of a particular class

11.2 : A List Class

In this section, we will design and implement a general-purpose class that represents a list of items. Let's think in terms of a to-do list. Before we begin to brainstorm, however, we must ask an important question: For whom are we designing the class? We may be designing the class for ourselves to keep in our library of classes. Alternatively, we may be designing it for others to use in a team project. When we create a class, the software that uses it is called the **client** of the class. In our discussion, we will use the terms "client" and "user" interchangeably, as we sometimes think of them as referring to the people who are writing the software that uses the class, rather than the software itself.

---

1. At the implementation level, a relationship also exists between the elements, but the physical relationship may not be the same as the logical one.

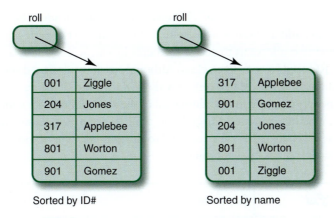

FIGURE 11.1   List Sorted by Two Different Keys

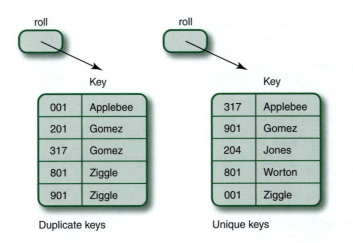

FIGURE 11.2   List with Duplicate Keys and List with Unique Keys

■ Brainstorming

Because we are designing a general-purpose class, our brainstorming must be more speculative. We don't have a specific problem to solve; instead, we have to think in terms of what we currently do with our to-do lists as well as what other things we might like to do if we could. Ideally, we will start with an empty list each morning and add things to it. Of course, there may also be unfinished items remaining from the previous day. As we accomplish a task on the list, we will cross it off. We will check whether an item is already on the list. We will check whether we can add one more item to the list. We will check whether the list is empty (we wish!). We will ask how many items we have left to do. We will go through the list one item at a time.

Let's translate these observations into responsibilities for the list, in the form of a CRC card. Notice that constructors are obvious because they are prefaced by "create," whereas observers are identified by "get" or "is". Likewise, the choice of identifier for transformers gives their type away: add and remove. Note that this is our first experience with using an iterator, an operation that allows us to access the items in a structure one at a time.

Here is the CRC card for our `List` class. Although we have designed our CRC card for a to-do list, the responsibilities outlined remain valid for any kind of list. For example, if we are creating a list of people to invite to a wedding, all of these operations are valid. We add names to the list, check whether a name is already on the list, count the names on the list, check whether the list is full (that is, the length is equal to the number of invitations bought), remove names, and review the names one at a time.

Class Name: *List*	Superclass:	Subclasses:
Responsibilities	Collaborations	
Create(maxItems)		
Is list full? return Boolean		
Is list empty? return Boolean		
Get length. return int		
Is an item in the list? return Boolean		
Add item to the list (item)		
Remove item from the list (item)		
Set up for iteration		
Has next? return Boolean		
Get next item. return item		

To make the rest of the discussion more concrete, let's assume that the items on the list are strings. Later, we will see how the items can be made more general.

■ Refining Responsibilities

Let's go back through the responsibilities, refining them, and converting them into method headings. Because we are designing a general-purpose class, we will consider simplified scenarios that exemplify how we believe the class may be employed. Because the class is intended for widespread use, we should pay special attention to the documentation beginning at the design stage.

The observers, which test for full and empty lists, and returning the number of items, need no further discussion, other than to note that the Get length responsibility in the CRC card becomes a method called `size` to be consistent with Java class library uage. Here are their method headings:

```
public boolean isFull()
// Returns true if no room to add a component; false otherwise
```

```
public boolean isEmpty()
// Returns true if no components in the list; false otherwise
```

```
public int size()
// Returns the number of components in the list
```

The observer that checks whether an item is in the list must take the item as a parameter. Calling this method isThere would make sense, but we use the identifier contains instead because, once again, this terminology is consistent with Java usage.

```
public boolean contains(String item)
// Returns true if item is in the list; false otherwise
```

In designing the transformers, we must make some decisions. For example, will we allow duplicates in our list? This choice has implications for both removing items and adding items. If we allow duplicates, what do we mean by "removing an item"? Do we remove just one copy of the item or all of them? Because this chapter focuses on algorithms, for now we just make a decision and design our algorithms to fit it. We will examine the effects of other choices in the exercises.

Let's allow only one copy of an item in the list. This decision means that deleting an item removes just one copy. But do we assume that the item to be removed is in the list? Is it an error if it is not? Or does the remove operation mean "remove, if there"? Let's use the last meaning.

We now incorporate these decisions into the documentation for the method headings.

```
public void add(String item)
// Adds item to the list
// Assumption:  item is not already in the list
```

```
public void remove(String item)
// item is removed from the list if present
```

The iterator allows the user to see each item in the list one at a time. Let's call the method that implements the "Get next item" responsibility next. The list must keep track of the next item to return when the iterator is called. It does so with a state variable that records the position of the next item to be returned. The constructor initializes this position to 0, and it is incremented in next. The client could use the length of the list to control a loop. An alternative approach is to provide an observer hasNext that asks if there is another item in the list that has not been seen. Let's use this second approach and explore the first approach in the exercises. Because invoking next when hasNext is false causes an error, our documentation must make explicit our assumption that there is an item to be accessed when next is called. In an actual application, we might need a transformer iterator that goes through the list applying an operation to each item; for our general discussion here, we simply provide an observer iterator.

What happens if a user adds or removes an item in the middle of an iteration? Nothing good, you can be sure! Depending on whether an addition or deletion occurs before or after the iteration point, our iteration loop could end up skipping or repeating items.

We have several choices for how we handle this possibly dangerous situation: The list can throw an exception, reset the current position when adding or deleting an item, or disallow transformer operations while an iteration is taking place. We choose the latter option here by identifying this assumption in the documentation. In case the user wants to restart an iteration, let's provide a `resetList` method that reinitializes the current position.

```
public void resetList()
// The current position is reset

public boolean hasNext()
// Returns true if there is another item to be returned; false
// otherwise

public String next()
// Assumptions:  No transformers are called during the iteration.
// There is an item to be returned; that is, hasNext is true when
// this method is invoked
```

■ A Sample Scenario

Before moving on to the implementation phase, let's consider a scenario that illustrates how we might use `next`. Suppose the client code wants to print out the items in the list. The client application cannot directly access the list items, but it can use `next` to iterate through the list. The following code fragment prints the string values in `list`:

```
while (list.hasNext())
  System.out.println(list.next());   // Print current item and advance to next
                                      // item
```

Why do we call this method `next` and not `getNext`, which would follow the Java use of "get" as a prefix for an observer method? Java makes an exception to the "get" prefix when referring to the next item in a collection of items. Recall that the `Scanner` class uses `next`, `nextInt`, and so forth, rather than `getNext` or `getNextInt`. Thus we will conform to the Java naming convention here.

Now we must review the CRC card and see whether we need to add any responsibilities. For example, do we need to provide an equals test? If we want to perform a deep comparison of two lists, we must provide equals; however, comparing lists is not a particularly useful operation, and we have provided the client with the tools needed to write a comparison operation if necessary. In fact, here is the algorithm to compare two lists. It determines whether the sizes match; if they do, it iterates through the lists checking whether corresponding items are the same.

```
boolean isDuplicate

if sizes are not the same
  return false
else
  Set same to true
  while they are still the same AND more items
    Set same to result of seeing if list1.next.compareTo(list2.next) is 0
return same
```

We can implement this algorithm without having to know anything about the list. We just use the instance methods supplied in the interface.

```java
private boolean isDuplicate(List list1, List list2)
// Returns true if the lists are identical
{
  boolean same = true;                    // True if lists are equal
  if (list1.size() != list2.size())       // Number of items is not the same
    return false;
  else
  {
    list1.resetList();                     // Set up for iteration
    list2.resetList();
    while (list1.hasNext() && same)
      same = list1.next().compareTo(list2.next()) == 0;
  }
  return same;
}
```

This method was included in the following driver, which was run twice with two different versions of `list1.dat`. We can write this driver without knowing anything about the list's implementation. All we have to do is `import` the package `list`, where the class `List` is stored.

```java
import list.*;
import java.io.*;
public class ListDriver
{
  public static void main(String[] args) throws IOException
  {
    Scanner inFile;
    Scanner inFile2;
    inFile = new Scanner(new FileReader("list1.dat"));
    inFile2 = new Scanner(new FileReader("list2.dat"));
    // Instantiate the lists
    List list1 = new List(20);
    List list2 = new List(20);
    String line;      // Used for reading input
    // Read values and add into lists
    while (inFile.hasNextLine())
      list1.add(inFile.nextLine());
    while (inFile2.hasNextLine())
      list2.add(inFile2.nextLine());
    if (isDuplicate(list1, list2))
      System.out.println("Lists are the same.");
    else
      System.out.println("Lists are not the same.");
    inFile.close();
    inFile2.close();
  }
  private boolean isDuplicate(List list1, List list2)
  // Returns true if the lists are identical
  { . . . }
}
```

Result from the first run:

`Lists are the same.`

Result from the second run:

`Lists are not the same.`

Now we are ready to choose an internal representation, code the algorithms, and test the implementation.

Attributes   How will we represent the items in the list? As mentioned previously, we are assuming that the items are strings, so an array of strings is the obvious answer. What other data fields do we need? We need to keep track of the number of items in our list, and we need a state variable that tells us where we are in the list during an iteration. Because we are creating a concrete implementation where the items on the list are `String` objects, let's call the class `ListOfStrings`. The same CRC card interface could be implemented using integers, real numbers, or any class that provides a `compareTo` method.

```
public class ListOfStrings
{
  // Data fields
  protected String[] listItems;   // Array to hold list items
  protected int numItems;         // Number of items in the list
  protected int currentPos;       // State variable for iteration
  ...
}
```

In Chapter 9, we introduced the concept of subarray processing. At that time, we pointed out that every Java array object has a final field called `length` that contains the number of components defined for the array object. The literature for lists uses the identifier "length" to refer to the number of items that have been put into the list; Java uses "size" for the same identifier. Faced with this ambiguity in terminology, we still talk about the length of the list, but we use `size` as the name of the method that returns this value. We refer to the field that contains the number of items in the list as `numItems`.

It is very important to understand the distinction made between the array object that contains the list items and the list itself. The array object is `listItems[0]..listItems[listItems.length - 1]`; the items in the list are `listItems[0]..listItems[numItems - 1]`. Figure 11.3 illustrates

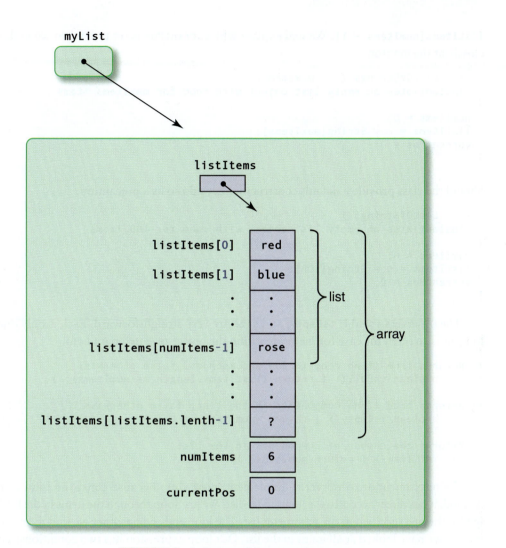

FIGURE 11.3 An Instance of Class `ListOfStrings`

this distinction. In the figure, six items are stored in the list, which was originally instantiated with the following statement:

```
ListOfStrings myList = new ListOfStrings(10);
```

■ Responsibility Algorithms

As Figure 11.3 shows, the list exists in the array elements `listItems[0]` through `listItems[numItems - 1]`. To create an empty list, it is sufficient to set the `numItems` field to 0. We do not need to store any special values into the data array to make the list empty, because the list algorithms process only those values stored in `listItems[0]` through `listItems[numItems - 1]`. We will explain why `currentPos` is set to 0 when we look more closely at the iterator.

```java
public ListOfStrings (int maxItems)
// Instantiates an empty list object with room for maxItems items
{
  numItems = 0;
  listItems = new String[maxItems];
  currentPos = 0;
}
```

Should the class provide a default constructor? Let's do so as a precaution.

```java
public ListOfStrings()
// Instantiates an empty list object with room for 100 items
{
  numItems = 0;
  listItems = new String[100];
  currentPos = 0;
}
```

The observers `isFull`, `isEmpty`, and `size` are very straightforward. Each is only one line long, as is so often the case for methods within the object-oriented paradigm.

```java
// Returns true if no room to add a component; false otherwise
public boolean isFull() { return (listItems.length == numItems); }

// Returns true if no components in the list; false otherwise
public boolean isEmpty() { return (numItems == 0); }

// Returns the number of components in the list
public int size() { return numItems; }
```

We have one more observer to implement: `contains`. Because `contains` is an instance method, it has direct access to the items in the list. We just loop through the items in the list looking for the one specified in the parameter list. The loop ends when either we find the matching item or we have looked at all items in the list. Our loop expression has two conditions: The index is within the list, and the corresponding list item is not equal to the one for which we are searching. After exiting the loop, we return the assertion that the index is still within the list. If this assertion is `true`, then the search item was found.

---

boolean contains

Set index to 0
while more to examine and item not found
    Increment index
return (index is within the list)

We can code this algorithm directly into Java, using the `compareTo` method of class `String`:

```java
public boolean contains(String item)
// Returns true if item is in the list; false otherwise
{
  int index = 0;
  while (index < numItems && listItems[index].compareTo(item) != 0)
    index++;
  return (index < numItems);
}
```

This algorithm is called a *sequential* or *linear search* because we start at the beginning of the list and look at each item in sequence. We halt the search as soon as we find the item we are seeking (or when we reach the end of the list, at which point we conclude that the desired item is not in the list). We can use this algorithm in any application requiring a list search. In the form shown, it searches a list of `String` components; however, the algorithm actually works for any class that has a `compareTo` method.

Let's look again at the heading for the operation that puts an item into the list:

```java
public void add(String item)
// Adds item to the list
// Assumption:  item is not already in the list
```

Does anything in the documentation say where each new item should go? No, this is an un-sorted list. Where we put each new item is up to the implementer. In this case, let's put each new item in the easiest place to reach: the next free slot in the array. Therefore, we can store a new item into `listItems[numItems]` and then increment `numItems`.

This algorithm brings up a question: Do we need to check whether the list has room for the new item? We have two choices. The **add** method can test `numItems` against `listItems.length` and throw an exception if there isn't room, or we can let the client code perform this test before calling **add**. Our documentation is incomplete because it does not specify what occurs in this situation. A third option is to test for `isFull` and leave the list unchanged if the list is full. Let's use this option. The client can check before the call if he or she wishes to do something else in this situation.

This algorithm is so simple that we just go directly to code.

```java
public void add(String item)
// Adds item to the list
// Assumptions:  item is not already in the list.
// If the list is not full, puts item in the
// list; otherwise, list is unchanged
{
  if (!isFull())
  {
    listItems[numItems] = item;
    numItems++;
  }
}
```

Removing a component from a list consists of two parts: finding the item and removing it from the list. We can use the same algorithm we used for `contains` to look for the item. We know from the documentation that the item may or may not be in the list. If we find the item, how do we remove it? We shift each item that comes after the one being removed forward by one array slot.

---

remove

> Set index to location of item to be removed if found
> `if` found
>   Shift remainder of list up
> Decrement numItems

---

shiftUp

> (index is the location of the item to be removed)
> `for` count going from index through numItems − 2
>   Set listItems[count] to listItems[count + 1]

```java
public void remove(String item)
// Removes item from the list if it is there
// Implements "remove, if there" semantics
{
  int index = 0;
  boolean found = false;
  while (index < numItems && !found)
  {
    if (listItems[index].compareTo(item) == 0)
      found = true;
    else
      index++;
  }
  if (found)
  {
    for (int count = index; count < numItems-1; count++)
      listItems[count] = listItems[count+1];
    numItems--;
  }
}
```

The `resetList` method is analogous to the open operation for a file in which the file pointer is positioned at the beginning of the file, so that the first input operation accesses the first component of the file. Each successive call to an input operation gets the next item in the file. Therefore `resetList` must initialize `currentPos` to the first item in the list. Where is the first item in an array-based list? In position `0`. The `next` operation is analogous to an input operation; it accesses the current item and then increments `currentPos`.

We mentioned earlier that we must keep the client from performing deletions and additions during an iteration. Let's review how methods within a class might interact to change the state of the list and, therefore, cause problems. In Chapter 3, we discussed the concept of mutable and immutable objects. Clearly, a `ListOfStrings` object is a mutable object, because transformer methods are defined for it. That is, `resetList` changes the state variable `currentPos`.

The **add** and **remove** methods change not only the contents of the list structure, but also the state variable **numItems**. Likewise, **next** changes the internal state of **currentPos**.

We need to monitor the interactions of these transformers carefully. If **currentPos** is reset during successive calls to **next**, the iteration just begins again. If **add** or **remove** is invoked during an iteration, however, several things could happen. For example, **currentPos** could now be greater than **numItems**, causing **next** to send back an item that is no longer in the list. To solve this problem of interacting transformers, we have chosen to place a precondition on the method **next**: No transformer methods have been called since the last call to **next**.

```
// The iteration is initialized by setting currentPos to 0
public void resetList() { currentPos = 0; }

// Returns true if there is another item in the list; false otherwise
public boolean hasNext() { return (currentPos != numItems); }

public String next()
// Returns the item at the currentPos position
// Assumptions:  No transformers are called during the iteration
// There is an item to be returned; that is, hasNext returns true
{
  String next = listItems[currentPos];
  currentPos++;
  return next;
}
```

Both of the methods change **currentPos**. Shouldn't we consider them to be transformers? We could certainly argue that they are, but their intention is to set up an iteration through the items in the list, returning one item at a time to the client.

Here is the UML diagram for class **ListOfStrings**. The UML symbol for protected attributes is the hash mark (#).

ListOfStrings
#listItems: String()   #numItems: int   #currentPos: int
+ListOfStrings()   +ListOfStrings(maxItems: int)   +isFull(): boolean   +isEmpty(): boolean   +size(): int   +contains(): boolean   +add(item: String)   +remove(item: String)   +resetList(): void   +hasNext(): boolean   +next(): String

■ Test Driver

Our usual procedure is to create a test plan and then write a driver to carry out the test plan. This time, we will write the driver first. How can that be? We will write a *command-driven* test driver. That is, we will enter commands from the keyboard telling the program which operations to execute. We can write a test driver within the context of our to-do list. Because our to-do list is surely an ongoing list, we'll keep it in a text file. As a consequence of that decision, the first thing our driver does is to read in the current list from a file. We then set up a menu with the methods to be tested, much like the interface used in the case study in Chapter 10. The last step is to write the changed list to a file. This is a slightly more elaborate test driver than we have used before, but will serve as a model for test drivers in the future.

Let's call our driver class `ToDoList`. We must define an enumerated type to represent the operations to be tested. Because this type will be used only within this driver, we can declare it within the class.

```
enum Operations {ADD, REMOVE, SIZE, ISEMPTY, ISFULL, CONTAINS, PRINT, QUIT}
```

We need a method `inOperation` that prompts for and reads in strings and converts them to `Operations`. We can use the same algorithm that we used in the case study in Chapter 8. The top-level algorithm for the driver is summarized below.

Main

Read file into list
Set operation to inOperation()
Set keepGoing to true
while
    Execute operation
    Set operation to inOperation
Write list to file

fileToList

while toDoFile.hasNext()
    list.add(toDoFile.nextLine())

listToFile

while (list.hasNext())
    toDoFileSave.println(list.next())

executeOperation

switch (operation)
    case ADD :
        Print "Enter item to add."
        Set item to in.nextLine()
        if !list.contains(item)
            list.add(item)

executeOperation (continued)

```
        case REMOVE:
            Print "Enter item to remove."
            Set item to in.nextLine()
            list.remove(item)
        case SIZE:
            Print "Length of list is " + list.size()
        case ISEMPTY:
            if list.isEmpty()
                    Print "List is empty."
            else    Print "List is not empty."
        case ISFULL:
            if list.isFull()
                    Print "List is full."
            else    Print "List is not full."
        case CONTAINS:
            Print "Enter item to check."
            Set item to in.nextLine()
            if list.contains(item)
                    Print item + " is in the list."
            else    Print item + " is not in the list."
        case PRINT:
            Print "The to-do list contains the following items."
            while list.hasNext()
                    Print list.next()
        case QUIT:
            Set keepGoing to false
```

Here is the code for class `ToDoList`, the driver for class `ListOfStrings`:

```java
//*************************************************************************
// Class ToDoList is the driver for class ListOfStrings
//*************************************************************************
import java.io.*;
import java.util.*;

public class ToDoList
{
  public static void main (String[] args)
    throws IllegalArgumentException, FileNotFoundException
  {
    Scanner toDoFile = new Scanner(new FileReader("toDoList"));
    Scanner in = new Scanner(System.in);
    Operations operation;
    String item;
    boolean keepGoing = true;
    ListOfStrings list = new ListOfStrings(4);
    while (toDoFile.hasNext())
      list.add(toDoFile.nextLine());
```

```java
        toDoFile.close();
        operation = inOperation(in);
        while (keepGoing)
        {
          switch (operation)
          {
            case ADD:
                System.out.println("Enter item to add.");
                item = in.nextLine();
                if (!list.contains(item))
                  list.add(item);
                break;
            case REMOVE:
                System.out.println("Enter item to remove.");
                item = in.nextLine();
                list.remove(item);
                break;
            case SIZE:
                System.out.println("Length of list is " + list.size());
                break;
            case ISEMPTY:
                if (list.isEmpty())
                  System.out.println("List is empty.");
                else
                  System.out.println("List is not empty.");
                break;
            case ISFULL:
                if (list.isFull())
                  System.out.println("List is full.");
                else
                  System.out.println("List is not full.");
                break;
            case CONTAINS:
                System.out.println("Enter item to check.");
                item = in.nextLine();
                if (list.contains(item))
                  System.out.println(item + " is in the list.");
                else
                  System.out.println(item + " is not in the list.");
                break;
            case PRINT:
                System.out.println("The to-do list contains the following
                                    items:");
                list.resetList();
                while (list.hasNext())
                  System.out.println(list.next());
                break;
            case QUIT:
                keepGoing = false;
                break;
          }
          if (keepGoing)
            operation  = inOperation(in);
        }
        PrintWriter toDoFileSave = new PrintWriter("toDoList");
        list.resetList();
        while (list.hasNext())
```

```
        toDoFileSave.println(list.next());
    toDoFileSave.close();
}

public static Operations inOperation(Scanner in)
{
    boolean invalidOperation;
    Operations operation = Operations.QUIT;
    do
    {
        System.out.println("Enter the operation you wish "
            + "to apply from the following list:");
        for (Operations command : Operations.values())
            System.out.print(command + " ");
        System.out.println();
        try                          // Read string and convert to enum
        {
            operation = Operations.valueOf(in.nextLine().toUpperCase());
            invalidOperation = false;
        }
        catch (IllegalArgumentException ex)
        // User entered invalid Operation
        {
            invalidOperation = true;
            System.out.println("Invalid operation name entered.");
        }
    }
    while (invalidOperation);    // Try again until Operation is valid
    return operation;
}
}
```

■ Test Plan

The documentation for the methods in the class List identifies the tests necessary for a black-box testing strategy. The code of the methods indicates a need for a clear-box testing strategy. Thus, to test the List class implementation, we use a combination of black-box and clear-box strategies. We first test the constructor by seeing whether the list is empty.

The methods size, add, and remove can be tested together. That is, we add several items and check the length of the list; we remove several items and check the length. How do we know that the add and remove methods work correctly? We iterate through the list using hasNext and next to print out the values. We check the status of the list after a series of additions and deletions. Because we have made the assumption that the items in the list are unique, the test driver invokes contains before each add operation and does not call add if the item is in the list. To test the isFull and isEmpty operations, we must call them both when the list is full and when it is not, and both when it is empty and when it is not. We must also call add when the list is full to confirm that the list remains unchanged.

Do we need to test any special cases for remove and contains? We look first at the end cases—that is, when the item is in the first position in the list, when the item is in the last position in the list, and when the item is the only one in the list. We must verify that remove can correctly remove items in these positions. We must check that contains can find items in these same positions and correctly determine that the items are not in the list.

But what about testing methods `hasNext`, `resetList`, and `next`? They will be tested each time we call the code to print the contents of the list.

Before we run our test driver, we need a detailed test plan. First we create a beginning to-do list:

```
Pick up laundry
Buy milk
Buy flowers
Put gas in the car
```

Below is a test plan. Note that the driver instantiates the list with `maxItems` set to 4 so that we can more easily perform the test that depends on the list being full.

TEST PLAN

Number	Method	Input	Expected Output
1	print	PRINT	The to-do list contains the following items: Pick up laundry Buy milk Buy flowers Put gas in the car
2	size	SIZE	Length of list is 4
3	isFull	ISFULL	List is full.
4	add	ADD Return library book PRINT	The to-do list contains the following items: Pick up laundry Buy milk Buy flowers Put gas in the car
5	contains	Pick up laundry	Pick up laundry is in the list.
6	remove	REMOVE Buy milk REMOVE Buy flowers REMOVE Pick up laundry PRINT	The to-do list contains the following items: Put gas in the car
7	Remove isEmpty	REMOVE Put gas in the car ISEMPTY	List is empty
8	add	ADD Return library book ADD Buy flowers ADD Call home at 3 PRINT	The to-do list contains the following items: Return library book Buy flowers Call home at 3

Here is the output from running the driver according to this plan. To save space, we show only the output, rather than the entire dialog with the user.

Output from Test 1

```
The to-do list contains the following items:
Pick up laundry
Buy milk
Buy flowers
Put gas in the car
```

Output from Test 2

```
Length of list is 4
```

Output from Test 3

```
List is full.
```

Output from Test 4

```
The to-do list contains the following items:
Pick up laundry
Buy milk
Buy flowers
Put gas in the car
```

Output from Test 5

```
Pick up laundry is in the list.
```

Output from Test 6

```
The to-do list contains the following items:
Put gas in the car
```

Output from Test 7

```
List is empty.
```

Output from Test 8

```
The to-do list contains the following items:
Return library book
Buy flowers
Call home at 3
```

SOFTWARE MAINTENANCE CASE STUDY

Software Maintenance in Action: Enhancing Class ListOfStrings with a Sort

Maintenance Task Method **next** presents the items to the user in the order in which they were added. Rearrange the list components so that an iteration presents the items in order.

Solution This task requires some background work. What do we mean by "order"? If the list holds names for wedding invitations, we might want to put the names in alphabetic order. If the list holds **StudentRec** objects (see Chapter 9), we might want to put the names in order by

> **Sorting** Arranging the components of a list into order (for instance, words into alphabetical order or numbers into ascending or descending order)

GPA. Arranging list items into order is a very common operation and is known in software terminology as **sorting**. Clearly, this particular maintenance problem means "alphabetic order" because the items are strings. But let's step back and look at sorting in general before we tackle our specific problem.

If you were given a sheet of paper with a column of 20 names on it and asked to write the names in ascending order, you would probably do the following:

1. Make a pass through the list, looking for the lowest name (the one that comes first alphabetically).
2. Write it on the paper in a second column.
3. Cross the name off the original list.
4. Repeat the process, always looking for the lowest name remaining in the original list.
5. Stop when all names have been crossed off.

We could implement this algorithm as client code, using `next` to go through the list searching for the lowest value. When we found it, we could add it into another list and remove it from the original. However, we would need two lists—one to hold the original list and a second to hold the sorted list. In addition, the client would have destroyed the original list. If the list is large, we might not have enough memory to maintain two copies, even if one is empty. A better solution is to derive a class from `ListOfStrings` that has a sort method that rearranges the values in the list. Because the data fields in `ListOfStrings` are declared as protected, the new class can inherit them. By accessing the values directly within the list, we can avoid maintaining two lists.

Let's call our derived class `ListOfStringsWithSort`. The constructor takes the maximum number of items and calls the `ListOfStrings`'s constructor. None of the other methods needs to be overridden.

Class Name: *ListWithSort*	Superclass: *List*	Subclasses:
Responsibilities	**Collaborations**	
Create itself (maxItems)	super	
Sort the items in the list	String	

Going back to our by-hand algorithm, we can search `listItems` for the smallest value, but how do we "cross off" a list component? We could simulate crossing off a value by replacing it with `null`. In this way, we set the value of the crossed-off item to something that doesn't interfere with the processing of the rest of the components. However, a slight variation of our by-hand algorithm allows us to sort the components *in place*. We do not have to use a second list; we can, instead, put a value into its proper place in the list by having it swap places with the component currently in that list position.

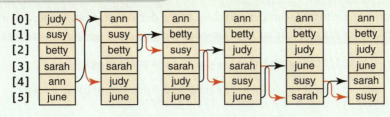

[0]	judy	ann	ann	ann	ann	ann
[1]	susy	susy	betty	betty	betty	betty
[2]	betty	betty	susy	judy	judy	judy
[3]	sarah	sarah	sarah	sarah	june	june
[4]	ann	judy	judy	susy	susy	sarah
[5]	june	june	june	june	sarah	susy

FIGURE 11.4 Straight Selection Sort

We can state this algorithm as follows: We search for the smallest value in the array holding the items and exchange that element with the component in the first position in the array. We search for the next-smallest value in the array and exchange that element with the component in the second position in the array. This process continues until all components are in their proper places.

> **selectSort**
>
> **for** count going from 0 through numItems – 2
>   Find the minimum value in listItems[count]..listItems[numItems – 1]
>   Swap minimum value with listItems[count]

Figure 11.4 illustrates how this algorithm works.

Observe that we perform **numItems – 1** passes through the list because **count** runs from **0** through **numItems – 2**. The loop does not need to be executed when **count** equals **numItems – 1** because the last value, **listItems[numItems – 1]**, is in its proper place after the preceding components have been sorted.

This algorithm, known as the *straight selection sort*, belongs to a class of sorts called *selection sorts*. Many types of sorting algorithms exist. Selection sorts are characterized by their practice of finding the smallest (or largest) value left in the unsorted portion at each iteration and swapping it with the value indexed by the iteration counter. Swapping the contents of two variables requires a temporary variable so that no values are lost (see Figure 11.5).

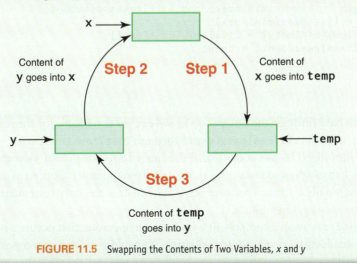

FIGURE 11.5 Swapping the Contents of Two Variables, *x* and *y*

We are now ready to code our derived class. In the documentation, we need to indicate that the alphabetic order may be lost with future additions.

```java
public class ListOfStringsWithSort extends ListOfStrings
{
  // The items in the list can be rearranged into ascending order
  // This order is not preserved in future additions

  public ListOfStringsWithSort()
  { // Default constructor
    super();
  }

  public ListOfStringsWithSort(int maxItems)
  { // Constructor
    super(maxItems);
  }

  public void selectSort()
  // Arranges list items in ascending order;
  //    selection sort algorithm is used
  {
    String temp;              // Temporary variable
    int passCount;            // Loop control variable for outer loop
    int searchIndex;          // Loop control variable for inner loop
    int minIndex;             // Index of minimum so far

    for (passCount = 0; passCount < numItems - 1; passCount++)
    {
      minIndex = passCount;
      // Find the index of the smallest component
      // in listItems[passCount]..listItems[numItems - 1]
      for (searchIndex = passCount + 1; searchIndex < numItems;
           searchIndex++)
        if (listItems[searchIndex].compareTo(listItems[minIndex]) < 0)
          minIndex = searchIndex;
      // Swap listItems[minIndex] and listItems[passCount]
      temp = listItems[minIndex];
      listItems[minIndex] = listItems[passCount];
      listItems[passCount] = temp;
    }
  }
}
```

With each pass through the outer loop in `selectSort`, we look for the minimum value in the rest of the array (`listItems[passCount]` through `listItems[numItems - 1]`). Therefore, `minIndex` is initialized to `passCount` and the inner loop runs from `searchIndex` equal to `passCount + 1` through `numItems - 1`. Upon exit from the inner loop, `minIndex` contains the position of the smallest value. (Because the *if* statement is the only statement in the loop, we do not have to enclose it in a block.)

This method may swap a component with itself, an operation that occurs if no value in the remaining list is smaller than `listItems[passCount]`. We could avoid this unnecessary swap by check-

Original File	Sorted File
red	black
blue	blue
yellow	brown
brown	crimson
black	green
pink	orange
green	pink
orange	red
white	rose
violet	violet
crimson	white
rose	yellow

TABLE 11.1 File Sorting

ing whether `minIndex` is equal to `passCount`. Because this comparison would occur in every iteration of the outer loop, it is more efficient not to check for this possibility and just to swap something with itself occasionally. For example, if our list contains 10,000 elements, then making this comparison adds 10,000 operations to the execution of the loop, yet we might save just a few dozen unnecessary swap operations as a result. Table 11.1 shows an input file and the results of sorting the file.

Our algorithm sorts the components into ascending order. To sort them into descending order, we must scan for the maximum value instead of the minimum value. Simply changing the test in the inner loop from "less than" to "greater than" accomplishes this goal. Of course, in this case `minIndex` would no longer be an appropriate identifier and hence should be changed to `maxIndex`.

Here are the UML diagrams for `ListOfStrings` and `ListOfStringsWithSort`. The triangular arrow shows the inheritance relationship between them.

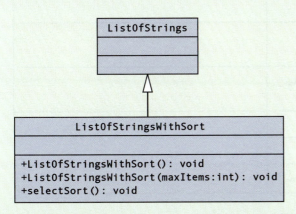

11.3 : A Sorted List

Adding a sorting method to a list does not provide the user with a sorted list class. That is, the **add** and **remove** algorithms do not preserve ordering by value. The **add** operation places a new item at the end of the list, regardless of its value. After sorting a list, the list items remain in sorted order only until the next addition takes place. Of course, the client could sort the list after every addition, but this technique is inefficient. Here we look at a sorted list design in which all of the list operations cooperate to preserve the sorted order of the list components. Keep in mind that a sorted list is just a list in which the items remain sorted by value.

   Once we have a list in sorted order, we can devise more efficient algorithms to search for items in the list. After developing the sorted list algorithms, we look at linear searching in a sorted list and binary searching. Both of these algorithms represent an improvement over the algorithm used in the previous section.

■ Brainstorming

The interface for class **List** as represented in the CRC card says nothing about the order of its items. If we want to keep the list items in sorted order, we need to specify this criterion. Let's go back to the CRC card design for **List** and indicate that we want the list to be sorted.

Class Name: *List*	Superclass:	Subclasses:
Responsibilities	**Collaborations**	
Create(maxItems)		
Is list full? return Boolean		
Is list empty? return Boolean		
Get length. return int		
Is an item in the list? return Boolean		
Add item to the list (item), keeping list sorted		
Remove item from the list (item), keeping list sorted		
Set up for iteration		
Has next? return Boolean		
Get next item in sorted order. return item		

   The first thing we notice is that the observers do not change. They remain the same whether the list is sorted by value or not. The transformers **add** and **remove** and the iterator have new constraints, however. Rather than designing an entirely new class, we can derive `SortedList` from `List`, overriding those methods whose implementations need changing.

Class Name: *SortedList*	Superclass: *List*	Subclasses:
Responsibilities	**Collaborations**	
Create(maxItems)		
Add item to the list (item), keeping list sorted		
Remove item from the list (item), keeping list sorted		
Get next item in sorted order. return item		

■ Responsibility Algorithms

Let's look first at method **add**. Figure 11.6 illustrates how it should work for three different initial states and each possible new arrangement, based on the value being added.

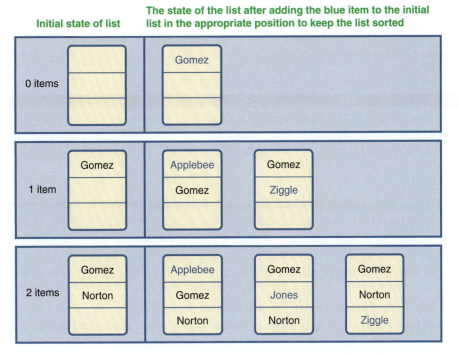

FIGURE 11.6 Different Cases of Adding Items into a List so that Ordering Is Preserved

The first item added into an empty list can go into the first position. Because there is only one item, the list is sorted. If a second item being added is less than the first item, the first item must be moved into the second position and the new item put into the first position. If the second item is larger, it goes into the second position. If we add a third item that is smaller than the first item, the other two items shift down by one and the third item goes into the first position. If the third item is greater than the first item but less than the second, the second item shifts down and the new item goes into the second position. If the third item is greater than the second item, it goes into the third position.

To generalize, we start at the beginning of the list and scan until we find an item greater than the one we are adding. We shift that item and the rest of the items in the list down by one position to make room for the new item. The new item goes in the list at that point.

```
add

if (list is not full)
    while place not found AND more places to look
        if item > current item in the list
            Increment current position
        else
            Place found
    Shift remainder of the list down
    Add item
    Increment numItems
```

Assuming that **index** is the place where item is to be added, the algorithm for shifting the remainder of the list down is as follows:

```
shiftDown

for count going from numItems down to index + 1
    Set listItems[count] to listItems[count − 1]
```

This algorithm is illustrated in Figure 11.7. It is based on how we would accomplish the task by hand. Often, such an adaptation is the best way to solve a problem. However, in this case, further thought reveals a slightly better approach. Notice that we search from the front of the list (people always do), and we shift down from the end of the list upward. We can, in fact, combine the searching and shifting operations by beginning at the *end* of the list.

If **item** is the new item to be added, we can compare **item** to the value in **listItems[numItems - 1]**. If **item** is less, we put **listItems[numItems - 1]** into

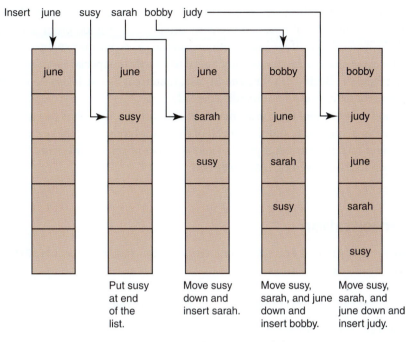

FIGURE 11.7 Adding into a Sorted List

`listItems[numItems]` and compare `item` to the value in `listItems[numItems - 2]`. This process continues until we find the place where `item` is greater than or equal to the list item. We then store `item` directly after it. Here is the algorithm:

```
add (revised)

if (list is not full)
    Set index to numItems – 1
    while index >= 0 && (item.compareTo(listItems[index]) < 0)
        Set listItems[index + 1] to listItems[index]
        Decrement index
    Set listItems[index + 1] to item
    Increment numItems
```

Notice that this algorithm works even if the list is empty. When the list is empty, `numItems` is 0 and the body of the *while* loop is not entered. Thus `item` is stored into `listItems[0]`, and `numItems` is incremented to 1. Does the algorithm work if `item` is the smallest value? What about the largest value? Let's see. If `item` is the smallest value, the loop body executes `numItems` times and `index` is −1. Thus `item` is stored into position 0, where it belongs. If `item` is the largest value, the loop body is not entered. The value of `index` remains `numItems - 1`, so `item` is stored into `listItems[numItems]`, where it belongs.

Are you surprised that the general case also takes care of the special cases? This situation does not always happen, but it occurs sufficiently often that it is good programming practice to start with the general case. If we begin with the special cases, we may still generate a correct solution, but we may not realize that we don't need to handle the special cases separately. Thus we have this guideline: Begin with the general case, then treat as special cases only those situations that the general case does not handle correctly.

The methods **remove** and **next** must maintain the sorted order—but they already do! An item is removed by removing it and shifting all of the items larger than the one removed up by one position; **next** merely returns a copy of an item—it does not change the item. Only **add** needs to be overridden in the derived class **SortedList**.

■ Implementation

Now that we are ready to make our class concrete, we should call it **SortedListOfStrings** and have it inherit from **ListOfStrings**.

```java
public class SortedListOfStrings extends ListOfStrings
{
  public SortedListOfStrings()
  {
    super();
  }
  public SortedListOfStrings(int maxItems)
  {
    super(maxItems);
  }
  public void add(String item)
  // If the list is not full, puts item in its proper place in
  //  the list; otherwise, list is unchanged
  // Assumption:  item is not already in the list
  {
    if (!isFull())
    {
      int index = numItems - 1;            // Loop control variable
      while (index >= 0 && (item.compareTo(listItems[index]) < 0))
      { // Find addition point
        listItems[index+1] = listItems[index];
        index--;
      }
      listItems[index+1] = item;           // Add item
      numItems++;                          // Increment number of items
    }
  }
}
```

Here is the UML diagram that represents this class and its superclass:

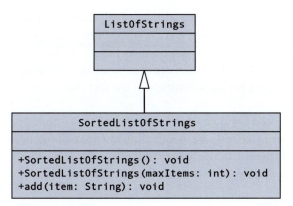

■ Test Plan

We can use the same test plan for the sorted list that we used for the unsorted version of the to-do list. The only difference is that in the expected output, the list items should appear in sorted order. Alternatively, we could use the same input file that was used to test `ListOfStringsWithSort` to test `SortedListOfStrings`.

11.4 ⋮ Searching

In our `SortedListOfStrings` class, we overrode the **add** method—the only method that we had to rewrite to keep the list in sorted order. We found the place to put the item by looking at each successive item until we found where the item belonged. However, if the list is already sorted, we can perform a more efficient search. In this section, we look at two searching algorithms that depend on the list items being in sorted order.

■ Sequential Search

The `contains` algorithm assumes that the list to be searched is unsorted. A drawback to searching an unsorted list is that we must scan the entire list to discover that the search item is *not* present. Think what it would be like if your city telephone book contained people's names in random order rather than alphabetical order. To look up Marcus Anthony's phone number, you would have to start with the first name in the phone book and scan sequentially, page after page, until you found Marcus's name. In the worst case, you might examine tens of thousands of names, only to find out that his name is not in the book.

Of course, telephone books are alphabetized, and the alphabetical ordering makes searching easier. If Marcus Anthony's name is not in the book, you can discover this fact quickly by starting with the A's and stopping the search as soon as you pass the place where his name should be. Although the sequential search algorithm in `contains` works in a sorted list, we can make the algorithm more efficient by taking advantage of the fact that the items are sorted.

How does sequential searching in a sorted list differ from searching in an unordered list? When we search for an item in an unsorted list, we won't discover that the item is missing until we reach the end of the list. If the list is already sorted, we know that an item is missing when we pass the place where it should be in the list. For example, if a list contains the values

becca

bobby

june

phil

robert

tomas

and we are looking for judy, we need simply compare judy with becca, bobby, and june to know that judy is not in the list.

If the search item is greater than the current list component, we move on to the next component. If the item is equal to the current component, we have found the desired element. If the item is less than the current component, then we know that the search item is not in the list. In either of the last two cases, we stop looking. In our original algorithm, the loop conditions stated that the index was within the list and the corresponding list item was not the one sought. In this algorithm, the second condition must be that the item being sought is less than the corresponding list item. However, determining whether the item is found is a little more complex. We must first assert that the index is within the list and, if that is true, assert that the search item is equal to the corresponding list item.

```
contains (in a sorted list)

Set index to 0
while index is within the list AND item is greater than listItems[index]
        Increment index
return (index is within the list AND item is equal to listItems[index])
```

Why can't we just test whether `item` is equal to `listItems[index]` after we exit the loop? This strategy works in all cases except one: if `item` is larger than the last element in the list. In that case, we would exit the loop with `index` equal to `numItems`. Trying to access `listItems[index]` would then cause the code to crash with an "index out of range" error. Therefore, we must check the value of index first.

```
public boolean contains(String item)
// Returns true if item is in the list; false otherwise
// Assumption:  List items are in ascending order
{
  int index = 0;
  while (index < numItems && item.compareTo(listItems[index]) > 0)
    index++;
  return (index < numItems && item.compareTo(listItems[index]) == 0);
}
```

On average, searching a sorted list in this way takes the same number of iterations to find an item as searching an unsorted list. The advantage of this new algorithm is that we find out sooner if an item is missing. Thus the revised algorithm is slightly more efficient. Another search algorithm exists that works only on a sorted list, but it is more complex: a binary search. In this case, the extra complexity is worth the trouble.

■ Binary Search

The binary search algorithm on a sorted list works considerably faster both for finding an item and for discovering that an item is missing. A binary search is based on the principle of successive approximation. The algorithm divides the list in half (divides by 2—that's why it's called a binary search) and decides which half to look in next. Division of the selected portion of the list is repeated until the item is found or it is determined that the item is not present in the list.

This searching method is analogous to the way in which we look up a name in a phone book (or a word in a dictionary). We open the phone book in the middle and compare the desired name with one on the page that we turned to. If the name we're seeking comes before this name, we continue our search in the left-hand section of the phone book. Otherwise, we continue our search in the right-hand section of the phone book. We repeat this process until we find the name. If it is not present, we realize that either we have misspelled the name or our phone book isn't complete. See Figure 11.8 on page 616.

With this approach, we start with the whole list (indexes 0 through `numItems - 1`) and compare our search value to the middle list item. If the search item is less than the middle list item, we continue the search in the first half of the list. If the search item is greater than the middle list item, we continue the search in the second half of the list. Otherwise, we have found a match. We keep comparing and redefining the part of the list in which to look (the search area) until we find the item or the search area is empty.

Let's write the algorithm bounding the search area by the indexes `first` and `last`. Figure 11.9 illustrates the algorithm.

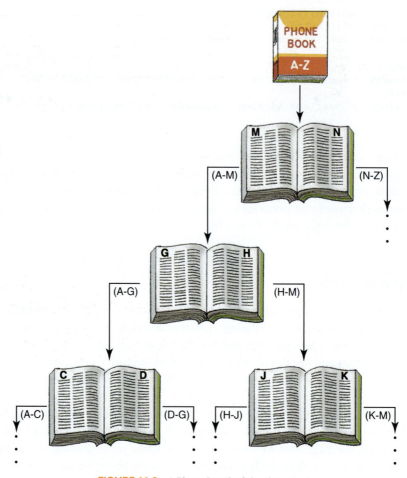

FIGURE 11.8 A Binary Search of the Phone Book

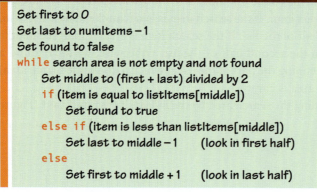

This algorithm should make sense. With each comparison, at best, we find the item for which we are searching; at worst, we eliminate half of the remaining list from consideration.

listItems

[first]   [middle]   [last]

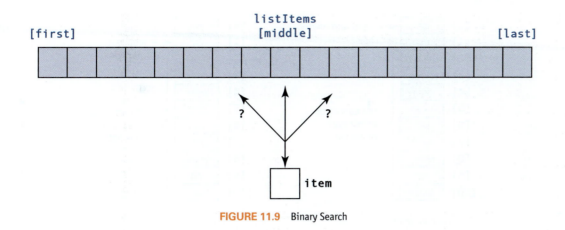

FIGURE 11.9   Binary Search

Before coding this algorithm, we need to determine when the search area is empty. If the search area is between listItems[first] and listItems[last], then the area is empty if last is less than first.

Let's do a walkthrough of the binary search algorithm. The item we are searching for is "bat". Figure 11.10 a shows the values of first, last, and middle during the first iteration. In this iteration, "bat" is compared with "dog", the value in listItems[middle]. Because "bat" is less than (comes before) "dog", last becomes middle – 1 and first stays the same.

Figure 11.10b shows the situation during the second iteration. This time, "bat" is compared with "chicken", the value in listItems[middle]. Because "bat" is less than (comes before) "chicken", last becomes middle – 1 and first again stays the same.

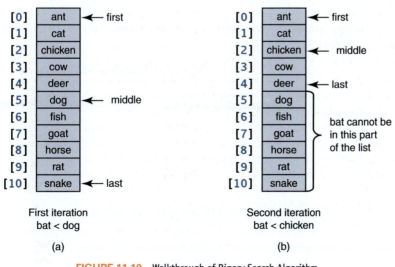

FIGURE 11.10   Walkthrough of Binary Search Algorithm

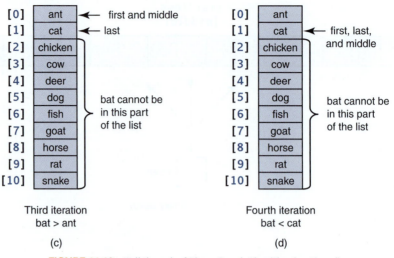

FIGURE 11.10 Walkthrough of Binary Search Algorithm (continued)

In the third iteration (Figure 11.10c), `middle` and `first` are both 0. The item `"bat"` is compared with `"ant"`, the item in `listItems[middle]`. Because `"bat"` is greater than (comes after) `"ant"`, `first` becomes `middle + 1`.

In the fourth iteration (Figure 11.10d), `first`, `last`, and `middle` are all the same. Again, `"bat"` is compared with the item in `listItems[middle]`. Because `"bat"` is less than `"cat"`, `last` becomes `middle - 1`. Now that `last` is less than `first`, the process stops; `found` is `false`.

The binary search is the most complex algorithm that we have examined so far. Table 11.2 shows `first`, `last`, `middle`, and `listItems[middle]` for searches for the items `"fish"`, `"snake"`, and `"zebra"`, using the same data as in the previous example. Examine the results in this table carefully.

Notice in Table 11.2 that no matter whether we searched for `"fish"`, `"snake"`, or `"zebra"`, the loop body never executed more than four times. It never executes more than four times in a list of 11 components because the list is cut in half each time through the loop. The following table compares a sequential search and a binary search in terms of the average number of iterations needed to find an item:

	Average Number of Iterations	
Length	**Sequential Search**	**Binary Search**
10	5.5	2.9
100	50.5	5.8
1,000	500.5	9.0
10,000	5000.5	12.0

If the binary search is so much faster, why not use it all the time? This strategy certainly is faster in terms of the number of times we go through the loop, but it requires more computations within the binary search loop than the other search algorithms do. Thus, if the number

Iteration	first	last	middle	listItems[middle]	Terminating Condition
item : fish					
First	0	10	5	dog	
Second	6	10	8	horse	
Third	6	7	6	fish	found is true
item : snake					
First	0	10	5	dog	
Second	6	10	8	horse	
Third	9	10	9	rat	
Fourth	10	10	10	snake	found is true
item : zebra					
First	0	10	5	dog	
Second	6	10	8	horse	
Third	9	10	9	rat	
Fourth	10	10	10	snake	
Fifth	11	10			last < first

TABLE 11.2 Binary Searching

of components in the list is small (say, fewer than 20), the sequential search algorithms are faster because they perform less work during each iteration. As the number of components in the list increases, the binary search algorithm becomes relatively more efficient.

Here is the code for **contains** that uses the binary search algorithm:

```
public boolean contains(String item)
// Returns true if item is in the list; false otherwise
//    Binary search algorithm is used
// Assumption:  List items are in ascending order
{
  int first = 0;             // Lowest position in search area
  int last = numItems - 1;   // Highest position in search area
  int middle;                // Middle position in search area
  boolean found = false;
  while (last >= first && !found)
  {
    middle = (first + last) / 2;
    if (item.compareTo(listItems[middle]) == 0)
      found = true;
    else if (item.compareTo(listItems[middle]) < 0)
      // item not in listItems[middle]..listItems[last]
      last = middle - 1;
    else
      // item not in listItems[first]..listItems[middle]
      first = middle + 1;
  }
  return found;
}
```

Theoretical Foundations

Complexity of Searching and Sorting

We introduced Big-O notation in Chapter 7 as a way of comparing the work done by different algorithms. Let's apply it to the algorithms that we've developed in this chapter and see how they compare with each other. In each algorithm, we start with a list containing some number of items, N.

In the worst case, the `contains` sequential-search method scans all N components to locate an item. That is, it requires N steps to execute. On average, `contains` takes roughly $N/2$ steps to find an item; however, recall that in Big-O notation, we ignore constant factors (as well as lower-order terms). Thus the method `contains` is an order N—that is, an $O(N)$—algorithm.

What about the algorithm we presented for a sequential search in a sorted list? The number of iterations is decreased for the case in which the item is missing from the list. In this approach, however, we have simply taken a case that would require N steps and reduced its time, on average, to $N/2$ steps. Therefore, this algorithm is also $O(N)$.

Now consider what happens to `contains` when we use the binary search algorithm. In the worst case, `contains` eliminates half of the remaining list components on each iteration. Thus the worst-case number of iterations equal to the number of times N must be divided by 2 to eliminate all but one value. This number is computed by taking the logarithm, base 2, of N (written $\log_2 N$). Here are some examples of $\log_2 N$ for different values of N:

N	$\log_2 N$
2	1
4	2
8	3
16	4
32	5
1024	10
32,768	15
1,048,576	20
33,554,432	25
1,073,741,824	30

As you can see, for a list of more than 1 billion values, the binary search algorithm takes only 30 iterations. It is definitely the best choice for searching large lists. Algorithms such as the binary search algorithm are said to be of logarithmic order.

Now let's turn to sorting. The method `selectSort` contains nested *for* loops. The total number of iterations is the product of the iterations performed by the two loops. The outer loop executes $N - 1$ times. The inner loop also starts out executing $N - 1$ times, but

Theoretical Foundations

steadily decreases until it performs just one iteration: The inner loop executes $N/2$ iterations. The total number of iterations is thus

$$(N - 1) \times N/2$$

Ignoring the constant factor and lower-order term, this is N^2 iterations, and `selectSort` is an $O(N^2)$ algorithm. Whereas `contains`, when coded using the binary search algorithm, takes only 30 iterations to search a sorted array of 1 billion values, putting the array into order takes `selectSort` approximately 1 billion times 1 billion iterations!

Our **add** algorithm for a sorted list forms the basis for an insertion sort, in which values are inserted into a sorted list as they are input. On average, **add** must shift down half of the values ($N/2$) in the list; thus it is an $O(N)$ algorithm. If we call **add** for each input value, we execute an $O(N)$ algorithm N times; therefore, an insertion sort is an $O(N^2)$ algorithm.

Is every sorting algorithm of complexity $O(N^2)$? Most of the simpler ones are, but some $O(N \log_2 N)$ sorting algorithms do exist. Algorithms that are $O(N \log_2 N)$ are much closer in performance to $O(N)$ algorithms than are $O(N^2)$ algorithms. For example, if N is 1 million, then an $O(N^2)$ algorithm takes 1 million times 1 million (1 trillion) iterations, but an $O(N \log_2 N)$ algorithm takes only 20 million iterations—that is, it is 20 times slower than the $O(N)$ algorithm but 50,000 times faster than the $O(N^2)$ algorithm.

PROBLEM SOLVING CASE STUDY

Grade Statistics Revisited

Problem In Chapter 9, we implemented class **Statistics**, which calculated statistics on a file of grades. We must now upgrade this application because the input file has changed: Each line in the file contains a grade, which may be in either integer or real form, and a name. Three additional outputs must be provided: the names of the students with the maximum grade, the names of the students above the average, and the names of the students below the average.

Discussion In Chapter 9, we used an array data structure in which each slot in the array served as a counter for the number of students who made that grade. For example, `grades[85]` was a counter for the number of students who made 85 on the exam. This structure made the implementation of the methods very easy. However, the scheme depends on the grades falling between 0 and 100 inclusive. Although any grade can be scaled to fall within the range of 0 to 100, the scaling can lose accuracy. Also, this structure has no way of keeping a name associated with a grade. These additional constraints require an entirely different implementation. We begin by going back to the CRC card for class `Statistics`. The added responsibilities are highlighted in the CRC card.

Class Name: *Statistics*	Superclass:		Subclasses:
Responsibilities		**Collaborations**	
Create (file of grades)		*Scanner*	
Get average			
Get maximum grade			
Get minimum grade			
Get number above average			
Get number below average			
Print students with maximum grade		*System.out*	
Print students above the average		*System.out*	
Print students below the average		*System.out*	

We have just designed and implemented several variations of a `List` class. Let's think of this problem in terms of a list of grades. The first five tasks remain the same, but let's look at them in terms of list operations. We need to average the values in the list, find the maximum value in the list, find the minimum value in the list, count the number of values above the average, and count the number of values below the average. We know how to calculate an average: We sum the list of grades and divide by the number of grades. To find the maximum and minimum values in a list, we go through the list "remembering" the largest (smallest) value so far. When the last value has been examined, the largest (smallest) value so far is the correct value. The fourth and fifth tasks involve looking at each grade, comparing it to the average, and incrementing a counter.

If all we had to do was find the average and the minimum and maximum grades, we could perform the processing at the same time that we read the data values. The tasks of calculating the number of grades above and below the average, however, require that each grade be examined more than once because we can't determine the average until all values have been read. We suggested in Chapter 9 that the statistics could be calculated in the constructor and stored for later use. Given that we are rewriting this application, let's do it that way this time.

What about the new responsibilities? Without knowing the exact attributes, it looks like each responsibility requires a loop through the list comparing a grade to a value, and printing a name depending on the result of the comparison. When we get to the implementation, we may be able to make one or more of these operations more efficient.

Attributes In the previous implementation, we used an integer array `grades` and two integer variables `numGrades` and `intAverage`. Our input has now changed: We must accept a name and either an integer or a real value. We already have a `Name` class, so our list items must be a name object and a grade. We can make the grade a `float` value. Recall that an `int` and a `float` can both be read with method `nextFloat`. But wait—do we really need to use class `Name`? All we do is print the name as written on the file. Let's just read the name as a string and print it as a string.

Do we want the list to be sorted or unsorted? If sorted, by name or by grade? Does it matter? Yes. This decision determines which algorithm we will use for several of the methods. If the list is unsorted, we must search for the minimum and maximum grades. If the list is sorted by grade, the minimum grade is the first value. If the list is unsorted, we must search the entire list to determine how many values are below and above the average. If the list is sorted, we have to search only part of the list to determine how many grades are below the average; those above the average are the total number minus the number below the average. Printing those below the average becomes more efficient as well.

Which fields do we need? We do not need a field for the number of grades, because this value is part of the list. We do need to keep the average, but it does not need to be an integer value. We do not need a field for the minimum grade because it is the first item in the list, but we do need a field for the maximum grade. We do not need a field for the number of grades above the average, but we do need a field for the number below the average. Because this is a different application, let's give our class a new name `StatisticsList`.

```
public class StatisticsList
{
   SortedListOfGrades list;
   float average;
   float maxGrade;
   int numBelow;

...
```

Later in this chapter, we describe how to implement a list in which the items on the list can be of any class. For now, we just take the `SortedListOfStrings` as a model and "borrow" most of the code. All we have to change is the type of the item on the list. We create a class `Student` containing a name and a grade, provide `get` methods for the values, and provide a `compareTo` method that compares grades (which means that `Student` implements `Comparable`).

```
public class Student implements Comparable
{
   String name;
   float grade;
   public Student(float newGrade, String newName)
   {
```

```
      name = newName;
      grade = newGrade;
    }
  public int compareTo(Object aStudent)
  {
      Student anotherStudent = (Student)aStudent;
      if (grade < anotherStudent.grade)
        return - 1;
      else if (grade > anotherStudent.grade)
        return 1;
      else
        return 0;
  }
  public float getGrade() { return grade; }
  public String getName() { return name; }
}
```

Responsibility Algorithms The constructor takes a `Scanner` object as a parameter, reads the items, and stores them in the list. It calculates the average and maximum grade as the grades are read.

```
Statistics(Scanner gradeFile)

  Instantiate list, a SortedListOfGrades
  Set sum to 0.0
  Set maxGrade to 0.0
  Set numBelow to 0
  while gradeFile.hasNext ()
       Set grade to gradeFile.nextFloat()
       Set name to (gradeFile.nextLine())
       Set student to new Student(grade, name)
       list.add(student)
       Set sum to sum + grade
       if (grade > maxGrade)
           Set maxGrade to grade

  Set average to sum / list.size()
  list.resetList()
  while ((list.next()).getGrade() – average) < 0
       Increment numBelow
```

As we said earlier, keeping the list sorted means that we have direct access to the minimum grade.

Get minimum grade

```
list.resetList()
return (list.next().getGrade())
```

Get maximum grade

```
return maxGrade
```

Get number below average

```
return numBelow
```

Get number above average

```
return list.size() – numBelow
```

Students with max grade

```
list.resetList()
Set item to list.next()
while (maxGrade > item.getGrade())
    Set item to list.next()
Write item.getName() + " had the maximum score."
while (list.hasNext())
    Write list.next().getName() + " had the maximum score."
```

Students above average

```
list.resetList()
for count going from 1 through numBelow
    Set item to list.next()
Write "Students who scored above the average: "
for count going from numBelow + 1 to list.size()
    Write list.next().getName()
```

Students below the average

```
Write "Students who scored below the average: "
list.resetList()
for count going from 1 through numBelow
    Write list.next().getName()
```

The UML diagram and the code for class `StatisticsList` follow.

```
┌─────────────────────────────────────┐
│            StatisticsList            │
├─────────────────────────────────────┤
│ -list: SortedListOfGrades            │
│ -average: float                      │
│ -maxGrade: float                     │
│ -numBelow: int                       │
├─────────────────────────────────────┤
│ +Statistics(gradeFile: Scanner)      │
│ +getAverage(): float                 │
│ +getMinGrade(): float                │
│ +getMaxGrade(): float                │
│ +getAboveAverage(): int              │
│ +getBelowAverage(): int              │
│ +studentMaxGrade(): void             │
│ +studentsAbove(): void               │
│ +studentsBelow(): void               │
└─────────────────────────────────────┘
```

```java
//****************************************************************
// Class StatisticsList provides methods to calculate statistics
//    on a file of grades.
//****************************************************************
import java.util.Scanner;
import java.io.*;
public class StatisticsList
{
  SortedListOfGrades list = new SortedListOfGrades();
  float average = 0.0;
  float maxGrade = 0.0;
  int numBelow = 0;
  // Scanner-based constructor
  public StatisticsList(Scanner gradeFile)
  {
    Student student;
    float sum = 0.0;
    float grade;
    String name;
    while (gradeFile.hasNext())
    {
      grade = gradeFile.nextFloat();
      name = gradeFile.nextLine();
      student = new Student(grade, name);
      list.add(student);
      sum = sum + grade;
      if (grade > maxGrade)
        maxGrade = grade;
    }
```

```java
    average = sum / list.size();
    list.resetList();
    while ((list.next().getGrade() < average))
      numBelow++;
}
// Simple observers
public float getAverage() { return average; }
public float getMaxGrade() { return maxGrade; }
public int getAboveAverage() { return (list.size() - numBelow); }
public int getBelowAverage() { return numBelow; }
// Return first grade on list (minimum grade)
public float getMinGrade()
{
  list.resetList();
  return (list.next().getGrade());
}
// Print names of students with the highest score
public void studentMaxGrade()
{
  list.resetList();
  Student item;
  item = list.next();
  while (maxGrade > item.getGrade())
    item = list.next();
  System.out.println("The following student(s) had the maximum score.");
  System.out.println(item.getName());
  while (list.hasNext())
    System.out.println(list.next().getName());
}
// Print names of students who are above average
public void studentsAbove( )
{
  Student item;
  list.resetList();
  for (int count = 1; count <= numBelow; count++)
    item = list.next();
  System.out.println("Students who scored above the average: ");
  for (int count = numBelow + 1; count <= list.size(); count++)
    System.out.println(list.next().getName());
}
// Print names of students who are below average
public void studentsBelow()
{
  Student item;
  System.out.println("Students who scored below the average: ");
  list.resetList();
  for (int count = 1; count <= numBelow; count++)
    System.out.println(list.next().getName());
}
}
```

Testing Because the input has changed, we cannot use the same test driver that we used in Chapter 9. However, we can add names to the same scores, and compare the answers to the original set of methods.

```
0 Bill Bly
100 Mary Jones
7 Anne Margaret
9 Susy Sunshine
78 Jim Jones
99 Alex Dale
67 Claire Clear
44 Allen Aldridge
```

Here is the driver, followed by the output:

```java
import java.io.*;
import java.util.Scanner;
public class StatisticsDriver
{
  public static void main(String[] args) throws IOException
  {
    StatisticsList statistics;
    Scanner in = new Scanner(System.in);
    System.out.println("Enter the file name.");
    String fileName = in.next();
    Scanner gradeFile = new Scanner(new FileReader(fileName));
    statistics = new StatisticsList(gradeFile);
    System.out.println("average " + statistics.getAverage());
    System.out.println("minimum grade " + statistics.getMinGrade());
    System.out.println("maximum grade " + statistics.getMaxGrade());
    System.out.println("number above average " +
                  statistics.getAboveAverage());
    System.out.println("number below average " +
                  statistics.getBelowAverage());
    statistics.studentMaxGrade();
    statistics.studentsAbove();
    statistics.studentsBelow();
  }
}
```

```
Console X
<terminated> StatisticsDriver [Java Application] /opt/sun-jdk-1.5.0.08/
Enter the file name.
Statistics.in
average 50.5
minimum grade 0.0
maximum grade 100.0
number above average 4
number below average 4
The following student(s) had the maximum score.
 Mary Jones
Students who scored above the average:
 Claire Clear
 Jim Jones
 Alex Dale
 Mary Jones
Students who scored below the average:
 Bill Bly
 Anne Margaret
 Susy Sunshine
 Allen Aldridge
```

It is comforting to see that the answers are the same as those obtained by the common methods. Nevertheless, the application has not been thoroughly tested. This implementation is based on a list of values, so a complete test plan should be based on list parameters. To thoroughly test this application, we must test for cases in which there are no grades, one grade, a few grades, and exactly the maximum number of grades. We took care of the case in which there are more grades to be stored than there are slots in the list by checking for **isFull** in method **add** in class **SortedListOfGrades**. You are asked to write a comprehensive test plan in the exercises.

11.5 : Refactoring the List Hierarchy

As we have noted in our discussions of maintenance, sometimes software evolves into a form that is so difficult to maintain that we just need to rewrite it. Reorganizing a class hierarchy may be one way to clean up the problem. When the goal of a maintenance project is to improve maintainability without changing functionality, we refer to the process as code **refactoring**. In this section we review the list hierarchy that we have created and refactor it for easier maintenance.

Refactoring Modifying code to improve its quality without changing its functionality

The `List` Class Hierarchy

We have discussed the abstract design of a `List`, a `ListWithSort`, and a `SortedList` in terms of data structures. In reality, we have created a parallel hierarchy of concrete classes with `ListOfStrings` at the top and two derived classes. We can visualize these parallel hierarchies as follows:

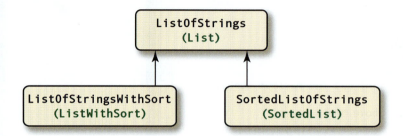

At the logical level, a `ListWithSort` is a `List`, as is a `SortedList`, but `ListWithSort` and `SortedList` are not derived from each other. At the implementation level, the same relationships exist.

There is something unappealing about the idea that a `SortedList` is a subclass of a `List` that isn't sorted. It would seem more logical if both classes were derived from a common ancestor, rather than making one a superclass over the other.

Turning to the implementations of these lists, suppose we want to provide a new **add** method in `ListOfStrings` that adds an item at a given location in the list. That's a nice feature, and it's probably useful for `ListOfStringsWithSort`, which automatically inherits it. Of course, `SortedListOfStrings` will also inherit that new method. Such a method doesn't make sense in a sorted list, because it is likely to disrupt the ordering of the items.

How did we get into this situation? We began with the idea of a general list class, then decided to implement it for a specific item type, and proceeded to derive our other classes from that implementation. With the benefit of hindsight, we can see that this seemingly reasonable approach is leading us down a path to future problems. It's time to refactor the hierarchy.

Using an Abstract Class

As an alternative, we could have originally implemented the observers and iterator in an abstract class and left the implementation of the transformers to the derived classes. Then the unsorted and sorted versions of the list could both inherit from the abstract class. The documentation for the classes would be as follows:

```
public abstract class AbstractList
{
  public AbstractList()
  public AbstractList(int maxItems)
  public boolean isFull()
  public boolean isEmpty()
  public int size()
  public void resetList()
```

```
    public boolean hasNext()
    public String next()
    public boolean contains(String item)
    public abstract void remove(String item)
    public abstract void add(String item)
}

public class ListOfStrings extends AbstractList
{
    public ListOfStrings()
    public ListOfStrings(int maxItems)
    public void remove(String item)
    public void add(String item)
}

public class SortedListOfStrings extends AbstractList
{
    public SortedListOfStrings()
    public SortedListOfStrings(int maxItems)
    public void remove(String item)
    public void add(String item)
}

public class ListOfStringsWithSort extends ListOfStrings
{
    public ListOfStringsWithSort()
    public ListOfStringsWithSort(int maxItems)
    public void selectSort()
}
```

As you can see, we still gain the benefits of reuse through inheritance for the common methods. But those methods that have different semantics are defined as **abstract**, and can be implemented differently by the concrete subclasses. Under these conditions, the class hierarchy would look like this:

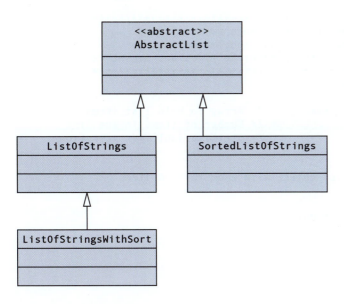

As you can see, `SortedListOfStrings` is no longer a subclass of `ListOfStrings`. Now it is safe to implement that new **add** method, because only `ListOfStringsWithSort` will inherit it.

11.6 ⋮ From Lists of Strings to Lists of Comparable Objects

In an ideal world, we would like to write the code for a list's operations but wait until later to define the types of the objects on the list. Although we called the components of our logical lists "items," they are actually implemented as `String` objects. Could we construct a truly general-purpose list where the items can be of any type? For example, could we have a list that could hold either `Name` objects or `Entry` objects? To a certain degree, we can.

One strategy is to declare the objects on the list to be `Comparable`. Let's see how we can use this approach to make our lists more general. (In Chapter 12, we present another way, using the Java generic type construct to obtain this generality in a manner that is more flexible and less prone to error.)

In Chapter 10, we examined the `Comparable` interface, which is part of the Java library. Any class that implements this interface must implement the method `compareTo`. For example, we made our `Name` class implement `Comparable`. The `String` class also implements `Comparable`. We had our `Student` class do so as well.

To make our list classes as general as possible, we replace `String` with `Comparable` throughout the `AbstractList` class. As a consequence, any object of a class that implements the `Comparable` interface can be passed as an argument to **add**, **remove**, or **contains**. In addition, the type of the array elements must be declared as implementing `Comparable`, and **next** must return a value of type `Comparable`. (These changes are highlighted below.)

The following version of class `AbstractList` is built around `Comparable`. Because the implementation of **contains** involves a comparison of values that depends on their types, we also make it abstract so that each subclass of `AbstractList` must supply a class-specific implementation.

```
//*****************************************************************
// Class AbstractList provides common methods to create and
// maintain a list of Comparable objects. Subclasses must
// implement its transformers with appropriate types and semantics.
//*****************************************************************
public abstract class AbstractList
{
  protected Comparable[] listItems;      // Array to hold list items
  protected int numItems;                // Number of items in the list
  protected int currentPos;              // State variable for iteration

  public AbstractList()
  // Instantiates an empty list object with room for 100 items
  {
    numItems = 0;
    listItems = new Comparable[100];
    currentPos = 0;
  }
```

```java
public AbstractList(int maxItems)
// Instantiates an empty list object with room for maxItems items
{
  numItems = 0;
  listItems = new Comparable[maxItems];
  currentPos = 0;
}

// Returns true if there is no room for another component; false otherwise
public boolean isFull() { return (listItems.length == numItems); }

// Returns true if there are no components in the list; false otherwise
public boolean isEmpty() { return (numItems == 0); }

// Returns the number of components in the list
public int size() { return numItems; }

// Returns true if item is in the list; false otherwise
public abstract boolean contains(Comparable otherItem);

// Abstract transformers to be implemented by subclasses
public abstract void add(Comparable item);
public abstract void remove(Comparable otherItem);

// Prepare list for iteration
public void resetList() { currentPos = 0; }

// Returns true if there is another item in the list; false otherwise
public boolean hasNext() { return (currentPos < numItems); }

public Comparable next()
// Returns the item at the currentPos position and increments currentPos
// Assumption:  no transformers have been invoked since last call
{
  Comparable next = listItems[currentPos];
  currentPos++;
  return next;
}
}
```

Here is a class that extends `AbstractList` to create a list of strings. Notice that the method signatures must use `Comparable` so that they are compatible with `AbstractList`, but in each case we cast the parameter to a `String`. When we are comparing list items to another value, we also have to cast the list items to `String`, because technically they can be of any `Comparable` class.

```java
public class ListOfStrings extends AbstractList
{
  public ListOfStrings() { super(); }
  public ListOfStrings(int maxItems) { super(maxItems); }
```

```java
public boolean contains(Comparable otherItem)
// Returns true if item is in the list; false otherwise
{
  String item = (String)otherItem;
  int index = 0;
  while (index < numItems &&
         ((String)listItems[index]).compareTo(item) != 0)
    index++;
  return (index < numItems);
}

public void add(Comparable item)
// If the list is not full, puts item in the last position in the
//  list; otherwise list is unchanged
{
  if (!isFull())
  {
    listItems[numItems] = (String)item;
    numItems++;
  }
}

public void remove(Comparable otherItem)
// Removes item from the list if it is there; implements "remove, if there"
// semantics; maintains ordering of elements
{
  String item = (String)otherItem;
  int index = 0;
  boolean found = false;
  while (index < numItems && !found)
  {
    if (((String)listItems[index]).compareTo(item) == 0)
      found = true;
    else
      index++;
  }
  if (found)
  {
    for (int count = index; count < numItems-1; count++)
      listItems[count] = listItems[count+1];
    numItems--;
  }
}
}
```

To test this new implementation of class `ListOfStrings`, we ran the same driver that we used previously, with slightly abbreviated input. To save space, we do not show the command-entry prompts.

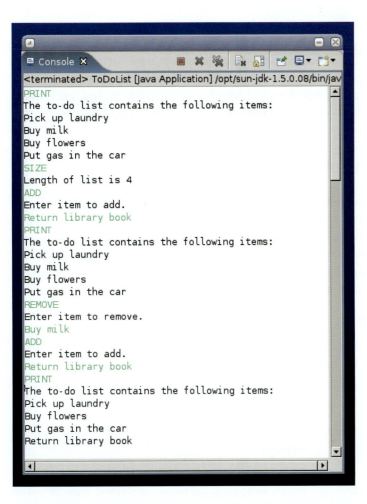

There is an important point to note about this approach to making a general list. Although the derived class diligently casts all of its parameter values to `String` objects, that doesn't prevent client code from passing other kinds of `Comparable` objects through those parameters. They simply get converted to some string representation, which may be meaningless. Thus the class works correctly as long as we assume that the client code is careful to only pass in strings. That's not a safe assumption, and it could lead to some difficult-to-understand errors.

Also, because `add` is abstract, the compiler cannot verify that it adds only objects of a single class. Therefore we can potentially create a subclass of `AbstractList` that fills the list with a mixture of any kind of `Comparable` objects. That's a perfect example of dynamic binding polymorphism, which can be highly inefficient (assuming that the client code overcomes all of the complexities involved in making this approach work).

While it is true that we've succeeded in creating an abstract class that can be easily extended to provide a list that contains any of a wide variety of objects, the result is susceptible to errors and poor performance. Nor have we completely achieved our goal of having a general list that can contain a value of a given type, simply by specifying it. That is why the Java designers extended Java 5 with language features to support generic types, which we present in Chapter 12.

At this point you may be wondering why we put so much effort into developing list classes that have so many shortcomings. Our purpose was to show you the underlying algorithms and also the many issues that must be considered in creating a general-purpose list class. Armed with this knowledge, you are now prepared to appreciate the presentation of the Java library classes in Chapter 12 to a much deeper level than if we had directly introduced them. Your understanding of the algorithms also enables you to more effectively extend the library classes or develop your own list classes in the future.

11.7 : A Preview of Java Collections

In this chapter, we have shown you how to build your own list data structure. The `java.util` package includes many interfaces, abstract classes, and classes that describe data structures available for you to use. The `Vector` class is one of these; we described it briefly in Chapter 9. In Chapter 12, we delve into the structures provided in this package in some depth. In this section, we provide a preview by introducing the class `ArrayList`, which has operations much like the classes that we have just written.

■ `ArrayList` Class

Class `ArrayList` provides many methods that allow the client to manipulate the underlying array as a list. Here are some of the methods:

Method	Meaning
`ArrayList<type>()`	Returns an empty list
`ArrayList<type>(int number)`	Returns an array with an initial capacity of `number` elements
`add(Object anObject)`	`anObject` is appended to the end of the list
`add(int index, Object anObject)`	Inserts `anObject` at the `index` position and shifts the rest of the elements down one position
`contains(Object anObject)`	Returns `true` if `anObject` is in the collection; `false` otherwise
`isEmpty()`	Returns `true` if the list contains no elements
`set(int index, Object anObject)`	Sets the `index` position to `anObject` (no objects are shifted down)
`size()`	Returns the number of elements in the list
`remove(int index)`	Removes and returns the object at the `index` position and shifts the rest of the elements up one position
`remove(Object anObject)`	Removes one instance of `anObject` if it is there
`get(int index)`	Returns object at the `index` position (no objects are shifted)
`indexOf(Object anObject)`	Returns the index within the list of `anObject`
`iterator()`	Returns an `Iterator` over the elements of the list

Are you surprised that the method names look familiar? These operations are common to most lists. The only method that looks strange is `iterator()`, a method that returns an `Iterator`. What is an `Iterator`? For our list classes we defined methods `resetList`, `hasNext`, and `next`, so that we could iterate through the list. The Java library takes a different approach (which we explain more fully in Chapter 12).

In essence, an `Iterator` is an object that is created by an `ArrayList` to allow us to iterate through it. Each `Iterator` object has its own `currentPos` field, and supplies methods `next` and `hasNext`. We show how this approach works when we look at an implementation using `ArrayList`. Why does the Java library do this? As we note in Chapter 12, it allows a list to have more than one iteration in progress at a time, which is useful in some advanced list processing algorithms.

You should also note a bit of new syntax in the constructors for `ArrayList`: `<type>`. In Chapter 12, we see how Java supports generic classes and uses the angle brackets to indicate the type to be used for a generic class. Thus we can write

```
ArrayList<String> stringList = new ArrayList<String>();
```

to declare an `ArrayList` that holds strings. We can write

```
ArrayList<Name> nameList = new ArrayList<Name>();
```

to declare an `ArrayList` that contains values of our class `Name`.

Class `ArrayList` is also expandable. If the number of items put into the list exceeds the number of spaces initially assigned to the list, the list is expanded automatically. Thus an `isFull` method is unnecessary. In the following demonstration application, the initial capacity is set to 4 in the constructor; 13 values are inserted as shown by the output. For this application, we declare the `ArrayList` to hold strings (as highlighted), but any class that implements the `Comparable` interface is acceptable.

```java
//***********************************************************
// This application uses the ArrayList class
//***********************************************************
import java.util.*;
import java.io.*;
public class ListDriver
{
  private static Scanner inFile;
  private static PrintWriter outFile;

  public static void main(String[] args) throws IOException
  {
    inFile = new Scanner(new FileReader("list.dat"));
    // Instantiate the list
    ArrayList<String> list = new ArrayList<String>(4);
```

```
    // Read values and insert in list1
    while (inFile.hasNextLine())
      list.add(inFile.nextLine());
    inFile.close();
    // Print file using an iterator
    Iterator listIterator = list.iterator();        // Instantiate iterator
    while (listIterator.hasNext())
      System.out.println(listIterator.next());
  }
}
```

Let's take a closer look at the iterator. The `Iterator` class object `listIterator` (shaded in yellow) is instantiated and then used in the loop and in the output statement:

```
Iterator listIterator = list.iterator();        // Instantiate iterator
while (listIterator.hasNext())
  System.out.println(listIterator.next());
```

As you can see, this loop is functionally equivalent to the one we wrote for going from 0 through `list.size()` - `1`. The call to `listIterator.next` is functionally equivalent to `list.next` in our loop implementation.

SOFTWARE MAINTENANCE CASE STUDY

Refactoring `StatisticsDriver`

Maintenance Task When we wrote the `StatisticsDriver` application, we said that it would be necessary to implement a `SortedListOfGrades` by borrowing code from `SortedListOfStrings`. While that approach is effective, it means that the new class is not part of our list hierarchy. Now that we've developed a general-purpose `AbstractList` class, let's see what it takes to implement `SortedListOfGrades` as a subclass, and what effect this has on the application.

Discussion To extend `AbstractList`, we create a concrete class that provides methods `contains`, `add`, and `remove`. We've seen how to create such a class for an unsorted list of strings, but in this case we need to provide a sorted list of `Student` objects. Fortunately, we had the foresight to make `Student` implement the `Comparable` interface. All we really need to do now is reuse the code for these methods from `SortedListOfStrings`, replacing `String` with `Comparable`, and casting parameters and array values to `Student` as necessary.

Revised Code Here is the new version of `SortedListOfGrades`, derived from `AbstractList`. The changes made to the `SortedListOfStrings` methods are highlighted.

```java
public class SortedListOfGrades extends AbstractList
{
  public SortedListOfGrades() { super(); }
  public SortedListOfGrades(int maxItems) { super(maxItems); }

  public boolean contains(Comparable otherItem)
  // Returns true if item is in the list; false otherwise
  {
    Student item = (Student) otherItem;
    int index = 0;
    while (index < numItems &&
           ((Student)listItems[index]).compareTo(item)> 0)
      index++;
    return (index < numItems &&
           ((Student)listItems[index]).compareTo(item)== 0);
  }

  public void add(Comparable item)
  // If the list is not full, puts item in its proper place in
  //   the list; otherwise, list is unchanged
  // Assumption:  item is not already in the list
  {
    if (!isFull())
    {
      int index = numItems - 1;             // Loop control variable
      while (index >= 0 &&
             (((Student)item).compareTo((Student)listItems[index]) < 0))
      { // Find addition point
        listItems[index+1] = listItems[index];
```

```
        index--;
      }
      listItems[index+1] = item;          // Add item
      numItems++;                         // Increment number of items
    }
  }

  public void remove(Comparable otherItem)
  // Removes item from the list if it is there; implements "remove, if there"
  // semantics; maintains ordering of elements
  {
    int index = 0;
    boolean found = false;
    Student item = (Student) otherItem;
    while (index < numItems && !found)
    {
      if (((Student)listItems[index]).compareTo(item) == 0)
        found = true;
      else
        index++;
    }
    if (found)
    {
      for (int count = index; count < numItems-1; count++)
        listItems[count] = listItems[count+1];
      numItems--;
    }
  }
}
```

As you can see, the changes are fairly modest, and they essentially follow the same pattern that we saw with the ListOfStrings derived from AbstractList. No changes were required for the Student and AbstractList classes. What about StatisticsList and StatisticsDriver? While the latter can be used unchanged, StatisticsList uses the next method that SortedListOfGrades inherits from AbstractList. That method returns Comparable objects rather than the Student objects that StatisticsList expects to have returned by next.

Two approaches can be employed to deal with this incompatibility. The first strategy is to search through StatisticsList, inserting a cast to Student in front of every call to next. That works, but it is tedious. And, if possible, we would really like to have SortedListOfGrades be a direct replacement that doesn't require changes to client code. We can achieve this goal by using the second approach: we can create another next method in SortedListOfGrades that returns a Student object. Then StatisticsList can call the version of next whose return type is Student.

To implement this new version of next, we simply call next from the superclass and then cast its result to Student before returning it. This implementation is just a one-line method that we insert into SortedListOfGrades:

```
public Student next() { return (Student)super.next(); }
```

We've managed to concentrate all of the changes into one class. That's just what we like to see when refactoring an object-oriented design.

11.8 : Testing and Debugging

We have written test plans for both the unsorted list and the sorted list, but we have not tested the sort method that was used in the class `ListOfStringsWithSort`. The method `selectSort` takes a list of items and rearranges the items so that they are in ascending order. If we write a black-box testing plan, which end cases should we test in addition to the general case? These cases fall into two categories, based on the length of the list of items and on the order of the items in the original list:

1. The list is empty.
2. The list contains one item.
3. The list contains more than one item.
4. The list contains the maximum number of items.
5. The list is already sorted in ascending order.
6. The list is already sorted in descending order.

We leave the conversion of this list into a complete test plan for you as an exercise.

Testing and Debugging Hints

1. Review the testing and debugging hints from Chapter 9.
2. When the objects on the list are of simple types, their type names must be on the parameter lists for `contains, add,` and `remove`.
3. When the objects on the list are of composite types, use `Comparable` in the parameter lists for the class name.
4. Verify that any argument to a list method with a `Comparable` parameter belongs to a class that has implemented the `Comparable` interface.
5. Be careful: Arguments of primitive types cannot be passed to a method whose parameter implements the `Comparable` interface.
6. Test general-purpose methods outside the context of a particular application, using a test driver.
7. Choose test data carefully so that you test all end conditions and some conditions in the middle. End conditions reach the limits of the structure used to store them. For example, a list test plan should include test data in which the number of components is zero, one, and the array size, as well as somewhere in between.

Graphical User Interfaces

Handling Events from Multiple Sources

In Chapter 10, we saw how to add a button to a user interface and handle the events that it generates. Many user interfaces contain multiple buttons, each of which generates a different event. In this chapter, we see how to handle an interface that has multiple event sources. We'll also see how we can build an interface that includes a repeated element, using a component called a panel.

Figure 11.11 summarizes the event-handling process for a button. When the user clicks a button, the current thread of control suspends execution, and control jumps to an event handler method within an event listener object. Prior to putting a button on the screen, we register an event listener object with it. When the user clicks a button, it calls the `actionPerformed` method within the registered event listener.

Thus one way to handle events from different buttons is to register a different event listener with each one. If a user interface has buttons marked Yes, No, and Cancel, we could declare classes `YesListener`, `NoListener`, and `CancelListener`, and instantiate an object of each of these classes to register with the corresponding button. In some

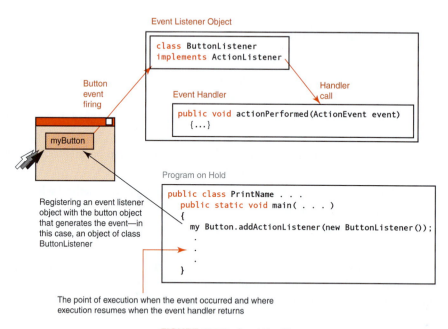

FIGURE 11.11   Event Handling

cases, we can just use multiple instances of the same event listener to respond to different buttons. Let's take a look at an example.

Suppose you are working for a research project that is keeping track of the total rainfall in your area. Observers from different stations call you to report how much rain has fallen at the end of a storm. You need to enter the values for these stations as they come in and display the running total for each station. It's safe to assume that we'll have a `Station` class, and that we'll use instances of this class to represent the different stations.

How does this choice affect the user interface? We want to enter the rainfall amount for the particular station and then click a button to get the new total rainfall amount. Thus, a station needs to have a button, a data entry field, and a label for output. It also needs to label the field and the output with descriptions. Here's what the portion of the interface for one station looks like:

Station xxxxxxxxxx: | 0.0 | Enter | Total Rainfall: 123.05

Let's make a `Station` object be responsible for creating its own portion of the interface and returning it for `main` to add as a unit to the frame. How can we do this? We use a panel, which is a self-contained section of a user interface. In Java, we create panels with the `JPanel` class. Like a `JFrame`, a `JPanel` can have a layout manager, and we can add user interface elements to it. For example, if our `Station` class has a `JPanel` instance variable called `panel`, we can write the following in the `Station` constructor:

```
panel = new JPanel();               // Instantiate a panel
panel.setLayout(new FlowLayout()); // Set layout for the panel
enter = new JButton("Enter");       // Instantiate an Enter button
panel.add(enter);                   // Add the Enter button to the panel
```

The user can instantiate a station and then get its panel by calling a `getPanel` method as declared here:

```
public JPanel getPanel() { return panel;}
```

We can then add the returned panel directly to the content pane of the user interface frame:

```
inputPane.add((new Station("Austin")).getPanel());  // Station for
                                                     // Austin
```

We now have the ability to create a panel for a station, and then return that panel to the client so it can be placed in a frame. Of course, we also need to handle the event from our Enter button. We know how to write an event listener class to supply the event handler. However, there will be multiple stations in the frame, and hence multiple Enter buttons. How do we uniquely associate a handler with each station?

To solve this problem, we declare the event listener class within the `Station` class. We make this so-called inner class `private` because it is used only within the enclosing class. Here is the code for the `Station` class, showing the inner `StationHandler` class at the end:

```java
//*************************************************************************
// This class represents individual rainfall reporting stations. Each
// station has its own user interface panel that contains its specific
// user interface elements.
//*************************************************************************
package station;
import java.awt.*;                        // Layout manager
import java.awt.event.*;                  // Event-handling classes
import javax.swing.*;                     // User interface classes
public class Station
{
  JButton enter;                          // Enter data button
  JTextField amountField;                 // Data entry field
  JLabel outputLabel;                     // Result display label
  JPanel panel;                           // Panel for user interface
  StationHandler action;                  // Event handler
  double total = 0.0;                     // Total rainfall

  public Station (String name)            // Station constructor
  {
    // Set up panel to hold user interface elements
    panel = new JPanel();                 // Get a panel
    panel.setLayout(new FlowLayout());    // Set layout for the panel
    // Create user interface elements
    amountField = new JTextField("0.0", 10); // Field for data entry
    enter = new JButton("Enter");         // Enter button
    action = new StationHandler();        // Create an event handler
    enter.addActionListener(action);      // Register handler with
                                          // button

    outputLabel = new JLabel("Total Rainfall: "  // Label for output
                      + total);
    // Add user interface elements to panel
    panel.add(new JLabel("Station " + name +":"));
    panel.add(amountField);
    panel.add(enter);
    panel.add(outputLabel);
  }

  public JPanel getPanel() { return panel; } // Return the filled panel

  // Define an action handler with an instance of a Station
  private class StationHandler implements ActionListener
  {
    public void actionPerformed(ActionEvent event)
```

```java
    // Handles events from the Enter button in this station's panel
    {
      double value;                           // Holds input value
      // Convert string in inputField to a double value
      value = Double.parseDouble(amountField.getText());  // Get value
                                              // from field
      total = total + value;                  // Add amount to sum
      outputLabel.setText("Total Rainfall: " + total);    // Display
                                                          // total
      amountField.setText("0.0");             // Clear input field
    }
  }
}
```

As you can see, each time the `actionPerformed` method within `StationHandler` is called by the user clicking the Enter button, it gets the text from the `amountField` field, converts the string to a `double` value, adds it to the total rainfall for this station, and updates the total amount in the display. When we instantiate a `Station` object, a `StationHandler` object is instantiated within it when the constructor instantiates `action`. Because this event listener class is declared as part of the `Station` class, its objects have access to the instance fields of the enclosing class. As a result, the client code can instantiate several `Station` objects, each one of which has its own dedicated `StationHandler`. Let's see how this is done in the driver:

```java
//************************************************************************
// This application keeps track of rainfall amounts for three stations
//************************************************************************
import java.awt.*;                            // Layout manager
import java.awt.event.*;                      // Event-handling classes
import javax.swing.*;                         // User interface classes
import station.*;                             // Rainfall station
public class Rainfall
{
  public static void main(String[] args)
  {
    JFrame inputFrame;                        // User interface frame
    Container inputPane;                      // Content pane
    // Set up the frame
    inputFrame = new JFrame();
    inputPane = inputFrame.getContentPane();
    inputFrame.setSize(500, 150);
    // End event loop
    inputFrame.setDefaultCloseOperation(JFrame.EXIT_ON_CLOSE);
    inputPane.setLayout(new GridLayout(0, 1));
    // Add components to frame - start of event loop
    // In each case, create a Station object and
    // directly get its panel to add to the frame
```

```
    inputPane.add((new Station("Austin")).getPanel());    // Station
                                                           // for Austin
    inputPane.add((new Station("Amherst")).getPanel());   // Station
                                                           // for
                                                           // Amherst
    inputPane.add((new Station("LaCrosse")).getPanel());  // Station
                                                           // for
                                                           // LaCrosse

    inputFrame.setVisible(true);                           // Show the
                                                           // frame
  }
}
```

Here is the user interface during a sample run:

Each of the **Station** panels creates a separate event loop. You can click on any of the buttons at any time and the appropriate action listener is called. The user interface then waits for another operation. How do we end these event loops? In this case, we use a feature of the **JFrame** that allows us to specify that the application should quit when the window is closed. If you look closely at the application, you'll notice these lines:

```
// End event loop
inputFrame.setDefaultCloseOperation(JFrame.EXIT_ON_CLOSE);
```

The method **setDefaultCloseOperation** specifies what should happen when the window is closed. The **JFrame** class defines several public constants that we can pass to this method, including **EXIT_ON_CLOSE**. If we don't specify a different action by calling this method, then the default action is to hide the window without exiting the application.

We've just seen one way of handling events from different buttons—each button can have a different event listener registered with it (in our example, the different listeners were separate instances of the same class, but they can also be of different classes). In many cases, however, the actions of several buttons may be related in a way that makes it easier if a single listener handles all of them.

When we instantiate a button with **new**, we pass a string as an argument to its constructor. The string is used to label the button on the screen; it also identifies an event from the button. Suppose we need a user interface with two buttons, Copy and Done. We can create one `ButtonHandler` listener object and register both buttons with it as follows:

```
buttonAction = new ButtonHandler();        // Instantiate a ButtonHandler
                                           // object
copy = new JButton("Copy");                // Create a button marked "Copy"
copy.addActionListener(buttonAction);      // Register buttonAction with
                                           // copy
done = new JButton("Done");                // Create a button marked "Done"
done.addActionListener(buttonAction);      // Register buttonAction with
                                           // done
```

When the user clicks either of these buttons, `actionPerformed` is called, just as we saw previously. How does `actionPerformed` decide which button was clicked? Recall that when we write the heading for the `actionPerformed` method, we include a parameter of type `ActionEvent`. The source event passes an object to the method through that parameter. That object has a field containing the string we gave to the button to identify it. We access the string by calling the value-returning method `getActionCommand` associated with the parameter object.

For example, if the heading for `actionPerformed` is written this way:

```
public void actionPerformed(ActionEvent someButton)
```

then we obtain the string that identifies which button was clicked using the following statement (`command` is a `String` variable):

```
command = someButton.getActionCommand();
```

Within our declaration of the method, we use string comparisons and branches to perform the necessary action for the particular button. For example, we might write a handler that copies the value in a field to an output label when the user clicks the Copy button, but exits the application if the user clicks the Done button.

```
private static class ButtonHandler implements ActionListener
{
  public void actionPerformed(ActionEvent buttonEvent) // Event handler
                                                       // method
  {
    String command;                          // String to hold
                                             // button name
    command = buttonEvent.getActionCommand(); // Get the button's
                                             // name
    if (command.equals("Copy"))              // When the name is
                                             // "Copy"
      outputLabel.setText(inputField.getText()); // Copy the field
    else if (command.equals("Done"))         // When the name is
                                             // "Done"
```

```
    {
      dataFrame.dispose();               // Close the frame
      System.exit(0);                    // Quit the application
    }
    else                                 // Otherwise, it's an
                                         // error
      outputLabel.setText("An unexpected event occurred.");
  }
}
```

When the event source calls `actionPerformed`, the method gets the button's name using `getActionCommand`. It then uses an *if-else-if* structure to decide which button was clicked and execute the appropriate statements. Although `getActionCommand` should never return a name other than "Copy" or "Done," we provide a branch for other names just to be safe. After all, at some point in the future, the program might be changed to add another button. If the programmer forgets to add a corresponding branch to handle that event, the program displays an error message instead of crashing.

In the preceding example, we introduced two new methods, `dispose` and `exit`. The `dispose` method is an instance method associated with a `JFrame` object; it permanently removes the frame from the screen. We could also have called `setVisible(false)`, but `dispose` does some extra work in the background that saves the JVM from having to clean up after us. The `exit` method is a class method associated with the `System` class; it causes the JVM to terminate execution of the application. Passing it an argument of 0 indicates that the application was intentionally ended in a normal manner.

We have now seen how to handle multiple button events in a single handler. In the Rainfall application, we saw how to handle events from different buttons using a handler for each one. How do we decide which approach to take for a given problem?

When a user interface contains buttons that perform tasks associated with a specific object, it makes sense to combine the handling of their events into a single method. If clicking a button requires processing that is unrelated to other buttons, then it should have its own event handler. For example, in our `Rainfall` application, each station has its own Enter button plus a handler that is dedicated to that particular button. Both the button and its handling are integral to a `Station` object. It would not make sense to create a single button handler that responds to the buttons for all of the stations. If we added a Reset button to each station, however, we would want the `actionPerformed` method in `StationHandler` to respond to both the Enter and the Reset buttons. It would do so by using `getActionCommand` and comparing the return value with `"Enter"` and `"Reset"` to select the appropriate action.

As a demonstration of combining both approaches, the following application implements a simple calculator with add and subtract operations (you can easily see how to add more operations, starting from this basic version). It also permits the user to clear the display. All of the arithmetic operations are handled by one listener class, and the clear operation is handled by a separate class. In this case, we declared both listener classes as inner classes.

```java
//*********************************************************************
// This application implements a simple on-screen calculator
//*********************************************************************
import java.awt.*;
import java.awt.event.*;
import javax.swing.*;
public class Calculator
{
  static JTextField inputField;          // Data entry field
  static JLabel register;                // Result shown on screen
  static double result;                  // Keeps current value
  static JFrame calcFrame;               // Declare a frame
  static Container calcPane;             // Content pane of frame
  static NumericHandler operation;       // Declare numeric
                                         // listener
  static ClearHandler clearOperation;    // Declare clear listener
  static JLabel resultLabel;             // Labels output area
  static JLabel entryLabel;              // Label for input field
  static JButton add;                    // Add button
  static JButton subtract;               // Subtract button
  static JButton clear;                  // Clear button

  // Listener for operation buttons
  static class NumericHandler implements ActionListener
  {
    public void actionPerformed(ActionEvent event)
    {
      double secondOperand;              // Holds input value
      String whichButton;                // Holds the button's
                                         // name

      // Get the operand
      secondOperand =
        Double.valueOf(inputField.getText()).doubleValue();
      whichButton = event.getActionCommand(); // Get the button's name
      if (whichButton.equals("+"))       // When the name is "add"
        result = result + secondOperand; //    add the operand
      else                               // Otherwise,
        result = result - secondOperand; //    subtract the operand
      register.setText("" + result);     // Display result
      inputField.setText("");            // Clear input
    }
  }
  // Listener for clear button
  static class ClearHandler implements ActionListener
  {
    public void actionPerformed(ActionEvent event)
    {
      result = 0.0;                      // Set result back to
                                         // zero
      register.setText("0.0");           // Reset value in display
      inputField.setText("");            // Clear input
    }
  }
```

```java
public static void main(String[] args)
{
  operation = new NumericHandler();         // Instantiate operation
                                            // listener
  clearOperation = new ClearHandler();      // Instantiate clear
                                            // listener

  result = 0.0;                             // Initialize result
  // Instantiate labels and initialize input field
  resultLabel = new JLabel("Result:");
  register = new JLabel("0.0", JLabel.RIGHT);
  entryLabel = new JLabel("Enter #:");
  inputField = new JTextField("", 10);
  // Instantiate button objects
  add = new JButton("+");
  subtract = new JButton("-");
  clear = new JButton("Clear");
  // Register the button listeners
  add.addActionListener(operation);
  subtract.addActionListener(operation);
  clear.addActionListener(clearOperation);
  calcFrame = new JFrame();                 // Give the frame a value
  calcFrame.setSize(300, 200);              // Specify size of frame
  calcFrame.setDefaultCloseOperation(JFrame.EXIT_ON_CLOSE);
  calcPane = calcFrame.getContentPane();    // Get the content pane
  calcPane.setLayout(new GridLayout(4, 2)); // Set the layout manager
  // Add interface elements to calcPane
  calcPane.add(resultLabel);
  calcPane.add(register);
  calcPane.add(entryLabel);
  calcPane.add(inputField);
  calcPane.add(add);
  calcPane.add(subtract);
  calcPane.add(clear);
  calcFrame.setVisible(true);               // Show the frame
  }
}
```

Here is the user interface that the application displays:

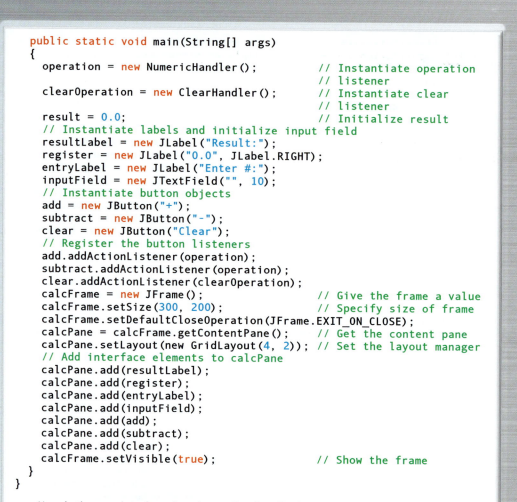

Summary

This chapter provided practice in working with lists, where the items on the list are stored in a one-dimensional array. We examined algorithms that add, remove, and search data stored in an array-based unsorted list, and we wrote methods to implement these algorithms. We also examined an algorithm that takes the array in which the list items are stored and sorts them into ascending order.

Sorting a list does not make it a "sorted list," because the next insertion might put the items out of order again. We defined a class where the list items are stored in order based on some function of the value of the items. We found that the only method that needed to be changed from the unsorted version was the **add** method.

We examined several search algorithms: sequential search in an unsorted list, sequential search in a sorted list, and binary search. The sequential search in an unsorted list compares each item in the list to the search item. We must examine all items before we can determine that the search item is not present in the list. The sequential search in a sorted list can determine that the search item is not in the list when it passes the place where the item belongs. The binary search looks for the search item in the middle of the list. If it is not there, the search then continues in the half where the item should be. This process continues to cut the search area in half until either the item is found or the search area is empty.

We introduced the concept of a command-driven test driver for a class in which the tester inputs operations and associated data and the operations are executed. The operations in the test plan become input to the test driver.

We generalized the list in an abstract class called **AbstractList**, which we extended by **ListOfStrings**. We then implemented and tested the new class using the command-driven tester implemented earlier. We saw how replacing **String** with **Comparable in the AbstractList** can make the list items more general. Finally, we looked briefly at **ArrayList** from the Java library.

LEARNING / Portfolio

Quick Check

1. What is the difference between a list and an array? (pp. 592–593)
2. If the list is unsorted, does it matter where a new item is added? (p. 608)
3. The following code fragment implements the "remove, if there" meaning for the remove operation in an unsorted list. Change it so that the other meaning is implemented—that is, the assumption states that the item is in the list. (pp. 595–598)

```
while (index < numItems && !found)
{
  if (listItems[index].compareTo(item) == 0)
    found = true;
```

```
    else
      index++;
}
if (found)
{
   for (int count = index; count < numItems-1; count++)
      listItems[count] = listItems[count+1];
   numItems--;
}
```

4. In a sequential search of an unsorted array containing 1000 values, what is the average number of loop iterations required to find a value? What is the maximum number of iterations? (pp. 613–619)

5. The following code fragment sorts list items into ascending order. Change it to sort the items into descending order. (pp. 603–607)

```
for (passCount = 0; passCount < numItems; passCount++)
{
   minIndex = passCount;
   for (searchIndex = passCount + 1; searchIndex < numItems;
         searchIndex++)
     if (listItems[searchIndex].compareTo(listItems[minIndex]) < 0)
       minIndex = searchIndex;
   temp = listItems[minIndex];                     // Swap
   listItems[minIndex] = listItems[passCount];
   listItems[passCount] = temp;
}
```

6. Describe how the **add** operation can be used to build a sorted list from unsorted input data. (pp. 608–612)

7. Explain the following statement: "Sorting the elements in a list does not make the list a sorted list." (pp. 608–612)

8. Describe the basic principle behind the linear search in a sorted list. (pp. 613–619)

9. Describe the basic principle behind the binary search algorithm. (pp. 613–619)

10. What methods were marked **abstract** in our class **AbstractList**? (pp. 629–632)

11. What determines which methods are left **abstract**? (p. 631)

12. Which two methods are supplied by an **Iterator** as used with **ArrayList**? (pp. 636–638)

Answers

1. A list is a variable-sized structured data type; an array is a built-in type often used to implement a list.
2. No.

3.
```
index = 0;
  while (listItems[index].compareTo(item) != 0)
    index++;
  for (int count = index; count < numItems-1; count++)
    listItems[count] = listItems[count+1];
  numItems--;
```
4. The average number is 500.5 iterations; the maximum number is 1000 iterations. 5. The only change required is to replace the `< 0` with `> 0` in the inner loop. As a matter of style, the name `minIndex` should be changed to `maxIndex`. 6. The list initially has a length of zero. Each time a value is read, `add` puts the value in the list in its correct position. When all of the data values have been read, they are in the array in sorted order. 7. A sorted list is one that is always sorted. Sorting a list makes the list temporarily sorted; the next time an item is added, the list is no longer sorted. 8. A linear search in a sorted list can determine that an element is not there when the search passes the place it would belong. 9. The binary search takes advantage of sorted list values, looking at a component in the middle of the list and deciding whether the search value precedes or follows the midpoint. The search is then repeated on the appropriate half (quarter, eighth, and so on) of the list until the value is located. 10. `contains`, `remove`, and `add` 11. Methods that depend on a knowledge of the elements in the list are left `abstract`. 12. `next` and `hasNext`

Exam Preparation Exercises

1. A binary search can be applied to integers as well as to objects. Suppose the following values are stored in an array in ascending order:

   28 45 97 103 107 162 196 202 257

   Applying the binary search algorithm to this array, search for the following values and indicate how many array-component comparisons are required either to find the number or to find that it is not present in the list.

   a. 28

   b. 32

   c. 196

   d. 202

2. Repeat Exercise 1, applying the algorithm for a sequential search in a sorted list.

3. The following values are stored in an array in ascending order:

   29 57 63 72 79 83 96 104 114 136

   Apply the binary search algorithm looking for 114 in this list, and trace the values of `first`, `last`, and `middle`. Indicate any undefined values with a U.

4. A binary search is always a better choice than a sequential search. (True or False?)

5. If `resetList` initializes `currentPos` to −1 rather than 0, what corresponding change would have to be made in `next`?

6. Why does the outer loop of the sorting method run from 0 through `numItems - 2` rather than `numItems - 1`?

7. A method that adds a constant to the salary of everyone in a list is an example of (a) a constructor, (b) an observer, (c) an iterator, or (d) a transformer.

8. A method that stores values into a list is an example of (a) a constructor, (b) an observer, (c) an iterator, or (d) a transformer.

9. Is it slower to remove an item from the end of a list or from the beginning of a list?

10. Why does the remove operation have to shift elements in the array?

11. Which interface contains the method `compareTo`? What does `compareTo` return?

12. The class `ListOfStrings` assumes that no duplicate items appear in the list.

    a. Which method algorithms would have to be changed to permit duplicates?

    b. Would there still be options for the remove operation? Explain.

13. In the version of `ListOfStrings` derived from `AbstractList`, why did we have to cast items from the array to `String`?

14. Compare and contrast the functionality of the `ListOfStrings` class that we defined with the Java library's `ArrayList`.

Programming Warm-Up Exercises

1. Complete the implementation of `SortedListOfStrings` as a class derived from the original class `ListOfStrings`.

2. Complete the implementation of `ListOfStringsWithSort` as a class derived from the original class `ListOfStrings`.

3. Derive a subclass of `ListOfStrings` that has the following additional methods:

    a. A value-returning instance method named `position` that receives a single parameter, `item`, and returns the position where `item` occurs in the list.

    b. A Boolean instance method named `greaterFound` that receives a single argument, `item`, and searches the list for a value greater than `item`. If such a value is found, the method returns `true`; otherwise, it returns `false`.

    c. An instance method named `component` that returns a component of the list given a position number (`pos`). The position number must be within the range 0 through `numItems - 1`.

    d. A copy constructor for the class that takes an argument that specifies how much to expand the array holding the items. Implement the copy constructor by creating a larger array and copying all of the items in the list into the new array.

4. Implement `SortedListOfStrings` as a class derived from `AbstractList`.

5. Derive a subclass of `SortedListOfStrings` that has the additional methods outlined in Programming Warm-Up Exercise 3.

6. Write a Java **boolean** method named **exclusive** that takes three arguments: **item**, **list1**, and **list2** (the latter two arguments are of class **ListOfStrings** as defined in this chapter). The method returns **true** if **item** is present in either **list1** or **list2** but not both.

7. The **add** method in the class **SortedListOfStrings** adds items into the list in ascending order. Derive a new class from **SortedListOfStrings** that sorts the items into descending order.

8. Exam Preparation Exercise 12 asked you to examine the implication of a list with duplicates.

   a. Design an abstract class **ListWithDuplicates** that allows duplicate keys.

   b. How does your design differ from that of **AbstractList**?

   c. Implement your design, such that the items are unsorted and **remove** removes all of the duplicate items.

   d. Implement your design where the items are sorted and **remove** removes all of the duplicate items.

   e. Did you use a binary search in part (d)? If not, why not?

9. Rewrite the method **add** in the class **SortedListOfStrings** so that it implements the first addition algorithm discussed for sorted lists. That is, the place where the item should be added is found by searching from the beginning of the list. When this place is found, all of the items from the addition point to the end of the list shift down by one position.

10. Fill in the requested statements or code fragments for an **ArrayList** object.

    a. Instantiate an **ArrayList** object that is equivalent to our **ListOfStrings** object with room for 100 strings.

    b. Write a statement that instantiates an **ArrayList** object with no size specified. How many slots are allocated?

    c. Write a statement that adds **item** to the end of the **ArrayList** object **list**.

    d. Write a statement that returns the index of the last occurrence of a specified object in a list.

    e. Write a statement that instantiates an **ArrayList** iterator.

    f. Write a loop that iterates through the **ListOfStrings** class.

    g. Write a loop that iterates through an **ArrayList<String>** class.

11. Write a loop that uses the size of the list to access and print each item.

Programming Problems

1. A company wants to know the percentages of total sales and total expenses attributable to each salesperson. Each salesperson has a pair of data lines. The first line contains his or her name, with the last name coming first. The second line contains his or her sales (**int**) and expenses (**float**). Write an application that produces a report with a header

line containing the total sales and total expenses. Follow this header with a table containing each salesperson's name, percentage of total sales, and percentage of total expenses, sorted by the salesperson's name. Use one of the list classes developed in this chapter to implement your solution.

2. Only authorized shareholders are allowed to attend a company stockholders' meeting. Write an application to read a person's name from the keyboard, check it against a list of shareholders, and print a message on the screen saying whether the person may attend the meeting. The list of shareholders is in a file called `owners`, with one name per line, in the following format: first name, blank, last name. Use the end-of-file condition to stop reading the file. The maximum number of shareholders is 1000.

   As a stockholder enters the meeting, he or she enters his or her name. If the name does not appear on the list, the code should repeat the instructions on how to enter the name and then tell the user to try again. A message saying that the person may not participate in the meeting should be printed only after he or she has been given a second chance to enter the name.

3. Enhance the application in Problem 2 as follows:

   a. Print a report file showing the number of stockholders at the time of the meeting, the number present at the meeting, and the number of people who tried to participate in the meeting but were denied permission to attend.

   b. Follow this summary report with a list of the names of the stockholders, with either "Present" or "Absent" appearing after each name.

4. An advertising company wants to send a letter to its clients announcing a new fee schedule. The clients' names appear on several different lists in the company. The various lists are merged to form one file, called `clients`, but the company does not want to send a letter twice to anyone.

   Write an application that removes any names appearing on the list more than once. Each data line contains a four-digit code number, followed by a blank, and then the client's name. For example, Amalgamated Steel is listed as

   0231 Amalgamated Steel

Your code should output each client's code and name, but should not print any duplicates. Use one of the list classes developed in this chapter to implement your solution.

LEARNING / Portfolio

Case Study Follow-Up

1. Complete coding of the original version of `SortedListOfGrades`, which was to be implemented by borrowing code from `SortedListOfStrings`. How does this compare with the version derived from `AbstractList`?

2. Did you include method `contains` in your answer to Exercise 1? It is not needed in this application. Discuss the pros and cons of including an unnecessary method to make the list implementation consistent with other lists.

3. Complete the test plan for class `StatisticsList`.

4. Complete the test plan for the method `selectSort`.

5. In the version of `SortedListOfGrades` derived from `AbstractList`, we used the linear search for `add`. Replace it with a binary search.

12 Data Structures and Collections

Goals

Knowledge Goals

To:

- Understand the difference between array and linked implementations of a list
- Know how a stack works
- Know how a queue works
- Know how a binary tree works
- Know how a hash table works
- Understand the concepts behind the Java collections framework

Skill Goals

To be able to:

- Develop a linked data structure
- Use the `ArrayList` and `LinkedList` classes
- Use the `HashSet` and `TreeSet` classes
- Use the `Stack` class
- Use the `LinkedList` class to implement a queue
- Choose when to use an array-based versus a linked implementation of a data structure

1983
Bjarne Stroustrup works on the development of the programming language C++ at AT&T Bell Labs

1984
Apple introduces its 32-bit Macintosh computer through a famous Orwellian-themed advertising campaign that premiers during the Super Bowl

1984
Sony and Philips introduce the CD-ROM, a new means of storing digital data that far exceeds the floppy disk's potential

1984
The Last Starfighter revolutionizes the use of supercomputer-generated graphics in movies, and the term "cyberspace" is coined by William Gibson

1984
Intel's 16-bit 80286 chip, created in 1982, will be installed in 15 million PCs within 6 years

1985
The Cray 2 and Thinking Machines' parallel processor Connection Machine take speed to a new level: 1 billion operations per second

Introduction

In Chapter 11, we saw how to implement a list using an array. The array stores the list elements in a contiguous block of memory. Access to the array occurs through an index that indicates a memory location relative to the base address of the array. Because the computer can quickly look up values in an array, most list operations are very efficient when an array is used as the implementation structure.

As we saw, however, some list operations (such as `remove`) may require moving many elements of the array, which can be very slow. Also, the fixed size of the array limits the length of the list. In this chapter, we consider an alternative implementation approach—using references to connect the elements of a list. We call this structure a linked list, and it addresses these problems although it introduces some new issues.

Using the linking approach, we also examine some common ways of structuring data: stacks, queues, trees, and chained hash tables. We then look at a rich set of classes supplied by Java that implement various ways of managing collections of data using both arrays and linked structures.

1985
Microsoft releases Windows 1.0. It is their first in a series of widely-used operating systems

1985
Intel introduces the 80386, a 32-bit processing chip with on-chip memory management

1985
Paul Brainard creates PageMaker, and launches the world of PC desktop publishing

1986
The Cray XMP supercomputer executes 713 million floating-point calculations per second

1988
Microprocessor speeds reach 17 million instructions per second with Motorola's 88000 chip

1988
Robert Morris Jr. releases a worm program into the Internet, demonstrating the need for greater network security

12.1 ፧ Linked Structures

We begin this chapter by considering the differences between using an array or linking to implement a data structure. It is important throughout this chapter to keep in mind that any data structure can be implemented with either an array or links. We choose the implementation based on the needs of the problem we are solving. Just as each kind of object has a logical representation and an implementation, each type of data structure can be considered independently from a logical perspective and an implementation perspective. Later in the chapter we encounter some structures that are naturally considered, from the logical perspective, as being formed with links. However, from the implementation perspective, we still have the option to choose whether to use an array or links in building them.

■ Contiguous Versus Linked Structuring

As we have already pointed out, many problems in computing involve lists of items. In Chapter 11, we used the array to store the items in the list. The size of an array is fixed at instantiation time. Yet when we are working with lists, many times we don't know how many components we will ultimately have. The typical solution in this situation is to instantiate the array to be large enough to hold the maximum amount of data we expect. Because we usually have less data than the maximum, the length of the array is sometimes much larger than the number of components stored in the list. The length of the list varies during execution, but the array declared to hold the components doesn't vary in size (see Figure 12.1).

There is another technique for representing a list, however. With this alternative method, the list components are objects that are instantiated only as they are needed. Rather than being physically next to each other, as in an array, the components are logically next to each other (see Figure 12.2). Each component contains information about the location of the next component—a reference to the next component in the list is stored with each component.

Such a list can expand or contract as the program executes. As a consequence, we don't have to know in advance how long the list will be (see Figure 12.3). The only limitation is the amount of memory space available. Data structures built using this technique are called **dynamic data structures**. A dynamic data structure is built out of nodes, where each node is made up of a component (the data) and a reference (the **link**). Let's look at how we can use Java references to create dynamic data structures.

> **Dynamic data structure** A data structure that can expand and contract during execution
>
> **Link** A reference to an item that is logically adjacent to the current item

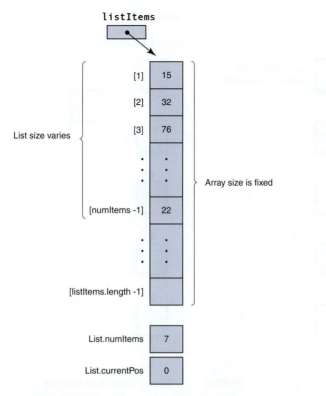

listItems

[1] 15
[2] 32
[3] 76

List size varies

.
.
.

Array size is fixed

[numItems -1] 22

.
.
.

[listItems.length -1]

List.numItems 7

List.currentPos 0

FIGURE 12.1   Array `listItems` is of Fixed Size

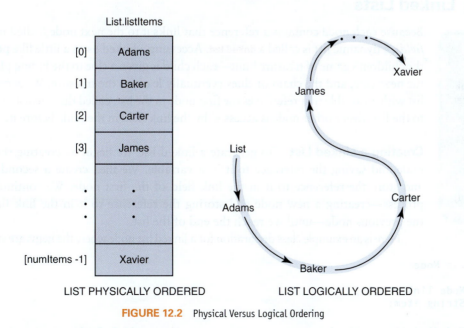

List.listItems

[0] Adams
[1] Baker
[2] Carter
[3] James

.
.
.

[numItems -1] Xavier

LIST PHYSICALLY ORDERED

Xavier
James
List
Adams
Baker
Carter

LIST LOGICALLY ORDERED

FIGURE 12.2   Physical Versus Logical Ordering

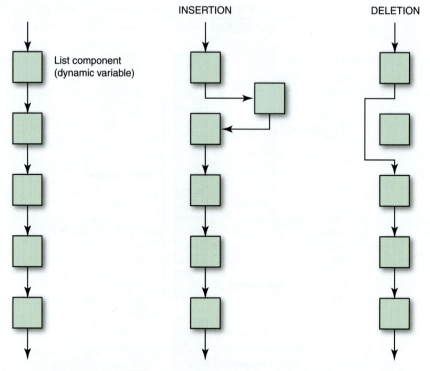

FIGURE 12.3 Dynamic Linked Data Structure

■ Linked Lists

> **Linked list** A list in which the order of the components is determined by an explicit link field in each node, rather than by the sequential order of the components in memory
>
> **External reference** A named variable that references the first node (also known as the head) of a linked list

Because each node contains a reference that links it to the next node (called its *link field*), a dynamic list is called a **linked list**. Accessing a linked list is a little like playing the children's game of treasure hunt—each child is given a clue to the hiding place of the next clue, and the chain of clues eventually leads to the treasure. We access the list with a variable that references the first node in the list, called the **external reference** to the list. Every other node is accessed by the link field in the node before it.

Creating a Linked List To generate a linked list, we begin by creating the first node and saving the reference to it in a variable. We then create a second node and store the reference to it in the link field of the first node. We continue this process—creating a new node and storing the reference to it in the link field of the previous node—until we reach the end of the list.

Here is an example class declaration for a linked list node where the items are strings:

```
class Node
{
  Node link = null;
  String item;

  Node() { item = ""; }                    // Default constructor
  Node(String newItem) { item = newItem; }  // Constructor
}
```

The only methods that we include in this code are the constructors. We could easily provide get and set methods for the fields, but this class is declared at the package level of access and will be used only by classes within the package that are designed to directly access the fields of nodes. Our use of linked nodes rather than arrays is an example of abstraction at work: Client code should not be aware of which approach is used to implement a list.

The following code fragment creates a linked list with the names Adams, Baker, and Carter as the items in the nodes (note that the fragment is in the same package and, therefore, has direct access to the fields of a node):

```
Node current;                              // Current end of list
Node list;                                 // External list reference
list = new Node("Adams");
current = list;
current.link = new Node("Baker");
current = current.link;
current.link = new Node("Carter");
current = current.link;
```

Let's go through each of these statements, describing what is happening and showing the list as it appears after each statement executes. First we create two variables that can refer to a node:

```
Node current;
Node list;
```

current

| null |

list

| null |

Next, we create a node, and set `list` and `current` to refer to it:

```
list = new Node("Adams");
current = list;
```

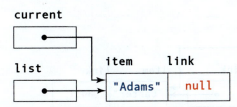

We then create a new node and set the `link` field of the existing node to refer to it:

```
current.link = new Node("Baker");
```

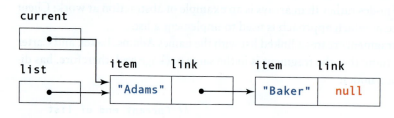

The next step is to make `current` refer to the new node by assigning its own `link` field to itself:

```
current = current.link;
```

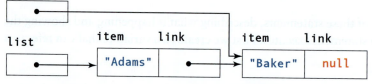

Now we can create another new node and set the `link` field of the node referenced by `current` to refer to it:

```
current.link = new Node("Carter");
```

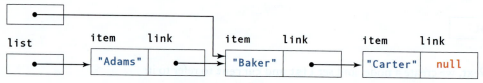

Once again, we make `current` refer to the new node:

```
current = current.link;
```

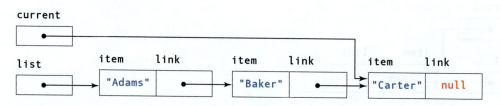

The last two steps can be applied any number of times to create a list of precisely the required length. Notice that `list` continues to refer to the first node in the list. It is through this external reference variable that we subsequently access the items in the list. We use `current` to keep track of the last element in the list (called the *tail*), which is where we add new elements.

Here is a demonstration application that builds a linked list from a file, and then shows how we can run through the list, printing the items out on the screen. Notice that we keep a count of the number of nodes in the list, just as we did with the array-based list in Chapter 11.

```java
import java.util.*;
import java.io.*;
public class LinkDemo
{
  // Create a linked list from lines on a file and then print the list
  public static void main (String args[]) throws IOException
  {
    Node current = null;                    // Create empty list
    Node list = null;
    int numItems = 0;
    Scanner in = new Scanner(new FileReader("linkdemo.txt"));

    if (in.hasNext())                       // Insert first node
    {
      list = new Node(in.nextLine());       //    Create first node
      current = list;                       //    Set current to first node
      numItems++;                           //    Increment count of nodes
    }

    while (in.hasNext())                    // Insert remaining nodes
    {                                       // Append new node
      current.link = new Node(in.nextLine());
      current = current.link;               //    Advance current to new node
      numItems++;                           //    Increment count of nodes
    }
    in.close();

    current = list;                         // Set current to first node
    for (int count = 0; count < numItems; count++)
    {                                       // Print nodes in list
      System.out.println(current.item);     // Print current node
      current = current.link;               // Set current to next node
    }
  }
}
```

Take a close look at the pattern for accessing the list, associated with the *for* loop in this application. Access to the list is initialized by resetting `current` to the first element of the list (the *head*). Each iteration of the loop then outputs the `item` field of the node, and advances `current` to the next node by assigning the `link` field of the `current` node to `current`. Thus, when the next iteration begins, `current` refers to the node following the one that was just output.

Be sure that you understand how assigning the `current.link` field to `current` causes `current` to advance through the list. In contrast, advancing to the next element in an array-based list involves simply incrementing the current position variable.

What would happen if the *for* loop tested for `count <= numItems`? At the end of the next-to-last iteration, `current` is set equal to the `link` field of the last node in the list. Because there is no successor node, the last node's `link` field is `null`. On the last iteration, attempting to output the `item` field of the node results in a `NullPointerException` being thrown, and the application crashes. Thus, when you use the number of items in the list to control a loop that runs through all of the nodes, you must be careful to avoid going one node too far.

With a linked list, there is another possibility for handling this situation. We can end the loop when the `link` field of the `current` node is `null`:

```
current = list;                           // Set current to first node
while (current.link != null)
{
  System.out.println(current.item);       // Print current node
  current = current.link;                 // Set current to next node
}
```

In this *while* loop, the continuation condition depends on the `link` field referring to a node that follows it. When we reach the last node, the `null` link indicates that we are done. As a result, we don't have to be concerned with the loop accidentally running off the end of the list.

As you can see, with a linked list, we don't need to use `numItems` to control the loop. That attribute is really needed only to support subarray processing in the array-based list implementation.

Traversal To visit every node in a data structure following an organized pattern of access

Running through an entire data structure in this kind of organized manner is called a **traversal**. In an array-based list, a traversal involves running through every item from index 0 to index `numItems-1`.

Now that we have a sense of how a linked list works, let's reimplement our `ListOfStrings` class from Chapter 11, this time using a linked structure instead of an array. We'll call the new class `LinkedListOfStrings`. We know from the preceding discussion that we need a variable, `list`, to reference the head of the list. We also need a variable, `current`, to use in traversing the list.

Even though a linked list doesn't need to keep track of the number of entries, the `ListOfStrings` class provides a method that returns that value. We can keep this value in a field, or we could compute it whenever it is needed by traversing the list and counting the nodes. Let's take the latter approach, because doing so will simplify the `add` and `remove` methods.

In our earlier example, the list was filled before any processing was done. Thus `current` did double duty: It kept track of the end of the list as it was built, and it then traversed the list from head to tail. In the general case, items may be added to a list at any time, and we may wish to traverse the list before it is completely filled. Because `current` is used for running through the list, we need another variable, which we call `tail`, to keep track of where items should be added to the list.

Here is the code for the class heading and its attributes:

```
public class LinkedListOfStrings
{
  // Data fields
  protected Node list = null;        // Reference to first node
  protected Node tail = null;        // Reference to end node
  protected Node current = null;     // Variable for traversal with an
                                     // iterator
```

Next we turn our attention to the operations on the linked list. Let's review the operations supplied by `ListOfStrings`:

ListOfStrings
#listItems: String() #numItems: int #currentPos: int
+ListOfStrings() +ListOfStrings(maxItems: int) +isFull(): boolean +isEmpty(): boolean +size(): int +contains(item: String): boolean +add(item: String) +remove(item: String) +resetList(): void +hasNext(): boolean +next(): String

Because a linked list is always just the right size, we no longer need a constructor that specifies the maximum number of items in the list. A default constructor will do just fine. Also, `isFull` is never **true**, so we can delete it from the interface. The other operations are common to both implementations. Here are the UML diagrams for our new **Node** and `LinkedListOfStrings` classes:

Node
~link: Node ~item: String
~Node() ~Node(String)

LinkedListOfStrings
#list: Node #tail: Node #current: Node
+ListOfStrings() +isEmpty(): boolean +size(): int +contains(item: String): boolean +add(item: String) +remove(item: String) +resetList(): void +hasNext(): boolean +next(): String

Now we are ready to look at each of the operations in turn.

Operations on Linked Lists   The default constructor is trivial because all of the fields are properly initialized by their declarations. Thus it does nothing (we could omit it, but we prefer to document its nature by including it):

```java
public LinkedListOfStrings() {}
```

How do we tell if a linked list is empty? We simply check for `list == null`:

```java
public boolean isEmpty() { return list == null;}
```

We have decided to compute the size of the list by traversing it, so we use a *while* loop that tests for the current node being `null`:

```java
public int size()
{
  Node current = list;
  int numItems = 0;
  while (current != null)        // Done when there is no next node
  {
    numItems++;
    current = current.link;      // Advance to the next node
  }
  return numItems;
}
```

The `contains` operation requires that we traverse the list until we find a matching value in an `item` field. In the array-based implementation, we used a *while* loop that tested for the end of the list and for a matching item. We'll use the same approach here, except that we test for the end of the list by looking for a `null` `link` field. In the following code, we declare a local `current` variable, which allows us to call `contains` without disturbing the value in the instance field `current`. Keep in mind that `current` (the instance field) is reserved for use in conjunction with the iterator `next`.

```java
public boolean contains(String item)
{
  Node current = list;
  while (current != null && current.item.compareTo(item) != 0)
    current = current.link;
  return current != null;
}
```

Look closely at the test in the *while* loop. We are taking advantage of the partial evaluation that Java uses for a logical `&&` operation. If `current == null`, then the right-hand side of the expression is not evaluated. That's a good thing, because if `current` is `null`, it doesn't refer to a node, there wouldn't be an `item` field to compare with, and an exception would be

Next-to-last iteration of `contains`

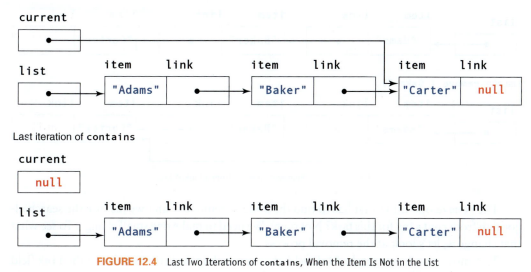

Last iteration of `contains`

FIGURE 12.4   Last Two Iterations of `contains`, When the Item Is Not in the List

thrown. Figure 12.4 shows the state of the list in the next-to-last and last iterations of this loop when `item` isn't found:

By arranging the loop condition in this manner, we check every item in the list. Only if none of them matches `item` do we end up with `current` equal to `null`. When the loop exits, we simply return the result of testing for `current != null`.

Next we turn to the **add** operation. Two situations must be considered when adding an item to the list. If the list is currently empty, we need to assign the new item to `list` as well as to `tail`. If this item is not the first item in the list, we append it to the last node in the list and set `tail` to refer to it. Keep in mind that when we enter the method, `tail` refers to the item that is currently the last in the list. Appending the new item therefore involves setting `tail.link` to the new item.

```java
public void add(String newItem)
{
  Node item = new Node(newItem);
  if (list == null)              // List empty
  {
    list = item;                 // Refer list to this new node
    tail = item;                 // Tail is also this new node
  }
  else                           // List not empty
  {
    tail.link = item;            // Append new node to tail
    tail = tail.link;            // Advance tail to new node
  }
}
```

Original list

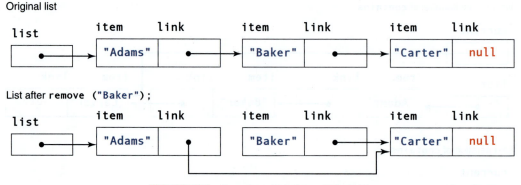

List after `remove` (`"Baker"`);

FIGURE 12.5 Removing a Node from a Linked List

The `remove` operation first has to find the node to remove. Can't we just use the search algorithm from `contains` for this task? Not quite. We need to make one small change. To see what that change is, let's look at the removal process.

To remove a node, we set the `link` field of the preceding node to the value of the `link` field of the matching node so that the preceding node then refers to the node following the match. This process is illustrated in Figure 12.5 for a call to `remove`(`"Baker"`). Thus, as we search for the matching node, we also must keep track of the node preceding the one that is currently being compared.

As you can see in Figure 12.5, the removed node still exists, but no other node or variable refers to it. Thus the JVM's garbage collection process will sweep it up and return the node to the free memory pool, as shown in Figure 12.6.

In languages such as C++, we must explicitly dispose of such nodes. When we first discussed garbage collection, we described an error called a memory leak, in which a programmer forgets to get rid of objects when they are no longer being used. Failing to dispose of nodes as they are removed from a linked list is a classic example of a memory leak bug. Java's use of garbage collection both avoids such errors and saves us the extra work of explicit disposal of the nodes.

The algorithm for the general case of `remove` is quite simple. First we search for the node to delete (note that we've used *prior* to designate "the preceding node"):

```
Find node matching item

Set current to list
Set prior to null
while (current != null && current.item.compareTo(item) != 0)
    Set prior to current
    Set current to next node (current.link)
```

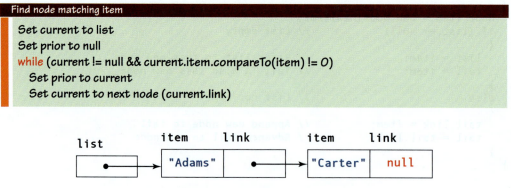

FIGURE 12.6 The List After Garbage Collection

As with `contains`, `current` will equal `null` if the item isn't found. Thus we should guard the operation to remove the node by checking that the node was found. Given that `current` refers to the matching node, and `prior` refers to the node before it, removing a node is just a matter of setting the `link` field of the `prior` node to refer to the node following the match. The `link` field of the matching node contains the reference to the node that follows it, so the guarded assignment is

---
remove node (general case)

if a match was found (current != null)
    Set prior.link to current.link

That takes care of the general case. But there are some special cases to consider:

1. The list is empty.
2. The item is the first in the list: We need to adjust `list`.
3. The item is the last in the list: We need to adjust `tail`.
4. The item is the only one in the list: We need to adjust both `list` and `tail`.

Let's consider each of these cases in turn.

First, what happens if the list is empty? The search algorithm ends with `prior` and `current` both equal to `null`. Because no match was found, nothing is done.

To understand the case where the item is the first in the list, let's look at an illustration. Figure 12.7a shows the list when the search has found a match in the first node. When the item matches the first node in the list, we have to explicitly change the value of `list`. In Figure 12.7b, you can see that `current` still refers to the removed node. Thus you might think that the node won't be subject to garbage collection. But keep in mind that this version of `current` is local to the method. Therefore, when the method returns, the JVM disposes of `current`, and the node can be collected.

We test for the match being the first node by checking whether `prior == null`. Once `list` is updated, no further action is required. In the following algorithm, notice that the test for whether a match was found now guards both cases:

List after search

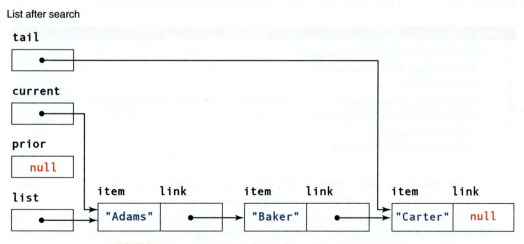

FIGURE 12.7a   Removing the First Node in a List: `remove("Adams")`

List after first item is removed

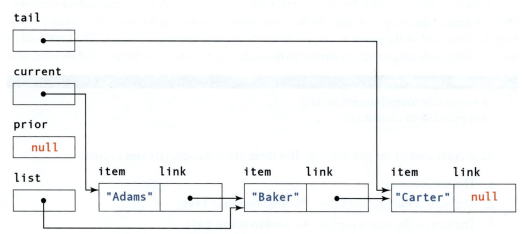

FIGURE 12.7b Removing the First Node in a List: `remove("Adams")` (cont.)

remove node (general and first node cases)

> if a match was found (current != null)
>   if node is first (prior == null)
>   Set list to next node (list.link)
>   else (general case)
>   Set prior.link to current.link

To see what happens when the item is at the end of the list, let's look at another illustration. Figure 12.8 shows what happens when we call `remove("Carter")`. There are two changes to the list in this case. We adjust `tail` to equal `prior`, and we treat the node itself like the general case by setting its `link` field to the value of the `link` field in the matching node (which happens to be `null`). Here is the algorithm that incorporates this special case:

remove node

> if a match was found (current != null)
>   if node is last (current == tail)
>   Set tail to prior
>   if node is first (prior == null)
>   Set list to next node (list.link)
>   else (general case)
>   Set prior.link to current.link

Our last special case is the situation when the matching node is the only one on the list. As Figure 12.9 shows, we must set both `list` and `tail` to `null`.

If you look at the current algorithm carefully, you'll see that the special cases already take care of setting `list` and `tail` to `null`. Because `current` is the same as `tail`, `tail` is set to `prior`, which is `null`. Because `prior` is `null`, `list` is set to the contents of its `link` field (which is also `null`). Thus no changes to the algorithm are needed, and we are ready to code the method.

List after search

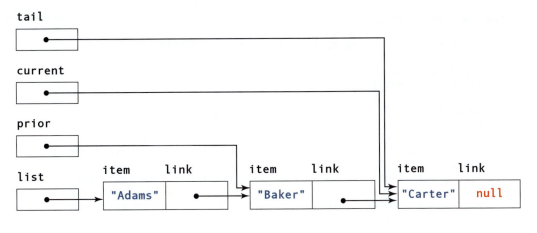

List after last item is removed

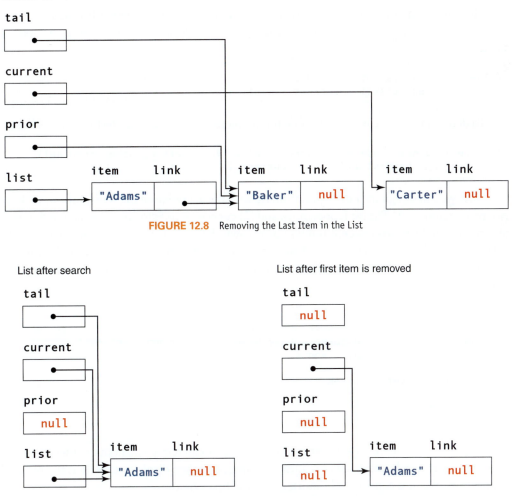

FIGURE 12.8 Removing the Last Item in the List

List after search

List after first item is removed

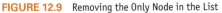

FIGURE 12.9 Removing the Only Node in the List

```
public void remove(String item)
{
  Node current = list;
  Node prior = null;
  while (current != null && current.item.compareTo(item) != 0)
  {
    prior = current;
    current = current.link;
  }
  if (current != null)                    // Item found
  {
    if (current == tail)                  // Removing last item
      tail = prior;                       //    Refer tail to prior node
    if (prior == null)                    // Removing first item
      list = list.link;                   //    Refer list to next node
    else                                  // Match isn't the first item
      prior.link = current.link;          //    Refer prior to next node
  }
}
```

The only remaining operations are those related to our iterator: resetList, hasNext, and next. To reset the list, we merely set current (the version declared as an instance variable) to list:

```
// The iteration is initialized by setting current to list
public void resetList() { current = list; }
```

To determine if there is another node following the current one, we test for a null link:

```
// There is a next node when current refers to something other than null
public boolean hasNext() { return current != null; }
```

Now we can design the next operation. As with the array-based implementation, we have two preconditions: (1) The list is not empty, and (2) current is not already at the end of the list—otherwise, a NullPointerException will be thrown. Before advancing current, we save the current item value in a variable. To advance current to the next item, we set it to the value of its link field. After advancing current, we can return the saved item value. Here is the code that implements these steps:

```
public String next()
// Returns the item at the next position
// Assumptions:  no transformers have been invoked since last call,
//    the list is not empty, and current is not at tail
{
  String item = current.item;
  current = current.link;
  return item;
}
```

Now that we have a LinkedListOfStrings class, we can reimplement our earlier LinkDemo application that reads a text file into a list of strings, and then displays it. Here is the recoded application, which is considerably shorter than the first version:

```java
import java.util.*;
import java.io.*;
public class LinkedListOfStringsDemo
{
  // Create a linked list from lines on a file and then print the list
  public static void main (String args[]) throws IOException
  {
    LinkedListOfStrings list = new LinkedListOfStrings();   // Make an
                                                            // empty list
    Scanner in = new Scanner(new FileReader("linkdemo.txt"));
    while (in.hasNext())                                    // Fill the list
      list.add(in.nextLine());
    in.close();
    list.resetList();
    while (list.hasNext())                                  // Print the list
      System.out.println(list.next());
  }
}
```

Comparison of Array-Based and Linked Lists How do we choose between our different implementations of a list of strings? One approach uses the array as its underlying structure, and the other uses a linked list. Which strategy is better? As usual, it depends on the situation. It is more informative to ask: When is each implementation more appropriate?

The array-based list has the advantage of providing rapid access to its elements. Modern computer memory has been designed to provide faster access to groups of values stored in adjacent memory locations, as is done with an array. In contrast, the nodes of a linked list do not have to be adjacent, so it can take longer to fetch them from RAM. Also, at the machine code level, it takes fewer instructions to increment an index and fetch the corresponding array value than it does to fetch an address from a link field and then fetch the next node and retrieve its item field.

If you refer back to the `remove` operation for the `ListOfStrings` class, you will notice that we used a *for* loop to move all of the remaining elements up by one place to fill the vacated slot in the array. With a linked list, we merely adjust some references to delete a node. In terms of efficiency, we say deletion in an array-based list can take a maximum of N operations, where N is the number of elements in the list. In a linked list, however, it never takes more than two assignments to perform a deletion. Thus, in addition to the advantage that a linked list is always just the right size, node deletion is faster in a linked list. Notice that we did not say that the `remove` operation is faster. We have defined `remove` to include a linear search, so the operation may take as many as N operations in both implementations. Nevertheless, once we have found the node to delete, the linked version is generally faster.[1]

If the removals occur near the head of the list, then removing from a linked list is much faster. For example, if we are simulating people arriving to and departing from a long line at an airport ticket counter, all of the additions occur at the tail and all of the deletions occur at the head, which is faster in a linked list. Conversely, if the deletions occur near the tail, the search in the

---

1. In terms of algorithmic complexity, we say that array-based deletion is $O(N)$ and linked list deletion is $O(1)$.

array-based list is faster (because accessing memory is faster with an array), and the deletion time is similar for the two implementations.

When you are trying to decide whether to use an array representation or a linked representation, determine which of the operations are applied most frequently. Use your analysis to choose the implementation that would be better in the context of your particular problem.

There is an additional point to consider when deciding whether to use an array-based list or a linked list. How accurately can you predict the maximum number of components in the list? Does the number of components in the list fluctuate widely? If you know the maximum and it remains fairly constant, an array representation is probably more useful. Otherwise, it would be better to choose a linked representation to use memory more efficiently. When the size of the list is expected to remain small, an array-based implementation is almost always faster.

SOFTWARE MAINTENANCE CASE STUDY

Linked Implementation of `ToDoList`

Maintenance Task Our job is to change the `ToDoList` application from Chapter 11 so that it uses the `LinkedListOfStrings` in place of the original array-based `ListOfStrings`.

Discussion Whenever you are presented with the task of replacing an underlying class in an application with a different implementation, the place to begin is by comparing the interfaces of the two classes. If they are identical, then your job may be as simple as changing the class name in a few declarations. In that case, we say that the new class is **backward compatible** with the old one.

Backward compatible A property of a new piece of software that enables it to be used in place of an existing piece of software, with no changes to any client code. The new software may add features, but must fully support all existing features.

Perfect backward compatibility is a rare scenario. Instead, we typically replace a class with another because the new class provides some additional features. In doing so, it may also eliminate some operations if they are redundant or unnecessary in the context of the improvements.

Let's review the UML diagrams for our two classes. Here is the diagram for the new class:

```
            LinkedListOfStrings
#list: Node
#tail: Node
#current: Node

+ListOfStrings()
+isEmpty(): boolean
+size(): int
+contains(item: String): boolean
+add(item: String)
+remove(item: String)
+resetList(): void
+hasNext(): boolean
+next(): String
```

Now we look at the UML diagram for the existing class. We've highlighted the methods in `ListOfStrings` that aren't provided in the linked implementation—namely, the constructor that sets the maximum size of the list and the `isFull` method. Because the linked version of the list isn't limited in size, these methods are no longer relevant.

```
              ListOfStrings
#listItems: String()
#numItems: int
#currentPos: int

+ListOfStrings()
+ListOfStrings(maxItems: int)
+isFull(): boolean
+isEmpty(): boolean
+size(): int
+contains(item: String): boolean
+add(item: String)
+remove(item: String)
+resetList(): void
+hasNext(): boolean
+next(): String
```

Existing Code Once we have identified the interface differences, the next step is to search through the existing code to locate all statements that depend on these differences. Here is the code, with these places highlighted:

```java
//**************************************************************************
// Class ToDoList is the driver for class ListOfStrings
//**************************************************************************
import java.io.*;
import java.util.*;

public class ToDoList
{
enum Operations {ADD, REMOVE, SIZE, ISEMPTY, ISFULL, CONTAINS, PRINT, QUIT}

  public static void main (String[] args)
    throws IllegalArgumentException, FileNotFoundException
  {
    Scanner toDoFile = new Scanner(new FileReader("toDoList"));
    Scanner in = new Scanner(System.in);
    Operations operation;
    String item;
    boolean keepGoing = true;
    ListOfStrings list = new ListOfStrings(4);
    while (toDoFile.hasNext())
      list.add(toDoFile.nextLine());

    toDoFile.close();
    operation = inOperation(in);
    while (keepGoing)
    {
      switch (operation)
      {
        case ADD:
            System.out.println("Enter item to add.");
            item = in.nextLine();
            if (!list.contains(item))
              list.add(item);
            break;
        case REMOVE:
            System.out.println("Enter item to remove.");
            item = in.nextLine();
            list.remove(item);
            break;
        case SIZE:
            System.out.println("Length of list is " + list.size());
            break;
        case ISEMPTY:
            if (list.isEmpty())
              System.out.println("List is empty.");
            else
              System.out.println("List is not empty.");
            break;
```

```
            case ISFULL:
                if (list.isFull())
                    System.out.println("List is full.");
                else
                    System.out.println("List is not full.");
                break;
            case CONTAINS:
                System.out.println("Enter item to check.");
                item = in.nextLine();
                if (list.contains(item))
                    System.out.println(item + " is in the list.");
                else
                    System.out.println(item + " is not in the list.");
                break;
            case PRINT:
                System.out.println
                    ("The to-do list contains the following items:");
                list.resetList();
                while (list.hasNext())
                    System.out.println(list.next());
                break;
            case QUIT    :
                keepGoing = false;
                break;
        }
        if (keepGoing)
            operation  = inOperation(in);
    }
    PrintWriter toDoFileSave = new PrintWriter("toDoList");
    list.resetList();
    while (list.hasNext())
        toDoFileSave.println(list.next());
    toDoFileSave.close();
}
```

There are no statements in the `inOperation` method that depend on the differences, so we do not repeat the code here.

Obviously, the declaration of `list` depends directly on the class from which it is instantiated. It is straightforward to make that change:

```
LinkedListOfStrings list = new LinkedListOfStrings();
```

But what about the case that calls the `isFull` method, and the presence of a corresponding value in the `Operations` `enum`? One simple approach would be to replace that case with the following code:

```
case ISFULL:
    System.out.println("List is not full.");
    break;
```

The list is never full, so we can always print the same message. (Actually, the computer could potentially run out of memory, in which case it will throw an exception. Of course, if our to-do list ever gets that long, we have bigger problems to worry about!) Our original test plan assumed a list of limited size for testing `isFull`, so that test will always fail with this new implementation. Thus it is essentially pointless to retain this aspect of the application.

The alternative is to entirely remove the command from the driver. To do so, we delete `ISFULL` from the enum, and we delete the whole `ISFULL` case from the *switch* statement. By deleting the highlighted code and replacing the name of the class that we use to declare `list`, our application has now been converted to use `LinkedListOfStrings`.

■ Other Data Structures

We can use links (or arrays) to implement many other data structures. The study of data structures forms a major topic in computer science. Indeed, entire books and courses cover the subject. Our purpose in this section is not to turn you into an expert in data structures but rather to describe some commonly used structures at an abstract level. We mention briefly four of the most useful structures: stacks, queues, binary trees, and chained hash tables. A thorough treatment is left to a data structures text.

> **Stack** A data structure in which insertions and deletions can be made from only one end

Stacks　A **stack** is a data structure that can be accessed from only one end. We can insert an element at the top (as the first item) and we can remove the top (first) element. This structure models a property commonly encountered in real life. Accountants call it LIFO, which stands for "last in, first out." The plate holder in a cafeteria has this property. You can take only the top plate. When you do, the plate below it rises to the top so the next person can take one. Cars in a noncircular driveway also exhibit this property: The last car in must be the first car out. The term **push** is used for the insertion operation, and the term **pop** is used for the deletion operation. Figure 12.10 shows what happens when you **push** an element on a linked implementation of a stack and then **pop** the stack.

Stacks are used frequently in systems software. The JVM, for example, uses a stack to keep track of method calls. The Java compiler uses a stack to translate arithmetic expressions. Stacks are used whenever we wish to remember a sequence of objects or actions in the reverse order from their original occurrence. An algorithm to read in a file of lines and print it out in reverse order using a stack of strings is shown here:

Reverse File

```
Create stack
Create Scanner in
while in.hasNext
    stack.push(in.nextLine())
while not stack.empty
    println stack.pop
```

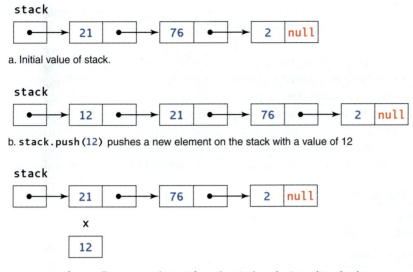

a. Initial value of stack.

b. `stack.push(12)` pushes a new element on the stack with a value of 12

c. `x = stack.pop()` pops an element from the stack and returns its value in `x`

FIGURE 12.10   A Linked Implementation of a Stack, Showing **push** and **pop** Operations

We can implement a stack using a linked structure. The **push** and **pop** operations merely add and remove elements from the head of the structure. Here is the algorithm for **push**:

```
push (String newItem)

   Create newNode(newItem)
   Set newNode.link to stack
   Set stack to newNode
```

The **pop** algorithm is similarly simple, although we do need to check for an empty stack:

```
pop () returns String

   if stack != null
      Set top to stack.item;
      Set stack to stack.link
      return top
   else
      return null
```

Queues   A **queue** (pronounced like the letter Q) is a data structure in which elements are entered at one end and removed from the other. Accountants call the property FIFO, meaning "first in, first out." A waiting line in a bank or supermarket and a line of cars on a one-way street are types of queues. Indeed, queues often are used in computer simulations of similar situations.

Whereas the terminology for the insert and remove operations on stacks is standard (**push, pop**), no such standardization exists with queues. The operation of

> **Queue**   A data structure in which insertions are made at one end and deletions are made at the other end

inserting at the rear of the queue has many names in the literature; insert, add, and enqueue are three common ones. Correspondingly, the operation for removing from the front of the queue is variously called delete, remove, and dequeue.

We have chosen to call our procedures **add** and **remove**. We are accessing both ends, so we need two external pointers: **front** and **rear**. For a linked implementation, Figure 12.11 shows an empty queue (a), insertion into a queue (b), and deletion from a queue (c).

We have already seen the algorithms for both **add** and **remove**. The queue **add** operation is identical to the **add** operation that appends the new node to the tail of a linked list; **remove** is the same as the stack **pop** operation, which removes a node from the head of a list. In fact, it is quite common to implement stack and queue classes using a linked list class as the underlying structure.

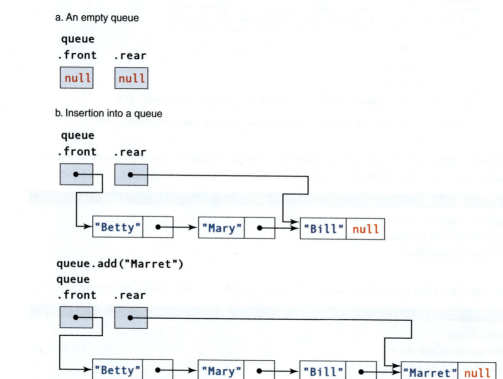

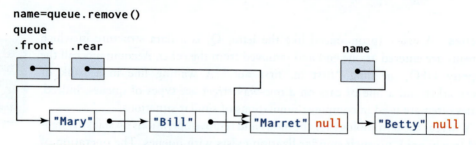

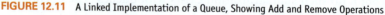

FIGURE 12.11   A Linked Implementation of a Queue, Showing Add and Remove Operations

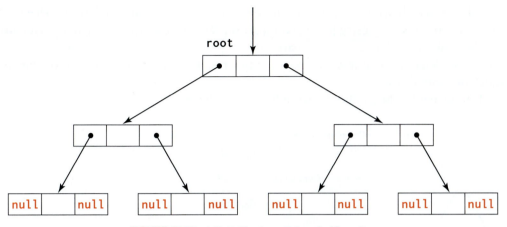

FIGURE 12.12 A Linked Implementation of a Binary Tree

Binary Trees We can expand the concept of a linked list to structures containing nodes with more than one link field. One of these structures is known as a **binary tree** (Figure 12.12). The tree is referenced by an external pointer to a specific node, called the *root* of the tree. The root has two pointers: one to its *left child* and one to its *right child*. Each child also has two pointers: one to its left child and one to its right child. The left and right children of a node are called *siblings*. Note that we can also implement this logical structure with an array, but it is most easily visualized using links.

For any node in a tree, the left child of the node is the root of the *left subtree* of the node. Likewise, the right child is the root of the *right subtree*. Nodes whose left and right children are both `null` are called *leaf nodes*.

Although Figure 12.12 shows a binary tree with only seven nodes, there is no theoretical limit on the number of nodes in a tree. It is easy to see why this structure is called "binary"—each node can have two branches. If you turn the figure upside down, you can see why it is called a tree.

A **binary search tree** is a special kind of binary tree. In a binary search tree, the component in any node is greater than the component in its left child and any of its children (left subtree) and less than the component in its right child and any of its children (right subtree). This definition assumes no duplicates. The tree illustrated below is an example of a binary search tree.

> **Binary tree** A data structure, each of whose nodes refers to left and right child nodes
>
> **Binary search tree** A binary tree in which the value in any node is greater than the value in its left child and any of its children and less than the value in its right child and any of its children

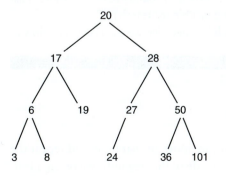

A binary search tree is useful because, if we are looking for a certain item, we can tell which half of the tree it is in by using just one comparison. We then can tell which half of that half-tree the item is in with one more comparison. This process continues until either we find the item or we determine that it is not present in the tree. The process is analogous to a binary search of a sorted array.

Let's search for the number 50 in our binary search tree.

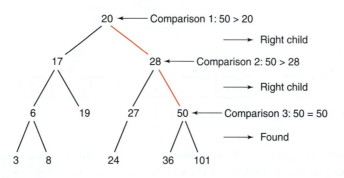

Now let's look for 18, a number that is not there.

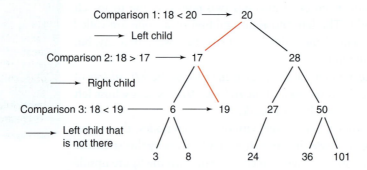

The left child of 19 is `null`, so we know that 18 isn't in the tree. Not only do we know that 18 is not present, but we are also at the right place to insert 18 if we want to do so.

To summarize, we compared the value we were looking for with the item in the tree and took the appropriate branch if the value and the item were not the same. When we started to take a branch that was `null`, we knew that the value was not in the tree. Just as the binary search of a sorted list with N items takes at most $\log_2 N$ steps, so does searching in a binary search tree.

If we want to print all of the values in a binary search tree in order, we traverse it as follows:

Tree Traversal

If the left child isn't null, traverse the left subtree
Print the current item
If the right child isn't null, traverse the right subtree

We start at the root of the tree. If it has a left child, we move to that node and repeat the process. We continue in the same manner down the left side of the tree until we reach a leaf, which we print. Then we move back up to the parent of that leaf and print it before traversing the subtree to its right. For example, given the binary search tree

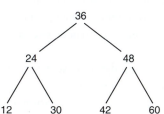

traversal begins with the root (36), proceeds to its left child (24), and then moves to the left child of 24, which is 12. Because 12 is a leaf, it is printed, and we back up to 24, which we also print. Then we traverse its right subtree, which is the leaf 30. After printing 30 we go back to 24. Since we are done with this subtree, we back up to 36 and print it. Then the process repeats with the right subtree, printing 42, 48, and 60.

As we see in Chapter 13, an algorithm such as this one, which calls itself to process a smaller portion of the problem, is said to be *recursive*. In that chapter, we'll also see that a stack is the natural choice of data structure for keeping track of where we are in the tree.

This particular form of traversal (visit left subtree, then root, then right subtree) is called an **in-order traversal**. Two other traversal patterns are commonly used for a tree as well:

> **In-order traversal**   A traversal of a binary tree that proceeds in the pattern of "visit the left subtree, visit the root, then visit the right subtree"

Pre-order Traversal

Visit the root.
Visit the left subtree.
Visit the right subtree.

Post-order Traversal

Visit the left subtree.
Visit the right subtree.
Visit the root.

The names of these patterns reflect the place within the order of traversal that we visit the root. If we visit the root before we visit the subtrees, then it is **pre-order traversal**. If we visit the root after the subtrees, then it is **post-order traversal**. Depending on the data stored in a binary tree, each order of traversal may have a particular use.

Trees are not limited to a binary branching factor. If we define a node to have three children, for example, we get a tree that has three branches per node. Nor are trees limited to having the same number of branches in each node. For example, we can construct a tree that represents a family genealogy, where the number of links from a node depends on the number of children who were born to a given set of parents. To implement a variable number of child links, we might use a list of nodes as a field within a tree node.

> **Pre-order traversal**   A traversal of a binary tree that proceeds in the pattern of "visit the root, then visit the left and right subtrees"
>
> **Post-order traversal**   A traversal of a binary tree that proceeds in the pattern of "visit the left and right subtrees, then visit the root"

Graph A data structure in which the nodes can be arranged in any pattern

Hashing A technique used to perform insertion of and access to elements in a data structure in approximately constant time, by using the value of each element to identify its location in the structure

Hash function A function used to manipulate the value of an element to produce an index that identifies its location in a data structure

Lists, stacks, queues, and trees all share the property that the logical adjacency is in one direction (from head to tail, from root to leaf, and so on). We can form even more sophisticated structures, called **graphs**, in which logical connections can be in any direction. We might use a graph to represent the roads connecting a set of cities or the network connecting a set of computers. As you can see, data structures can become quite complex.

Just as we were able to implement a list as an array or a dynamic structure, so we can implement stacks, queues, trees, and graphs with dynamic structures or arrays. Always keep in mind that a data structure has both a logical organization and an implementation structure. The two are distinct, and the choice of each depends on the requirements of any given problem.

Next we look at a different kind of logical structure that provides very fast searching under certain conditions. We'll again see that this structure can have multiple implementations.

Hash Tables Your summer job at a drive-in theater includes changing the movie title on the sign each week. The letters are kept in a box in the projection booth. During your first day on the job, you discover that the letters are in random order, so you have to search through nearly all of them to find the ones you need. You sort the letters into alphabetical order, which allows you to use a binary search to locate each letter, but that's still tedious. Finally, you make a set of 26 cards to separate the letters, and then you are able to directly pull each letter from its place in the box.

Because you are searching for values within a known range, you've divided up the space so that you can directly locate them. In general, if the items you are searching have this property, you can merely use an index to access the corresponding section of an array, based on their values, and retrieve them. Given a set of N values, the searching algorithms we've seen up to now have had a maximum of either N steps (linear search) or $\log_2 N$ steps (binary search). This new technique typically takes just a few steps, regardless of the amount of data. We refer to this approach as **hashing**.

Our letter-finding example is a perfect situation for using hashing because there are a small number of possible values. Unfortunately, most data are not so well behaved. For example, if our data values are real numbers representing temperatures, then the number of potential values is immense. Java does not let us create an array big enough to use a **float** value as an index.

In a given application, however, temperatures might have a very limited range, such as 90.0 to 110.0. If we are interested in precision to only one-tenth of a degree, then there are actually just 201 distinct values. We could develop a method that takes a temperature and returns an index in the range of 0 to 200, thereby storing temperatures using hashing. Such a method is called a **hash function**. Assuming that the hash function takes a small amount of time to compute, then searching with hashing is still a very fast operation.

In the preceding discussion we have ignored the problem of dealing with duplicates in the data set. Also, some data sets contain an irregular distribution of values. For example, if you are sorting by names, you will find that many more begin with A, M, or S than with Q, X, or Z (although those frequencies change depending on where you are in the world). As a consequence, we may end up trying to store multiple values into the same place in the array, a condition that we call a **collision**.

Several approaches to dealing with collisions are possible. For example, when we attempt to store a value into a location that's already full, we can simply increment the index until we find an empty location. Unfortunately, that strategy tends to produce clusters of filled locations. In the worst case, it can take as many accesses to find an empty slot as there are elements in the array. Another approach is known as rehashing—we feed the output of the hash function back into the function (or into another function) to select a new index.

Until now, we've assumed a simple linear array implementation. Hashing, however, isn't limited to such a structure. We could, for example, use an array of linked lists. The hash function indexes into this array and adds the item to the linked list at that location. With each collision on a given array slot, the associated list simply grows one node longer. If the hash function is well designed, the lists remain reasonably short (few collisions), so the search still takes just a few operations. Figure 12.13 shows such a structure, called a chained hash table.

The efficiency of hashing depends on having an array or table that is large enough to hold the data set with enough extra room to keep collisions to a minimum. Sometimes this is an impractical condition to satisfy, but for many problems hashing is a very effective means of organizing data. For example, we could use a hash table to implement a list that has fast insertion, deletion, and access operations.

Developing a good hash function can require a considerable amount of data analysis. Our goal here is not to show you how to develop such functions, but merely to help you appreciate hashing and its limitations. As we see later in the chapter, the Java library supports several classes that use hashing to implement data structures.

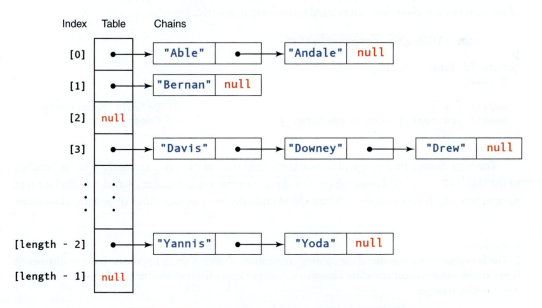

FIGURE 12.13 A Linked Implementation of a Chained Hash Table

12.2 ⋮ Generic Types in Java

In all of our discussions of data structures, we have typically assumed that items have a specific type or class (such as `String`). In Chapter 11, we also saw how a list item could be an object of any class that implements `Comparable`, enabling many different classes of items to be stored in a list.

There is, however, a risk associated with using `Comparable` to support a general-purpose list type: A client may try to insert items of different classes into such a list. Our `compareTo` operation may then throw an exception when we try to search the list, because we would be comparing the search value against different classes of items.

For example, the `Name` and `String` classes both implement `Comparable`. Thus we could add a mix of these objects to the list. If we then try to search for a name among this mix of `String` and `Name` objects, the `compareTo` method provided by `Name` tries to compare the search value (a `Name`) with each item on the list. When the search comes to the first `String` object, the argument to `compareTo` will be incompatible.

What we really want to do is create a generic list class that can operate on any type of data without having to change the code, while avoiding the potential problems of using a list of `Comparable` items. For example, suppose we declare a variable that holds the name of a data type, which we then pass as an argument to the constructor for our list, so that it would be specialized to hold a list of that type of item. Java does, indeed, support such type variables, and here we see how to use them to make a generic linked list.

■ A Generic Linked List

Let's start by looking at the implementation of a generic version of class `Node`. We highlight all of the parts of the class that are related to making it generic.

```
class Node <T extends Comparable<T>>
{
  Node<T> link = null;
  T item;

  Node() { }                              // Default constructor
  Node(T newItem) { item = newItem; }     // Constructor
}
```

The first change that you will notice is the declaration of type parameter `T` in the heading of the class: `<T extends Comparable<T>>`. Java uses the angle brackets < and > to declare type parameters and type variables.[2] When client code declares an identifier of generic class `Node`,

---

2. The Java designers recommend the naming convention of using a single uppercase letter to distinguish type variables from object and class identifiers. Another approach is to use the word `Type` in the name— for example, `ItemType`.

it will supply a type as an argument that is passed to this parameter. In the following example, we declare a `protected` variable `current` to be a `Node` whose type variable is specified as `String`:

```
protected Node<String> current;
```

We can instantiate a value for this variable by passing the type to the constructor:

```
current = new Node<String>();
```

Let's take a closer look at type parameter declarations. For a simple declaration of a type parameter, we could just write `<T>`. We can then pass any class as an argument to that parameter. We call this an *unrestricted* type parameter.

For our list, however, we want to restrict the user to specifying only classes that implement `Comparable`, because items in a list must have a `compareTo` method that can be used in operations that search a list. To specify this restriction in a type parameter declaration, we write `<T extends Comparable>`. The formulation `<X extends Y>` means that we want to declare a type parameter `X` whose arguments are restricted to subclasses of `Y`. Any class that implements a Java interface is considered a subclass of the interface. Thus, any class that implements `Comparable` is a subclass of `Comparable` and can be passed as an argument to `T`.

What about the final appearance of `<T>` in the heading, after `Comparable`? It turns out that `Comparable` itself is generic—it has a type parameter. Previously, when we implemented `Comparable`, we did so without specifying the type. Here, however, we want to be certain that items don't just implement `Comparable` for some arbitrary type—we want to ensure that they implement it for the same type as `T`. Thus the declaration

```
<T extends Comparable<T>>
```

says, "Declare a type parameter `T`, and restrict its arguments to types that implement `Comparable`, where `compareTo` is defined for the same type `T`."

Within the class, we simply write `T` wherever we would normally write the name of the type. For example, we can use it as the type of a field (as highlighted here):

```
T item;      // Item field will be whatever type the user specifies in the
             // type argument
```

Now that `Node` takes a type parameter, when client code declares a field of class `Node`, it must also specify the type to be used for the item within the node. Here's another example of declaring a `Node` that holds a `String`:

```
Node<String> someStringNodeField = new Node<String>("Default string");
```

If we want a `Node` that holds a value of the wrapper class, `Integer`, we would write[3]

```
Node<Integer> someIntegerNodeField = new Node<Integer>(0);
```

---

3. See the discussion of wrapper classes, auto-boxing, and auto-unboxing in the "Graphical User Interfaces" section of Chapter 10 for more information about `Integer` and related classes in the Java library that allow us to represent primitive type values as objects.

We've shown arguments that are class names, but we can also pass a type variable as an argument. For example, within the **Node** class, we want links to refer only to nodes of the same type, so we use <T> to specify the node type for the **link** field:

```
Node<T> link = null;
```

Now let's see how the generic linked list is implemented. Changes from **LinkedListOfStrings** are highlighted:

```java
public class LinkedList <S extends Comparable<S>>
{
  // Data fields
  protected Node<S> list = null;          // Reference to first node
  protected Node<S> tail = null;          // Reference to end node
  protected Node<S> current = null;       // Variable for traversal with an
                                          // iterator

  public LinkedList() {}

  public boolean isEmpty() { return list == null;}

  public int size()
  {
    Node<S> current = list;
    int numItems = 0;
    while (current != null)      // Done when the prior link was null
    {
      numItems++;
      current = current.link;    // Advance to the next node
    }
    return numItems;
  }

  public boolean contains(S item)
  {
    Node<S> current = list;
    while (current != null && current.item.compareTo(item) != 0)
      current = current.link;
    return current != null;
  }

  public void add(S newItem)
  {
    Node<S> item = new Node<S>(newItem);
    if (list == null)            // List empty
    {
      list = item;               // Refer list to this new node
      tail = item;               // Tail is also this new node
    }
    else                         // List not empty
```

```
    {
      tail.link = item;        // Append new node to tail
      tail = tail.link;        // Advance tail to new node
    }
  }

  public void remove(S item)
  {
    Node<S> current = list;
    Node<S> prior = null;
    while (current != null && current.item.compareTo(item) != 0)
    {
      prior = current;
      current = current.link;
    }
    if (current != null)             // Item found
    {
      if (current == tail)           // Removing last item
        tail = prior;                //    Refer tail to prior node
      if (prior == null)             // Removing first item
        list = list.link;            //    Refer list to next node
      else                           // Match isn't the first item
        prior.link = current.link;   //    Refer prior to next node
    }
  }

  // The iteration is initialized by setting current to list
  public void resetList() { current = list; }

  // There is a next node when current refers to something other than null
  public boolean hasNext() { return current != null; }

  public S next()
  // Returns the item at the current position; null if empty list. Resets
  //    current position to first item after the last item is returned.
  // Assumptions:  no transformers have been invoked since last call,
  //    and the list is not empty
  {
    S item = current.item;
    current = current.link;
    return item;
  }
}
```

As you can see, we made three kinds of changes to the class:

1. Add the declaration of type parameter **S**, with the same restrictions as for the type parameter of **Node**.

2. Follow each use of **Node** with **<S>**, to specify that **S** is the type argument for **Node**.

3. Use **S** in place of **String** throughout.

The reason that we declare S with the same restrictions that we used for T in the Node class is that we use S to instantiate the nodes. If S doesn't have the same restrictions, we can't pass it as the type argument to Node.

■ Using the Generic Linked List

We now have a generic linked list class that accepts a type argument. Let's rewrite the **LinkedListOfStringsDemo** to use this generic class. In the revised application, we specify that the list contains items of class **String**, as highlighted.

```java
import java.util.*;
import java.io.*;
public class GenericLinkedListDemo
{
  public static void main (String args[]) throws IOException
  {
    LinkedList<String> list = new LinkedList<String>();
    Scanner in = new Scanner(new FileReader("linkdemo.txt"));
    while (in.hasNext())
      list.add(in.nextLine());
    in.close();
    list.resetList();
    while (list.hasNext())
      System.out.println(list.next());
  }
}
```

Here is the output from reading a six-line file of text:

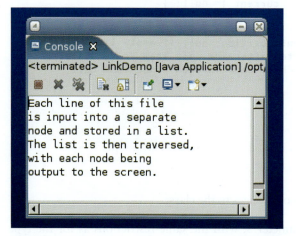

Now, let's have the demo program read a file of integers. The changes are highlighted:

```java
import java.util.*;
import java.io.*;
public class GenericLinkedListDemo
{
  public static void main (String args[]) throws IOException
```

```
{
  LinkedList<Integer> list = new LinkedList<Integer>();
  Scanner in = new Scanner(new FileReader("linkdemo2.txt"));
  while (in.hasNext())
    list.add(in.nextInt());
  in.close();
  list.resetList();
  while (list.hasNext())
    System.out.println(list.next());
}
}
```

All we did to convert the generic linked list from a list of strings to a list of integer values was change the type argument from `String` to `Integer`. Of course, we also changed the input method from `nextLine` to `nextInt`. Here is its output, when the file contains six integers on two lines:

■ Some Limitations on Generics

There are several aspects of Java's generic types that we have not covered as yet. We briefly mention some key limitations on their use here, but leave further coverage to a more advanced course.

When one class is a subclass of another class, it is tempting to think that generic types created with these classes would also have the same superclass–subclass relationship. For example, you might expect that `Node<BusinessPhone>` is a subclass of `Node<Phone>`. But it is not. Put simply, a `Node` is a `Node` is a `Node`! The type parameter is just used within `Node` to determine the type of the item field. It is not defining a new class.

One repercussion of the fact that Java treats all instantiations of the `Node` class as being the same is that if you try to determine the class of a `Node` variable with `instanceof` or `getClass`, you will find that it is just `Node`. Java uses type parameters to check the compatibility of generic types during compilation; type parameter values do not exist at run time.

Because type values aren't present at run time, another side effect is that arrays cannot be instantiated with generic elements. For example, you cannot declare and instantiate an array variable as follows:

```
Node<T>[] nodeArray = new Node<T>[100];        // Doesn't work
```

The compiler will warn you that this declaration is unsafe, and it may lead to a run-time error because the array could end up holding elements of different types of nodes. The compiler cannot check that operations on these nodes are always correct. Also, you would receive a compiler error if you tried to create an array of type variables, because type variables do not exist at run time.

Yet more advanced features of generic types exist that are beyond the scope of this text. Our goal here is just to show you how generics can be used in a simple context to create a generic class. Understanding the basic concepts of generics also enables you to appreciate how they are used in the Java library to implement generic data structure classes, which are the subject of the remainder of this chapter.

May We Introduce

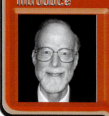

Sir Charles Antony Richard Hoare

Tony Hoare's interest in computing was awakened in the early fifties, when he studied philosophy (together with Latin and Greek) at Oxford University, under the tutelage of John Lucas. He was fascinated by the power of mathematical logic as an explanation of the apparent certainty of mathematical truth. During his National Service (1956–1958), he studied Russian in the Royal Navy. Then he took a qualification in statistics (and incidentally) a course in programming given by Leslie Fox. In 1959, as a graduate student at Moscow State University, he studied the machine translation of languages (together with probability theory) in the school of Kolmogorov. To assist in efficient look-up of words in a dictionary, he discovered the well-known sorting algorithm Quicksort.

On return to England in 1960, he worked as a programmer for Elliott Brothers, a small scientific computer manufacturer. He led a team (including his later wife Jill) in the design and delivery of the first commercial compiler for the programming language Algol 60. He attributes the success of the project to the use of Algol itself as the design language for the compiler, although the implementation used decimal machine code. Promoted to the rank of Chief Engineer, he then led a larger team on a disastrous project to implement an operating system. After managing a recovery from the failure, he moved as Chief Scientist to the computing research division, where he worked on the hardware and software architecture for future machines.

These machines were cancelled when the company merged with its rivals, and in 1968 Tony took a chance to apply for the Professorship of Computing Science at the Queen's University, Belfast. His research goal was to understand why operating systems were so much more difficult than compilers, and to see if advances in programming theory and languages could help with the problems of concurrency. In spite of civil disturbances, he built up a strong teaching and research department, and published a series of papers on the use of assertions to prove correctness of computer programs. He knew that this was long-term research, unlikely to achieve industrial application within the span of his academic career.

In 1977 he moved to Oxford University, and undertook to build up the Programming Research Group, founded by Christopher Strachey. With the aid of external funding from government initiatives, industrial collaborations, and charitable donations, Oxford now teaches a range of degree courses in Computer Science, including an external Master's degree for software engineers from industry. The research of his teams at Oxford pursued an ideal that takes provable correctness as the driving force for the accurate specification, design, and development of computing systems, both critical and non-critical. Well-known results of the research include the Z specification language, and the CSP concurrent programming model. A recent personal research goal has been the unification of a diverse range of theories applying to different programming languages, paradigms, and implementation technologies.

Throughout more than thirty years as an academic, Tony has maintained strong contacts with industry, through consultancy, teaching, and collaborative research projects. He took a particular interest in the sustenance of legacy code, where assertions are now playing a vital role, not for his original purpose of program proof, but rather in instrumentation of code for testing purposes. On reaching retirement age at Oxford, he welcomed an opportunity to go back to industry as a senior researcher with Microsoft Research in Cambridge. He hopes to expand the opportunities for industrial application of good academic research, and to encourage academic researchers to continue the pursuit of deep and interesting questions in areas of long-term interest to the software industry and its customers.

The preceding biographical sketch was written by Sir Tony Hoare himself and reprinted with his permission. What he does not say is that he received the Turing Award in 1980, at the age of 46, for his fundamental contributions to the definition and design of programming languages and was awarded a Knighthood in 1999 for his services to education and computer science.

12.3 : Java Collections Framework

From the very beginning, the Java library has supplied a variety of classes that implement common data structures, such as the `Vector` class that we saw in Chapter 9. However, when generics were added in Java 5, the library designers decided to rework data structure support into a more coherent and comprehensive organization called the *collections framework*.

■ Framework Organization

The collections framework is divided into two parts, depending on which of two main interfaces is being implemented: `Collection` or `Map`. Recall that a Java `interface` specifies headings for methods that must be supplied by any class declared to implement it. Thus some of the classes in the framework implement `Collection` and some implement `Map`.

A class that implements `Collection` is a data structure that holds elements in some organized manner, such as a list, stack, queue, or set. (In Java, a set is simply a list that does not allow duplicate elements; it can be used as the basis for implementing mathematical sets.) A class that implements `Map`, on the other hand, holds value objects in association with objects called keys. Maps are meant to support the construction of discrete mathematical functions in which

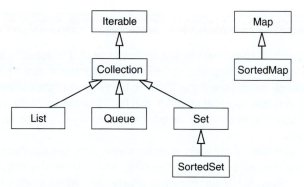

FIGURE 12.14 Collections Framework Interface Hierarchy

an input value is mapped to an output value. Although they can be used as a kind of data structure and are loosely connected with the structures that implement the `Collection` interface, we won't cover maps further. Each of the main interfaces has one or more subinterfaces, as shown in Figure 12.14.

Each interface or subinterface is implemented by one or more classes, using different underlying structures. For example, the `List` interface is implemented by `ArrayList` and `LinkedList` classes, allowing us to choose the version that offers better performance for a given problem. In most cases, abstract classes are used to define common operations.

Figure 12.15 shows the portion of the collections framework class hierarchy that we will examine. The figure also indicates which interfaces are implemented by each class, using color to distinguish the interfaces. To keep the figure simple, we do not show the connections between an interface and subclasses of classes that implement it. The implementation is automatically inherited by the subclasses.

If you look carefully at Figure 12.15, you will notice that the `Queue` interface is implemented by both `AbstractQueue` and `LinkedList`. Also, we have not shown any classes derived from `AbstractQueue`, even though the library provides multiple `AbstractQueue` subclasses. The subclasses of `AbstractQueue` implement forms of queues that are specialized in ways that are more

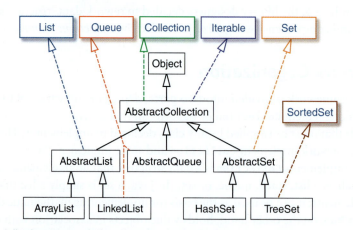

FIGURE 12.15 Collections Framework Class Hierarchy, Showing Implemented Interfaces (Interfaces are in color, classes are in black)

advanced than we are ready to cover. For more general purposes, the `LinkedList` class supports the operations defined by the `Queue` interface, enabling us to use that class as a list or a queue.

Next we look at the operations commonly supported by all collections derived from `AbstractCollection`. Keep in mind that all of the classes we will be considering are generic, so they can be specialized to hold a given class of element. Thus, where we show a method taking or returning `Object`, we really mean that it takes or returns an object of whatever class has been specified as the type argument when the structure was instantiated.

AbstractCollection Class The `AbstractCollection` class specifies that its subclasses must support the following observer methods:

Method	Meaning
`boolean contains(Object)`	Returns **true** if the collection contains the object.
`boolean containsAll(Collection)`	Returns **true** if this collection contains matches of all of the elements in the given collection.
`boolean isEmpty()`	Returns **true** if the collection has no elements.
`int size()`	Returns the number of elements in the collection.
`Object[] toArray()`	Returns an array containing all of the elements of the collection.
`String toString()`	Returns a string representation all of the elements of the collection.
`Iterator iterator()`	Returns an `Iterator` object for the collection.

This class also defines several optional operations, such as **add** and **remove**. We'll see how these operations are implemented later.

Iterator Interface The effect of most of the `AbstractCollection` methods should be fairly obvious. The `iterator` method, which we described briefly in Chapter 11, requires further explanation. In the list classes we have written, we have supplied the ability to iterate through the list using `resetList`, `hasNext`, and `next`. There can be just one iteration in progress on such a list at any given time. In some problems, however, multiple iterators may be needed that refer to different places in a collection. The Java library supplies a generic interface, called `Iterator` for this purpose. When you call the `iterator` method, it returns an `Iterator` object that keeps track of an iteration over the collection. An `Iterator` object has at least the methods `hasNext`, `next`, and `remove` (later we'll see that additional methods are available for specific types of collections).

As you would expect, `hasNext` returns **true** if there is a next element in the collection, and `next` returns that next element and advances the iterator to the next position. Thus, if we have a list object called `myList`, with elements that support `toString`, we would iterate through it in the following manner to print it out:

```
Iterator myIter = myList.iterator();
while (myIter.hasNext())
  System.out.println(myIter.next());
```

The **remove** operation, however, is different from the one we are familiar with—it removes the element that was last returned by **next**. This approach allows the iteration to proceed after the element is removed. In contrast, the **remove** method that we wrote for our list classes deletes the given element. As a result, we documented that it could not be used during iteration because it could potentially change the structure of the list in a manner that causes **hasNext** and **next** to behave incorrectly.

The **remove** method associated with the **Iterator** object avoids this problem, so it can be used to safely change a list in mid-iteration. The **Iterator** object is aware of the actions of its own **remove** method, and it adjusts the iteration accordingly to compensate for such changes. An **Iterator** still cannot tolerate changes that are made with methods other than its own. For example, even using the **remove** operation associated with another **Iterator** object for the same collection isn't safe. Many of Java's collection classes also support the same kind of **remove** operation as we used in our own list classes, which should likewise never be applied during iteration through the collection.

Collections Class   In addition to the methods defined in the interfaces and implemented by the framework's classes, the Java library provides a class called **Collections** that contains a large number of static helper methods for use with collections. Here are just a few of them, to give you an idea of what is available:

Method	Meaning
`void sort(List)`	Sorts the list elements into ascending order.
`int binarySearch(List, key)`	Uses a binary search on a sorted list. Returns the index of the key object in the list. If the key isn't found, returns a negative number that, when negated, gives the location where the item should be inserted.
`void reverse(List)`	Reverses the order of the elements in a list.
`void shuffle(List)`	Randomly reorders the elements in a list.
`void copy(DestinationList, SourceList)`	Copies the source list into the destination list.
`Object min(Collection)`	Returns the minimum value in the collection.
`Object max(Collection)`	Returns the maximum value in the collection.
`boolean replaceAll(List, OldValueObject, NewValueObject)`	Replaces all occurrences of the old value in a list with the new value. Returns **true** if any values were replaced.
`boolean disjoint(Collection, Collection)`	Returns **true** if the two collections do not have any common elements.

Now that we've seen the general structure of the framework, let's look at some specific implementations. We start with the familiar list, and then move on to other structures.

■ Lists

The `AbstractList` subclass specifies the basic operations to be implemented by a list class. Here we list those that are most commonly used. Keep in mind that this class also inherits the methods specified by the `AbstractCollection` class.

Method	Meaning
`void clear()`	Deletes all of the elements from the list.
`Object get(int)`	Returns the element at the given index. Throws `IndexOutOfBoundsException` if the argument isn't >= 0 and < size of list.
`int indexOf(Object)`	Returns the index where the first match of the given object is found (-1 if not found).
`ListIterator listIterator()`	Returns a `ListIterator` object for the list.
`Object removeRange(int start, int end)`	Deletes the specified range of elements, from `start` through `end-1`.
`List subList(int start, int end)`	Returns the sublist from index `start` to index `end-1`.

The `listIterator` method deserves some additional explanation. A `ListIterator` is an object of a class that implements the `ListIterator` interface, which extends the `Iterator` interface. Thus a `ListIterator` has all of the methods of an `Iterator` plus some extra list-specific methods. In particular, a `ListIterator` supports reverse iteration with the methods `hasPrevious` and `previous`, which are analogous to `hasNext` and `next`, respectively. The `remove` operation is also redefined to delete the element most recently returned by either `next` or `previous`.

Given these abstract classes, the actual implementations of a list are already mostly defined. We look at two of them here: `ArrayList` (which we introduced briefly in Chapter 11) and `LinkedList`.

ArrayList   As its name implies, an `ArrayList` is a list that uses an array as its underlying implementation. Unlike our array-based lists in Chapter 11, an `ArrayList` automatically adjusts its size to fit the number of elements that it holds. It achieves this by noticing when an **add** operation will exceed the bounds of the current array, whereupon it instantiates a new, larger array and copies the current array into it. As a consequence, adding to an `ArrayList` can sometimes be a very slow process. Otherwise, this is a very fast list implementation for most operations except removing elements near the start of the list.

Also, unlike our array-based list classes, `ArrayList` is generic, so we instantiate it with a type argument. For example:

```
ArrayList<String> list1 = new ArrayList<String>();   // An ArrayList with
                                                     // String elements
ArrayList<Name> list2 = new ArrayList<Name>();       // An ArrayList with Name
                                                     // elements
```

In addition to the default constructor that creates an empty list, `ArrayList` supplies a constructor that takes a collection as its argument, which builds a new `ArrayList` by iterating through the given collection and adding each of its elements to the list.

Here are some of the more commonly used `ArrayList` methods. Keep in mind that they are provided in addition to the methods inherited from `AbstractCollection` and `AbstractList` (`contains`, `containsAll`, `isEmpty`, `size`, `toArray`, `toString`, `iterator`, `listIterator`, `clear`, `get`, `indexOf`, `removeRange`, and `subList`).

Method	Meaning
`boolean add(Object)`	Adds the object at the end of the list. Returns `true`.
`void add(int, Object)`	Inserts the object at the given index. Throws `IndexOutOfBoundsException` if the index argument isn't `>= 0` and `<` size of list.
`boolean addAll(Collection)`	Adds the elements in the collection to the end of the list. Returns `true` if any items are added.
`Object remove(int)`	Deletes and returns the list element at the given index. Throws `IndexOutOfBoundsException` if the argument isn't `>= 0` and `<` size of list.
`boolean remove(Object)`	Deletes first matching object. Returns `true` if an element was deleted.
`void removeAll(Collection)`	Removes from the list all elements that match elements of the given collection.
`boolean retainAll(Collection)`	Removes from the list all elements that do not have a match in the given collection.
`Object set(int, Object)`	Replaces the element at the given index with the given object. Returns the element that was replaced.
`void ensureCapacity(int)`	Ensures that the underlying array has the specified number of element slots. May be used to avoid a series of array instantiation and copy operations when adding a large number of elements to an `ArrayList`.
`void trimToSize()`	Reduces the size of the underlying array to match the number of elements in the list. May be used after deleting many elements to enable garbage collection of the unused elements.

You might wonder why the **add** operation always returns `true`. The reason is that it is an optional method specified by the `AbstractCollection` class, which has a `boolean` return value. In subclasses of `AbstractCollection` that do not allow duplicate entries, such as `Set`, the **add** operation returns `false` if the element is already in the list. Because we can always add to a list, the **add** method always returns `true`.

It is also interesting to note that the Java library designers chose to mix array-like indexed access into `ArrayList`. In particular, the **add**(`int`, `Object`), **set**(`int`, `Object`), and **remove**(`int`) methods provide this array-like quality. As a result, `ArrayList` isn't purely a list in the abstract sense. As we see in the next section, the designers gave the same behavior to `LinkedList` to enhance its compatibility with `ArrayList`.

LinkedList   A `LinkedList` is, of course, an implementation of `List` that uses a linked structure. As we've seen, this approach is more efficient when the length of the list grows and shrinks by large amounts, or when a large fraction of the `remove` operations delete elements near the head of the list. Like `ArrayList`, `LinkedList` is generic, so it is instantiated with a type argument. Also like `ArrayList`, it supplies a default constructor as well as a constructor that builds the list from a given collection.

Here are some of the more commonly used `LinkedList` methods, which are extensions beyond the methods inherited from `AbstractCollection` and `AbstractList`. Notice that several methods give different names to the same operations, because `LinkedList` also provides one of the implementations of queues in the collections framework.

Method	Meaning
`boolean add(Object)`	Adds the object to the end of the list. Returns `true`.
`void add(int, Object)`	Inserts the object at the given index. Throws `IndexOutOfBoundsException` if the index argument isn't `>= 0` and `<` size of list.
`void addLast(Object)`	Adds the object to the end of the list. No return value.
`boolean offer(Object)`	Adds the object to the end of the list. Returns `false` if the element cannot be added.
`boolean addAll(Collection)`	Adds the elements in the collection to the end of the list. Returns `true` if any items are added.
`void addFirst(Object)`	Adds the object to the head of the list.
`Object getFirst()`	Returns the first element of the list. Throws `NoSuchElementException` if list is empty.
`Object peek()`	Returns a reference to the first element of the list. Returns `null` if the list is empty.
`Object getLast()`	Returns a reference to the last element of the list. Throws `NoSuchElementException` if the list is empty.
`Object remove()`	Deletes and returns the first element of the list. Throws `NoSuchElementException` if the list is empty.
`Object removeFirst()`	Deletes and returns the first element of the list. A synonym for `remove`.
`Object poll()`	Deletes and returns the first element of the list. Returns `null` if the list is empty.
`Object removeLast()`	Deletes and returns the last element of the list. Throws `NoSuchElementException` if the list is empty.

Method	Meaning
`Object remove(int)`	Deletes and returns the list element at the given index. Throws `IndexOutOfBoundsException` if the argument isn't `>= 0` and `<` size of list.
`boolean remove(Object)`	Deletes the first matching object. Returns `true` if an element was deleted.
`void removeAll(Collection)`	Removes from the list all elements that match elements of the given collection.
`boolean retainAll(Collection)`	Removes from the list all elements that do not have a match in the given collection.
`Object set(int, Object)`	Replaces the element at the given index with the given object. Returns the element that was replaced. Throws `IndexOutOfBoundsException` if the argument isn't `>= 0` and `<` size of list.

Before we move on to other structures, let's see how we can use the library `LinkedList` class to implement our linked list demo application. We highlight the changes that we made to the `GenericLinkedListDemo` application to create this new demo.

```
import java.util.*;
import java.io.*;
public class LinkedListDemo
{
  public static void main (String args[]) throws IOException
  {
    LinkedList<String> list = new LinkedList<String>();
    Scanner in = new Scanner(new FileReader("linkdemo.txt"));
    while (in.hasNext())
      list.add(in.nextLine());
    in.close();
    Iterator listIter = list.iterator();
    while (listIter.hasNext())
      System.out.println(listIter.next());
  }
}
```

Is that all? Just changing the iteration to create an `Iterator` object instead of calling `resetList`, and then applying `hasNext` and `next` to the iterator instead of the list? Actually, the biggest change is one that you don't see. With the `GenericLinkedListDemo`, we included class `Node` and our own `LinkedList` class in the default package. This new application doesn't need those classes. It is complete all by itself.

If the library supplies an equivalent `LinkedList` class, why did we go to the trouble of writing our own `Node` and `LinkedList` classes? As a computing professional, it is important that you understand how your tools operate. Given that understanding, you now know how the library `List` classes work, and you have a good idea of how the other collections function. We could have simply explained them in the abstract and then given you the class specifications, but then they would seem more like magic.

What would we have to change to make this application use `ArrayList` instead of `LinkedList`? Only the name of the list class!

```
ArrayList<String> list = new ArrayList<String>();
```

Everything else remains the same because we have used only methods that they have in common. This is a perfect example of the value of data and control abstraction.

■ Sets

In the Java collections framework, a set is a list that doesn't allow duplicate elements. It is so named because it can be used to represent a mathematical set. Of course, because the elements can be any type of object that implements `Comparable`, a set can actually do much more. Java defines `AbstractSet` as a subclass of `AbstractCollection`, so it inherits `contains`, `containsAll`, `isEmpty`, `size`, `iterator`, `toArray`, and `toString`. It reimplements two methods from `Object` and one optional method from `AbstractCollection`. We do not discuss this subclass further.

It is interesting to note, however, that the `containsAll` method, when its argument is also a set, is equivalent to the mathematical subset $\subseteq$ comparison operation. Also, the `Collections.addAll` method, when applied to two sets, is a set union $\cup$ operation; the `Collections.disjoint` method is a set inequality test. `Collections.emptySet` is a helper method that returns the empty set for use in other set operations.

HashSet   As its name implies, a `HashSet` is a set implemented by a hash table, so it provides fast access. Unfortunately, its reliance on a hash table means that iteration through the set doesn't follow any specific order. If the set changes, the new iteration order may not be at all consistent with an iteration that preceded the change. Even so, iteration will access every one of the set's elements in some order.

As with the list classes, a default constructor is supplied together with a constructor that creates the new `HashSet` from a given collection. `HashSet` also provides the following operations (some of which are implementations of optional methods inherited from its superclasses).

Method	Meaning
`boolean add(Object)`	Adds the given object to the set. Returns `true` if the object wasn't already in the set.
`void addAll(Collection)`	Adds all of the elements of the given collection to the set (set union).
`void clear()`	Removes all elements from the set.
`boolean remove(Object)`	Removes the specified object from the set. Returns `true` if the object was present.
`void removeAll(Collection)`	Removes from the set all elements that match elements of the given collection (set difference).
`boolean retainAll(Collection)`	Removes from the set all elements that do not have a match in the given collection (set intersection).

As you can see, the library provides all of the operations that would be needed to program set algebra expressions using `HashSet` objects.

TreeSet   You can probably guess that a `TreeSet` is a set implemented by a binary search tree. This definition, together with the fact that it implements the `SortedSet` interface, means that iteration through the set returns the elements in order. `TreeSet` provides additional methods that take advantage of this property, but the extra functionality is obtained at the cost of not being as fast as a `HashSet`. The additional methods beyond those of `HashSet` are described here:

Method	Meaning
`Object first()`	Returns a reference to the first object in the set. Throws `NoSuchElementException` if the set is empty.
`Object last()`	Returns a reference to the last object in the set. Throws `NoSuchElementException` if the set is empty.
`SortedSet headSet(Object)`	Returns a set containing the elements of this set that are less than the given object.
`SortedSet tailSet(Object)`	Returns a set containing the elements of this set that are greater than or equal to the given object.
`SortedSet subSet(Object from, Object to)`	Returns a set containing elements that are greater than or equal to the `from` object and less than the `to` object.

The `headSet`, `tailSet`, and `subSet` operations all return a set whose elements are aliases of the elements in the original set. If you want a new set containing the same elements, you must use the copy constructor for `TreeSet`, which takes a `TreeSet` as its only argument. Thus we can write

```
TreeSet newTreeSubSet = new TreeSet(oldSet.subSet(from, to));
```

to achieve the goal of obtaining a subset whose elements aren't aliases of the original set. Note that `TreeSet` also provides constructors equivalent to the pair we described for `HashSet`.

As a demonstration of using `TreeSet`, consider the following problem. You and friend have been collecting signatures for a petition. Unfortunately, both of you canvassed the same streets in some cases. As a consequence, duplicate signatures appear on some of your petitions. You want to output two lists, one of which merges the two input lists, but without the duplicates. You also want to output a list of all of the signatures that are duplicates, so that you can cross them off of one of the petitions. The first list is the set union of the signatures, and the second list is the set intersection. Thus, with each input list on a separate file, you can simply read each one into a `TreeSet`, and then print out the union and intersection.

```
import java.util.*;
import java.io.*;
public class SetDemo
{
  public static void main (String args[]) throws IOException
```

```
{
  TreeSet<String> union = new TreeSet<String>();
  TreeSet<String> intersection = new TreeSet<String>();
  String line;
  Scanner in = new Scanner(new FileReader("setdemo1.txt"));
  while (in.hasNext())
  {
    line = in.nextLine();
    union.add(line);          // Create separate sets to eventually hold
                              // union and
    intersection.add(line);   // intersection, adding first file's values
                              // to each
  }
  in.close();

  TreeSet<String> set2 = new TreeSet<String>();
  in = new Scanner(new FileReader("setdemo2.txt"));
  while (in.hasNext())
    set2.add(in.nextLine());  // Create a set holding values from second
  in.close();                 // file

  union.addAll(set2);              // Compute union of the two sets
  intersection.retainAll(set2); // Compute intersection of the two sets
  System.out.println("Combined lists: " + union);
  System.out.println("Duplicates: " + intersection);
  }
}
```

Given the following two test data files

setdemo1.txt	setdemo2.txt
James Jones	April Boyce
Sally Smith	Donald Vole
David Paul	Amy Tessar
Mary Day	Toby Black
Frank Holmes	Sally Smith
Dora Welch	Frank Holmes

the program outputs

```
Console ×
<terminated> SetDemo [Java Application] /opt/sun-jdk-1.5.0.08/bin/java (Oct 29, 2006 3:10:08 PM)
Combined lists: [Amy Tessar, April Boyce, David Paul, Donald Vole, Dora Welch, Frank Holmes, James Jones, Mary Day, Sally Smith, Toby Black]
Duplicates: [Frank Holmes, Sally Smith]
```

We could have used an iterator to print each set element on a separate line, but it is informative to see the format that the **toString** method uses to convert a **TreeSet** to a string. The set elements are ordered using normal string comparison. If we want them to be sorted by last name, then we could input the data into a `Name` object and use `<Name>` as the type argument for instantiating the sets.

■ Stacks

You may have noticed that Figure 12.15 doesn't show a `Stack` class. The Java library does supply one, but it is a subclass of `Vector`, which we mentioned in Chapter 9. `Vector` itself is a subclass of `AbstractList`. Clearly, the `Stack` class inherits a rich set of methods. Here, we will examine only the ones that `Stack` adds to support traditional stack processing. Keep in mind that `Stack` is generic, so we instantiate it with a type argument, and its methods return objects of that type.

Method	Meaning
`boolean empty()`	Returns `true` if the stack is empty.
`Object peek()`	Returns the element on the top of the stack without deleting it.
`Object pop()`	Returns the element on the top of the stack, and deletes it from the stack.
`Object push(Object)`	Adds the given object to the top of the stack, and returns the same value.
`int search(Object)`	Returns the distance to the uppermost match of the given object in the stack. The distance is defined as the number of **pop** operations required to retrieve the value; thus, if the match is the top of the stack, the return value is 1. If no match is found, returns −1.

Earlier we saw a stack algorithm for reading a file and printing its lines in reverse order. Here is that algorithm, implemented as a demo program:

```java
import java.util.*;
import java.io.*;
public class StackDemo
{
  public static void main (String args[]) throws IOException
  {
    Stack<String> stack = new Stack<String>();
    Scanner in = new Scanner(new FileReader("stackdemo.txt"));
    while (in.hasNext())
      stack.push(in.nextLine());
    in.close();
    while (!stack.empty())
      System.out.println(stack.pop());
  }
}
```

Given the input file

```
This is the first line.
This is the second line.
This is not the last line.
This is the last line.
```

the program outputs

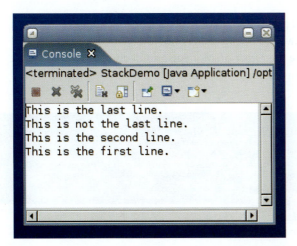

■ Queues

Earlier, we said that the **AbstractQueue** class is the basis for implementing more sophisticated queues with capabilities that go beyond the scope of this text. The **LinkedList** class, however, implements the **Queue** interface to provide a simple, traditional queue structure. The following methods are defined by the interface:

Method	Meaning
Object element()	Retrieves but doesn't remove the head element of the queue. Throws a **NoSuchElementException** if the queue is empty.
Object peek()	Retrieves but doesn't remove the head element of the queue. Returns **null** if the queue is empty.
Object remove()	Retrieves and removes the head element of the queue. Throws a **NoSuchElementException** if the queue is empty.
Object poll()	Retrieves and removes the head element of the queue. Returns **null** if the queue is empty.
boolean offer(Object)	Adds the object to the tail of the queue, returning **true**. (There are other implementations of **AbstractQueue** that can return **false**.)

Notice the pattern in the first four methods: Each pair performs the same operation, but one returns a value and the other throws an exception if the queue is empty. The `offer` operation also returns a value. Its exception-throwing counterpart is the normal `LinkedList add` operation:

Method	Meaning
`void add(Object)`	Adds the object to the tail of the queue.

All of these methods are implemented as part of `LinkedList`. Hence, this implementation of a queue is simply a linked list in which we use the methods that add elements to the tail and remove elements from the head to achieve the effect of enqueue and dequeue operations. We explore the use of queueing in the Problem-Solving Case Study.

PROBLEM SOLVING CASE STUDY

Average Waiting Time

Problem A local bank would like you to write a program to determine the average waiting time for a customer at its drive-up window. The bank has gathered data on a minute-by-minute basis. Each minute, a customer arrives with a task that takes some number of minutes once he or she reaches the head of the line. Additional customers wait in the line behind the customer being served. Time spent at the front of the line doesn't count toward the average because then the customer's request is being satisfied. Only the time spent in line, while not being served, is considered "waiting." The average waiting time is the total waiting time for all customers, divided by the number of customers served. The data file is a series of integer numbers, each of which represents the service time required by the customer arriving during that minute. Initially, we'll assume that customers arrive every minute. In the exercises, we'll ask you to explore cases in which customers arrive at different intervals.

Discussion In the United Kingdom, a waiting line is actually known as a queue, and people are said to "queue up." This is a good hint that a queue can be used to model a waiting line. Because the Java library's `LinkedList` class can be used as a queue, we don't need to develop any new classes. Even so, we'll walk through a scenario to ensure that we have the process correct.

Scenario We start with a priming read to put the first customer in the queue. By definition, the first customer never waits. Each minute we check whether the customer at the head of the line will complete his or her business during this period (time ≤ 1 minute). If so, we remove the customer, and everyone else advances; if not, then we decrement the remaining service time for the customer. Also during each minute we add a new customer (if any) to the tail of the queue. Each customer behind the customer being served is waiting 1 minute, so we add as many minutes to the total waiting time as there are customers behind the head (which is the queue size − 1). Once the queue is empty, we divide the total waiting time by the number of customers to get the average time.

Here is an example, showing the state of the queue and the total during each minute, for a data file with the values 3, 2, and 1. The data mean that the first customer has a 3-minute task for the teller, the second customer has a 2-minute task, and the third customer has a 1-minute task. We color code the first customer red, the second customer green, and the third customer blue.

Queue	Total	Comment
3	0	First customer arrives and is immediately served
2 2	0	Second customer arrives; first customer has been served for 1 minute
1 2 1	1	Second customer has waited 1 minute; third customer arrives
2 1	3	Second customer is served after waiting 2 minutes; third customer has waited 1 minute
1 1	4	Third customer has waited 2 minutes; second customer has been served for 1 minute
1	5	Third customer waited 3 minutes before being served

Average = 1.666666 minutes

How do we instantiate a `LinkedList` queue to hold integer values? As we saw earlier, we can use the wrapper class `Integer` as a type argument. Java allows us to assign `int` values to `Integer` objects, and `Integer` objects can be assigned to `int` variables because Java automatically converts between this class and the primitive type `int`.

To check the remaining time for the customer being served, we can use the **peek** operation, which retrieves the value of the head element. Then, if the head value is greater than 1, we simply decrement it and use the **set** operation to change the value in the first element of the list. The algorithm that we've described can be summarized as follows:

Average Waiting Time

```
Set total to 0
Set customers to 1
if in.hasNext
   Add next int from in to queue
while queue isn't empty
   Add queue.size - 1 to total
   peek at head of queue
   if head > 1
      Decrement head
      Set queue element 0 to head
   else
      remove head
   if in.hasNext
      Add next int from in to queue
      Increment customers
Output average = (float)total/(float)customers
```

Here is the application:

```java
import java.util.*;
import java.io.*;
public class AverageWaitTime
{
  public static void main (String args[]) throws IOException
  {
    LinkedList<Integer> queue = new LinkedList<Integer>();
    Scanner in = new Scanner(new FileReader("queuedemo.txt"));
    int total = 0;                   // First customer never waits
    int customers = 1;
    int head;
    if (in.hasNext())
      queue.add(in.nextInt());       // Put the first customer in the queue
    while (!queue.isEmpty())
    {
      total= total + queue.size() - 1;   // Add one minute per waiting
                                         // customer
      head = queue.peek();           // Convert first element to int
      if (head > 1)                  // If head customer still being serviced
      {
        head--;                      //    Decrement head customer's waiting time
        queue.set(0, head);
      }
      else                           // Otherwise head customer is done
        head = queue.remove();       //    Remove head customer
      if (in.hasNext())              // If there's a next customer
      {
        queue.add(in.nextInt());     //    Add the new customer to the queue
        customers++;                 //    Increment customer count
      }
    }
```

```
        in.close();
        System.out.println("Average wait: " + ((float)total/(float)customers) +
                            " minutes.");
    }
}
```

For a file containing

5 4 3 2 1

the application outputs

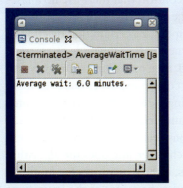

Here's a test plan for this application:

Number	Input	Expected Output
1	<empty file>	Average wait: 0.0 minutes.
2	5	Average wait: 0.0 minutes.
3	1 1 1 1 1 1 1	Average wait: 0.0 minutes.
4	2 1	Average wait: 0.5 minutes.
5	5 4 3 2 1	Average wait: 6.0 minutes.

TEST PLAN

The purpose of test 1 is to check for proper handling of an empty file. Test 2 ensures that the first customer doesn't cause any waiting time to be added and that the application works for a single value. Test 3 is a special case in which there are multiple customers, but none waits. In Test 4, we check the simplest scenario that causes waiting for the minimal amount of time. The last test ensures that the application works for a normal set of values for which the outcome is easy to verify by hand.

12.4 : Testing and Debugging

When we test code that uses a data structure, it is important that the class implementing the structure has gone through thorough unit testing. That frees us to test our use of it under the assumption that it behaves according to the abstraction it implements. It can be very frustrating to spend hours attempting to debug a client class or application, only to discover that the underlying data structure isn't implemented correctly.

When testing linked implementations of data structures, confirm that there are no aliases of deleted elements that could prevent them from being garbage collected. Also, test for proper deletion of the head or root of a structure, and of tail or leaf nodes. Be certain that deletion of a node doesn't accidentally delete the entire portion of the structure that the node refers to.

If we know that the data structure is properly implemented, then our testing strategy is similar to that for arrays. We need to especially test the boundary conditions: Does our code function properly for an empty structure, a full structure, and a single-element structure? In some cases, we need to test the behavior when elements are added and deleted in different orders.

For the Java collections classes, some special considerations arise related to how iteration occurs. If we are using multiple iterators, can they run past each other, and does the algorithm operate correctly in that case? While an iteration is in progress, is the structure being modified in a way that causes the iterator to malfunction? We also need to be aware of the limitations of generic types in declaring and working with the collections classes.

Testing and Debugging Hints

1. When traversing a linked data structure, be certain that you do not try to go past a `null` link field.

2. Be careful about passing tail or leaf elements to methods. If the method tries to access the successor node, it will throw an exception.

3. Make sure that you do not change the value of the external reference variable in a manner that causes the entire structure to become inaccessible.

4. When deleting an element, make sure that you have first set another element or the external reference to its link field; otherwise, you could lose the ability to access the structure beyond that point.

5. Remember that Java doesn't allow instantiation of generic arrays.

6. Keep in mind that sets cannot contain duplicate elements.

7. The collections classes all support `toString`, which is an easy way to print out a snapshot of the contents of a structure during debugging.

Graphical User Interfaces

Radio Buttons

In Chapter 11, we used a command-driven test driver (`ToDoList`) that allowed us to enter a command from a list of choices. The prompting message included a list of the commands, and it became somewhat annoying to see such a long prompt displayed repeatedly. Also, the interface required the user to type out each command in full, which becomes tiring after the first few times.

Java's library includes a graphical user interface component that is designed for this common input chore, called a radio button. The name comes from old-fashioned car radios that sported a row of buttons for selecting preset stations. Pressing one of these buttons made any other pressed button pop out. Thus only one button (station) could be pushed in at any given time. You've probably encountered this interface component many times before. Here is an example, showing buttons for four radio stations, with the third one selected:

Just like a `JButton`, a `JRadioButton` fires an event that calls the `actionPerformed` method in whatever action listener is registered with the button. The name of the button is passed to the method, so that we can use `getActionCommand` to determine which button the user clicked. There are two main differences between `JButton` and `JRadioButton` objects. The first relates to the appearance: a `JButton` has its name within its border, while the name of a `JRadioButton` appears beside it. The second difference is that a `JRadioButton` belongs to a `ButtonGroup`. The `ButtonGroup` object automatically deselects the currently selected button when the user clicks another button.

To create a radio button user interface component, we must therefore make four calls for each button:

1. Instantiate it with a name.
2. Add it to a `ButtonGroup` object.
3. Register an `ActionListener` with it.
4. Add it to the user interface.

The following code segment implements these steps for a single button. The name of the `ButtonGroup` object is `radioGroup`. As is typically done, we'll put the radio button in a `JPanel`, which we call `radioPanel`.

```java
JRadioButton mine = new JRadioButton("Mine!");
radioGroup.add(mine);
mine.addActionListener(this);
radioPanel.add(mine);
```

We can repeat these steps with different buttons as many times as necessary to place the desired series of buttons in this panel. Then we add the panel to the content pane of the frame. In this example, we've assumed that the `actionPerformed` method is defined in the same class.

Let's take a look at a demo application that has four radio buttons: Three select different tests and the fourth quits the application. To keep the example short, we'll just have it display a label indicating which Test button was clicked. The action for the Quit button will close the frame and exit the application. Here is the code for the user interface class:

```java
import java.awt.*;
import java.awt.event.*;
import javax.swing.*;
import javax.swing.border.*;
class GUI implements ActionListener
{
  JFrame userFrame = new JFrame();              // Create a frame
  Container userPane = userFrame.getContentPane(); // Get content pane
  JRadioButton test1 = new JRadioButton("Test1"); // Create radio
                                                  // buttons

  JRadioButton test2 = new JRadioButton("Test2");
  JRadioButton test3 = new JRadioButton("Test3");
  JRadioButton quit = new JRadioButton("Quit");
  ButtonGroup testGroup = new ButtonGroup();    // Create group for
                                                // buttons
  JPanel testPanel = new JPanel();              // Panel for radio
                                                // buttons
  JLabel out = new JLabel();                    // Label for output
  // Constructor builds and displays the interface
  public GUI()
  {
    userFrame.setSize(310, 120);                // Set frame size
    userPane.setLayout(new FlowLayout());       // Flow layout
                                                // manager in frame
```

```
      testPanel.setBorder(
        new EmptyBorder(15, 15, 15, 15)); // Make empty border for panel
      testPanel.setLayout(new GridLayout(1, 4));    // Grid layout
                                                    // manager in panel

      testGroup.add(test1);                         // Add buttons to
      testGroup.add(test2);                         // group
      testGroup.add(test3);
      testGroup.add(quit);

      test1.addActionListener(this);                // Register action
      test2.addActionListener(this);                // listeners
      test3.addActionListener(this);
      quit.addActionListener(this);

      testPanel.add(test1);                         // Add buttons to
      testPanel.add(test2);                         // panel
      testPanel.add(test3);
      testPanel.add(quit);

      userPane.add(testPanel);                      // Add panel to
                                                    // content pane
      userPane.add(out);                            // Add output label
                                                    // to pane
      userFrame.setVisible(true);                   // Show on screen
    }

  public void actionPerformed(ActionEvent event)    // Action event
  {                                                 // handler
    if (event.getActionCommand().equals("Quit"))
    {
      userFrame.dispose();                          // Remove the frame
      System.exit(0);                               // Exit the
    }                                               // application
    else                                            // Display button
    {                                               // clicked
      out.setText("You selected " + event.getActionCommand());
      userFrame.setVisible(true);
    }
  }
}
```

There's one other new bit of code in this demo that you should note:

```
testPanel.setBorder(new EmptyBorder(15, 15, 15, 15)); // Make empty
                                                      // border for
                                                      // panel
```

The `setBorder` method tells a `JPanel` that it should have a border around it. In this case, we use an `EmptyBorder` object that is 15 pixels wide on each side just to provide some space around the panel that prevents it from bumping into other interface components. The library provides other kinds of borders, such as `LineBorder`, that allow you to achieve other visual effects. Borders are just one of many ways that Java enables us to fine-tune the appearance of a user interface to make it more appealing. Borders are defined in the `javax.swing.border` package, so we must also import that package at the beginning of the class.

The code for the driver is just a few lines to create an instance of the `GUI` class. After that, the event loop with the action handler takes over.

```java
public class GUIRadioButtonDemo
{
  public static void main(String[] args)
  {
    GUI gui = new GUI();
  }
}
```

Here is an example of this user interface in action:

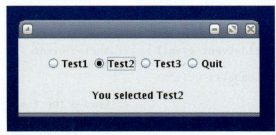

Of course, Java supports many more aspects of graphical user interfaces. We have merely scratched the surface in this text. With this understanding, however, you should be able to read the library documentation and figure out how to make use of the rich set of possibilities that exist for building sophisticated GUI-based applications.

Summary

Using references to link the elements of a data structure is an alternative to using an array to organize collections of data. Linked structures have the advantage of being dynamically allocated so that they are always, as Goldilocks would say, "just right." Access to array-based data structures is generally faster than access to a linked structure. If the application calls for many operations that require shifting a significant fraction of the array elements, such as adding and removing elements near the front of a list, then a linked implementation will offer a speed advantage, however.

We can use linking to implement a list structure. A named variable, called the external reference, is used to gain access to the first node of the list. Each node in the linked list contains a reference to the next node in the list, and the last node has a `null` reference. Similarly, a stack provides a linear arrangement of nodes, but one in which elements are added and deleted from the same end (the top). In other words, a stack is a "last in, first out" (LIFO) structure. The queue is another linear structure, but in this case elements are added at one end (the tail) and removed from the other end (the head). Therefore, a queue is a "first in, first out" (FIFO) structure.

By supplying two links per node, we can implement a binary tree, which is a branching data structure containing a root node with left and right subtrees. Each subtree has a pair of links to its own subtrees, and so on. Nodes that have two `null` links are called leaves. A node with non-`null` links is said to be a parent, and the nodes directly below it are called its children. By arranging the values in a binary tree so that every left child's value is less than its parent's value, and every right child's value is greater than its parent's value, we create a binary search tree. Finding a value in a binary search tree containing N values takes $\log_2 N$ steps. An in-order traversal of the tree will visit all of the elements in order. A binary tree may also be traversed in pre-order or post-order.

Hashing is a technique that computes an index for storing and retrieving values in a structure in roughly constant time. The keys to effective hashing are developing a good hash function and having enough extra space in the structure to minimize collisions. A chained hash table uses an array of linked lists, where a collision results in a node being added to the list associated with the array element where the collision occurred.

Java provides the ability to declare variables whose type is specified by a type variable. When the object containing this generic variable is instantiated, a type is provided as an argument to the constructor, and the type of the generic variable is then fixed. The use of generics in Java is limited to cases in which the compiler can check that the code works correctly for all potential types. If such checking isn't possible, then the code may not compile, or it may compile with a warning that an operation isn't safe. When used properly, generics enable us to define data structures that can be applied to a wide range of classes. For example, we can write a generic linked list class that can hold a list of strings, or a list of names, or a list of integers, without changing the code for the class. The only change involves how the client code instantiates the class.

The Java library includes a rich set of classes that implement common data structures using a variety of underlying structures. For example, both a linked implementation and an array-based implementation of a list are provided so that we can choose the version that will perform best in a given application. Other structures that are supported include sets, stacks, queues, and maps. Implementation structures include arrays, linked lists, binary search trees, and chained hash tables.

Using the Java library's collections classes enables us to write applications that solve complex problems with ease. At the same time, it is important to understand the operational advantages and disadvantages of each kind of structure and its underlying implementation so that we can choose the one that will be most efficient for a given problem.

LEARNING Portfolio

Quick Check

1. What are two advantages of using a linked implementation of a list instead of an array-based list? (pp. 660–662)
2. What are the two basic operations on a stack? (pp. 680–681)
3. Is a queue a LIFO structure or a FIFO structure? (pp. 681–682)
4. In what order does post-order traversal visit the nodes of a binary tree? (pp. 683–686)
5. What is a collision in a hash table? (pp. 686–687)
6. Which is the root of the class hierarchy in the Java collections framework, `AbstractCollection` or `Collection`? (pp. 695–698)
7. What is the class of the `link` field in a `Node` object? (pp. 662–667)
8. Write the declaration of an `ArrayList` variable, `names`, that will hold a list of `Name` objects. (pp. 699–701)
9. Given two `TreeSet` objects, `setA` and `setB`, write a statement that makes `setA` the union of the two sets. (pp. 703–706)
10. Write the expression that removes and returns the top element of the stack `myStack`. (pp. 706–707)
11. Write the declaration of a queue variable, called `movieLine`, that contains elements of class `Ticket`. (pp. 707–708)
12. When would you choose to use an `ArrayList` instead of a `LinkedList`? (pp. 699–701)

Answers

1. The linked list can grow and shrink dynamically, and removing items near the front of the list is faster. 2. `push` and `pop`. 3. FIFO. 4. Left subtree, right subtree, and then root. 5. The condition in which the hash function maps two values to the same place in the structure. 6. `AbstractCollection`; `Collection` is an interface rather than a class. 7. `Node`. 8. `ArrayList<Name> names`; 9. `setA.addAll(setB)`; 10. `myStack.pop()` 11. `LinkedList <Ticket> movieLine`; 12. When the approximate number of elements is known in advance; when the operations on the list involve frequently indexing elements at random; when few operations will add or remove values near the head of the list.

LEARNING / Portfolio

Exam Preparation Exercises

1. **a.** Linked lists can vary in size. (True or False?)

   b. Accessing an element in the middle of a linked list is as fast as accessing the same element in an array-based list. (True or False?)

   c. Removing an element from the tail of an array-based list is as fast as for a linked list. (True or False?)

   d. Removing an element from the head of an array-based list is as fast as for a linked list. (True or False?)

   e. A linked list has only one link field with a `null` reference. (True or False?)

2. **a.** What is the purpose of the external reference in a linked list?

   b. What is the value of the external reference when a list is empty?

   c. Why do we need a variable that refers to the tail of a linked list?

   d. Under what conditions do we need to perform special-case processing for removing a node from a linked list?

3. **a.** If the current element isn't the tail of the list, is the following algorithm for returning the current item and advancing to the next element correct? If not, then correct it.

   ```
   Set current to current.link
   Return current.item
   ```

   b. If the list is empty, is the following algorithm for adding a node correct? If not, correct it. Note that itemNode is the node to be added.

   ```
   Set tail to itemNode
   Set list to itemNode
   ```

   c. If the list is not empty, is the following algorithm for adding a node to the tail of the list correct? If not, correct it. Note that itemNode is the node to be added.

   ```
   Set tail.link to itemNode
   Set tail to itemNode
   ```

4. **a.** Write an algorithm for removing a node from the tail of a linked list.

   b. Write an algorithm for removing a node from the head of a linked list.

   c. Write an algorithm for removing a node from the middle of a linked list.

5. a. What expression is used to return a `boolean` value indicating whether there is a next item following the node that `current` refers to?

b. Write the conditional expression for the *while* loop that is used to traverse a list in determining its current size.

c. Write the conditional expression for the *while* loop that is used to traverse a list in determining whether the value in the variable `match` is contained in the list.

6. a. Given the following operations on a stack that is initially empty:

$$\texttt{push(5), push(4), push(3), pop(), push(2), push(1), pop(), pop()}$$

How many elements are on the stack, and what is the value at the top of the stack?

b. Write the algorithm for popping an element from the top of a stack and returning it, when a linked list is used as the underlying implementation for the stack.

7. a. Given the following operations on a queue:

$$\texttt{add(5), add(4), add(3), remove(), add(2), add(1), remove(), remove()}$$

How many elements are in the queue, and what is the value at the head of the queue?

b. Write the algorithm for removing an element from the head of a queue and returning it, when a linked list is used as the underlying implementation for the queue.

8. a. Write an algorithm to perform in-order traversal of a binary tree.

b. Write an algorithm to perform pre-order traversal of a binary tree.

c. Write an algorithm to perform post-order traversal of a binary tree.

9. a. What is the relationship between the values in the parent node and in its two children in a binary search tree?

b. If a binary search tree contains 63 nodes, what is the maximum time required to search for a matching value among its nodes?

10. a. What problem can result from resolving a collision in a hash table by incrementing the index and using the next location in the table?

b. What do we mean by the "chain" in a chained hash table?

11. a. Generic type variables are always enclosed in angle braces (<>). (True or False?)

b. Writing `extends` and the name of an interface in the declaration of a type variable means that the variable can hold only types that implement the interface. (True or False?)

c. If we instantiate a `Stack<Phone>` and a `Stack<BusinessPhone>` the second stack is a subclass of the first because `BusinessPhone` is a subclass of `Phone`. (True or False?)

d. Java allows us to declare and instantiate a generic array. (True or False?)

12. **a.** What are the three abstract subclasses of `AbstractCollection`?

   b. Which interfaces are implemented by `AbstractCollection`?

   c. What is the direct superclass of `HashSet` and `TreeSet`?

   d. What is the direct superclass of `ArrayList` and `LinkedList`?

13. **a.** What does the `Iterator` interface do?

   b. What does the `remove` operation on a `Iterator` do that is different from the remove operation on a list?

   c. How is the `Collections` class related to the collections framework?

   d. What does the `Collections.shuffle` operation do?

14. The following code segment uses a `LinkedList<String>` as an implementation structure for a queue. What does it output?

```
queueLL.add("Able");
queueLL.add("Delta");
queueLL.add("Charlie");
queueLL.remove();
queueLL.add("Baker");
queueLL.add("Echo");
queueLL.remove();
queueLL.add("Charlie");
System.out.println(queueLL);
```

15. Given a `TreeSet<String>` called `mySet`, what does the following code segment output?

```
mySet.add("Able");
mySet.add("Delta");
mySet.add("Charlie");
boolean present = mySet.remove("Able");
mySet.add("Baker");
mySet.add("Echo");
present = mySet.remove("Delta");
mySet.add("Charlie");
System.out.println(mySet);
```

Programming Warm-Up Exercises

1. Create a `stack` class with `push` and `pop` methods, copying code, as necessary, from the generic `LinkedList` class developed in this chapter.

2. Create a queue class with a `removeFirst` method by extending the generic `LinkedList` class developed in this chapter.

3. Add a `reverse` method to the generic `LinkedList` class developed in this chapter. The effect of the method is to reverse the order of the elements in the list.

4. Add a `copy` method to the generic `LinkedList` class developed in this chapter. This method returns a copy of the list. The nodes will not be aliases of the nodes in the original list, but the `item` fields will `alias` the item fields of the original list.

5. Add a `sort` method to the generic `LinkedList` class developed in this chapter that orders the elements in the list. You can adapt an exchange sort, like the one in Chapter 11, to work with a linked list.

6. Write a method that takes a `LinkedList<Integer>` as a parameter, and returns `true` if the elements are the same in reverse order. For example, 1 2 3 is not the same as 3 2 1, but 1 3 1 is the same in reverse order.

7. Write a method that fills an `ArrayList<Integer>` with the numbers 1 through 52, and then shuffles its contents before returning the list.

8. Write a method that takes an `ArrayList<Integer>` containing the numbers 1 though 52 in random order, and prints it as representing deck of playing cards, using the following convention: 1–13 are hearts, 14–26 are clubs, 27–39 are diamonds, and 40–52 are spades. The first 10 numbers in each range are the corresponding number cards, and the last 3 are the jack, queen, and king. For example, the number 38 represents a queen of diamonds.

9. Given two `HashSet<Integer>` variables, how would you determine whether they contain all different values?

10. Write a method that takes two `HashSet<Integer>` variables as parameters, and returns a set containing the union of the values that they do not have in common. The result should exclude any values that appear in both sets.

11. Write a method that takes three `LinkedList<Integer>` variables as parameters, and returns a sorted linked list containing all of the distinct values in the three lists, without any duplicates.

12. Write a method that takes a `Stack<Integer>` and a `char` as arguments. The allowable `char` values are +, -, *, /, and R. If the `char` is one of the arithmetic operators, then the method pops the top two values from the stack, performs the indicated operation, and pushes the result back onto the stack. If the `char` is R, then it pops the top two values from the stack and pushes them back onto the stack in reverse order. If the stack has fewer than two values, then the method should throw an exception.

13. How would you sort the values in a queue using the Java collections framework? (*Hint:* Remember that a queue in the collections framework is actually a `LinkedList`.)

LEARNING / Portfolio

14. Write a method that takes a `Stack<String>` as a parameter, and returns a `LinkedList<String>` containing the values in the stack such that the top of the stack is the first element in the list. When the method returns, the stack should still contain all of the same values, in their original order.

Programming Problems

1. A doubly linked list has nodes that refer to both the following and the prior nodes in the list. It is therefore possible to easily traverse the list in either direction. Modify the generic `LinkedList` class developed in this chapter to create a `DoublyLinkedList` class. Add operation `hasPrevious` that indicates whether an element appears before the current element, and operation `previous` that returns the prior element if there is one. If `previous` is called when the current element is the head, it should return the value of the tail element. If it is called when the list is empty, it should return `null`. Write a test driver that fills the list with strings from a file, and then outputs the symmetric pairs of nodes (that is, the first and last nodes, then the second and next-to-last nodes, and so on). If the list contains an odd number of nodes, the middle node should be output as its own partner.

2. You are registering people for a campus club that charges dues. New members receive a discount, and returning members pay the full fee. You have a file that contains the ID numbers (integers) of existing members, and a file that contains the ID numbers of people who have signed up for the club this year. Write an application that determines which of the people who have signed up for this year are new and which are returning. The application should combine the two files so as to eliminate duplicates and then write them out as a new file of existing members. It should also write out three additional files: the first contains the ID numbers of past members who did not return, the second contains the ID numbers of returning members, and the third contains the ID numbers of new members.

3. Write a class, called `Deck`, that represents a deck of playing cards. Each card has a rank and a suit. The ranks are 1 through 13, with 11, 12, and 13 being equal to the jack, queen, and king, respectively. Suits are hearts, clubs, diamonds, and spades, with spades having the highest value and hearts the lowest value. Thus you can write a `Card` class that implements `Comparable`, whose objects are the elements of a `Deck`. The `Deck` class should support an `add` operation that puts a card in a deck, a `remove` operation that takes a card from the top of the deck, and a `shuffle` operation that randomly rearranges the cards in the deck. It should be possible to construct either an empty `Deck` or one that contains the standard set of 52 cards. Because some card games involve multiple decks of cards, and piles that contain cards from more than one deck, a `Deck` object (which is

also useful for representing piles of cards in a game) should allow duplicates to be added. Write a driver for the class that deals out a deck of cards in the initial arrangement for a game of Solitaire (you can choose the particular version of Solitaire), indicating which cards are visible and which are hidden in each stack.

4. A local movie theater has three ticket windows and two computerized ticket kiosks. Some transactions, such as group discounts, can be handled only at the ticket windows. An arriving customer looks at the lines and chooses to stand in the shortest one that can handle his or her transaction. Group sales take 4 minutes to process. Normal ticket sales take 2 minutes at a window and 3 minutes at a kiosk. Internet ticket sales pickups take only 1 minute at a kiosk but 2 minutes at a window. Write a simulation of this process, using queues to represent the five lines. The data set should consist of randomly arranged customer arrivals, with 5% group sales, 20% Internet ticket sales pickups, and 75% regular ticket sales. A data set will contain 200 customers. All of the customers tend to arrive shortly before the beginning of a movie, so we are simplifying the simulation to say that they all arrive at the same time. From this simulation, the theater wants you to determine the maximum length of each line, the average waiting time for each line, and the time required for each line to empty.

   (*Hint:* You can use an `ArrayList` to create the data set by adding 10 group, 40 Internet, and 150 regular customers and then shuffling the list. After that, the list is traversed, transferring each customer to the shortest queue that can handle his or her transaction.)

LEARNING / Portfolio

Case Study Follow-Up

1. Write and implement the test plan described for the `AverageWaitingTime` case study.

2. Sometimes minutes go by without any customers driving to the bank. These times can be represented by data values of zero. In that case, no element is added to the queue, and the number of customers doesn't increase. Modify the application so that it properly handles input with values of zero.

3. During rush periods, multiple customers may drive up to the bank during a single minute. Modify the input and the application to allow this kind of situation to be modeled. One approach is to shorten the time period to seconds, but then there may be many seconds with no arrivals. Another approach is to have each customer record include a time of arrival. The application then reads input values and adds them to the queue until an input value is found that comes after the current minute. When a customer record specifies an arrival time that occurs in the future, it is held until the simulation reaches that time before it is added to the queue.

4. The bank is evaluating the benefit of adding a second drive-up lane with an ATM. It wants you to determine the average waiting times for the two lines. You can assume that when a customer arrives, he or she chooses to enter the shortest line. If the lines are equal, the customer chooses the window over the ATM. The data file is the same format as for the original problem.

13 Recursion

Goals

Knowledge Goals

To:

- Understand the concept of a recursive definition
- Understand the difference between iteration and recursion
- Understand when recursion is appropriate

Skill Goals

To be able to:

- Identify the base cases and the general case in a recursive definition
- Identify the size of the problem—that is, the aspect that must become smaller
- Write a recursive algorithm for a problem involving only simple variables
- Write a recursive algorithm for a problem involving structured variables

Introduction

Recursion is a unique problem-solving approach supported by many computer languages (Java included). With recursion, we solve a problem by repeatedly breaking it into smaller versions of the same problem, until the problem is reduced to a trivial size that can be easily solved. We repeatedly combine our solutions to the subproblems until we arrive at a solution to the original problem.

In the first part of this chapter, we define recursion and apply the techniques to problems with simple variables. In the second part, we apply the technique to problems with structured data.

1992
The first 64-bit chip is introduced by DEC

1993
Apple Computer announces the Newton, a personal digital assistant (PDA) with handwriting recognition capabilities

1993
Intel introduces the Pentium Chip

1994
Jim Clark and Marc Andreesen create Netscape Communications (their first browser), contributing to a growing population of Web surfers

1995
Toy Story is produced from the Pixar division of Disney and is the first full-length computer-generated feature film. It receives rave reviews

1995
Sun Microsystems introduces the object-oriented programming language Java™

JAVA™

727

13.1 ⋮ Simple Variables

In Java, any method can call another method. A method can even call itself! When a method calls itself, it makes a **recursive call**. The word *recursive* means "having the characteristic of coming up again, or repeating." In this case, a method call is repeated by the method itself. Recursion is a powerful technique that can be used in place of iteration (looping).

Recursive solutions may be less efficient than iterative solutions to the same problem. However, some problems lend themselves to simple, elegant, recursive solutions; these same problems may sometimes be very cumbersome to solve iteratively. Some older programming languages—for example, early versions of FORTRAN, Basic, and COBOL—do not support recursion. Other languages are especially oriented to recursive algorithms—Lisp, for example. Java lets us take our choice: We can implement both iterative and recursive algorithms.

> **Recursive call** A method call in which the method being called is the same as the one making the call

Our examples in this chapter are broken into two groups: problems that use only simple variables and problems that use structured variables. If you are studying recursion before reading about arrays in Chapter 9, then you should cover only the first set of examples and leave the rest until you have completed Chapters 9 and 11.

■ What Is Recursion?

You may have seen a set of gaily painted Russian dolls that fit inside one another. Inside the first doll is a smaller doll, inside of which is an even smaller doll, inside of which is yet a smaller doll, and so on. A recursive algorithm is like such a set of Russian dolls. It reproduces itself with smaller and smaller examples of itself until a solution is found—that is, until no more dolls remain. The recursive algorithm is implemented by using a method that makes recursive calls to itself.

■ Power Function Definition

Let's examine a method that calculates the result of raising an integer to a positive power. If x is an integer and n is a positive integer, then

$$x^n = \underbrace{x \times x \times x \times x \times x \times \cdots \times x}_{n \text{ times}}$$

We could also write this formula as

$$x^n = x \times \underbrace{(x \times x \times x \times x \times \cdots \times x)}_{n-1 \text{ times}}$$

or even as

$$x^n = x \times x \times \underbrace{(x \times x \times x \times \cdots \times x)}_{n-2 \text{ times}}$$

In fact, we can write the formula most concisely as

$$x^n = x \times x^{n-1}$$

This definition of x^n is a classic **recursive definition**—that is, a definition given in terms of a smaller version of itself. x^n is defined in terms of multiplying x times x^{n-1}. How is x^{n-1} defined? Why, as $x \times x^{n-2}$, of course! And x^{n-2} is $x \times x^{n-3}$; x^{n-3} is $x \times x^{n-4}$; and so on. In this example, "in terms of smaller versions of itself" means that the exponent is decremented each time.

When does the process stop? When we reach a case for which we know the answer without resorting to a recursive definition. In this example, it is the case where n equals 1: x^1 is x. The case (or cases) for which an answer is explicitly known is called the **base case**. The case for which the solution is expressed in terms of a smaller version of itself is called the recursive or **general case**. A **recursive algorithm** expresses the solution in terms of a call to itself, a recursive call. A recursive algorithm must terminate; that is, it must have a base case.

> **Recursive definition** A definition in which something is defined in terms of smaller versions of itself
>
> **Base case** The case for which the solution can be stated non-recursively
>
> **General case** The case for which the solution is expressed in terms of a smaller version of itself
>
> **Recursive algorithm** A solution that is expressed in terms of (1) smaller instances of itself and (2) a base case

■ Power Function Implementation

We use an *if* statement to determine which case is being executed. The following method implements the power function with the general case and the base case marked in the comments:

```
public static int power(int x, int n)
// Returns x raised to the power n
// Assumption:  x is a valid integer and n is greater than 0
// Note: Large exponents may result in integer overflow
{
  if (n == 1)
    return x;                   // Base case
  else
    return x * power(x, n - 1); // Recursive call
}
```

We can think of each recursive call to **power** as creating a completely new copy of the method, with each copy having its own copies of the parameters x and n. The value of x remains the same for each version of **power**, but the value of n decreases by 1 for each call until it becomes 1.

Let's trace the execution of this recursive method, with the following initial call:

```
xToN = power(2, 3);
```

We will use a new format to trace recursive routines: We number the calls and then discuss what is happening in paragraph form. This trace is also summarized in Figure 13.1, where each box represents a call to the power method. The values for the parameters for that call are shown in each box. Refer to the figure while you work through the trace in paragraph form.

Call 1: power is called with the number equal to 2 and the exponent equal to 3. Within power, the parameters x and n are initialized to 2 and 3, respectively. Because n is not equal to 1, power is called recursively with x and n - 1 as arguments. Execution of Call 1 pauses until an answer is sent back from this recursive call.

Call 2: x is equal to 2 and n is equal to 2. Because n is not equal to 1, the method power is called again, this time with x and n - 1 as arguments. Execution of Call 2 pauses until an answer is sent back from this recursive call.

Call 3: x is equal to 2 and n is equal to 1. Because n equals 1, the value of x is returned. This call to the method has finished executing, and the method return value (which is 2) is passed back to the place in the statement from which the call was made in Call 2.

Call 2: This call to the method can now complete the statement that contained the recursive call because the recursive call has returned. Call 3's return value (which is 2) is multiplied by x. This call to the method has finished executing, and the method return value (which is 4) is passed back to the place in the statement from which the call was made in Call 1.

Call 1: This call to the method can now complete the statement that contained the recursive call because the recursive call has returned. Call 2's return value (which is 4) is multiplied by x. This call to the method has finished executing, and the method return value (which is 8) is passed back to the place in the statement from which the call was made. Because the first call (the nonrecursive call) has now completed, 8 is the final value of the method power.

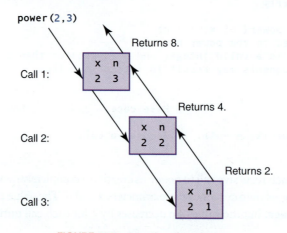

FIGURE 13.1 Execution of power(2,3)

What happens if no base case exists? We have **infinite recursion**, the recursive equivalent of an infinite loop.

For example, if the condition

```
if (n == 1)
```

were omitted, `power` would be called over and over again forever. Theoretically, infinite recursion also occurs if we call `power` with n less than or equal to 0. Because integers in Java are finite, recursion will eventually stop in this case, but only after a very long time.

In actuality, recursive calls can't go on forever in any case. When we call a method, either recursively or nonrecursively, the computer system creates temporary storage for the parameters and the method's (automatic) local variables. This temporary storage is a region of memory called the run-time stack. When the method returns, its parameters and local variables are released from the run-time stack. With infinite recursion, the recursive method calls never return. Each time the method calls itself, a little more of the run-time stack is used to store the new copies of the variables. Eventually, the memory space on the stack runs out. At that point, the program crashes with an error message such as "Run-time stack overflow" (or the application may simply freeze).

13.2 : More Examples with Simple Variables

For some people, thinking recursively is intuitive; for others, it is a mysterious process verging on the supernatural. The objective of the rest of this chapter is to demystify the recursive process by working through a collection of examples.

▪ Calculating the Factorial Function

Let's look at another example: calculating a factorial. The factorial of a number n (written $n!$) is n multiplied by $n - 1$, $n - 2$, $n - 3$, and so on. Another way of expressing a factorial is

$$n! = n \times (n - 1)!$$

This expression looks like a recursive definition. The term $(n - 1)!$ is a smaller instance of $n!$—that is, it takes one less multiplication to calculate $(n - 1)!$ than it does to calculate $n!$. If we can find a base case, we can write a recursive algorithm. Fortunately, we don't have to look too far: 0! is defined in mathematics to be 1.

```
factorial(number)

if number is 0
    return 1
else
    return number * factorial(number – 1)
```

We can code this algorithm directly as follows:

```
public static int factorial(int number)
// Returns the factorial of number
// Assumption: number is greater than or equal to 0
// Note: Large values of number may cause integer overflow
{
  if (number == 0)
    return 1;                                      // Base case
  else
    return number * factorial(number - 1); // General case
}
```

Let's trace this method with an original number of 4.

Call 1: number is 4. Because number is not 0, the *else* branch is taken. The *return* statement cannot be completed until the recursive call to factorial with number - 1 as the argument has been completed.

Call 2: number is 3. Because number is not 0, the *else* branch is taken. The *return* statement cannot be completed until the recursive call to factorial with number - 1 as the argument has been completed.

Call 3: number is 2. Because number is not 0, the *else* branch is taken. The *return* statement cannot be completed until the recursive call to factorial with number - 1 as the argument has been completed.

Call 4: number is 1. Because number is not 0, the *else* branch is taken. The *return* statement cannot be completed until the recursive call to factorial with number - 1 as the argument has been completed.

Call 5: number is 0. Because number equals 0, this call to the method returns, sending back 1 as the result.

Call 4: The *return* statement in this copy can now be completed. The value to be returned is number (which is 1) times 1. This call to the method returns, sending back 1 as the result.

Call 3: The *return* statement in this copy can now be completed. The value to be returned is number (which is 2) times 1. This call to the method returns, sending back 2 as the result.

Call 2: The *return* statement in this copy can now be completed. The value to be returned is number (which is 3) times 2. This call to the method returns, sending back 6 as the result.

Call 1: The *return* statement in this copy can now be completed. The value to be returned is number (which is 4) times 6. This call to the method returns, sending back 24 as the result. Because this is the last of the calls to factorial, the recursive process ends. The value 24 is returned as the final value of the call to factorial with an argument of 4.

Figure 13.2 summarizes the execution of the factorial method with an argument of 4.

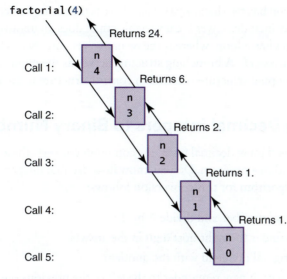

factorial(4)

Returns 24.

Call 1: n 4

Returns 6.

Call 2: n 3

Returns 2.

Call 3: n 2

Returns 1.

Call 4: n 1

Returns 1.

Call 5: n 0

FIGURE 13.2 Execution of `factorial(4)`

Let's organize what we have done in the preceding examples into an outline for writing recursive algorithms:

1. Understand the problem. (We threw this task in for good measure; it is always the first step.)
2. Determine the base case(s). A base case is the problem for which you know the answer. It does not involve any further recursion.
3. Determine the recursive case(s). A recursive case is one in which you can express the solution in terms of a smaller version of itself.

We have used the `factorial` and `power` algorithms to demonstrate recursion because they are easy to visualize. In practice, we would never want to calculate either of these values using the recursive solution. In both cases, the iterative solutions are actually simpler and much more efficient because starting a new iteration of a loop is a faster operation than calling a method. Let's compare the code for the iterative and recursive versions of the factorial problem.

Iterative Solution

```
public static int factorial(int number)
{
  int factor = 1;
  int count;
  for (count = 2; count <= number; count++)
    factor = factor * count;
  return factor;
}
```

Recursive Solution

```
public static int factorial(int number)
{
  if (number == 0)
    return 1;
  else
    return number *
           factorial(number - 1);
}
```

The iterative version has two local variables, whereas the recursive version has none. A recursive method usually includes fewer local variables than does an iterative method. Also, the iterative version always has a loop, whereas the recursive version always has a selection statement—either an *if* or a *switch*. A branching structure serves as the main control structure in a recursive method; a looping structure is the main control structure in an iterative method.

■ Converting Decimal Integers to Binary Numbers

When you enter integer data in decimal form, the computer converts these decimal numbers to binary form for use within a program. Do you know how decimal integers are converted to binary numbers? The algorithm for this conversion follows:

1. Take the decimal number and divide it by 2.
2. Make the remainder the rightmost digit in the answer.
3. Replace the original dividend with the quotient.
4. Repeat, placing each new remainder to the left of the previous one.
5. Stop when the quotient is 0.

This algorithm is clearly meant for a calculator and paper and pencil. Certainly, we cannot implement expressions such as "to the left of" in Java as yet. Let's do an example—convert 42 from base 10 to base 2—to get a feel for the algorithm before we try to write a computer solution. Remember, the quotient in one step becomes the dividend in the next step.

Step 1

```
        21    ← Quotient
     2)‾4‾2‾
        4
        2
        2
        0     ← Remainder
```

Step 2

```
        10    ← Quotient
     2)‾2‾1‾
        2
        1
        0
        1     ← Remainder
```

Step 3

```
         5    ← Quotient
     2)‾1‾0‾
        10
         0    ← Remainder
```

Step 4

```
         2    ← Quotient
     2)‾5‾
         4
         1    ← Remainder
```

Step 5

```
         1    ← Quotient
     2)‾2‾
         2
         0    ← Remainder
```

Step 6

```
         0    ← Quotient
     2)‾1‾
         0
         1    ← Remainder
```

The answer is the sequence of remainders from last to first. Therefore, the decimal number 42 is 101010 in binary.

It looks as though we can implement the solution to this problem with a straightforward iterative algorithm. Each remainder is obtained from the remainder operation (% in Java), and each quotient is the result of the / operation.

```
convert(number)

while number > 0
    Set remainder to number % 2
    Print remainder
    Set number to number / 2
```

Let's do a walk-through to test this algorithm.

Iteration	Number	Remainder
1	42	0
2	21	1
3	10	0
4	5	1
5	2	0
6	1	1
Answer:		0 1 0 1 0 1

The answer is backward! An iterative solution (using only simple variables) doesn't work. We need to print the last remainder first. The first remainder should be printed only after the rest of the remainders have been calculated and printed.

In our example, we should print 42 % 2 after (42 / 2) % 2 has been printed. This, in turn, means that we should print (42 / 2) % 2 after [(42 / 2) / 2] % 2 has been printed. Now our solution begins to look like a recursive definition. We can summarize by saying that, for any given number, we should print number % 2 after (number / 2) % 2 has been printed.

What is the base case? We know the answer when number is zero: We have finished and have nothing left to do. What is the recursive case? Convert number divided by 2. When this conversion is complete, print the remainder of number divided by 2 (number % 2). This solution leads to the following algorithm:

```
convert (number)

if number > 0
    convert(number / 2)
    Print number % 2
```

If **number** is 0, we have called **convert** as many times as necessary and can begin printing the answer. The base case occurs when we do nothing. The recursive solution to this problem is encoded in the following **convert** method:

```java
public static void convert(int number)
// Converts number to binary and prints it
// Assumption:  number >= 0
{
  if (number > 0)
  {
    convert(number / 2);    // Recursive call
    System.out.print(number % 2);
  }
  // Empty else clause is the base case
}
```

Let's do a code walk-through of **convert(10)**. We pick up our original example at Step 3, where the dividend is 10.

Call 1: **convert** is called with an argument of 10. Because **number** is not equal to 0, the *then* clause is executed. Execution pauses until the recursive call to **convert** with an argument of (**number** / 2) has completed.

Call 2: **number** is 5. Because **number** is not equal to 0, execution of this call pauses until the recursive call with an argument of (**number** / 2) has completed.

Call 3: **number** is 2. Because **number** is not equal to 0, execution of this call pauses until the recursive call with an argument of (**number** / 2) has completed.

Call 4: **number** is 1. Because **number** is not equal to 0, execution of this call pauses until the recursive call with an argument of (**number** / 2) has completed.

Call 5: **number** is 0. Execution of this call to **convert** is complete. Control returns to the preceding call.

Call 4: Execution of this call resumes with the statement following the recursive call to **convert**. The value of **number** % 2 (which is 1) is printed. Execution of this call is complete.

Call 3: Execution of this call resumes with the statement following the recursive call to **convert**. The value of **number** % 2 (which is 0) is printed. Execution of this call is complete.

Call 2: Execution of this call resumes with the statement following the recursive call to **convert**. The value of **number** % 2 (which is 1) is printed. Execution of this call is complete.

Call 1: Execution of this call resumes with the statement following the recursive call to **convert**. The value of **number** % 2 (which is 0) is printed. Execution of this call is complete. Because this is the nonrecursive call, execution resumes with the statement immediately following the original call.

Figure 13.3 shows the execution of the **convert** method with the values of the parameters.

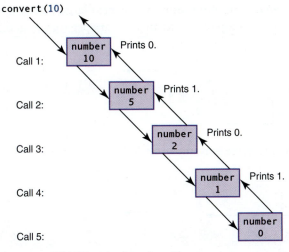

FIGURE 13.3 Execution of `convert (10)`

Next, we examine a more complicated problem—one in which the recursive solution is not immediately apparent.

■ Towers of Hanoi

One of your first toys may have been a board with three pegs holding colored circles of different diameters. If so, you probably spent countless hours moving the circles from one peg to another. If we put some constraints on how the circles or discs can be moved, we have an adult game called the Towers of Hanoi.

When the game begins, all the circles are on the first peg in order by size, with the smallest circle on the top. The object of the game is to move the circles, one at a time, to the third peg. But there is a catch: A circle cannot be placed on top of one that is smaller in diameter. We can use the middle peg as an auxiliary peg, but it must be empty at the beginning and end of the game.

To get a feel for how this problem might be resolved, let's look at some sketches of what the configuration must be at certain points if a solution is possible. We use four circles or discs. The beginning configuration is

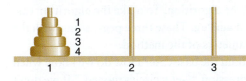

To move the largest circle (circle 4) to peg 3, we must move the three smaller circles to peg 2. Then we can move circle 4 into its final place:

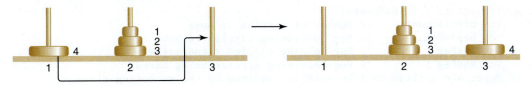

Let's assume we can do this. Now, to move the next largest circle (circle 3) into place, we must move the two circles on top of it onto an auxiliary peg (peg 1, in this case):

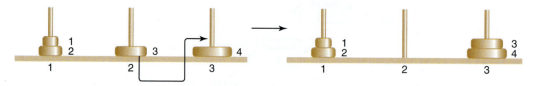

To get circle 2 into place, we must move circle 1 to another peg, freeing circle 2 to be moved to its place on peg 3:

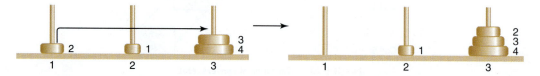

The last circle (circle 1) can now be moved into its final place, and we are finished:

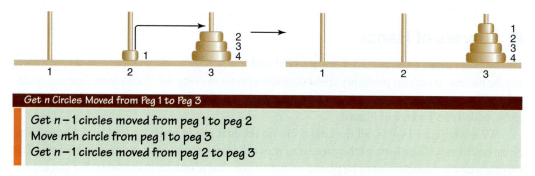

Get n Circles Moved from Peg 1 to Peg 3

Get n − 1 circles moved from peg 1 to peg 2
Move nth circle from peg 1 to peg 3
Get n − 1 circles moved from peg 2 to peg 3

This algorithm certainly sounds simple—surely there must be more to it! But this solution really is all there is.

Let's write a recursive method that implements this algorithm. We can't actually move discs, of course, but we can print out a message to do so. Notice that the beginning peg, the ending peg, and the auxiliary peg keep changing during the algorithm. To make the algorithm easier to follow, we call the pegs `beginPeg`, `endPeg`, and `auxPeg`. These three pegs, along with the number of circles on the beginning peg, are the parameters of the method.

We have the recursive (general) case, but what about the base case? How do we know when to stop the recursive process? The clue lies in the expression "Get *n* circles moved." If we don't have any circles to move, then we don't have anything to do. We are finished with that stage. Therefore, when the number of circles equals zero, we do nothing (that is, we simply return).

```java
public static void doTowers(
    int circleCount,     // Number of circles to move
    int beginPeg,        // Peg containing circles to move
    int auxPeg,          // Peg holding circles temporarily
    int endPeg )         // Peg receiving circles being moved
// Moves are written on file outFile, defined by the enclosing class
```

```
{
  if (circleCount > 0)
  {
   // Move n - 1 circles from beginning peg to auxiliary peg

     doTowers(circleCount - 1, beginPeg, endPeg, auxPeg);
     outFile.println("Move circle from peg " + beginPeg
             + " to peg " + endPeg);
     // Move n - 1 circles from auxiliary peg to ending peg
     doTowers(circleCount - 1, auxPeg, beginPeg, endPeg);
  }
}
```

It's difficult to believe that such a simple algorithm actually works, but we can prove it. We enclose the method within a driver class that invokes the **doTowers** method. We have added output statements so that we can see the values of the arguments with each recursive call. Because two recursive calls are made within the method, we have indicated which recursive statement issued the call.

```
//**********************************************************************
// Driver class for doTowers method
// Reads the number of circles from a file and calls doTowers
//**********************************************************************
import java.io.*;              // File types
import java.util.Scanner;
public class Towers
{
  static Scanner inFile = new Scanner(System.in);       // Input data file
  public static void main(String[] args) throws IOException
  {
    // Prepare files
    int circleCount;           // Number of circles on starting peg
    System.out.println("Input the number of circles: ");
    circleCount = inFile.nextInt();
    System.out.println("Input number of circles: " + circleCount);
    System.out.println("OUTPUT WITH " + circleCount + " CIRCLES");
    System.out.print("From original: ");
    doTowers(circleCount, 1, 2, 3);
    inFile.close();
  }

  public static void doTowers(
    int circleCount,          // Number of circles to move
    int beginPeg,             // Peg containing circles to move
    int auxPeg,               // Peg holding circles temporarily
    int endPeg       )        // Peg receiving circles being moved
  // Moves are written on file outFile.
  // This recursive method moves circleCount circles from beginPeg
  // to endPeg. All but one of the circles are moved from beginPeg
  // to auxPeg, then the last circle is moved from beginPeg to
  // endPeg, and then the circles are moved from auxPeg to endPeg.
  // The subgoals of moving circles to and from auxPeg involve recursion.
  {
    System.out.println("#circles: " + circleCount + " Begin: " +
       beginPeg + " Auxil: " + auxPeg + " End: " + endPeg);
    if (circleCount > 0)
    {
      // Move n - 1 circles from beginning peg to auxiliary peg
```

```
        System.out.print("From first:      ");
        doTowers(circleCount - 1, beginPeg, endPeg, auxPeg);

        System.out.println("Move circle " +  circleCount + " from peg "
          + beginPeg + " to peg " + endPeg);

        // Move n - 1 circles from auxiliary peg to ending peg
        System.out.print("From second:     ");
        doTowers(circleCount - 1, auxPeg, beginPeg, endPeg);
      }
    }
  }
```

The output from a run with three circles follows. "Original" means that the parameters listed beside it are from the nonrecursive call, which is the first call to **doTowers**. "From first" means that the parameters listed are for a call issued from the first recursive statement. "From second" means that the parameters listed are for a call issued from the second recursive statement. Notice that a call cannot be issued from the second recursive statement until the preceding call from the first recursive statement has completed its execution.

```
Console ✕
<terminated> Towers [Java Application] /opt/sun-jdk-1.5.0.08/bin/java (Oct
Input the number of circles:
3
Input number of circles: 3
OUTPUT WITH 3 CIRCLES
From original: #circles: 3 Begin: 1 Auxil: 2 End: 3
From first:    #circles: 2 Begin: 1 Auxil: 3 End: 2
From first:    #circles: 1 Begin: 1 Auxil: 2 End: 3
From first:    #circles: 0 Begin: 1 Auxil: 3 End: 2
Move circle 1 from peg 1 to peg 3
From second:   #circles: 0 Begin: 2 Auxil: 1 End: 3
Move circle 2 from peg 1 to peg 2
From second:   #circles: 1 Begin: 3 Auxil: 1 End: 2
From first:    #circles: 0 Begin: 3 Auxil: 2 End: 1
Move circle 1 from peg 3 to peg 2
From second:   #circles: 0 Begin: 1 Auxil: 3 End: 2
Move circle 3 from peg 1 to peg 3
From second:   #circles: 2 Begin: 2 Auxil: 1 End: 3
From first:    #circles: 1 Begin: 2 Auxil: 3 End: 1
From first:    #circles: 0 Begin: 2 Auxil: 1 End: 3
Move circle 1 from peg 2 to peg 1
From second:   #circles: 0 Begin: 3 Auxil: 2 End: 1
Move circle 2 from peg 2 to peg 3
From second:   #circles: 1 Begin: 1 Auxil: 2 End: 3
From first:    #circles: 0 Begin: 1 Auxil: 3 End: 2
Move circle 1 from peg 1 to peg 3
From second:   #circles: 0 Begin: 2 Auxil: 1 End: 3
```

In the examples we have seen so far, the values of the variables kept getting smaller until a base case was reached, in which the answers were known. In the next examples, the size of a structure gets smaller until a solution is known.

13.3 : Structured Variables

In our definition of a recursive algorithm, we identified two cases: the recursive (general) case and the base case for which an answer can be expressed nonrecursively. In the general case for all our algorithms so far, we expressed one argument in terms of a smaller value each time. When we use structured variables, however, we often state the recursive case in terms of a smaller structure rather than a smaller value; the base case occurs when there are no values left to process in the structure.

■ Printing the Values in an Array

Let's write a recursive algorithm for printing the contents of a one-dimensional array of *n* elements to show what we mean. What is the base case? We have no elements left to print. What is the general case? We print the item in the first position in the array, and then print the rest of the items.

> **Print Array**
>
> **if** more elements
>   Print the item in the first position
>   Print the rest of the array

The recursive case is to print the values in an array that is one element "smaller"; that is, the size of the array decreases by 1 with each recursive call. The base case occurs when the size of the array becomes 0—that is, when we have no more elements left to print.

Our arguments must include the index of the first element (the one to be printed). How do we know when no more elements are left to print (that is, when the size of the array to be printed is 0)? We have printed the last element in the array when the index of the next element to be printed is beyond the index of the last element in the array. Therefore, we must pass the index of the last array element as an argument. We call the indexes `first` and `last`. When `first` is greater than `last`, we are finished. The name of the array is `data`.

```
public static void print(int[] data,    // Array to be printed
                         int first,      // Index of first element
                         int last  )     // Index of last element
// Prints an array
{
  if (first <= last)
  {                                      // Recursive case
    outFile.println(data[first]+ " ");
    printArray(data, first + 1, last);
  }
  // Empty else clause is the base case
}
```

Here is a code walk-through of the method call

```
print(data, 0, 4);
```

using the pictured array:

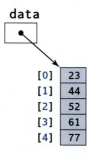

Call 1: `first` is 0 and `last` is 4. Because `first` is less than `last`, the value in `data[first]` (which is 23) is printed. Execution of this call pauses while the array from `first + 1` through `last` is printed.

Call 2: `first` is 1 and `last` is 4. Because `first` is less than `last`, the value in `data[first]` (which is 44) is printed. Execution of this call pauses while the array from `first + 1` through `last` is printed.

Call 3: `first` is 2 and `last` is 4. Because `first` is less than `last`, the value in `data[first]` (which is 52) is printed. Execution of this call pauses while the array from `first + 1` through `last` is printed.

Call 4: `first` is 3 and `last` is 4. Because `first` is less than `last`, the value in `data[first]` (which is 61) is printed. Execution of this call pauses while the array from `first + 1` through `last` is printed.

Call 5: `first` is 4 and `last` is 4. Because `first` is equal to `last`, the value in `data[first]` (which is 77) is printed. Execution of this call pauses while the array from `first + 1` through `last` is printed.

Call 6: `first` is 5 and `last` is 4. Because `first` is greater than `last`, the execution of this call is complete. Control returns to the preceding call.

Call 5: Execution of this call is complete. Control returns to the preceding call.

Calls 4, 3, 2, and 1: Each execution is completed in turn, and control returns to the preceding call.

Tail recursion   A recursive algorithm in which no statements execute after the return from the recursive call

Notice that once the deepest call (the call with the highest number) was reached, each of the calls before it returned without doing anything. When no statements execute after the return from the recursive call to the method, the recursion is known as tail recursion. **Tail recursion** often indicates that we could solve the problem more easily by using iteration. We used a recursive solution in the array example because it made the recursive process easy to visualize; in practice, an array should be printed iteratively.

Figure 13.4 shows the execution of the `print` method along with the values of the parameters for each call. Notice that the subarray being processed becomes smaller with each recursive call (`data[first]` through `data[last]`). If we want to print the array elements in reverse order recursively, we simply swap the two statements within the *if* statement.

`print(data, 0, 4)`

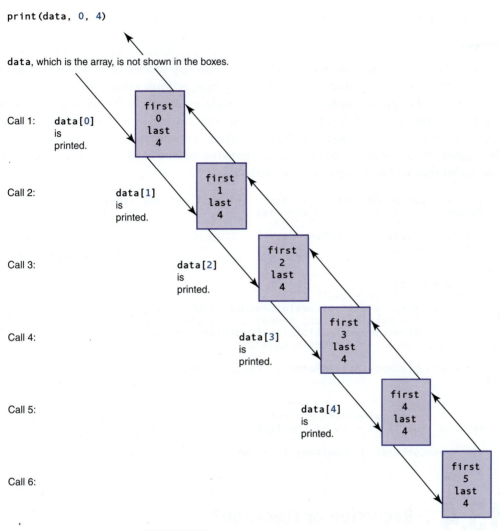

data, which is the array, is not shown in the boxes.

Call 1:   `data[0]`
           is
           printed.

           first
           0
           last
           4

Call 2:   `data[1]`
           is
           printed.

           first
           1
           last
           4

Call 3:   `data[2]`
           is
           printed.

           first
           2
           last
           4

Call 4:   `data[3]`
           is
           printed.

           first
           3
           last
           4

Call 5:   `data[4]`
           is
           printed.

           first
           4
           last
           4

Call 6:

           first
           5
           last
           4

FIGURE 13.4   Execution of `print(data, 0, 4)`

In Chapter 12, we used a stack to print lines from a file in reverse order. Here, we accomplished the same process with recursion. Thus, it shouldn't come as a surprise that recursion and stacks are closely related. Each recursive call effectively pushes the method's local variables and parameters onto a stack, and each return pops a set of local variables and parameters off the top of this stack. Java calls this the *run-time stack*. (Recall that when infinite recursion occurs, the error message from the JVM is "Run-time stack overflow.")

■ Binary Search

Do you remember the binary search in Chapter 11? Here is the description of the algorithm: "The algorithm divides the list in half (divides by 2—that's why it's called a binary search) and decides which half to look in next. Division of the selected portion of the list is repeated until the item is found or it is determined that the item is not in the list." There is something inherently recursive about this description.

Although the method that we wrote in Chapter 11 was iterative, it is really a recursive algorithm. The solution is expressed in terms of increasingly smaller versions of the original problem: If the answer isn't found in the middle position, perform a binary search (a recursive call) to search the appropriate half of the list (a smaller problem). In the iterative version, we kept track of the bounds of the current search area with two local variables, `first` and `last`. In the recursive version, we call the method with these two values as arguments. We must call the recursive binary search method from the `contains` method of the `SortedListOfStrings` class rather than writing it as part of that method.

```java
private boolean binContains(int first, int last, String item)
// Returns true if item is in the list
{
  if (first > last)        // Base case 1
    return false;
  else
  {
    int midPoint;
    midPoint = (first + last) / 2;
    if (item.compareTo(listItems[midPoint]) < 0)
      return binContains(first, midPoint-1, item);
    else if (item.compareTo(listItems[midPoint]) == 0)
      return true;         // Base case 2
    else
      return binContains(midPoint+1, last, item);
  }
}

public boolean contains(String item)
// Returns true if item is in the list
{
  return binContains(0, numItems-1, item);
}
```

13.4 : Recursion or Iteration?

Recursion and iteration are alternative ways of expressing repetition in an algorithm. When iterative control structures are used, processes repeat because we embed code in a looping structure such as a *while*, *for*, or *do* statement. In recursion, a process repeats because a method calls itself. A selection statement controls the repeated calls.

Which technique is better to use—recursion or iteration? This question has no simple answer. The choice usually depends on two issues: efficiency and the nature of the problem at hand.

Historically, the quest for efficiency, in terms of both execution speed and memory usage, has favored iteration over recursion. Each time a recursive call is made, the system must allocate stack space for all parameters and local variables. The overhead involved in any method call is time-consuming. On early, slow computers with limited memory capacity, recursive algorithms were visibly—sometimes painfully—slower than the iterative versions. On modern, fast computers, however, the overhead associated with recursion is often so small that the difference in computation time is almost invisible to the user. Except in cases where efficiency is absolutely critical, then, the choice between recursion and iteration more often depends on the second issue—the nature of the problem at hand.

Consider the `factorial` and `power` algorithms discussed earlier in this chapter. In both cases, iterative solutions were obvious and easy to devise. We imposed recursive solutions on these problems merely to demonstrate how recursion works. As a rule of thumb, if an iterative solution is more obvious or easier to understand, use it; it is probably more efficient. For other problems, the recursive solution is more obvious or easier to devise, such as in the Towers of Hanoi problem. (It turns out that the Towers of Hanoi problem is surprisingly difficult to solve using iteration.) Computer science students should be aware of the power of recursion. If the definition of a problem is inherently recursive, then a recursive solution should certainly be considered.

13.5 : Testing and Debugging

Recursion is a powerful technique when used correctly. When used incorrectly, however, it can result in errors that are difficult to diagnose. The best way to debug a recursive algorithm is to construct it correctly in the first place. To be realistic, we give a few hints about where to look if an error crops up.

Testing and Debugging Hints

1. Be sure that a base case exists. If there is no base case, the algorithm will continue to issue recursive calls until all memory has been used. Each time the method is called, either recursively or nonrecursively, stack space is allocated for the parameters and local variables. If no base case is available to end the recursive calls, the run-time stack will eventually overflow. An error message such as "Run-time stack overflow" indicates that the base case is missing.

2. Be sure that you have not used a *while* statement. The basic structure in a recursive algorithm is the *if* statement. At least two cases must be provided: the recursive case and the base case. If the base case does nothing, the *else* clause is omitted. The selection structure, however, must be present. If a *while* statement is used in a recursive algorithm, it usually should not contain a recursive call.

3. Use your system's debugger program (or use debug output statements) to trace a series of recursive calls. Inspecting the values of parameters and local variables often helps to locate errors in a recursive algorithm.

Summary

A recursive algorithm is expressed in terms of a smaller instance of itself. It must include a recursive (general) case, for which the algorithm is expressed in terms of itself, and a base case, for which the algorithm is expressed in nonrecursive terms.

In many recursive problems, the smaller instance refers to a numeric argument that is reduced with each call. In other problems, the smaller instance refers to the size of the data structure being manipulated. In the base case, the size of the problem (value or structure) reaches a point for which an explicit answer is known.

In the conversion of decimal integers to binary numbers, the size of the problem is the number to be converted. When it is zero, the conversion is finished. In the Towers of Hanoi game, the size of the problem is the number of discs to be moved. When only one is left on the beginning peg, it can be moved to its final destination.

In the example of printing an array using recursion, the size of the problem is the size of the array being printed. When the array size reaches 1, the solution is known. In the binary search algorithm, the size of the problem is the size of the search area. This algorithm has two base cases: (1) when the search item is found and (2) when the search area becomes empty and you know that the search value is not there.

LEARNING / Portfolio

Quick Check

1. What is the essential ingredient in a recursive definition? (pp. 728–729)

2. What distinguishes the base case from the recursive case in a recursive algorithm? (pp. 728–729)

3. What is the size of the problem in the recursive power algorithm? (pp. 729–731)

4. What is the base case in the Towers of Hanoi algorithm? (pp. 737–740)

5. In working with simple variables, the recursive case is often stated in terms of a smaller value. What is typical of the recursive case when you are working with structured variables? (pp. 741–743)

6. Which control structures are used to implement recursion? (pp. 744–745)

7. Which control structures are used to implement iteration? (pp. 744–745)

8. In the binary search algorithm, what is the base case? (pp. 743–744)

9. Which of the algorithms presented in this chapter are better implemented using iteration? (pp. 744–745)

Answers

1. The essential ingredient in a recursive definition is the repetition of the problem in terms of a smaller version of itself. 2. The base case is the simplest case—that is, the case for which the solution can be stated nonrecursively. 3. The size of the problem is the power to which the number is taken. It is decreased by 1 in each call. 4. There are no more circles left to move. 5. It is often stated in terms of a smaller structure. 6. Selection 7. Looping 8. The search area is empty or the item is found. 9. `factorial`, `power`, printing values in an array

LEARNING / Portfolio

Exam Preparation Exercises

1. Recursion is an example of _____.

   a. selection

   b. a data structure

   c. repetition

   d. data-flow programming

2. A `void` method can be recursive, but a value-returning method cannot. (True or False?)

3. When a method is called recursively, the arguments and local variables of the calling version are saved until its execution resumes. (True or False?)

4. Given the recursive formula $F(N) = -F(N - 2)$, with a base case of $F(0) = 1$, what are the values of $F(4)$, $F(6)$, and $F(5)$? (If any of the values are undefined, say so.)

5. Which algorithm error(s) leads to infinite recursion?

6. Which control structure appears most commonly in a recursive method?

7. If you develop a recursive algorithm that employs tail recursion, what should you consider?

8. A recursive algorithm depends on making something smaller. When the algorithm works on a data structure, what may become smaller?

   a. Distance from a position in the structure

   b. The data structure

   c. The number of variables in the recursive method

9. What is the name of the memory area used by the computer system to store a method's parameters and local variables?

10. Given the following data on an input file:

```
15
23
21
19
```

What is the output of the following method?

```java
public void printNums()
{
  int n;
  if (inFile.hasNextInt())              // If not EOF . . .
  {
    n = inFile.nextInt();
    System.out.print(n + " ");
    printNums();
    System.out.print(n + " ");
  }
}
```

Programming Warm-Up Exercises

1. Write a Java value-returning method that implements the recursive formula $f(n) = f(n-1) + f(n-2)$ with base cases of $f(0) = 1$ and $f(1) = 1$.

2. Add whatever is necessary to fix the following method so that `func(3)` equals 10.

```java
public static int func(int n)
{
    return func(n - 1) + 3;
}
```

3. Rewrite the following `printSquares` method using recursion.

```java
public static void printSquares()
{
    int count;
    for (count = 1; count <= 10; count++)
        outFile.println(count + " " + count * count);
}
```

4. Modify the `factorial` method discussed in this chapter to print its parameter and returned value indented two spaces for each level of call to the method. For example, the call `factorial(3)` should produce the following output on `System.out`:

```
3
  2
    1
      0
      1
    1
  2
6
```

5. Write a recursive value-returning method that sums the integers from 1 through n.

6. Rewrite the following method so that it is recursive.

```java
public static void printSqRoots(int n)
{
    int i;
    for (i = n; i > 0; i--)
        outFile.println(i + " " + Math.sqrt((double)i));
}
```

7. The `print` method discussed in this chapter prints the contents of an array from first element to last. Write a recursive method that prints the array contents from last element to first.

8. Write a `contains` method that takes an array as a parameter and performs a recursive linear search.

9. Rewrite the `power` method using another base case.

10. Rewrite the `power` method using the following formula:

```
if n == 0, return 1
if n == 1, return x
if n is even, return power(x*x, n/2)
else return x*power(x, n-1)
```

Programming Problems

1. Use recursion to solve the following problem:

   A palindrome is a string of characters that reads the same forward and backward. Write a program that reads in strings of characters and determines whether each string is a palindrome. Each string appears on a separate input line. Echo-print each string, followed by "Is a palindrome" if the string is a palindrome or "Is not a palindrome" if the string is not a palindrome. For example, given the input string

   `Able was I, ere I saw Elba.`

   the program should print "Is a palindrome." In determining whether a string is a palindrome, consider uppercase and lowercase letters to be the same and ignore punctuation characters.

2. Write a program to place eight queens on a chessboard in such a way that no queen attacks any other queen. This classic problem lends itself well to a recursive solution. Represent the chessboard as an 8 × 8 Boolean array. If a square is occupied by a queen, the value is `true`; otherwise, the value is `false`. The status of the chessboard when all eight queens have been placed is the solution.

3. A maze is to be represented by a 10 × 10 array of characters: P (for path), H (for hedge), or E (for Exit). The maze has one exit. Write a program to determine whether it is possible to exit the maze from a given starting point. You may move vertically or horizontally in any direction to a square that contains P; you may not move to a square that contains H. If you move into a square that contains E, you have exited.

   The input data consist of two parts: the maze and a series of starting points. The maze is entered as 10 lines of 10 characters (P, H, and E). Each succeeding line contains a pair of integers that represents a starting point (that is, row and column numbers). Continue processing entry points until end-of-file occurs.

14 Applets

Goals

Knowledge Goals

To:
- Understand the differing roles of applications and applets
- Understand how a browser operates
- Understand the role of HTML

Skill Goals

To be able to:
- Write an applet to perform a simple task
- Embed Bytecode within a web page
- Construct a simple HTML web page that executes an applet

1995
E-commerce sites Ebay and Amazon.com open, forecasting a revolution in the way goods are bought and sold

1997
In a legendary match, IBM's Deep Blue computer defeats Garry Kasparov, the world champion chess player

1999
Shawn Fanning, while at Northeastern University, founds Napster. The easy trading of music in MP3 format raises copyright issues

1999
Membership to the Internet Service Provider AOL exceeds 20 million, signifying an explosion of personal computer use for the Internet

2001
Apple introduces the iPod, and replaces MacOS with a Unix variant, OSX

2001
Microsoft releases Windows XP, successor to Windows 2000 and Windows 95

Introduction

So far in this text, we have written all of our programs as Java applications. That is, we have written a class that contains a method called `main` that acts as the driver for whatever set of responsibilities our objects support. Java provides a second type of program called an applet. As its name implies, it is intended to be a small application. An applet doesn't stand on its own but rather is run in a web browser.

From an educational viewpoint, we have presented only applications to this point because they enable us to use all of Java's features. They also do not require the use of a browser or a separate program (called an applet viewer) to run compiled code. Now that you are comfortable with Java, we end this book with a chapter on applets. We describe what they are, how to write them, and how to run them.

2002
Microsoft releases the .NET development environment partially in response to the success of Java

2004
Microsoft releases Service Pack 2, an update to Windows XP designed to address security and reliability concerns

2005
IBM sells its PC business to Chinese computer maker Lenovo

2006
Apple switches from IBM and Motorola PowerPC processors to chips made by Intel

2007
Apple announces the iPhone, which is meant to do for the cell phone what the iPod did for music players

2007
Microsoft releases Vista, the first new version of Windows in five years

14.1 ⋮ What Is an Applet?

Applets are a kind of mini-application designed to be distributed along with web pages and run under a browser or applet viewer. They are typically used as elements of web pages. Most web browsers include a special JVM that can execute the Bytecode version of an applet. When the browser encounters a link to an applet Bytecode file, it copies the file into memory and calls its JVM to execute the Bytecode.

The browser's ability to execute applets enables us to create web pages that are as sophisticated as almost any program we can write in Java. We say "almost" because applets are subject to certain limitations that do not apply to Java applications. For example, you would not want your browser to run an applet that destroys the files on your computer. As a consequence, applets are generally prohibited from accessing files except under certain conditions. Likewise, an applet cannot send messages to other computers from your computer (except the one from which it was loaded). These security restrictions are included in Java to prevent the creation of harmful applets (malware) by malicious programmers.

Applets differ from applications in several ways:

- An applet doesn't have a `main` method. It is much more like a windowing component than a stand-alone application.
- An applet is not invoked in the same fashion as an application. Instead, it is embedded within an HTML document. HTML is the language used to create web pages. We describe HTML briefly later in this chapter.
- Applets are subjected to more security constraints than an application because they are distributed over the Internet.
- Applets are not in control of their own execution. They simply respond when told to do so by the browser or viewer.

Because of the way applets are executed, they do not have constructors. Instead, the operations that we would normally place into a constructor (such as initializing fields or setting up the user interface) are written into the applet's `init` method. When a browser first downloads an applet, its JVM executes this method. In this chapter, we use the `init` method not only to serve as a constructor but also to play the role of `main` in an application. It contains the main block of code that begins the work of the applet.

Whereas applications are derived implicitly from `Object`, applets must be explicitly derived from the `Applet` or `JApplet` class, both of which are descendants of the `Container` class. These classes contain additional methods called `start`, `stop`, and `destroy` that are used with more sophisticated applets that employ features of Java not covered in this text. For example, if an applet is showing a graphics animation, we may want the animation to stop when the user moves to a different web page and resume (start) when the user returns to the page with the applet.

In the "Graphical User Interfaces" sections of Chapters 9–12, we showed how to create GUIs using the `awt` and `swing` packages, which are GUI toolkits provided as part of the Java library.

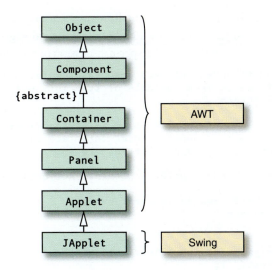

FIGURE 14.1　Applet Inheritance Hierarchy for AWT and Swing

Many of the Swing classes have the letter "J" in front of them—for example, `JButton`, `JLabel`, and `JTextField`. The "J" distinguishes the class from the AWT class of the same name. Both AWT and Swing support applets. Figure 14.1 shows the inheritance hierarchy. As you can see, the `JApplet` class is derived from `Applet`.

In our applications, we had to instantiate a `JFrame`. Given a frame, we obtained a reference to its content pane (an object of class `Container`). We then added our user interface components to that container. Because `Applet` is derived from `Container`, we can simply call methods such as `add` and `setLayout` to directly create a user interface within an applet. Thus, in some ways, writing applets is easier than writing user interfaces with frames.

14.2 : How Do We Write an Applet?

Let's demonstrate how to write an applet by returning to two examples that appeared earlier in the book. The first is the factorial function developed in Chapter 13, which originally did not use a GUI, and the second is the calculator application from Chapter 11, which we created using a `JFrame`.

■ Factorial Applet

Let's consider how to write an applet in the context of a specific problem. In Chapter 13, we wrote the factorial function. What we didn't mention there is that the factorial of a number becomes very large very fast. Let's write an applet that lets us enter a number and then displays the factorial of that number. This process continues until the user closes the window in the browser. Thus the applet sets up an event loop, allowing the user to continue to enter a value for which the factorial is computed and to watch how fast the value grows.

We display the code for the applet and intersperse discussion of this code at the different parts.

```java
// Applet FactInt on file FactInt.java computes the factorial of
// its input and stores it in a variable of type int, which is
// displayed on the screen.

import javax.swing.*;      // Supplies user interface classes
import java.awt.*;         // Supplies user interface classes
import java.awt.event.*;   // Supplies event classes

public class FactInt extends JApplet implements ActionListener
{
  public void actionPerformed(ActionEvent event)
  // Event handler method
  {
    int value;
    value = Integer.parseInt(inputField.getText());
    inputField.setText("");
    outLabel.setText(value + " factorial is " + factorial(value));
  }
```

The class heading is just like that of an application, except the phrase `extends JApplet im-plements ActionListener` follows the class name. This phrase tells the compiler that we are working with an applet and not an application: Our class is derived from `JApplet`. This applet also implements the `ActionListener` interface, so we should expect a `public` method `actionPerformed` to be part of the class. The event handler takes a string as input, converts it to an integer value, resets the text field to the empty string, and invokes the `factorial` method within the output statement. The `factorial` method that follows is identical to the one used in Chapter 13:

```java
private int factorial(int n)
// Assumption:  n is not negative
{
  if (n == 0)
    return 1;        // Base case
  else
    return (n * factorial(n-1)); // General case
}
```

The next sections of code set up a button, a label, and a text input field:

```java
// Set up a button, label, and input field
private JTextField inputField;
private JLabel label;
private JLabel outLabel;
private JButton button;
```

In an application, execution begins in the `main` method. By contrast, in an applet, execution begins in the `init` method. Thus the initializations that are carried out in `main` in an application are carried out in `init` in an applet. Note the use of `this` as the argument to `addActionListener`; the applet is its own listener.

```java
public void init()
{
  // Instantiate components
```

```
        label = new JLabel("Enter an integer; click Enter.");
        outLabel = new JLabel("Answer");
        button = new JButton("Enter");
        button.addActionListener(this);
        inputField = new JTextField("Value here");
        // Add components
        add(label);
        add(inputField);
        add(button);
        add(outLabel);
        // Specify a layout manager for the window
        setLayout(new GridLayout(4,1));
    }
}
```

Here is a series of screen shots showing the initial window and the results from various input values.

To stop execution, the user closes the applet window (or browser window).

See what we mean about the factorial becoming very large very fast? 16! is 10 digits. 17! cannot possibly be a negative number. What happened? The result was too large to store in an integer variable, so overflow occurred. The JVM just kept going with a "garbage" value for the number, which in this case was displayed as a negative number.

■ Calculator Applet

Now let's look at a somewhat more complex example. In Chapter 11, we created a calculator that performs addition and subtraction. Let's write an applet that does the same thing. You may want to compare our approach here with that program. When we wrote the calculator application in Chapter 11, we used separate event handlers for the Clear button and the arithmetic operations. In this version, we demonstrate how the applet can respond to all of the buttons through a single event handler.

The applet class both extends the class **JApplet** and implements the **ActionListener** interface. Thus **Calculator2** is its own listener class. This fact is reflected in the heading and in the code, where **this** is the argument for the **addActionListener** method. Within the event handler, the string-to-numeric conversion operation is enclosed within a *try-catch* statement that handles numeric input errors.

```java
import javax.swing.*;                      // User interface classes
import java.awt.*;                         // User interface classes
import java.awt.event.*;                   // Event-handling classes
public class Calculator2 extends JApplet implements ActionListener
{
  // Field, label, and variable for use by the event handler
  private JTextField inputField;           // Data field
  private JLabel register;                 // Result shown on screen
  private double result;                   // Keeps current value

  // Event handler for buttons in the applet
  public void actionPerformed(ActionEvent event)
  {
    double secondOperand;                  // Holds input value
    String whichButton;                    // Holds the button's name
    // Get the operand, checking for numeric format error
    try
    {
      secondOperand = Double.parseDouble(inputField.getText());
    }
    catch (NumberFormatException except)
    {
      secondOperand = 0.0;                 // If error, set to zero
    }
    whichButton = event.getActionCommand();  // Get the button's name
    if (whichButton.equals("+"))           // When the name is "+"
      result = result + secondOperand;     //   add the operand
    else if (whichButton.equals("-"))      // When the name is "-"
      result = result - secondOperand;     //   subtract the operand
    else
      result = 0.0;                        // Clear result to zero
    register.setText("" + result);         // Display result
    inputField.setText("");                // Clear input
  }
```

Notice that no **JFrame** has been declared or instantiated in the following **init** method. The applet already has its own window.

```java
// Applet initialization method
public void init()
```

```
{
    JLabel resultLabel;                             // Indicates output area
    JLabel entryLabel;                              // Label for input field
    JButton add;
    JButton subtract;
    JButton clear;
    result = 0.0;
    // Instantiate labels and initialize input field
    resultLabel = new JLabel("Result:");
    register = new JLabel("0.0", JLabel.RIGHT);
    entryLabel = new JLabel("Enter #:");
    inputField = new JTextField("", 10);
    // Instantiate button objects
    add = new JButton("+");
    subtract = new JButton("-");
    clear = new JButton("Clear");
    // Register the button listener with the buttons
    add.addActionListener(this);
    subtract.addActionListener(this);
    clear.addActionListener(this);
    // Add interface elements to applet window
    setLayout(new GridLayout(4,2));                 // Set the layout manager
    add(resultLabel);
    add(register);
    add(entryLabel);
    add(inputField);
    add(add);
    add(subtract);
    add(clear);
  }
}
```

Here is how this applet appears on the screen.

14.3 : How Do You Run an Applet?

As we said earlier, an applet must be run within a web browser or an applet viewer. The browser recognizes a link to a Bytecode file, and the JVM within the browser executes the code. Most Java systems provide an applet viewer that runs the Bytecode version of the applet so that you can see the results. Although each system is different, there is usually an HTML file associated with each applet that gives the name of the compiled class to the viewer. The name of the class is typically the name of the `public` class with a `.class` extension. Recall that the JVM executes Bytecode—not Java code or machine language code.

Let's review a few fundamental facts about web browsers. We'll then look at HTML, the language in which web pages are written.

■ Web Browsers

The terms *Internet* and *Web* are often used as synonyms, but they are not. The Internet is a **network**. A network is a collection of computing devices connected so that they can communicate and share resources. A **local area network (LAN)** is a network that connects a small number of nodes located within a close geographic area. A wide area network (WAN) is a network that connects two or more local area networks. The **Internet** is a wide area network that spans the planet. In contrast, the **Web** (short for World Wide Web) is an infrastructure of information and the network software used to access it.

A web page is a document that contains or references various kinds of data, including links to other web pages. Web pages are referenced by their **Uniform Resource Locator (URL)**, such as `http://www.jbpub.com`. When you access a web page in your browser by entering a URL, the browser goes to that page and brings a copy back to you. Thus the expression "visit a web page" is somewhat misleading: Your browser actually visits the other site and brings back a copy for you to view. If the web page contains a link to an applet, this code is brought to your browser and runs on your browser's JVM.

■ HTML

Both browsers and applet viewers read web pages. To create or build web pages, we use the **Hypertext Markup Language (HTML)**. The term *hypertext* means that the information is not organized linearly, like a book. Instead, links to other information are embedded within the text, enabling the viewer to jump from one place to another as needed within the text. These days, a more accurate term would be *hypermedia*, because web pages deal with many types of information in addition to text, including images, audio, and video.

The term **markup language** means that the primary elements of the language take the form of **tags** that we insert into a document to annotate the information stored there. In the case of HTML, the tags indicate how the information should be dis-

Network A collection of connected computing devices that communicate and share resources

Local area network (LAN) A network in a close geographic area

Wide area network (WAN) A network that connects two or more local area networks

Internet A wide area network that spans the planet

Web An infrastructure of information and the network software used to access it

Uniform Resource Locator (URL) The address of a web page on the Internet

Hypertext Markup Language (HTML) The language used to create or build web pages

Markup language A language that uses tags to annotate the information in a document

Tags The syntactic element in a markup language that indicates how information should be displayed

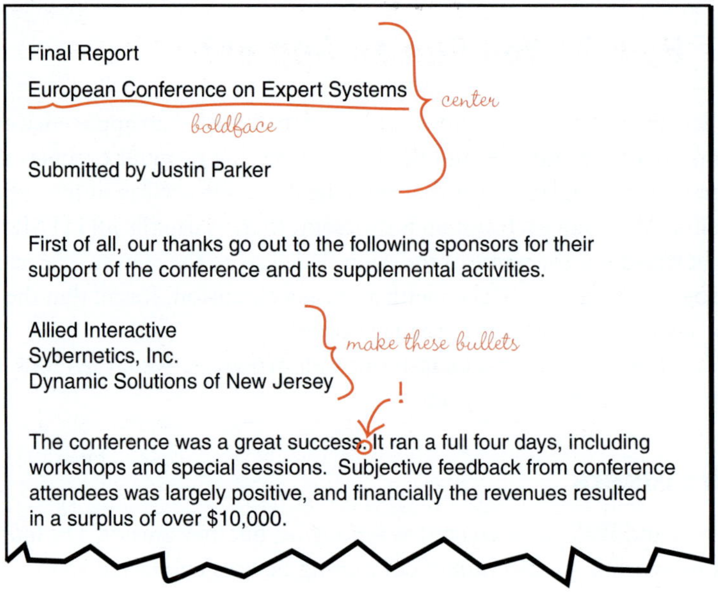

FIGURE 14.2   A Marked-Up Document

played. It's as if you took a printed document and marked it up with extra notation to specify other details, as shown in Figure 14.2.

■ Factorial HTML

Figure 14.3 shows the HTML document that contains the link to the Bytecode version of `FactInt`.

```
<HTML>
<HEAD>
<TITLE>Factorial Labs</TITLE>
</HEAD>
<BODY>
<H1>Factorial with Int Result</H1>
<P>Enter increasing values beginning with 0 and record the results of the factorial
of your input.  At some point, the answer will seem strange.  Record what seems
strange about the answer and return to the previous page.</P>
<P><HR></P>
<P><APPLET code = "FactInt.class" width=250 height=150></APPLET></P>
</BODY>
</HTML>
```

FIGURE 14.3   An HTML Document That Causes the Applet `FactInt` to Be Executed

Although we will not try to teach you HTML in this chapter, we do want to point out which features cause the execution of the applet. Tags are enclosed in angled brackets and are not case sensitive. Most of them come in pairs, with the second or closing tag preceded by a "/". At the beginning and the end of the document, you will see `<HTML>` . . . `</HTML>`; at the beginning and the end of the title, you will see `<TITLE>` . . . `</TITLE>`. The body of the HTML code is enclosed in `<BODY>` . . . `</BODY>`. `<H1>` . . . `</H1>` indicates that the information between the tags is a type 1 heading, and `<P>` . . . `</P>` encloses a paragraph. `<HR>` inserts a horizontal rule (line) and has no ending tag.

The following HTML code runs the factorial; applet:

```
<APPLET code = "FactInt.class" width=250 height=150></APPLET>
```

Between `<APPLET` and `</APPLET>` lie the keywords that cause the applet to be executed. The JVM starts executing the Bytecode from the file `FactInt.class`. The applet is in an event loop that keeps executing as long as the browser remains on the web page containing the applet.

■ Calculator HTML

We ran the calculator applet within a viewer provided by our particular Java system. Figure 14.4 shows the `.html` file that our Java system automatically generated when it compiled the calculator applet.

Although this HTML document is a little different, the important element is the applet tag enclosing the name of the file with a `.class` extension. Notice the two-stage process:

1. Compile the Java code into Bytecode.
2. Create an HTML document with a link to the Bytecode file in the web page.

```
<title>Calculator2.class</title>
<hr>
<applet codebase="Java Classes" code="Calculator2.class" width=200 height=200>
</applet>
<hr>
<a href="Calculator2.java">The source.</a>
```

FIGURE 14.4   `.html` File for Running the Calculator Applet

PROBLEM SOLVING CASE STUDY

Searching Experiments

Problem: Write an applet that lets the user experiment with looking for items in a list and trying to determine which searching algorithm is being used. The number of comparisons is a metric that is often employed to measure searching efficiency, so the applet should display the number of comparisons performed in determining whether the value was present in the list.

Background: Chapter 11 presented and discussed three searching algorithms: a sequential search in a sorted list, a sequential search in an unsorted list, and a binary search. A sequential search begins by looking at the first item in the list and continues looking at each successive item until it finds the item or reaches the end of the list. A sequential search in a sorted list can recognize when the search has reached the place where the item would be if it were present and, therefore, stops at that point. A binary search assumes that the list items are sorted; it begins by looking in the middle of the list and successively throws away half of the list with each comparison until it finds the item or there is nowhere else to look.

Brainstorming: The problem doesn't state which of the three algorithms we must use. Thus we can wait to make that decision later, because the primary processing does not depend on the algorithm. The classes in this solution are found in the problem statement: a list of items, an item, and a counter to keep track of the number of comparisons. Because the applet runs from a web page, we know that the input and output will rely on the GUI components on the screen. Thus we must have an input text field and an output label. Where there is an input text field, a button is always lurking nearby.

List
Item
GUI components (label, textfield, button)
Applet

The user enters an item, and the applet reports whether the item is in the list and how many comparisons were required to make that determination. Where there is a button, there are a listener and an event loop. Which actions must be executed within the event handler? The item must be read, the list must be searched, and the results must be given to the user. The user may input another item or quit the process by closing the applet window (if an applet viewer is being used) or going to another web page.

What must the applet do to set up this situation within the event handler? For one thing, it must generate a list to be searched. Because the problem statement says nothing about the types of items in the list, let's make them be integers. We can then use a random-number generator to create the items in the list.

Class Name: *Search*	Superclass: *Applet*	Subclasses:
Responsibilities	**Collaborations**	
Prepare GUI components	*Label, TextField, Button*	
Generate list values	*Random*	
Get an item		
Search the list (item) *return boolean*	*List*	
Report results		

Responsibility Algorithms: The first responsibility—preparing the GUI components—is very straightforward. We need an input label, an output label, a text field, and a button.

Generating the list requires a little more thought. The CRC card says that this operation collaborates with the class `Random`. This Java class supplies a method that generates a random number. We can call this method to give us an integer—say, between 0 and 999. Here is how the method works:

```java
Random rand = new Random();
value = Math.abs(rand.nextInt()) % 1000;
```

The first line initializes the random-number generator. Each time it is called, the `nextInt` method returns a random number within the range of the `int` data type. The `Math.abs` method converts the result to a nonnegative integer, and the `% 1000` limits the values to three digits. `Random` can be found in `java.util`.

Which kind of list shall we use? Does the list need to be sorted? It must be sorted only if we decide to use the searching strategies that require a sorted list. Abstraction lets us write the primary algorithms without having to make this decision right away. What size shall we make the list? Let's set a constant `SIZE` to be 100. This way it will be easy to change later.

Generate values

for counter going from 1 to SIZE
    Generate random number
    Insert number into list

The next three responsibilities should be placed within the event handler and can be grouped together:

Event handler

```
Get item
Search list for item
if found
    Write item, " is in list found with ", count, " comparisons"
else
    Write item, " is not in list, determined with ", count, " comparisons"
```

Have we forgotten anything? Yes—how will we count the number of comparisons? We can derive a class from one of the list classes and have it override the `contains` method. Before we do that, let's spend a minute thinking about the processing that we need to do. We don't delete an item, and we don't use any of the observers. In fact, we aren't really dealing with a list at all, because the number of items is a constant. It would be much more efficient to just generate the random numbers directly into an array, and then write a `contains` method that searches the array and counts the number of comparisons. We can borrow the code for these operations from one of our list classes. We use the linear search because the array items are not in sorted order.

Generate list (revised)

```
for counter going from 0 to SIZE – 1
    values[counter] = Math.abs(rand.nextInt()) % 1000
```

Contains (item)

```
Set location to 0
Set found to false
Set count to 0
Set moreToSearch to (location less than SIZE)
while moreToSearch and !found
    Increment count
    if item equals values[location]
        Set found to true
    else
        Increment location
        Set moreToSearch to (location less than SIZE)
return found
```

We have to make `count` be a field in the applet class. We need two outputs from our `contains` method (`found` and `count`), yet the *return* statement can return only one value. Therefore, we must make `count` be a field that other methods can access. Here is the code for our applet, followed by a screen shot showing execution by the applet viewer, where the value 12 has just been searched for, and 68 has been entered for the next search.

```java
//*************************************************************
// This applet prompts a user to input an integer value and
// reports whether the value is in a list and how many comparisons
// it took to make that determination
//*************************************************************
import javax.swing.*;        // Supplies user interface classes
import java.awt.*;           // Supplies user interface classes
import java.awt.event.*;     // Supplies event classes
import java.util.*;          // Supplies Random class

public class Search extends JApplet implements ActionListener
{

  private int[] values;              // Values to be searched
  private int count = 0;             // Comparison count
  private final int SIZE = 100;      // Size of the array

  // Event handler method
  public void actionPerformed(ActionEvent event)
  {
    int value;
    value = Integer.parseInt(inputField.getText());
    inputField.setText("");
    if (contains(value))
      outLabel.setText(value + " is in list found with "
        + count + " comparisons");
    else
      outLabel.setText(value + " is not in list determined with "
      + count + " comparisons");
  }

  private boolean contains (int item)
  // Returns true if the item is in the array;
  //   otherwise, returns false
  {
    boolean moreToSearch;
    int location = 0;
    boolean found = false;
    count = 0;
    moreToSearch = (location < SIZE);

    while (moreToSearch && !found)
    {
      count++;
      if (item == values[location])
        found = true;
      else
      {
        location++;
        moreToSearch = (location < SIZE);
      }
    }
    return found;
  }
```

```java
private void generateValues(int size)
// Initializes the values array with random integers
//   from 0 to 999
{
  values = new int[size];
  Random rand = new Random();
  for (int index = 0; index < size; index++)
    values[index] = Math.abs(rand.nextInt()) % 1000;
}

private static JTextField inputField;
private static JLabel label;
private static JLabel outLabel;
private static JButton button;

public void init()
{
  // Instantiate the GUI components
  label = new JLabel("Enter a value between 0 and 999; click Enter.");
  outLabel = new JLabel("Results");
  button = new JButton("Enter");
  inputField = new JTextField("Value here");

  // Finish processing GUI components
  button.addActionListener(this);
  add(label);
  add(inputField);
  add(button);
  add(outLabel);

  // Generate the array of integers
  generateValues(SIZE);
  setLayout(new GridLayout(4,1));
}
}
```

Applet Viewer: chapter14.Search.cl

Applet

Enter a value between 0 and 999; click Enter.

68

Enter

12 is not in list determined with 100 compari...

Applet started.

14.4 : Testing and Debugging

Testing an applet is much like testing an application. Because an applet is usually smaller, however, there is less code to test. In contrast, the steps involved in getting an applet to run are more involved because you have to set up a web page.

Testing and Debugging Hints

1. Be sure that all of your initializations take place within the `init` method.
2. An applet is often its own event listener. In such a case, confirm that the `addActionListener` method has `this` as its argument.
3. The spelling of the file name in the viewer or web page must be identical to the name of the file containing the Bytecode version of the applet.

Summary

A Java application must have a method named `main`, and all of the included classes should have constructors. A Java applet, by contrast, is a class derived from the class `Applet` that implements `ActionListener`; here, the class is its own listener, and initializations occur within the init method. Most applets appear in event loops that continue running until the applet window is closed or you exit the web page in which the applet is embedded.

The link to the Bytecode version of the applet is found within a web page. An example of HTML code that provides the link is `<APPLET code = "FactInt.class" width=250 height=150></APPLET>`. Using the keyword `code` followed by the equals sign and a file name with a `.class` extension says to execute the Bytecode stored in that file.

LEARNING / Portfolio

Quick Check

1. How do applications and applets differ in terms of how they are used? (pp. 752–753)
2. Applets must be explicitly derived from which class(es)? (pp. 753–756)
3. What distinguishes AWT classes from Swing classes? (pp. 752–753)
4. Where does execution begin in an applet? (pp. 752–753)
5. In an applet class heading, which phrase must follow the applet class name? (pp. 753–756)

LEARNING / Portfolio

6. How does a web page get loaded into a browser? (pp. 759–761)

7. What is HTML used for? (pp. 759–761)

8. How is an applet linked within a web page? (pp. 759–761)

9. What is the meaning of the `.class` extension? (pp. 759–761)

Answers

1. An application is a stand-alone program that solves a problem. An applet is a small piece of code that runs under a browser. 2. `Applet` or `JApplet` 3. The letter "J" before the class. 4. Method `init`. 5. `extends JApplet implements ActionListener` 6. When you enter a URL into your browser, the browser goes to that place and brings back a copy of what is there for you to see, including any applets to which it links. 7. HTML is the language used to write web pages. 8. `<APPLET code = "appletName.class" . . . ></APPLET>` links the applet whose Bytecode is stored in the file `appletName.class` into the web page. 9. `.class` means that the file contains the Bytecode version of an applet.

Exam Preparation Exercises

1. Name four ways in which applets differ from applications.

2. Because applets do not have constructors, where are their initializations carried out?

3. Because applets do not have a `main` method, where does execution begin?

4. From which class must your applet be derived?

5. Why do we not need to instantiate a `JFrame` with an applet?

6. Why do you not need to append an object name to add components to the window?

7. What happens when an `int` variable overflows in Java?

8. What distinguishes a Swing component from an AWT component?

9. How do you run an applet?

10. What is HTML?

11. What is a markup language?

12. What is a tag?

13. What is the HTML tag that encloses a web page?

14. What does `<P> . . . </P>` enclose?

15. Distinguish between the Internet and the Web.

16. Describe what happens when you enter a URL in your browser.

17. Distinguish between a LAN and a WAN.

Programming Warm-Up Exercises

1. Write the Java statement that provides access to the `JApplet` class.

2. Write the class heading for an applet class named `Sorts`.

3. For the applet of Exercise 2, write the statements that declare, instantiate, and place a text field into the window.

4. For the applet of Exercise 2, write the statements that declare, instantiate, and place into the window a label with the phrase "Enter a real number between 0.0 and 1.99."

5. For the applet of Exercise 2, write the statements that declare, instantiate, and place a button object into the window.

6. Write the statement that registers a listener with the button of Exercise 5.

7. For the applet of Exercise 2, write the statement that sets the layout of the window.

8. Write the HTML tags that must appear in a web page to execute the following applets:

   a. `Sorts`

   b. `Search`

   c. `Calculator`

9. Write the HTML statements that create the following title: Now is the time!

10. Write the HTML tag(s) to place a horizontal rule on the page.

11. Which HTML symbols enclose a paragraph?

Programming Problems

1. a. Write an applet that calculates the factorial of a number using `byte` arithmetic. That is, the input value is a `byte`, and the value returned by the factorial function is a `byte`. Execute your applet by inputting increasing values beginning with 0. What is the largest factorial value that can be calculated? What happens when you enter a larger value?

   b. Modify the applet to use `short` arithmetic. That is, the input value is a `short`, and the value returned by the factorial function is a `short`. Execute your applet by inputting increasing values beginning with the largest value for which a factorial could be calculated using `byte` arithmetic. What is the largest factorial value that can be calculated? What happens when you enter a larger value?

   c. Modify the applet to use `long` arithmetic. Execute your applet by inputting increasing values beginning with 15. What is the largest factorial value that can be calculated? What happens when you enter a larger value?

d. Change the applet to use `float` arithmetic. Execute your applet by inputting increasing values beginning with 50. What is the largest factorial value that can be calculated? What happens when you enter a larger value?

e. Change the factorial applet to use `double` arithmetic. Execute your applet by inputting increasing values beginning with 100. What is the largest factorial value that can be calculated? What happens when you enter a larger value?

2. Write an applet that counts the number of comparisons required to sort a list of integers using the selection sort algorithm. The user should enter the size of the list, and the applet should report back the number of comparisons. Run your applet five times and record the size of the list and the number of comparisons required. Relate your findings to the discussion of Big-O complexity in Chapter 11.

3. Extend the calculator applet in this chapter to include functions for multiplication, division, square root, and exponent. Also add a "memory" register with operations to store the current value in the memory and recall the value in the memory to the main register. The memory should be displayed in a label field.

LEARNING Portfolio

Case Study Follow-Up

1. Rather than having the number of elements be a constant in the list-searching applet `Search`, ask the user to input the number of elements to be searched.

2. Create another applet exactly like the altered version of `Search` in Exercise 1, but replace the linear search with a linear search in a sorted list. Don't forget to sort the values before you search.

3. Create another applet exactly like the one in Exercise 2, but replace the linear search with a binary search. Be sure to sort the values before you search.

4. The output from each applet should give the user enough information to determine which search algorithm is being used. After the user runs the applet for a number of times, have the user enter which of the three algorithms he or she thinks is being used. If the answer is correct, congratulate the user; otherwise, suggest that he or she run the applet again at another time.

Appendix A

Java Reserved Words

These words appear in red when used in this book.

abstract	else	interface	switch
assert	enum	long	synchronized
boolean	extends	native	this
break	false*	new	throw
byte	final	null*	throws
case	finally	package	transient
catch	float	private	true*
char	for	protected	try
class	goto	public	void
const	if	return	volatile
continue	implements	short	while
default	import	static	
do	instanceof	strictfp	
double	int	super	

*false, null, and true are technically not reserved words. They are predefined literals. We list them here because, like reserved words, you cannot use them as identifiers.

Appendix B

Operator Precedence

In the following table, the operators are grouped by precedence level (hightest to lowest), and a horizontal line separates each precedence level from the next.

Precedence (highest to lowest)

Operator	Assoc.*	Operand Type(s)	Operation Performed
.	LR	object, member	object member access
[]	LR	array, int	array element access
(args)	LR	method, arglist	method invocation
++, --	LR	variable	post-increment, decrement
++, --	RL	variable	pre-increment, decrement
+, -	RL	number	unary plus, unary minus
~	RL	integer	bitwise complement
!	RL	boolean	boolean NOT
new	RL	class, arglist	object creation
(type)	RL	type, any	cast (type conversion)
*, /, %	LR	number, number	multiplication, division, remainder
+, -	LR	number, number	addition, subtraction
+	LR	string, any	string concatenation
<<	LR	integer, integer	left shift
>>	LR	integer, integer	right shift with sign extension
>>>	LR	integer, integer	right shift with zero extension
<, <=	LR	number, number	less than, less than or equal
>, >=	LR	number, number	greater than, greater than or equal
instanceof	LR	reference, type	type comparison
==	LR	primitive, primitive	equal (have identical values)
!=	LR	primitive, primitive	not equal (have different values)
==	LR	reference, reference	equal (refer to the same object)
!=	LR	reference, reference	not equal (refer to different objects)
&	LR	integer, integer	bitwise AND
&	LR	boolean, boolean	boolean AND
^	LR	integer, integer	bitwise XOR
^	LR	boolean, boolean	boolean XOR

*LR means left-to-right associativity; RL means right-to-left associativity.

Precedence (highest to lowest)

Operator	Assoc.*	Operand Type(s)	Operation Performed
|	LR	integer, integer	bitwise OR
|	LR	boolean, boolean	boolean OR
&&	LR	boolean, boolean	conditional AND (short-circuit evaluation)
||	LR	boolean, boolean	conditional OR (short-circuit evaluation)
?:	RL	boolean, any, any	conditional (ternary) operator
=	RL	variable, any	assignment
*=, /=, %=, +=, -=, <<=, >>=, >>>=, &=, ^=, |=	RL	variable, any	assignment with operation

*LR means left-to-right associativity; RL means right-to-left associativity.

Appendix C

Primitive Data Types

Type	Value Stored	Default Value	Size	Range of Values
char	Unicode character	Character code 0	16 bits	0 to 65535
byte	Integer value	0	8 bits	2128 to 127
short	Integer value	0	16 bits	-32768 to 32767
int	Integer value	0	32 bits	-2147483648 to 2147483647
long	Integer value	0	64 bits	-9223372036854775808 to 9223372036854775807
float	Real value	0.0	32 bits	$\pm1.4E\text{-}45$ to $\pm3.4028235E\text{+}38$
double	Real value	0.0	64 bits	$\pm4.9E\text{-}324$ to $\pm1.7976931348623157E\text{+}308$
boolean	true or false	false	1 bit	NA

Appendix D

ASCII Subset of Unicode

The following chart shows the ordering of characters in the ASCII (American Standard Code for Information Interchange) subset of Unicode. The internal representation for each character is shown in decimal. For example, the letter *A* is represented internally as the integer 65. The space (blank) character is denoted by a "□".

Left Digit(s) \ Right Digit	ASCII									
	0	1	2	3	4	5	6	7	8	9
0	NUL	SOH	STX	ETX	EOT	ENQ	ACK	BEL	BS	HT
1	LF	VT	FF	CR	SO	SI	DLE	DC1	DC2	DC3
2	DC4	NAK	SYN	ETB	CAN	EM	SUB	ESC	FS	GS
3	RS	US	□	!	"	#	$	%	&	´
4	(	)	*	+	,	–	.	/	0	1
5	2	3	4	5	6	7	8	9	:	;
6	<	=	>	?	@	A	B	C	D	E
7	F	G	H	I	J	K	L	M	N	O
8	P	Q	R	S	T	U	V	W	X	Y
9	Z	[	\	]	^	_	`	a	b	c
10	d	e	f	g	h	i	j	k	l	m
11	n	o	p	q	r	s	t	u	v	w
12	x	y	z	{	|	}	~	DEL		

Codes 00–31 and 127 are the following nonprintable control characters:

NUL	Null character	VT	Vertical tab	SYN	Synchronous idle
SOH	Start of header	FF	Form feed	ETB	End of transmitted block
STX	Start of text	CR	Carriage return	CAN	Cancel
ETX	End of text	SO	Shift out	EM	End of medium
EOT	End of transmission	SI	Shift in	SUB	Substitute
ENQ	Enquiry	DLE	Data link escape	ESC	Escape
ACK	Acknowledge	DC1	Device control one	FS	File separator
BEL	Bell character (beep)	DC2	Device control two	GS	Group separator
BS	Back space	DC3	Device control three	RS	Record separator
HT	Horizontal tab	DC4	Device control four	US	Unit separator
LF	Line feed	NAK	Negative acknowledge	DEL	Delete

Appendix E

Decimal Format Type

To give more precise control over the formatting of numbers, Java provides a class called `DecimalFormat` that is part of a package called `java.text`. The `DecimalFormat` class allows us to create patterns that can be used to format numbers for output. These patterns are in the form of strings, made up of characters that represent the parts of a formatted number. For example, the pattern

```
"###,###"
```

indicates that a number should be formatted with up to six decimal digits, and when there are more than three digits in the number, a comma should be used to separate the thousands from the rest of the number.

There are four steps we must follow to use `DecimalFormat` patterns to format numbers:

- `import java.text.*;`
- Declare a variable of type `DecimalFormat` for each number format we wish to use.
- For each variable, instantiate a `DecimalFormat` object that contains the pattern.
- Format each number using the `format` method associated with each of the `DecimalFormat` class.

Let's examine each of these steps in turn. You are familiar with writing `import` declarations, so all you need to do for the first step is remember to put the declaration at the start of your program. Declaring variables of type `DecimalFormat` is done in the same way as declaring object variables of any other class. For example:

```
DecimalFormat dollar;        // Format for dollar amounts
DecimalFormat percent;       // Format for percentages
DecimalFormat accounting;    // Format for negative values in ()
```

The third step involves using `new` and the `DecimalFormat` constructor to create an object whose address we can assign to the variable. The call to the constructor contains the string representing the pattern. Here are statements that associate patterns with each of the variables declared previously. Don't be concerned yet with trying to interpret the specific patterns shown; we explain them shortly.

```
dollar = new DecimalFormat("$###,##0.00");
percent = new DecimalFormat("##0.00%");
accounting = new DecimalFormat("$###,##0.00;($###,##0.00)");
```

The last step is to format the number using a method called **format**, which is a value-returning method associated with each of the **DecimalFormat** objects. The **format** method takes as its parameter a numeric value and returns a value of type **String** that contains the formatted number. For example, if we write

```
System.out.println(dollar.format(2893.67));
```

then a line is output that contains a string of the form

```
$2,893.67
```

Now that we have seen the process for using patterns to format numeric values, let's look at how to write the patterns themselves. The following table shows the characters that can appear in a pattern string and their meanings.

Character	Meaning
0	Display one digit here. If no digit is present in this place, display a zero.
#	Display one digit here. If no digit is present in this place, display nothing here (not even a blank).
,	If there are digits on both sides of this place, insert a comma to separate them. The comma is only meaningful in the integer part of the pattern (the part to the left of the decimal point).
.	Put the decimal point here. If the pattern doesn't have any digit symbols (0 or #) to the right of the period, and the number doesn't have a fractional part, don't insert the decimal point.
%	When used anywhere to the right of the rightmost digit in the pattern, this indicates that the number is a percentage. Multiply it by 100 before displaying it, and put the % sign here.
;	The pattern to the left of ; is for nonnegative numbers. The pattern to the right is for negative numbers.
'	The character following is one of the special pattern characters, but should be printed literally (For example, use '# to show a # in the formatted number.)
other	Anything else is inserted exactly as it appears.

Now we can interpret the patterns we associate with the **DecimalFormat** variables. The pattern we gave to **dollar** is `"$###,##0.00"`, which means the number should have a decimal point with at least two fractional digits and one digit in the integer part. When the integer part has more than three digits, use a comma as a separator. The number should start with a dollar sign to the left of the first digit.

We use the pattern `"##0.00%"` to tell `format` that the number is a percentage that should first be multiplied by 100. After that, it is formatted with fractional digits and at least two digits in the integer part. The percent sign is to be placed to the right of the last digit.

The third pattern, `"$###,##0.00; ($###,##0.00)"`, is the most complex of the three, but is really just a minor variation on the `dollar` format. The semicolon indicates that the pattern on the left, which is the same as the pattern we gave to `dollar`, is to be used when the number is nonnegative. The pattern on the right (the same pattern but in parentheses) is to be used when the number is negative.

Here is a code segment that shows the definition and use of these patterns:

```
dollar = new DecimalFormat("$###,##0.00");
percent = new DecimalFormat("##0.00%");
accounting = new DecimalFormat("$###,##0.00; ($###,##0.00)");

System.out.println(dollar.format(2893.67));
System.out.println(dollar.format(-2893.67));
System.out.println(dollar.format(4312893.6));
System.out.println(dollar.format(0));
System.out.println(percent.format(0.23679));
System.out.println(percent.format(1));
System.out.println(accounting.format(2893.67));
System.out.println(accounting.format(-2893.67));
```

and here is the output:

```
$2,893.67
-$2,893.67
$4,312,893.60
$0.00
23.68%
100.00%
$2,893.67
($2,893.67)
```

Let's take a closer look at each of these output lines. The first line demonstrates what happens when a positive floating-point value is formatted with the dollar format. Only as many digits are used as are necessary, and the dollar sign is immediately adjacent to the leftmost digit. The second line shows the result of formatting a negative number. The format is the same as in the first case, but a minus sign precedes the dollar sign.

The third line is an example of formatting a number with more digits than the pattern specifies. Notice that the pattern is expanded to fit. The separation between the decimal point (or the rightmost digit, in the case of an integer) and the comma closest to it are used as a guide to the placement of additional commas. In this case, the comma is three places to the left of the decimal point, so additional commas are inserted every three places. We can't split up the fractional part of a number with a separator character such as a comma or period. If you try to use a comma in the fractional part, it simply ends up being pushed to the right end of the number.

The fourth line demonstrates that an integer value can be formatted to look like a floating-point value. It also shows that placing a zero in the pattern forces a zero to appear in the resulting string when there is no corresponding digit in the number.

The fifth line shows the use of the **percent** format. Notice that the value is multiplied by 100 before it is formatted. This example also shows that when there are more digits of precision in the fractional part than in the pattern, it is not expanded to show the additional fractional digits. The sixth line shows the application of the **percent** format to an integer.

The last two lines demonstrate the use of the pattern we associated with **accounting**. When the number is nonnegative, it is formatted normally, and when it is negative, it is enclosed in parentheses. Using two different patterns separated by a semicolon suppresses the automatic insertion of the minus sign and allows us to use other characters to indicate that the number is negative. As a safeguard, however, if we mistakenly use the same pattern on both sides of the semicolon, **format** ignores the semicolon and reverts to using the minus sign.

DecimalFormat gives us a powerful mechanism to format numbers in the patterns we typically use in our programs. However, it has some limitations. For example, when printing a dollar amount on a check, it is typical to fill the extra space around the number with asterisks or dashes to prevent tampering. **DecimalFormat** doesn't enable us to do this directly. However, because the **format** method returns its value as a string, we can store a formatted number into a **String** object and then use string operations to further refine its formatting.

Suppose we write the assignments

```
dollar = new DecimalFormat("###,##0.00");
value = 8239.41;
```

then the expression

```
dollar.format(value)
```

has the value `"8,239.41"`. Further suppose that we want to display this in a fixed space of thirteen character positions, where the first character is the dollar sign and the spaces between the dollar sign and the first digit are filled with stars: `"$****8,239.41"`. If the number has more digits, fewer stars are needed, and if it has fewer digits then more stars must be concatenated. The number of stars to add is

```
12 - dollar.format(value).length
```

because the dollar sign takes up one of the thirteen character positions. The maximum value of this expression is 8, because the format requires at least three decimal digits and a decimal point. Thus, if we use a string constant called **STARS** that contains eight stars, we can write

```
STARS.substring(0, 12 - dollar.format(value).length)
```

to get a string with the proper number of stars. All we have left to do is to concatenate the pieces to form the desired string.

```
"$" + STARS.substring(0, 12 - dollar.format(value).length) +
   dollar.format(value)
```

   Look closely at this expression to be certain that you understand how it works. Many programming problems require that output values be precisely formatted. In such cases, you may need to use complex combinations of the string operations that Java provides. Breaking an output format into its component pieces and deciding how to format each piece before concatenating them together is a common strategy for dealing with this complexity.

Appendix F

Program Style, Formatting, and Documentation

Useful programs have very long lifetimes, during which they must be modified and updated. Good style and documentation are essential if another programmer is to understand and work with your program.

General Guidelines

Style is of benefit only for a human reader of your programs—differences in style make no difference to the computer. Good style includes the use of meaningful identifiers, comments, and indentation of control structures, all of which help others to understand and work with your program. Perhaps the most important aspect of program style is consistency. If the style within a program is not consistent, it then becomes misleading and confusing.

Comments

Comments are extra information included to make a program easier to understand. You should include a comment anywhere the code is difficult to understand. However, don't overcomment. Too many comments in a program can obscure the code and be a source of distraction.

In our style, there are four basic types of comments: headers, declarations, in-line, and sidebar.

Header comments appear at the top of a class, method, or package and should include your name, the date that the code was written, and its purpose. It is also useful to include sections describing the input, output, and assumptions that form the basis for the design of the code. The header comments serve as the reader's introduction to your code. Here is an example:

```
// This method computes the sidereal time for a given date and solar time
//
// Written by: Your Name
//
// Date completed: 4/8/03
//
// Input: java.util.calendar object for the date and solar time
//
// Output: a java.util.calendar object containing the corresponding
//   sidereal time
//
// Assumptions: Solar time is specified for a longitude of 0 degrees
```

Declaration comments accompany the field declarations in a class. Anywhere that an identifier is declared, it is helpful to include a comment that explains its purpose. For example:

```java
// Class constants
static final String FIRST  = "Herman";      // Person's first name
static final String LAST   = "Herrmann";    // Person's last name
static final char   MIDDLE = 'G';           // Person's middle initial
// Instance variables
String firstLast;                            // Name in first-last format
String lastFirst;                            // Name in last-first format
int studentCount;                            // Number of students
int sumOfScores;                             // Sum of their scores
long sumOfSquares;                           // Sum of squared scores
double average;                              // Average of the scores
float deviation;                             // Standard deviation of scores
char grade;                                  // Student's letter grade
String stuName;                              // Student's name
```

Notice that aligning the comments gives the code a neater appearance and is less distracting.

In-line comments are used to break long sections of code into shorter, more comprehensible fragments. It is generally a good idea to surround in-line comments with blank lines to make them stand out. In this text we save space by printing the in-line comments in color rather than using blank lines. Some editors also color comments automatically, which makes it easier to spot them on the screen. However, blank lines are still helpful because code is often printed on paper in black and white. Here is an example:

```java
// Instantiate labels and input field

resultLabel = new JLabel("Result:");
register = new JLabel("0.0", Label.RIGHT);
entryLabel = new JLabel("Enter #:");
inputField = new JTextField("", 10);


//Instantiate button objects

add = new JButton("+");
subtract = new JButton("-");
clear = new JButton("Clear");


// Register the button listeners

add.addActionListener(operation);
subtract.addActionListener(operation);
clear.addActionListener(clearOperation);
```

Even if comments aren't needed, blank lines can be inserted wherever there is a logical break in the code that you would like to emphasize.

Sidebar comments appear to the right of executable statements and are used to shed light on the purpose of the statement. Sidebar comments are often just pseudocode statements from your responsibility algorithms. If a complicated Java statement requires some explanations, the pseudocode statement should be written to its right. For example:

```java
while ((line = dataFile.readLine()) != null) // Get a line if not EOF
```

Because the page of a textbook has a fixed width, it is sometimes difficult to fit a sidebar comment next to a long line of code. In those cases, we place the sidebar comment before the statement to which it refers. Most computer screens can now display more characters on a line than fit across a page, so this situation is less common in practice. However, if lines of code become too long, they are hard to read. It is then better to place the sidebar comment before the line of code.

In addition to the four main types of comments that we have discussed, there are some miscellaneous comments that we should mention. Although we do not do this in the text, to conserve space, we recommend that classes and methods be separated in a compilation unit file by a row of asterisks.

```java
//**********************************************************************
```

Programmers also sometimes place a comment after the right brace of a block to indicate which control structure the block belongs to. This is especially helpful in a package file where there may be multiple classes. Indicating where a class or long method ends helps readers keep track of where they are looking in scanning the code.

```java
        return noCorrect;
    }
} // End of class TheKey
```

Identifiers

The most important consideration in choosing a name for a field or method is that the name convey as much information as possible about what the field is or what the method does. The name should also be readable in the context in which it is used. For example, the following names convey the same information, but one is more readable than the other:

```java
datOfInvc        invoiceDate
```

Although an identifier may be a series of words, very long identifiers can become quite tedious and can make the program harder to read. The best approach to designing an identifier is to try writing out different names until you reach an acceptable compromise—and then write an especially informative declaration comment next to the declaration.

Formatting Lines and Expressions

Java allows you to break a long statement in the middle and continue onto the next line. The split can occur at any point where it would be possible to insert spaces without affecting the behavior of the code. When a line is so long that it must be split, it's important to choose a breaking point that is logical and reasonable. Compare the readability of the following code fragments:

```java
outFile.println(" for a radius of " + radius + " the diameter of the cir"
                + "cle is " + diameter);
outFile.println(" for a radius of " + radius +
                " the diameter of the circle is " + diameter);
```

When writing expressions, keep in mind that spaces improve readability. Usually you should include one space on either side of the == operator as well as most other operators. Occasionally, spaces are left out to emphasize the order in which operations are performed. Here are some examples:

```java
if (x+y > y+z)
   maximum = x + y;
else
   maximum = y + z;
hypotenuse = Math.sqrt(a*a + b*b);
```

Indentation

The purpose of indenting statements in a program is to provide visual cues to the reader and to make the program easier to debug. When a program is properly indented, the way the statements are grouped is immediately obvious. Compare the following two program fragments:

```java
while (count <= 10)
{
num = Integer.parseInt(in.readLine());
if (num == 0)
{
count++;
num = 1;
}
out.println(num);
out.println(count);
}
```

```java
while (count <= 10)
{
  num = Integer.parseInt(in.readLine());
  if (num == 0)
  {
    count++;
    num = 1;
  }
  out.println(num);
  out.println(count);
}
```

As a basic rule in this text, each nested or lower level item is indented by two spaces. Exceptions to this rule are parameter declarations and statements that are split across two or more lines. Indenting by two spaces is a matter of personal preference. Some people prefer to indent by more spaces.

In this text, we prefer to place the braces on separate lines so that it is easy to scan down the left edge of a block of code and find them. Placing them on separate lines also reminds us to consider whether the beginning or the end of a block would benefit from an in-line comment and automatically gives us a place to write one. This is just one style of placement, and you will encounter other styles as you examine code written by other programmers.

As we noted at the beginning of this appendix, the most important aspect of code formatting is consistency. You may frequently find it necessary to adopt the style of another programmer in order to update his or her code in a consistent manner. Even when you believe your own favorite style to be superior, resist the temptation to mix your style with a different, existing style. The mixture is likely to be more confusing than either style alone.

Abstract   A modifier of a class or field that indicates it is incomplete and must be fully defined in a derived class

Abstract step   A step for which some implementation details remain unspecified

Abstraction   The separation of the logical properties (interface and specification) of an object from its implementation

Access modifiers   Reserved words in Java that specify where a class, method, or field may be accessed; two examples are `public` and `private`

Algorithm   Instructions for solving a problem in a finite amount of time using a finite amount of data

Alias   When multiple variables refer to the same object, acting as synonyms of one another

Argument   An expression used for communicating values to a method

Arithmetic/logic unit (ALU)   The component of the central processing unit that performs arithmetic and logical operations

Array   A collection of components, all of the same type, structured in N dimensions ($N \geq 1$). Each component is accessed by N indexes, each of which represents the component's position within that dimension

Assembler   A program that translates an assembly language program into machine code

Assembly language   A low-level programming language in which a mnemonic represents each machine language instruction for a particular computer

Assignment expression   A Java expression with (1) a value and (2) the side effect of storing the expression value into a memory location

Assignment statement   A statement that stores the value of an expression into a variable

Atomic   A property of a data type that its values have no component parts

Attributes   The values defined by a class that are used to represent its objects; the combination of instance and class values

Auto-boxing   Automatic instantiation of a primitive type wrapper class object from a primitive type value

Auto-unboxing   Automatic conversion of an object of one of the primitive type wrapper classes to the corresponding primitive type value

Auxiliary storage device   A device that stores data and programs in encoded form outside the computer's main memory

Backward compatible   A property of a new piece of software that enables it to be used in place of an existing piece of software, with no changes to any client code. The new software may add features, but must fully support all existing features.

Base address   The memory address of the first element of an array

Base case   The case for which the solution to a recursive algorithm can be stated non-recursively

Binary operator   An operator that has two operands

Binary search tree   A binary tree in which the value in any node is greater than the value in its left child and any of its children and less than the value in its right child and any of its children

Binary tree   A data structure, each of whose nodes refers to left and right child nodes

Brainstorming   Freely listing all the objects that may contribute to the solution of a problem

Bytecode   A standardized machine language into which Java source code is compiled

Call   A statement that causes a method to be executed; in Java we call a method by writing its name, followed by a list of arguments enclosed in parentheses

Central processing unit (CPU)   The part of the computer that executes the instructions (object code) stored in memory; made up of the arithmetic/logic unit and the control unit

Character set   A list of letters, digits, and symbols with corresponding binary representations in the computer

Checked exception   An exception in Java that must either be caught with a *catch* statement or explicitly thrown to the next level

Class (general sense)   A description of the attributes and behavior of a group of objects with similar properties and behaviors

class (Java construct)   A pattern for an object, containing fields and methods

Class method   A method that implements a class responsibility

Class responsibility   An operation performed with respect to a class of objects

Class value   A value that is associated with a class and is the same for every object of that class

Client   Software that declares and manipulates objects of a particular class

Clock   An electrical circuit that sends out a train of pulses to coordinate the actions of the computer's hardware components; its speed is measured in hertz (cycles per second)

Code   Instructions for a computer that are written in a programming language

Collaboration   An interaction between objects in which one object requests that another object carry out one of its responsibilities

Collaborations   The interactions between the classes that are needed to solve a problem

Collating sequence   The ordering of characters, with respect to one another, within a character set

Collision   The condition resulting when a hash function maps multiple values to the same location

Compilation unit   A file containing Java code that can be compiled

Compiler   A program that translates code written in a high-level language into machine code

Complexity   A measure of the effort expended by the computer in performing a computation, relative to the size of the computation

Composite data type   A data type that allows a collection of values to be associated with an identifier of that type

Computer   A programmable device that can store, retrieve, and process data

Computer program   Instructions defining a set of objects and orchestrating their interactions to solve a problem

Computer programming   The process of specifying objects and the ways in which those objects interact to solve a problem

Concrete step   A step for which the implementation details are fully specified

Constructor   An operation that creates a new instance of a class

Control abstraction   The separation of an object's behavioral specification from the implementation of the specification

Control structure   A statement used to alter the normally sequential flow of control

Control unit   The component of the central processing unit that controls the actions of the other components so that instructions (the object code) execute in the correct sequence

Copy constructor   An operation that creates a new instance of a class by copying an existing instance, possibly altering some or all of its state in the process

Count-controlled loop   A loop that executes a specified number of times

Counter A variable that is incremented repeatedly

Data Information in a form that a computer can use

Data abstraction The separation of the logical representation of an object's attributes from its implementation

Data structure The implementation of a composite data type

Data type The specification in a programming language of how information is represented in the computer as data and the set of operations that can be applied to it

Declaration A statement that associates an identifier with a field, a method, a class, or a package so that the programmer can refer to the item by name

Default constructor A constructor that has no parameters; Java automatically supplies one for each class if we do not do so

Deserializing Translating a serialized stream of bytes back into an object

Desk checking Tracing the execution of a design on paper

Dialog box A small temporary panel that appears on the screen, with which a user can interact

Direct execution The process by which a computer performs the actions specified in a machine language program

Documentation The written text and comments that make an application easier for others to understand, use, and modify

Driver A program for creating the objects and coordinating their collaborations to solve the problem

Dynamic binding The situation in which Java resolves a polymorphic method call to a specific version of a method at run time

Dynamic data structure A data structure that can expand and contract during execution

Encapsulation Designing a class so that its attributes are isolated from the actions of external code except through the formal interface

Enumeration A data type in which the elements are a set of identifiers that are ordered so that each element (except the first) has a unique predecessor in the ordering and each (except the last) has a unique successor

Evaluate To compute a new value by performing a specified set of operations on given values

Event-controlled loop A loop that terminates when something happens inside the loop body to signal that the loop should be exited

Event counter A variable that is incremented each time a particular event occurs

Event loop A situation in which an event handler can be called repeatedly

Exception An unusual condition in execution of Java code that causes control to be transferred to statements that are designed to handle the condition. The exception is thrown when the condition is detected and is caught by the handling code

Exception handler A section of code that is executed when a particular exception occurs; in Java, an exception handler appears within the *catch* clause of a *try* control structure

Execution trace Going through the code with actual values, recording the state of the variables

Explicit memory management Recycling of object memory that must be manually coded

Expression An arrangement of identifiers, values, and operators that can be evaluated to compute a value of a given type

Expression statement A statement formed by appending a semicolon to an assignment expression, an increment expression, or a decrement expression

Extensible language   A procedural programming language that allows the definition of new data types

External reference   A named variable that references the first node (also known as the head) of a linked list

Field   A named place in memory that holds data

Filtering   Reviewing the initial list of objects to identify duplicate and unnecessary objects

Flow of control   The order in which the computer executes statements

Formal interface   The components of a class that are externally accessible, which consist of its nonprivate fields and methods

Functional decomposition   A technique for developing software in which the problem is divided into more easily handled subproblems, whose solutions are combined to create a solution to the overall problem

Garbage collection   Automatic recycling of memory when objects are no longer needed

General case   The case for which a recursive solution is expressed in terms of a smaller version of itself

Graph   A data structure in which the nodes can be arranged in any pattern

Hardware   The physical components of a computer

Hash function   A function used to manipulate the value of an element to produce an index that identifies its location in a data structure

Hashing   A technique used to perform insertion of and access to elements in a data structure in approximately constant time, by using the value of each element to identify its location in the structure

Helper method   A method that is private to a class and called from within other methods of the class. Typically used to simplify code or supply an operation that is used at multiple points in the class

Hide   To provide a field in a derived class that has the same name as a field in its superclass; to provide a class method that has the same form of heading as a class method in its superclass. The field or class method is said to hide the corresponding component of the superclass.

Hypertext Markup Language (HTML)   The language used to create or build web pages

Identifier   A name associated with a package, class, method, or field and used to refer to that element

Immutability   The property of a class that its instances cannot be modified once they are created

Implementation (in Java)   A class containing the definitions of the methods specified in an interface

Infinite recursion   The situation in which a method calls itself over and over endlessly

Information   Any knowledge that can be communicated

Inheritance   A mechanism by which one class (a subclass) acquires the properties—the data fields and methods—of another class (its superclass)

In-order traversal   A traversal of a binary tree that proceeds in the pattern of "visit the left subtree, visit the root, then visit the right subtrees"

Input/output (I/O) devices   The parts of the computer that accept data to be processed (input) and present the results of that processing (output)

Inspection   A verification method in which one member of a team reads the code or design line by line and the other team members point out errors

Instance   A way of referring to an object as being an example of its class

Instance method   A method that implements an instance responsibility

Instance responsibility   An operation performed with respect to a specific object

Instance value   A value that is associated with a specific object

Instantiation   Creating an object, which is an instance of a class

Interactive system   A system that supports direct communication between the user and the computer

Interface (in Java)   A model for a class that specifies the fields and methods that must be present in a class that implements the interface

Internet   A wide area network that spans the planet

Interpretation   The translation, while a program is running, of non-machine language instructions (such as Bytecode) into executable operations

Iteration   An individual pass through, or repetition of, the body of a loop

Iteration counter   A counter variable that is incremented in each iteration of a loop

Key   A member of a class whose value is used to determine the logical and/or physical order of the items in a list

Length (size in Java)   The number of items in a list; it can vary over time

Linear relationship (in a data structure)   Every element except the first has a unique predecessor, and every element except the last has a unique successor

Link   A reference to an item that is logically adjacent to the current item

Linked list   A list in which the order of the components is determined by an explicit link field in each node, rather than by the sequential order of the components in memory

Literal constant   Any value written directly in Java

Local area network (LAN)   A network in a close geographic area

Local declaration   A declaration that appears within a method

Loop   A control structure that causes statement or group of statements to be executed repeatedly

Loop entry   The point at which the flow of control reaches the first statement inside a loop

Loop exit   The point at which the repetition of the loop body ends and control passes to the first statement following the loop

Loop test   The point at which the *while* expression is evaluated and the decision is made either to begin a new iteration or to skip to the statement immediately following the loop

Machine language   The language, made up of binary-coded instructions, that is used directly by the computer

Malware   Software written with malicious purposes in mind

Markup language   A language that uses tags to annotate the information in a document

Memory leak   Failure to recycle memory when explicit memory management is being used

Memory unit   Internal data storage in a computer

Metalanguage   A language that is used to write the syntax rules for another language

Method   A subprogram in Java

Method   A subprogram that defines one aspect of the behavior of a class

Mixed type (mixed mode) expression   An expression that contains operands of different data types

Modifiability   The property of an encapsulated class definition that allows the implementation to be changed without having an effect on code that uses it (except in terms of speed or memory space)

Module   A self-contained collection of steps that solves a problem or subproblem; it can contain both concrete and abstract steps

Mutate   Changing the value(s) of an object's attribute(s) after it is created

Named (symbolic) constant   A location in memory, referenced by an identifier, that contains a data value that cannot be changed

Narrowing conversion   A type conversion that may result in a loss of some information, as in converting a value of type `double` to type `float`

Network   A collection of connected computing devices that communicate and share resources

Object   A collection of data values and associated operations

Object (general sense)   An entity or thing that is relevant in the context of a problem

Object (Java)   An entity containing data in fields, with associated operations

Object code   A machine language version derived from source code

Object-oriented design (OOD)   A technique for developing software in which the solution is expressed in terms of objects that interact with one another

Object-oriented language   A programming language in which new data types can be defined so that they include the data representation and the operations for the type in a self-contained unit called an object

Observer   An operation that returns information from an object without changing the content of the object

One-dimensional array   A structured collection of components, all of the same type, that is given a single name; each component (array element) is accessed by an index that indicates the component's position within the collection

Operating system   A set of programs that manages all of the computer's resources

Ordinal   A property of a data type in which each value (except the first) has a unique predecessor and each value (except the last) has a unique successor

Out-of-bounds array index   An index value that is either less than 0 or greater than the array size minus 1

Override   To provide an instance method in a derived class that has the same form of heading as an instance method in its superclass. The method in the derived class redefines (overrides) the method in its superclass. We cannot override class methods.

Package   A named collection of classes in Java that can be imported by a program

Peripheral device   An input, output, or auxiliary storage device attached to a computer

Polymorphic   An operation that has multiple meanings depending on the class of object to which it is bound

Post-order traversal   A traversal of a binary tree that proceeds in the pattern of "visit the left and right subtrees, then visit the root"

Pre-order traversal   A traversal of a binary tree that proceeds in the pattern of "visit the root, then visit the left and right subtrees"

Priming read   An input operation preceding an event-controlled loop that gets an initial value to be tested as part of the termination condition of the loop

Primitive type   Any of the built-in types that represent integral, real, character, or Boolean values

Procedural language   A programming language that focuses on the processing procedures that are applied to built-in types of data (unlike languages that facilitate the representation of new types of data)

Programming   Writing out instructions for solving a problem or performing a task

Programming language   A set of rules, symbols, and special words used to construct a computer program

Queue   A data structure in which insertions are made at one end and deletions are made at the other end

Recursive algorithm   A solution that is expressed in terms of (1) smaller instances of itself and (2) a base case

Recursive call   A method call in which the method being called is the same as the one making the call

Recursive definition   A definition in which something is defined in terms of smaller versions of itself

Refactoring   Modifying code to improve its quality without changing its functionality

Registering a listener   Connecting an event handler object to an event source object by calling a method associated with the event source. The method adds the handler to the event source's list of listeners, which are called whenever the event happens

Reliable   A property of a unit of software such that it always operates consistently, according to the specification of its interface

Reserved word   A word that has a specific pre-defined meaning in Java

Responsibility   An action that an implementation of an object must be capable of performing

Reuse   The ability to import a class into code that uses it, without additional modification to either the class or the user code; the ability to extend the definition of a class

Scalar   A property of a data type in which the values are ordered and each value is atomic (indivisible)

Scope of access (scope)   The region of program code where it is legal to reference (use) an identifier

Scope rules   The rules that determine where in a program an identifier may be referenced, given the point where the identifier is declared and its specific access modifiers

Self-documenting code   Program code that contains meaningful identifiers as well as judiciously used clarifying comments

Semantics   The set of rules that determines the meaning of instructions written in a programming language

Serializing   Translating an object into a stream of bytes

Shadowing   A scope rule specifying that a local identifier declaration blocks access to an identifier declared with the same name outside the block containing the local declaration

Short-circuit (conditional) evaluation   Evaluation of a logical expression in left-to-right order with evaluation stopping as soon as the final Boolean value can be determined

Signature   The distinguishing features of a method heading; the combination of the method name with the number and type(s) of its parameter in their given order

Software   Computer programs; the set of all programs available on a computer

Software engineering   The application of traditional engineering methodologies and techniques to the development of software

Software piracy   The unauthorized copying of software for either personal use or use by others

Sorted list   A list whose predecessor and successor relationships are determined by the content of the keys of the items in the list; a semantic relationship exists among the keys of the items in the list

Sorting   Arranging the components of a list into order (for instance, words into alphabetical order or numbers into ascending or descending order)

Source code   Instructions written in a high-level programming language

Specification   The written description of the behavior of a class with respect to its interface

Stack   A data structure in which insertions and deletions can be made from only one end

Standard (built-in) type   A data type that is automatically available for use in every Java program

Statements   Specific combinations of symbols and special words that are defined by a programming language to be complete units within a program; analogous to sentences in a human language

Static binding   The situation in which Java resolves a polymorphic method call to a specific version of the method at compile time

Strongly typed   A property of a programming language in which the language allows a variable to contain only values of the specified type or class

Structured data type   An organized collection of components; the organization determines the means used to access individual components

Subclass   A class that is derived from another class (its superclass)

Superclass   A class that is extended by one or more derived classes (its subclasses)

switch **expression**   The expression whose value determines which *switch* label is selected

Syntax   The formal rules governing how valid instructions are written in a programming language

System software   The set of programs that simplifies the user/computer interface and improves the efficiency of processing

Tags   The syntactic element in a markup language that indicates how information should be displayed

Tail recursion   A recursive algorithm in which no statements execute after the return from the recursive call

Termination condition   The condition that causes a loop to be exited

Test plan   A document that specifies how a class is to be tested

Test plan implementation   Writing and running a driver that implements the test cases specified in a test plan to verify that the class methods produce the predicted results

Transformer (mutator)   An operation that changes the internal state of an object; a method that changes the information contained in an object

Traversal   To visit every node in a data structure following an organized pattern of access

Two-dimensional array   A collection of components, all of the same type, structured in two dimensions; each component is accessed by a pair of indexes that represent the component's position in each dimension

Type casting   The explicit conversion of a value from one data type to another

Type conversion   The implicit (automatic) conversion of a value from one data type to another

Unary operator   An operator that has just one operand

Unchecked exception   An exception in Java that can optionally be caught or allowed to propagate automatically to the next level

Uniform Resource Locator (URL)   The address of a web page on the Internet

Unsorted list   A list in which data items are placed in no particular order with respect to their content; the only relationships between data elements consist of the list predecessor and successor relationships

Unstructured data type   A collection of components that are not organized with respect to one another

User/computer interface   A connecting link that translates between the computer's internal representation of data and representations that humans are able to work with

Value-returning method A method that is called from within an expression and returns a value that can be used in the expression

Variable A location in memory, referenced by an identifier, that contains a data value that can be changed

Virtual machine A program that makes one computer act like another

Virus Malicious code that replicates and spreads to other computers through email messages and file sharing, without authorization, and possibly with the intent of doing harm

void method A method that is called as a separate statement; when it returns, processing continues with the next statement

Walkthrough A verification method in which a team performs a manual simulation of the code or design

Web An infrastructure of information and the network software used to access it

Wide area network (WAN) A network that connects two or more local area networks

Widening conversion A type conversion that does not result in a loss of information

Worm Malicious code that replicates and spreads to other computers through security gaps in the computer's operating system, without authorization, and possibly with the intent of doing harm

Wrapper class A class that provides additional operations for a primitive type by enclosing a primitive type value in an object

Zombie A computer that has been taken over for unauthorized use, such as sending spam email

Italicized page locators indicate a figure; tables are indicated with a *t*; notes are indicated with an *n*.

A

We would like to thank the following people and organizations who generously contributed the photographs and images found in our Timeline. We also thank the IEEE Computing Society for publishing their Timeline of Computing History, which proved a valuable resource as we created a chronology of significant events and developments in the history of computer technology.

Chapter 1
Abacus – © Photodisc
Blaise Pascal – © Mary Evans Picture Library/Alamy Images
Augusta Ada Lovelace – © The Print Collector/Alamy Images
Typewriter – © Photodisc

Chapter 2
Herman Hollerith Tabulating Machine – IBM Corporate Archives
Punched Card – Courtesy of Douglas W. Jones at the University of Iowa
Computer Chip – © Photodisc
1924 IBM Logo – IBM Corporate Archives
Blaise Pascal – © Mary Evans Picture Library/Alamy Images

Chapter 3
Television – © Photodisc
Service Technicians – IBM Corporate Archives
ENIAC – Courtesy of U.S. Army
Robot Arm – Courtesy of Adept
Augusta Ada Byron – © Mary Evans Picture Library/Alamy Images

Chapter 4
EDVAC – Courtesy of U.S. Army
Grace Murray Hopper – Naval Historical Center
World's First Transistor – Lucent Technologies Inc./Bell Labs
Charles Babbage – © Popperfoto/Alamy Images

Chapter 5
EDVAC – Courtesy of U.S. Army
First Silicon Transistor – Courtesy of Texas Instruments
Sputnik I – Courtesy of NASA
George Boole – © Mary Evans Picture Library/Alamy Images

Chapter 6
Integrated Circuit – Courtesy of Texas Instruments
John McCarthy – Courtesy of John McCarthy
Xerox Copier – Courtesy of Xerox Corporation
IBM 7030 – IBM Corporate Archives
USB Flash Stick – © Alex Kotlov/ShutterStock, Inc.
DVD in Laptop Tray – © Adrian Hughes/ShutterStock, Inc.

Chapter 7
Telstar Communications Satellite – IBM Corporate Archives
Bob Bemer – Courtesy of Bob Bemer
Engelbart's Mouse – Courtesy of Douglas Engelbart and Bootstrap Institute/Alliance
Electronic Calculator – Courtesy of Texas Instruments
Augustus de Morgan – © Mary Evans Picture Library/Alamy Images

Chapter 8
Edsger Dijkstra – Courtesy of The University of Texas at Austin
Grove, Noyce, and Moore – Courtesy of Intel Corporation. Reprinted with permission.
Unix Creators – Lucent Technologies Inc./Bell Labs
Microprocessor – © Photodisc
John von Neumann – Courtesy of Los Alamos National Laboratory

Chapter 9
Pong Image – Courtesy of the Atari Museum
Vincent Atanasoff – University Archives, Iowa State University Library
Chess – © Photodisc
Grace Murray Hopper – Naval Historical Center

Chapter 10
PET Commodore Computer – Courtesy of the Commodore History Web Site,
    www.commodore.ca
Key – © Photodisc
Bob Frankston and Dan Bricklin – Louis Fabian Bachrach/Dan Bricklin
Alan Turing – © King's College Library, Cambridge, <AMT/K/7/13>

Chapter 11
Cell Phone – © Photodisc
IBM PC – IBM Corporate Archives
John Warnock and Charles Geschke – Courtesy of Adobe Systems, Inc. Reprinted with
    permission.

Chapter 12
CD-ROM – © Photodisc
Intel 286 Microprocessor – Courtesy of Intel Corporation. Reprinted with permission.
Intel 386 Microprocessor – Courtesy of Intel Corporation. Reprinted with permission.
Seymour Cray – Courtesy of Cray Inc.
Sir Charles Antony Richard Hoare – Courtesy of Inamori Foundation of Kyoto, Japan

Chapter 13
Intel Pentium Chip – Courtesy of Intel Corporation. Reprinted with permission.
Java Logo – Copyright 2006 Sun Microsystems, Inc. All rights reserved. Used by permission.

Chapter 14
.COM – © AbleStock
Kasparov and Deep Blue – IBM Corporate Archives
Windows Vista Logo – Courtesy of Microsoft Corporation